Order this book online at www.trafford.com
or email orders@trafford.com

Most Trafford titles are also available at major online book retailers.

Printed in the United States of America.

ISBN: 978-1-4269-3006-5 (soft)
ISBN: 978-1-4269-3007-2 (hard)

Library of Congress Control Number: 2010908023

Our mission is to efficiently provide the world's finest, most comprehensive book publishing service, enabling every author to experience success. To find out how to publish your book, your way, and have it available worldwide, visit us online at www.trafford.com

Trafford rev. 6/4/2010

www.trafford.com

North America & international
toll-free: 1 888 232 4444 (USA & Canada)
phone: 250 383 6864 • fax: 812 355 4082

POLITICAL SELF DESTRUCTION OF MOST AFRICAN AMERICANS

Ernest Lawson

The book is dedicated to my great grandfather

L S Campton &c. To Deed Dawan Jones Z/330	State of Alabama } For and in consideration of the sum of Marengo County } Four Hundred dollars to us in hand paid by Dawan Jones the receipt whereof is hereby acknowledged we the undersigned Levin S. & Irwin Campton have bargained and sold and by these presents do bargain sell and convey to the said Dawan Jones the following described real estate to wit, the South west quarter of the northeast quarter of Section Seven Township Seventeen Range two east containing forty acres. to have and to hold unto him his heirs or assigns forever, binding ourselves our heirs and executors forever to warrant the title of said land against the lawful claims of any one whatever Witness our signatures this first day of May 1883.
	The State of Alabama } L S Campton (L.S.) I P Campton (L.S.) Marengo County } I A Y Sharpe a Notary Public in & for said State & County hereby certify that L S Campton and I P Campton whose names are signed to the foregoing conveyance and who are known to me acknowledged before me on this day that being informed of the contents of the conveyance they executed the same voluntarily on the day the same bears date. Given under my hand this the 10 day of December A.D. 1881 A Y Sharpe Notary Public
	Filed for record Nov 3. 1887. James W. Taylor, Judge of Probate
James T Dye Adm To Deed R P Hollis	The State of Alabama } Whereas by an order heretofore Talladega County } made by the Probate Court of said County towit: on the 11th day of May 1886. I James T Dye as the administrator de bonis non cum testamento annex

THIS BOOK IS WRITTEN IN AN EFFORT TO OFFER AN EXPLICIT EXPLANATION TO THE PLIGHT OF AFRICANS FROM AFRICA TO AMERICA. DURING THE YEAR OF SIXTEEN NINETEEN, AND THEIR RESOLVE FROM THAT TIME PARTICULARLY WITH IN THE SOUTHERN STATES.

AND THEIR MIGRATION TO OTHER PARTS OF THE NATION. ALSO THEIR UNPREDICTABLE BEHAVIOR REGARDS TO SELF CONTROL AND INTENSE TURMOILS, BECAUSE DURING AND THE TRANSFORMATION FROM BONDAGE INTO A CIVIL FREE SOCIETY, WAS A RUDE AWAKENING, AND TRAUMATIZING FOR MANY. THE SOCIALISTIC SCARS ARE FOR EVER LASTING FOR MOST AFRICAN AMERICANS, BASED ON INHERITED GENETIC CONTROLLABILITY. WHICH IS A CARRY OVER INTO PRESENT DAY SOCIETY.

THAT IS BEING EXPLOITED FOR POLITICAL ACCOMODATIONS TO ENHANCE BOUNTY. HOWEVER THERE IS NO RECKONING TO JUSTIFY THESE OUTRAGIOUS NONSENSICAL OCCURRENCES. HOWEVER AFRICAN AMERICANS (MUST) STRIVE TO BECOME A INTRICATE PART OF THE RATIFIED LAWS THAT PREVAIL TO A DIVERSE SOCIETY OF PEOPLE, THAT RESIDE AS CITIZENS OF THE UNITED STATES OF AMERICA.

THE CONSTITUTION DID NOT HEAL THE WOUNDS FOR MANY, BUT PROVIDED THE (ONLY) RESOLUTION AVAILABLE THAT GRANTED THE SAME PRIVILEGES AS EQUALITY TO (ALL)

AND IF POLITICALLY UNDERSTOOD AND USED APPROPIATELY, YOU WILL ATTAIN PROSPERITY RELEGATED IN ACCORD TO YOUR•(OWN) AMBITIONS. HOWEVER IF YOU SHOULD (CHOOSE) TO INVEST YOUR ENERGY AND TALENT IN SOME NONSENSICAL HISTORICAL NOTION, THAT THERE IS A DEBT OF GRATITUDE TO BE SETTLED FOR YOUR

ANCESTORS TURMOILS, AND DEVELOP INCONGRUOUS BEHAVIOR PATTERNS THAT IS INCONSISTENT WITH INTELLECTUAL MORAL VALUES, I GOT YOUR BACK BLACK BROTHER, BACK SLAPPING HAND AND FINGER TWISTING, ALSO ADHERING TO THE DEMANDS OF BLACK SELF APPOINTED, LEADERS, THAT DENOUNCE THE PRAGMATIC APPROACH THROUGH EDUCATION AS A FUNDAMENTAL RESOLUTION TO THE MAJORITY OF REBELLIOUS INFLAMED PROBLEMS THAT EXIST WITH MOST AFRICAN AMERICANS FOR ANY SEGMENT OF PEOPLE TO REFRAIN FROM THE THERAPEUTIC AGENDA, OF WHAT THE UNITED STATES OF AMERICA WAS ESTABLISHED ON. AND THE STANDARDS OF THE EXISTING FORMALITIES, BASED ON INDIVIDUAL INTELLECT UNFORTUNATELY DESTITUTION IS INEVITABLE, AND YOU ARE GOING TO BE (WORSE) OFF THAN YOUR ANCESTORS, WITH YOUR FATE BEING DECIDED BY A JUDGE AND JURY.

THERE ARE MANY HIGHLY EDUCATED, SOPHISTICATED, INTELLECTUAL AFRICAN AMERICANS. UNFORTUNATELY SOME HAVE DECIDED TO DEVOTE THEIR ENTIRE LIVES TRYING TO EXPLAIN AWAY THE FAILURE OF OTHERS, WITH ADVERSE RHETORIC FROM THE PAST, TO NO AVAIL.

AND SOME OF THE MOST PATHETIC STATEMENTS ARE DIVULGED AND COMMONLY USED, ARE. THE PLAYING FIELD NEED TO BE LEVELED WITH PRIVILEGES EQUAL TO WHITES. UNFORTUNATELY (NOT) REALIZING THAT APPROXIMATELY SEVENTY PERCENT OF AFRICAN AMERICANS, HAVE ALREADY LEVELED THE PLAYING FIELD FOR THEMSELVES. BASED ON INTELLECT, HARD WORK AND PRINCIPLES. RELATED TO THEIR INDIVIDUAL AMBITIONS TO SUCCEED. CHRONOLOGICAL RECORDS OF SIGNIFICANT EVENTS, DICTATE THIS HAS (ALWAYS) BEEN A CRUSADE FOR MOST ASTUTE AFRICAN AMERICANS AND BECAME MORE PREVALENT AFTER THE RATIFYING OF THE CIVIL AND VOTING RIGHTS ACT AMENDMENT TO THE CONSTUTION DURING NINETEEN SIXTY FOUR AND SIXTY FIVE.

HOWEVER UNFORTUNATELY THERE IS APPROXIMATELY THIRTY PERCENT OF AFRICAN AMERICANS, THAT IS

OBSESSED WITH A DELUSION OF HERDING BEHIND SELF APPOINTED BLACK LEADERS, THAT IS (DISTORTING) REALITY AND INSTIGATING TO THEM WHAT THEY WANT TO HEAR, INSTEAD OF WHAT THEY SHOULD KNOW.

SO AS LONG AS THERE ARE POLITICAL ASPIRATIONS FOR PERSONAL NOTORIETY GAINED THROUGH THIS KIND OF DISTORTED PROPAGANDA. THERE WILL ALWAYS BE A SEGMENTED AUDIENCE OF AFRICAN AMERICANS OBSESSED WITH THIS FAILED AGENDA.

THAT IS DENOUNCED BY THE CONSTITUTION, AND THE JURISDICTION OF LAW ENFORCEMENT, AND THE AUTHORITY OF THE COURTS, PLAYING FIELDS ARE LEVELED BY ONES (OWN) INDIVIDUAL AMBITIONS TO SUCCEED (NOT) BY PROMISES FROM SELF PROCLAIMED POLITICAL ADVOCATES. POLITICAL ASPIRATIONS, AND THE FUNDAMENTAL ADVOCACY TO ENLIGHTEN REGARDS TO HYPERCRITICAL DISTORTION, IS THE FUNDAMENTAL PRINCIPLE FOR THESE WRITINGS.

IN AN EFFORT TO DEFEND ACCURACIES PERTAINING TO TITLE OF BOOK, POLITICAL SELFDESTRUCTION.

I LIST EXAMPLES OF AFRICAN AMERICANS RELATED TO THE SUBJECT. THE PINNACLE OF POLITICAL SUCCESS FOR (REPUBLICAN) AFRICAN AMERICANS BEGAN IN EIGHTEEN SEVENTY FOUR..

WHEN BLANCHE K. BRUCE, WAS ELECTED AS THE FIRST AFRICAN AMERICAN TO SERVE A FULL TERM AS U.S. SENATOR. TWENTY ONE WERE ELECTED TO THE HOUSE OF REPRESENTATIVES, AND THAT WAS THE VERY BEGINNING OF POLITICAL SELF DESTRUCTION RELATED TO AFRICAN AMERICANS. BASED ON CONTEMPT, GREEDAND EXPLOITATION.

WHEN MANY WOULD STROLL INTO THE CHAMBERS WITH BARE FEET, HAVING WHITE WOMEN CLUTCHED AT THEIR SIDES.

UNFORTUNATELY ONE OF THE MOST DEVASTATING ATROCITIES OCCURRED IN EIGHTEEN THIRTY ONE, PERTAINING TO AFRICAN AMERICAN POLITICAL EXPEDIENCY. WHEN NAT TURNER. STAGED A REBELLIOUS

REVOLUTION AGAINST SOUTHERN WHITES IN VIRGINIA AS REPORTED.

THIS WAS ONE OF THE BLOODIEST REVOLTS IN THE HISTORY OF AMERICA. PERPETRATED BY AFRICAN AMERICANS, FOR POLITICAL CONTROL OF OTHERS BY RAIDING, PILLAGING, AND MURDERING WHITES AT THEIR CONVENIENCE. UNFORTUNATELY THERE WERE (DIRE) CONSEQUENCES PERTAINING TO INNOCENT BLACKS, BECAUSE WHITES RETALIATED BY PARADING FROM RICHMOND, THROUGH SOUTHHAMPTON COUNTY, KILLING EVERY AFRICAN AMERICAN IN SIGHT, BY TOTURE, BURNING, AND SHOOTING TO DEATH. ONE HUNDRED AND TWENTY BLACKS WERE SLAUGHTERED IN ONE DAY. ALTHOUGH THIS TRAGEDY WAS ONE HUNDRED AND SEVENTY EIGHT YEARS AGO THE REASONING IS DEEMED TO BE POLITICAL SELF DESTRUCTION, BY SOME RADICAL AFRICAN AMERICANS, DUE TO COMPULSIVE GREED.

WE ARE NOW CURRENTLY INTO THE TWENTY FIRST CENTURY, AND THIS GENETIC STIGMATIZATION IS QUITE PREVALENT AMONG BLACKS IN POLITICS. MINAS WHOLESALE (VIOLENCE)

FOR INSTANCE POLITICAL SELF DESTRUCTION IN RECENT TIMES, REGARDS TO SOME POLITICALLY ASPIRED AFRICAN AMERICANS, (NAMELY)

ERTHA KITT, ENTERTAINER
CAROL MOSELY BRAUN, FORMER U.S. SENATOR
JOYCELYN ELDERS, FORMER SURGEON GENERAL
COLEN POWELL, FORMER SECRETARY OF STATE
MARION BERRY, FORMER MAYOR
WILLIAM JEFFERSON, FORMER CONGRESS MEMBER
JOHN FORD, FORMER STATE SENATOR
RON BROWN, (PRIOR TO HIS DEMISE) COMMERCE SEC.
KAWME KILPATRICK, FORMER MAYOR
CYNTHIA MCKINNEY, FORMER CONGRESS MEMBER
ROLAND BURRIS, U.S. SENATOR
CHARLIE RANGLE, CONGRESS MEMBER
VAN JONES, FORMER GREEN CZAR

(JUST.TO NAME A FEW)

CHRONOLOGICAL RECORDS OF SIGNIFICANT EVENTS, AND THE GENERAL CONSENSUS OF GENETIC HERITAGE, PERTAINING TO AFRICAN AMERICANS, ASSOCIATED WITH THE POLITICAL ARENA, DICTATE THERE (WILL) BE OTHERS TO FOLLOW THIS INEPT AGENDA OF POLITICAL SELF DESTRUCTION (SOON)

POLITICAL ARCHAIC EXCEPT IN POLITIC, HAVING PRACTICAL WISDOM PRUDENT SHREWD DIPLOMATIC, CRAFTY UNSCRUPULOUS, PRUDENTLY OR ARTFULLY CONTRIVED EXPEDIENT, AS A PLAN, ACTION, REMARK ECT, TO ENGAGE IN POLITICAL CAMPAGINING, (VOTEGETTING), ETC. (SUAVE).

SO IT IS QUITE OBVIOUS AS GOD CREATED US TO BE, AND BASED ON INDIVIDUAL CENSUS, WE ARE AFFECTED BY THIS SINGLE WORD ONE WAY OR ANOTHER, EACH AND EVERY DAY OF OUR LIVES, BUT MOSTLY WHEN ASSEMBLED WITH OTHER PEOPLE.

WITH OUT QUESTION THIS IS THE GREATEST COUNTRY ON GODS GLOBE, AND I THINK PRESIDENT JOHN F. KENNEDY, PHRASED IT WITH REMARKABLE LOYAL DIPLOMACY, WHEN HE STATED ASK (NOT) WHAT YOUR COUNTRY CAN DO FOR YOU, BUT WHAT YOU CAN DO FOR YOUR COUNTRY.

THESE WORDS WILL FOR EVER BE A CORNER STONE OF HIS LEGACY, THAT EPITOMOZE THE GLAMOUR OF THE UNITED STATES OF AMERICA. THIS BOOK IS (NOT) ABOUT RACISM IT IS ABOUT PEOPLE GENERALLY EMBROILED IN A STRUGGLE FOR SURVIVAL, AND BASED ON THEIR ABILITY TO VENT INGENUITY FOR NOTORIETY AND PERSONAL GAIN, ALSO MAINTAIN POLITICAL CONTROL OVER OTHERS, THAT IS SUTIABLE FOR THEIR AGENDA OF IDEOLOGY.

I AM HOPEFUL THAT YOU WILL READ AND CONCLUDE BASED ON THE GIST OF (REALITY)

THE EXTENSIVE JOURNEY COMMENCE IN AFRICA, AND IS OPEN ENDED IN THE UNITED STATES OF AMERICA.

SLAVE TRADING BEGAN BETWEEN EUROPE AND AFRICA CENTURIES AGO, IN THE WEST AFRICAN COSTAL NATIONS.

FROM WEST AFRICA TO THE MEDITERRANEAN. THE SENTIMENTS REGARDS TO THE RELATIONSHIP BETWEEN THE TWO COUNTRIES,WAS THE EPITOME OF SLAVE TRADING FOR PROFIT.

GUINEA CONTROLLED THE AFRICAN EUROPEAN TRADE ROUTES, WHICH CONSIST OF OVER THREE HUNDRED MILES OF COAST.

THERE WERE GREAT DEMANDS FOR SLAVES, BECAUSE OF THE SUGAR PLANTATIONS. SLAVES WERE TRADED FOR SUCH GOODS AS GOLD, TEXTILES, IVORY SPOONS, BEADS, BED COVERS, AND GUNS.

SLAVES WERE CAPTURED FROM GUINA TO NIGERIA, WHICH WERE THE TWO MAJOR TRADING PLACES BEFORE THE EUROPEANS WERE INVOLVED IN SLAVE TRADE IN NORTH AND WEST AFRICA, IT HAD BEEN ESTABLISHED AS A ANCIENT INSTUTION BY THEIR OWN PEOPLE. SO MOST AFRICANS UNDERSTOOD SLAVERY.

IN WEST AFRICA THE OWNERSHIP OF HUMAN BEINGS WAS CONSIDERED TO BE MAJOR WEALTH FOR CENTURIES, OWINING AND TRADING SLAVES WAS A COMMODITY AND RICH COMMERCE.

AFRICAN KINGS WERE THE FOUNDERS OF SLAVERY AND OWINING PEOPLE. I SUSPECT THERE ARE MANY AFRICAN AMERICANS, THINK THAT THE WHITE MAN VOYAGED OFF TO AFRICA, ROUNDED UP SOME AFRICANS, PUT THEM ON A SHIP AND BROUGHT TO AMERICA.

(NOT SO) LETS EVALUATE THE POLITICAL PLANNING OF THE CULPRITS, AFRICAN KINGS ESTABLISHED EMPIRES, WHICH THEY WERE SLAVE OWNERS. THEY SELECTED CAPABLE SLAVES TO INVADE OTHER TRIBES. THEIR TITLE WAS SLAVE WARRIORS A SPECIAL ARMED FORCE, THEY WORE LONG BRAIDED HAIR, SOME MATTED THEIR HAIR WITH HUMAN DUNG IN ORDER FOR PLACEMENT, HOWEVER THEIR SOLE RESPONSIBILITY WAS TO RAID OTHER TRIBES, AND CAPTURE OTHER AFRICANS FOR SLAVE TRADE, ALSO

WHAT VALUABLES THEY HAD, ALONG WITH THEIR FAMILIES AND DELIVER THEM TO THE KINGS.

THESE AFRICANS WERE SAVAGE, AND VIOLENTLY ILLITERATE, SOME HAD DEVELOPED TRIBAL CUSTOMS REGARDS TO BRUTAL CAINING UNTIL DEATH, BONES THROUGH THEIR NOSE, DRINKING COWS MILK UNTIL THEIR STOMACH WOULD SPLIT OPEN, AUCTIONING THEIR FAMILY MEMBERS AT AGE TWELVE THROUGH FIFTEEN MOSTLY FEMALES FOR PIGS.. AND CATTLE, SLASHING THEIR BODY WITH SHARP OBJECTS FOR TRIBAL MARKINGS, HERDING LITTLE BOYS AT A CERTIAN AGE INTO GROUPS AND CIRCUMCISING THEM WITH BLADED OBJECTS, SOME TRIBES PRACTICE CANNIBALISM. JUST TO MENTION A FEW UNCIVILIZED ATROCITIES. THIS WAS THE GENETIC HERITAGE INTRODUCED TO AMERICA IN SIXTEEN NINETEEN. (NOT CIVIL EDUCATORS). THE SLAVE WORRIOES JOB WAS FARILY EASY IN RADING OTHER TRIBES, BECAUSE THEY HAD GUNS SUPPLIED BY THE EUROPEANS, THE AFRICAN TRIBSMEN REFUSED TO USE GUNS THEY CONSIDERED THOSE WEAPONS WAS FOR COWARDS, THE WEST COAST OF AFRICA WAS CONTROLLED BY AFRICAN KINGS FOR THE SOLE PURPOSE OF AFRICAN CAPTIVES TO BE SOLD INTO SLAVERY, TO VARIOUS EUROPEAN NATIONS. THEY WERE BROUGHT TO THE SLAVE MARKET YOKED TOGATHER WITH FORKETED YOKES FROM TREE LIMBS. AND HELD IN SLAVE FORTS UNTIL THE BRITISH SLAVE SHIPS ARRIVED. THEY WERE PACKED IN THE BOWELS OF THE SHIP LIKE SARDINES, A VERY INHUMANE METHOD OF HUMAN CARGO. HOWEVER THEY WERE TRANSPORTED TO DIFFERENT PARTS OF THE CONTINENT, TRANSPORTING SLAVES WAS A DANGEROUS BUISNESS, BUT IT WAS SUCH A LUCRATIVE BUISNESS SHIP CAPTIANS WAS WILLLING TO CHANCE IT.

IN THE SEVENTEENTH CENTURY ONE SUCH SHIP WAS COMMANDEERED BY SLAVES THEY KILLED A PORTION OF THE CREW HELD THE CAPTIAN HOSTAGE AND SAILED THE SHIP BACK AND NEGOTIATED THEIR FREEDOM, THERE WERE BRUTAL ATROCITIES OCCURRED AT SEA , MANY AFRICANS LITERALLY COMITTED SUICIDE BASED ON CONDITIONS IN

THE HOLE OF THE SHOP, HUMAN FECES ALL ABOUT , SO WHEN THEY WERE LET ON SHIP DECK THEY JUMPED OVER BOARD, SOME BECAUSE OF THEIR APPREHENSIVE TO BEING INCARCERATED , THERE WERE OTHER ATROCITIES WHERE ONE SLAVE SHIP DELIBERATELY THREW APPROXIMATELY ONE HUNDRED FIFTY TO TWO HUNDRED AFRCANS OVER BOARD BECAUSE OF FOOD SHORTAGES, THESE BARBARIC ACTS OCCURED NOT BECAUSE SOME AFRICANS WERE NEEDED IN AMERICA, THE SLAVE TRADE WAS A LUCRATIVE BUISNESS PRACTICALLY ALL OVER THE WORLD FOR AFRICANS,ALSO OTHER NATIONALLY OF PEOPLE, YOU SEE THE SLAVE TRADERS WERE NOT STUPID PEOPLE, THEY SHIPPED PEOPLE TO POTENTIAL PLACES WHERE THEY WERE MOST ADAPTABLE, FOR INSTANT AFRRICANS WERE SHIPPED TO THE SOUTHERN PART OF AMERICA BASED ON THE PIGMENTATION OF THEIR SKIN TO WITH STAND HEAT, TO WORK THE CAIN AND RICE FIELDS, LATER THE COTTON FIELDS, ALSO THEY WERE IMMUNE TO CERTAIN DISEASES IN THE SOUTH.

THE FIRST AFRICANS ARRIVED AT THE COLONY IN VIRGINIA, THE YEAR SIXTEEN NINETEEN, ABOARD A DUTCH WARSHIP, THE SHIP PORTED IN JAMESTOWN, AFRICANS HAD CAME WITH THE EUROPEANS TO OTHER PARTS OF AMERICA, HOWEVER THIS WAS THE FIRST INTROUDUCTION TO ,THE BRITISH COLONIAL IN NORTH AMERICA, THE SHIP CAPTIAN WAS IN DIRE NEED OF SUPPLIES, SO HE TRADED APPROXIMATELY TWENTY AFRICANS FOR FOOD, AND SUPPLIES, BONDAGE HAS NOW BEGAN IN NORTH AMERICA, SUGARCANE AND SUGAR, WAS THE MAJOR CROP IN PARTS OF LATIN AMERICA, AND THE CARIBBEAN, SO APPROXIMATELY 40% OF ANGOLAN AND CONGOLESE AFRICANS WERE TRANSPORTED THERE TO WORK THE CAIN FIELDS, OPPOSE TO APPROXIMATELY 68% TO THE COLONY OF VIRGINIA, ON THE NORTH AMERICA MAINLAND, THE AFRICANS BROUGHT TO JAMESTOWN WORK LONG HARD HOURS IN THE FIELDS, AND IN THE HOMES OF WHITE VIRGINIANS, THERE WERE WHITE INDENTURED SLAVES, NOT ALL AFRICANS WERE TREATED AS SLAVES, IN SOME

CASES AFRICANS SERVED IN SPECIFIED RESPONSIBILITY, AS MUCH AS THEIR WHITE COUNTERPART DID.

AFTER A NUMBER YEARS SERVED, THEY WERE RELEASED FROM BONDAGE, FOR THEIR SERVICES MOST WERE AWARDED FORTY TO FIFTY ACRES OF LAND OVER A PEROID OF TIME SOME INCREASED THEIR LAND HOLDINGS TO TWO THREE HUNDRED ACRES OR MORE.

SOME ACCUMULATED ENOUGH WEALTH TO OWN SLAVES THEM SELVES. SLAVERY WAS A VERY EXTREME COMPLEX ISSURE, SIMPLY BECAUSE YOU ARE DEALING WITH PEOPLE THAT ARE PREDOMINANTLY ILLITERATE, AS A RESULT THEY GAMBLE, BOOZE, AND WAS POLITICALLY CHEATED OUT OF THEIR LAND, ONCE THAT HAPPENED SOME WOULD PLAN A INTEGRATED EXCAPE WHEN THEY WERE APPREHENDED THEIR PUNISHMENT WAS TO SERVE THEIR MASTERS FOR LIFE. DUE TO INEPTNESS, MOST BLACKS CREATED (SELF) DILEMMAS. HOWEVER SLAVE MASTERS OFTEN MARRIED AFRICAN WIVES, AND USED SOME AS MISTRESSES, THERE WERE TIMES HE WAS INVOLVED WITH MORE THAN ONE WIFE OR MISTRESS, FREEDOM WAS GRANTED TO A LOT OF THOSE AFRICAN WOMEN, ALONG WITH LAND, AND THEY BECAME SLAVE OWNERS THEM SELVES THE ESTABLISHED DUTCH WEST INDIA COMPANY HELD AFRICAN SLAVES IN NEW AMSTERDAM, WHICH CONSTITUTED A FLEXIABLE SYSTEM LABELED HALF FREE BONDAGE, UNDER THIS SYSTEM AFRICANS COULD PAY A YEARLY TAX AND LIVE INDEPENDENTLY OF THEIR MASTERS, UNDER THIS AGREEMENT THEY WERE REQUIRED TO REPORT TO THE COMPANY WHEN CALLED IN THE NEW NETHERLAND, AFRICANS COULD OWN PROPERTY, PERSUE TRADES AND EVEN INTERMARRY WITH WHITES.

DURING THE LATE SIXTEEN HUNDREDS, COMPASSIONATE BEHAVIOR BETWEEN WHITES, AND AFRICAN SLAVES WAS CAUSE FOR CONCERN , COLOINAL VIRGINIA, AUTHORITIES FORMULATED REGULATIONS TO RESTRICT CERTIAN INVOLMENTS UNDER TRADITIONAL ENGLISH LAW, WHERE A CHILD TOOK THE FATHERS STATUS, VIRGINIA CHANGED THE LAW, IN ORDER TO ALLOW STATUS THROUGH LINE

^MATERIAL, BASED ON UNIONS BETWEEN AFRICAN SLAVE WOMEN AND THEIR WHITE MASTERS, MEANING ANY CHILD PRODUCED BY THE SLAVE MASTER, THE CHILD WOULD CONTINUE TO BE A SLAVE IN LINE. THEY ALSO ATTEMPTED TO DISCOURAGE INTERRACIAL MARRIAGE RELATIONSHIP, THERE ALSO WERE LAWS STIPULATING ANY ANY WHITE WOMAN MARRYING AN AFRICAN SLAVECOULD BE FORCED TO SERVE HER HUSBAND MASTER FOR ETERNITY, IN THE EARLY SEVENTEEN HUNDREDS MASSACHUSETTS BANDED INTERRACIAL MARRIAGE, STIPULATING THAT ANY AFRICAN SLAVE DISOBEYING THE ORDER WOULD BE FLOGGED, AND SOLD OUTSIDE INTO SLAVERY OUTSIDE THE COLONY, WHITE MEN WERE TO BE FLOGGED,, FINED, AND ANY CHILDREN PRODUCED FROM THE RELATIONSHIP WOULD BE HIS SOLE RESPONSIBILITY.

WHITE WOMEN WERE TO BE FLOGGED AND BOUND INTO INDENTURE. THEIR CONCERNS REGARDS TO INTERRAICAL SEXUAL BEHAVIOR IT MIGHT COMPLICATE RACIAL DEFINITIONS, UNFORTUNATELY THESE LAWS DID NOT SERVE AS A DETERENT.

LATE IN THE SIXTEEN CENTUARY, AN ALLIANCE BETWEEN AFRICAN SLAVES AND WHITES, FORMED A REBELLION TO APPROPRIATE NATIVE AMERICANS LAND IN WESTERN VIGINIA, THEY BURN THE COLONIAL CAPITAL, THE GOVERNOR WAS REPELLED FROM HIS RESIDENT, THE GROUP OF INVADERS WERE LABELED CRIMINALS, EIGHT OR NINETY AFRICAN SLAVES AND TWENTY OR THIRTY WHITES PARTICIPATED IN THAT REBELLION. THE VIRGINIA MOLITIA WAS CALLED ON AND THEIR PLOT WAS SOON ELIMINATED.

IN THE MID SEVENTEENTH CENTURY MORE THAN ONE HUNDRED AFRICAN SLAVES STAGED A REBELLION, SOME OF THOSE SLAVES WERE KONGOLESE SOLDIERS CAPTURED IN CENTRAL AFRICA IN BATTLE. AND BRAUGHT TO SOUTH CAROLINA, THEIR LEADER HAD MILITARY SRILLS FROM THE KONGO IN AFRICA,

HE PLANNED THEIR STRATEGIES, THEY BROKE INTO STORES CONFISCATED GUNS, AND AMMUNITION, KILLING SHOPKEEPERS IN THE PROCESS, THEY MARCHED

IN MILITARY RANKS, THEY CARRIED FLAGS , AND BEAT DRUMS. THE AUTHORITES OF SOUTH CAROLINA CALLED OUT THE MILITIA AND THEIR FATE DEATH, BY THE LATE SEVENTEENTH CENTURY THE POPULATION OF AFRICAN SLAVES INCREASED DRAMATICALLY, MANY OF THE AFRICANS CAME FROM DIFFERENT ETHNIC GROUPS, A LOT OF THEM SPOKE DIFFERENT LANGUAGES, THE REBELLION OCCURED IN SOUTH CAROLINA SPREAD LIKE WILDFIRE.

SOON AFTER A REBELLION AROSE IN NEWYORK CITY, AFRICAN SLAVES AND AND INDIANS, SET FIRES AND KILLED A NUMBER OF WHITES, THE AUTHORITIES CAPTURED THE REBELS, THEY WERE TORTURED AND HANGED, OTHERS WERE BURNED AT THE STEAK, AFRICAN SLAVES AND WHITES WERE SCREAMING FOR THEIR FREEDOM.

IN THE INTREM LAWS WERE BEING LEGISLATED IN ATTEMPT TO PROVENT THIS KIND OF BARBARIC BEHAVIOR.

UNFORTUNATELLY THE VIOLENCE PERSISTED, IN THE EARLY EIGHTEEN HUNDREDS THERE WAS ANOTHER UPRISING AFRICAN SLAVES FORMED A MAKESHIFT MILITARY, BEATING DRUMS, BURNING PLANTATIONS, MOVING THROUGH THE COUNTRYSIDE KILLING WHITES, THE STATE MILITIA WAS CALLED ON TO HALT THE UPRISING, AT LEAST SEVENTY TO EIGHTY AFRICAN SLAVES WERE KILLED, SOME OF THEIR BODYS WERE BEHEADED, PLACED ON POLES ALONG THE MISSISSIPPI RIVER, WHITES WERE ON THE ALERT, WITH HIGH ANXIETY, THERE WERE SOME WHITES INVOLVED IN THIS SCHEME, THEY SUPPLIED GUNS AND AMMUNITION TO THE INSURGENTS, THEY WERE FINALLY CAUGHT, AND THEIR FATE WAS PRISON, AFTERWARDS CITIZENS ARMED THEMSELVES TO PROTECT THEIR LIVES AND PROPERTY, HOWEVER DURING ALL THE VIOLENCE SOME PROGRESS WERE MADE, THE FIRST AFRICAN AMERICAN NEWS PAPER BOURN, (THE FREEDONS JOURNAL) DURING THIS TIME AFRICAN AMERICANS REJECTED THE TERM AFRICAN, THEY OPPOSED THAT TERMINOLOGY, THEY JUST WANTED TO BE CALLED AMERICANS, SO THE NAME WAS CHANGED TO COLORED AMERICANS, AROUND THIS TIME SUGAR PROFITS ESCALATED STATEHOOD WAS GRANTED TO LOUISIANA, IN 1812. MISSISSIPPI, IN 1817. ALABAMA, IN 1819. THE SLAVE TRADE WAS SERGING INTO TENNESSEE, AND KENTUCKY, SLAVE TRADEING IN THE SOUTH WAS A LUCRATIVE BUISNESS, SOME WHITES BECAME EXTREMELY WEALTHY, HOWEVER CONTROVERSY AROSE REGARDS TO THE BALANCINGACT OF THE TWENTY TWO STATES, ELEVEN FREE STATES, AND ELEVEN SLAVE STATES, THERE WAS A DEBATE IN CONGRESS REGARDS TO BOUNDRY, BETWEEN FUTURE SLAVE STATES , AND FREE STATES, SLAVERY WAS NOT TO EXCEED NORTH OF THE MISSOURI, SOUTHERN BORDER.

THOMAS JEFFERSON, RELUCTANT TO ENDORSE THIS POLICY HE LABELED IT A POWDER KEG, UNFORNATELY THE SOUTHERN SLAVEHOLDERS WON THAT ROUND , BASED ON INCREASING PROFITS FROM COTTON, WHICH INSTITUTED GREAT POLITICAL POWER FOR THE SLAVEHOLDERS, SO AS A RESULT THE THE SLAVE TRADE FLOURISHED, SOME SLAVEHOLDERS FELT SOME GUILT BY THE INHUMANE WAY FAMILES AND THEIR MARRIAGES WERE BROKEN UP, OTHRS ARGUED THAT IT WAS A TRADITION FROM AFRICA, SO IT REALLYDIDNTMATTERTHATMUCH,CHRISTIANMORALITY CAME INTO QUESTION PERTAINING TO MARRIAGE OF SLAVES, BASED ON MORALITY AND IMMORALITY THE BAPTIS ASSOCIATION DEBATED THIS DILEMMA, THE CHURCH ELDERS DECIDED THAT IF A OLD MARRIAGE WAS BROKEN BY SALE, THEY ENTERATED IT WOULD BE EQUIVALENT TO DEATH, THUS A NEW MARRIAGE WAS ACCEPTABLE IN THE SIGHT OF GOD, THIS WAS A POLITICAL PLOY BECAUSE SOUTHERN LAWS DID NOT RECOGNIZE SLAVE MARRIAGES ANY WAY. HOWEVER ON SOUTHRN PLANTATIONS THE RELATIONSHIP BETWEEN MASTERS AND SLAVES WERE CORDIAL EVEN FAMILY LIKE MOST OF THE TIME, THE PLANTATIONS WERE A ORGANIZED BUISNESS, RAN BY SLAVE MASTERS AND SLAVE DRIVERS, SLAVES HAD THEIR OWN PRIVATE QUARTERS, THEY ALL HAD CHOSEN RESPONSIBILITIES, SOME WORKED IN THE MASTERS HOME WITH CHORES OF CLEANING, COOKING, AND TENDING THEIR MASTERS CHILDREN, MANY MANY TIMES AS THE CHILDREN GREW OLDER, THEY TAUGHT MANY SLAVES TO READ AND WRITE, ALSO THE ADULT WHITE FEMALES WERE INSTRUMENTAL! THEIR LEARNING, SOME TIME ON WEEKENDS THE WOMEN WOULD GO TO THE SLAVE QUARTERS AND TEACH READING AND WRITING, THERE ALSO WERE OTHER CHORES, SUCH AS TAKING CARE OF THE COTTON FIELDS, WATCHINNG AND TAKING CARE OF THE DIFFERENT ANIMALS.

WITH OUT A DOUBT SOUTHERN WHITE CULTURE WAS SHAPED BY THE RELATIONSHIP THEY HAD WITH THEIR PLANTATION SLAVES, SOME OF THE SLAVES WORKED WELL WITH THEIR HANDS, CULTIVATING THE SOIL, SOME

WERE CAPENTERS, BUILDING HOMES IN COMMUNITIES, BASED ON THEIR SKILLS AND THEIR LOYALTY, SOME WERE GIVEN THEIR OWN LAND, ON CONDITION THEY WOULD CONTINUE TO ASSIST WITH THE PLANTATION CHORES, WHAT PROFITS THEY MADE ON THE GIVEN LAND THEY WERE ALLOWED TO KEEP FOR THEMSELVES AND THEIR FAMILES, THE SLAVE POPULATION GREW AT AN ALARMING RATE, UNRELATED SLAVES WERE RAPIDLY FORMING FAMILIES, THIS WAS MOSTLY DUE TO THE DEBACLE SLAVE TRADE IN TENNESSEE. THE SLAVE POPULATION GREW AT AN ALARMING RATE.

RELATED TO FREE AFRICAN AMERICANS, AND SLAVES, REGARDS TO THEIR BUISNESS INVOLVEMENTS WERE CIRCUMSCRIBED BY SLAVERY IN THE SOUTH, ALSO THEIR BUISNESS ORGANIZATION KNODLEDGE, HOWEVER IN THE NORTH IT DID EXIST, FALLING INTO CATEGORIES, ONE GROUP COMPOSED OF OF THE FREE AFRICAN AMERICAN, WHO ACCUMILATED SUFFICIENT CAPIAL TO SET UP BUISSNESSES, AND THE OTHER COMPRISED OF SLAVES THROUGH THRIFT INDURSTY NATIVE INTELLIGENCE, AND SOMETIMES THE LIBERAL PATERNALISM OF THEIR MASTERS,THEY MANAGED TO DEVELOP SMALL BUISNESSES, THEIR GREATEST SUCCESS WERE MAINLY LABOR, ILLITERACY UNFORNATELLY WAS A GRAVE HANDICAP, HOWEVER THEY WERE DETERMINE TO UTILIZE WHAT SKILLS THEY HAD TO EMBRACE THE FABRIC OF AMERICA, JUST TO ELABORATE ON A FIEW OF THEIR SKILLS, THERE WERE MACHANICS RESTURANT AND HOTEL OPERATORS, BARBERS, ON A SMALL SCALE THEY MANUFACTURED BOOTS, SHOES, CLOTHING, TAILORING, PICKLE MAKING, BED MANUFACTURING, CATERING, SALE MAKING, LUMBER, ALSO COAL, SOME WERE INDIVIDUAL THINKERS, THEY APPLIED THEIR SKILLS TO INVENTIONS, SUCH AS RAZOR STROPS, THE COTTON GIN, STRAIGHTENING COMBS, SOME WORKED AS APPRENTICES IN TAILORING SHOPS, AND TAUGHT THEMSELVES TO READ AND RITE, WITH HELP FROM OTHERS, AND BECAME SUCCESSFUL BUISNESS PEOPLE IN THE NORTHERN STATES, SOME FREE AFERICAN AMERICANS WERE COLLEGE EDUCATED THEY ORGANIZED

BANKS, AND OPENED CEMETERYS FOR THE GENERAL PUBLIC, IN THE NORTHERN STATES, SOME REVOLUTIONIZED THE SOUTHERN ARGILUCTURE, BY UTILIZING RAW MATERIALS SUCH AS, PEANUTS, SWEET POTATOES, SOYBEANS, AND RED CLAY, TO PRODUCE BLEACH, SHAMPOO, FLOUR, OIL, COFFEE, AND HOUSE PAINT, BY THE WAY LETS NOT FORGET THE ONES THAT PARTICIPATED IN THE UNDER GROUND SLAVE MOVEMENT.

THESE INDIVIDUAL PEOPLE WERE TRAIL BLAZING PIONEERS, EMBEDED INTO THE FABRIC OF THIS GREAT COUNTRY CALLED AMERICA, THESE.GREAT-PEOPLE CAME UNDER THE HEADING OF ASK NOT WHAT YOUR YOUR COUNTRY CAN DO FOR YOU, BUT WHAT YOU CAN DO FOR YOUR COUNTRY, THEIR AGENDA WAS TO BE SUCCESSFUL, NOT TO BE NONSENSICAL MISGUIDED BY TRIBAL THINKING, REGARDS TO POLITICS, WHICH RELATES TO POVITY , FOR A LARGE MAJORITY OF MINORITES.

HOWEVER DURING THE EIGHTEENTH CENTURY,THERE WAS TRAGITY LOOMING OVER THE HORIZON, ANTISLAVERY SENTIMENT WAS BECOMING STRONGER, IN THE NORTHERN STATES, TAKING ON A RADICAL TONE, FREE AFRICAN AMERICANS, IN BOSTON ESTABLISHED A ABOLITIONIST GROUP LABELED THE MASSACHUSETTS GENERAL COLERED ASSOCIATION PROCLAMATION TO FIGHT FOR THE IMMEDIATE END TO SLAVERY, IN THE NATION, ONE AFRICAN AMERICAN FROM A SOUTHERN STATE HAD RECENTLY MOVED TO BOSTON, HE ADDRESSED THE ASSOCIATION, SOME OF HIS REMARKS EXACERBATED SOUTHERN FEARS, HIS REMARKS WERE VIOLENT AND MILITIANT STATEMENTS, WHICH WERE DIRECTED AT WHITES, REGARDS TO THEIR ASSERTIONS BASED ON INFERIORITY, SOME OF HIS INSIDIOUS REMARKS . WERE TO ATTACK AFRICAN AMERICAN COLONIZATION AND CLAIM THEIR RIGHTS AS AMERICANS, HE STATED WE MUST STAND AS ONE HE COMMANDED THE SLAVE MASTERS WILL HAVE TO BEAT US FROM OUR COUNTRY AMERICA, THIS COUNTRY BELONG TO US, NOT THE WHITE MAN, HE STATED THIS COUNTRY IS ENRICHED WITH OUR BLOOD AND TEARS, HE SAW WHITE AND BLACK SPIRITS ENGAGED BATTLE, THE

SUN DARKEN, THUNDER ROLLED IN THE HEAVEN, AND BLOOD FLOWED IN THE RIVERS, HE BELIEVED IT WAS A SIGN OF GOD.

THEN THE REBELS COMMENCED THEIR ATTACK RAIDING PLANTATIONS ONE AFTER ANOTHER, KILLING ALL WHITE IN THE HOUSEHOLD TAKING GUNS AND AMMUNITION,AND FREEING OTHER SLAVES, TO JOIN THEIR REBELLION THE CONFISCATED, HORSES, GUNS, SWORDS, AND AXES, THEY RAUTED ONE SMALL WHITE MILITIA GROUP, BUT OTHER WHITES REINFORCEMENT FROM THE THE TOWN PREVALED, TO HALT THIS SLAUGHTER, THE LEADER OF THE REBEL GROUP AND A FIEW OTHERS TOOK TO REFUGE IN THE SWAMPY WOODS, HOWEVER THERE WAS A HEAVY PRICE TO PAY FOR THE PLANTATION SLAVES, BECAUSE APPROXIMATELY SEVENTY OR EIGHTY WHITES WERE KILLED, OTHER WHITES WERE STUNNED BY THE MAGNITUDE OF THIS REBELLION, THEY BEGAN TO TAKE REPRISAL ON INNOCENT SLAVES, BECAUSE THIS WAS THE BLOODIEST REVOLT IN AMERICAN HISTORY, AT THAT TIME, ALL SLAVES PAID A ASTRONOMICAL PRICE WITH THEIR LIVES, MOST SLAVES WERE INNOCENT, BUT THEY WERE TORTURED, BURNED TO DEATH, SHOT, BRUTALLY MURDERED IN EVERY FASHION, IN ONE DAY OVER ONE OR TWO HUNDRED SLAVES WERE SLAUGHTED, WHITE INDIVIDUALS WERE ELATED EVEN BRAGGED ABOUT THE NUMBERS KILLED,THROUGH OUT THE COUNTRY SIDE FREE AFRICAN AMERICANS AND SLAVES WOULD BE ASKED IF THEY AROUND THE AREA ON THAT DAY IF THEIR ANSWER WAS YES THEY WERE SHOT DEAD, THE SOUTHERN WHITES ATTEMOTED COLONIZATION, TO PROVENT FURTHER REBELLION, THEY WERE LITERALLY FILLED WITH FEAR,SOME WHITE WOMEN PETITION THE LEGISLATURE EXPRESSING CONCERN CLAMING KNOWING THEIR LOVE ONES WERE NOT SAFE, THAT THEIR RESPONSIBILITY REGARDS TO THEIR DUTY HAD BEEN HALTED, AS A RESULT HEAVY RESTRICTIONS WERE PLACED SLAVES, THE LEGISLATURE PASSED A NUMBER OF MEASURES TO ADDRESS THE FEARS OF THE WHITES, EVEN CONSIDERED THE REMOVAL OF ALL SLAVES FROM THE STATE HOWEVER

THAT PROGNOSIS WAS SUSPENDED INDEFINITELY, AFTER THE VIOLENT ATTACK ON SLAVES BY WHITES THE REVOLT BY SLAVES WAS REMOTE, HOWEVER ADDITIONAL CONTROL LAWS WERE IMPLEMENTED, SUCH AS A PASS SYSTEM THAT REQUIRED SLAVES TO CARRY WRITTEN PERMISSION TO MOVE ABOUT, SLAVES WERE FORBIDDEN TO GATHER , PREACHERS WERE PROHIBITED FROM MOVING ABOUT TO PREACH, THEY WERE BARRED FROM HOLDING RELIGOUS SERVICE OR MEETING AT NIGHT, MASTERS PROHIBITED TEACHING SLAVES TO READ OR WRITE, MASTERS AND THEIR MALE FAMILY MEMBERS BECAME MORE AGRESSIVE TO ALL FEMALE SLAVES, REGARDS TO SUBMISSION, WHITES PARTICIPATED IN SLAVE CONTROL GUARD THE CONSTITUTION GUARANTEED SLAVEHOLDERS THE RIGHT TO HUMAN PROPERTY, ALSO ANY UPRISING WOULD BE EXTINGUISHED BY LOCAL EHITE VOLUNTEERS, OR THE UNITED STATES MILITARY, WEEKS LATER THE AUTHORITIES APPREHENDED THE MILITANT LEADER THAT INITIATED THAT WHOLE DEBACLE OF MURDERING WHITES, THEY TRIED HIM, FOUND HIM GUILTY , AND HE WAS HANGED, A CROUD GATHERSD INCLUDING SLAVES, AFTER HANGING HIS BODY WAS SKINNED AND DISSECTED, AND PASSED OUT PORTIONS OF HIS BODY PARTS FOR SOUVENIRS, FOR THE ACCASION .

THE SKIN WAS TANNED TO MAKE PERSES AND SHOES, THE BONES WERE CARVED INTO TROPHIES, FOR SOUTHERN FAMILYS HEIRLOOMS, I WOULD SUSPECT THIS HORRIFYING ACT HAUNTED PEOPLE IN THAT AERA ESPECIALLLY WHITES FOR YEARS.

AFTER A WHILE THINGS STARTED TO NORMALIZE ON THE PLANTATIONS, THE WHITE FAMILIES BEGAN TO VISIT THE SLAVE QUARTERS AGAINFTHE,SLAVES THE SLAVES WOULD DANCE AND PUT ON A SHOW, THE OLDER SLAVES WOULD SHOUT OUT GOD BLESS YOU MISSA YOU FEED US AND CLOTHE US , YOU SEE THAT WE ARE NURSED WHEN WE ARE SICK, WHEN WE ARE TO OLD WE DONT HAVE TO WORRY ABOUT ANYTHING, YOU TAKE OF US, IT IS WELL UNDERSTOOD THE ELDERS OF THE SLAVE QUARTERS WERE

CONSIDERED TO BE THE WISE MEN, SOME EVEN PRACTICE WITCH CRAFT, THEIR POLITICAL AGENDA WAS STRICKLY TO CONTROL THE HERD OF SLAVES, THEIR NONSENSICAL VIEW WAS DO NOT LEARN TO READ AND WRITE BECAUSE THAT WAS EDUCATION, AND IF YOU WERE EDUICATED THE MASSA MEANING MASTER WOULD THINK YOU WERE A SMART NIGGER, AND THEY WOULD NOT FEED AND CLOTHE YOU AND GIVE YOU A PLACE TO STAY, SO FORGET ABOUT THAT READING AND RITEING BUISNESS, THE MASTERS RULED THE PLANTATION, THEY HAD HEROM OF WOMEN TO CHOOSE FROM, SLAVE WOMEN HAD NO CHOICE BUT TO SUBMIT TO THEIR MASTERS, SOME OF THEIR WIVES KNEW OF THEIR SEXUAL LIASONS WITH SLAVE WOMEN BUT IN THOSE TIMES THE MASTERS RULED. THE WIVES WOULD ACCEPT THE FACT THAT THEIR HUSBANDS HAD FATHERED ILLEGITIMATE CHILDREN BY SLAVE WOMEN, IN THE MID EIGHTEENTH CENTURY SLAVE MASTERS ORGANIZED HIERARCHY IN ORDER FOR BETTER CONTROL HE HAND PICKED LOYAL MALE SLAVES, SUPPLIED THEM WITH HIGH BOOTS, AND A WHIP, THEY WERE CALLED SLAVE DRIVERS, THEY KEPT THE OTHER SLAVES IN LINE, SOME TIME THEY WERE SO BRUTAL TO OTHER SLAVES THE MASTER WOULD CHASTISE THEM, THEY WERE THE EYES AND EARS. UNDER THE SLAVE DRIVER AUTHORITY, THE FARMS WERE CULTIVATED IN UNISON, MOST EVERY CHORE WAS PERFORMED IN UNISON, CHOPPING COTTON HOEING COTTON, PICKING COTTON, GATHERING SUGAR CANE, HARVESTING CORN, THIS WAS SUCH A COMMON PRACTICE UNTIL THE SLAVE MASTERS CALLED IT HERDING.

SLAVERY WAS A WAY OF LIFE, WEATHER YOU AGREE OR NOT, IT WAS SOME WHAT RELAXED IN THE NORTHERN STATES, BUT WERE AGGRESSIVELY PURSUED IN THE DEMOCRATIC CONFEDERACY SOUTHER STATES, SIMPLY BECAUSE OF THE LUCRATIVE GROTH OF COTTON ON THE PLANTATIONS, WHICH REQUIRED LARGE HERDS OF PEOPLE TO MAINTAIN, IT IS A VERY DISTINCT POSSIBILITY SLAVERY WOULD NOT HAVE EXISTED IN AMERICA IF NOT FOR MASS GROUP OF PEOPLE NEEDED TO FARM THE PLANTATIONS, OF SUGAR CAIN, RICE AND WHEAT, AND THE LARGEST

COMMODITY OF ALL IN THE SOUTH, COTTON, PROFITS WERE SO GREAT UNTIL POLITICAL POWER LEGISLATED LAWS THROUGH FEDERAL AND STATE TO ENHANCE THE PLANTATION MASTERS INHERENT POWER OVER THEIR SLAVES, IN ORDER TO EFFECTIVELY MAINTAIN THIS VALUABLE COMMODITY, SO BASED ON THAT POLITICAL AGENDA, GREED, ILLITERACY, TORTURE, MURDER, MOLESTATION, ASSASSINATIONS, BETRAYAL, INEPTITUDE, WERE ESCUALATED TO THE HIGHEST LEVEL, LATS DEFINE THE CLEVER THINKING OF THE SLAVE MASTERS, COTTON WAS THEIR MAIN SOURCE OF FINANCIAL SURVIVAL, THEY WERE TO SLAVE LABOR AND WOULD STOP AT NOTHING TO KEEP IT.

SO WITH THEIR HUGE PROFITS FROM PLANTATION COTTON THEY CORRUPTED POLITICAL OFFICIALS, EVEN PRESIDENTS, TO STRENGTHEN THEIR HOLD ON SLAVERY, ONCE ACCOMPLISHED THEY POLITICIZED THEIR PLANTATIONS SLAVES WITHOUT THE SLAVES BEING AWARE OF THE INTENT.

FOR INSTANT THE SLAVE DRIVERS WERE THE MOST IMPORTANT TO HIM BECAUSE OF THEIR LOYALTY AND DECEITFUL MANNERISM THEY TILD EVERY YHING THAT TRANSPIRED AMONG THE OTHER SLAVES, ALSO THE SLAVE DRIVERS DELEGATED AUTHORITY TO THE ELDERS OF THE HERD, SOME WERE WITCH DOCTERS, THAT PRACTICED HEALING AND DELIVERING BABIES, DEPENDING ON THE SIZE OF THE HERD , DETERMINED HOW MANY DRIVERS WERE NEEDED, THE DRIVERS FROM TIME TO TIME WERE INSTRUTED TO BRING MISTRESSES AT HIS COMMAND, ALSO COMMUNICATE TO THE ELDERS THAT EDUCATION WAS NOT NECESSARY BECAUSE HE WOULD ALWAYS BE THERE FOR THEM, THE STRATEGY WAS IF YOU CANT READ AND WRITE YOUR CHANCES OF ESCAPE IS ALMOST NIL.

BY THE WAY HERD WAS COMMONLY USED BY THE MASTERS, THE NEWLY FORMED REPUBLICAN CONGRESS SAUGHT TO HALT WESTERN TERRITORIES FROM EXPANDING SLAVERY, BASED ON A SLAVE SEEKING HIS FREEDOM, THE CASE HEARD BY THE SUPREME COURT, THEY RULED SEVEN

OUT OF NINE IN FAVOR OF MAINTAINING SLAVERY, THE CHIEF JUSTICE READ OPINION, HE STATED THAT CONGRESS HAD ON NO AUTHORITY TO EXCLUDE SLAVERY FROM THE TERRITORIES, DECLARING THAT AFERICAN AMERICANS WERE NOT, HAVE NEVER BEEN, AND COULD NEVER BE AMERICAN CITIZENS, AND HAD NO RIGHT UNDER UNDER THE CONSTITUTION EQUAL TO THE WHITE MAN.

COTTON HAD BECAME THE MOST VALUABLE EXPORT IN AMERICA, NOTHING WAS MORE VALUABLE THAN COTTON, COTTON TRANSLATED INTO POLITICAL SOUTHERN POLITICAL POWER, THE SLAVE MASTERS AND THEIR SYMPATHIZERS CONTROLLED THE SUPREME COURT, AND A MAJORITY OF THE COMMITTIES IN CONGRESS, AND A STRONG SUPPORT FROM THE PRESIDENT. HOWEVER MOST OF THE SOUTHERN BUREAUCRATS FELT UNEASY THEY SENSED THEIR WAY OF LIFE REGARDS TO SLAVERY COULD BE THREATENED, THEY STARTED TO DISCUSS THE POSSISSIBILITY OF A INDEPENDENT NATION. IN THE INTERIM A GROUP OF INTIGRATED VIGILANTES WERE RAMPAGING THROUGH THE COUNTRY SIDE FREEING SLAVES, HOWEVER THE WHITE LEADER WAS CAUGHT AND EXECUTED FOR TREASON, TENSIONS WERE RUNNING EXTREMELY HIGH DURING THIS TIME, PRESIDENTAL ELECTIONS WERE IN FULL BLOOM, THE YEAR WAS EIGHTEEN SIXTY, FOR SOME REASON THE CONFEDERATE DEMOCRATICS FROM THE DEEP SOUTH, HELD THEIR CONVENTION CHARLESTON ALL OF A SUDDEN SOME WALKED OUT, OTHERS MOVE THEIR CONVENTION TO BALTIMORE, THE DEMOCRATS WERE IN DISARRAY, THEY SPLIT THE PARTY AND FORMED ANOTHER, WHICH THEY CALLED THE UNION PARTY, THAT NOMINATED JOHN BELL, FOR THEIR CANIDATE, THE DEMOCRATS SETTLED FOR STEPHEN A. DOUGLAS, THE REPUBLICANS NOMINATED ABRAHAM LINCOLN, DURING THE PRESIDENTAL ELECTION ONLY THE REPUBLICANS OPPOSED SLAVERY AND CONDEMMED THE EXPANSION, THE THE DEMOCRATS TOOK THE RADICAL SOUTHERN VIEW, UNLESS SLAVERY BE CONTINUED SECESSION MOST LIKE WOULD PREVAIL, THE UNION PARTY, WAS A LITTLE MORE MODERATE, EXCISING SOME COMPROMISE

WITH THE SOUTH REGARDS TO PROTECTING SLAVERY, THERE WERE APPROXIMATELY ONE HALF MILLION FREE AFERICAN AMERICANS, IN AMERICA, THEIR SUPPORT FOR THE REPUBLICAN PARTY WAS OVERWHELMING, THE DEMOCRATS VERBALLY ATTACKED THE SOON TO BE PRESIDENT LINCOLN, WITH AN ATTEMPT TO SMEAR CHARACTER, IMPUGN HIS INTEGORTY, SPOUT OUT DEROGATORY REMARKS LIKE BLACK PRESIDENT, NIGGER LOVER, AND THREATENED THAT HE WOULD PAY THE PRICE IF SLAVERY WAS ABOLISHED, THEIR FEARS WERE IF HE WAS ELECTED TO BE PRESIDENT, SLAVERY WOULD BE ABOLISHED. PRIOR TO BECOMING PRESIDENT WHILE IN THE LEGISLATURE, LINCOLN DENOUCED SLAVERY, SOME OF HIS STATEMENTS WERE SLAVE MASTERS, GOVERNS THEIR SLAVES WITHOUT THEIR CONCENT,THEIR RULES ALTOGETHER IS DIFFERENT FROM THOSE PRESCRIBED FOR THEM SELVES.

ABRAHAM LINCOLN, WAS NEVER A SUPPORTER OF SLAVERY, ANY TIME IN HIS ENTIRE LIFE, POLITICS HAD NOTHING TO DO WITH HIS LOYALTY TO MEN BEING FREE TO CONTROL THEIR OWN DESTINY REGARDS TO INDIVIDUAL LIFE, THESE IDEALS WAS LONG EMBEDED IN HIS SOLE,BEFORE HIS PRESIS DENCY, HE WAS A SUCCESSFUL ATTORNEY, PARTLY SELF TAUGHT ALONG WITH FORMAL SCHOOLING, BEFORE HIS POLITICAL CAREER AS A CONGRESSMAN HE WAS BELONG TO THE PARTY OF THE WHIGS, BEFORE HELPING FORM THE REPUBLICAN PARTY, AND BECOMING A MEMBER, HE ONCE STATED IN 1858, THE REPUBLICAN PARTY HOLD THAT THIS GOVERNMENT WAS INSTUTED TO SECURE THE BLESSING OF FREEDOM, AND SLAVERY IS AN UNQUALIFIED EVIL TO ALL MEN, TO THE SOIL, AND STSTES, AND THERE IS NO REASON IN THE WORLD WHY AFRICAN AMERICANS, SHOULD NOT BE ENTILED TO ALL THE NATURAL RIGHTS ENUMERATED IN THE DECLARATION OF INDPENDENCE, THE RIGHT TO LIFE LIBERTY, AND THE PERSUIT OF HAPPINESS, AND HE HELD THAT THHEY ARE AS MUCH ENTILED TO THESE RIGHTS AS THE WHITE MAN, LINCOLN AND HIS COLLEAGUES

DEPLORED SLAVERY, HE ALSO STATED WHERE THERE IS SLAVERY THERE AS NO HOPE,IN THE SOUTH IT WAS A FIXED CONDITION, WHICH PREVENTED THE SLAVES FROM EATING THE FOOD THEY GREW AND HARVESTED WITH THEIR OWN HANDS SLAVERY NOT ONLY BESMIRCHED THE IDEALS OF THE DECLARATION, BUT VIOLATED PRINCPLES OF SELF HELP, SOCIAL MOBILITY, AND ECONOMIC INDEPENDANCE, ALL OF WHICH LAY AT THE CENTER OF REPUBLICAN IDEOLOGY.

PRESIDENT JAMES BUCHANAN, A STAUNCH DEMOCRAT, ENDORSED THE DRED SCOTT DESISION RULED ON BY THE SUPREME COURT, EDITED BY CHIEF JUSTICE ROGER BROOKE TANEY, THE COURT CONSISTING OF SEVEN DEMOCRATS AND TWO REPUBLICANS, THE TWO REPUBLICANS VIGOROUSLY DISSENTED, THE CHIEF JUSTICE DECLARED, THAT FREE AFRICAN AMERICANS, WERE NOT AND NEVER HAD BEEN U,S. CITIZENS, THAT THE CONSTUTION AND THE LANGUAGE OF THE DECLARATION OF INDENPENDANCE DID NOT EMBRACE THEM AS PART OF THE AMERICAN PEOPLE AT THAT TIME THESE DOCUMENTS WERE FRAMED, HE REPLIED BLACKS WERE REGARDED AS BEING OF INFERIOR ORDER AND ALTOGATHER UNFIT TO ASSOCIATE WITH THE WHITE RACE, EITHER IN SOCIAL OR POLITICAL RELATIONS, AND SO FAR INFERIOR THAT THEY HAD NO RIGHTS WHICH THE WHITE MAN WAS BOUND TO RESPECT, SO AS A CONSEQUENCE THE DECLARATION IT SELF WAS A WHITE MAN DOCUEMENT WHICH HAD NEVER APPLIED TO BLACKS.

BY THE WAY JUSTICE TANEY, WAS A GAUNT DEMOCRAT AND FORMER SLAVE OWNER, THIS DECISION BY THE SUPREME COURT ROCKED THE REPUBLICANS, BECAUSE THEIR IDEALS OF FREEDOM FOR AFRICAN AMERICANS HAD BEEN DANGEROUSLY SABOTAGED.

DEMOCRAT U.S. SENATOR STEPHEN A. DOUGLAS, LET HIS FEELINGS BE KNOWN, HIS COMMENTS WERE,THAT HE OPPOSED AFRICAN AMERICANS CITIZENSHIP IN ANY AND EVERY SHAPE OR FORM, AND HE BELIVE THIS GOVERNMEK NT WAS MADE,ON THE WHITE BASIS, ANT IT WAS MADE BY WHITE MEN FOR THE BENEFIT OF WHITE MEN, AND

THEIR POSTERITY FOREVER, ABRAHAM LINCOLN HAD RAN AGAINST DIUGLAS FOR HIS SENATE SEAT IN 1859, UNEORTUNATELF HE LOST, HOWEVER THE REPUBLICANS RALLIED BEHIND HIM TO RUN FOR THE PRESIDENCY IN 1860, ALL THE REPUBLICANS STOOD TOGATHER THEY ALL OPPOSED THE DRED SCOTT DECISION, RENDERED BY THE SUPREME COURTFOR POPULAR SOVEREIGNTY AND THE SINISTER DESIGNS OF THE SLAVE POWERS, THE DOUGLAS SOUTHERN DEMOCRATS WERE DOING EVERY THING THEY COULD TO SMEAR AND BELITTLE REPUBLICANS AND LINCOLN, THE DEMOCRATIC JOURNALS INSISTED LINCOLN HAD DONE NOTHING IN ALL THE HISTORY OF HIS LIFE PERTAINING TO LEGISLATIVE OR EXECUTIVE CAPICITY, THAT HE LIKE EXECUTIVE CAPACITY THAT ENTILED HIM TO BE PRESIDENT, AND ON THE CONTRAY HE WAS ILLITERATE, COARSE AND VULGAR, AND A PETTIFOGGING ABLOITIONIST WHO LUSTER FOR THE EMANCIPATION AND EQUALITY OF NIGGERS, LIKE THE REST OF THE REPUBLICAN PARTY.

HOWEVER IN THE FEW NORTHERN STATES WHERE AFRICAN AMERICANS, COULD VOTE, THE SUPPORTERS OF LINCOLN EVEN FORMED BLACK REPUBLICANS CLUBS, BECAUSE LINCOLN WAS THEIR ONLY HOPE FOR FREEDOM, BUT NOT ALL BLACKS WAS FOR LINCOLN, SOME BLACK LEADERS SUGGESTED LINCOLN WAS ODIOUS TO ANTISLAVERY, THEY WERE EMINET BLACKS IN THE NORTH, HOWEVER LINCOLN COULD NOT BELIEVE THE TUMULT, AND VIOLENT BEHAVIOR HIS CANDIDACY FOR THE PRESIDENCY HAD CAUSED, PIRATICALLY IN THE SOUTHERN STSTES, HE WAS BURNED IN EFFIGY IN PUBLIC PLACES, THEY CALLED HIM ANOTHER JOHN BROWN, A LUNATIC, CHIMPANZEE, A BLOOD THIRSTY TYRANT, THEY SUGGESTED HE HAD UNITED AND ORGANIZED PEOPLE THE LIKES OF NAT TURNER, AND JOHN BROWN, AND THAT THE REPUBLICAN PARTY WAS FOR FREE LOVE FOR NIGGERS, AND IF ELECTED PRESIDENT HE WOULD FREE ALL THE SLAVES AND GIVE THE NIGGERS ALL THE JOBS THAT HAD BEEN FOR WHITES, AND URGE THEM TO COPULATE AND MARRY WHITE WOMEN, THEY SHOUTED IF THE REPUBLICANS TOOK POWER THE NEXT THING WOULD BE THE INVASION OF THEIR PLANTATIONS, LIBERATING THEIR SLAVES AT GUN POINT, AND THERE WOULD BE ROBBRIES, RAPES, AND MURDERS OF WHITE PEOPLE BY THE EMANCIPATED SLAVES, BUT LINCOLN DID NOT TAKE THE SOUTHERN DEMOCRATS BIGOTS SERIOUSLY, HE WAS DETERMINE TO SUCCEEDE ON HIS MISSION TO EMANCIPIATE SLAVERY, WASHINGTON WAS UZZING WITH PLOTS TO ASSASSINATE HIM AT HIS INAUGURATION, AND THERE WERE THE IRRIATE SOUTHENERS SEEMED TO THINK HE SHOULD APOLOGIZE FOR HIS VICTORY, FORTUNATELY FOR HIM AND AFRICAN AMERICANS, HE.CHOOSE TO FOR GO THE SENATE AND PERSUE THE PRESIDENCY,

THIS GRUELING TASK BELIEVED TO HAVE EFFECTED HIS HEALTH, HOWEVER HE BECAME THE GRACIOUS LEADER OF ALL TIMES, IN A PRESIDENT AND HE HAD NO INTENTIONS OF BEING DOCILE, BECAUSE NO DEMOCRATIC PRESIDENT HAD BARGIN FOR THE RIGHT TO TAKE OFFICE, HOWEVER HE WOULD BE RESTRAINED, BUT WOULD NOT SURRENDER THE GOVERNMENT OR THE REPUBLICAN PRINCIPLES OF FREEDOM AND LIBERTY FOR ALL, MOST OF ALL EDUCATION, AND TO FORMAT PROGRAMS TO INSURE AFRICAN AMERICANS, COULD BE EDUCATED AND INTRODUCED TO A VIABLE UNDERSTANDING OF THE NECESSITY TO SUSTAIN MENTALITY AND POLITICALLY. ABRAHAM LINCOLN WAS SWORN IN BT THE CHIEF JUSTICE TANEY, THE JUSTICE OF THE DRED SCOTT DEBACLE, AND SO ABRAHAM LINCOLN TOOK THE OATH AS THE SIXTEENTH PRESIDENT OF THE UNITED STATES OF AMERICA.

AS I FOCUS ON PRESIDENT LINCOLN, I BECOME SOME WHAT EMOTIONAL ALSO ANGRY, HERE IS A COMPASSIONATE MAN REGARDS TO A NATIONALLY OF PEOPLE, AFRICAN AMERICANS ANCESTRY BROUGHT HERE FROM AFRICA, TOTALLY SAVAGELY AND ILLITERATE TO CUSTOMS OF AMERICA, HE KNEW YOU WERE NOT A ANIMAL AS THE SOUTHERN DEMOCRATS PLANTATION SLAVE MASTERS PORTRAYED YOU TO BE, HE GAVE HIS LIFE FOR AFRICAN AMERICANS TO BE FREE AND EDUCATE THEM SELVES, AND PROVE TO NOT ONLY THE SOUTHERN RACIST DEMOCRATS,BUT TO THE WORLD THAT THEY COULD INCORPORATE THEM SELVES INTO A DIVERSE SOCIETY OF PEOPLE AND BECOME PRODUCTIVE CITIZENS OF THIS GREAT COUNTRY AT THEIR INDIVIDUAL FREE WILL, AND BECOME SUCCESSFUL IN YOUR OWN RIGHT.

REGRETFULLY ONLY A MINIUM AMOUNT OF AFRICAN AMERICANS, SUPPORTED THIS THEORY, AND IT IS VERY UNFORTUNATE BECAUSE THE MAJORITY EITHER CHOOSE NOT TO EDUCATE THEM SELVES, AND THOSE THAT ARE EDUCATED CHOOSE TO FOLLOW A HERD LEADER DOWN THE ROAD TO POLITICAL DESTRUCTION RELATED TO A POLITICAL PARTY THAT HAS PULVERIZED THEIR SANITY INTO OMISSION BASED ON BRUTALITY, LIES AND

DECEIT, ON MARCH 4, 1861, ABRAHAM LINCOLN, BECAME PRESIDENT, THE SOUTHERN CONFEDRATE DEMOCRATIC PARTY WAS ENRAGED, THE SOUTH CAROLINIANS .HELD A CONVENTION IN COLUMBIA, AFTER THREE OR FOUR DAYS THEY CONCLUDED TO DISSOLVE FROM THE UNION OF THE UNITED STATES, AND FORM A INDEPENDANT SOUTHERN DEMOCRATIC CONFEDRATE GOVERNMENT,CONSISTING OF SOUTH CAROLINA, MISSISSIPPI, FLORDIA, ALABAMA, GEORGIA, LOUISANA, AFTER A REFRENDUM WAS HELD IN TEXAS, THEY JOINED, THEN A CONFEDRATE CONSTITUTION WAS ADOPTED, A CARBON COPY OF THE U.S. CONSTITUTION, EXCEPT THE STATES WERE GIVEN POWER OVER THE FEDERAL CONSTITUTION REGARDS TO SLAVERY, THIS WAS IN ORDER FOR THE STATES TO MAINTAIN SLAVERY, THE CONFEDERATE CONSTITUTION EXPLICITY PROTECTED THE RIGHTS OF THE SLAVE MASTERS, TO MAINTAIN SLAVERY, JEFFERSON DAVIS DECLARED PRESIDENT, OF THE SOUTHERN CONFEDERECY, THERE WERE A FIEW STATES PONDERING THEIR LOYALTY, FINALLY VIRGINIA, ARKANSAS, TENNESSEE, AND NORTH CAROLINA, JOINED THE CONFEDERCY. MOST LIKELY THIS DECISION WAS INSTIGATED BECAUSE THE CONFEDERATE BATTERIES ATTACAKED THE FEDERAL FORT SUMTER IN CHARLESTON HARBOR THE REPUBLICAN PARTY, WERE COMITTED TO THE FREEDOM OF SLAVES IN THE UNITED STATES OF AMERICA AS CITIZENS.

IN THIS SEGEMENT OF THE BOOK I AM GOING TO PAY TRIBUTE TO ONE OF THE GREATEST PRESIDENTS EVER LIVED, REGARDS TO EQUAL LIBERTIES, I WILL RESPECTFULLY BEGIN WITH THE ATTACK ON FORT SUMPTER IN CHARLESTON AFTER THIS DESERVING TRIBUTE.

AT AGE NINETEEN ABARAHAM LINCOLN WAS VISITING NEW ORLEANS, HE WITNESSED A TRUMATIC EXPERIENCE PERTAINING TO A MULATT WOMAN BEING AUCTION OFF BY NABOBS, WITH NO CONCERN FOR PEOPLE IN GENERA RAL THE GROUP THAT HE WAS WITH HE EXPLICATED, BY GOD IF I EVER GET THE CHANCE TO DISMANTLE SLAVERY, I WILL HIT IT HARD, AT SUCH EARLY AGE THIS TRULY EXEMPLIFYED THE TRUE HEART FEELING OF HIS

CONVICTIONS, APPARENTLY TO WITNESS THIS BARBARIC ACT FUELED HIS MOTIVATIONS TO ABOLISH SLAVERY,YEARS LATER HE SUCCEEDED. HOWEVER AS THE DEMOCRATS PRODICTED HE PAID A HEAVY PRICE, WITH HIS LIFE.

AS I SET MY MIND TO CONCENTRATE THERE ARE TIMES I BECOME EMOTIONAL BASED ON MORAL POLITICAL BETRAYAL, RELATED TO AFRICAN AMERICAANS.

LINCOLN RESPONDED TO THIS VICIOUS ATTACK WITH A CALL FOR ALMOST A HUNDRED THOUSAND VOLUNTEERS, AS THE WAR BETWEEN BEGAN, NORTHERN AFRICAN AMERICANS DESPERATELY OFFERED THEIR SERVICES AS VOLUNTEERS, BUT WAS REJECTED, MANY TIMES THEY WERE APPROACHED BY WHITES AND INSULTED WITH VERBAGE LIKE YOU NIGGERS KEEP OUT OF THIS, THIS IS THE WHITE MANS WAR, THE ADMINISTRATION INCLUDING LINCOLN BELIEVED THEY WOULD NOT MAKE GOOD SOLDIERS BECAUSE THEY WOULD BE TO SUBMISSIVE AND COWARDLY TO FIGHT THEIR FORMER SLAVE MASTERS, THESE COMMENTS DREW OUTRAGE AND INDIGNATION FROM THE AFRICAN AMERICANS, APPARENTLY SOME HAD FORGOTTEN WHAT DISTINGITION THEY FAUGHT WITH IN THE WAR OF 1812, TO HELP WIN AMERICAN INDEPENDENCE FROM THE BRITISH.

DURING THE FIRST YEAR OF THE WAR, THE UNITED STATES LOST OVER TWO HUNDRED THOUSAND TROOPS, THE SOUTHERN STATES HAD THE ADVANTAGE, BECAUSE SLAVES COULD MAINTAIN THE PLANTATIONS WHILE MASTERS FAUGHT THE UNITED STATES TROOPS, FEDERAL CASUALTIES WERE MOUNTING,AT BULL RUN IN VIRGINIA OVER THREE HUNDRED THOUSAND WERE LOST, BASED ON THE RICH COTTON STATES OF THE SOUTH, THE CONFEDERACY ATTRACTED THE ATTENTION OF WESTERN EUROPE AND BRITIAN, THIS WOULD SPELL TROUBLE FOR THE UNITED STATES, FINALLY CONGRESS AUTHORIZED PRESIDENT LINCOLN TO INLIST AFERICAN AMERICANS INTO THE MILITARY, TO SUPPRESS THE REBELLION, MANY WHITES EXPRESSED THEIR TRUE FEELINGS, THAT THEY WERE A SUPERIOR RACE AND TO GOOD TO FIGHT ALONG BESIDE NIGGERS, GENERAL RUFUS SAXTON, ORGANIZED

THE FIRST FIVE REGIMENTS OF ALL AFRICAN AMERICAN SOLDIERS, AND LATER THOMAS WENTWORTH HIGGINSON PROCEDED SAXTON, AND LED THE AFRICAN AMERICANS INTO BATTLE HE WAS SO IMPRESSED HE WROTE, NO BODY KNOWS ANYTHING ABOUT THESE MEN, WHO HAS NOT SEEN THEM IN BATTLE, NO OFFICER IN THIS REGIMENT NOW DOUBTS THAT THE KEY TO THE SUCCESSFUL PROSECUTION OF THIS WAR LIES IN THE UNLIMITED EMPLOYMENT OF THE AFRICAN AMERICAN TROOPS. THERE WERE SOME POLITICALLY MOTIVATED WHITES IN WASHINGTON AND THE NORTHERN STATES, COMPLAINING THAT PRESIDENT LINCOLN, SHOULD NOT HAVE GONE TO WAR TO DISPEL SLAVERY.

OVER A HUNDRED AND FORTY YEARS LATER, THERE ARE THOSE SAME KIND OF POLITICAL, MISGUIDED, BUFFOONISH, MIS-FITS, HAVING NO COMPASSION REGARDS TO FREEDOM FOR OTHERS, SCREAMING ABOUT PRESEDENT GEORGE BUSH SHOULD NEVER HAVE GONE INTO IRAQ.

MUST BE AN ANCESTORY DEBACLE, THE COMPARISON BETWEEN SLAVERY AND IRAQ, IS ALMOST IDENTICAL, ONE EXCEPTION THE DEMOCRATIC SOUTHERN PLANTATION MASTERS, WERE BRUTALITLY MURDERING AFRICAN AMERICAN SLAVES, AND A BRUTIAL DICTATOR IN IRAQ, WAS DOING THE SAME THING, TO HIS OWN PEOPLE, THESE BRAVE AFRECIAN AMERICANS, FOUGHT BRAVELY AND SOME DIED TO BE FREE, AN AS HISTORY WILL BE THE JUDGE, THE UNITED STATES, COULD HAVE NEVER, REPEAT COULD HAVE NEVER,DEFEATED THE SOUTHERN CONFEDERACY, IF NOT FOR BRAVERY AND FIGHTING TENACITY OF THE AFRICAN AMERICAN SOLDIERS.

THEY WERER REWARDED FOR THEIR BRAVERY SOME RECEIVED THE MEDAL OF HONOR, IN SEPTEMBER 22, 1862, PRESIDENT ABRAHAM LINCOLN, ISSURED THE EMANCIPATION PROCLAMATION DECLARING FREEDOM FOR ALL ENSLAVED AFRICAN AMERICANS, THEY REGARDED PRESIDENT LINCOLN, AS A EMANCIPATOR AND MASTER OF SYMBOLIC EXPRESSION, HE WALKED THE STREETS GREETING AFERICAN AMERICAN SOLDIERS.

THIS WAS THE MOST BRUTAL WAR ON AMERICAN SOIL EVER, APPROXIMATELY TWO HUNDRED FIFTYTHOUSAND CONFEDRATEJMEN LIST. THEIR LIVES£APPROXIMATELY THREE HUNDRED EIGHTY THOUSAND UNITED STATES FORCES LOST THEIR LIVES, INCLUDING THIRTY SEVEN OR THIRTY EIGHT THOUSAND WERE AFRICAN AMERICANS.

IN 1865, A VOTE OF ONE HUNDRED TWENTY ONE, TO TWENTY FOUR IN CONGRESS, PASSED THE THIRTEENTH AMENDENT TO THE UNITED STATES CONSTITUTION PROVIDING FOR THE TOTAL END TO THE ABOLISHMENT TO SLAVERY IN AMERICA, RATIFIED DECEMBER 6,1865.

THE SOUTHERN ECONOMY WAS DESTROYED, WORTHLESS MONEY, AND THE MOST IMPORTANT ASSET TO THE SOUTH WAS OWNERSHIP OF SLAVES, HAD BEEN ABOLISHED, COTTON PRODUCTION WAS CUT IN HALF, BECAUSE ALMOST FOUR MILLION SLAVES WERE FREE, AFTER THE SURRENDER OF THE SOUTH PRESIDENT ABRAHAM LINCOLN ADDRESSED THE NATION, HE SPOKE OF A NEW GOVERNMENT IN THE SOUTH, AND HOW HE WANTED EXSLAVES TO GO TO SCHOOL AND BE TAUGHT HOW TO READ AND WRITE, JOHN WILKES BOOTH, WAS IN THE AUDIENCE, A SOUTHERN CONFEDRATE DEMOCRAT, A STERN HATER OF OF THE REPUBLICAN PARTY AND PRESIDENT LINCOLN, HE CONSIDERED THEM TO BE RADICAL, BECAUSE OF THEY EMBRACED THE FREEDOM OF SLAVES, HE QUOTED TO ONE OF HIS FRIENDS, NOE THE NIGGERS WILL BECOME CITIZENS, AND PREDICTED THAT THIS WOULD BE THE LAST SPEECH FOR PRESIDENT LINCOLN, AND THAT WAS NO IDLE THREAT.

ON APRIL 14, AT FORD THEATER, PRESIDENT ABRAHAM LINCOLN WAS ASSASSINATED BY JOHN WILKES BOOTH WITH A PISTOL, SHOT TO THE HEAD, BOOTH LEAPED TO THE STAGE, AND YELLED OUT, NOW THE SOUTH IS AVEGEND, BE IT SO TO ALL TYRANTS, TO CLARIFY ONE THING, IT WAS THE REPUBLICAN PARTY ALONG WITH LINCOLN THAT ABOLISHED SLAVERY, BECAUSE THE CONGRESS HAD TO RATIFY THE PROCLAMATION, UNLIKE THE SOUTHERN DEMOCRATIC CONFEDERACY PARTY, REPUBLICANS BELIEVE IN EQUAL JUSTICE FOR ALL MAN KIND.

BEING FREE WAS COMPLETE CHAOS FOR SLAVES, UNEDUCATED TRYING TO TRACK DOWN THEIR RELATIVES, AND LOVEONES, THAT WAS SOLD INTO SLAVERY NOT TO MENTION FINANCES, SO LAND OWNERSHIP WAS ESSENTIAL FOR THEIR SURVIVAL, PRESIDENT LINCOLN HAD PLANS FOR THIS CRISIS BASED ON REAERVED SOUTHERN LAND FROM SLAVE OWNERS CONFISCATED DURING THE CIVIL WAR, THAT LAND WAS TO BE SAT ASIDE FOR SLAVES, BY THE ACT OF WAR AND THE EMANCIPATION PROCLAMATION, OF THE PRESIDENT, OF THE UNITED STATES, EACH FAMILY WAS TO RECEIVE FORTY ACRES OF LAND AND A ARMY NULE, TO USE IN THE CULTIVATION OF THE LAND, THE LATTER PART OF 1865, VICE PRESIDENT ANDREW JOHNSON, REPLACED THE ASSASSINATED PRESIDENT LINCOLN, WHICH HAD BEEN HIS CHOICE TO GET SOUTHERN VOTES DURING THE ELECTION, THEIR RELATIONSHIP WERE NEVER THAT GREAT, BECAUSE JOHNSON WAS A SOUTHERNER FROM TENNESSEE, WITH IDEAS TOTALLY THE OPPOSITE OF PRESIDENT LINCOLN, REGARDS TO SLAVERY HIS IDEALS WERE OF THE DEMOCRATIC CONFEDERATE, BECAUSE IMMEDIATELY HE SET ASIDE THE LINCOLN IDEA OF FORTY ACRES AND A MULE. AND RETURNED ALL THE SOUTHERN CONFISCATED LAND TO THE SLAVE MASTERS.AS A RESULT EXSLAVES WITH NO SKILLS, OTHER THAN FARMING, AND NO EDUCATION HAD TO RETURN TO THEIR MASTERS, HOWEVER IT WAS A DIFFERENT ANGLE BASED ON THE ABOLISHMENT OF SLAVERY, AND WITH THE DEMAND FOR COTTON, SO THE LAND OWNERS DEVISED A POLITICAL DIABOOLIICAL PLAN CALL SHEAR CROPPING, THIS PLAN WAS DESIGNED FOR TO CONTINUE SLAVERY WITHOUT THE EXSLAVES KNODLEDGE, THEY OFFERED FORTY TO FIFTY ACRES OF LAND TO FAMILIES PROVIDING THEY WOULD OPERATE THEIR PLANTATION, AND THEY ACCUMULATED ENOUGH FUNDS THEY COULD PURCHASE THE LAND, SOME SURVIVED THIS FIENDISH TASK, UNFORTUNATELY THE MAJORITY STUMBLE AND FELL BY THE WAY SIDE, BECAUSE ILLITERACY, GREED, HABITS UNBECOMING, NOT ONLY THAT THE LAND OWNERS, OWNED THE STORES, WHERE THEY HAD TO GET THEIR SUPPLIES, SUCH AS, FOOD; GRAIN,

MULES, HORSES FOR TRANSPORTATION, WAGONS, TOOLS, SO AT THE END OF THE YEAR THEY WOULD STILL BE IN DEBT. AND LATER THEIR CREDIT WOULD BE SHUT OFF, THEY WOULD LOOSE THE LAND THEY NEVER HAD, ONCE THAT OCCURED THE MASTER WOULD TELL THEM NO PROBLEM, YOU STILL HAVE A HOME, I WILL TAKE CARE OF YOU JUST WORK THE PLANTATION.

GUESS WHAT, A WELL PLANNED POLITICAL SCHEME TO ADOPT HERDING AND SLAVERY, ALL OVER AGAIN, AND BE CHEATED FOR ETERNITY. THEY WERE FREE BUT STILL A SLAVE BY THEIR OWN CONVICTIONS, THIS IS THE GREATIST COUNTRY IN THE WORLD, IT IS HERE FOR EVERYONE, AND ALWAYS WILL BE, BUT IF YOU FAIL TO UNDERSTAND THE POLITICAL STRUCTURE THAT IS EMBEDDED INTO THE FABRIC OF THIS COUNTRY, HAVING TO DO WITH EDUCATION, AND COMMITMENT TO THE WHOLE COUNTRY,WITH INDIVIDUAL THINKING, THAT THIS IS A DIVERSE COUNTRY, OF APPROXIMATELY THREE HUNDRED MILLION PEOPLE, INCLUDED IN THAT NUMBER AFRICAN AMERICANS REPRESENT ABOUT 12%, SO IF YOU CAN COUNT THAT REPRSENT A SMALL MINORITY, SO UNTIL YOU STOP LISTERNING TO THE PROVERBAL RADICAL, LEFT WING SLAVE DRIVER, AND START THINKING FOR YOUR SELF YOU ARE ALWAYS GOING TO BLAME SOMEONE ELSE FOR YOUR INABILITY TO SUSTAIN POLITICALLY, THE WAY THIS LOVELY COUNTRY WAS AUTHENTICATED BY THE FORE FATHERS,IF YOU REMAIN ISOLATED FROM INDIVIDUAL THINKING AND REMAIN WITH THE HERDS, MOST LIKELY YOUR FATE THE REPUBLICAN CONTROLLED CONGRESS TRIED DESPERATELY TO PROTECT THE RIGHTS OF AFERICAN AMERICANS, PRESIDENT JOHNSON, FOUGHT ANY EFFORT HAD TO DO WITH CIVIL RIGHTS, FOR PROVIDING CITIZENSHIP TO AFRICAN AMERICANS, JOHNSON CAMPAIGNED WIDELY FOR DEMOCRATIC CANIDATESTO CONGRESS, IN 1866, HE BASHED THE REPUBLICAN CANIDATES ATTACKED PROGRAMS TO AIDE FORMER SLAVES, THE REPUBLICANS WERE OUTRAGED, HOWEVER THEY GAINS IN THE ELECTIONS, THE REPUBLICAN CONGRESS PASSED THE CIVIL RIGHTS ACT OF 1866, AND THE FOURTEENTH AMENDMENT WHICH

WROTE PROVISIONS, GUARANTEING AFERICAN AMERICANS CITIZENSHIP, INTO THE CONSTITUTION, THE REPUBLICANS WAS SO OUTRAGED WITH PRESIDENT JOHNSON BEHAVIOR THE CINGRESS PASSED SEVERAL MEASURES TO LIMIT JOHNSONS POWER, ONE OF THESE MEASURES WERE THE TENUE OF OFFICE ACT, WHICH PROHIBITED THE PRESIDENT FROM DISMISSING ANY CABINET MEMBER APPOINTED WITH ADVICE AND CONSENT TO THE SENATE UNTIL THE SENATE APPROVE A SUCCESSOR, JOHNSON DID NOT FOLLOW THOSE PROCEDURES OF THE LAW, SO THE REPUBLICANS VOTED TO IMEACH HIM, HE WAS LUCKY TO BE SAVED BY ONE VOTE IN THE SENATE, HIS PRESIDENCY WAS SEVERELY DAMAGED, BECAUSE HIS ATTEMPT TO RECONSTRUCT SLAVERY IN THE SOUTH FAILED, UNDER THE REPUBLICAN LED CONGRESS, AFRICAN AMERICANS ATTAIN POLITICAL POWER, WHICH ALLOWED THEM TO VOTE,IN SOUTH CAROLINA, MISSISSIPPI, LOUISANA, THEY WERE ALLOWED TO OFFER THEIR OPIONS REGARDS TO CONSTITUTION LAWS, SUCH AS THE SOUTHERN HOHESTEAD ACT, WHICH GAVE SLAVES AND WHITES WHO WAS LOYAL TO THE UNITED STATES, ACCESS TO FORTY FOUR MILLION ACRES OF PUBLIC LAND, IN FIVE STATES, THE CONGRESS RATIFIED THE FIFTEENTH AMENDMENT TO THE UNITED STATES CONSTITUTION, OUTLAWING THE USE OF RACE TO DISENFRANCHISE VOTERS, AFRICAN AMERICANS GAINED SIGNIFICANT POLITICAL POWER THROUGH THE REPUBLICAN PARTY, THEY ATTENDED POLITICAL MEETINGS, AFRICAN AMERICANS WERE THE MAJORITY OF THE ELECTORATE IN FIVE SOUTHERN STATES, THEY WERE THE FOUNDATION POLITICALLY FOR THE REPUBLICAN PARTY IN THE SOUTH RELATED TO VOTING. THEY AND THE WHITE REPUBLICANS WERE ALLIES, SOMETHING THAT HAD NEVER EXISTED, WHITE REPUBLICANS FROM THE NORTHERN STATES CAME IN GREAT NUMBERS, TEACHERS, NURSES, TO AID IN EUDCATING FORMER SLAVES, THERE ALSO WERE EDUCATED AFRICAN AMERICANS, ONE BECAME A SENATOR IN 1870, THE VERY FIRST, A REPUBLICAN FROM MISSISSIPPI, HE FILLED THE VACATED SEAT OF JEFFERSON DAVIS.

WHEN THERE WAS VOTING AFRICAN AMERICANS , HAD TO PROTECT THE REPUBLICAN VOTERS, FROM DEMOCRATIC VIGILANTE GROUPS, THE NORTHERN REPUBLICANS WERE HUMILIATED BY DEMOCRAT VIGILANTE TERROIST GROUPS YELLING OUT, NIGGER LOVERS, CARPETBAGGERS, THEIR CLAIM WAS WE WILL NEVER ALLOW Y.OUL TO EDUCATE NIGGERS, THEY ARE SUBSERVIENT THE PLANTATION IS WHERE THEY BELING.

THE DEMOCRATS BECAME SO INFURIATED, THEY FORMED THE KU KLUX KLAN, IN TENNESSEE, THE YEAR 1866.

TO EXCLUSIVELY VIOLENTLY TERRORIZE, THE FORMER SLAVES AND DRIVE AWAY THE NORTHERN REPUBLICANS HELPING EDUCATE THE AFRICAN AMERICANS, AND INTIMIDATE ALL VOTERS IN THE REPUBLICAN RACES, THEY ALSO RAIDED , AND MOLESTED AFRICAN AMERICAN WOMEN, AND HUNG THEIR MEN, BURNED THEIR CHURCHES, AND HOMES.

SPRAYED THEM WITH POWERFUL WATER HOSES, THIS POLITICAL TERROISM LASTED INTO THE TWENTIETH CENTURY, ALL IN HOPES OF REVIVING SLAVERY.

IN 1866, ONE OF THE MOST BARBARIC ACTS OF THE DEMOCRATIC AGONIZED KU-KLUX-KLAN, HAPPENED IN MEMPHIS TENNESSEE, WHITE AND AFERICAN AMERICANS, REPUBLICANS, DELEGATES WERE IN A HALL MEETING, A RUKUS STARTED OUTSIDE, THE POLICE AND A GROUP OF WHITE BIGOTS, ATTACKED THE CROWD OF REPUBLICAN BY STANDERS, KILLING AT WILL, SOME TRIED TO FIGHT BACK BUT TO NO AVAIL, THEN THEY INVADED THE HALL, DELEGATES PLEADED FOR THEIR LIVES, THE POLICE CONTINUED TO SHOOT EVERYONE IN THEIR WAY, ONE DELIGATE WAVED A WHITE HANDKERCHIEF AND YELLED OUT FOR GOD SAKE ARREST ME WHAT EVER, BUT PLEASE DONT SHOOOT ME, BUT TO NO AVAIL HE WAS SHOT DEAD, THE UNMERCIFULLY KILLIING CINTINUED SOME ESCAPED TO THE STREETS THEY WERE TRACKED DOWN AND KILLED, THE VICIOUS MOB KILLED APPROXIMATELY FORTY TO FIFTY AFERICAN AMERICANS, ASSOCIATED WITH THE REPUBLICAN CONVENTION. THIS WAS A BARBARAC

MASSACRE BY THE DEMOCRATIC PARTY FOUNDED KU-KLUX-KLAN.

REPUBLICAN ULYSSES S. GRANT BECAME PRESIDENT IN EIGHTEEN SIXTY EIGHT, REPLACING ANDREW JOHNSON, IMMEDIATELY CONGRESS REACTED TO QUELLING THE VIOLENCE BEING COMMITTED BY THE VIGILANTI,, DEMOCRATS. THEY PASSED INTO LAW A NUMBER OF MEASURES, PRESIDENT GRANT SUSPENDED THE WRIT OF HABEHS CORPUS, IN NINE SOUTHERN SOUTH CAROLINA COUNTIES WHERE THE KLAN WAS MOST INTENSIFIED, THERE WAS A INTENSIVE INVESTIGATION BYOCONGRESS REGARDSCTO THESE SENSLESS KILLINGS THE FEDERAL OFFICIALS ARRESTED AND INDITED HUNDREDS OF WHITES. FROM MISSISSIPPI, SOUTH CAROLINA, AND NORTH CAROLINA, AMONG THE GROUP WERE DOCTERS, LAWYERS, MINISTERS, COLLEGE PROFSSORS, AND POOR WHITES.

UNDER THE REPUBLICAN ADMINISTRATION THE RECONSTRUCTION OF THE SOUTH HAD BEGIN, HUNDREDS IF NOT THOUSANDS, OF AFERICAN AMERICANS AND WHITES OF PROFESSIONAL STATUS LAWYERS, TEACHERS, MINESTERS, POURED INTO THE SOUTH TO TAKE ADVANTAGE OF THESE UNPRECEDENTED OPPORTUNITIES,THEY WORKED WITH LOCAL REPUBLICANS, TO REBUILD THE SOUTH, UNDER THE REPUBLICAN ADMINISTRATION MORE THAN SEVEN HUNDRED AFRICAN AMERICANS SERVED IN THE STATE LEGISLATURE, OVER TWENTY WERE ELECTED TO THE UNITED STATES,HOUSE HOUSE OF REPRESENTATIVES AND TWO WAS ELECTED TO THE SENATE, THE MAJORITY OF THE DELIGATES TO THE SOUTH CAROLINA CONSTITUTION WEREAFRICANAMERICANS,CONSISTINGOFONEHUNDRED TWENTYFOUR,FIFTYSEVENWEREFORMERSLAVES,ALOTOF MEASURES WERE PASSED BY THIS REPUBLICAN LEGISLATED BODY, SUCH AS ABOLISHING RACIAL DISCRIMINATION IN VOTING. PROTECTING MARRIED WOMEN PROPERTY RIGHTS, ESTABLISHING THE STATES FIRST DIVORCE LAW, THE FIRST FREE PUBLIC SCHOOL SYSTEM, THE ELECTION OF JUDGES RATHER THAN APPOINTED, ABOLISHING DUELING, ESTABLISHED THOUSANDS OF SCHOOLS OPEN TO WHITES AND MINORITIES, SOME OF SCHOOLS WERE

IN AREAS WHERE THERE HAD NEVER BEEN ANY, THESE SCHOOLS EDUCATED STUDENTS FROM KINDERGARTEN TOO COLLEGE, EDUCATION IS THE IMPORTANT HALL MARK FOR FREEDOM, AND REPRESENT HOPE FOR A BETTER FUTURE, BECAUSE MOST ALL SLAVES WERE FORBIDDEN FROM LEARNING TO READ AND WRITE 95% OF SLAVES WERE ILLITERATE, BUT UNDER THAT ADMINISTRATION OVER THREE QUARTERS OF A MILLION FORMER SLAVES CHILDREN WERE IN ELEMENTARY SCHOOL, HOWEVER THE DEMOCRATS WERE FURIOUS REGARDS TO THIS PROGRESS, THEIR AGENDA WAS TO REINSTATE RACIAL CONTROL, OF THE PREWAR SOUTH, THEIR MAIN GOAL WAS TO PROHIBIT EDUCATION TO AFRICAN AMERICANS, AND RETURN THEM TO PLANTATION SLAVERY.

SO THE DEMOCRATS CALLED OUT THEIR BIG GUNS, THE KU-KLUX-KLAN TO VALIDATE THEIR HEINOUS CRIME POLITICAL AGENDA, WHICH INCLUDE MURDERING INNOCENT PEOPLE, THEIR BATTLE CRY WAS HELP SAVE SOUTHERN CIVILIZATION, AND ANY ILLEGAL ACTION EVEN MURDER WAS ACCEPTABLE IF DONE IN THE NAME OF WHITE SUPREMACY, ONE OF THEIR MAIN INTENTIONS WERE TO CONTROL VOTING POWER, ONE ARMED DEMOCRAT FORCE CALLED THE WHITE LEAGUE, KU-KLU-KLAN, MARCHED ON THE STATE HOUSE IN NEW ORLEANS, TO INTIMIDATE REPUBLICANS, WHITES AND AFERICAN AMERICANS, IN AN ATTEMPT TO OVERTHROW THE GOVERNMENT, AND OPENLY ADMITTED ANY METHOD WOULD BE INCLUDING ASSASSINATION, THE DEMOCRATIC PARTY MADE THEIR COMMITMENT TO WHITE SUPREMACY, IN VICKSBURG MISSISSIPPI, WHITE DEMOCRAT TERROIST SLAUGHTED OVER THREE HUNDRED AFRICAN AMERICANS, AS PART OF A POLITICAL PLOY TO UNDERMINE THEIR SUPPORT FOR THE REPUBLICAN PARTY, IN ORDER TO INSTALL DEMOCRATIC POLITICAL RULED POWER IN THE SOUTH.

THE KU-KLUX-KLAN PATROLLED THE POLING PLACES, IN ORDER TO KEEP WHITES AND AFRICAN AMERICANS FROM VOTING, IN ATTEMPT TO OBTAIN POLITICAL POWER TO OVERTHROW THE GOVERNMENT, THEY USED ANY AND EVERY TACTIC TO PREVENT REPUBLICANS FROM VOTING,

EVEN FIRING CANNONS TO AID IN THEIR .VICIOUS. ASSAULT, THEY LOOTED AND VANDALIZED AFRICAN AMERICANS AND BUISNESSES, IN THEIR RELENTLESS PERSUIT FOR POLITICAL POWER, A LOT OF THE PEOPLE , WHITE AND AFRICAN AMERICANS, STARTED TO MIGRATE TO OTHER PARTS OF THE COUNTRY, AND LEAVING THEIR POLITICAL HOPES AND ASPIRATION BEHIND.

BUT MOST AFRICAN AMERICANS, AND FAMILYS COULD NOT LEAVE THE SOUTH BECAUSE OF FINANCIAL STABILITY AND ILLITERCY.

DURING THE PRESIDENTAL ELECTION BETWEEN DEMOCRAT SAMUEL J. TILDEN AND REPUBLICAN, RUTHERFORD B. HAYES, IT WAS A TIGHT RACE EACH CANDIDATE CLAIM VICTORY, IN LOUISIANA, SOUTH CAROLINA, AND FLORDIA, HOWEVER THE ELECTORAL COMMISSION VOTED TO AWARD THE PRESIDENCY TO HAYES, THE DEMOCRATS IN THE CONGRESS REVOLTED AND REFUSED TO CERTIFY THE ELECTION, THERE WAS PANDEMONIUM, AND POLITICAL UNCERTAINTY, THE NATION BECAME RESTLESS, BUISNESS INTEREST, STATE AND LOCAL GOVERNMENTS, CHURCHES, AND UNIVERSITES, PRESSURED FOR CLOSURE OF THIS MATTER, UNDER EXTREME PRESSURE THE DEMOCRATS OUT FLANKED THE REPUBLICANS, WITH A POLITICAL PLOY TO SUIT THEIR AGENDA, IT WAS AGREED, THAT THE DEMOCRATS WOULD CERTIFY HAYES AS PRESIDENT, AND WOULD NOT INTERFERE WITH POLICIES BENEFITTING REPUBLICANS INTEREST, IN RETURN THE ADMINISTRATION WOULD REMOVE FEDERAL TROOPS FROM THE SOUTH, LEAVING SOUTHNERS TO HANDLE CIVIL STABILITY, AND CIVIL RIGHTS, IN THEIR PROSPECTIVE STATES. THROUGH VIOLENCE AND UTALIZING THE KU-KLUX-KLAN, TO INTIMIDATE REPUBLICANS VOTERS FROM THE POLLS, THE DEMOCRATS HAD BARGAIN THEMSELVES BACK IN CONTROL OF THE SOUTHERN STATES, AND WOULD FOREVER RUIN THE LIVES OF AFRICAN AMERICANS.

MEANING LATER YEARS THEY OVER CAME THE PHYSICAL ABUSE, BUT THEIR MORAL POLITICAL GENERAL CHARACTOR, ASSUMED SHAPED FOREVER. THE DEMOCRATS

THROUGH VIOLENCE UTALIZED THE KU-KLUX-KLAN TO INTIMIDATE REPUBLICANS VOTERS FROM THE POLLS, THAT ACT IT SELF MOST LIKELY PRECIPITATED THE RUNOFF BETWEEN SAMUEL J. TILDEN AND RUTHERFORD B. HAYES, WHICH HAD TO BE RULED ON BY THE ELECTORAL COMCOMMISSION, BECAUSE BASED ON THAT RULING AND THE ACCOLADES TO FOLLOW, MOST LIKELY DROVE AFRICAN AMERICANS INTO A FRENZY,MOST OF THEM NOT AWARE OF THEIR POLITICAL FATE

BECAUSE DURING THE FOLLOWING YEARS, THE DEMOCRATS WERE SUCCESSFUL IN THEIR SLICK, CLEAVER, PERSUASIVE WAY OF POLITICKING, TO CONVINCE THE COURTS, PRINCIPALLY THE SUPREME COURT, EITHER TO WEAKEN OR STRIKE DOWN DECADES OF CIVIL RIGHTS LEGISLATION, THE MOST DAMMING AND MEAININGFUL WAS TO ALLOW THE RESPONSIBILITY OF THE FOURTEENTH AND FIFTEENTH AMENDMENTS,BE ENFORCED BY THE SOUTHERN STATES. DEMOCRATS ESCALATED INTO POSITIONS OF POLITICAL POWER AT ALL LEVELS OF STATE GOVERNMENT, THE RECOURSE TO DETER WAS SIMPLY REMOTE, THEIR PREHISTORIC IDEALS AND AGENDA TO REINTRODUCE SLAVERY ACROSS THE SOUTH HAD BEGIN, STARTING IN MISSISSIPPI, THE YEAR 1890. THE DEMOCRATS IMPLEMENTENTED FRANCHISES FOR WHITES ONLY. AFRICAN AMERICANS, SUDDENLY FOUND THEIR VOTING RIGHTS RESTRICTED, AND HOLPELESSLY TO DO ANYTHING ABOUT IT BECAUSE OF DEMOCRAT STATE LAWS, THEY CREATED A POLL TAX, WHICH AFFECTED POOR AFRICAN, AMERICANS, BECAUSE MOST WERE SHARECROPPERS AND FINANCIALLY DESTITUTE, THEY DEVISED A LITERACY REQUIREMENT, THIS TACTIC ELIMINIATED SOME WHITES AND PRACTICALLY ALL AFRICAN ALL AFRICAN AMERICANS, FROM PRECIPITATING IN THE VOTING PROCESS, HOWEVER FOR ILLITORATE WHITES, A SAFEGUARD WAS IMPLEMENTED TO PROTECT THEIR VOTING RIGHTS, BY WAVING THE LITERACY REQUIREMENTS FOR VOTERS CONSIDERED TO BE OF GOOD CONDUCT, WHOSE GRANDFATHERS VOTED IN THE PAST YEARS, KNOWING THAT MOST AFRICAN AMERICANS IN THE SOUTH WERE SLAVES, AND FJFQT

ELIGIBLE TO VOTE, ALSO THEIR LAWS PROVIDED FOR RACIAL SEGREGATION IN PUBLIC PLACES, INCLUDING TRANSPORTATION, MEANING THE BACK OF THE SYNDROME, AND A MULTITUDE OF OTHER RESTRICTIONS PERTAINING TO AFRICAN AMERICANS ONLY.

THE DEMOCRATS ARE EXTREMELY SKILLED AT LOCATING AND SUPPORTING SUCCESSFUL AFRICAN AMERICANS, AND POLITICALLY SEDUCING THEM INTO SPREADING THEIR RADICAL IDEOLOGY , KNOWING FULL WELL THAT MOST AFRICAN AMERICANS INSTINCTIVELY HERD, AND FOLLOW A LEADER, THIS PRACTICE IS EMBEDED IN OUR CULTURE FROM THE TRIBES OF OUR ANCESTORS FROM AFRICA, WHERE THEY LIVED UNDER THE SOLE GUIDANCE OF A KING, OR A CHIEF WITCH DOCTOR.

SO THIS SILLY BEHAVIOR OF HERDING HAS COST THE MAJORITY OF AFRICAN AMERICANS A LIFECTIME OF PROGRESS PERTAINIG TO POLITICAL AND FINANCIAL STABILITY, BECAUSE WHEN YOU HERD YOUR INSTINCTS ARE TO FOLLOW A LEADER OTHER THAN WHAT THE FOREFATHERS INTENDED, THAT ALL CITIZENS OF THE UNITED STATES OF AMERICA , BE GUIDED BY A ELECTED PRESIDENT, CONGRESS, SENATE, AND A JUDICIAL SYSTEM AND OF COURSE THE CONSTITUTION, IF YOU ARE UNABLE TO DISTINGUISH ACKNOWLEDGE THE IMPORTANCE OF THE ADOPTIONS PERTAINING TO OUR GOVERNMENT, M. THEN IT IS QUITE OBVIOUS YOU ARE NOT A INDIVIDUAL THINKER, AND REGARDLESS TO YOUR EDUCATIONAL BACK GROUND YOU BECOME A HERD LEADER OR A FOLLOWER, WITH THE STRUCTURE OF THE GOVERNMENT BEING DICTATED TO YOU BY A INDIVIDUAL,THAT IS MUCH SMARTER THAN YOU ARE, AND HE, SHE, OR THEY SEDUCE YOU INTO THEIR WAY OF THINKING PERTAINING TO POLITICS, AND THEIR CYNICAL EXPLOITATIONS OF WHAT SOME ONE IS DOING TO IMPEDE YOUR PROGRESS IN LIFE, AND YOU ARE OFF TO CONVINCE THE HERD THAT YOU ARE ON TO SOMETHING, AND THEY SHOULD CONTINUE VOTING IN A BLOC, BECAUSE THIS IS THE ONLY WAY TO CLIMB OUT OF POVITY, MOST LIKELY YOU ARE UNAWARE THAT YOU ARE CARRYING A

CONVOLUTED MESSAGE FROM SLAVE MASTERS THAT .WAS FORMULATED YEARS AGO,

THE DEMOCRATS ANCESTRY GO BACK HUDREDS OF YEARS THEY ARE EXTREMELY SKILLFULLY AT WHAT THEY DO REGARDS TO POLITICS, THEY ARE THE BEST AT MANIPULATING PEOPLE, INTO THEIR POSSESSIVE WAY OF THINKING, THEY ARE GENIUSES AT DISTORTING THE TRUTH, YOU HAVE TO GIVE THESE PEOPLE CREDIT, FOR APPROXIMATELY FOUR HUNDRED YEARS, THE DEMOCRATS HAVE VIOLATED, ASSAULTED, MURDERED, HUNG, SKINNED, CHEATED, MASS SLAUGHTERED, AFRICAN AMERICANS, ACCORDING TO HISTORY, PRIMARILY FOR SLAVE LABOR, IN THE PAST YEARS, AND TODAY THEIR POLITICAL VOTING BLOC, SO EITHER THE DEMOCRATS, ARE EXTREMEMLY SMART OR THE MAJORITY OF AFRICAN AMERICANS, EDUCATED AND ILLITERATE, ARE JUST PLAIN STUPID, BECAUSE THEY STILL SUPPORT THE DEMOCRATS, POLITICALLY WITH THEIR VOTING BLOCK, ESTIMATED TO BE APPROXIMATELY 95%, THIS IS A BRIEF SYNOPSIS OF DEMOCRATS SKILLS AT ITS BEST REGARDS TO THEIR POLITICAL AGENDA, RELATED TO AFRICAN AMERICANS, SUPPORTING THEIR RADICAL CAUSES, IN 1985, THEY HAND PICKED ONE OF THE MOST RECOGIZED INFLUENCTIAL AFRICAN AMERICAN, IN THE SOUTH IF NOT THE UNITED STATES, AND CONVICED HIM TO SUPPORT THEIR PATHETIC IDEOLOGY THAT SEGREGATION SHOULD BE A WAY OF LIFE, AND THAT SEPARATE IS BENEFICIAL, AND SHARECROPPING IS THE FURURE, AND BEENTAL AFRICAN AMERICAN, DID PUBLIC EXHIBITIONS IN MOSTLY RICH COTTON STATES IN THE SOUTH, HEAVILY POPULATED WITH AFRICAN AMERICANS, BECAUE OF HIS INFLUENCE AND STATUS, A LARGE MAJORITY APPLAUDED IN ACCEPTANCE TO THIS BUFFOONISH DEMAGOGUREY.

SOME WERE STUNNED AND OUTRAGED, HOWEVER BASED ON THESE HIDEOUS LAWS ENDORSED BY THE FOUNDER AND PRESIDENT, OF TUSKEEGEE INSTITUTE, SOME AFRICAN AMERICANS CHALLENGED THE VALIDITY THROUGH THE COURTS, THEY LOST THEIR COMPLAINT IN THE SUPREME COURT, MOST LIKELY BECAUE OF THE

COMPASSIONATE SPEECHES INSTIGATING ACCEPTANCE TO THE DEMOCRATS WELL ORGANIZED ATTEMPT TO PROVENT AFRICAN AMERICANS, FROM POLITICAL IN VOLVEMENT IN THE PROCESS OF STATE AND FEDERAL DECISION REGARDS TO LAWS.

THE SUPREME COURT ENDORSED THE DEMOCRATS SADISTIC LAWS, RULING THAT THE SEPARATING OF PEOPLE WAS CONSTITUTIONAL, AS LONG AS EACH RACE WAS PROVIDED EQUAL FACILITIES OF SAME QUALITY.

SO THE SEPRATE BUT EQUAL DOCTRINE WAS BORN, SO THE DEMOCRATS COULD NOT REINVENT THE WHEEL OF SLAVERY, BUT CLUNG TO AN ABUNDANT AMOUNT THAT THE SLAVE SYSTEM HAD PROVIDED, THERE IS NO QUESTION THE DEMOCRATS HAD DEPRIVED AFERICAN AMERICANS OF POLITICAL POWER, HOWEVER SLAVERY NO LONGER EXISTED, AFRICAN AMERICAN FAMILES COULD REST AT EASE BECAUSE THEY WOULD NO LONGER BE STRIPPED AWAY FROM THEIR FAMILES AND SOLD INTO SLAVE LABOR, SOME MADE STRIDES IN EDUCATION, AND SOME PURCHASED LAND, THE N.A.A.C.P. WAS FOUNDED, THE SUPREME COURT REVISITED THE FIFTEENTH AMENDMENT AND REMOVED THE THE GRANDFATHER CLAUSE, REGARDS TO VOTING RIGHTS, AND DEEMED IT TO BE A VIOLATION, TO THE CONSTITUTION, SOME POSITIVE SIGNS WERE BEING MADE , THROUGH OUT THE SOUTH REGARDS TO RACIAL TENSION, HOWEVER SLAVERY DID EXIST AND THAT IS A FACT.

A SMART PEOPLE, WILL EXAMINE THE CAUSES AND ON A INDIVIDUAL BASIS COME TO CONCLUSION TO PUT THIS RADICAL DEMOCRATIC PARTY, INHUMANE BEHAVIOR TO REST, UNFORTUNATELY THIS IS NOT TO BE, BECAUSE FOR A MAJORITY OF AFRICAN AMERICANS, BECAUSE OF LIBERAL DEMOCRATIC VAIN STRATEGY IN THE SOUTH, THEY BRUTALIZED YOU IN ORDER TO DESTROY YOUR MORAL SELF ESTEEM, ONCE THAT HAD BEEN ACCOMPOLISHED, THEN THE PHYSIOLOGICAL TACTICS BEGAN, IT WAS THEIR INTENTION TO HAVE YOU THINK YOU WERE A AMINAL SIMPLY BECAUSE YOU WERE SOLD LIKE ONE ONCE AN INDIVIDUAL WILL IS BROKEN THEY BECOME DOCILE, AND YOU BECOME A VICTOM OF THEIR THINKING MANNERISM,

THEIRMAINOBJECTIVEWASCONVINCEYOUTHATTHEYARE SUPERIOR, BUT IN ORDER TO ACCOMPLISH THAT MISSION THEY NEEDED STRONG LEADERS OF THE HERD OF PEOPLE AND THATS WHERE THE SLAVE DRIVERS CAME IN,AND WAS SO IMPORTANT. THEY WERENT MISTREATED BECAUSE OF BEING AFRICAN AMERICAN, THIS BRUTAL FATE WAS CAST UPON SLAVES TO WORK THE PLANTATIONS WITH FREE LABOR, TO GROW COTTON AND CONTROL THE ECONOMY REGARDS TO WEALTH FOR POLITICAL POWER, SOME OF THESE FUNDS WERE USED TO SOLICIT CONGRESSMANS, LAWYERS, JUDGES, AND OTHER INFLUENTIAL AFRICAN AMERICANS, WHICH A GREAT DEAL OF THEM WERE MULATTOS, THEYWERE/1 ALWAYS FIRST IN LINE BECAUSE OF THEIR LIGHT COLOR, YOU SEE THE SLAVE MASTER WAS A BRILLIANT VICIOUS INDIVIDUAL, HE KNEW MORE ABOUT SLAVES THAN THEY KNEW ABOUT THEM SELVES, HE KNEW IF A AFRICAN AMERICAN WAS LIGHT SKINNED MOST LIKELY IN HIS OR HER ANCESTRY THERE WHITE BLOOD AND MOSTLIKELY THEY WERE SMARTER THAN OTHERS, NOT TO SAY OTHER AFRICAN AMERICANS WERENT SMART BUT MOST NEVER GOT THE CHANCE TO PROVE IT, LETS NOT FORGET THE FIRST CHOICE FOR SLAVERY WAS THE INDIAN AFTER THE WAR, HOWEVER THEY REFUSED TO SUBMITT TO DOCILITY MANY WHITES LOST THEIR LIVES IN ATTEMPT TO ENSLAVE INDIANS, HOW EVER THIS WAS NOT TO BE, TO TEST YOUR MEMORY BOOKER T. WASHINGTON, ADAM CLAYTON POWELL, ROSA PARKS, THESE PEOPLE WERE PIONEERS, TO INCLUDE MY ANCESTRIE THERE IS A PHOTO OF MY GREAT GRAND FATHER ALONG WITH HIS DEED TO HIS FORTY ACRES OF LAND, THIS IS FOR THOSE WHO SPREAD RADICAL BUFFOONISH LIES ABOUR FORTY ACRES OF LAND AND AND WHERE IS IT, BY THE WAY ITS STILL THERE IN ALABAMA, IT WAS NOT FOOLISHLY GAMBLED AWAY OR CHEATED OUT OF LIKE MANY MANY AFRICAN AMERICANS DID, MOSTLY BECAUSE OF ILLITERACY, WE ARE A NATIONALLY OF PEOPLE THAT THE MAJORITY HAS DONE LITTLE FOR OURSELVES SENSE SLAVERY, YOU ALWAYS LOOK TO BLAME SOME ONE ELSE, FOR YOUR INABILITY TO BE SUCCESSFUL, I FEAR THAT THIS IS A TRAGEDY INHERENTLY

PASSED ON FROM GENERATIONS PERTAINIG TO CULTURE MEANING HERDING BEHIND LEADERS THAT IS TIED TO THE PATHETIC SYSTEM INVENTED BY THE SLAVE MASTERS AND THEIR MAIN INTENT WAS TO CONTROL AND OWN OTHER PEOPLE.

THAT SYSTEM DEVELOPED BY THE DEMOCRATIC PARTY WAS ABOLISHED IN 1865, HOWEVER IT STILL EXIST TODAY ITS CALLED BEING IN BONDAGE BY MIND CONTROL, AND JUST AS YOU WERE THERE TO WORK THE PLANTATIONS FOR THE SLAVE MASTERS, TO KEEP THEM IN POLITICAL POWER, FROM THE WEALTH OF COTTON,

YOU ARE TODAY BEING SEDUCED BY SLICK DEVISED PLANNING BY DEMOCRATS TO KEEP THEM IN POLITICAL POWER WITH YOUR VOTES, BUT IN ORDER TO ACCOMPLISH THIS WELL ORGANIZED PLAN THEY SABOTAGED THE ABRAHAM LINCOLN PLAN, WHICH MEANT SCHOOLS, FREEDOM AND LIBERTY FOR ALL, MANY TIMES BEFORE HE WAS ASSASSINATED HE STATED THESE PEOPLE MUST BE EDUCATED, MEANING AFRICAN AMERICANS AND WHITES, BECAUSE IF YOU EDUCATE THE WHITES HOPEFULLY THAT WOULD LESSEN BIGOTRY, AND THIS IS THE MAIN. REASON THE DEMOCRATS PLOTTED AND TOOK HIS LIFE, HOWEVER IN HIS LEGACY AFRICAN AMERICANS WERE FREED, THE DEMOCRATS WERE OUT FOR REVENGE, THEY HAD WORKED SO DILIGENTLY TO RESTRICT VOTING AND SCHOOLING FOR AFRICAN AMERICANS THAT WERE IN THE PARTY OF LINCOLN, THE REPUBLICAN PARTY SO THEY DEVISED A PLAN TO TEAR DOWN THE PARTY AFFILIATIONS RELATED TO AFRICAN AMERICANS, THEIR STATEMENTS WERE,NO THIS CANT BE NO NIGGERS SHOULD BE EDUCATED, THAT MEAN THEY WILL BE ABLE TO VOTE IN THE REPUBLICAN PARTY, AND MOVE INTO POLITICS, WE ARE THE SUPERIOR WHITE RACE.

AMERICAN SLAVERY COULD BE BRUTAL, BUT SELDOM EMERGED INTO DEATH FROM THEIR MASTERS, FORMER SLAVE ROBERT SMALLS IN 1863, BECAME AN AFRICAN AMERICAN HERO, HE WAS A SECOND LIEUTENANT IN THE NAVY AND ASSIGNED AS PIOLET OF THE PLANTER DURING THE CIVIL WAR. IT ALL BEGAN WHEN SMALLS WAS

HIRED OUT BY HIS MASTER IN SOUTH CAROLINA, HE AND SEVERAL OTHER SLAVES WERE USED BY THE SOUTHERN CONFEDERATES AS STEAM POWERS TO CLEAN AND READY THE SHIP FOR BATTLE THE SHIP WOULD RETURN TO PORT FOR SUPPLIES, AND REPLENISH WITH AMMUNITION AND OTHER EXPLOSIVES, DURING THE STOCKING THE CAPTIAN AND CREW WOULD VACATE TO THE CITY FOR SOME DOWN TIME, DURING ONE OF THESE ESCAPADES ROBERT SMALLS AND HIS SLAVE FOLLOWERS DECIDED TO RAISE THE CONFEDERATE FLAG AND SAIL OUT OF PORT THROUGH THE CONFEDERATE GUARDED LINES, INTO NORTHERN U.S. CONTROLLED TERRITOTY PRIOR TO ENTERING HE RAISED A WHITE FLAG, ONCE THERE HE STATED TIS WAS A PRESENT FOR UNCLE ABRAHAM LINCOLN, FOR HIS STAND ON FREEDOM FOR SLAVES, FOR HIS COURAGE THE NAVY PROMOTED SMALLS TO SECOND LIEUTENANT, AND ASSIGNED HIM AS PIOLET OF THE SHIP HE HANDILY RELIEVED THE SOUTHERN CONFEDERATES OF, DURING THE CIVIL WAR THE CAPTAIN OF THE PLANTER WAS ENGAGED IN BATTLE AND CONTEMPLATED SURRENDOR, BUT ROBERT SMALLS URGED THE CREW TO FIGHT ON WITH ALL TEIR GOD GIVEN STRENGTH, AND THEY SAVED THE PLANTER FROM CAPTURE, BY THE SOUTHERN CONFEDERACY.

AFTER HIS TOUR OF DUTY AND THE END TO THE CIVIL WAR, ROBERT SMALLS RETURNED TO HIS NATIVE STATE OF SOUTH CAROLINA,HE BECAME A MEMBER OF THE BEAUFORT COUNTY SCHOOL DISTRIC BOARD, HE WAS ESPICALLY INTERESTED IN DEVELOPING THE EDUCATION SYSTEM, IN IN A STATE THAT OFFERED VERY LITTLE EDUCATION FOR IT CITIZENS BLACK OR WHITE HE SAT AS A DELIGATE TO THE 1868, STATE CONSTITUTION CONVENTION, HE SPONSERED A RESOLUTION FOR PUBLIC SCHOOLS, HE SERVED IN THE SOUTH CAROLINA HOUSE OF REPRESENTIVES, AND IN THE STATE SENATE, EDUCATION WAS ONE OF HIS TOP PRIORITY AND PRIMARY CONCERNS. FRANCIS LOUIS CARDOZO, A BLACK RECONSTRUCTION POLITICIAN, BORN FREE IN CHARLESTON, CARDOZO WAS A DELIGATE TO SOUTH CAROLINAS STATE CONSTITUTION CONVENTION IN 1868, AND SERVED AS SOUTH CAROLINA SECRETARY OF STATE

UNTIL 1872, HE ALSO WAS STATE TREASUER FOR FIVE YEARS UNTIL 1878, WHEN HE RECIEVED AN APPOINTMENT TO THE TREASURY DEPARTMENT IN WASHINGTON D.C.

ALSO IN LOUISANA PICKNEY BENTON STEWART PINCHBACK, BECAME THE NATION FIRST AFRICAN AMERICAN GOVERNOR OF THAT STATE. EGBERT SAMMIS, WAS ELECTED TO THE FLORDIA STATE SENATE IN 1884. JONATHAN GIBBS, SERVED AS FLORDIAS SECETARY OF STATE FROM 1868, TO 1872, LATER SERVED AS FLORIDAS STATE SUPERINTENDENT OF EUDCATION.

OSCAR J. DUNN AN EXSLAVE BECAME LIEUTENANT GOVERNOR OF LOUISANA. HIRMAN RHODES REVELS, A NORTH CAROLINIAN WAS AMERICA FIRST BLACK U.S. SENATOR IN 1870, A REPUBLICAN THAT REPRESENTED MISSISSIPPI FOR ONE YEAR, COMPLETING THE TERM OF JEFFERSON DAVIS, WHO GAVE UP SENATE POSITION IN 1861, TO BECOME PRESIDENT OF THE CONFEDRACY, AFTER HIS TERM IN THE SENATE REVELS SERVED AS PRESIDENT OF MISSISSIPPI ALCORN AGRICULTURAL COLLEGE FOR BLACK STUDENTS. BLANCHE K. BRUCE, A REPUBLICAN WAS THE FIRST AFRICAN AMERICAN TO SERVE A FULL TERM AS A U.S. SENATOR, ELECTED IN LOUISIANA IN 1874 THE DEMOCRATS CRUSHED THIS ADVANCEMENT BY AFRICAN AMERICANS IN THE SOUTH, BECAUSE THEIR IDEOLOGY IS THAT NO NIGGER SHOULD BE EDCATED AND IN CHARGE OF ANYTHING, SO ALONG WITH THEIR FOUNDED KU-KLUX-KLAN, THEY VIOLENTLY ATTACKED VOTING AND POLITICAL ORGANIZING PLACES THROUGH THE SOUTH, KILLING AND SLAUGHTERING BLACK AND WHITE REPUBLICANS, ONE SUCH HORRIBLE KILLING WAS THE REVEREND DR. NORTON OF MEMPHIS TENNESSEE, SHOT DEAD PLEADING FOR HIS LIFE AT A REPUBLICAN STRATEGY POLLING HALL.

THE FREEING OF AFRICAN AMERICANS FROM SLAVERY WAS ONE OF THE TROUBLING AND COMPLEX ISSURES THE DEMOCRATS FACED IN DECADES, BECAUSE THEIR HOLD AND CONTROL REGARDS TO SLAVERY HAD BEEN ABOLISHED, AND THE AFFILIATIONS OF AFRICAN AMERICANS WITH THE REPUBLICAN PARTY WAS A DISASTER FOR THEM BECAUSE THEY KNEW ALING WITH THEIR VOTING BLOC AND IN THE

PROCESS OF BECOMING EDUCATED, WHICH IS ONE OF THE BASIC FOUNDATIONS OF THE REPUBLICANS, AND EQUALITY, IF THIS SHOULD HAPPEN AND AS THE POPULATION GREW, BEING EDUCATED AND HAVING FREEDOM THE SAME AS EVERY ONE ELSE THEY COULD BECOME MORE FAMILIAR WITH THE POLITICAL SYSTEM AND HOW IT WORK, AND MOST OF ALL DEFEAT THEIR INSANE IDEA OF DEMOCRATIC WHITE SUPREMACY RULE, SO THEIR ONLY HOPE WAS TO RELUCTANTLY LURE AFRICAN AMERICANS TO THEIR SIDE NOT FOR THEIR CAUSE PERTAINING TO PROGRESS, BUT FOR THEIR VOTES ONLY.

SO THE POLITICAL TRICKERY BEGAN BUT NOT UNTIL THE NINETEEN CENTURY, THEY RELEASED A BOMBSHELL OF DECEIT, THERE ARE TIMES I BECOME A LITTLE EMOTIONAL EXPLAINING THE FACTS PERTAINING TO THE DEMOCRATIC PARTY, BECAUSE THERE ARE SUCH SENSITIVES ISSURES AS AFRICAN AMERICANS, OUR ANCESTORS FOUGHT AND DIED FOR FREEDOM FIRST THE WAR OF 1812, THIS WAS FOR WHITE AND THEIR OWN FREEDOM FROM BONDAGE OF OF BRITISH RULE, THE SECOND MAJOR WAR WAS BETWEEN THE STATES TO BE FREE THEMSELVES, IN THIS WONDERFUL COUNTRY UNDER THE GUIDANCE OF PRESIDENT ABRAHAM LINCOLN, THAT HAD A VISION THAT IF YOU WERE FREE YOU COULD EDUCATR YOURSELF AND FUNDALISM WOULD BE YOUR REWARD, IN ORDER TO BECOME INDIPENDANT IN YOUR OWN RIGHT, AND INTERGRATE INTO A POLITICALLY DIVERSE SOCIETY OF ALL PEOPLE THAT MAKE THIS GREAT COUNTRY OF AMERICA WHAT IT IS TODAY. BUT UNFORTUNATELY AND SADLY THE DEMOCRATS SEDUCED THE MAJORITY OF AFRICAN AMERICANS INTO THEIR RADICAL IDEOLOGY WAY OF THINKING SEPARATE AND NOT EQUAL, THIS DOCTRINE HAS BEEN TAUGHT BY THE DEMOCRATS SENSE AFRICAN AMERICANS FIRST SRRIVAL IN AMERICA, AND IT IS MORE PRONOUNCED TODAY THAN EVER, THEIR IDEOLOGY FRUSTRATE MANY WHITES, SLAVERY NO LONGER EXIST THEY CANT REALISTICALLY SHOVE PEOPLE AROUND AT THE BALLOT BOX THE COURTS ARE SLOWLY ESCAPING FROM THEIR GRASP AND THE MOST AGONIZING OF ALL, THE REPUBLICANS PARTY HAVE

POSITION SOME AFRICAN AMERICANS TO POTENTIALLY BECOME PRESIDENT OF THE UNITED STATES OF AMERICA, THEIR VIOLENCE THROUGH HISTORY PORTRAY THAT IF THEY CANT REMAIN IN POLITICAL POWER THROUGH INTIMIDATION THEY WILL ATTEMPT TO DESTROY WHO EVER OR WHAT EVER STAND IN THEIR WAY, AND THIS COUNTRY IS TO LOVELY TO ALLOW SOME OF THESE BUFFOONISH, NIT-WITS, WHITH HIDDEN CONVOLUTED WHITE SUPREMACY IDEALS, ANY OPPERTUNITY TO DEPRIVE ALL CITIZENS WHITE AND AFRICAN AMERICAN , THE FREEDOM THAT WE HAVE SHARED FOR SO LONG SO WE AS A NATION BETTER UNDERSTAND THAT WE FACE ONE THE MOST SERIOUS CHALLENGES OF ALL TIMES, AND IF WE DONT DEFEAT THESE RADICAL NUTS AT THE BALLOT BOX, WE AS A NATION WILL SUFFER THE CONSEQUENCES.

BECAUSE THEY HAVE THEIR POLITICAL SLAVE DRIVERS OUT IN FORCE, AND AND THE POLITICAL MASTERS ARE SITTING BACK EGGING THEM ON BEHIND CLOSE DOORS.

THERE ARE SOME SUPPOSEDLY EDUCATED AFRICAN AMERICANS, SOME ARE COLLEGE PROFESSORS ADVOCATING REAPPORATION FOR SLAVERY, THIS IS ANOTHER ATTEMPT TO HERD IGNORANCE INTO A CORALLAND EXPOUND ON DEMOCRATIC NONSENSICAL ISSURES, AND PROBABLY INSITE VIOLENCE, CLAIMING THAT AFRICAN AMERICANS ARE OWED SOMETHING BY THE WHITE BUISNESS OWNERS IN THIS COUNTRY, WOULD SOMEONE PLEASE ATTEMPT TO ADVISE THESE IDIOTS THAT THE WAR OF 1812, WAS ABOUT FREEING WHITES AND AFRICAN AMERICANS, SOME WERE INDENTURED, HOWEVER I WANT TO OPEN THE DOOR REGARDS TO YOUR INDIVIDUAL THINKING, SO PLEASE BE ADVISED THAT THIS COUNTRY WAS HERE LONG BEFORE THE ARRIVAL OF OF AFRICANS TO AMERICÀ,THEIR PART WAS SIGNIFICANT WITH OUT DOUBT IN THE STABILITY REGARDS TO BUILDING, BUT TO FABRICATE THIS OUTRAGEOUS DEMAGOGUREY THERE IS SOMETHING OWED FOR BUILDING THIS COUNTRY IS LUDICROUS, I AM SURE THESE POLITICAL SLAVE DRIVERS NEVER HEARD OF THE KINGSLEYS, THE MASTER MARRIED HIS AFRICAN SLAVE WOMEN AND SHE INHERITED THOUSANDS OF ACRES OF

LAND AND ALL THE SLAVES NOT TO MENTION SOME SLAVES WORKED HARD AND EARN THEIR FREEDOM AND WITH THE HELP OF THEIR MASTERS ACCUMULATED THEIR OWN FORTUNE MEANING LAND, AND HAD SLAVES OF THEIR OWN, LAND WAS GIVEN TO THOSE THAT WORKED HARD AND CAUSE PROBLEMS, AFRICAN AMERICANS OWNED LAND SLAVES THROUGH THE SOUTH, SO WOULD SOME ONE PLEASE PASS ON TO THESE EDUCATED IDIOTS,THAT IF THEY WANT REAPPORATION FOR SLAVERY GO TO AFRICA WHERE OWNING PEOPLE WAS ORIGNATED BY AFRICAN KINGS.

FIRST OF ALL AFRICANS WERE A SAVAGE ILLITERATE HUMAN BEING WHEN THEY WERE BROUGHT HERE FROM AFRICA, THEY BROUGHT A CULTURE OF VIOLENT ACTIVITIES ALONG WITH THEM, WHICH THEY CLUNG TO THROUGH THE SEVENTEENTH AND EIGHTEENTH CENTURY, SO THERE IS NO QUESTION IT HAD TO BE DELT WITH THROUGH VIOLENT ACTS, BY THEIR SLAVE MASTER OR THE GOVERNMENT MILITIA, OTHER THAN THAT THE WHITE POPULATION WOULD HAVE SLAUGHTERED, EXAMPLE SOME IDIOT WAS ON NATIONAL TELEVISION ADMIRING NAT TURNER, BRAGGING THAT MORE AFRICAN AMERICANS SHOULD BE LIKE NAT, BY THE WAY HE CLAIM TO BE A MINISTER, I CAN IMAGINE WHAT HE TEACH , HOWEVER SOME ONE SHOULD ADVISE THIS MINISTER THAT NAT TURNER, WAS A PLANTATION SLAVE FROM VIRGINIA THAT FORMED A REBELLIOUS GROUP OF THUGSH AND PARADED THROUGH THE SOUTH KILLING WHITES, AND FREEING SLAVES^LOOTING, THE MILITIA WAS CALLED ON THEY PUT THEM DOWN, AND LATER FOUND NAT TURNER, TRIED AND HUNG HIM, AND CALLED ON DOCTORS TO SKIN HIM, AND MADE SOUVENIRS FROM HIS SKIN, SUCH AS PURSES, SHOES, AND TABLE MOUNTS FROM HIS BONES.

JUST THINK THIS PERSON IS ON NATIONAL TELEVISION, CLAIMING TO BE A MINISTER, IF SO HE HAS A FOLLOWING YOUNG AND OLD AFRICAN AMERICANS, LISTEN TO THIS KIND OF FOOLISH SCATTER BRAIN TALK AND BECOME BELLIGERENT THEIR FATE IS JAIL, SOME TIME DEATH, BUT MOST OF ALL POVITY,

BENJAMIN RUSH, THE SIGNER OF THE DECLARATION OF INDEPENDENCE STATED AFRICANS WERE THE MORAL AND INTELLECTUAL EQUAL OF WHITES, THAT SLAVERY AND THE ALAVE TRADE MUST BE ENDED, IN AN EFFORT TO EDUCATE AFRICANS IN ORDER THAT THEY MAY BECOME USEFUL CITIZENS, AND AMERICA COULD BECOME A BEACON OF FREEDOM FOR ALL. I JUST HAPPEN TO BE WALKING THROUGH MY LIVING ROOM, AND CAUGHT A SHOT OF SENATOR OBAMA, GIVING SOME KIND OF SPEECH ON NATIONAL TELEVISION, WITH A LARGE PHOTO OF PRESIDENT ABRAHAM LINCOLN IN THE BACK GROUND, I WAS STUNNED IN DISBELIEF, JUST LIKE THE SEVENTEEN AND EIGHTEENTH CENTURY THE DEMOCRATIC SLAVE MASTERS AND THEIR SLVE DRIVERS WILL USE ANY TACTIC IF THEY THINK IT WILL BENIFIT THE TR IDEOLOGY OF CONTROL OVER OTHER PEOPLE, NOW HERE IS A DEMOCRAT SENATOR, AND AN ATTORNEY, PORTRAYING A BACK DROP PHOTO OF A REPULICAN PRESIDENT THAT FREED THE SLAVES FROM BONDAGE, AND HE USE THIS PHOTO TO BESMIRCH THIS FINE PRESIDENT INTEGRITY, IN ORDER TO PROMOTE THE IDEOLOGY OF THE DEMOCRATIC PARTY, WHICH PLOTTED AND ASSASSINATED HIM FOR HIS IDEALS REGARIDS TO SLAVERY, AND FORMED THE KU-KLUX-KLAN TO MAINTAIN THEIR WHITE SUPREMACY OVER AFRICAN AMERICANS

SO FOR THIS CONFUSED MISGUIDED SENATOR, TO USE PRESIDENT LINCOLN PHOTO, AS A BACK DROP IN ORDER TO SUGGEST THEIR IDEALS ARE COMPATIBLE IS ABSURD, BECAUSE HE REPRESENT THE DEMOCRATIC PARTY AND ALL THEY STAND FOR.

NOW IT WOULD HAVE BEEN APPROPRIATE TO USE A PHOTO OF PRESIDENT ANDRED JOHNSON, VICE PRESIDENT TO ABRAHAM LINCOLN WHICH ASSUMED THE PRESIDENCY AFTER HIS DEATH, AND DISMANTLED EVERY EFFORT THAT THE REPUBLICAN PARTY AND LINCOLN HAD INVESTED IN AND SET ASIDE IN ORDER THAT EVERY AFRICAN AMERICAN COULD PROSPER THAT WANTED TO, HIS IDEA WAS TO UTALIZE THE LAND THAT THE UNION ARMY CONFISCATED FROM THE SOUTHERN SLAVE MASTERS, AND DIVIDE INTO

FORTY ACRES FOR EACH AFRICAN AMERICAN FAMILY ALONG WITH A GOVERNMENT MULE.

ANDRED JOHNSON A SOUTHERN TURNCOAT DEMOCRAT FROM TENNESSEE, VOIDED THESE PLANS AND RETURNED ALL THE LAND BACK TO THE SLAVE MASTERS WAS THE BEGINNING OF THE SHARECROPPING FIASCO, BECAUSE SLAVERY WAS ABOLISHED,THE SOUTHERN ARISTOCRATS WITH THEIR WHITE POWER AGENDA COULD NOT FORCE AFRICAN AMERICANS BACK IN SLAVERY, BUT UNFORTUNATELY THEY HAD NO PLACE TO GO, THE ONLY THING THEY KNEW WAS FARMING AND MOST BEING ILLITERATE THIS WAS THEIR ONLY CHOICE, TO SURVIVE IN A SOCIETY OF SOUTHERN BIGOTS INSTITUTING RADICAL DEMOCRATIC IDEOLOGY, THAT YOU WERE BORN TO SERVE AND FARM THE PLANTATIONS, MOST AFRICAN AMERICANS HAVE NO IDEA HOW THE WELL OILED POLITICAL MACHINE WORK, REGARDS TO DECEIT.

ON FEBRUARY 8, 2006, ON A NATIONAL TELEVISION NET WORK, ONE RED BLOODED FEMALE AMERICAN HAD THE COURAGE TO GIVE A BRIEF SYNOPSIS OF THE SERIOUS PROBLEM WITH THE MAJORITY OF AFRICAN AMERICANS SHE DIDNT EXACTLY PHRASE IT IN THIS MANNER, HOWEVER I WILL. ILLITERACY, A POPULATION EXPLOSION OUT OF WEDLOCK, ALSO NO CONTROL OVER THE AMOUNT OF CHILDREN THEY HAVE BEING MARRIED, AND MOST OF ALL HERDING BEHIND LEADERS THAT ARE CARRYING THE CONFEDERATE FLAG FOR THEIR SOUTHERN PLANTATION SLAVE MASTERS, SPREADING THEIR POVITY DRIVEN PROPAGANDA THAT THE ONLY REASON YOU ARE POOR, ITS THE WHITE MAN FAULT THAT IS AFFILIATED WITH THE REPUBLICANS, THIS IS A TACTIC THE DEMOCRATS HAVE USED SENSE AFRICAN AMERICANS BECAME ELIGIBLE TO VOTE, AND THIS IS TO KEEP THEM IN LINE REGARDS TO THEIR VOTING BLOC, AND THEIR VOTES ONLY.

BECAUSE THEY KNOW HOW POLITICAL IGNORANT AFRICAN AMERICANS ARE. THIS LADY WAS FOLLOWED BY A FAT FACE BUFFOON CARRYING THE CONFEDERATE FLAG FOR HIS SLAVE MASTERS, FOAMING AT THE MOUTH WITH DEMOCRAT SEWAGE DEFENDING FOOLISH IGNORANT

POWER GRABBING REMARKS SPEWED OUT BY A POLITICAL SLAVE DRIVER FOR HIS MASTERS.

THE SKILLS PORTRAYED BY DEMOCRATS, ARE SO CAMOUFLAGED UNTIL IT KEEP SOME REPUBLICANS BACK ON THEIR HELLS, SO YOU KNOW HOW AFRICAN AMERICANS DEAL WITH THIS ISSURE.

THE DEMOCRATS CONTROLLED THE CONGRESS FOR FORTY YEARS AND NEVER ELEVATED ANY MINORITIES SUCH AS THE CURRANT ADMINISTRATION HAS. I AM GOING TO MAKE A PREDICTION REGARDS TO SENATOR OBAMA, FUTURE AS A DEMOCRATIC POLITICIAN, THIS IS AN ELECTION YEAR THE DEMOCRATS NEED AFRICAN AMERICAN VOTES, SENATOR OBAMA IS THEIR BEST CHOICE AT THIS TIME BECAUSE AFRICAN AMERICANS FEEL THAT SOME DAY HE WILL BE PRESIDENT,SO THEY ARE GOING TO HERD BEHIND HIM HOPING HE CAN BR A RUNNING MATE FOR SOME DEMOCRAT THAT WIN THE NOMINATION YOU SEE THIS IS AN OLD TRICK OF THE DEMOCRATS STRONG HOLD TO GET BLOC VOTES.

YOU SEE HE HAS ALREADY STARTED THEIR THEME, WITH THE LINCOLN BACK DROP PHOTO, THEY ARE GOING TO RUN HIM RAGGED WITH DEMOCRATIC DEMAGOGY HE IS GOING TO CARRY THIS ON THROUGH THE YEAR, BUT LITTLE DOES HE KNOW HIS POLITICAL ASPIRATIONS IS SMOLDERING DEEP INSIDE LIKE A VOLCANO, THIS IS DEMOCRAT POLITICS AT ITS BEST TUST REMEMBER HE AGREED TO SUPPORT A BIPARTISAN PROJECT WITH SENATOR MCCAIN, THE DEMOCRATS SAW THEIR CHANCE TO CUT HIM TO PEICES AFTER HE DELIVER THE AFRICAN AMERICAN VOTES, OF COURSE THEY ARE GOING TO SIT ON THEIR DEVIOUS PLAN UNTIL HE DELIVER THE HERD VOTES, YOU SEE AFTER HE AGREED TO SUPPORT SENATOR MCCAIN, THE DEMOCRATS CALLED HIM BEHIND CLOSED DOORS AND SEDUCED HIM INTO RENEGING ON ONE OF THE MOST POWERFUL REPUBLICANS SENATOR IN WASHINGTON, SPARKS WERE FLING ALL OVER THE NATIONAL NEWS, AND THE DEMOCRATS ARE SITTING BACK LICKING THEIR CHOPS, NOT ALL THE DEMOCRATS BUT THE WHITE SUPREMACIST NO NIGGERS ALLOWED

ROTTWEILERS,I WANT YOUR VOTES,BUT I STILL THINK LIKE MY ANCESTORS DO WHAT EVER IT TAKE FOR YOU TO KEEP ME IN POLITICAL POWER, BUT YOU WILL NEVER MEASURE UP TO HAVE A SEAT AT THE TABLE, BECAUSE WE ARE SUPREME. TO PICK A FIGHT WITH SENATOR MCCAIN,BEING A JUNIOR SENATOR IS POITICAL ANARCHY PARTICALLY WHEN YOU GAVE YOUR WORD, HOWEVER ITS NOT SENATOR MCCAIN GOING TO BESMIRCH HIM IT IS HIS OWN PARTY, AND BLAME IT ON MCCAIN, ONCE THEY HAVE USED HIM TO BRING IN THE HERD VOTES, THEY WILL FIND SOMETHING IN HIS BACKGROUND LEAK IT TO THE PRESS, AND WHEN IT COME TIME FOR CHOOSING A RUNNING MATE FOR THE DEMOCRATIC PRESIDENT CANIDATE THE DEMOCRATI POLITICAL MASTERS WILL ADVISE HIM THAT THEY ARE SO SORRY BUT MCCAIN MESSED HIM UP OVER THAT RENEGE THING.

AND THAT IS DEMOCRATS AT THEIR BEST,USE THE HERD LEADER TO GET VOTES, AND ONCE IT OVER THROW HIM OUT AND LEAVE HIM OR HER LICKING THEIR WOUNDS,AND IGNORANT OF THE WHOLE ORDEAL, AND WHAT THIS DOES IS CAUSE HIM TO GO ON NATIONAL TELEVISION AND RADIO BLASTING SENATOR MCCAIN, STATEING MCCAIN COST HIM A POTENTIAL RUN FOR THE PRESIDENCY ONE DAY, AND GUESS WHAT THE MAJORITY OF HERDING AFRICAN AMERICANS THROUGH THE COUNTRY WILL BLAST THE REPUBLICAN PARTY, AS THEY USUALLY DO, FOR CAUSING ONE OF THEIR POLITICAL LEADERS HIS CAREER, AND THEY WILL CONTINUE FLOCKING TO THE DEMOCRATIC PARTY WITH THEIR VOTES,IN AN EFFORT TO KEEP THEM IN POWER,OR PUT THEM IN POWER.

AND THAT MY FRIENDS IS DEMOCRAT STRATEGY, THAT HAS HAD AFRICAN AMERICANS POLITICALLY BRAIN DEAD FOR YEARS, AND IS CALLED POLITICAL SELF DESTRUCTION, BECAUSE THE MAJORITY OF AFRICAN AMERICANS DO NOT UNDER POLITICS.

IF THE DEMOCRATS COULD REORGANIZE THE KU-KLUK-KLAN THEY WOULD, BECAUSE THEY SENSE THEY ARE LOOSING THEIR HOLD ON POLITICAL POWER AND THIS IS WHY THEY ARE DISPLAYING TEMPERS OF A ENRAGED

ROTTWEILER, BECAUSE FHE HISPANIC VOTES,HAVE SENT THEM INTO A SPIN,BECAUH SE THEY HAVE OFFSET THAT MAJORITY AFRICAN AMERICAN VOTE. BY SPLITTING THEIR VOTES BY APPROXIMATELY 40%, FOR REPUBLICANS, THIS IS DRIVING THE DEMOCRATS CRAZY, DID YOU WATCH MRS. CORETTA SCOTT KING FUNERAL, THIS WAS A FINE EXAMPLE OF DEMOCRATIC LUNACY, FOR POLITICAL POWER.

THE DEMOCRATIC POLITICAL MASTERS, AND THEIR POLITICAL DRIVERS WERE OUT IN FORCE SPREAD,ING THEIR HIDDEN SLAVE MASTER IDEOLOGY TO A HUGE CROWD OF AFRICAN AMERICANS, ONE WHITE AND ONE AFRICAN AMERICAN, SHOULD HAVE BEEN GIVEN A OSCAR FOR THEIR PERFORMANCE TRYING TO CONVINCE THIS ALMOST NINETY FIVE PRECENT MINORITIE CROWD THAT THEY ARE THE PARTY OF THE FUTURE, THEY WERE THE PARTY FOR FORTY YEARS, INSTEAD OF HAVING THEIR POLITICAL SLAVE DRIVERS INITIATE LEADER SHIP REGARDS TO EDUCATION, SELF ASTEEM, INDEPENDENT ..THINKING, BECAUSE GOD GAVE YOU THE SAME FIVE SENSES THAT HE GAVE EVERY ONE ELSE, TO USE AT YOUR LEISURE, SO IF YOU CHOOSE TO INCORPORATE YOUR THINKING INTO A HERD, AND HAVE SOME ONE ELSE THINK FOR YOU THERE IS A PRICE TO PAY PERTAINING TO POLITICKS, AND ANY THING ELSE, BECAUSE THE MAJORITY OF THE TIME YOU HAVE SOLD YOURSELF OUT TO SOME MONEY GRUBBING SLICK TALKING DEMOCRATIC POLITICAL SLAVE DRIVING INDIVIDUAL, FOR YOUR VOTE,TO KEEP POLITICIANS IN POWER. AND THE PRICE YOU PAY IS POVITY, THE IDEOLOGY OF THE DEMOCRATS AS RE SOCIAL PROGRAMS, TO KEEP YOU THINKING THEY ARE HELPING YOU BUT IT IS ALL FOR POLITICAL CONTROL, THROUGH THEIR POLITICAL SLAVE DRIVING COMPANIONS AS THEY DID DURING SLAVERY, BECAUSE A ILLITERATE PERSON HAVE NO OTHER CHOICE BUT SERVE SOME ONE, FINE EXAMPLE AFTER AFRICAN AMERICANS WERE FREED FROM SLAVERY, MOST BEING ILLITERATE HAD NO OTHER CHOICE BUT BE REINTRODUCED INTO THE HALL OF FAME RELATED TO SOPHISTICATED SLAVERY, CALLED SHARECROPPING, THE ONLY DIFFERENCE, THEN THE SUPREME SLAVE MASTERS, AND THEIR DRIVERS NEEDED

YOUR LABOR TO SUPPORT THEIR POLITICAL THIRST FOR POWER AND WEALTH, TODAY YOU RESERVE THE RIGHT TO VOTE,SAME ISSURE YOU ARE HERDED INTO POVITY STRIKEN HIGH RISE BUILDINGS AROUND THE COUNTRY AND GIVEN A GOVERNMENT CHECK, AND THE ILLITERACY RATE IS STARTLING, SOME DONT EVEN KNOW WHO THE PRESIDENT OF THE UNITED STATES IS AND EVEN DR. MARTIN LUTHER KING, AND REALLY DONT CARE, BUT WHEN IT IS. VOTING TIME, THE POLITICAL, SLAVE DRIVERS, LOCATE AND ADVISE THEM WHOM THEY SHOULD VOTE FOR, SO WHEN THESE TALKING POLITICAL SLAVE DRIVING MOUTH PEICES FOR THE DEMOCRATIC PARTY GO ON NATIONAL TELEVISION THROW THEIR HANDS UP AND BLAME THIS DISASTROUS DILEMMA ON CHURCHES, THIS IS PURE DEMOCRAT POLITICAL DEMAGOGUERY SPUED OUT BY THEIR POLITICAL SLAVE DRIVERS,SOME OF THE MINISTERS ARE JUST AS BAD BUT THEY ARE NOT ON NATIONAL TELEVISION AS REGULAR, THESE DEMOCRATIC POLITICAL SLAVE DRIVERS IS LARGELY RESPONSIBLE FOR THE JAILS, BUSTING AT THE SEAMS, ILLITERACY, AND POVITY, AND SOME ARE SO STUPID THEY ARE UNAWARE THAT THEY ARE A MAJOR PART OF THE PROBLEM, BY CONSTANTLY SPREADING PREHISTORIC SLAVE MASTER IDEOLOGY, AND INDICATING YOU ARE OWED SOMETHING, FOR YOUR SERVICES, AND THEY BEING A STAUNCH SUPPORTER OF THE DEMOCRAT PARTY, AND YOU THINKING THAT IF YOU CAST YOUR VOTE, FOR THE DEMOCRATS YOUR SHIP IS GOING TO COME IN,I GOT NEWS FOR THE MAJORITY OF AFRICAN AMERICANS, THAT FOLLOW THESE SILLY BUFFOONS, YOUR SHIP WAS SUNK IN 1865,

GETTING BACK TO MRS. CORETTA SCOTT KING, FUNERAL I WATCHED THE MOST DISGUSTING DEMOCRATIC DISPLAY OF DEMAGOGUERY I HAVE EVER SEEN, SOME OF THESE VOTE HUNGRY POWER GRUBBING, POLITICAL SLAVE MASTERS AND THEIR DRIVERS USED THIS PIONEER OF A WOMAN FUNERAL TO PROMOTE THEIR POLITICAL AGENDA, ONE ELECTED THE NEXT PRESIDENT ONE SPEWED OUT FOOLISH DEROGATORY REMARKS, AIMED AT A SITTING PRESIDENT, THE OTHER RATHER FOOLISHLY ADDRESSED

WIRE TAPPING ON DR. MARTIN LUTHER KING, BUT HE DID NOT DISCUSS,IT WAS THE DEMOCRATS, ORDED THE WIRE TAPPING, WHICH HE IS A AVID MEMBER/SOME SUSPECT THE DEMOCRATS MAY HAVE APPROVED HIS ASSASSINATION.

I FEEL THOSE WHO BELITTLE A SITTING PRESIDENT, BECAUSE HE IS THE PEOPLES CHOICE, THEY HAVE NO COMPASSION FOR THEIR OWN COUNTRY, AND LUST FOR POLITICAL POWER, HAVE ADDLED THEIR SENSE OF THINKING. AND THOSE ACCUSE A SITTING PRESIDENT OF KNOWING OF TERROIST ACTS, AND CALLING HIM A TERROIST, SHOULD BE SEDATED, SHIPPED TO AFRICA STRIPPED NAKED, PLASTER HUMAN DUNG ON THEIR HEADS, AND RELEASED THEM AMID HYENAS, AND SEND A FIEW NEWS REPOTERS ALONG FOR SNAKS, ESPECIALLY SOME FROM ATLANTA, BECAUSE SOME WERE SYMPATHETIC TO THIS FOOLISH DEMAGOGUERY DISPLAYED AT MRS. CORETTA SCOTT KING FUNERAL, I SAT AND WATCHED PART OF AN INTERVIEW ON ONE OF THE MAJOR NETWORKS, WITH A NOTED AFRICAN AMERICAN, I HONESTLY COULD NOT TAKE IT ANY MORE, BECAUSE ANY SANE PERSON REFUSE TO ACKNOWLEDGE REALITY EITHER SHE OR HE IS SENILE OR A DAMN FOOL, I AM FULLY COVINCED THAT THERE ARE SO MANY OF THESE PEOPLE WAVING THE CONFEDERATE FLAG FOR THE DEMOCRATIC PARTY, THAT YOU ARE SUPPOSE TO TAKE FROM THE RICH AND GIVE TO THE POOR, YOU COULD GIVE A LAZY EDUCATED AND A ILLITERATE PERSON A MILLION DOLLARS TODAY,IN A FIEW DAYS THEY WOULD BE BACK FOR MORE, BECAUSE ONE IS TO LAZY TO WORK, AND THE OTHER IS TO DUMD TO FIND GOOD EMPLOYMENT, HOWEVER YOU FIND THESE SPOON FED POLITICAL SLAVE DRIVERS SCREAMING, THE GOVERNMENT IS NOT DOING ENOUGH FOR THE POOR, THIS IS INSANE, PARENTS THAT ARE RESPECTABLE AND CARE ABOUT THEIR CHILDREN FUTURE THEY ENTER THEM INTO SCHOOL, BE VERY OBSERVANT OF THEIR ACTIVITIES MAKE SURE THEY ARE OUT TO SCHOOL EVERY DAY HAVE THEM KNOW THAT ANY STRANGE ACTIVITIES OCCUR IN SCHOOL THEY BETTER ADVISE YOU, HOME WORK IS MANDATORY,LIES WILL NOT BE TOLERATED, AT ALL WHEN THEY BECOME TEEN AGERS

AT THE APPROPRIATE TIME GET PART TIME JOBS, TEACH THEM THE VALUE OF A DOLLAR, AND FOREVER RESPECT YOU AS A PARENT. AND FORMAL EDUCATION IS ABSOLUTELY NECESSARY, AND THAT THIS A DIVERSE COUNTRY YOU HAVE TO BE OPEN MINDED TO ALL PEOPLE, AND FOR GOD SAKE THINK FOR YOUR SELF, AND TEACH THEM ABOUT THE HERD SLAVE DRIVERS, IF YOU DO HALF THESE THINGS, MOST LIKELY YOU HAVE SENT A INDIVIDUAL OFF INTO THE WORLD WILL MAKE YOU PROUD.

ON THE OTHER HAND IF YOU ALLOW YOUR CHILD TO DITCH SCHOOL, MAKE INAPPROPRIATE DESISIONS ON HIS OR HER OWN DISRESPECTFUL CANT GET ALONG PEOPLE SELFISH, DROP OUT OF SCHOOL, THEN MOST LIKELY YOU HAVE ADDED TO THAT HERD COMPLAINING THAT THE WHITE MAN IS KEEPING HIM DOWN, BECAUSE HE IS AFRICAN AMERICAN.

THEN HE OR SHE BECOME PRIME IDIOT FOR THE DEMOCRATIC POLITICAL SLAVE DRIVERS, TO SEDUCE HIM INTO JUST VOTE DEMOCRATIC, AND THEY WILL STRAITEN ALL THIS OUT, BECAUSE THIS NEVER WOULD HAVE HAPPEN IF THE REPUBLICANS WASNT GIVING SO MUCH MONEY TO THE RICH, AND NOT LOOKING OUT FOR YOU, JUST HANG IN THERE THE DEMOCRATS ARE WORKING ON YOUR CASE JUST KEEP VOITNG TO KEEP THEM IN POLITICAL POWER, AND WHILE HE IS WAITING HE NEED FINANCES BECAUSE HE CANT KEEP A JOB BECAUSE HE HOLD THE WHITE MAN RESPONSIBLE FOR HIS CONDITIONS, SO NOW HE IS GOING TO TAKE WHAT HE FEEL BELONG TO HIM HE GET A GUN ROB A STORE GET EIGHTEEN DOLLARS, IN THE PROCESS HE SHOOT THE CLERK BECAUSE HE IS ANGRY WITH WHITE PEOPLE FOR WHAT THE POLITICAL SLAVE DRIVERS SUDECED HIM INTO THINKING, HE GET TEN TO TWENTY, HE GO TO DO HIS TIME, HE IS ABUSED BY HARDEN CRIMINALS, AND ALL BECAUSE HIS FAMILY DIDNT MAKE HIM RESPECT THE GOLDEN RULE, AND THE DEMOCRATIC POLITICAL SLAVE DRIVERS TOOK HIM OVER FOR HIS VOTE.

THE WEALTHY IS THE FOUNDATION FOR ANY COUNTRY, THESE ARE THE PEOPLE THAT FAUGHT THEIR WAY TO SUCCESS,BASED ON THE TRADITIONS OF WHAT

AMERICA, AND THE ESTABLISH FORMAT THAT IS HERE FOR EVERYONE, TO COMPREHEND, IF YOUR DESIRE IS TO FORGO THIS STANDARD PROCEDURE THEN I THINK IT IS QUITE OBVIOUS YOUR IDEALS PERTAIN TO MALAISE, REGARDLESS OF YOUR RACE.

LETS EXPLORE THE RENDITION, IN THE BEGINNING GOD CREATED MAN EQUAL, MEANING THAT YOU HAVE ALL THE ATTRIBUTES OF ANY ONE ELSE, WHICH MEAN A BRAIN, THAT CONTROL YOUR BODY, IN THAT BRAIN CONSIST FIVE SENSES, THERE IS NO WHERE IN THE BIBLE YOU WILL FIND THAT GOD INDICATED HE WOULD TELL YOU HOW TO USE THE FIVE SENSES THAT HE GAVE YOU, THAT WAS LEFT UP TO YOUR PURGATIVE, BECAUSE I SUPECT THAT IF HE WAS GOING TO BE IN CONTROL OF YOUR DESTINATION, THE FIVE SENSSES WOULD HAVE BEEN LEFT OUT, PERTAINING TO AFFAIRS ON EARTH.

I TRULY BELIVE THAT ALL THAT GOD HAS GIVEN YOU IN YOUR PERFECT DESIGENED BODY, AND YOU ARE A WITNESS TO THIS EXTRAORDINARY PERFECTION ON A DAILY BASIS ,IT IS IGNOMINIOUS TO PLEAD FOR MORE, MEANING THATYOU ARETHE SOLE ALLOWABLE INDIVIDUAL HERE ON EARTH RESPONSIBLE FOR YOUR ACTIONS.

HOWEVER IF YOU SHOULD CHOOSE TO TRUST SOME ONE ELSE WITH THIS PRECIOUS GIFT FROM GOD, YOU ARE DOOMED FOR FAILURE, IN ALL ASPECTS OF LIFE, BECAUSE YOUR SENSE OF DIRECTIONS IS MIRED BEYOND APPROACH, RICH PEOPLE ALL OVER THE WORLD CONTROL THEIR OWN DESTINY, IF A POOR PRESIDENT IS ELECTED THE WHOLE COUNTRY IS IN TROUBLE, REMEMBER MILK SOME YEARS AGO, LOBBYST RUN THE COUNTRY, IT IS A VERY DISTINCT POSSIBILITY POOR WHITES AND THE MAJORITY OF AFRICAN AMERICANS, ARE TOTALLY CONFUSED REGARDS TO WEALTHY PEOPLE,THEY ARE NOT THERE TO ASSIST YOUR IGNORANCE FOR BEING POOR, THEY ARE THERE FOR THE BASE OF THE COUNTRY, THEY ARE THERE TO SUPPLY YOU WITH EVERY THING YOU NEED, BEING POOR SUCH AS JOBS, AND ALL THE ECONOMICS OF LIVING, THEY PAY THE SALARIES OF PROFESSIONALS PERSONELL, SUCH AS DOCTORS, LAWYERS, FOOT BALL, BASKET BALL,

HOCKEY, BASE BALL, SOCKER, GOLF, ECT. ALSO THEY ARE RESPONSIBLE FOR INDORSEMENTS AND SUPPLY OF THOSE, $150-200, SNEAKERS YOU LUST FOR PERTAINING TO MICHAEL JORDAN, AND KOBE BRYANT, WEAR, SO IT IS HIGHLY IMPOSSIBLE TO CORALL THE RICH AND FAMOUS, YOUR BEST EFFORT IS TO STAY IN SCHOOL , AND TRY TO FIGURE OUT THE SECRET TO THEIR SUCCESS.

DESPITE MY FRUSTRATION AND ANGER OVER THE DEMOCRATS ANTICS AT MRS KING FUNERAL MUST GET BACK TO ISSURES PERTAINING TO POLITICAL CONTROL OF THE MAJORITY OF AFRICAN AMERICANS BY THE DEMOCRATS,I AM MOVING INTO THE NINETEENTH CENTURY, IT WAS THAT CENTURY SOME ONE , SOME HOW DECIDED TO LABEL AFRICAN AMERICANS AS BLACK, TO ME IT NEVER MADE MUCH SENSE, BECAUSE MOST PEOPLE EDUCATED OR ILLITERATE CAN OR SHOULD BE ABLE TO DISTINGUISH COLOR, PIRATICALLY WHEN YOU ARE LOCKING AT IT, IT SEEM PRETTY SILLY FOR AN INDIVIDUAL TO PURCHASE A BLACK AUTOMOBILE DRIVE INTO A PICNIC AREA WHERE LOTS OF PEOPLE ARE STANDING AROUND, GET OUT AND SHOUT LOOK YOU ALL I DRIVING A BLACK CAR, HOWEVER IF AFRICAN AMERICANS WANT TO ADOPT BLACK, INSTEAD OF COLORED, WHICH THEY ADOPTED IN THE EIGHTEEN CENTURY, SO BE IT, I WILL ROLL INTO THE NINETEENTH CENTURY WITH BLACK, HOWEVER I AM AN INDEPENDANT THINKER, I DO NOT BELONG TO A HERD, SO I SHALL REMAIN A AFRICAN AMERICANOF AFRICAN HERITAGE, THAT IS A CITIZEN OF THE UNITED STATES OF AMERICA THANK GOD. IN 1932, FRANKLIN DELANO ROOSEVELT WAS ELECTED TO BECOME THE MOST POWERFUL PRESIDENT OF THE UNITED STATES EVER, HE WASNT JUST THE THE PRESIDENT OF THE UNITED STATES, HE WAS PRESIDENT OF THE WORLD HE WAS THE GRAND OF POLITICS, THERE WAS NONE BEFORE HIM AND THERE WILL NOT BE ANY AFTER HIM, HE WAS TRULY A GENIUS REGARDS TO DEMOCRATIC POLITICS, HE CONTROLLED THE CONGRESS, THE SENATE, AND THE SUPREME COURT, ALSO THE BRITISH, THE FRENCH, POLAND, YOU NAME IT HE SERVED APPROXIMATELY SIXTEEN YEARS IN OFFICE, AS PRESIDENT, HE HAD A ABLE SUPPORTING

PARTNER IN HIS WIFE FIRST LADY ELENOR, WAS A POLITICAL DRIVING FORCE, SHE WAS EXTREMELY GOOD AT HER RESPONSIBILITIES AT QUELLING RACIAL TENDENCIES, IT WAS THE EARLY NINETEEN HUNDREDS AND BLACKS AND POOR WHITES, WERE FEELING THEIR WAY AROUND REGARDS TO EQUALITY, BLACK ACTIVIST AND SOME WHITE PROGRESSIVES CREATED THE NIAGRA MOVEMENT IN ORDER TO CARRY ON THE STRUGGLE AGAINST RACIAL INJUSTICE, LATER THIS ORGANIZATION WAS SUPERSEDED BY THE NAACP, THERE WAS A MOVIE PRODUCED, CALLED THE BIRTH OF A NATION SYMPATHETIC TO THE DEMOCRATS FOUNDED KU-KLUX-KLAN OF LYNCHING OF THOUSAND OF BLACKS IN THE SOUTH, DESPITE THE PROGRESS MADE AGAINST RACIAL INJUSTICE, AS AMERICANS WE MUST UNDERSTAND SLAVERY AND THE CONSEQUENCES, IF WE ARE EVER TO BE EMANCIPATED, FROM ITS GRASP,

PRESIDENT FRANKLIN D. ROSEVELT WAS LIKE A GOOD POKER PLAYER, HE NEVER REVEALED HIS HAND , HE WAS A DISSEMBLER AND WAS A NATURAL CONCENTRATOR, AND EXTREMELY PROUD OF HIS DEVIOUSNESS, AND IT SERVED WELL, HOWEVER THERE SOME CHALLENGING TIMES AHEAD , MOST OF THE COUNTRY WERE OPTIMISTIC , SOME ON THE RIGHT WERE JUGDMENTAL WITH SUSPECTS OF THE PRESIDENT BEING A SOCIALIST SYMPATHIZER, THOSE ON THE LEFT REGARDED HIM AS AN ALLY, JUNE 1934, THE PRESIDENT WAS SOME WHAT ELATED IN HAVING HELPED ESCALATE AGRICULTURE WHICH HAD BEEN POUNDED BY PROSTRATION, NEXT ON THE AGENDA WAS TO PROMOTE GENERAL WELFARE, AND TO PAY FOR IT ONA CONTRIBUTORY BASIS, HE SENT A PLAN TO THE CONGRESS COVERING BOTH UNEMPLOYMENT AND OLDAGE INSURANCE, AND INCREASING AID FOR STATES DEPENDANT CHILDREN, ALSO HEALTH ASSISTANCE, THE BILL FAILED THE PRESIDENT WAS DISCREETLY ANNOYED, HOWEVER THE PRESIDENT WOULD LATER PREVAIL, AND RANTED NO DAMN POLITICAN IS GOING TO STOP MY, SOCIAL PROGRAMS, THERE WAS A OMPETUOUS MOVE THAT STRUCK AN EXECUTIVE ORDER IN 1935, SETTING UP THE RESETTLEMENT ADMINISTRATION TO RESETTLE POOR

URBAN AND RURAL FAMILIES, THE PRESIDENT AIMED TO RESETTLE ONE HALF MILLION RURAL FAMILIES, HE HOPED TO BUY TEN MILLION ACRES OF PRIME LAND TO OF SETT THE BARREN LAND PRODUCTION, THE IDEA WAS TO MOVE A NUMBER OF DISADVANTAGE FAMLIES INTO A AREA, HOWEVER A NUMBER OF PROBLEMS OCCURED WITH THIS PLAN, SUCH AS INADEQUATE HOUSING, TERRIBLY COLD WINTERS , THE FIRST LADY ELEANOR TRIED DESPERATELY TO PERSUADE COMPNIES TO LOCATE AND INVEST, BUT TO NO AVAIL, THE CONGRESS BALKED AT FINACING A POST OFFICE SUPPLY FACTORY, THIS PROJECT BECAME A ALBATROSS FOR THE FIRST LADY, HOWEVER THE WELFARE DEPENDENCE WITH EXAGGERATED EXPECTATIONS MOVED ON CONTRAY TO HIS WIFE EXPECTATIONS, THE PRESIDENT WAS NOT OVERLY PERTURBED, AND HE WOULD CONTINUE ON WITH HIS LEGISLATURE PLANS, THERE WERE MANY ALPHABETIICAL PROGRAMS THAT ASSISTED THE UNEMPLOYED,AND A LOT OF WERE ABOUT TO RECEIVE ASSISTANCE FROM THE SOCIAL SECURITY SYSTEM, DURING THESE TIMES THERE WERE BRUISING CONTEMPTUOUS LEGISLATIVE BATTLES, IN FACT , SUPPOSABLY A NATION WIDE RUMOR THAT THE PRESIDENT WAS INSANE, BUT LITTLE DID THE COUNTRY KNOW THIS POLITICAL GENIUS WAS STRATEGICALLY PLOTTING TO SPREAD A RUMOR THAT HE WAS GOING TO TAKE FROM THE WEALTHY AND GIVE TO THE POOR, ASSUMEDLY FOR VOTING RECIPIENTS, THIS WAS PIRATICALLY GEARED AT BLACKS, BECAUSE THEY WERE CONSIDERED TO BE THE PARTY THAT LINCOLN BUILT.

FOR AT LEAST SEVENTY YEARS, PRESIDENT ROSEVELT APPROVED THROUGH THE EMPLOYMENT RELIEF PROGRAM, AND IT WAS HIGHLIGHTED THAT BLACKS WAS RECEVING THE SAME AMOUNT OF EMPLOYMENT RELIEF AS WHITES, BLACKS EXPLOITED THIS POLITICAL TACTIC AS THE PRESIDENT HELPING THEM BECOME EQUAL TO WHITES, ALTHOUGH THEY WERE STILL SEGREGATED, THIS CLEVELY PLANNED DEMOCRATIC PLOY, WAS^O SEDUCE BLACKS AWAY FROM THE PARTY THAT LINCOLN BUILT IN FAVOR OF BLACKS, PERTAINING TO THEIR LIBERTY AND FREEDOM, DESPITE THE DISENFRANCHISEMENT IN THE SOUTHERN

STATES, THIS POLITICAL PLOY WAS TO HERD BLACK VOTES, NATION WIDE JUST ONE NAIL IN THE COFFIN TO DEPRIVE BLACKS OF THEIR FREEDOM, THE PRESIDENT ARRANGED FOR A FIRST TO HAVE A BLACK CONGRESSMAN ARTHUR MITCHELL, FROM ILLINOIS TO ADDRESS THE DEMOCRATIC CONVENTION, HIS MAJOR TOPIC WAS TO PRAISE THE PRESIDENT IN HIS EFFORT TO BENIFIT BLACKS REGARDS TO HIS POLITICAL PROGRAMS, THIS TACTIC HAS WORKED AGAINST BLACKS, ALL THEIR LIVES IN AMERICA, EITHER FOR THEIR SLAVE LABOR ON THE PLANTATIONS, AND FOR THEIR VOTES AFTER THEY BECAME ELIGIBLE TO VOTE.

BLACKS ARE DEMOCRATICALLY ILLADVISED, BY SLICK POLITICAL MASTERS OF THE DEMOCRAT PARTY TO ACCESS THIS RUTHLESS TACTIC USED BY DEMOCRATS FOR VALUED PARTY LINE VOTES.

THEY KNOW IF THEY FIND A PROMINENT BLACK THE REST WILL HERD AND FOLLOW HIS OR HER INSTRUCTIONS, ON HOW THEY SHOULD VOTE, REMEMBER BOOKER T. WASHINGTON IN THE EIGHTEENTH CENTURY, SUPPOSEDLY ADVOCATING AT PLANTATIONS IN THE SOUTH THAT SECOND CLASS CITIZENSHIP WAS OK AND THEY CHEERED, SIMPLY BECAUSE OF HIS STATURE, THE PRESIDENT CLEVER TACTICS WORKED IN 1936, THE PARTY OF LINCOLN WAS DISOLVING LIKE ICE FROM SALT, ONE OF THE MOST DEMOCRATIC GENIUS ACTS WAS EXECUTED BY THE FIRST LADY ELEANOR, IN 1939, CONTRALTO MARIAN ANDERSON, WAS DENIED FROM PERFORMING AT CONSTITUTION HALL, MRS. ROSEVELT PUBLICY RESIGNED FROM THE DAUGHTERS OF THE AMECRICAN REVOLUTION, AND ORGANIZED A CONCERT FOR MS. ANDERSON AT THE LINCOLN MEMORIAL, CAN YOU IMAGINE HOW MANY BLACKS ATTENDED THERE WERE ALMOST ONE HUNDRED THOUSAND, MOST LIKELY SHE KNEW THE ORGANIZATION SHE RESIGNED FROM WAS RACIST WHEN SHE JOINED, HOWEVER THI IS WAS A GLORIFYING OPPORTUNITY TO EXPLODE THE WHEELS OF THE PARTY THAT LINCOLN BUILT,JUST THINK THE PRESIDENT WIFE PERSONALLY ORGANIZE THIS CONSERT, THEEMAJORITY OFCSTUPID BLACKS WILL ADOGT HER AS A SOALMOTHER,THATGOINGTOLEADTHEMTOTHEPROMISE

LAND SOLVE ALL THE RACIAL INJUSTICE, BRING THEM OUT OF POVITY, BLACKS NOT REALIZING THIS IS A MASTERFUL PLAN TO HERD BLACK VOTES BACK TO THE DEMOCRATIC PARTY, THESE CLEVER TACTICS WORKED IN 1936, HE WON REELECTION HANDILY HIS PERCENTAGE OF BLACK VOTERS WAS 25% IN 1932, IN 1936, PRECENTAGE ROSE TO OVER 50%, THE PARTY THAT PRESIDENT ABRAHAM LINCOLN BUILT PERTAINING TO BLACKS STRESSING EDUCATION, DIGNETY, RESPONSIBILITY, SELF PRESERVATION, POLITICALLY ALERT, AND EQUALCJUSTLOEEPSR ALL, HAD BEEN MANIPULATED FROM THE MAJORITY OF BLACKS FOREVER.

PRESIDENT ROSEVELT, NOMINATED HUGO BLACK, OF ALABAMA TO THE SUPREME COURT, AND NO ONE REVEALED THAT HE WAS A KLKLUXKLAN MEMBER, UNTIL HE WAS CONFIRMED, HE HUGO BLACK, PUBLICALLY ADDRESSED THE MATTER AND CLAIMED HE HAD RESIGNED, AND THE MATTER WAS SUPPRESSED THE SUPREME COURT WAS THE PRESIDENT PRIZE PROCESSION,HE APPOINTED SEVEN OF THE NINE JUSTICES, TO THE SUPREME COURT.

PRESIDENT ROSEVELT, REASSURED THE AFRICAN AMERICAN CONSTITUENCY THAT HAD BEEN LARGELY WON OVER FROM THE LINCOLN PARTY, THROUGH WELFARE AND PROGRAMS WHICH WAS PROVIDING RELIEF FOR OVER AN ESTIMATED ONE MILLION BLACK FAMILES.

FIRST LADY ELEANOR ADDRESSED THE CONVENTION OF THE SLEEPING CARPORTERS, IN 1940, THIS UNION WAS FOUNDED BY PHILIP RANDOLPH, A HIGHLY DISTINGUISH BLACK LEADER, AND OTHER BLACKS LEADERS, OF ORGANIZATIONS, THE URBAN LEAGUE, AND THE N,A.A.C.P. ALONG WITH WALTER WHITE, AND ARNOLD HILL, SHE ARRANGED A MEETING FOR THEM WITH THE PRESIDENT, THIS MEETING WAS SUPPOSABLY FOR TO DISCUSS THE CODITIONS OF AFERICAN AMERICANS, IN THE ARMED FORCES, AND THE FACT WAS EMPHASIZED THAT BLACKS WOULD BE PUT INTO PRORATED UNITS, AND WOULD BE ELIGIBLE FOR COMBAT, HE LED THEM TO BELIEVE HE WAS GOING TO INTERGRATE THE ARM FORCES, AND PROMISED SCHEDULE ANOTHER MEETING, I SUSPECT THIS WAS NOTHING MORE THAN A DEMOCRATIC POLITICAL PLOY,

TO INSULATE THE FACT THAT FIFTEEN BLACK CREWMAN ABOARD THE U.S.S. PHILADELOHIA, HAD CAUSED CONTROVERSEY BY RELEASING INFORMATION TO THE PITTSBURGH COURIER, ABOUT SLAVE MENTALITY ABORD SHIP THEY HAD TO ENDURE , THEY WERE THROWN INTO THE BRIG AND DISHONORABLE DISCHARGED AS UNFIT FOR SERVICE, BECAUSE THEY EXPOSED THE IDEALS OF THE PRESIDENT, PRESS SECRETARY STEVE EARLY, A SOUTHERN WHITE SUPREMACIST AND SEGREGATIONST, FORTUNATELY THIS RENDITION OF POLITICAL APPEASEMENT STARTED TO FALL APART, BECAUSE TWO AFRIW CAN AMERICANS WERE TORTURED AND BURNED TO DEATH WITH BLOW TORCHES IN FRONT OF A CHEERING CROWD OF WHITES, IN DUCK HILL MISSISSIPPI. LETS REVIEW THE CIRCUMSTANCES REGARDS TO THE MEETING WITH THE CIVIL RIGHTS LEADERS, IF YOU ARE THE PRESIDENT OF THE UNITED STATES OF AMERICA, THE ENTIRE MILITARY IS AT YOUR DISPOSAL, ACCORDING TO THE CONSTITUON, ALSO STATES CIVIL RIGHTS, WHY WOULD YOU REFER TO POWERLESS CIVIL RIGHTS LEADERS CONCERNING THE SOLE AUTHORITY INVESTED IN YOU.

THIS IS A VERY CLEVER TACTIC USED BY DEMOCRATS, USED THEN AND STILL BEING USED TODAY, IF YOU ARE A IMPORTANT DEMOCRAT LEADER, ALL YOU HAVE TO DO TO MAINTAIN BLACKS VOTING BLOC, IS SOCIALIZE WITH THEIR SUPPOSEDELY LEADERS, AND A NINE ELEVEN COULD HAPPEN THEY ARE GOING TO SUPPORT THE DEMOCRATIC IDEOLOGY OF REPRESSING EDUCATION FOR SOCIAL PROGRAMS, AND POVITY AMONG BLACKS WILL CONTINUE TO ESCALATE, DURING PRESIDENT ROSEVELT REIGN,THE FIRST SEVEN YEARS OF HIS PRESIDENCY AT LEAST EIGHTEEN AFRICAN AMERICANS WERE LYNCHED ANUALLY, THERE HAD BEEN ANTILYNCHING LEGISLATION SUBMITTED TO THE CONGRESS REGARDS TO PROTECTION TO FORBID THESE BARBARIC ACTS AGAINST BLACKS, FROM 1934, TO 1936, HOWEVER THE SOUTHERN DEMOCRATS WOULD FILIBUSTER IN AN EFFORT TO PREVENT IT FROM PASSING, THERE WAS HEAVY DEBATE IN THE CONGRESS OVER PASSING THIS LEGISLATION, REGARDS TO ANTILYNCHING, ONCE IT CAME VERY CLOSE TO PASSING AND THE PRESIDENT WAS

SOME WHAT RELUCTANT TO ENDORSE THIS SOUTHERN BUREAUCRATIC BEHAVIOR, AND STATED THE TIME JUST WASNT RIGHT, THERE WERE SOME LYNCHINGS DURING PRESIDENT HOOVER TERM APPROXIMATELY FORTY, UNFORTUNATELY SOUTHERN DEMOCRATS ALONG WITH THEIR KUKLUX KLAN, SUPPRESSED THE REPORTING THROUGH INTIMIDATION, AND VIOLENCE AGAINST BLACKS, THE CONGRESS FAILED TO ACT REGARDS TO THESE CRIMES.

PRESIDENT ROSEVELT,WAS DEEPLY CONCERNED ABOUT THE BLACK VOTERS, BECAUSE THE BLACK POPULATION HAD GROWN TO 5% OVERALL IN THE NATION MOSTLY FROM THE NORTHEN STATES, THROUGH EMIGRATION OF BLACKS WHICH COULD DETERMINE ELECTORIAL VOTES, SO HE COMMISSION A RESERCH TEAM THROUGH OUT THE UNITED STATES, PARATICALLY THE NORTHEN STATES, THE REPORT SUGGESTED THAT BLACKS ALWAYS VOTED IN A BLOC, PRIMARY TO SUPPORT A PROMINANT BLACK LEADER, IMMEDIATELY THE WHEEELS WAS SET IN MOTION, THERE WAS A COLONEL IN THE ARMED FORCES, THE HIGHEST RANKING BLACK IN THE MILITARY, THE GRANDSON OF A SLAVE , BENJAMIN C. DAVIS, HE WAS PROMOTED TO GENERAL, AND THE DEAN OF HOWARD LAW SCHOOL WILLIAM HASTIE, WAS GIVEN A POSITION AS STAFF OF WAR SECRETARY, ATTACHED TO STIMSON, AFRICAN AMERICANS AROUND THE NATION APPLAUDED GRACIOUSLY, AND ASSUMED THIS WAS THE END TO WHITE SUPREMACY AND SEGREGATION IN THE SOUTH, STINSON WROTE T THIS WAS A TERRIBLE IDEA OF THESE PROMOTIONS, AND BLAMED THEM ON THE IMPULSIVE BUFFOONISH INTERVENTION OF THE FIRST LADY, BUT THIS WAS THE DUO AT THEIR BEST, HERDING BLACK VOTES, AND DESTROYING T.\ THE PARTY THAT LINCOLN BUILT AT THE SAME TIME, AND THEY WERE VERY SUCCESSFUL.

TO CONNECT THE DOTS TO THEIR WELL PLANNED SCHEME RELATED TO POLIP TICAL SELF DISTRUCTION OF BLACKS CONTROLLED BY POLITICAL MASTERS, THROUGH POLITICAL SLAVE DRIVERS,

HENRY FORD HAD A LURCATIVE CONTRACT FROM THE GOVERNMENT TO BUILD P AIRPLANE ENGINES, HE WAS APPOSE TO UNIONS ALL WORKERS WENT ON STV RIKE EXCEPT BLACKS, THEY REMAINED ON THE^JOB DESPITE OTHER STRIKE ERS APPROXIMATELY TWO OR THREE THOUSAND REMAINED LOYAL TO THE COMPANY, ANY INDIVIDUAL TRYING TO ORGANIZE A UNION WAS FIRED, TO AFRICAN AMERICANS LEADERS WHICH HAD VISITED THE WHITE HOUSE PREPREVIOUSLY, PHILIP RANDOLPH AND WALTER WHITE, THEY WERE APPEAL TO BY THE WHITEHOUSE, TO GET THESE WORKERS TO JOIN THE OTHER STRIKERS, AND THEY CONVINCED THE ENTIRE HERD TO WALK OUT AND JOINED THE OTHER STRIKERS.

PRESIDENT ROOSEVELT AND THE FIRST LADY, MASTERED AMERICAN POLITICS IN EVERY ASPECT HE WAS A MASTER AT MANEUVING THE CONGRESS LEAADERS AND THEY WERE THE BEST AT MOBILIZING PUBLIC OPINION ALL THEIR EFFORTS PERTAINING TO LEGISLATION WERE TIMED TO PERFECTION, HOWEVER THE SOUTHERN DEMOCRATS WHITE SUPREMACIST WERE A SERIOUS PROBLEM, AFRICAN AMERICANS WERE DESPERATELY TRYING TO OBTAIN EQUALITY FROM THE LONG BONDAGE OF SEGREGATION PARTICALLY IN THE SOUTHERN STATES, IN 1943, THERE WAS A TERRIBLE FLARE UP IN MOBILE ALABAMA, AT LEAST ELEVEN BLACKS WERE INJURED IN AN ATTEMPT TO INTERGRATE WITH WHITE WELDERS, IN THE CITY SHIPYARD, ALSO A RACE RIOT OCCURED IN DETROIT MICHIGAN, THIRTY TO FORTY PEOPLE WERE KILLED, TWENTY OR THIRTY AFRICAN AMERICANS, THE PRESIDENT HAD EFFECTIVELY DISMANTLED THE PARTY THAT LINCOLN BUILT TO ASSIST BLACKS, HOWEVER THE SOUTHERN DEMOCRATS WERE ENRAGED BECAUSE THE PRESIDENT WAS TOYING AROUND WITH BLACKS BECOMING ELIGIBLE TO VOTE, THE SOUTHERN BIGOTED DEMOCRATS FEARED IF BLACKS WERE ALLOWED TO VOTE FREELY THEY WOULD BECOME BESIDE THEM SELVES AND NEVER BE DOCILE AGAIN, SO THERE WAS AN ALL OUT EFFORT BY THE DEMOCRATS THROUGH OUT THE SOUTHERN STATES TO PROVENT AFRICAN AMERICANS FROM VOTING.

THEY ORGANIZED ALL KINDS OF RACIS RESTRICTIONS INCLUDING A POLL TAX, THE PRESIDENT WITH DREW HIS EFFORTS TO PUSH FOR CIVIL RIGHTS, DUE TO THE STRONG DISCOURAGEMENT FROM THE SOUTHERN DEMOCRATS. SO THE WHITE SUPREMACIST POSTSLAVERY SYSTEM IN THE SOUTHERN STATES PERSUADED BY DEMOCRATS WAS IN FULL BLOOM, THE PRESIDENT WAS MIRED IN THE POWER OF THE RACIST SOUTHERN CONGRESSIONAL POLITICAL LEADERS WITH LITTLE CHANCE TO EMANCIPATE.

IN 1944, HOLLYWOOD JOINED WITH WRITERS AND SCIENTIST, WITH OVER FORTY JOURNALIST IN A SPLENDID ORGANIZED UMBRELLA ORGANIZATION CALLED ARTS AND SCIENCES FOR THE PRESIDENT, THE LETTER HEAD WAS VERY EXTENSIVE THAT IT FILLED A ENTIRE PAGE, THERE ALSO WERE NONAMERICANS THERE, WITH HOLLYWOOD CUSTOMARY ELITE, ENERGIZED BY UNITS FROM THE INTELLECTUAL COMMUNITY, THIS AFFAIR WAS BROADCAST ACROSS THE COUNTRY CONSTANTLY IN THE PRESS, AND RADIO, UNIFORMLY HELPFUL TO THE PRESIDENT.

ROOSEVELT RAN FOR PRESIDENT A THIRD CONSECUTIVE TERM, SENATOR HARRY S. TRUMAN, WAS CHOSEN AND ELECTED TO BE HIS RUNNING MATE,THEY WON THE DEMOCRATIC ELECTION OVER REPUBLICANS TO A THIRD TERM, AS PRESIDENT OF THE UNITED STATES OF AMERICA, DURING HIS THIRD TERM HE WAS BEFALL BY ILLNESS WHICH CAUSED HIS DEMISE, PRESIDENT FRANKLIN DELANO ROOSEVELT, WAS LAID TO REST AT HYDE PARK, APRIL 15, 1945, HIS SUCCESOR WAS HIS VICE PRESIDENT HARRY S. TRUMAN, HOMETOWN INDEPENDENCE MISSOURI, THE ENTIRE TOWN WAS AFRICAN AMERICAN BORN PERTAINING TO THEIR POPULATION, PRATICALLY ALL OVER FORTY, WAS BORN INTO SLAVERY.

THERE WERE OTHER NATIONALLYS THERE ALSO, THE IRISH, TALIANS, CR^ OATIANS, AND OTHER FOREIGNERS THEY ALL WERE MOSTLY POVITY STRICKEN, MOST OF THESE NATIONALS CONGREGATED AROUND KANSAS CITY, VERY SELDOM SEEN IN INDEPENDENCE, BLACKS HERDED IN A PLACE CALLED NIGGER NECK, AND LIVED IN DILAPIDATED HOUSING, AND BASED ON THEIR CYNICAL DISPOSITION,

THEY WERE NOT WELCOME AT MOST OF THE STORES, ALSO THE LIBARYS. IN TOWN, HOWEVER THE TRUMANS HAD SERVANTS WHICH THEY WERE KIND TO, AND ADDRESSED THEMAMOST COMMONLYAS--NIGGERS OR COONS, AS A MATTER OF POLITE SOCIETY, AND NO BLACK WAS ALLOWED TO PROTEST OR GET OUT OF PLACE, BECAUSE THROUGH OUT THE SOUTH LYNCHINGS WAS IN ORDER, AND ANY TIME THIS HAPPENED SOME PLACE ELSE THE LOCAL PAPERS WOULD REPORT HE GOT WHAT HE DESERVED, THE AT LAGE COMMUNITY AROUND INDEPENDENCE WERE NEVER ALARMED WHEN THERE WAS A LYNCHING BECAUSE OF THE LOITERING AND THIEVERY OF WORTHLESS YOUNG BLACK MEN IN TOWN WHO DID NOTHING, THEY REFUSED TO WORK FOR FOR ANY ONE REGARDS TO WAGES, ALL THEY DID WAS CONGREGATE AND STAND AROUND AND MAKE DEROGATORY REMARKS ABOUT LADIES AND AND OTHERS PEOPLE THAT HAD JOBS, AND HERD INTO ELECTRIC CARS AND INSULT AND INTIMIDATE OTHER PASSENGERS.

HARRY TRUMAN, FINISHED HIGH SCHOOL IN 1901, THIS WAS TRULY A REMARKABLE INDIVIDUAL TENACITY TO SUCCEED BECAUSE AMERICA OFFER EVERY ONE THE OPPORTUNITY TO BE SUCCESSFUL AND THE ONLY PRICE TO PAY IS COMMON SENSE PERSEVERANCE AND HARD WORK, AND BE INDIVIDUAL JUDGE OF YOUR OWN CONVICTIONS AS HE DID, HE WAS TAUGHT BY HIS PARENTS HONESTY IS THE BEST POLICY, AND IF YOU TELL THE TRUTH YOU DO NOT HAVE TO CONSTANTLY HAVE TO REMEMBER WHAT YOU SAID, AND ALWAYS MAKE YOUR SELF USEFUL, BECAUSE ANYTHING WORTHWHILE REQUIRE EFFORT AND AT FIRST YOU DO NOT SUCCEED KEEP TRYING AND NEVER GIVE UP,AND THAT CHILDREN IS A REFLECTION OF THEIR PARENTS, PRIOR TO GRADUATING FROM HIGH SCHOOL HE WORKED FOR THE LOCAL DRUGGIST, AFTER HIGH SCHOOL HE WANTED TO ATTEND WEST POINT, BUT WAS REJECTED BECAUSE OF HIS EYESITE, HE FOUND A JOB AS A CONSTRUCTION TIME KEEPER WHICH WAS NOT THE MOST IDEAL BECAUSE OF ALL THE DRUNKEN VULGARITY, AND THE SADISTIC BEHAVIOR AMONG THE WORKERS, IN 1903, HE LANDED A JOB AS A BANK CLERK, IN 1905, HARRY

SIGNED UP WITH A NATIONAL GUARD UNIT, HE DID FARM WORK SOME TIME FROM DUST TO DAWN, HE JOINED THE MASONIC AS HE WORKED HARD HOURS ON THE FARM, HOWEVER HE HAD A INKLING FOR POLITICS HE HAD SEEN PITFALLS AND SEDUCTION OF POLITICS HE TOOK IT UPON HIMSELF TO BUY AND SELL OIL LEASES, IN 1917, HE JOINED THE MILITARY NATIONAL GUARD,AND OVER A PEROID OF TIME WAS PROMOTED TO OFFICER, LATER SHIPPED OF TO FRANCE, HE LATER DECIDED TO ATTEND ARTILLERY SCHOOL, AND LATER WAS PROMOTED TO CAPTIAIN AND BATTERY COMMANDER, HIS UNIT WAS ENGAGED IN PHYSICAL COMBAT AND SERVED IN A HEROIC MANNER.

AFTER RETURNING HOME HE INVESTED IN A HABERDASHERY BUISNESS WHICH FAILED LATER,

HARRY TRUMAN WAS APPROACHED BY A POLITICIAN AND OFFERED AN OPPORTUNITY TO RUN FOR A JUDICIAL ADMINISTRATION POSITION, HE ACCEPTED THEIR OFFER, HE WON THE ELECTION, HE WAS ELATED WITH HIS TITLE JUDGE TRUMAN, HOWEVER IT WAS ONLY FOR TWO YEARS, HE LOST THE REELECTION FOR JUDGE, HE PURSUED BECOMING PRESIDENT OF THE NATIONAL OLD TRAILS ASSOCAITION BUILDING HISTORIC TRAILS, HE ALSO SPENT SOME TIME IN LAW SCHOOL AND DROPPED OUT, HE EXPERMINTED WITH SELLING STOCK STOCK IN THE NEW COMMUNITY SAVINGS AND LOAN ASSOCATION, IN 1927, HARRY TRUMAN RAN FOR PRESIDING JUDGE AND WON,HE SERVED IN THAT CAPACITY FOR EIGHT YEARS, PRIOR TO THAT HE TOTTERED THE CITIZANS SECURITY OF BANKS, IN HIS JUDGE CAPACITY HE WAS THE CHIIEF EXECUTIVE OFFICER, WITH NO PRIOR POLITICAL EXPERIENCE, BEING THE PRESIDING JUDGE HE WAS ELECTED TO THE PRESIDENT OF THE GRATER KANSAS CITY PLAN ASSOCATION, THE DIRECTOR OF NATIONAL CONFERENCE OF CITY PLANNING, HE ALSO SERVED IN A FEDERAL POST TRAVELING TO WASHINGTON ON GOVRRNMENT BUISNESS, HE WAS SOLOCITED TO PERSUE THE THE SENATE, HE ACCEPTED AND WON, HE TOOK THE OATH IN 1935. AND WON A SECOND TERM TO THE SENATE IN 1944, LATER WAS CHOSEN AND ELECTED AS VICE PRESIDENT TO PRESIDENT

FRANKLIN DELANO ROOSEVELT, AFTER A LONG DEBATING PROCESS OF WHICH CANIDATE COULD SOLIDIFY THE AFRICAN AMERICAN VOTERS, HARRY TRUMAN WAS A STRAIGHT FORWARD INDIPENDANT INDIVIDUAL, THAT MADE CHOICES PERTAINING TO HIS PERSONAL LIFE THAT PROPELLED HIM INTO A SPECIAL ACCOLADE THAT MOST LIKELY WILL NEVER BE DUPLICATED, HE WAS GUIDED BY HIS INTEGRITY AND GOOD SOUND THINKING ONCE THE KU-KLUX-KLAN SOLICITED HIM IN HIS HOME TOWN PRIOR TO HIS ROLE IN THE WHITE HOUSE, AND ONCE HE LEARNED OF THEIR AGENDA, PERTAINING TO JEWS AND BLACKS HE REJECTED THEIR APPROACH AND MOVED ON.

ON APRIL 12, 1945, PRESIDENT FRANKLIN DELANO ROOSEVELT LOST HIS BID FOR LIFE, LITTLE OVER TWO HOURS AFTER HIS DEMISE, HARRY S. TRUMAN WAS SWORN IN AS PRESIDENT OF THE UNITED STATES OF AMERICA, PRESIDENT HARRY S, TRUMAN, WAS A RENOWNED INDIVIDUAL AND SHOULD BE AN INSPIRATION FOR ALL RACES OF PEOPLE, BECAUSE HE HAD NO PRIOR FORMAL EDUCATION FRON ANY NOTED UNIVERSITY, JUST A HIGH SCHOOL DIPLOMA, HOWEVER HE HELD ON TO HIS BIAS RACIAL TENDENCIES OCCASIONALLY SURFACING PRIVATELY, HE WOULD SPEAK OF NIGGERS, ONCE HIS SISTER BLURTED OUT WITH GLEE, HARRY IS NO MORE FOR NIGGERS EQUALITY THAN ANY OF US, ONCE HE WAS IN A MEETING WITH SOUTHERN DEMOCRATS PRIVATELY AND THERE WERE COMMENTS REGARDS TO.HIS PERSONAL VIEWS, PERTAINING TO RACE,AND HE RESPONDED THAT HIS FOREBEARS WE RE CONFEDRATES AND HE CAME FROM AT PART OF MISSOURI WHERE JIM CROW STILL PREVAILED.

THERE WERE RACIALLY MOTIVATED HORRIFYING OCCURRENCES,ONCE ON THE LOUISIANA AND ARKANSAS RAILWAY LOCOMOTIVES THAT BURN COAL FOR ENERGY THE COAL STOKING WAS RESERVED FOR AFRICAN AMERICANS BECAUSE IT WAS A BACK BREAKING CHORE AND FILTHY, BUT AS SOON AS THE LOCOMOTIVES CONVERTED TO OIL AND FUEL, BLACKS WERE SHOT AND MURDERED BECAUSE NOW IT WAS CONSIDERED A WHITE MAN JOB, THERE WERE FOUR BLACKS MURDERED IN MONROE GEORGIA IN 1946,

TWO MEN AND THEIR WIVES WERE DRAGGED FROM A AUTOMOBILE AND GUNNED DOWN, IT WAS SUCH A BRUTAL ATTACAK THEIR BODYS WEWE NOT IDENTIFIABLE, IN THE FALL OF 1945, AN INVITATION FROM THE DAUGHTERS OF THE AMERICAN REVOLUTION AT CINSTUTION HALL WAS SUBMITTED TO FIRST LADY BESS SHE ACCEPTED AND WAS NOT A MEMBER.

HOWEVER ADAM CLAYTON POWELL A MINISTER AND CONGRESSMAN RAISED THE ISSURE AND DID SOME SABER RATTLING BECAUSE HIS WIFE WAS A PIANIST AND WAS DENIED PERMISSION TO PERFORM AT CONSTUTION HALL, HE PUBLICICLY DENOUNCED THE FIRST LADY AND REFERRED TO HER AS THE LAST, LADY OF THE LAND, AT A STAFF MEETING THE PRESIDENT EXPLODED AND CALLED ADAM CLAYTON POWELL A DAM NIGGER PREACHER AND DECLARED POWELL WOULD NEVER BE INVITED TO THE WHITE HOUSE AGAIN. DURING PRESIDENT TRUMAN BID FOR A SECOND TERM HE HAD LEARNED WELL FROM THE POLITICAL PROFESSIONALS REGARDS TO BLACK VOTING SUPPORT, HE BLASTED INTO HARLEM , THIS WAS ONLY CIVIL RIGHTS SPEECH OF HIS CAMPAGIN, IT WAS NO DECLARATION OF IMPRESSION, HOWEVER HE FOCUSED ON CIVIL RIGHTS COMMISSION AND MOMENTOUS, IT WAS THE FIRST TIME A MAJOR PARTY CANIDATE FOR PRESIDENT HAD STOPPED IN HARLEM AND HISHISTORICALLY REMINDED THE 95% AFRICAN AMERICAN AUDIENCE THAT HE WAS TO ESTABLISH EQUAL OPPORTUNITY, HE PRIMISED TO KEEP WORKING FOR EQUAL RIGHTS AND EQUAL OPPORTUNITY WITH EVERY OUNCE OF HIS STRENGTH AND DETERMINATION.

THE CHEERING WAS SO LOUD YOU THOUGHT BABE RUTH WAS THERE AND HIT HIS SIXTIETH HOME RUN, HE SPOKE AT THE BROOKLYN ACADEMY OF MUSIC THAT EVENING, THE AUDIENCE APPLAUDED FOR TWELVEFIFTEEN MINUTES, THE MAJORITY OF AFRICAN AMERICANS HAS DEMONSTRATED OVER THE YEARS THAT THEIR DESIRE TO COMPREHEND POLITICAL VIEWS IS PRACTICALLY NONEXISTENCE ALONG WITH OTHER AULTURAL UNDESIRABLE TRAITS SUCH AS VIRULENCY PERTAINING TO OTHER NATIONALLY OF PEOPLE WITHOUT CAUSE, IT IS ASTOUNDING THAT THE

MAJORITY OF BLACKS CAN NOT OR WILL REEVALUATE THEIR IDEOLOGY PERTAINING TO PRODUCTIVE ISSURES AND REALIZE THAT THEY ARE THE CULPRIT PERTAINING TO THEIR FAILURE IN THIS COUNTRY AND NO ONE ELSE.

LETS REVISIT HARRY TRUMAN, HIGH SCHOOL DAYS IN INDEPENDANCE THE YEAR 1901, IT WAS STATED THEN THAT MOST NEGRO MEN WERE WORTHLESS AND HAD NO INTENTIONS OF GOING TO SCHOOL OR WORKING, ALL THEY DID WAS STAND AROUND ON STREET CORNERS AND STRESS THEIR OPENION ABOUT LADIES, AND OTHERS MAY PASS BY, AND CROUD INTO ELECTRIC CARS AND INTIMIDATE PASSANGERS ON THEIR WAY TO WORK, HOWEVER THERE WERE MANY LAWABIDING NEGRO CITIZENS THAT UNDERSTOOD THE TRUTH ABOUT THOSE MIS-FITS THE SAME AS EVERYONE ELSE, LETS NOT FORGET THERE WERE OTHER IMPOVISHED IMMIGRANTS, SUCH AS THE IRISH, ITALIANS, AND CROATIANS ALSO OTHER NATIONALS, HARRY TRUMAN GREW UP VERY POOR, HIM SELF, HOWEVER OVER ONE HUNDRED YEARS LATER, IT IS ONLY THE AFRICAN AMERICANS ARE COMPLAINING ABOUT FAILED5 SUCCESS IN A HERD FASHION, RAGING ABOUT WHAT SOME ONE NEED TO DO FOR THEM, OR DIDNT DO.

THIS INSANITY HAS BLOSSOMED INTO EPIDEMIC PROPORTIONS, THE ONLY WAY TO HEAD OFF THIS MADNESS THAT IS BEING FULED BY THE DEMOCRAT PARTY AND SOME OF THEIR BUREAUCRATIC POLITICAL POWER HUNGRY, POLITICAL MASTERS AND THEIR BLACK POLITICAL SLAVE DRIVERS, IN AN EFFORT TO LURE STUPID AFRICAN AMERICANS, INTO A NET OF VOTING THEM INTO POLITICAL POWER, SO THEY MAY CONTINUE TO CONTROL YOU AS THEY DID DURING SLAVERY, BUT NOW ITS FOR YOUR VOTING BLOC, THIS INSANE PHANTASM DEMONSTRATED BY SOME AFRICAN AMERICANS AND INDORSED BY SOME IN THE DEMOCRAT PARTY MUST BE BROUGHT TO A HALT, AND ONLY WAY IS TO REVEAL THEIR INTENTIONS TO THE NATION, THE DEMOCRATS COULD GIVE A DAMN ABOUT THE WELL FARE OF BLACKS AND THEY SHOULD NOT , BECAUSE EVERY ADULT SHOULD BE IN CONTROL OF HIS OR HER OWN DESTINY.

UNFORTUNATELY THE MAIN STREAM DEMOCRATIC MASTERS HAS FORMATED A MALICIOUS POLITICAL TACTIC WITH STRONG ASSISTANCE FROM THEIR BLACK POLITICAL SLAVE DRIVERS STRATEGIST TO SUBSTANTIATE THEIR CLAIM OF BUFFOONERY BRAIN WASH THAT AFRICAN AMERICANS HAVE BEEN MARRED IN FOR CENTURIES, THERE IS NO LOGICAL EXPLANATION HOW 95% OF A NATIONALLY OF PEOPLE CAN FOR SOME STRANGE REASON BE DUPED POLITICALLY FOR SO MANY YEARS, OTHER THAN HERDING BEHIND A TYRANNICAL MIS-FITS THAT IS STUPID ENOUGH TO THINK THAT THEY WILL BE RECOGNIZED AS SOME KIND OF SPECIAL GOVERNING FORCE THAT WILL BE ATTACHED TO OUR EXISTING GOVERNMENT AND RAN EXCLUSIVE BY RADICAL EXTREMIST BLACKS, WHICH HAVENT THE KNOWLEDGE TO UNDERSTAND THAT THEY ARE THE PROBLEM, PERTAINING TO POVITY, AMONG AFRICAN AMERICANS IF THE SYSTEM IS SO BAD HOW IS IT THAT TWO PUFFY AND HARRY FACE GOONS GO ON NATIONAL TELEVISION AND CLAIN TO SPEAK FOR BLACK AMERICA, SOME ONE NEED TO EXPLAIN TO THESE TWO PEOPLE THAT NEITHER HAS BENN ELECTED TO ASSOCIATE PRESIDENT OF THESE UNITED STATES IT IS ALL TO OFTEN AFRICAN AMERICANS ARE MADE TO THINK THEY NEED A SPOKESMAN TO GUIDE THEM INTO SUCCESS, THIS IS INSANE, AND AS LONG AS BLACKS LISTEN TO SUPPOSEDELY LEADERS THEY ARE GOING TO CONTINUE SINK INTO OBLIVION, SOME OF THESE OBNOXIOUS SO CALLED BLACK LEADERS ARE AS PHONY AND DECEVING AS THEIR POLITICAL MASTERS MOST NEVER OFFER AN EXPLANATION AS TO THEIR SUCCESS, BECAUSE THEY RODE IN ON THE WHITE MAN COAT TAIL, AND ONCE THEY ARE THERE THEY WOULD LIKE FOR ALL AFRICAN AMERICANS TO THINK THE REASON YOU ARE NOT WHERE THEY ARE IS BECAUSE THE WHITE MAN IS KEEPING YOU DOWN, AND MOST OF THEIR COMMENTS ARE DIRECTED AT WHITES THAT ARE NONE DEMOCRATS, THIS NATION NEED TO UNDERSTAND THAT THERE IS A PREHOSTRIC POLITICAL ISSURE THAT HAS BEEN SMOULDERING FOR YEARS INITIATED BY THE DEMOCRATS TO CONTROL AFRICAN AMERICAN VOTING BLOC, WHICH

HAS BEEN DETRIMENTAL TO THE MAJORITY OF BLACKS, BECAUSE IT ALLOW A FIEW TO CONTROL MANY, REGARDS TO MAKING POLITICAL DECISIONS, WHICH MOST OF THE TIME IS NOT IN THEIR BEST INTEREST, PERTAINING TO ECONOMICS HAVING TO DO WITH SUCCESS.

THE ONLY WAY TO OVER-RIDE THIS INSIDIOUS DELIMMA,IS THAT OTHER SANE RED BLOODED AMERICANS THAT LOVE THIS COUNTRY, FLOCK TO THE POOLS AND DEFEAT THIS DEMOCRATIC CONFEDRATE POLITICAL FASCISM, THAT IS DISGUISED IN THE NAME OF HELP FOR THE UNDER PRIVILEGE, WHICH HAVE NO MERIT PERTAINING TO ANY AMERICAN.

BUT PREDOMINATELY THIS POLITICAL AGGRESSION IS GEARED FOR AFRICAN AMERICANS, TO CONTINUE ASSUME THEIRVOTING BLOC, HOWEVER FOR SOME BLACKS THERE IS NO HOPE, LIKE DURING THE HARRY TRUMAN YEARS 1901, SOME UNDERSTOOD THE FUNDAMENTALS OF LIFE BUT OFTEN THEY FAIL TO VOICE THEIR OPENION FEAR OF POLITICAL REPRISAL FROM BLACK POLITICAL SLAVE DRIVING BOOT LICKERS JOINED AT THE HIP WITH THE DEMOCRATIC IDEOLOGY.

BECAUSE THERE IS NO HOPE FOR ANY INDIVIDUAL THAT GO AGAINST THE GRAIN OF WHAT THIS COUNTRY WAS BUILT ON, EDUCATION, HARD WORK, BELIEVING IN ONE SELF, HAVING A OPEN MIND, AND UNDERSTANDING THE MEANING OF DIVERSITY, IF FOR SOME REASON YOU DO NOT COMPREHEND THESE IMPORTANT ATTRIBUTES YOUR DESTINATION IS DOOMED FOR POVITY, AND THERE IS NO OTHER CHOICE REGARDLESS TO WHAT THE POLITICAL SLAVE DRIVING BOOT LICKERS TRY AND TELL YOU ABOUT WHY YOU ARE LESS FORTUNATE THAN OTHERS.

DWIGHT D. EISENHOWER, SOLIDER AND PRESIDENT OF THE UNITED STATES, PRIOR TO HIS PRESIDENCY , THE DEMOCRATS HELD POLITICAL POWER FOR SEVERAL YEARS IN THE CONGRESS , THE ADVANCEMENT OF AFRICAN AMERICANS WAS ON THE BACK BURNER, AND NOT ONE OF HIS STRONG POINTS,HIS INVOLVEMENT WITH BLACKS WHILE GROWING UP IN ABILENE WAS NIL, BECAUSE THERE WERE NONE THERE IN HIS HOME TOWN, ALSO LATER IN

YEARS NONE AT WEST POINT, AND HE DEPARTED THE MILATARY PRIOR TO DESEGREGATION, HOWEVER HE HAD SOUTHERN FRIENDS AND SEEMED TO SHARE THEIR RACIST VIEWS, OCCASIONALLY VISITING THE SOUTHERN STATES, SOME OF THE PLANTATION OWNERS WOULD TELL STORIES ABOUT DARKIES, AFTER HIS PRESIDENCY HE ENDORSED THE FACT THAT ALL PEOPLE REGARDLESS TO RACE RESERVE THE RIGHT TO BE REPRESENTED, DURING HIS STATE OF THE UNION ADDRESS HE ANNOUNCED THAT HE WAS GOING TO PUT FORTH HIS BEST EFFORT TO PUT AN END TO SEGREGATION IN THE DISTRICT OF COLUMBIA AND THE ARMED FORCES , HE DID ACCOMPLISH THAT TO HIS CREDIT. HOWEVER IT HAD LITTLE AFFECT FOR SIXTEEN MILLION OF AFRICAN AMERICANS OUT SIDE OF THE FEDERAL ESTABLISHMENT, BECAUSE THE THE SOUTHERN DEMOCRAT GOVERNERS HAD A STRANGLE HOLD ON WHITE SUPREMACY AND SEGREGATION, BECAUSE THEY WERE ELECTED BY ALL WHITE ELECTORATE AND A MAJORITY OF WHITE CONSTITUANCE, IN 1954, THE SUPREME COURT RULED ON BROWN V. TOPEKA, AND ALESSY V. FERGUSON, PERTAINING TO SCHOOL INTERGRATION, AND DECLARED SEGREGATION BY RACE IN PUBLIC SCHOOLS WAS UNCONSTITUTIONAL, BY A UNANIMOUS OPENION NINE TO ZERO, EISENHOWER RESPONDED TO THE DESION THAT THE SUPREME COURT HAD SPOKEN AND HE WAS SWON TO UPHOLD THE CONSTITUTION IN THIS COUNTRY, AND MOST CERTAINTLY WOULD OBEY, HOWEVER HE REFUSED TO ENDORSE THE RULING PUBLICLY, AND HE CALLED FOR A BIPARTSAN COMMISSION TO INVESTIGATE RACIAL SITUATIONS AND ADVISE WITH APPROPIATE LEGISLATION,AND SUGGESTED THEY STAY ON TOP OF THIS MATTER, BECAUSE CIVIL RIGHTS HAD BEEN IDLE FOR EIGHTY FIVE YEARS PRESIDENT EISENHOWER KNEW RACE RELATIONS AT THIS TIME WAS LIKE CROSSING THE GRAND CANYON ON A TIGHT ROPE.

BECAUSE OF THE DEMOCRATIC CONTROLLED SOUTHERN STATES, AND THE MOST CERTAIN FILIBUSTERS IN THE CONGRESS, BECAUSE MODERATION WAS NONE EXISTENCE WITH DEMOCRATS, THE AFRICAN AMERICANS

WERE SOME MODERATE BUT GRADUAL MEANT NEVER, WHICH THE MAJORITY OF THE WHITE RACIST IN THE SOUTH WANTED, VIOLENCE INCREASED TO ALMOST EPIDEMIC PROPORTIONS ALWAYS WHITES AGAINST BLACKS, IN 1956, REPUBLICAN PRESIDENT EISENHOWER, HAD A TEAM OF EXPERTS DO A STUDY ON AFRICAN AMERICAN VOTERS NATIONALLY, THE RESULTS REVEALED THAT THE MAJORITY OF AFRICAN AMERICANS NATION WIDE VOTED TO SUPPORT THE DEMOCRATS, HE WAS DEEPLEY DISAPPOINTED AND SADDEN, TO THINK HE WAS OBLIGATED TO CARRY OUT THE SUPREME COURT RULING REGARDS TO INTERGRATION AND WAS TOTALLY FRUSTRATED THAT HE WAS TAKING A POUNDING FROM SOUTHERN DEMOCRATIC CONSTITUENTS, INSISTING THEY WANTED NO BIG STUPID NIGGER SITTING NEXT TO THEIR WHITE CHILDREN IN SCHOOL. WHILE THE AFRICAN AMERICANS, WERE CONSISTENTLY VOTING IN A BLOC SUPPORTING DEMOCRATS EFFORTS TO REMAIN IN POLITICAL POWER, IN ORDER FOR DEMOCRATS TOUSUPBRESS CIVIL RIGHTS ISSURES PERTAINING TO THEIR OWN CAUSE.

THE PRESIDENT VENTED HIS FRUSTRATION TO THIS COMPLEX BEHAVIOR REGARDS TO BLACKS, BY SPEAKING OUT THAT ALL THE REPUBLICANS HAVE TRIED TO DO FOR THEM AS FAR BACK AS ABRAHAM LINCOLN, THEY LIKE THE ABILITY TO EVALUATE WHAT IS IN THEIR BEST INTEREST REGARDS TO POLITICAL ISSURES.

THE SOUTHERN DEMOCRATS LAUNCHED A VIGOROUS ATTACK AGAINST THE SUPREME COURT RULING TO INTERGRATE SCHOOLS IN 1956, THEY CLAIMED THE SUPREME COURT DECISION HAD NO ATHORITY OF AFFECT IN THEIR STATES, IN THE INTERIM A FEDERAL JUDGE ORDERED THE UNIVERSITY OF ALABAMA TO ENROLL AUTHERINE LUCY, THE UNIVERSITY OFFICIALS EXPELLED HER ON GROUNDS THAT SHE LIED IN HER LAW SUIT AGAINST THE UNIVERSITY, CLAIMING THE REASON SHE WAS DENIED ADMITTANCE WAS BECAUSE OF RACE, THIS WAS A CLEVER CASE OF DEFIANCE OF FEDERAL COURT ORDERS TO INTERGRATE,THE COUNTER ATTACK FROM THE SOUTHERN DEMOCRATS ESCULATED FROM STATED FEDERAL LEVEL, A ONE HUNDRED AND

ONE SOUTHERN DEMOCRATIC MANIFESTO WAS SIGNED BY THE HOUSE OF REPRESENTIVES AND THE SENATE, IN AN EFFORT TO OVERTURN THE DECISION OF THE SUPREME COURT RULING, IT WAS SUSPECTED THE PRESIDENT HAD BECAME SOMEWHAT SYMPATHETIC FOR THE SOUTHNERS, BECAUSE OF THE DISAPPOINTING VOTING BEHAVIOR OF AFRICAN AMERICANS ON A NATIONAL LEVEL SUPPORTING THE DEMOCRATS AND THEIR RACIST IDEOLOGY, WHICH HAD REJECTED EVERY CIVIL RIGHTS BILL PRESENTED TO THE CONGRESS AND SENATE FOR AN ETERNITY, MARTIN LUTHER JR. WAS LEADING BUS BOYCOTTS IN MONTGOMERY. ALABAMA, INSISTING BUS SEATING SHOULD NOT BE SEGREGATED, BLACK CITIZENS WERE SHOT, HOMES AND CHURCHES WERE BOMBED, J. EDGAR HOOVER WAS ON TOP OF THIS RACIAL UNREST, HE SUBMITTED A TWENTY FOUR PAGE BREFING TO THE PRESIDENT AND STRESSED HE BE DAMNED THE EXTRMIST ON BOTH SIDES THE N.A.A.C.P. AND THE WHITE CITIZENS COUNCEL, BETTER KNOWN AS THE KU-KLUX-KLAN, HE STATED THAT BLACK CITIZENS WAS SO TERRFIED THEY REFUSED TO TESTIFY TO THE VIOLENCE WAGED AGAINST THEM, AFTER HOOVER MADE HIS PRESENTATION AND OUTLINED THE CIVIL RIGHTS BILL, IT CALLED FOR FOR A BIPARTISAN COMMISION TO BE CREATED BY CONGRESS, WITH THE POWER TO SUBPOENA AND INVESTIGATE ALLEGED CIVIL RIGHTS VIOLATIONS, AND TO POSITION A ASSISTANT ATTORNEY GENERAL TO BE IN CHARGE OF CIVIL RIGHTS IN THE JUSTICE DEPARTMENT, IN ORDER TO ENFORCE NEW LAWS FOR VOTING RIGHTS, AND STRENGTHEN EXISTING CIVIL RIGHTS STATUTES, AND PROTECT PRIVLEGES OF CITIZENS, THE PRESIDENT WAS ELATED WITH THIS PROPOSAL AND ADVISED TO MOVE FORWARD WITH .THE PROJECT, HOWEVER HE WAS VERY CONCERNED ABOUT THE SOUTH ABANDON POBLIC EDUCATION ALTOGATHER, THE WHITES WOULD HAVE THEIR OWN PRIVATE CHURCH RELATED SCHOOLS, AND THE AFRICAN AMERICANS WOULD HAVE NO EDUCATION AT ALL, HOWEVER HE INSISTED THE LAW MUST BE ENFORCED, HE CAME TO THE CONCLUSION THAT HE SHOULD FORCE THE UNIVERSITY OF ALABAMA, TO ACCEPT LUCY, BUT IT

WAS NOT IN HIS POWER TO DO SO, BECAUSE EDUCATION WAS A STATE LOCAL MATTER, SO AS A RESULT HIS HANDS WAS TIED, HOWEVER HE WAS COMITTED TO THE CAUSE OF CIVIL RIGHTS, IN THE MEANTIME THE DEMOCRATS WERE UP TO THEIR OLD TRICKS CLEVERLY PLANNING ISSURES TO USE AGAINST EISENHOWER IN THE UP COMING PRESIDENTAL CAMPAIGN SO THEY DECIDED ON THE MISSLE GAP DEBACLE, AND TRIED TO BLAME THE THE PRESIDENT, BUT IT WAS THEIR OWN ADMINISTRATION THAT HAD CUT COST FOR THE PROGRAM, UNDER PRESIDENT HARRY TRUMAN, THE AMERICAN BALLISTIC MISSLE PROGRAM STARTED AFTER WORLD WAR TWO, AND THERE WERE ONLY A FIEW MILLION DOLLARS ALLOCATED BY TRUMAN, AS A COST CUTTING FACTOR.

THE SUMMER OF 1956, THE REPUBLICANS INTRODUCED THE CIVIL RIGHTS BILL TO THE CONGRESS PERTAINING TO THE HOOVER PRESENTATION, THE SOUTHERN DEMOCRATS DENOUCED THE BILL WITHOUT BOTHERING TO READ IT AND OPINIONATED THAT THE PRESIDENT COULD SEND IN THE MILITARY BUT HE COULD NOT MAKE THEM OPERATE THE SCHOOLS, AFTER A LONG HAGGLING DEBATE AND INFIGHTING THE HOUSE PASSED TWO MILD PROVISIONS OF THE BILL.

ONE CREATING A BIPARTISAN COMISSION, AND ESTABLISHING A CIVIL RIGHTS DIVISION IN THE JUSTICE DEPARTMENT, ALL THE REST WAS REJECTED THIS WAS A SMOKE SCREEN, BECAUSE THE ENTIRE BILL WAS DISPOSED OF IN THE SENATE JUDICIARY COMMITTEE, LED BY SENATE DEMOCRAT CHAIRMIAN JAMES EASTLAND, OF MISSISSIPPI, THERE WERE MANY AFRICAN AMERIANS THROUGH THE SOUTHERN STATES VOICING THEIR POLITICAL ILLITERATE VIEWS,REGARDS TO THEIR CIVIL RIGHTS AND VOTING, THEY WERE OF THE OPENION THAT THE NORTHERN NIGGERS WERE STEERING UP A LOT OF MESS ABOUT VOTING AND GOING TO SCHOOL WITH WHITES, THEY NEEDED TO JUST LEAVE IT ALONE BEFORE THEY GET THEM ALL KILLED IN THE SOUTH, APPARENTLY THIS WAS SWEET MUSIC TO THE SOUTHERN DEMOCRATS IN THE CONGRESS, BECAUSE THE EISENHOWER CIVIL RIGHTS BILL WAS REINTRODUCED

SEPTEMBER 1957, AND A WATERED DOWN VERSION WAS PASSED TO ADOPT A JURY TRIAL AMENDMENT WHICH GAVE A JUDGE THE RIGHT TO DETERMINE JURY TRIALS FOR DEFENDANTS, AND TO EMPOWER THE ATTORNEY GENERAL TO SEEK INJUNCTIONS WHEN PEOPLE WERE DENIED THE RIGHT TO VOTE CIVIL RIGHTS PROBLEMS WERE BURNING LIKE PROPANE, THE GOVENOR OF ARKANSAS ORVAL FAUBUS, CALLED OUT THE NATIONAL GUARD TROOPS TO PREVENT BLACKS FROM ENTERING GENERAL HIGH SCHOOL IN LITTLE ROCK, A RACIST BELLOWING MOB ASSEMBLED AROUND THE SCHOOL, THEY ASSULTED AND BEAT NEWS REPORTERS VOWING TO LYNCH NIGGERS, PRESIDENT EISENHOWER CALLED IN FEDERAL TROOPS, ALONG WITH NATIONAL GUARDSMEN AND DISPERSED THE MOB, BLACKS ENTERED THE SCHOOL UNDER MILATERY GUARD SLOWLY THE CHRISIS FADED.

IN NOVEMBER 1958, THE DEMOCRATS ALONG WITH SUPPORT FROM AFRICAN AMERICAN VOTERS, DEMOLISHED THE REPUBLICANS IN THE HOUSE OF REPRSENTIVES AND THE CENATE, NEARLY TWO TO ONE IN THE HOUSE AND CENATE, THEY WERE IN CONTROL OF COMMITTIES AND INVESTIGATIONS,THEY LAUNCHED A BRUTAL ATTACK AGAINST THE PRESIDENT, CLAIMING WITH EMPHASIS, THAT HE WAS GUILTY OF MORAL EQUIVOCATION, AND HAD NOT PRVIDED LEADERSHIP, AND DID NOT SEE DESEGREGATION AS A CRISIS, AND BROUGHT IN ARMY CHIEF OF STAFF MAXWELL TAYLOR, WITH CRITICISM OF HIS DEFENSE PROGRAMS, ALSO SIX YEARS OF LEADERSHIP HAVE LED THE UNITED STATES TO THE BRINK OF HAVING TO FIGHT A NUCELAR WAR, INADEQUATELY PREPARED AND ALONE, AND ALLOWED A MISSLE GAP TO BE SET BACK, WHICH JEOPARDIZE THE SAFETY OF AMERICANS, AFRICAN AMERICANS CLAIM HE HAD DONE NOTHING FOR THEM REGARDS TO CIVIL RIGHTS, AND SCHOOL DESEGREGATION, HOWEVER IN CONTRAST TO HIS DEMOCRATIC CRITICS PRESIDENT EISENHOWER, KEPT THE PEACE AND BALANCED THE BUDGET, AND STOPPED INFLATION, AND THAT WAS A SUCCESS NO TWENTIETH CENTURY PRESIDENT COULD LAY CLAIM TO, AND ALTHOUGH THE CIVIL RIGHTS

BILL PRESENTED TO THE DEMOCRATIC CONGRESS WAS REJECTED, IT WAS THE PRAGMATIC ATTEMPT TO RESOLVE.

1960, WAS A PRESIDENTAL ELECTION YEAR, SENATOR JOHN F. KENNEDY, WAS SELECTED BY HIS PARTY THE DEMOCRATS TO PERSUE THE PRESIDENCY BEING FULLY AWARE THAT THE CENATE AND THE HOUSE WERE CONTROLLED BY THE DEMOCRATS, MEANING NO CHANCE OF ANY CIVIL RIGHTS LEGISLATION BEING TALKED ABOUT LET ALONE PASSING, HOWEVER IN HIS PERSUIT FOR PRESIDENT AGAINST RICHARD NIXON, HE MET PRIVATELY WITH MARTIN LUTHER KING, AND PUBLICLY ADDRESSED THE NAACP, AND ASSURED THEM THAT HE WANTED NO COMPROMISE OF BASIC PRINCIPLES, HE GAVE A ROUSING SPEECH AND SAID IT WAS NOT ENOUGH TO FIGHT SEGREGATION ONLY IN SOUTH BUT HE INTENDED TO PERSUE MORE SUBTLE BUT EQUALLY VICIOUS FORMS OF DISCRIMINATION, MEANING IN CLUBS, CHURCHES, AND IN NEIGHBORHOODS AROUND THE COUNTRY.

AND THAT HE PLANNED TO USE VAST AUTHORITY OF THE WHITE HOUSE, ALSO THE LEGAL AUTHORITY OF THE WHITE HOUSE TO PROTECT VOTING RIGHTS, AND PUT AN END TO SCHOOL SEGREGATION, AND ASSURE EQUAL OPPORTUNITY IN FEDERALLY FUNDED JOBS, AND HOUSING.

THIS SPEECH WAS GIVEN DAYS BEFORE HIS NOMINATION (HINT) AFRICAN AMERICAN VOTES, BEING A SENATOR AND RESPECTED FOR HIS POLITICAL ABILITIES, HE MOST CERTAINLY WAS AWARE OF THE ANTIQUATED NOTION IN THE HOUSE AND CENATE PERTAINING TO CIVIL RIGHTS, AND SCHOOL DESEGREGATION, BECAUSE IN HIS INAUGURAL ADDRESS HE BRIEFLY TUCHED ON CIVIL RIGHTS, IN A SENTENCE DESCRIBING HOW AMERICA WAS COMMITTED TO HUMAN RIGHTS AT HOME AND AROUND THE WORLD, BECAUSE HE VERY WELL UNDERSTOOD THAT THAT A SOUTHREN DONIMATED CONGRESS WAS PRONE NOT TO MOVE ON EQUALITY FOR AFRICAN AMERICANS, BY LEGISLATIVE ACTIONS, BY MID FEBRUARY HE WAS SOUNDLY CONVINCED BY THE CONGRESS HE

COULD NOT GET A CIVIL RIGHTS BILL PASSED IN THAT SESSION, PRESIDENT JOHN F. KENNEDY INABILITY TO GET CONGRESS ATTENTION ON SOIAL NEEDS AND ON ISSURES THAT COULD GIVE THE DEMOCRATS AN ADVANTAGE HE THOUGHT ON CONGRESSIONAL ADVANTAGES IN 1962, SO HE DECIDED NOT TO BRING EITHER BILL TO THE ATTENTION OF CONGRESS IN THE FALL HOWEVER HE WOULD PURSUE ANOTHER EFFORT THE NEXT YEAR, IT WAS EVIDENT THAT KENNEDY WAS BECOMING FRUSTRATED REGARDS TO CIVIL RIGHTS BECAUSE HE WAS THINKING THROUGHOUT HIS 1960, CAMPAIGN AND MOST OF HIS PRESIDENCY, HE FELT NOT ENOUGH APPRECIATION WAS SHOWN BY CIVIL RIGHTS ACTVIST REGARDS TO HIS COMMITMENTS, IN THE INTERIM MARTIN LUTHER KING WAS PREDICTING THAT THE PRESENT ADMINISTRATION WOULD DO NO MORE FOR INTERGRATION BUT TREAT IT AS A TOKEN, BECAUSE DURING THE ELECTION HE HAD GIVEN HIS TESTIMONY FOR KENNEDY, AND HIS IMPRESSION THEN WAS THAT HE HAD THE INTELLIGENCE AND SKILLS, ALSO MORAL FERVOR TO GIVE LEADERSHIP THAT AFRICAN AMERICANS HAD BEEN WATING FOR, AND PERFORM A MIRACLE THAT NO OTHER PRESIDENT HAD EVER ACCOMPLISHED, NOW AFTER WATCHING HIM IN OFFICE HE WAS CONVINCED THAT HE UNDERSTOOD AND HAD THE POLITICAL SKILLS BUT LIKED MORAL PASSION, THERE WAS MUCH RESENTMENT DURING THE FIRST SIX MONTHS OF KENNEDY TERM, IN THE CONGRESS WHERE HE WOULD NEITHER SIGN A PROMISED EXECUTIVE ORDER DESEGREGATING FEDERALLY FINACED HOUSING,NOR ASK CONGRESS FOR CIVIL RIGHTS LAWS, BECAUSE HE WAS CERTAIN THIS ACTION WOULD ANGER THE SOUTHERN DEMOCRATIC CONTROLLED CONGRESS, AND LOOSE SUPPORT FOR ANY OTHER LEGISLATION HOWEVER DURING HIS CAMPAIGN HE HAD PUBLICLY CRITICIZED EISENHOWER FOR REFUSING TO ACT ON HOUSING, BY EMPHASIZING THAT ONLY A STROKE OF A PEN WAS NECSSSARY, THE GENERAL PUBLIC REMINDED HIM OF HIS PROMISE PERTAINING TO ONE STROKE OF A PEN, HIS RESPONSE WAS HOW IN THE WORLD HE COULD HAVE SAID SUCH A THING, PRESIDENT KENNEDY RELATIONSHIP

WITH MARTIN LUTHER KING IN 1961, REVOLVED INTO AN ENTANGLEMENT OF ISSURES BURDEN WITH PROMISES RELEGATED TO BEING ELECTED, ALMOST BEYOND COMPROMISE, THE MAJORITY OF AFRICAN AMERICANS HERDED BEHIND MARTIN LUTHSG KING, AND BELIEVED THE ADMINSTRATION WOULD LEAD THEM TO THE PROMISE LAND OF FREEDOM,SUDDENLY THEY SENSED THEIR HOPES WERE BEING DASHED, AND REALIZED THAT ALL THE KENNEDY PROMISES WERE ONLY FOR THEIR VOTES, AND THE ADMINISTRATION WAS DOING AS LITTLE AS IT COULD, AND LESS AS POSSIBLE. SO PEACFUL RETRIBUTION STARTED TO PREVAIL, A BUS LOAD OF FREEDOM RIDERS WAS ARRESTED IN JACKSON MISSISSIPPI, AND AFTER SERVING JAIL TIME, THEY RETURNED TO WASHINGTON, THE PRESIDENT REFUSED TO SEE THEM AT THE WHITE HOUSE, BLACK LEADERS AND THE NEWS MEDIA WAS COMPLAINING THAT HE HAD CHOSEN TO ATTACK AND CRITICIZE EISENHOWER ON THESE SAME ISSURES, AND NOW HE HAS CHOSEN NOT TO ADDRESS ANY RIGHTS OF AFRICAN AMERICANS TO TRAVEL WITHOUT DISCRIMINATION, MANY CIVIL RIGHTS ACTIVIST CONCLUDED THAT KENNEDY DID NOT HAVE THE MORAL COMMITMENT TO THE CIVIL RIGHTS CAUSE, THAT HIS BACKGROUND AS A RICH MAN INSULATED HIM FROM SOCALIZING WITH AFRICAN AMERICAN AND THAT HE WAS MORE OF A SIDELINE OBSERVER THAN A VISCERAL PROPONENT, KENNEDY NEEDED THE SOUTHERN CONGRESS AND SENATORS VOTES TO INCREASE APPROPRIATIONS FOR NATIONAL DEFENSE, SO HE DID NOT FEEL COMPELLED TO INCLUDE TO INCLUDE CIVIL RIGHTS AS PART OF THE STRUGGLE AGAINST INJUSTICE TYRANNY AND EXPLOITATION, SO IT DEEMED A TRADE OFF TO CONGRESS AND THE SENATE BECAUSE THEIR CONCERNS WAS NATIONAL DEFENSE, IN 1962, MARTIN LUTHER KING STIRRED THE POT OF DIFFICULTIES WITH PUBLIC STATEMENTS, THAT THE PRESIDENT COULD DO MORE TO ENDORSE SEGREGATION BY SPEAKING OUT AND COUNSELING THE NATION ON MORAL PROBLEMS, KENNEDY FIRED BACK ENIGMATICALLY THAT HIS COMMITMENTS WERE TO FULL CONSTITUTONAL RIGHTS FOR ALL AMERICANS, AND WAS VERY CLEAR THAT

HIS ADMINISTRATION HAD A VARIETY OF AFFECTIVE MEASURES TO IMPROVE EQUAL OPPORTUNITIES FOR ALL AMERICANS, AND WOULD CONTINUE ON THAT COURSE.

UNFORTUNATELY THERE WAS A SMOLDERING VOLCANO ABOUT TO ERUPT PERTAINING TO EQUAL RIGHTS, THERE WAS A REVOLUTIONARY MOVEMENT LED BY MARTIN LUTHER KING AND OTHER CIVIL RIGHTS ACTIVIST,AND THEY ACCUSED THE PRESIDENT OF BEING RELUCTANT TO BECOME INVOLVED OR TAKE POLITICAL RISK FOR AFRICAN AMERICANS EQUALITY, KING FORWARDED A TELEGRAM TO KENNEDY ASKING FOR FEDERAL PROTECTION AGAINST ANTIBLACK TERRORISM IN THE SOUTH, SOME CIVIL RIGHTS ACTIVISTS THREATENED TO PICKET THE WHITE HOUSE, BECAUSE THERE WERE BURNING OF CHURCHES, BLACKS WERE BEING SHOT BECAUSE OF TRYING TO VOTE, THE PRESIDENT PROMISED THAT THE F.B.I. WOULD PERSUE JUSTICE FOR THESE HORRENDOUS CRIMES, JAMES MEREDITH WAS TRYING TO BE ADMITTED TO THE UNIVERSITY IN OXFORD TO NO AVAIL, HE WON AN APPEAL TO THE U.S SUPREME COURTGWHICH ORDERED THE UNIVERSITY TO ADMIT HIM, THE MISSISSIPPI GOVENOR ROSS BARNETT A STAUNCH SEGREGATIONIST SPOKE ON NATIONAL TELEVISION AND DENOUNCED THE FEDERAL RULING THAT MEREDITH SHOULD BE ADMITTED, THE GOVERNOR INVOCKED THE PRECIVIL WAR DOCTRINE OF THE RIGHT OF A STATE TO INTERPOSE ITSELF BETWEEN THE U.S. GOVERNMENT AND THE CITIZENS OF A STATE, PROMISING NOT TO SURRENDOR TO EVIL AND ILLEGAL FORCES OF TYRANNY, HE DECLARED EITHER WE MUST SUBMIT TO UNLAWFUL DICTATES OF THE FEDERAL GOVERNMENT OR STAND LIKE MEN AND REJECT THEIR NOTION AND SAY NEVER.

SO THE GOVERNOR SUPPORTED BY RHE STATE LEGISLATURE BLOCKED MEREDITH REGISTRATION, THE PRESIDENT WAS PERSUING AN EFFORT TO GET MEREDITH ENROLLED WITHOUT VIOLENCE, PRESIDENT KENNEDY WIRED GOVERNOR BARNETT WITH QUESTIONS OF IF HE INTENDED TO KEEP THE PEACE UNSATISFIED WITH BARNETT RESPONCE, HE SIGNED AN ORDER FEDERALIZING

THE MISSISSIPPI NATIONAL GUARD, AS EISENHOWER HAD SIGNED IN THE LITTLE ROCK CRISIS, IN 1957, HOWEVER BARNETT RENEGED ON HIS PROMISE, AND KENNEDY SENT REGULAR ARMY TROOPS TO GET MEREDITH ENROLLED, PRESIDENT JOHN F. KENNEDY HAD HIS SIGHT ON THE UPCOMING ELECTION OF 1964, HE CRISSCROSED THE COUNTRY IN SUPPORT FOR A DEMOCRATIC CONGRESS, HE STATED THE NATION WELLBEING DEPEND ON ELECTING MORE DEMOCRATS WHO WOULD PRESENT NO PROBLEMS FOR ANY OF HIS PROGRAMS, AND HE BLAMED THE REPUBLICANS FOR MOST OF HIS LEGISLATION PROBLEMS, SUCH AS EXTENDING UNEMPLOYMENT BENEFITS, AND RESISTING INCREASING MINIUM WAGE, AND HIS AREA REDEVELOPMENT OF PUBLIC HOUSING BILLS, HE KNEW AFRICAN AMERICANS VOTERS WERE AMONG DEMOCRATS STAUNCH SUPPORTERS FOR BOTH MORAL AND POLITICAL REASONS, IN NOVEMBER HE SIGNED AN EXECUTIVE ORDER SUPPORTING INTEGRATING FEDERAL POBLIC HOUSING, AND BRAGGED THAT CONGRESS LOOKED MORE POWERFUL THAN WHEN HE WAS THERE.

THE FIRST SIX MONTHS OF 1963, HIS APPROACH TO CIVIL RIGHTS WAS PUT IN NEUTRAL, BECAUSE AFTER ISSURING A LIMITED ORDER IN 1962, HE REFUSED TO PERSUE ANY CIVIL RIGHTS PROGRAMS, ESPECIALLY LEGISLATION REGARDS TO SEGREGATION, HE WAS PRODDED ABOUT HIS REFUSAL TO ACCEPT A CIVIL RIGHTS COMMISSION RECOMMENDING THAT THE FEDERAL GOVERNMENT CUT OF FUNDS TO MISSISSIPPI UNLESS IT COMPLIED WITH COURT ORDERS PROTECTING BLACKS FROM VIOLENCE AND DISCRIMINATION, HIS RESPONSE WAS HIS ADMINISTRATION HAD INSTUTED LAWSUITS TO TAKE CARE OF THESE PROBLEMS, CIVIL RIGHTS ACTVIST WAS DEMONSTRATING IN BIRMINGHAM ALABAMA, AND WAS ATTACKED BY POLICE, CIVIL RIGHTS EXPLODED INTO THE HEADLINES AGAIN, THE CITY ADMINSTRATION HAD NO AFRICAN AMERICANS POLICEMAN, FIREMAN, OR ELECTED REPRESENTIVES, AND WAS LABELED ONE OF THE MOST RACIST COMMUNITIES IN THE ENTIRE SOUTH, RAN BY EUGENE BULL CONNOR CITY POLICE COMMISSIONER, HE

WAS THE DRIVING FORCE BEHIND THE ATTACK DOGS, AND HIGH PRESSURE FIRE HOSES ON AFRICAN AMERICANS, THAT TORE OF THEIR CLOTHING AND BITTEN BY VICIOUS DOGS, KENNEDY RESPONSE TO THIS BARBARIC ACT WAS MODERATE, AND URGED COMPROMISE FOR THE SAKE OF CIVIL PEACE.

AT A PRESS CONFERENCE PRESIDENT KENNEDY RESPONDED THAT VIOLATION OF FEDERAL CIVIL RIGHTS OR OTHER STATUTES, HE WAS WORKING TO BRING BOTH SIDES TOGATHER TO SETTLE IN A PEACEFUL FASHION, MARTIN LUTHER KING TOOK ISSURE WITH THE PRESIDENT PASSIVE CONCERNS, THAT THERE WERE NO FEDERAL STATUTES INVOLVED IN MOST ASPECTS OF THIS STRUGGLE, HE FELT THERE WERE BLATANT VIOLATIONS OF CONSTITUTIONAL PRINCIPALS, KU-KLUX-KLANSMEN FROM ALABAMA, AND GEORGIA, STAGED A VICIOUS ASSULT IN BIRMINGHAM PARK, BOMBING HOMES, AND BUISNESSES OF AFRICAN AMERICANS, BLACKS RETALIATED BY ATTACKING POLICES, AND FIREMAN, IT WAS THE MOST HORRIFYING DISPLAY OF VIOLENCE IN THE TWENTIETH CENTURY, IT LEFT ALMOST TWO SQUARE MILES OF DEVASTATION RELATED TO RACIAL VIOLANCE, IT CHANGED THE SCOPE OF RACE RELATION IN BIRMINGHAM, PRESIDENT KENNEDY WAS FORCED TO RESPOND TO THIS CRISIS, HE KNEW ALABAMA GOVERNOR GEORGE WALLACE, WOULD BE OF LITTILE ASSISTANCE BECAUSE HE WAS A DEVOUT RACIST HIMSELF, WHICH HAD TIES TO THE KU-KLUX-KLAN, HE HAD WON THE GOVERNORSHIP IN 1962, BY PROMISING SEGREGATION NOW, SEGREGATION TOMARROW, AND SEGREGATION FOREVER, HE ALSO PROMISED TO STAND IN THE DOOR OF SCHOOLS IN ORDER TO BLOCK ANY ILLEGAL FEDERAL COURT ORDER DEMANDING INTEGRATION PRESIDENT KENNEDY , WAS AFRAID THAT IF HE PASSED ON THIS ILLEGAL ACT AND DID NOTHING, THE COUNTRY WOULD BE IN A UPROAR, AND INSISTING THAT HE TAKE ACTION, SO THE PRESIDENT WAS BETWEEN A ROCK AND A HARD PLACE, IF HE CHOOSE TO FEDERALIZE THE ALABAMA NATIONAL GUARD , AND SEND TROOPS TO BIRMINGHAM, HE WAS OF THE OPENION IT WOULD ANTAGONIZE MOST OF THE LOCALS BECAUSE IF

THE BLACKS RETURNED TO THE STREETS WITH VIOLENCE, THEIR FATE WOULD BE MET OCCORDINGLY FROM THE FEDERAL TROOPS, AND COULD STIMULATE ADDITIONAL VIOLENCE FROM WHITES, AND THE SITUATION WOULD BE UNCONTROLABLE.

THE PRESIDENT BEGAN TO ACCESS THE DANGER BIRMINGHAM COULD CAUSE TO CIVIL PEACE ACROSS THE ENTIRE SOUTH, AND THE FUTURE OF HIS PRESIDENCY, SO HE HOPED TO FIND A SATISFACTORY SOLUTION TO THIS CRISIS, HE CONSULTED WITH SOME OF HIS CABNIET MEMBERS, AND COMPLAINED THAT SOME OF THEIR SUGGESTIONS LEANED TO MUCH IN FAVOR ON THE SIDE OF THE BLACKS, SOME OF THE WAITE MODERATS HAD ALLINED THEM SELVES TO A PEACFUL SOLUTION, SO KENNEDY KNEW HE HAD TO WORK EXTREMELY HARD AND CAREFUL NOT TO DAMAGE THAT RELATIONSHIP, SO HE ADDRESSED THE NATION FROM THE OVAL OFFICE ON TELEVISION, HE EXPOUNDED ON THE PEACFUL AGREEMENT BY SOME OF THE PEOPLE OF BIRMINGHAM, HE PRAISED THEIR EFFORTS AND STATED THAT FUNDERMENTAL RIGHTS OF ALL CITIZENS SHOULD ACCORDED EQUAL, HE PROMISED THAT THE FEDERAL GOVERNMENT WOULD NOT PERMIT A FIEW EXTREMIST ON BOTH SIDES TO SABOTAGE ANY SETTLEMENT THAT HIS INTENTIONS WERE TO DISPATCH RIOT CONTROL FORCES TO MILATARY BASES NEAR THE CITY AND FEDERALIZE THE ALABAMA NATIONAL GUARD, SHOULD THEY BE NEEDED FOR PEACE KEEPING, GOVERNOR WALLACE WAS WARNED OF THESE POSSIBILITES THAT THE PRESIDENT POSSESSED THIS AUTHOTITY, TO DEFEAT DOMESTIC VIOLENCE, IN THE INTERIM MARTIN LURTHE KING WAS APPELING TO THE AFRICAN AMERICAN COMMUNITY TO REFRAIN FROM VIOLENCE SO A DUO APPEAL FROM THE PRESIDENT, AND KING, A PEACEFUL SOLUTION TO THIS HORRIBLE CRISIS WAS DISPOSED OF.

HOWEVER GOVERNOR GEORGE WALLACE WAS PLEDGING THAT HE WOULD RATHER GO TO JAIL THAN ALLOW INTEGRATION AT THE UNIVERSITY OF ALABAMA, THE LAST SEGREGATED UNIVERSITY IN THE NATION, THE PRESIDENT PAID A VISIT TO GOVERNOR WALLACE,

THE ENCOUNTER PRODUCED NO HOPE, REGARDS TO HIS RADICAL RACIST BEHAVIOR, DURING A HELICOPTER RIDE WALLACE RESPONDED TO THE PRESIDENT QUESTIONS REGARDS TO BLACK EMPLOYMENT IN DEPARTMENT STORES, WALLACE VOICED HIS OPENION BY DENOUNCING MARTIN LUTHER KING, AND OTHER NIGGERS AS SELFINDULGENT CIGAR SMOKING WOMENIZERS, WHO DROVE CADILLACS AND LUSTERED FOR BLACK WHITE AND RED WOMEN, AFTER MEETING WITH THE GOVERNOR THE PRESIDENT WAS CONVINCED WITHOUT QUESTION HE HAD A MAJOR PROBLEM ON HIS HANDS, AND THERE WOULD BE NO OTHER CHOICE BUT GO TO CONGRESS FOR A MAJOR CIVIL RIGHTS BILL THAT WOULD OFFER A COMPREHENSIVE RESPONSE TO THESE RACIAL PROBLEMS, UNFORTUNATELY HE WAS UNCERTAIN HOW TO FORMAT SUCH A RECOMMENDATION TO THE CONGRESS.

THE PRESIDENT WAS FACED WITH COMPLEX DILEMMA, HE HAD ASSESED THE CRIPPLING NATURE OF THE HOPLESS CIVIL RIGHTS ORDEAL, HE ALSON KNEW CIVIL RIGHTS WAS A DIRTY WORD WITH THE CONGRESSIONAL DEMOCRATS THERE ARE SOMETIMES POLITICIANS ARE SO EAGER TO BECOME A LEADER FOR THEMSELVES AND THEIR PARTY THEY ARE FORCED INTO DIRE DECEITFUL DECISIONS, PARTICALLY THE PRESIDENCY, WHERE IF THEY MAKE A BAD CHOICE THE ENTIRE NATION CAN BE DAMAGED, KENNEDY CAMPAGINED THROUGH THE COUNTRY FOR A STRONG DEMOCRATIC CONTROLLED CONGRESS AND SENATE, WHICH HE MOST CERTIANALLY KNEW WAS APPOSED TO CIVIL RIGHTS, WHAT HE DID NOT EXPECT IS FOR AFRICAN AMERICANS TO RISE UP IN VIOLENCE AGAINST WHITES, NOW HE HAD TO FACE THE CONGRESS WHICH HE SPOKE SO PROUDELY OF AND ATTEMPT TO PERSUADE THEM TO SUPPORT HIS MUCH NEEDED CIVIL RIGHTS LEGESLATION.

AND WITHOUT QUESTION THE CONTROLLED DEMOCRATIC SENATE AND CONGRESS WOULD NEVER ALLOW A CIVIL RIGHTS BILL TO PASS, UNDER ANY CIRCUMSTANCES, BUT IN THE INTERIM THE COUNTRY COULD DEVELOPE INTO A BLOOD BATH, WITH PEOPLE BEING SLAUGHTED LIKE CHICKENS, BETWEEN BLACK AND

WHITES, AND MOSTLY AFRICAN AMERICANS, BECAUSE OF THEIR INABILITY TO COMPREHEND POLITICS, RECOURCES, AND SIMPLY THE POPULATION GAP, WHEN A REPORTER ASKED THE PRESIDENT WAS HE GOING TO TO CONGRESS WITH CIVIL RIGHTS LEGISLATION, HIS ANSWER WAS JUST SIMPLY YES, THERE WAS NO OTHER CHOICE BECAUSE HE WAS SITTING ON SMOLDERING VOLCANO OF HIS OWN MAKING, MEANING DURING HIS QUEST FOR PRESIDENT HE PROMOSED AFRICAN AMERICANS AND TOLD THEM WHAT THEY WANTED TO HEAR, REGARDS TO CIVIL RIGHTS, KNOWING FULL WELL THAT A DEMOCRATIC CONTROLLED CONGRESS AND SENATE TO GET CIVIL RIGHTS PASSED WOULD BE EQUAL TO GOVERNOR WALLACE STATEMENTS SEGREGATION TODAY, SEGREGATION TOMORROW, AND SEGREGATION FOREVER. HOWEVER THE PRESIDENT SENSED THE SERIOUS URGENCY REGARDS TO CIVIL RIGHTS LEGISLATION, THE TENSION WAS MOUNTING, AS ALWAYS WHEN WHEN AFRICAN AMERICANS IS INVOLVED REACH OUT THEIR TRIBAL LEADERS.

PRESIDENT JOHN F. KENNEDY, WAS IN A DIRE NEED TO FIND A SOLUTION TO THE FESTERING RACIAL PROBLEMS IN AMERICA, WHICH COULD ERUPT AT ANY TIME SO IT WAS SUGGESTED THAT HE MEET WITH AFRICAN AMERICAN. LEADERS SO HE SUMMONED HIS ATTORNEY GENERAL ROBERT KENNEDYTO THE CAUSE, IT WAS DECIDED THAT THE MEETING SHOULD TAKE PLACE IN NEWYORK, AT THE FAMILY APARTMENT CENTRAL PARK, SO AT THE ATTORNEY GENERAL JAMES BALWIN ORGANIZED THE WITH A GROUP OF ELITE BLACK ACTIVIST, THE MEETING TURNED INTO A PERSONAL VENTURE, WHICH HAD NO REALSTIC SUBSTANCE PERTAINING TO THE PROBLEMS FACING THE PRESIDENT AND AMERICA, SOME USED THE OPPORTUNITY TO VENT THEIR OWN FRUSTRATION WITH AMERICA, AND BLAMED THE PRESIDENT AND HIS BROTHER FOR ALL THESE RACIST PROBLEMS, THE ATTORNEY GENERAL BECAME FURIOUS AT SOME OF THE COMMENTS, WHICH WAS EXTREME AND RADICAL.

SO AFTER THE NEWYORK FIASCO, FINALLY THE PRESIDENT WAS GOING TO ASK CONGRESS FOR APPROVAL

OF A CIVIL RIGHTS LAW, VICE PRESIDENT LINDEN JOHNSON ADVISED HIM THAT HE HAD DOUBTS ABOUT THE BILL PASSING CONGRESS, AND ADVISED THE PRESIDENT THAT HE SHOULD TRAVEL TO THE SOUTHERN STATES HERD SOME AFRICAN AMERICAN LEADERS AND STROKE THEM THAT HE WAS ON THEIR SIDE, IT WORKED IN THE OLD DAYS. IN THE INTERIM THE PRESIDENT WAS DEBATING ON HOW TO MAKE A MORAL AGAINST GOVERNOR WALLACE, ON THE ADVICE OF SOME OF HIS STAFF, AND IT SHOULD BE MADE TO THE NATION, IT HAD TO DO WITH THE GOVERNOR BEHAVIOR AT THE UNIVERSITY OF ALABAMA, THE JUSTICE DEPARTMENT INTENDED TO SMEAR WALLACE WITH PROPAGANDA CONCERNING A NERVOUS DISABILITY HE SUFFERED IN THE AIR FORCE DURING WORLD WAR TWO, AND THIS COULD VERY WELL OFFER SOME LEAD WAY REGARDS TO TIME, HOWEVETHEY SCRUBBED THE WHOLE IDEA, FEARFUL OF A LAW SUIT. ON JUNE 19, THE PRESIDENT PRESENTED HIS CIVIL RIGHTS PROPOSAL TO THE CONGRESS, IT WAS THE DAY BEFORE MEDGAR EVERS ASSASSINATION, WITH A RIFLE SHOT TO THE BACK, AT THE DOOR OF HIS HOME, WIFE AND CHILDREN PRESENT, HE BEING A CIVIL RIGHTS ACTIVIST FROM MISSISSIPPI, SOME HINTED THIS INCIDENT COULD VERY WELL CONVINCE CONGRESS THAT IT WAS TIME FOR EQUAL RIGHTS.

THE PRESIDENT SUBMITTED HIS CIVIL RIGHTS BILL TO CONGRESS WITH WITH LAWS TO ENSURE ANY CITIZEN WITH A SIX GRADE EDUCATION THE RIGHT TO VOTE, AND WOULD BAN DISCRIMINATION IN ALL PUBLIC PLACES OF PUBLIC ACCOMMODATIONS, SUCH AS HOTELS,RESTAURANTS, AMUSEMENT FACILITIES, AND ESTABLISHMENT OF RETAIL, AND DECLARED THIS WAS CONSISTANT WITH THE FIFTEENTH AMENDMENT TO THE CONSTITUTION. THE PRESIDENT HAD STRONG SUSPICIONS THE DEMOCRATS WOULD REJECT THIS BILL, SO HE HAD TO APPEAL TO THE REPUBLICANS, KENNEDY MET WITH THE REPUBLICAN HOUSE AND SENATE LEADERS, AND ENLISTED FORER PRESIDENT EISENHOWER BACKING, AND REQUESTED THE DEMOCRATIC MEMBERS OF CONGRESS PUT ASSIDE RACISM AND POLITICS FOR THE GOOD OF THE

NATION, HOWEVER THE STAUNCH RACIST DEMOCRATS WERE SHARPENING THEIR KNIVES FOR A FILIBUSTER, ALSO IT WAS WIDELY CIRCULATD THAT VICE PRESIDENT LINDEN JOHNSON WOULD BE DROPPED FROM THE TICKET IN 1964, CAMPAGNE, THERE WERE SOUTHERN CONFEDRATE SENATORS CHOMPING AT THE BIT TO FILIBUSTER THE CIVIL RIGHTS BILL,AND THERE HAD NEVER BEN A SUCCESSFUL OVERRIDING WITH TWO THIRDS VOTES, THERE WERE PEACEFUL MARCHING DEMONSTRATED^BLACK AND WHITE TOGATHER AND THERE WAS NO OTHER CHOICE BUT MARCH NONE VIOLENT, BECAUSE THE KU-KLUX-KLAN AND THEIR COUNTERPARTS, WERE POISED TO RETALIATE WITH VICIOUS BRUTALITY EVERN MURDER.

MARTIN LUTHER KING GAVE HIS FAMOUS I HAVE A DREAM SPEECH AT LIEINCOLN MEMORIAL, BUT. TO NO AVAIL THE SOUTHERN DEMOCRATS WERE FROZEN IN TIME REGARDS TO CIVIL RIGHTS FOR AFRICAN AMERICANS.

PRESIDENT KENNEDY SENT A SECRET DELEGATION TO PLEAD WITH FORMER PRESIDENT EISENHOWER, IN ORDER TO SOLICIT REPUBLICAN BACKING FOR THE CIVIL RIGHTS BILL, HE KNEW REPUBLICANS WOULD BE SUPPORTAIVE OF CIVIL RIGHTS, HE TUCHED ON JUST THAT IN AN INTERVIEW WITH CBS ANCOR WALTER CRONKITE AND PROFESSED THAT THE REPUBLICAN PARTY IS THE PARTY THAT LINCOLN BUILT. ANDCHE KNEW THEY WERE PROUD OF IT AND HE FELT THEY WOULD SUPPORT EVERY CITIZEN TO HAVE EQUAL RIGHTS UNDER THE CONSTITUTION.

DURING THE RANGLING FOR CIVIL RIGHTS A CHURCH WAS BOMBED IN BIRMINGHAM ON SEPTEMBER 15, WHICH KILLED FOUR LITTLE YOUNG AFRICAN AMERICAN GIRLS, MOST LIKELY CARRIED OUT BY THE DEMOCRATIC FOUNDED KU-KLUX-KLAN, THIS BOMBING WAS HERD AROUND THE WORLD, THE AGITATION OF THIS BOMBING CAUSED PRESIDENT KENNEDY TO STATE IT WILL TAKE YEARS TO GET A HANDLE ON RACE RELATIONS IN THE SOUTH, HE SERCHED HIS SOLE FOR ANSWERS, HE SUSPECTED THE REPUBLICANS WERE THINKING OF AFRICAN AMERICANS IN A DISAPPOINTING MANNER,AND TOTALLY FRUSTRATED, BECAUSE FOR YEARS THEY HAD BEEN WORKING

DESPERATELY FOR THEIR PROSPERITY AND FREEDOM, BUT FOR SOME STRANGE REASON THEY CHOOSE TO VOTE TO KEEP DEMOCRATS IN OFFICE TO FILIBUSTER AND OVERIDE THEIR CIVIL RIGHTS LEGISLATION IN CONGRESS.

LEGISLATION BEGAN IN CONGRESS FOR THE KENNEDY CIVIL RIGHTS BILL, A COMPROMISE BILL PASSED THE JUDICARY COMMITTEE, BUT THERE WERE PROBLEMS IN THE RULES COMMITTEE, BECAUSE HOWARD SMITH WAS COMMITTEE CHAIRMAN A VIRGINIA SEGREGATIONST AND WAS GOING TO DO EVERY THING IN HIS POWER TO PREVENT THIS BILL FROM GETTING TO THE HOUSE FLOOR FOR A VOTE.

DURING THE SUMMER OF 1963, PRESIDENT JOHN F. KENNEDY LEFT MOST OF HIS LEGISLATIVE PROGRAMS INCLUDING THE CIVIL RIGHTS CHRISIS, WHICH THE DEMOCRATS HAD STALLED, TO HIS SUBORDINATES.

THE 1964, CAMPAIGN WAS GETTING ON THE WAY PRESIDENT KENNEDY HAD PLANNED TRIPS TO FLORDIA AND TEXAS, IN NOVEMBER, HIS INTENT WAS TO DISCUSS POLITICS, PIRATICALLY WITH THE GOVERNOR OF TEXAS JOHN CONALLY, BUT CONALLY WAS SOME WHAT EVASIVE BECAUSE HE WAS UP FOR ELECTION AND HE DID NOT WANT THE CIVIL RIGHTS ISSURE TO ALIENATE HIS TEXAS VOTERS.

UNFORTUNATELY THE TRIP TO TEXAS SILENCED PRESIDENT JOHN F. KENNEDY PRESIDENTAL CAREER AS LEADER AND COMMANDER AND CHIEF OF THE UNITED STATES OF AMERICA, CREDITED TO LEE HARVEY OSWALD ASSASSINATION.

NONE OF KENNEDYS MAJOR REFORM EXPECTATIONS BECAME LAW DURING HIS TIME IN OFFICE, TAX CUTS, FEDERAL AID TO EDUCATION, MEDICARE, AND MOST OF ALL CIVIL RIGHTS, HOWEVER HIS SIGNIFICANT PROPOSALS INCLDING PLANS FOR A HOUSING DEPARTMENT AND THE FIGHT AGAINST POVETY, RESPECTIVELY CAME TO BEAR UNDER PRESIDENT LYNDON JOHNSON, BASED ON THE SKILLS HE POESSED FROM BEING A CONGRESSMAN AND SENATE MAJORITY LEADER AND A SOUTHERNER,HE HAD SOME LEVERAGE ALSO HIS SENIOR STATUS AS A SENATOR,

BECAUSE HE WAS SUCCESSFUL IN GETTING PASSAGE OF THE TAX CUT, AND THE CIVIL RIGHTS BILL IN 1964, AND THE ANTIPPOVETY FEDERAL AID TO EDUCATION, AND VOTING RIGHTS FOR AFRICAN AFRICAN AMERICANS IN 1965, HOWEVER THERE WAS A KNOCK DOWN DRAG OUT FIGHT FROM THE DEMOCRATS, TO FILIBUSTER THESE BILLS, SENATOR ROBERT BIRD LED THE CHARGE, WHICH IS A FORMER MEMBER OF THE KU-KLUX-KLAN, AND PROUDLY SERVING IN THE SENATE TODAY.

FORTUNATELY THE REPUBLICANS RALLIED TOGATHER AND MADE IT POSSIBLE FOR THESE MAJOR BILLS TO BECOME LAW, WHICH VOTING AND EQUAL RIGHTS HAD BEEN RATIFIED BY THE CONSTUTION YEARS AGO, JULY 9, 1868. AND FEBRUARY 3, 1870.

FORMER SENATOR AND VICE PRESIDENT LYNDON JOHNSON, ASSUMED THE PRESIDENCY AFTER THE DEMISE OF PRESIDENT KENNEDY, JOHNSON LEADERSHIP WAS MOSTLY DEDICATED TO CREATING A NATIONAL EFFORT TO ACQUIRE SUPERIORITY PERTAINING TO THE POSSIBILITY OF SPACE EXPLORATION, HOWEVER IT IS SUSPECTED THAT THE SUCCESS WAS OVER SHADOWED BY NOT BEING SBLE TO GET CIVIL RIGHTS LAWS PASSED, THERE WERE SIX DIFFEERENT CIVIL RIGHTS BILLS DEFEATED BY THE MAJORITY DEMOCRATIC CONGRESS AND SENATE DURING THE FORTIES AND EARLY FIFTIES, HOWEVER THE SUPREME COURT RULED ON BROWN VERSUS BOARD OF EDUCATION, WHICH PROVIDED SOME CONSTITUTIONAL HOPE IN THE NASCENT OF THE CIVIL RIGHTS MOVEMENT, THE SOUTH WAS DEFIANT AND VIOLENT AND REFUSED TO COMPLY WITH CIVIL RIGHTS LAWS, HOWEVER THERE WERE MOUNTING SUPPORT IN OTHER PARTS OF THE COUNTRY, SOME AFRICAN AMERICANS WAS WILLING TO DESERT THE DEMOCRAT PARTY FOR REPUBLICANS, BECAUSE OF THE DEMOCRATIC CONTROLLED CONGRESSAND. /SENATE REJECTINGANYTHINGHAVEINGTODOWITHCIVILRIGHTS ACTION, FORMER PRESIDENT EISENHOWER A REPUBLICAN, SUBMITTED TO THE CONGRESS A ADMINISTRATIVE BILL THAT INCLUDED THREE PROVISIONS FOR CIVIL RIGHTS WITHIN THE JUSTICE DEPARTMENT REQUESTING THEIR

INTERVENTION ON BEHALF OF INDIVIDUALS CIVIL RIGHTS BEING VIOLATED IN HOUSING, EDUCATION AND VOTING ALSO THE APPOINTMENT OF A CIVIL RIGHTS COMMISSION TO RECOMMEND FURTHER LEGISLATION. AS ALWAYS THE DEMOCRATS KNOCKED THE BILL DOWN, IN 1957, SENATOR JOHNSON OBSERVED THE DEMOCRATS WAS STALLING, AND THE SIMPLY HAD TO ACT ON SOME OF THESE CIVIL RIGHTS BILLS, BECAUSE FOR A DEMOCRATIC CONTROLLED CONGRESS NOT TO ACT ON A REPUBLICAN CIVIL RIGHTS BILL WOULD CAUSE THE EROSION OF THE BLACK VTERS FOR THE DEMOCRATS, AND HE BEING THE MAJORITY LEADER FELT HIS CREDIBILITY COULD BE ON THE LINE, HE REALIZED THAT THE CIVIL RIGHTS ISSURE HAD CREATED A CRISIS OF LEGITIMACY FOR BOTH THE CENATE AND THE CONTROLLED DEMOCRATIC PARTY, BECAUSE ANY BILL REGARDS TO CIVIL RIGHTS INTRODUCED BY THE REPUBLICANS WAS FILIBUSTERED BY THE DEMOCRATS, AND THERE WERE STATEMENTS MADE REFERENCE TO CIVIL RIGHTS, THE NIGGERS ARE GETTING PRETTY UPPITY THESE DAYS, SINCE THEY HAVE GOT SOMETHING THEY NEVER HAD BEFORE THE POLITICAL PULL TO BACK THEIR UPPITYNESS, AND SOMETHING HAS TO BE DONE ABOUT THIS SO SENATOR JOHNSON DEVISED A PLAN TO HEAD OF THIS UNWARRANTED DILEMMA, WITH A BALANCING ACT TO PASS IN CIVIL RIGHTS LEGISLATION IN THE SENATE, HE BEGAN WITH SENATORS FROM THE MOUNTAIN STATES MST HAD NEVER SEEN A NEGRO ALONE CARED ABOUT THEIR WELFARE, HE KISSED ANKLES ALL OVER THE SENATE FINALLY IT CAME TO A DEBATE,AND VOTE IN AUGUST 1957, THE BILL WAS FINALLY PASSED BY THE SENATE, THE FIRST BILL APPROVED IN EIGHTY SEVEN YEARS, A FIED SENATORS WAS NOT IN FAVOR OF THIS BILL AND LET IT BE KNOWN, WAYNE MORSE, DISSENTED ON THE FLOOR AND ARGUED THAT HE DISAGREED WITH HIS MAJORITY LEADER ON THE NATURE OF THE BILL, THAT HE CONSIDERSD IT TO BE A CORPSE, HOWEVER SENATOR LYNDON JOHNSON HAD SOLIDIFIED THE AFRICAN AMERICAN VOTERS FOR THE DEMOCRAT PARTY, PRIMARILY IN THE NORTHERN STATES, BECAUSE HIS EFFORTS WAS NOT FOR CIVIL RIGHTS, BUT TO

LAY THE GROUND WORK FOR THE DEMOCRATS TO REMAIN IN POLITICAL POWER IN UPCOMING 1960, ELECTIONS, BECAUSE THEY HAD RULED FOR OVER TWENTY YEARS.

YOU MUST REMEMBER POLITICIANS WILL DO ANYTHING, SAY ANYTHING, SOSOMETIME EVEN KILL TO KEEP THEM SELVES AND THEIR PARTY IN POWER.

1960, WAS A ELECTION YEAR FOR PRESIDENT, THE DEMOCRATIC CONTROLLED SENATE WERE IN THE PROCESS OF MAKING A CHOICE TO REPRESENT THEIR PARTY, WITHOUT QUESTION LYNDON JOHNSON WOULD HAVE BEEN THEIR CHOICE, BUT FORTUNATELY THE SENATE DO NOT POSSESS THIS POWER, ONLY THE CITIZENS OF THE COUNTRY HAVE THAT RESPONSIBILITY, DURING THE DEMOCRAT PRIMARY JOHN F. KENNEDY CAME ON THE SCENE, SENATOR LYNDON JOHNSON CONFUSED THE NATIONAL CAMPAGIN WITH BARGANING IN THE SENATE AND ASSUMED EACH DEMOCRAT SENATOR CONTROLLED DELEGATES FROM HIS STATE, HE LOST HIS BID FOR THE NOMINATION TO SENATOR JOHN F. KENNEDY, SO IN ORDER TO MOVE UP IN POLITICAL POWER HE ACCEPTED KENNEDY OFFER AS RUNNING MATE REGARDS TO BECOMING VICE PRESIDENT, SENATOR JOHN F. KENNEDY WAS ELECTED PRESIDENT, THE VICE PRESIDENCY HAVE TWO MAJOR FUNCTIONS ONE IS TO PRESIDE OVER THE SENATE AND CAST A DECIDING VOTE WHICH IS RARELY NEEDED, AND THE OTHER IS TO REPLACE THE PRESIDENT IN CASE OF TRAGEDY,LYNDON JOHNSON HAD A STRONG DESIRE FOR POLITICAL POWER, AND HAD A UNCANNY WAY OF SHOWING IT, MOST LIKELY NO OTHER SENATOR COULD HAVE GOTTEN THAT CIVIL RIGHTS BILL THROUGH THE SENATE, BEING THE MAJORITY LEADER IN THE SENATE WAS SOMEWHAT APPLICABLE FOR HIS LING LUST FOR POLITICAL POWER, SO WHEN HE LOST IN THE PRIMARY TO JOHN F. KENNEDY HIS ASPIRATIONS WAS WATERED DOWN, HIS ACCEPTANCE OF VICE PRESIDENT WAS PRESTIGOUS BUT UNFORTUNATELY FOR HIM HE LOST POLITICAL POWER HE HAD IN THE SENATE TO SEDUCE, INTIMIDATE, AND DELEGATE. PRESIDENT JOHN KENNEDY MADE AN ALL OUT EFFORT TO APPEASE HIM BY DELEGATING IMPORTANT

FUNCTIONS TO HIM, BUT TO NO AVAIL, THERE WERE SUCH COMMENTS AS EVERY TIME HE CAME INTO THE PRESENCE OF KENNEDY HE FELT LIKE A GODDAMN RAVEN HOVERING OVER HIS SHOLDER, THE DEMOCRAT CAUCUS CONVENED IN 1961, THE NEW DEMOCRAT MAJORITY LEADER MIKE MANSFIELD, PROPOSED TO CHANGE THE RULES, AND ELECT VICE PRESIDENT JOHNSON, THE CHAIRMAN OF THE DEMOCRATIC CONFERENCE WHICH HE WOULD BE THE PRESIDING OFFICER OF FORMAL MEETINGS OF THE SENATE DEMOCRATS, THIS LUDICROUS MOVE WAS VOTED DOWN BECAUSE IT HAD THE INTENT TO VIOLATE THE SEPERATION OF POWERS, JOHNSON WAS DESPONDED BECAUSE IT DASHED ALL HOPES OF HIM LEADING THE CONGRESS FROM THE VICE PRESIDENT POSITION, VICE PRESIDENT JOHNSON WAS DISAPPOINTED HE RETIRED FROM THE HILL, HE BECAME NONE SUGGESTIVE IN MEETINGS WITH THE PRESIDENT, THE LOSS OF LEADERSHIP AMOUNTED TO POLITICAL DEFEAT, HE INDICATED THERE WERE TIMES HE FELT HE WOULD JUST SHRIVIL UP, HIS CRITICS PRONOUNCED HIM AS A DOCILE VICE PRESIDENT AN ONLOOKER IN OFFICE BUT OUT OF POWER, VICE PRESIDENT JOHNSON HAD TENDENCIES TO EMULATE HE LEARNED THE KENNEDIES LOVED SOUPS, AND INSISTED HIS PLANE BE STOCKED WITH A VARIETY OF SOUPS, HE NOTICED ROBERT MCNAMARA ORDERING LARGE SHRIMP ON A COCKTAILF HE BASICALLY DID THE SAME THING.

AFTER THE ASSASSINATION OF PRESIDENT JOHN F. KENNEDY HE BECAME OFFICIALLY THE PRESIDENT OF THE UNITED STSTESOF AMERICA, HOWEVER HE FELT AS A ILLEGIMATE PRESIDENT AN ILLEGAL RECIPIENT OF POWER, HOWEVER HE HAD THE POLITICAL POWER HE HAD SO DESPERATELY LONGED FOR, THE PRESIDENT ASSUMED THE RESPONSIBILITY OF TRANSFORMING KENNEDYS PROPOSALS INTO LEGISLATION VICTORIES, THE FIRST NINETY DAYS AS PRESIDENT, HE HELD MEETINGS WITH GOVERNORS, MAYORS, BUISNESS MEN, CIVIL RIGHTS LEADERS, HE REALIZED THE IMPORTANCE OF BEING PRESIDENT, JOHNSON GREATEST AMBITIONS IN HIS FIRST MONTHS IN OFFICE WERE RELATED TO CIVIL RIGHTS,

BECAUSE HE CLEARLY UNDERSTOOOD WITHOUT THE GENERAL CONSENSUS THAT EXISTED PERTAINING TO POLITICS, WITHOUT THE AFRICAN AMERICAN VOTING BLOC, SUPPORT IN THE UPCOMING ELECTION COULD BE JEOPARDIZED.

SO HE STARTED TO FLOAT RUMORS OF KENNEDYS CIVIL RIGHTS BILL, HOWEVER HIS GREATES FEAR WAS A FILIBUSTER BY THE SOUTHERN DEMOCRATS, BECAUSE HE HAD WITNESS THIS DISAPPOINTING PROCESS IN 1957,AND IN 1960, HE HIS PLAN IN MOTION, HE APPEALED TO THE SOUTHERN DEMOCRATS AND HOPED THEY WOULD RELENT TO STANDING AGAINST THE REST OF THE NATION, BUT TO NO AVAIL, THEY FILIBUSTERED IN AN ATTEMPT TO DFEAT THE CIVIL RIGHTS BILL, THE REPUBLICANS JOINED FORCES FOR CLOTURE AND DEFEATED THE FILIBUSTER AND OPEN THE WAY FOR CONGRESS TO PASS THE MOST OUTSTANDING CIVIL RIGHTS BILL FOR AFRICAN AMERICANS IN THE HISTORY OF THIS NATION, JULY 2, 1964. IF NOT FOR THE REPUBLICANS CONGRESS AND THEIR STERN BELIEF FOR JUSTICE AND FREEDOM FOR ALL, AND IT IS UNDENIABLE BECAUSE IT IS EMBEDDEB IN THE HISTORY OF THIS COUNTRY, THE UNITED STATES OF AMERICA, IF NOT FOR THEIR RALLYING TO BREAK THIS STRANGLE HOLD BY THE DEMOCRATS ON AFRICAN AMERICANS FREEDON, WE WOULD STILL BE SEATED ON THE BACK OF THE BUS, TREATED LIKE A ANIMAL WITH HOOF AND MOUTH DISEASE AT DRINKING FOUNTAINS, PREVENTED FROM ENTERING HOTELS, IN THE SOUTH, AND THERE WERE SO MANY OTHER DEGRADING AND HUHUMILIATING GUIDE LINES IMPOSED ON AFRICANS AMERICANS BY THE DEMCRATS AND THEIR COUNTERPART KU-KLUX-KLAN, IN THE SOUTH. PRESIDENT LYNDON JOHNSON WAS A SHREWD POLITICIAN DURING HIS YEARS IN SENATE AND BECOMING MAJORITY LEADER, WITH OUT A DOUBT HE KNEW POLITICS AND WAS AMONG THE BEST, HE KNEW ONCE HE TWISTED A FIEW ARMS AND PASSED A CIVIL RIGHTS BILL,AFRICAN AMERICAN VOTERS WOULD BE RAPPED IN A COCOON LABELED FOR DEMOCRAT USE ONLY.

BECAUSE HE OPENLY STATED SOMETHING HAD TO BE PUT IN THE WORKS REARDS TO CIVIL RIGHTS OTHER THAN THAT THE DEMOCRATS COULD LOOSE THE AFRICAN AMERICAN VOTERS TO THE REPUBLICANS, HE KNEW THAT LONG BEFORE HE BECAME PRESIDENT, HE ALSO ADMIRED THE ACHIEVEMENTS OF FOMER PRESIDENT ROOSEVELT, DERIVED FROM THE NEW DEAL, WHICH DOMINATED IN FORMER YEARS, MAINLY DISMANTLING THE PARTY THAT LINCOLN BUILT PERTAINING TO AFRICAN AMERICANS AND THEIR LIKE OF UNDERSTANDING OF SKILFUL PLANNED POLITICAL DEMOCRATIC IDEOLOGY WITH LIES PERPETRATED FOR THEIR BLOC VOTES, THERE WERE CONSISTENT RUMORS DEPICTING SUPPOSABLY PRESIDENT JOHNSON SINCERE DEDICATION TO CIVIL RIGHTS WITH TRUE MEANING, FOR MANY THAT NEW HIM OVER THE YEARS PROFOUNDLY FELT THIS SUDDEN CONVERSON OF NECESSITIES FOR CIVIL RIGHTS WERE PURLEY POLITICAL, IN ORDER TO HOLD AND WIN PRESIDENTAL OFFICE, PRESIDENTS AND THEIR CHOSEN STAFF WILL KEEP A SHARP EYE ON CONGRESS AND THE SENATE, THEY KNOW THE MEASURES THAT THEY SEND FOR DEBATE WILL PASS OR MOST LIKELY BE REJECTED, BECAUSE THEIR SUPPORTING CAST HAS ALREADY TESTED THE WATERS, PARTICALLY THOSE EECTED PRESIDENTS THAT HAVE SERVED LONG TERMS IN THE SENATE PRIOR TO BECOMING PRESIDENT, AS JOHNSON DID, DURING THE LATE FORTIES AND EARLY FIFTIES JOHNSON HAD PERSONALLY WITNESS CIVIL RIGHTS ISSURES DEFEATED IN THE CONGRESS, IN THOSE YEARS HE AVOIDED BEING IDENTIFIED WITH THE CIVIL RIGHT CAUSE FOR AFERICAN AMERICANS, BECAUSE SOUTHERN WHITE POLITICIANS AND SOME NORTHERNERS WERE INSENSITIVE TO AFRICAN AMERICANS WELFARE, THE ISSURE WAS REMOTE, POLL TAX OR ANTILYNCHING WAS CONSIDERED A SOUTHERN PROBLEM, THOSE FUNDAMENTAL TRAGEDIES WERE NEITHER CHALLENGED NOR DEBATED DURING THIS PEROID, SIX CIVIL RIGHTS BILLS MADE IT TO THE CONGRESS FLOOR, SIX WERE DEFEATED.

JOHNSON EXPLAINED HE WAS NOT A RACIST BUT CIVIL RIGHTS WAS NOT ONE OF HIS PRIORITIES, THAT OTHER

CINCERNS WERE MORE IMPORTANT, PERTAINING TO HIS RESPONSIBILITIES DURING HIS SENATE YEARS, AND HE WOULD NOT HAVE THE POWER TO DO ANY THING ABOUT IT ANY WAY.

JOHNSON KNEW THE CONGRESS VERY INTIMATELY IT HAD BEEN HIS LIFE AND LOVE FOR THIRTY FOUR YEARS, SO LYNDON JOHNSON AS PRESIDENT MOST LIKELY DREAMED OF FAME BUT THE POLITICAL WOUNDS INFLICTED DUELLING OVER CIVIL RIGHTS HAD MANIFESTED, SO THERE WERE SIXTY THREE DOCUEMENTS SUBMITTED TO CONGRESS FOR A VARIETY LEGISLATIVE APPROVALS, IT MAYBE INSTUTED BASED ON ACTIONS OF SUCCESS, PRESIDENT LYNDEN JOHNSON WANTED MANY THINGS, HOWEVER IT IS SUSPECT THAT MOST OF ALL HE WANTED TO EXCEED THE ACCOMPLISHMENTS OF FORMER PRESIDENT FRANKLIN DELANO ROOSEVELT RELATED TO SOCIAL PROGRAMS, HOWEVER UNDER HIS UNRELENTING OBSESSIONS , AFRICAN AMERICANS SQUEEZED THROUGH THE CRACK REGARDS TO VOTING AND CIVIL RIGHTS,BASED ON VIOLENT ACTIVITIES DEMONSTRATED IN ALABAMA, BY UNRELENTING RACIST DEMOCRATIC GOVERNOR GEORGE WALLACE, WITH AN ALL OUT EFFORT TO PRVENT AFRICAN AMERICANS FROM QUALITY EDUCATION AND CIVIL LIBERTIES IT WAS SO VICIOUS FEDERAL HAD TO BE DEPLOYED TO QUELL.

IN THE MIDDLE SIXTIES AFTER THE PASSAGE OF THE CIVIL RIGHTS BILL AND VOTING RIGHTS, THERE WAS A FRENZY OF FESTERED PROBLEMS ROOTED IN THE NORTHERN BIG CITIES, PERTAINING TO BLACKS SOME WERE BORN THERE AND A LARGE MIGRATION FROM THE SOUTHERN STATES, WHICH CREATED ATROCIOUS SLUMS, WITH BROKEN HOMES, A POPULATION EXPLOSION WITH BABIES OUT OF WEDLOCK, DISEASES, AND MOST OF ALL BIGOTRY TOWARD ALL WHITE PEOPLE, BECAUSE THEY CLAIMED WHITE PEOPLE WERE RESPONSIBLE FOR THEIR LIVING CONDITIONS, AND MOST WERE TO STUPID TO REALIZE THAT THEIR CIVIL AND VOTING RIGHTS WERE AVAILABLE ALMOST SENSE THE WAR OF 1812, IN THE NORTHERN STATES.

SO NOW THE NATION IS CONFRONTED WITH A MARAUDING BUNCH OF MIS-FITS THAT IS TOTALLY IGNORANT TO THE MEANING OF CIVIL RIGHTS, LOOKING FOR LEADERSHIP TO SUPPORT A CAUSE THAT HAS NO MERIT, AND HAS FORGOTTEN ABOUT THE REAL WARRIORS, SUCH AS MARTIN LUTHER KING, ROY WILKINS, CLARENCE MITCHELL, AND WHITNEY YOUNG, THAT UNDERSTOOD THE PRACTICAL ADVANTAGES AND DISADVANTAGES WERE SUDDENLY CONSIDERED OBSOLETE, BECAUSE IN ESSENCE THESE GROUPS OF MILITANT MOSTLY ILLETRATE YOUNG ANGRY BLACK MEN FROM THE GETTOS OF THE NORTHERN STATES, DID NOT HAVE THE SLIGHTEST IDEA OF THE CAREFUL AND PAINFUL ENDURANCE THESE OLD WARRIORS SUFFERED JUST TO CALL ATTENION TO CIVIL RIGHTS IN THE SOUTH, NOT TO MENTION THE LIVES LOST, BECAUSE THEIR COMMITMENT TO CIVIL RIGHTS HAD TO BE CAREFULLY ORCCHESTRATED TO SAVE LIVES IN THE SOUTH, A PROFOUND CHANGE TOOK PLACE IN SOME BLACK COMMUNITIES, SUCH AS VOCABULARY, HAIR AND LIFE STYLE, WHICH WOULD EVENTUALLY WOULD AFFECT A LARGE MAJORITY OF AFRICAN AMERICANS, IN THEIR QUEST FOR SUCCESS, OF COURSE THERE WERE THE RIOTS IN WATTS, IN LOS ANGLES OF AUGUST 1965, THERE IS NO QUESTION AFRICAN AMERICANS HAVE SUFFERED A GRAVE INJUSTICE PIRATICALLY IN THE SOUTHERN STATSE AS HISTORY WILL VARIFY, HOWEVER IT CAME TO PASS IN 1964, AND 1965, THE ACCEPTED FACT IS THATOVER FIRTY YEARS,AND AS IT WAS DURING RECONSTRUCTION WHEN AFRICAN AMERICANS WAS ELECTED TO CONGRESS THEY RAN INTO THE CHAMBERS IN BARE FEET, ACCOMPANIED WITH WHITE WOMEN, THEY WERE SIMPLY (NOT) PREPARED FOR THAT RESPONSIBILITY, AS OF TODAY MANY BLACKS ELECTED TO OFFICE ARE NOT PREPARED, BECAUSE POLITICS ARE ONE OF THE MOST RIGOROUS RESPONSIBILITY IN THE NATION, UNLESS YOU ARE A BUSHMAN FROM AFRICA,BECAUSE THE COUNTRY WAS FOUNDED ON POLITICS IF YOU DISAGREE , READ THE CONSTITUTION, IT IS THE LAND MARK FOR JUSTICE AND UNDERSTANDING OF RIGHTS FORMULATED BY A GROUP OF POLITICANS, AFRICAN

AMERICANS PREPAREDNESS IS LIMITED PERTAINING TO POLITICS BECAUSE OF THE INEGIBILITY TO PARTICIPATE UNTIL 1964, AND 1965, THAT IS APPROXIMATELY THREE HUNDRED AND FORTY YEARS OF POLITICAL ILLITERACY FOR THE MAJORITY OF BLACKS.

SOUTHERN DEMOCRATS IS ALL TO AWARE OF THIS DEFICIENCY WITH BLACKS BECAUSE THEY ARE THE PARTY THIS CATASTROPHIC DILEMMA SHOULD BE AWARDED TO AND EVEN TODAY THEY CONTINUE TO EXPLOIT THEIR DEVIOUS ACT, TO AGGRESSIVELY SEEK POLITICAL POWER USEING UNPREPARED AND POLITICALLY ILLADVISED AFRICAN AMERICANS VOTING BLOC, IN AN ATTEMPT TO SUSTAIN THEIR RADICAL IDEOLOGY, PRESIDENT LYNDON JOHNSON WAS A FINE EXAMPLE, HE WAS AN IDEALIST SUCCUMBED BY HIS OWN IMAGINATION HE WAS OF THE OPENION ALL AFRICAN AMERICANS THOUGHT ALIKE BECAUSE OF THEIR HERD VOTING, SO HE FIGURED THE MOST CONSTRUCTIVE THING TO DO WAS PUSH FOR THEIR VOTING RIGHTS, AND AFRICAN AMERICANS WOULD FLOCK TO THE POLLS, AND VOTE FOT THE PEOPLE RESPONSIBLE FOR THAT RIGHT, HE MET WITH BLACK ORGANIZATIONS IN ORDER TO IMPRESS AFRICAN AMERICANS BASED ON CONSTITUENCY ONLY, AND HE PROCLAIMED IF ONLY WHITNEY YOUNG, OR ROY WILKINS WOULD HANG A PORTRAIT OF HIM IN THEIR OFFICE, THAT WOULD BE GOOD FOR NOTORIETY ON HIS BEHALF AND HIS PARTY, HE APPOINTED THOURGOOD MARSHALL TO THE SUPREME COURT, THIS WOULD BE A FINE EXAMPLE, OF HIS DOCTRINE ABOUT AFRICAN AMERICANS IN GENERAL, PRESIDENT JOHNSON PERSONALLY FELT THAT UNDER HIS LEADERSHIP WITH CIVIL RIGHTS AND VOTING RIGHTS FOR AFRICAN AMERICANS AND THE APPOINTMENT OF THURGOOD MARSHALL TO THE SUPREME COURT, THIS COULD MARTYRIZE HIM AS A CHAMPION FOR AFRICAN AMERICANS, AND SURPASS FRANKLIN ROOSEVELT AS A PATROIT TO SUSTAIN THE AFRICAN AMERICAN VOTING BLOC, HE HAD SOME MARACLOUS IDEA OF AFRICAN AMERICANS NAMING THEIR CHILDREN AFTER THURGOOD, THE BUREAU OF BIRTH STATISTICS WERE CHECKED IN BOSTON AND NEW

YORK CITY, AND NOT A SINGLE THURGOOD WAS LISTED, CERTAIN CHANGES STARTED TO FORMULATE IN THE LATE SIXTIES REGARDS TO DEMOCRATIC STRATEGY,THEY STARTED TO EXERCISE THEIR PREROGATIVE OF CHOOSING AFRICAN AMERICANS THAT WERE MORE SUTIABLE FOR SPREADING THEIR DEMAGOGUREY TO INFLUENCE BLACKS TO REMAIN ON THE PLANTATION OF VOTING, AND NOW IT HAS DEVELOPED INTO EPIDEMIC PROPORTION, POLITICANS ARE A RARE BREED THEY WILL ALWAYS EXPLAIN THEIR ACCOMPLISHMENTS, BUT VERY SELDOM OFFER AN EXPLANATION TO THEIR REASONS, THINGS BEGAN TO SOUR FOR JOHNSON SO HE BLEW OF A LITTLE STEAM ON CERTAIN ISSUURES ONE BEING CIVIL RIGHTS, AND POUTED THAT A LOT OF PEOPLE WERE UNGREATFUL AND INDICATED THAT HE HAD FOUGHT FROM THE FIRST DAY HE ENTERED OFFICE FOR NEGROES AND THAT HE SPILLED HIS GUTS TO GET THE CIVIL RIGHTS ACT APPROVED IN 1964, APPARENTLY HE FORGOT TO MENTION HE HAD NO OTHER CHOICE BECAUSE OF UNSETTLING IN THE COUNTRY, REGARDS TO RACISM, BUT MOST OF ALL EVERY PRESIDENT AFTER PRESIDENT FRNKLIN DELANO ROOSEVELT,STUDIED HIS TACTICS INCLUDING SOME RPUBLICANS PRESIDENTS, AND MOST ADMIRED HIS POLITICAL SKILLS,PIRATICALLY PRESIDENT JOHNSON, A DEMOCRAT AND HAD AMBITIONS OF EMULATING HIS SUCCESS, SO IF HE ALLOWED AFRICAN AMERICAN VOTERS TO DESERT THE DEMOCRATIC PARTY THAT COULD MEAN POLITICAL SUICIDE FOR HIM AND HIS ADMINISTRATION,AND HAD TO RELY ON THE REPUBLICANS TO DO THE HEAVY LIFTING TO SUPPORT HIS DEVIOUS ACCOMPLISHMENTS, NOT THAT IT WASNT WARRANTED.

BUT FELT A DUTY. TO RELEASE PEOPLE FROM THIS BONDAGE OF DEMOCRATIC CONTROLLED SELF IMPOSED JIM CROW NONSENSENSICAL RULE, DURING 1968 PRESIDENT LYNDON JOHNSON WAS MARED IN CIVIL WAR BETWEEN SOUTH AND NORTH VIETNAM WITH HIS POLITICAL POLLING DECLINING,HIS SUPPORT IN HANDLING THE WAR DROPPED FROM FORTY TO TWENTY SIX PERCENT, THIS WAS A DRAMATIC DECLINE, THE MEDIA FOCUSED ON THE ISSURE, AMONG. THEM WERE THE WALL STREET JOURNAL,

THE NEW YORK POST, AND THE ST, LOUIS POST DISPATCH, LIFE, LOOK, TIME, NEWSWEEK, CBS, AND NBC, EACH CAME OUT AGAINST THE WAR.

THE EROSION OF SUPPORT AFFECTED CONGRESS AND THE DEMOCRATS, EVEN THE CABAINET, AND THE WHITE HOUSE STAFF, MEMBERS OF THE SENIOR AVISORY GROUP WHICH HAD SUPPORTED JOHNSON, TURNED AGAINST HIS POLICY OF WAR, WHEN THE AMERICAN PEOPLE WERE POLLED IN 1954, AND QUESTIONED WHICH PARTY WAS MOST LIKELY TO AVOID A LARGE WAR, THE MJORIETY AF AMERICANS RESPONDED IN FAVOR OF THE DEMOCRATS, AFTER APPROXAIMATELY FOUR YEARS OF INTENSIVE FIGHTING AND BOMBING IN VIETNAM IN 1968, THE SAME QUESTION WAS ASKED, THE MAJORITY RESPONDED IN FAVOR OF REPUBLICANS, THE UNREST ABOUT THE WAR AND PROTESTERS REGARDS TO BLACK AND WHITE! BIGOTS CRITICS BLAMED THE WHOLE OUTCRY INCLUDING RIOTS AND DEMONSTRATIONS IN THE NATION ON THE PRESIDENT, THIS STIMULATED SOME WHAT OF AN UNUSAL QUALITY IN POLITICAL THINKING OF THE PRESIDENT, WHICH CAUSED HIM TO BACK TRACK TO PREMONITIONS, HE WAS INSIDIOUSLY INTENSIFIED HIS BELIEF WAS HE WOULD HAVE A STROKE, OR BE PAROLIZED, BASED ON HIS FAMILY HISTORY THIS COULD BE THE WORST SITUATION IMAGINABLE, ALSO HE COULD NOT RID HIMSELF OF THE FACT THAT GOD WOULD PUNISH HIM IN THE CROULEST MANNER, DEPRESSION WAS MOUNTING, AND HE BELIEVED IT WAS THROBBING PAIN AND HE JUST WANTED RELIEF, PEACE AND QUIET, AND MOST OF ALL AN END TO THE PAIN, DURING THE FALL AND WINTER OF 1967, JOHNSON INSINUATED HIS WITHDRAWL FROM POLITICS, AND FELT HE WAS BEING CHASED BY A MARAUDING STAMPEED.

ONE BEING VETNAM, AND A INFLATIONARY ECONOMY, THE OTHER DEMONSTRATING AND RIOTING BLACKS, BUT MOST OF ALL ROBERT KENNEDY HAD ANNOUNCED HIS CANDIDACY FOR THE PRESIDENCY, AND THE AMERICAN PEOPLE WERE RECEPTIVE, HE PERSONALLY FELT HE WAS A FAILURE, AND AFTER THIRTY SEVEN YEARS OF SERVICE TO THE GENERAL PUBLIC HE DESERVED MORE THAN

WALLS COLLAPSING FROM ALL SIDES, THIS SITUATION WAS PROVOKING AN UNBEARABLE DILEMMA, AND HE SURMIZED THIS WAS THE GHOST OF FORMER PRESIDENT JOHN F. KENNEDY CHASING HIM THROUGH HIS BROTHER, ON MARCH 31, 1968, HE ADDRESSED THE NATION, TV, AUDIENCE PROPOSING A BOMBING HALT IN VIETNAM, THEN ANNOUNCED HE WOULD NOT ACCEPT NOMINATION OF HIS PARTY FOR ANOTHER TERM AS THEIR PRESIDENT, THE MOOD WAS EUPHORIA THE NEXT DAY IN THE CAPITAL, EVEN HE SEEMED RELIEVED,HOWEVER ROBERT KENNEDY QUEST FOR THE DEMOCRATIC NOMINATION FOR PRESIDENT, WAS CUT SHORT BY AN ASSASSIN BULLET, CREDITED TO SURHAN SURHAN.

AFTERWARDS PRESIDENT JOHNSON REFELECTED WITH SOME BITTERNESS,THAT IT WOULD HAVE BEEN HARD TO WATCH BOBBY MARCH TO HAIL TO THE CHIEF JOHNSON SIGNED THE OMNIBUS CRIME ACT, AGAINST HIS WILL, BECAUSE RICHARD NIXON WAS THE CHOSEN CANIDATE BY THE REPUBLICANS,TO LEAD THEIR PARTY IN AN EFFORT TO CAPTURE THE WHITE HOUSE AS PRESIDENT AND HE WAS EXPOSING THE DEMOCRATS AS BEING SOFT ON CRIME IN THE STREETS, AND JOHNSON STIPULATED NIXON WITH HIS BULLSHIT COULD CAUSE SERIOUS PROBLEMS FOR DEMOCRATS IN NOVEMBER.

ON JANUARY 20, 1969, RICHARD NIXON WAS SWORN IN AS THE THIRTY SEVENTH PRESIDENT OF THE UNITED STATES OF AMERICA.

AFTER 1965, AFRICAN AMERICANS FINALLY REACHED THAT PLATEAU THAT THE DEMOCRATS HAD DENIED THEM FOR SO LONG, THEIR FULL CIVIL AND VOTING RIGHTS, GUARANTEED UNDER THE CONSTITUTION OF THE UNITED STATES OF AMERICA, THIS WAS A SENSATIONAL ACCOMPLISHMENT, PIRATICALLY FOR SOUTHENERS, AFTER LIVING UNDER SLAVERY AND SOUTHERN DEMOCRAT JIM CROW RULE FOR SO MANY YEARS, HOWEVER AS I EXPLAINED DURING THE UNDER GROUND PLIGHT, AND THE BONDAGE FREEING IN 1865, MANY POLITICALLY ILLITERATE AFRICAN AMERICANS OVER CROWDED THE NORTHERN CITIES, PIRATICALLY CHICAGO, NEW YORK, DETROIT AND

PHIADELPHIA, AND BEING UNACCUSTOMED TO CITY LIFE ANDFRESHFROMTHESHARECROPPINGONTHEPLANTATION THEY STARTED TO GROW PIGS AND CHICKENS, IN WHAT SPACE THEY COULD FIND OUT DOORS, AND EVENTUALLY CREATED A DEVASTATING SLUM, OVER RAN BY RATS AND ACCUMULATED GARBBAGE, ALSO DRUG ABUSE AND HIGH CRIME, AND THE DEMOCRATIC ADMINISTRATION COMPOUNDED THE ISSURE BY APPROBATING FUNDS FOR LOW INCOME HOUSING, THAT CONSIST OF FOURTEEN AND FIFTEEN STORY BRICK BUILDINGS, WHICH TURNED INTO A SLUM EPIDEMIC, RUBBISH, GARBAGE, HUMAN FECES IN ELEVATORS, RAPES, MURDERS, IT IS SO BAD LAW ENFORCEMENT WAS AFRAID TO INVESTIGATE CRIME WITHOUT A GROUP OF PERSONELL, AND YOU COULD ASK A LARGE MAJORITY OF PEOPLE THAT LIVED UNDER THESE CONDITIONS, ABOUT THEIR CONSTITUTIONAL RIGHTS, AND THEY WOULD IMMEDIATELY ANSWER, THAT MUST BE SOME BULLSHIT FOR THE WHITE MAN NOT US, ALL THEY KNEW .WAS DR. MARTIN LUTHER KING SAY FREE, AT LAST, THANK GOD ALMIGHTY FREE AT LAST, AND THEY WANTED WHAT WAS COMING TO THEM FROM THE WHITE MAN, FINALLY THEY REALIZED THEY HAD NOTHING COMING MANY ACCUSED DR. MARTIN LUTHER KING OF LETTING THEM DOWN WITH LIES, AND STARTED TO SELF OPPOINT THEM SELVES AS LEADERS TO CLAIM THEIR PRIZE FROM THE WHITE MAN, BUT THERE WAS A SRIOUS PROBLEM, ONLY THEY LIVED IN THE SLUMS STACKED ON TOP OF EACH OTHER IN FOURTEEN STORY BRICK BUILDINGS IN THE INNER CITY, ALL OR MOST WHITES LIVED IN THE SUBURBS AND MOST SUBURBS WERE ALL WHITE, ONE IN PARTICULAR CICERO ILLINOIS, IF A BLACK WAS DRIVING THROUGH TO OR FROM WORK IT BETTER BE DAYTIME, AND BETTER HURRY,DURING THE LATE SIXTIES, AFRICAN AMERICANS WERE NOT THE ONLY PEOPLE TO MIGRATE FROM THE SOUTH, WHITES DID ALSO, BUT MOST WERE EDUCATED AND HAD AMPLE FUNDS TO BLEND IN AND GET JOBS ALL AROUND CHICAGO, AND CONTINUE THEIR LIVES ACCORDINGLY, OLDER BLACKS WHICH HAD LIVED IN THE INNER CITY FOR YEARS AND UNEUDCATED HAD

ESTABLISHED A WAY OF LIFE, THEY WOULD BUSS OR CATCH THE ELEVATOR TRAINS TO DOWN TOWN OR SUBURBAN AREAS AND OFFICES AND HOMES FOR A LIVING, WHICH THEY MOST COMMONLY DID IN THE SOUTH, AND THE LAZY GOOD FOR NOTHING GANG MEMBERS IN THE INNER CITY, WOULD STALK THE BUSS LINES AND ELEVATOR STATIONS,AND DOOR WAYS, IN AN ATTEMPT TO DEPRIVE THEM OF THEIR EARNINGS, PERSE SNATCHING IN MALLS AND ANY PLACE ELSE WAS THE MAIN OUT CRY, ALSO PICK POCKETS.

PRESIDENT LYNDON JOHNSON STATED NEAR THE END OF HIS TERM THAT WHITES ARE RESPONSIBLE FOR ILLITERACY AND THE RADICAL BEHAVIOR OF OF AFRICAN AMERICANS, QUITE TO THE CONTARY NOT ALL BLACKS ARE ILLITERATE, NOR IS ALL WHITES RESPONSIBLE FOR THIS TRAGEDY. IT WAS THE SOUTHERN DEMOCRATIC PARTY WITH THEIR FOUNDED KU-KLUX-KLAN, THAT DROVE THE THE EDUCATORS WHITE AND BLACK FROM THE SOUTH THAT CAME OUT IN FORCE TO ASSIST IN EDUCATING POOR WHITES AND BLACKS, THESE REPUBLICAN INTEGRATED EDUCATORS WERE BRUTALLY ATTACKED, AND SOME EVEN MURDERED, SO THEY HAD NO OTHER CHOICE BUT LEAVE THE SOUTH.

HOWEVER THE INTENT IS NOT TO PAINT ALL AFRICAN AMERICANS WITH THE SAME BROAD BRUSH, THERE ARE MANY LIVING AROUND AND SOMETIME CLOSE TO THE INNER CITIES IN NORTHERN STATES, THAT ARE SOME OF THE FINEST HONORABLE AND WELL EDUCATED AFRICAN AMERICANS IN THE COUNTRY, BUT THEIR LIFE STYLE IS TOTALLY UNIQUE IN A DIVERSE SOCIETY FROM THE INNER CITY SLUM DWELLERS, THEIR IDEALS ARE COMPATABLE WITH WHAT IT TAKE TO BE SUCCESSFUL IN AMERICA, AND IT IS SHOWN IN THEIR SURROUNDINGS, A CULTURE OF DIVERSITY BLACK AND WHITE LIVING AT PEACE WITH EACH OTHER, AND WORKING TOGATHER IN HARMONY, PROFESSIONAL AND COMMON LABORS, WILLING TO WORK IS THE SOLUTION TO POVITY, AND MOST OF ALL TO THINK FOR ONE SELF.

THERE WERE A HORRENDOUS AMOUNT OF AFRICAN AMERICANS CHOSE TO REMAIN IN THE SOUTH, THEIR DECISION MOST LIKELY WAS IN THEIR BEST INTEREST, IT WASNT THE MOST IDEAL PRIOR TO CIVIL RIGHTS, BUT MOST HAD NO SERIOUS PROBLEMS, AND KNEW EXACTLY WHARE THEY STOOD, THE MAJORITY LIVED RESPECTFUL LIVES AND WAS TREATED OCCORDINGLY BY WHITES, AND THEY HELPED EACH OTHER, AND THIS WAS LONG BEFORE CIVIL RIGHTS, MOST BLACKS IN THE SOUTH WERE HARD WORKING PEOPLE, THEY WORKED THEIR WAY INTO SUCCESS WITH VERY LITTLE EDUCATION IF ANY AT ALL, BUT THEY USED THEIR COMMON SENSE TO PREVAIL, THEY GREW MOST OF WHAT THEY ATE AND SOLD PRODUCE TO CITY FOLKS FROM THE FARM, AFTER THE ABOLISHMENT OF SLAVERY IN 1865, THEY WERE INVOLVED IN SHARE CROPPING, MOST WERE GIVEN LAND OR WORKED AND PURCHASED IT FROM THE PLANTATION OWNERS, AND BECAME INDPENDANT IN THEIR OWN RIGHT, MOST HAD SKILLS IN AUTO MACHANIC, GUN SMITH, WATCH REPAIR, BASKET MAKING, TRACTOR DRIVING, HORSE SHOEING, YOU NAME IT THEY COULD DO IT, THEY WERENT RICH NOR WERE THEY LIVING IN HORRIBLE SLUMS, MOST LIVED IN RURAL COUNTRY SIDE, AND CONSTANTLY INTERMINGLE WITH WHITES ON A DAILY BASIS, THERE WAS NOTHING WHITES WOULD NOT DO FOR PROMINENT RESPECTFUL AFRICAN AMERICANS, WHICH IS CONSIDERED TO BE THE COMMON BASIC STANDARDS OF LIFE, AND THIS WAS PREVALENT THROUGHOUT THE SOUTHERN STATES, SO WHEN CIVIL RIGHTS WAS PASSED IN 1964, THERE WERE ONLY A FIEW ADJUSTMENTS TO BE MADE THE END TO BACK OF THE BUS,ONE DRINKING FOUNTAIN,AND WASH ROOMS IN PUBLIC PLACES FOR ALL, YOUR CHOICE OF SEATING IN THEATERS, AND SCHOOL DESEGERATION, MOST OF THE SMALL TOWNS IN THE SOUTH THERE WERE NO PROBLEMS, HOWEVER THE MAIN CAUSE OF VIOLENCE WAS PREDICATED TO BLACK RADICALS LEAVING THE SHARE CROPPING FARMS, DRIVEN OFF BY HIS OR HER PARENTS OR LEFT ON THEIR OWN, AND MIGRATED TO LRGE CITIES AND JOINED THE SLUM FACTOR, MOST AFRICAN AMERICANS HAD A

CUSTOM , IN THE SOUTH IF HIS FAMILY HELPED WITH THE FARM HE OR SHE WAS CONSIDERED TO HAVE A SHARE, AND WHEN AND IF THEY CHOOSE TO LEAVE THEY WERE GIVEN THEIR SHARE, IF ONE LEFT AND WENT TO THE BIG CITY AND LOST HIS SHARE HE WOULD ENTICE SOME OF THE OTHERS TO LEAVE SO HE COULD HELP THEM LOOSE THEIRS, BECAUSE MOST HEAD OF FAMILIES HAD STRICT GUIDE-LINES IF YOU CHOOSE TO LEAVE AND WAS GIVEN YOUR SHARE, DO NOT COME BACK FOR MORE, AND MOST OF THE TIME IT WAS DONT COME BACK AT ALL, BECAUSE OLDER AFRICAN AMERICANS WERE EFFICIENT SAVERS, DEPENDING ON THE FAMILY SIZE SOME OF THESE SHARES COULD BE FIVE TO EIGHT THOUSAND DOLLARS, SOME TIME EVERN MOORE, SO NOW HE OR SHE IS HEADING FOR THE BRIGHT LIGHTS BIRMINGHAM, CHICAGO, DETROIT, MILWAUKEE, NEW YORK, OR PHILADELPHIA, ONCE HE ARRIVE THE GREETING IS WITH OPEN ARMS, AND BEFORE HE CAN RELAX HIS SISTER OR BROTHER OR BOTH WANT TO KNOW IF HE GOT HIS SHARE FROM THE FARM, HIS REPLY IS YES, SO NOW THEY STAGE A PARTY WITH THE REST OF THEIR FRIENDS FROM THE SLUM BRIGADE, BECAUSE HIS BROTHER IS ON DRUGS, AND HIS SISTER IS LIVING WITH A PIMP WITH TWO OR THREE KIDS, AND SHE IS PROSTITUTING TO SUPPORT HIS AND HER DRUG HABIT, NOW ONCE THEY USE ALL OF HIS FARM SHARES, THEY WILL INSTRUCT HIM EITHER HE HAS TO GO BACK HOME OR FIND SOME PLACE TO LIVE, DURING ALL THIS TIME LOCATING EMPLOYMENT WAS NEVER DISCUSSED, AND NOW ALL OF HIS FUNDS IS GONE, SO HE START TO HANG WITH SOME OF HIS SISTER AND BROTHER FRIENDS, BECAUSE THEY HAVE ASSURED HIM HE REALLY DID NOT HAVE A PROBLEM, JUST LISTEN TO THEM, IN THE INTERIM HE HAS GOTTEN HIMSELF ON DRUGS, SO HIS RADICAL FRIENDS TELL HIM THEY NEED MONEY AND THEY KNOW JUST THE PLACE TO GET IT, THERE IS A ARAB STORE NOT TO FAR, BECAUSE HE DONT BELONG IN THE NEIGHBORHOOD ANYWAY, NOW THE MOMENT OF TRUTH HAS ARRIVED, SOME TIME THEY HAVE SECOND THOUGHTS AND DECIDE NOT TO PARTICIPATE AND FEEL TO GO HOME IS IN THEIR BEST INTEREST, SO HE

WORK UP ENOUGH COURAGE TO CALL HOME, HIS FATHER ANSWER THE PHONE, HI PAPA, HIS FATHER BOY HOW YOU BEEN, JUST FINE PAPA, WHERE IS MAMA, LET ME SPEAK TO HER, HIS FATHER DID YOU FIND A JOB YET, OH YEA PAPA, START NEXT WEEK, WHERE IS MAMA, HIS FATHER THIS BOY WANT TO TALK TO YOU, HIS MOTHER, OH LORD MY BABY IS YOU ALLRIGHT, YES MAMA I DONT HAVE MUCH TIME, I AM IN A LITTLE TROUBLE, BUT DONT TELL PAPA, HIS MOTHER, WHAT IS THE MATTER IS YOU HIRT, NO MAMA, I HAD THIS JOB AND WE HAD TO WEAR UINFORMS, AND WHEN I CHANGED MY CLOTHES I FORGOT AND LEFT MY MONEY IN MY POCKET, AND SOME ONE STOLE IT, I JUST NEED YOU TO SEND ME ENOUGH FOR BUS FARE HOME, HIS MOTHER I WILL SEND YOU THE MONEY BUT YOU KNOW YOUR FATHER, IF I WERE YOU I WOULD NOT COME BACK TO THIS HOUSE, SO HE INQUIRE ABOUT HIS OTHER BROTHER, AND ASK WHERE IS HE, HIS MOTHER RESPOND YOU KNOW YOUR YOUNGER BROTHER WAS THE LAST TO LEAVE, AND HE IS IN BUNNINGHAM, DO YOU WANT HIS ADDRESS, YAA MAMA, SO WHEN HE RECEIVE THE FUNDS TO LEAVE HE HEAD TO BIRMINGHAM, TO JOIN HI!. YOUNGER BROTHER UPON ARRIVAL HE LEARN HIS BROTHER HAS A JOB, AND HIS OWN PLACE HIS FIRST QUESTION TO HIS BROTHER IS DID PAPA GIVE YOU YOUR SHARE FROM THE FARM, HIS BROTHER RESPONSE YES ITS IN THE BANK,HIS YOUNGER BROTHER ASK HIM WHERE ARE YOUR BAGS, CLOTHING AND ALL, HIS TALL TAIL IS THE BUILDING WHERE HE WAS LIVING CAUGHT FIRE AND ALL OF HIS CLOTHING WAS LOST, THE NEXT MORNING HIS BROTHER HEAD OFF TO WORK, THAT AFTERNOON HIS BROTHER ARRIVE HOME TO HIS APPARTMENT WITH TAR ALL OVER HIS CLOTHING, SO HE ASK HIS BROTHER MAN WHAT DO YOU DO, HIS BROTHER ANSWER I SPREAD TAR BEHIND A TAR TRUCK, HOW MUCH THEY PAY YOU FOR GETTING THAT SHIT ALL OVER YOU, HIS BROTHER SEVEN DOLLARS AND FIFTY CENT PER. HOUR, WHO IS DRIVING THE TRUCK HIS BROTHER SOME WHITE PERSON, MAN HAVE YOU LOST YOUR MIND, YOU ARE WALKING BEHIND A TRUCK SOME HONKEY IS DRIVING AND YOU ARE SPREADING HIS SHIT, IF YOU CANT

DRIVE THE TRUCK YOU NEED TO QUIT THAT JOB, SO THE NEXT EVENING WHEN HIS BROTHER ARRIVE HOME,HIS APPARTMENT IS FULL OF GROUPIES, DRUGGIES, AND WHORES, LATER HIS BROTHER GO TO BED BECAUSE HE HAS TO WORK, SO DURING THE NIGHT WHILE HIS BROTHER IS SLEEPING HE SCHOOL HIS FOLLOWERS, ABOUT HOW IT WAS DONE IN CHICAGO, THESE HONKEYS DONT KNOW SHIT DOWN HERE IN THE SOUTH, SO THE VERY NEXT DAY HE AND HIS NEW FOUND FRIENDS GO TO HIS BROTHER PLACE OF EMPLOYMENT AND VIRBALLY ABUSE THE TRUCK DRIVER, AND TELL HIM HE SHOULD HAVE HIS WHITE ASS BEHIND THIS TRCK, HIS BROTHER PLEAD WITH HIM TO LEAVE, FINALLY HE DEPART, AND TELL HIS FOLLOWERS HE IS GOING TO CHANGE THIS TOWN, LIKE THE WAY ITS, DONE IN CHICAGO, SO THEY DECIDE TO GO TO AN AFFLUNT WHITE RESTAURANT AND ASK TO BE SERVED, THE WAITRESS TELL THEM THIS IS FOR WHITE ONLY, THE MANAGER CALL THE POLICE, WHILE HE IS LEAVING HE CALL THE WAITRESS A WHITE BITCH, TWO DAYS LATER HE IS FOUND HANGING FROM A TREE IN A FOREST OF WOODS, HIS BROTHER CALL HIS PRENTS AT HOME, PAPA, BRO GOT HIS SELF HUNG NO BODY KNOW WHO DID IT, HIS FATHER RESPONDED I KNOWED IT DAT OLD BOY WOULD NOT TELL A MULE TO GET UP IF IT SAT IN HIS LAP, HE JUST WOULD NOT WORK FOR NOBODY.

THERE ARE PLURAL SCENARIOS PERTAINING TO AFRICAN AMERICANS THAT STILL LIVE IN AND MIGRATED FROM THE SOUTHERN STATES, THE HANGING OF THIS RADICAL MOST LIKELY FRIGHTEN HIS FOLLOWERS AND DURING THESE TIMES IN THE EARLY SIXTIES, THEIR PARENTS WOULD HARSHLY DEMAND THAT THEY LEAVE THE SOUTH FEAR OF REPRISAL, SO THEY WOULD GATHER WHAT FUNDS THEY COULD AFFORD AND SEND THEM ON THEIR WAY,AND WITHOUT QUESTION BASED ON THEIR BEHAVIORAL PATTERN DURING THEIR TIME IN THE SOUTH, THEY WERE HEADED FOR THE SLUMS IN THE NORTHERN STATES, TO ADD TO THE ALREADY DISMAL POVITY DEBACLE, AND MOST LIKELY END UP DURING HARD TIME IN JAIL, OR DEAD FROM OTHER GANG MEMBERS, OR A DRUG OVERDOSE.

OF COURSE THERE WERE SOME DECIDED TO STAY ON AND FARM, AND ALSO GET A JOB OUT SIDE OF THEIR FARM DUTIES, AND CHOOSE TO PURCHASE ADDITIONAL LAND, BUILT NICE HOMES, GOT MARRIED HAD CHILDREN AND AND INSISTED THEIR CHILDERN GET AN EDUCATION, SO WHEN THEY DECIDED TO GO ON THEIR OWN,IF THEY CHOOSE TO STAY OR LEAVE THEY WOULD BE WELL ARMED AND SUITED FOR A DIVERSE SOCIETY OF PEOPLE ANY PLACE IN THE COUNTRY, AND CARRY ON THEIR TRADITION OF SUCCESS AND MADE THEIR PARENTS AND GRAND PARENTS PROUD.

AND THERE IS ANOTHER DEBACLE PERTAINING TO AFRICAN AMERICAN WOMEN SOME FROM THE SHARE CROPPING PLANTATIONS OF THE SOUTHERN STATES, DURING SCHOOL SOME DECIDED TO FINISH AND GO ON TO COLLEGE, SOME CHOOSE TO FINISH HIGH SCHOOL, AND SOME DROPPED OUT, AND MANY AFTER SCHOLD DECIDED TO REMAIN ON THE FARM, WITH THEIR PARENTS, AND DATED MARRIED MEN, AND WOULD OFTEN HAVE SOME TIME FIVE CHILDREN EACH WITH A DIFFERENT FATHER, IN HER PARENTS HOME, SO ONE NIGHT IT IS JOY ON THE TOWN, AND SHE MEET SOME SLICK TALKING SLUM BUM, AND HE CONVINCE HER TO COME AWAY WITH HIM, SHE TELL HER PARENTS THAT SHE HAS BEEN OFFERED THIS HIGH PAYING JOB IN THE BIG CITY, AND IF THEY WOULD KEEP THE HER CHILDREN WHILE SHE WORKED, THAT SHE IS GOING TO SEND MONEY HOME, ONCE SHE ARRIVE IN THE BIG CITY, SHE LEARN THIS FELLOW LIVE IN A ONE ROOM APARTMENT,ANDLTHE CAR HE WAS DRIVING BELONG TO HIS FRIEND,AND NOT ONLY THAT HE IS ASSOCIATED WITH A LOT OF WOMEN WHICH IS ON PUBLIC ASSISTANCE, AND PAYING HIS RENT, SO SHE BECOME ENRAGED AND TELL HER STORY TO HIS FRIEND THAT LOANED, HIM THE CAR, SO HE TELL HER HE HAS A PLAN, AND THAT IS HE WILL TAKE HER TO GET HER KIDS, BECAUSE SHE CAN GET PUBLIC ASSISTANCE, SO SHE PICK UP HER KIDS AND TELL HER PARENTS SHE HAS TO GO BECAUSE SHE DONT WANT TO LOOSE HER JOB, AND THEY ARE OFF TO THE SLUMS WITH THE FIVE CHILDREN, THEY ALL PILE IN HIS ONE

ROOM APARTMENT UNTIL SHE FIND AN APARTMENT, AND GET ASSISTANCE, WITH JUST ENOUGH ROOM FOR THEM, HOWEVER HE DECIDED TO STAY OVER FOR A NIGHT OR TWO, BUT WHAT SHE DOSENT KNOW HE IS A DRUG PUSHER AND ON IT HIMSELF, AND IS LIVING FROM HOUSE TO HOUSE WITH OTHER WOMEN THAT IS ON PUBLIC ASSISTANCE, AND LATER SHE FIND OUT THAT HER THIRTEEN YEAR DAUGHTER IS PREGANAT BY HIM.

THESE STUPENDOUS NONE ISOLATED OCCURRENCES IS SIMPLY RESPONSIBLE FOR THE ESCALATING GROWTH OF POVITY, AND IT IS NOT DISCRIMINATING WHITES AND AFRICAN AMERICANS ARE SWALLOWED UP BY THIS DEVIOUS PHENOMENON ANUALLY BY THE THOUSANDS, BUT THERE IS A DIFFERENCE BETWEEN BLACK AND WHITE DISPARITY, POOR UNEDUCATED WHITES WILL MIGRATE TO A LARGE CITY, AND SPREAD OUT ALL OVER TO LIVE, AND LOCATE ANY KIND OF A JOB TO SURVIVE, IN CONTRAST AFRICAN AMERICANS IN THE SAME CATEGORY WILL RELY ON THEIR TRIBAL INSTINCTS FROM AFRICA, AND HERD INTO AN AREA THAT IS ALREADY OVER CROWDED AND COMPOUND THE ISSURE RELATED TO SLUMS, AND MOST HAVE NO INTENTIONS OF PERSUING EMPLOYMENT OF ANY KIND, AND SCREAM LIKE HELL THAT THE WHITE MAN IS KEEPING THEM DOWN, HOWEVER THERES.TIMES WHEN SOME BLACKS WILL LOCATE EMPLOYMENT AND HE OR SHE WILL BE QUESTIONED ABOUT THEIR WORK HISTORY AND EDUCATIONAL BACK GROUND, IT WILL BE ESTABLISHED HE OR SHE IS NEAR BEING ILLITERATE, HOWEVER HE OR SHE IS HIRED, AND PLACED IN A JOB THEY ARE MOST SUTABLE FOR, AFTER A FIEW DAYS OR WEEKS THEY LOUNGE AROUND AND FINALLY LOCATE A JOB, THAT SOME ONE ELSE IS RESPONSIBLE FOR DOING, BUT TO HE OR SHE IT LOOK EASY AND HAS SOME AUTHORITY, SO THE SUPERVISOR ACCOSTED AND SUGGESTIONS ARE MADE THAT THIS IS A JOB COULD BE PERFORMED BY HIM, AND HE IS TOLD BY HIS BOSS, THIS JOB REQUIRE SPECIAL SKILLS AND HE DO NOT QUALIFY, HOWEVER HE KEEP PESTERING HIS BOSS ABOUT THIS JOB, FINALLY ONE DAY THE TECHNICIAN IS AWAY FOR THE DAY,AND THE BOSS GIVE HIM A CHANCE,

HE IS ADVISED OF THE PROCEDUAL OPERATIONS ANS HIS SUPERVIOSER HAS TO STEP AWAY FOR A MOMENT, AND HE RUIN HNDREDS OF DOLLARS WORTH OF EQUIPMENT, THE BOSS REMOVE HIM FROM THE JOB AND SEND HIM BACK TO HIS JOB, IF HIS SUPERVISOR IS BLACK HE SUDDENLY BECOME A WHITE MAN NIGGER AND WILL NOT HELP HIS PEOPLE.

AND THAT IS WHAT WRONG WITH NIGGERS THEY DONT STICK TOGATHER FOR HIS BROTHERS, AND THAT HONKEY RUNNING THAT MACHINE DONT KNOW WHAT HE IS DOING HE IS THERE BECAUSE HE IS WHITE, AND GOD FORBID IF HIS SUPERVISOR IS WHITE, THE COMPLAINT WILL BE LARGED IN THIS MANNER, HE WAS GIVEN A JOB, AND REMOVED FOR A WHITE MAN, AND HE REALLY LIKED THAT JOB, AND THIS WHOLE COMPANY IS RACIST AGANIST BLACK, AND HE IS GOING TO SOLICIT JESSIE JACKSON OR AL SHARPETON IN THIS MATTER THEY WILL GET IT STRAIGHTEN OUT, BECAUSE THIS IS UNFAIR TO AFRICAN AMERICANS.

SO AS A REALITY THE COUNTRY IS INUNDATED WITH THESE KIND OF INTREPID EXTORTING TACTICS BY SOME AFRICAN AMERICANS, AND WILL EVENTUALLY DRASTICALLY REDUCE THEIR CHANCES OF OBTAINING NONE SKILL LABOR IN THE PRIVATE SECTOR, MANY AFRICAN AMERICANS ARE OF THE OPINION THAT EDUCATION IS NOT A NECESSITY TO BECOME FINANCIALLY STABLE, THAT THIS EDUCATION THING IS TO MUCH LIKE BEING WHITE, AND WHILE THEY ARE WAITING FOR JESSIE JACKSON, AL SHARPETON, OR TAVIS SMILEY TO RECTIFY THEIR STUPID IDEOLOGY, THE HISPANICS ARE MOVING INTO NONE SKILLED JOBS ALL OVER THE COUNTRY AND WORKING THEM SELVES INTO THEIR OWN BUISNESSES, AND BUYING HOMES, AND BECOMING PRODUCTIVE CITIZENS IN THE UNITED STATES OF AMERICA, AND SEEING THAT THEIR CHILDREN BECOME EDUCATED, AND HAS QUIETLY EXCEEDED THE AFRICAN AMERICAN POPULATION, AND AT THIS POINT ARE LEADING THE CHARGE IN OFF SETTING THE BLOC VOTE OF BLACKS FOR DEMOCRATS, BECAU?SE THEY HAVE THE INTELLIGENCES AND COMMON SENSE NOT TO FOLLOW SOME SELF OPPOINTED LEADER THAT IS POLITICALLY ILLITERATE, ADVISING THEM ON HOW THEY SHOULD CAST

THEIR VOTES, THE INITIATIVE OF HISPANICS IS TO THINK FOR THEM SELVES THEIR VOTING PATTERN IS EVIDENCE IT IS SPLIT SIXTY AND FORTY, THIS DEMONSTRATE SOME UNDERSTANDING OF CONSTITUTIONAL GOVERNMENTAL. CONTROL IN THE UNITED STATES OF AMERICA, UNLIKE AFRICAN AMERICANS,HURDING BEHIND SELF APPOINTED LEADERS WITH NO REGARD FOR THE CONSTITUTION AND HOW IT DICTATE THE EVERY DAY FEDERAL FUNCTIONS OF THIS COUNTRY, MEANING THE PRESIDENT, CONGRESS, AND THE SENATE, ALSO STATES ARE ORGANIZED WITH A CARBON COPY, STARTING WITH AN ELECTED GOVERNOR, ALL OF THESE POLITICIANS SIRE ELECTED BY THE VOTING CITIZENS OF THIS COUNTRY, THE YEARS 1964 AND 1965, GAVE AFRICAN AMERICANS THE RIGHT TO CHOOSE THEIR ELECTED OFFICIALS THROUGH VOTING, THE CONSTITUTION GIVE EVERY BONAFIDE CITIZEN OF THIS COUNTRY THAT RIGHT, SO IF YOU SHOULD CHOOSE TO FOLLOW A SELF APPOINTED LEADER IT IS YOUR PURGATIVE, BUT SOME TIME THERE CAN BE GRAVE CONSEQUENCES, BECAUSE THESELF. APPOINTED RADICALS ARE ONLY INTERESTED IN WHAT YOU CAN DO FOR THEM, LETS JUST USE THE MILLION MAN MARCH FOR EXAMPLE, THE ACCUMULATION OF THAT MANY PEOPLE,SO LETS ASSUME WITH ALL DONATIONS IT AVERAGED OUT TO TEN DALLARS A PERSON, YOU DO THE MATH, THEY LEAVE WITH MONEYS TO KEEP THEIR RADICAL AGENDA GOING, AND YOU LEAVE MINAS TEN DOLLARS, AND ACCORDING TO THE WAY OUR GOVERNMENT IS STRUCTURED UNDER THE CONSTITUTION THERE IS NOTHING, NOT ANY THING, NONE, NO WAY,THEY CAN DO ANYTHING FOR THE POVITY EXIST WITHIN THE AFRICAN AMERICAN SOCIETY, BECAUSE IT IS SELF IMPOSED.

AND THERE IS A MAJORITY OF AFRICAN AMERICANS EDUCATED, AND NONE EDUCATED, WEALTHY, AND POOR, BUY INTO THIS NONSENSICAL DEMAGOGY, BECAUSE AS LONG AS THERE IS A CONSTITUTION THERE WILL NEVER BE SOME KIND OF SPECIAL INCEPTION FOR BLACKS PERTAINING TO POVERTY. HOWEVER THERE IS A MOVEMENT BEING GENERATED BY SELF APPOINTED RDICAL LEADERS IN AN

EFFORT TO INCITE FOOLISH BLACKS TO REBEL, IF THIS SHOULD HAPPEN IT COULD BE DETRIMENTAL FOR MANY AFRICAN AMERICANS BASED ON THE ACCOMPLISHMENTS MADE OVER THE YEARS, NOT TO MENTION BEING SLAUGHTERED IN THE STREETS LIKE CHICKENS WITH THE BIRD FLU.

MOST OFTHESE SELF APPOINTED RADICAL LEADERS ARE TOTALLY UNAWARE OF WHAT RACIAL VIOLENCE WAS LIKE DURING THE EARLY SIXTIES IN BURMINGHAM ALABAMA, AND AROUND THE SOUTHERN STATES, IF THEY ONLY KNEW OR WAS THERE DURING THE MARTIN LUTHER KING ERA, THEY WOULD TONE THEIR BUFFOONISH DEMAGOGUERY, HIS CAUSE WAS FOR LIBERTY AND JUSTICE AND THE RIGHT TO BE JUDGED BY THE CONTENT OF YOUR CHARACTER, NOT BY THE COLOR OF YOUR SKIN, HIS TIRELESS EFFORT TO ACCOMPLISH THIS CUMBERSOME ENDEAVOR WAS MONUMENTAL, HE UNDERSTOOD THE CONSTITUTION AND THE IMPORTANCE OF RADIFICATION FOR AFRICAN AMERICANS PERTAINING TO CIVIL AND VOTING RIGHTS, HOWEVER THE SOUTHERN DEMOCRATS PERSECUTED THIS HONORABLE MAN FOR PROTESTING IN FAVOR OF THESE CONSTITUTIONAL RIGHTS, AND THERE IS NO QUESTION ABOUT WIRE TAPPING, IT WAS CONFIRMED BY FORMER PRESIDENT CARTER AT MRS. KING FUNERAL,NOT THAT WAS NOT WIDELY KNOWN, ONE SUCH INCIDENT OCCURRED AT THE WILLARD HOTEL IN WASHINGTON, WHICH COMPROMISING VERBIAGE WAS INTERCEPTED BY THE FBI, DR. MARTIN LUTHER KING DEDICATED MOST OF HIS LIFE TO ACCOMPLISH CIVIL AND VOTING RIGHTS FOR AFRICAN AMERICANS, AND MOST LIKELY GAVE HIS LIFE FOR THE CAUSE, HOWEVER AFTER 1964 AND 1965, HIS CRUSADE WAS FINISHED, AFRICAN AMERICANS SHOULD HAVE BEEN ON THEIR OWN, TO DEVERSIFY AND HEAL THE WOUNDS SUFFERED IN THEIR QUEST FOR EQUALITY WHICH ONLY CAN BE IMPROVED THROUGH INDIVIDUAL ENDEAVORS, UNFORTUNATELY THE MAJORITY OF BLACKS DECIDED TO FOLLOW JESSIE JACKSON, A SELF APPOINTED LEADER WITH TEACHINGS OF SAY IT LOUD I AM BLACK AND I AM PROUD, AND THERE IS ACAUSE FOR YOUR FAILURE

AND HE HAS THE ANSWER, JUST LEAVE EVERY THING TO HIM AND CROWD INTO RAIN BOW PUSH HALL, WITH YOUR FIEW HARD EARNED DOLLARS AND SUPPORT THE CAUSE, BUT GUESS WHAT. HE IS RICH AS HELL AND MOST OF YOU FOLLOWERS NATION WIDE IS STILL OBSESSED WITH HIS LOGIC SPENNING OUT DEMOCRATIC IDEOLOGY TO KEEP YOU THE POLITICAL PLANTATION REGARDS TO YOUR VOTING BLOC, AND MOST AFRICAN AMERICANS THAT IS LOYAL TO THIS MALARKY,ARE WORSE OFF TODAY THAN THEY WERE OVER FORTY YEARS AGO, HE HAS KEPT YOU SEALED IN THE TOMB OF IGNORANCE FOR OVER FORTY YEARS, OVER THE YEARS HE HAS LOST SOME OF HIS LUSTER, HIS APROPOS GENERATED HIS WEALTH AFTER THE DEMISE OF DR. MARTIN LUTHER KING, WITH THE INTERMEDIATING OF BUISNESSES BASED ON DISCRIMINATION ETHICS, MOST OF THE BUISNESSES DID NOT WANT THE NEWS COVERAGE AND THREATS OF PICKETING, SO THEY DOLED OUT FINANCES, AND THE PEOPLE THAT CAUSED THIS UP ROAR MOSTLIKELY LOST THEIR JOBS LATER ON,AND IF THERE WERE PICKETERS THEY WENT HOME WITH THEIR HANDS FROZEN TO THEIR SIGNS, AND HE WITH A FAT COMPENSATION, I DO NOT RECALL JESSIE JACKSON ENDORSING HARD CORE RADICALISM OUTWARDLY.

UNLIKE HIS WANT TO BE SUCCESSOR SELF APPOINTED PRESIDENT OF BLACK AMERICA TAVIS SMILEY, AND HIS CABNIET OF RADICALS, IF AFRICAN AMERICANS CHOOSE TO FOLLOW AND ENDORSE THEIR RADICAL THINKING, YOU AND YOUR FAMILIES AND LOVE ONES ARE IN FOR A RUDE AWAKENING, A LOT OF INNOCENT PEOPLE WILL SUFFER DRAMATICALLY, IN THAT RING OF FIRE THAT FARRAKHAN WISH ON AMERICA, ONE THING FOR CERTAIN JESSIE JACKSON AND TAVIS SMILEY, HAVE IN COMMON THEY EACH ARE PROFESSION NALS AT SABOTAGING THE AMERICAN ENGLISH.

THERE IS A PROVOCATIVE SCENARIO WITH SOME SUCCESSFUL AFRICAN AMERICANS, MOST ARE WHERE THEY ARE BECAUSE OF WHITES, BUT IN ESSENCE THEY WILL FORECAST TO OTHER BLACKSITHAT THE WHITE MAN IS HALTING THEIR BID FOR SUCCESS.

FORMER F.B.I. DIRECTOR J. EDGAR HOOVER ONCE STATED THAT HE FELT THE BRAINS OF AFRICAN AMERICANS WERE TWENTY PERCENT SMALLER THAN WHITES, I DISAGREE WITH HIS ANSLYSIS THEY ARE NOT SMALLER THAN WHITES BUT SOME ARE PROPORTIONALLY DYSFUNCTIONAL TO THE LEGITIMACY OF SELF CONTAIN REGULARITY, SIMPLY BECAUSE OF HERITAGE CHRONOLOGICALLY PASSED ON FROM EACH GENERATION, LETS REVERT BACK TO AFRICA THE ORIGINAL PLACE OF ANCESTRY AND PRIMARILY DEAL WITH CULTURAL BEHAVIOR, MANY SPORADIC TRIBES WERE CONTROLLED BY A SINGLE LEADER AND THE ENTIRE TRIBE HAS ONLY TWO CULTURAL AMBITIONS, AND THAT IS TO EAT AND SLEEP, AND THEIR FOOD IS BROUGHT TO THE THEM BY A FEW CHOSEN WARRIORS THAT HUNT, TO SUPPLY THE ENTIRE TRIBE WITH FOOD WHICH CONSIST OF MONKEYS, PARROTS, BABOONS, BEE HONEY, GAZELLES, ROOTS, NUTS AND POTATOES, NO OTHER RESPONSIBILITY, SO THEY ARE CAPTURED FROM DIFFERENT TRIBES,HERDED INTO HOLDING FACILITIES, LATER HERDED ON TO SHIPS, WHEN THEY REACH AMERICA THEY ARE SOLD AND HERDED TO PLANTATIONS IN THE SOUTHERN STATES, AND THEY LIVE ON PLANTATIONS WHICH CONSIST OF HERDING CONDITIONS,THAT IS SIMILAR TO WHERE THEY CAME FROM, ALSO WITH NO INDIVIDUAL RESPONSIBILITY BUT WORK THE RICE, CAIN, AND COTTON FIELDS, THEIR PLANTATION MASTERS SUPPLIED THEM WITH ALL OF THEIR NEEDS, SO THEIR CULTURAL OPPORTUNISM WAS A REPLICA OF THEIR LIFE STYLE IN AFRICA, SO IN 1865, WHEN SLAVERY WAS ABOLISHED,THEY HAD NO OTHER CHOICE BUT HERD BACK TO THE PLANTATIONS AND BE SUCCUMBED BY THEIR SLAVE MASTERS, UNDER SHARE CROPPING REGULATIONS, WHICH WAS A FORM OF SOPHISTICATED SLAVERY, HOWEVER THEY WERE CARED FOR, THESE CONDITIONS LINGERED ON UNTIL THE NINETEENTH CENTURY , AND THE NEW DEAL WAS PUT INTO AFFECT BY PRESIDENT ROOSEVELT, MEANING SOCIAL SECURITY, THIS WAS A GRATUITY OF A LIFE TIME FOR AFRICAN AMERICANS, THEY FRAUDULENTLY LOADED UP, DURING SLAVERY AFRICAN AMERICANS HAD NO DOCTORS FOR CHILD DELIVERY, AS IN AFRICA THERE

WERE SOME ONE IN THE TRIBE THAT COULD DELIVER BABIES, UNFORTUNATELY THERE WERE RECORDS OF BIRTH, BECAUSE THEY COULD NOT READ OR WRITE, LATER THERE WERE MIDWIVES REGISTERED BY RHE STATE, AND THERE WERE TIMES THEY WOULD GO TO DELIVER A BABY AND AFTERWARDS GET SOUSED ON MOONSHINE AND FORGET TO REGISTER THE BIRTH RECORD, THERE ARE HUNDREDSCOF THOUSANDS OF AFRICAN AMERICANS THROUGHOUT THE SOUTHERN STATES WITH NO BIRTH CERTIFIC, NOW COME ALONG THE NEW DEAL, SOCIAL SECURITY,AND NO APPROVAL OF AGE HOW DO YOU GET SOCIAL SECURITY, NO PROBLEM JUST GO THE OLDEST AND CREDIABLE WHITE MAN, THEY WERE CALLED VOUCHERS, CAN YOU IMAGINE SOME MAN OR WOMAN EIGHTY OR NINETY YEARS OLD AND SENILE TELLING YOU HOW OLD SOME ONE IS, AND BECAUSE OF THIS UNWITTINGLY DEBACLE THOUSANDS OF AFRICAN AMERICANS WERE RECEVING SOCIAL SECURITY BENIFITS AT AGE FORTY FIVE AND UP,BY THE WAY INCASE YOU ARE WONDERING WHITES HAD RECORDS OF THEIR BIRTH,BECAUSE BONAFIDE DOCTORS WENT TO THEIR HOMES AND DELIVERED THEIR BABIES, SO THIS WAS ANOTHER LEANING POST FOR SOME AFRICAN AMERICANS, WITH SOME BODY SUPPORT ME PLEASE WRITTEN ALL OVER IT,HOWEVER SOME DID WORK THE FIELDS PLOWING, CHOPPING AND-BICKING COTTON, IN THE INTERIM THEY WERE MIGRATING TO THE NORTHERN STATES WITH NO SKILLS AND NO EDUCATION,LOOKING FOR THE BIG CITY AND BRIGHT LIGHTS, AND NOT REALIZING THAT CHICAGO, NEW YORK, DETROIT, CLEVELAND, PHILADELPHIA, CINCINATTI, IS NOTHING MORE THAN A INTRODUCTION TO SLUM FOR MOST PEOPLE THAT ARE UNAWARE OF HOW TO SURVIVE, SO MOST OF THE TIME THEY ARE CHEWED UP AND SENT PACKING BACK HOME OR TO THE FOREVER CROWDED SLUMS, AND HOOKED ON DRUGS.

A FIEW YEARS LATER TWO THINGS OCCURED THAT SENT SOME FREE LOADING BLACKS IN SERCH OF A DIFFERENT SUPPORTING FACTOR, THE SMALL FARM BUSINESSES FOLDED, BECAUSE OF HIGH TECH EQUIPMENT, ALONG WITH CHEMICALS TO ELIMINATE GRASS ON THE BIG

PLANTATIONS, AND THE CIVIL AND VOTING RIGHTS ACT OF 1964, AND 1965, PASSED SO SOME AFRICAN AMERICANS BELIEVED IT WAS IN THEIR BEST INTEREST TO HEAD FOR THE NORTHERN STATES, TO LOOK FOR PROSPERITY NOT REALIZING THAT PROSPERITY WAS KNOCKING AT THEIR DOOR IN THE FORM OF CIVIL RIGHTS, AND THE RIGHT TO VOTE MOST OF ALL, BECAUSE THIS WAS THE MAJOR REASON THE CIVIL RIGHTS BILL WAS PASSED, PRESIDENT JOHNSON BEING FEARFUL THAT AFRICAN AMERICANS WOULD START TO SUPPORT THE REPUBLICAN PARTY AGAIN WITH THEIR BLOC VOTING.

IT IS ALL TO OFTEN SOME AFRICAN AMERICANS NEGLECT TO REALIZE HOW IMPORTANT IT IS TO UNDERSTAND THE STRUCTURE OF OUR GOVENMENT AND HOW IT IS FORMATTED, BASED ON THE CONSTITUTION.

ARTICLE (ONE)

SECTION (ONE)

SPECIFICALLY STATE (ALL) LEGISLATIVE POWERS HEREIN GRANTED SHALL BE VESTED IN A CONGRESS OF THE UNITED STATES, WHICH SHALL CONSIST OF A SENATE AND HOUSE OF REPRESENTATIVES.

LEGISLATE MEAN LAWS HAVING TO DO WITH ALL CITIZENS BLACK, AND WHITE, ALSO NONE CITIZENS OF THE UNITED STATES OF AMERICA,THERE IS NOTHING IN THE CONSTITUTION THAT ENDORSE SELF APPOINTED RADICAL LEADERS, MARTIN LUTHER KING, ENDURED TRAUMATIC EXPERIENCES IN THE SOUTHERN STATES, IN ORDER THAT AFRICAN AMERICANS COULD BE A PART OF THESE LAWS PROVIDED BY THE CONSTITUTION, FOR ALL AMERICAN CITIZENS, MEANING CONCLUSIVE RADIFICATION REGARDS TO CIVIL AND VOTING RIGHTS FOR ALL AMERICANS INCLUDING AFRICAN AMERICANS,INHERENTLY IT WAS ACCOMPLISHED IN 1964 AND 1965, HOWEVER THERE WILL ALWAYS BE A UNSETTLING MYSTERY IN MY HEART MIND AND SOUL, PERTAINING TO ARTICLE ONE AND SECTION ONE OF THE CONSTITUTION,WHICH SPECIFICALLY SPELL OUT THAT THE SENATE AND THE CONGRESS ARE THE

SOLE LEGISLATORS OF LAWS FOR THE UNITED STATES OF AMERICA, AND DURING THE SIXTIES MARTIN LUTHER KING WAS OUT THERE IN THE SOUTHERN STATES BEING BATTERED TO HELL, AND THE MAJORITY OF AFRICAN AMERICANS THROUGHOUT THE COUNTRY WERE VOTING FOR DEMOCRATS, TO HOLD THEIR SENATE SEATS IN ORDER SO THEY COULD DEPRIVE THEM OF THEIR CIVIL AND VOTING RIGHTS, AND THIS IS ONE OF THE REASONS I LABEL SOME AS HAVING A DYSFUNCTIONAL BRAIN, AND I THINK THE MAJORITY OF CIVILIZE CITIZENS IN THIS COUNTRY WOULD AGREE, HOWEVER THERE IS A MORE EGREGIOUS PHENOMENON THAT SOME AFRICAN AMERICANS IS TRANSFIXED ON, AND THAT IS TO SUPPORT THESE SELF APPOINTED SUPPOSEDLY LEADERS SPEWING OUT VILLAINOUS DEMAGOGUREY FOR PERSONSL GAIN FOR THEM SELVES AND THE DEMOCRATIC PARTY, WHICH THEY ALL SUPPORT.

THERE IS ANOTHER GOVERNMENTAL PROGRAM THAT HAS CREATED A MONUMENTAL SLUM THROUGHOUT THE NATION FOR MANY PEOPLE, BUT UNFORTUNATELY FOR AFRICAN AMERICANS IT IS BEYOND REPROACH AND MOST DAMING IN BIG NORTHERN CITIES, AND THAT IS A.D.C. AID FOR DEPENDABLE CHILDREN, I AM NOT ADVOCATING IT SHOULD NOT EXIST, BUT THE ABUSE HAS CREATED A UNIQUE SOCIETY OF PEOPLE IN THIS COUNTRY THAT IS DEVASTATING TO THE ENTIRE NATION, SOME OF THESE PEOPLE THAT ARE RECEIVING THIS ADE HAS NEVER HELD A JOB IN THEIR ENTIRE LIFE, AND HAVE NO INTENTION OF EVER BEING GAINFULLY EMPLOYED, THEY HERD INTO AREAS AND CREATE SLUMS OR MOVE INTO EXISTING SLUMS, AND MOST OF THESE PEOPLE HAVE NO REGARD FOR TRADITIONAL VALUES, BECAUSE THIS IS BEYOND THEIR COMPREHENSION, THE MODEL FOR THEIR IDEOLOGY IS LAWLESSNESS, REPRODUCTION, AND BEHAVIORAL PATTERNS THAT IS SO INSIGNIFICANT TO A CIVIL SOCIETY UNTIL IT IS PATHETIC, THEY HERD INTO THE SLUMS AND GENERATE THEIR OWN IDEALS ON HOW THE COUNTRY SHOULD BE RAN,AND THEIR ORCHESTRATED SUMMATION WOULD BE TO ACCOMMODATE THEIR WAY OF THINKING

WHICH IS PRIMITIVE AND EXTREMELY RADICAL AND RACIST, THEY ARE LIVING IN A SLUM GETTO, AND MOST HAS NEVER HAD A JOB IN THEIR LIFE, AND ILLITERACY IS PREVALENT, BUT THEY WANT TO SET THE AGENDA FOR THE ENTIRE NATION, MANY DONT KNOW WHO DR. MARTIN LUTHER KING WAS, AND IN FACT COULD CARE LESS, MANY HAVENT THE SLIGHTEST IDEA OF HOW THE GOVERNMENT FUNCTION IN THE NATION, THE REPUBLICANS IN THE SENATE DURING 1964, FAUGHT LIKE HELL TO OVER RIDE A DEMOCRATIC FILIBUSTER AGAINST AFRICAN AMERICANS TO HAVE THEIR CONSTITUTIONAL CIVIL RIGHTS, FINALLY IT PASSED PRESIDENT LYNDON JOHNSON SIGNED IT IN JULY 2, 1964, IN ATLANTIC CITY NEW JERSEY AUGUST 1964, AT THE DEMOCRATIC CONVENTION, AFRICAN AMERICANS FLOODED THE CONVENTION IN SUPPORT OF DEMOCRATS, IN AN EFFORT TO KEEP THEM IN POWER.

FOR SOME BRAIN DYSFUNCTIONAL REASON SOME AFRICANAMERICANSTHINKTHEPRESIDENTISRESPONSIBLE FOR THE GENERAL PUBLIC ACCOLADES HAVING TO DO WITH LEGISLATIVE APPROVAL OF LAW.

(IT IS THE CONGRESS)

MOST AFRICAN AMERICANS LIVING IN POVETY SPEND THEIR ENTIRE LIFE VENGEFULLY HATING ANY ONE THAT IS SUCCESSFUL MEANING BLACK AND WHITE PEOPLE, THEIR VERBAGE CONSIST OF WORDS OF THIS MANNER, THAT NIGGER THINK HE IS WHITE BECAUSE HE GOT A JOB, CAR, AND HOUSE,BUT HE AINT SHIT, HE THINK HE IS BETTER THAN US, HE AINT NOTHING BUT SOME WHITE MAN BOOT LICKER, AND NOW VERBAGE PERTAINING TO WHITES, THAT HONKEY GOT ALL THAT MONEY AND WANT GIVE US ANY OF IT, HE DONT KNOW WE WILL MESS HIM UP BECAUSE HE IS THE REASON WE ARE IN THE SHAPE THAT ALL OF US IS IN.

SOME OF THESE PEOPLE HAVE LIVED ON GOVERNMENT ASSISTANCE FOR SO IT HAS BECAME A FAMILY TRADITION THAT IS PASSED ON GENERATIONAL THEIR IDEOLOGY IS CONSISTENT THROUGH OUT THE NATION, SOME SPEND THEIR ENTIRE LIFE TRYING TO CONVINCE THE COUNTRY THEY HAVE THE BETTER IDEA, AND THEY HAVE BEEN HELD

BACK, BECAUSE PREJUDICE WHITE PEOPLE WONT GIVE THEM A BREAK BECAUSE THEY ARE BLACK, AND FEEL SOME DAY THEY WILL BE IN CHARGE OF THIS COUNTRY.

THE SICKENING ASPECTS OF THIS THEORY, IS THAT THERE ARE SELF APPOINTED SUPPOSEDLY BLACK LEADERS THAT ENDORSE THIS DECTIVE BUFFOONERY AND PUBLICLY INCITE THEIR THEORY, NAMELY TAVIS SMILEY, CORNELL WEST, LOUIS FARRAKHAN, AND HARRY BELAFONTE, THIS COULD PROVE TO BE VERY DANGEROUS FOR ALL AFRICAN AMERICANS IN THIS COUNTRY, SELF APPOINTED SPOKSEMAN FOR ALL AFRICAN AMERICANS, TAVIS SMILEY IS ON NATIONAL TELEVISION AND RADIO SUGGESTING THERE IS A MOVEMEMENT GOING ON IN THE COUNTRY, I AM CERTAIN HE IS REFERRINGTO ORGANIZING SOME AFRICAN AMERICANS IN ORDER TO GET THEM TO COMPREHEND THEIR OWN IDIOSYNCRASY,OR APPARENTLY HE HAVENT CHECK THE CENSUS LATELY, NOR DOES UNDERSTSND THAT THERE IS A SENATE AND HOUSE OF REPRESENTATIVE IN THE CONGRESS, AND A STATE NATIONAL GUARD, CITY LAW ENFORCEMENT, AND THE THE OVERWHELMING POPULATION OF WHITES THAT OUT NUMBER BLACKS IN THIS COUNTRY, BECAUSE IT WOULD IRRATIONALLY FOOLISH TO ATTEMPT ENCITEMENT OF SOME BRAIN DYSFUNCTIONAL SLUM GETTO BLACKS TO ORGANIZE A REBELLION.

BECAUSE IF SOMETHING OF THIS NAT TURNER NATURE SHOULD HAPPEN HIS FOLLOWERS SHOULD BE REMINDED THAT NAT TURNER SKIN AND BONES IS PROBABLY ON SOME ONE MANTLE IN IN SOUTHHAMPTON COUNTY VIRGINIA AS SOUVENIRS.

THIS POTENTIAL KIND OF REBELLIOUS INCITEMENT GOES AGAINST THE GRAIN OF HUMANITY, AND ANY ONE FOUND EMBROILED IN THIS ANCIENT STUPITIDY SHOULD BE DEALT WITH SEVERLEY, BECAUSE THIS IS A DIVERSE NATION, OPPORTUNITY HAS BEEN HERE FOR EVERY ONE DURING AND AFTER SLAVERY, BECAUSE HISTORY HOLDS THIS TO BE TRUE, SUCCESS DOES NOT COME EASY IF IT DID EVERY ONE WOULD HAVE IT, THE BOTTOM LINE IS FAMILY CULTIVATION OF CHILDREN, AND SOME TIME IS

EXTREMELY DIFFICULT, AND AFTER YOU HAVE POURED YOUR HEART OUT ANCESTRAL GENES WILL PREVAIL, ALONG WITH MISSELLANEOUS NEIGHBORHOOD COACHING, BUT THE BRUNT OF INITIAL GUIDANCE IS MANIFESTED IN THE FAMILY UNION, UNFORTUNATELY THERE ARE MILLIONS OF PEOPLE BLACK AND WHITE CHOOSE TO DISOBEY THE STANDARDIZED FORMULA THAT IS AVAILABLE TOI EVERYIINDIVIDUAL IN THIS NATION REGARDLESSQE RACE, THE CONSTITUTION GIVE EVERYONE THE RIGHT TO FREE SPEECH, AND THE RIGHT TO CONTROL THEIR OWN DESTINY, HOWEVER THERE ARE A FIEW BRAZEN ATTRIBUTES INDIGENCES RELATED TO A DETOUR FROM THE SLUMS, AND THAT IS TOLERENCE, DIVERSIFICATION AND EDUCATION, AND MOST LIKELY OFFER SOME INSITE ON SELF APPOINTED RADICAL BUFFON TRYING TO CONVINCE LESS FORTUNATE AFRICAN AMERICANS, THAT THE ERRONEOUS CHOICES THEY MADE IN LIFE IS TRULY NOT THEIR FAULT, THE BLAME SHOULD BE LAID AT THE DOOR STEP OF WHITE FOLKS, AND SUPPORT THE MOVEMENT AND JUSTICE WILL PREVAIL, SOME OF THESE IDIOTS NEED TO READ THE CONSTITUTION, ALSO STUDY SOME HISTORY FROM BIRMIMGHAM ALABAMA DURING THE SIXTIES. THERE WAS AN ESCAPADE PERFORMED DURING THE MONTH OF FEBRUARY, ON NATIONAL TELEVISION C-SPAN, THE STAGED AUDIENCE CONSIST OF SUCCESSFUL AFRICAN AMERICANS OFFERING AN EXPLANATION REGARDS TO THEIR STRATEGY AND GOALS PERTAINING TO THEIR PERSONAL SUCCESS, SOME WERE ENTHUSIASTICALLY CONCEITED, THIS WAS A POSITIVE ACCOLADE, BUT I WONDER HOW MANY SLUM BUMS WERE THERE, BECAUSE THE QUESTION WAS EXPRESSLY ASKED HOW MANY MILLION AIRS WERE ATTENDING AND TO RAISE THEIR HAND, I THOUGHT IT WAS IN POOR TASTE BECAUSE MOST SUCCESSFUL SENSIBLE PEOPLE DO NOT EXPLOIT THEIR WELTH, HOWEVER THERE IS ALWAYS A CLOWN AT THE SHOW, THEORETICALLY SUSPECT THIS WAS AT INDIGENOUS DISPLAY IN AN EFFORT TO BROADCAST AFRICAN AMERICANS SUCCESS IN AMERICA, AND INFORM THE LESS FORTUNATE OF WHAT THEY CAN ACCOMPLISH, BUT PRIOR TO NATIONALIZING ONE OF THESE EVENTS

YOUR DUCKS SHOULD BE IN A ROW ABOUT THE PEOPLE YOU HAVE CHOSEN TO PORTRAY AN LEAD, THERE HAVE BEEN EXTREMELY WEALTHY AFRICAN AMERICANS IN THIS COUNTRY ON A SMALL SCALE HUNDREDS OF YEARS, BUT YOU WOULD NEVER KNOW IT BECAUSE DURING SLAVERY IF THEY FOUND A POT OF GOLD, OR SOME OF THEIR SLAVE MASTERS GAVE THEM A FORTUNE, IT WAS THE BEST KEPT SECRET EVER, NOT EVEN THEIR CLOSE FAMILY KNEW ABOUT IT, BECAUSE OF REPRISAL FROM POOR WHITES, AND BRAIN DEAD FAMILY MEMBERS, SO AS A INHERITED FAMILY TRADITION AFRICAN AMERICANS DO NOT BROADCAST THEIR WEALTH, OFCOURSE THERE ARE A FIEW EXCEPTIONS.

HOWEVER I AM ALWAYS IMPRESSED WITH THE FACK THAT ANY AMERICAN BLACK OR WHITE HAS SHOWN RESPONSIBILITY TO THEM SELVES TO INTERGRATE INTO A DIVERSE SOCIETY AND UTILIZE THEIR GOD GIVEN TALENTS AND FACE LIFE HEAD ON AND MAKE THINGS HAPPEN FOR THEMSELVES, WITH INDIVIDUAL THINKING, ALSO IF IT WAS A DISPLAY TO IMPRESS THOSE THAT FEEL LEFT OUT OF THE SUCCESS CIRCLE, IT WAS A WASTE OF TIME FOR SOME,BECAUSE A LARGE SEGMENT OF BLACKS FEEL IF YOU SPEAK APPROPRIATE ENGLISH, AND RESPECTFULLY EARN A LIVING, BY OWNINING YOUR OWN BUISNESS, OR HAVE CLIMED THE CORPORATE LADDER, OR JUST PRIVATE SECTOR EMPLOYMENT, THEIR OPENION IS YOU ARE TRYING TO BE LIKE THE WHITE MAN, CASE CLOSED.

BY THE WAY THE POT OF GOLD HAS TO DO WITH THE CIVIL WAR BETWEEN THE STATES, RICH WHITE SOUTHERNERS WOULD BURY THEIR FORTUNES, PRIOR TO GOING OFF TO WAR OUT SIDE AROUND STUMPS, GARDENS, TREES, BARNS, OR THEIR WIVES WOULD, TO KEEP THE UNION SOLDIERS FROM LACATING IT IN THE HOUSE, AND THE SLAVES WOULD STUMBLE UPON THESE FORTUNES,EITHER THEY WOULD RUN AWAY TO THE NORTHERN STATES, OR HIDE IT ON THEIR OWN, AND MANY OF THE WHITES THAT HID THE FORTUNE WOULD BE KILLED DURING THE WAR SO AFTER SLAVERY WAS ABOLISHED SOME PURCHASED THOUSANSD OF ACRES

OF FARM LAND FROM THE PLANTATION OWNERS, SOME EVEN STARTED THEIR OWN BUISNESSES, AND OF COURSE SOME DECIDED TO GOOD TIME IT AWAY. AND THIS WAS ALL BEFORE CIVIL AND VOTING RIGHTS WAS AMENDED TO THE CONSTITUTION, IN 1964 AND 1965.

HOWEVER DURING THE CIVIL WAR THOUSANDS OF SLAVES ESCAPED FROM THE SOUTH, HOPING FOR A BETTER FUTURE IN THE NORTHERN STATES, MOST TRAVELED BY LAND, AND SOME FOUND TRANSPORTATION ON SHIPS, AND AS EXPECTED THEIR POSSESSIONS WAS CARRIED ALONG TO START A NEW LIFE, SO THIS LEFT WING LIBERALIZED HYPOCRISY BEING SPEWED OUT BY BLACK DEMOCRATIC STRATEGIST,THAT AFRICAN AMERICANS HAVE BEEN SPUN INTO A COCOON, BY WHITE SUPREMACIST,IS ONE OF THE MOST PROVOCATIVE,AND DISTURBING LIES PERPETRATED BY THESE POLITICAL DEMOCRATIC BLACK PARASITES KNOWN TO MAN KIND, FOR THE SOLE PURPOSE OF KEEPING AFRICAN AMERICANS IN FAVOR OF BLOC VOTING FOR THE DEMOCRATIC PARTY. THERE ARE MILLIONS OF AFRICAN AMERICANS CITIZENS IN THE UNITED STATES OF AMERICA, THAT NORMALLY GO ABOUT THEIR BUISNESS ON A DAILY BASIS, AND HAVE PAID AND ARE PAYING THEIR DUES TO SOCIETY BY BY WORKING AND OBTAINING OBJECTIVES TO BENEFIT THEIR OWN ACCORD, WHICH IS CONSISTENT WITH THE AMERICAN WAY, THESE FUNCTIONS ARE STANDARDIZE PERTAINING TO ALL PEOPLE IN THIS CIVILIZED COUNTRY, SO TO ADOPT SOME KIND OF NOTION THAT ALL AFRICAN AMERICANS NEED A SELF APPOINTED RADICAL SPOKESMAN THAT IS ADVERSE TO THE CONSTITUTION IS APPALLING, BECAUSE THERE IS NOTHING IN THE CONSTITUTION THAT RATIFY SEPRATE BUT EQUAL, HOWEVER THERE WAS A JIM CROW RULE ESTABLISHED AND ENDORSED BY THE SUPREME COURT IN 1896, IN AN EFFORT TO RECREATE CONTROL OVER AFRICAN AMERICANS BY SOUTHERN CONFEDERATE DEMOCRATIC RACIST WHITES, TO PROHIBIT INTEGRATION.

FORTUNATELY THIS DILEMMA WAS REEVALUATED BY THE SUPREME COURT IN 1954, AND THE CONCEPT OF SEPSRATE BUT EQUAL WAS OVER TURNED, IN EFFECT THE EARLIER

RULING SANCTIONED THE IMPOSITION OF SEPARATE AND UNEQUAL RACIAL CONDITIONS IN AMERICAN SOCIETY, PRIOR TO 1954, CIVIL RIGHTS RECEIVED A MAJOR BOOST FROM PRESIDENT HARRY TRUMAN, ISSURANCE OF AN EXECUTIVE ORDER INTEGRATIING THE U.S. ARMED FORCES IN 1947.

CHARLES HOUSTON WAS CHIEF COUNSEL FOR THE NAACP, WITH LEGAL FUNDS ESTABLISHED BY THURGOOD MARSHALL FOR THE NAACP LEGAL DEFENSE AND EDUCATION, WAS SUCCESSFUL IN GETTING THE SUPREME COURT TO ABOLISH THE SEPRATE BUT EQUAL LAW,ALSO IN 1956, THE FIRST CIVIL RIGHTS BILL WAS SENT TO CONGRESS IN 85 YEARS BY PRESIDENT EISENHOWER A RPUBLICAN, AND WAS DULY REJECTED BY A DEMOCRATIC SENATE,OTHER THAN THAT AFRICAN AMERICANS WOULD HAVE HAD CIVIL RIGNTS NINE YEARS EARLIER, THANKS TO AFRICAN AMERICANS BLOC VOTING, FOR STATE OFFICIALS TO SEND TO THE SENATE FOR DEMOCRATS.

APPROXIMATELY FIFTY TWO YEARS LATER A BUNCH OF OFFICIOUS SELF APOINTED LEADERS ON BEHALF OF AFRICAN AMERICANS IS SUSPECTED OF A MALICIOUS ATTEMPT TO REINSTATE THIS SEPARATE BUT EQUAL PREHISTORIC SUFFORCATING DOCTRINE OUT SIDE OF THE CONSTUTION IS APPALLING AND HAVENT THE SLIGHTEST IDEA OF THE CONSCIENCES, HOWEVER IT WILL NEVER HAPPEN, BUT IT DOES POSION THE MIND OF SOME AFRICAN AMERICANS.

FOR INSTANCE THE FAMILY FROM NEW YORK, WITH THE SEVEN YEAR OLD THAT WROTE THE REVERSE DISCRIMINATION POEM HAVING TO DO WITH COLUMBUS THAT WAS TELEVISED NATION WIDE, THIS IS A VERY INTERESTING SPECTACLE, BECAUSE IF THE CHILD IS SHELTERED FROM THE GENERAL PUBLIC AND TAUGHT THAT SHE IS SUPERIOR TO WHITES, I WONDER WHAT IS GOING TO HAPPEN WHEN SHE GROW UP AND FIGURE OUT THAT MOST ALL HUGE CORPORATIONS IS OWNED BY THE PEOPLE SHE HATE, AND LENDING INSTITUTIONS, PRODUCTION OF AUROMOBILES, FOOD CHAINS, GASOLINE, AND NOT TO MENTION IF SHE GO TO COLLEGE, EVEN

THE CLOTHES ON HER BACK I WONDER IF HER PARENTS HAVE ALL THIS FIGURED OUT, AND HOW SHETIS GOING TO AVOID CONTACT WITH THESE INSTITUTIONS AND BE SUCCESSFUL. IN ESSENCE THERE ARE MILLIONS OF HARD WORKING, SELF EDUCATED, FORMAL EDUCATED, SENSIBLE CONSTITUTION ABIDING AFRICAN AMERICAN CITIZENS IN THIS COUNTRY, THAT HAS CONDUCTED THEIR LIVES IN A CIVIL MANNER,AND ARE ASTUTELY COMMITTED TO MAINTAINING THE MORAL INFRASTRUCTURE OF THIS NATION.

HOWEVERTHEREAREAFIEWPOTENTIALSELFAPPOINTED LEADERS THAT IS SUSPECTED OF CONSTRUCTING AND CALCULATING A FEROCIOUS PLAN TO UNDER MIND THE INTEGRITY OF ALL AFRICAN AMERICANS, FOR A RADICAL DYSFUNCTIONAL MINDED FIEW, THAT HAS ELAPSED BACK INTO ANCESTRAL PREHISTORIC HISTORY, AND HAS ADOPTED THEIR TRAITS OF ILLITERACY, VIOLENT TACTICS, NONE EMPLOYMENT, HUGE HEADS OF HAIR, THAT A NEST OF MICE COULD HIDE IN,AND HAVE CULTIVATED THEIR OWN VIRBAGE TO COMMUNICATE, BAGGY PANTS HANGING BELOW THEIR BEHIND, NOSE, CHEEK, CHIN, TONG, EYE, AND EAR RINGS, THE ONLY THING MISSING IS THE ROUND SHAPED LIP DISK, AND THE BONE THROUGH THE NOSE, AND THATS PROBABLY PREDICTABLE FOR THE FUTURE, NOT TO MENTION THEIR UNDERWARE SHOWING AND THEIR PANT SEAT DOWN AROUND THEIR NEES, I AM SURE THERE WAS SOME PROBLEMS RUNNING WHEN KATRINA LANDED.

IT IS AN ESTABLISHED FACT IF YOU TAKE A TWO MONTH OLD BABY, AND HE OR SHE IS AFRICAN AMERICAN AND IS RAISED BY GERMAN SPEAKING POPLE THE CHILD IS GOING TO SPEAK GERMAN, THE SAME FOR FRENCH, AND OR ANY OTHER NATIONALLY OF PEOPLE, SO WHEN A CHILD GROW UP IN A SLUM GETTO THEY ARE GOING TO ADJUST TO THE ENVIROMENT AND CULTURE PREVAILING, SO FROM EIGHT, TEN, AND BEYOND, SOME ARE INNOCENT VICTOMS OF NEGLECT DEPRAVATIONS, AND INDUCTED INTO THE HALL OF FAME RELATED TO DRUG ABUSE, THEIR CHANCES OF BECOMING A CIVIL OBEDIENT INDIVIDUAL IN

A DIVERSE SOCIETY IS ALMOST NONEXISTENCE, BECAUSE CHILDREN AT A VERY EARLY AGE HAS TO BE TAUGHT THE FUNDAMENTALS OF A SYSTEMATIC COMPLEX SOCIETY THAT WE LIVE IN, IF THIS IS NEGATED THEY ARE BORN LOOSERS.BLACK OR WHITE.

HOWEVER IN THE AFRICAN AMERICAN SOCIETY THERE ARE SELF APPOINTED SYMPATHIZERS, AND SELF APPOINTED LEADERS, ALTHOUGH SOME OF THESE PEOPLE ARE CONTENTIOUS OBJECTORS OF CIVIL SOCIETY, BUT BLACK SYMPATHIZERS AND LEADERS WILL CONDONE THEIR MALICIOUS RADICAL BEHAVIOR, AND OFFER EXCUSES LIKE THEY ARE STILL FEELING THE AFFECTS OF SLAVERY,AND WE ARE GOING TO STAND TOGATHER UNTIL IT IS RECTIFIED, THESE BUFFOONISH INDULGENCES HAS BECAME PROBLEMATIC, BASED ON A RADICAL DISBURSEMENT OF FALSE HOPES, AND GENUINELY CAUSE THESE PEOPLE TO BECOME ENRAGED AND RESULT TO VIOLENCE.

AS A REAULT OF THESE DYSFUNCTIONAL BRAIN PROPAGANDA TACTICS, EVERY THING IS ADJUDICATED TO BE A BLACK AND WHITE ISSURE, AND AS THE SENSATIONALIZING ESCALATE EVENTUALLY IT WILL ERUPT INTO A POLITICIZING CHARADE THATSNOT GOOD FOR AFRICAN AMERICANS OR THE MAIM, PRIMARILY BASED ON PAST HISTORY.

THERE IS A INSIDIOUS DOUBLE STANDARD SPIRALLING OUT OF CONTROL REGARDS TO SOME AFRICAN AMERICANS BEHAVIOR, IT IS OK FOR HARRY BE LAFONTE AND OTHERS TO CALL THE PRESIDENT OF THE UNITED STATES A TERRORIST ON FOREGIN SOIL, WHILE EMBRACING DICTATORS THAT IS ADVERSE TO OUR CONSTITUTIONAL RIGHTS, AND WHEN QUESTIONED ABOUT THIS DESERTED RADICAL BEHAVIOR, THE BLACK DEMOCRATIC POLITICAL SLAVE DRIVERS BECOME DOCILE AND HERD TOGATHER AND HIDE BEHIND FREE SPEECH, AND LABEL THEMSELVES AS BROTHERS THAT IS HOODED TOGATHER,

HOWEVER WHEN A GROUP OF ANIMAL RIGHTS ACTVIST AT A UNIVERSITY IN

CALIFORNIA MENTION THE WORD SLAVERY, RELATED TO ANIMALS, THEY BE

COME ENRAGED AS IF SLAVERY WAS NOT AAREALITY TNTHIS COUNTRY, SL

AVERY WAS A WAY OF LIFE IN AMERICA FOR AFRICAN AMERICANS, IT WAS ABOLISHED AND RATIFIED TO THE CONSTITUTION ON DECEMBER 6, 1865, CREDITED TO REPUBLICAN PRESIDENT ABRAHAM LINCOLN, THAT IS APPROXIMATELY ONE HUNDRED AND FORTY ONE YEARS AGO, AND ACCORDING TO THE THIRTEENTH AMENDMENT, SECTION ONE IT READ LIKE THIS.

NEITHER SLAVERY NOR INVOLUNTARY SERVITUDE, EXCEPT AS A PUNISHMENT FOR CRIME WHERE OF THE PARTY SHALL HAVE BEEN DULY CONVICTED SHALL EXIST WITHIN THE UNITED STATES, OR ANY PLACE SUBJECT TO THEIR JURISDICTION.

(SECTION TWO)

CONGRESS SHALL HAVE POWER TO ENFORCE THIS ARTICLE BY APPROPIATE LEGISLATION.

AND LEGISLATION IS FURTHER ENDORSED BY THE FOURTEENTH AMENDMENT, RATIFIED JULY 9, 1868.

(SECTION ONE)

ALL PERSONS BORN OR NATURALIZED IN THE UNITED STATES AND SUBJECT TO THE JURISDICTION THERE OF ARE CITIZENS OF THE UNITED STATES AND OF THE STATE WHEREIN THEY RESIDE.

NO STATE SHALL MAKE OR ENFORCE ANY LAW WHICH SHALL ABRIDGE THE PRIVILEGES OR IMMUNITIES OF CITIZENS OF THE UNITED STATES, NOR SHALL ANY STATE DEPRIVE ANY PERSON OF LIFE, LIBERTY, OR PROPERTY WITHOUT DUE PROCESS OF LAW NOR DENY TO ANY PERSON WITHIN ITS JURISDICTION THE EQUAL PROTECTION OF THE LAWS.

FOR THE BENEFIT OF AFRICAN AMERICANS TO BE INCORPORATED TO THIS AMENDMENT BY CONGRESS IN 1964 AND1965, FOR THEIR CIVIL AND VOTING RIGHTS, APPROXIMATELY FORTY ONE YEARS AGO, CREDITED TO DR. MARTIN LUTHER KING,MARCHING AND GETTING HIS BRAINS BEAT OUT BY DEMOCRATIC RACIST ACTIVIST, AND

PRESIDENT LYNDON JOHNSON FEARFUL OF DESERTION OF AFRICAN AMERICANS VOTERS TO THE REPUBLICAN PARTY. THE FIRST AMENDMENT TO THE CONSTITUTION SPECIFICALLY STATE. CONGRESS SHALL MAKE NO LAW RESPECTING AN ESTABLISHMENT OF RELIGION, OR PROHIBITING THE (FREE) EXERCISE THEREOF OR ABRIDGING THE FREEDOM OF (SPEECH) OR OF PRESS, OR THE RIGHT OF THE PEOPLE PEACEABLE TO ASSEMBLE, AND TO PETITION THE GOVERNMENT FOR A REDRESS OF GRIEVANCE.

ALL LAW ABIDING AND INDIVIDUAL THINKING AMERICANS SHOULD BE CONCERNED ABOUT THIS RADICAL BEHAVIOR OF SOME AFRICAN AMERICAN, IN AN EFFORT TO PROHIBIT FREE SPEECH, THERE ARE BLACK HYPOCRITICAL SELF APPOINTED LIBERAL LEADERS AND SYMPATHIZERS JOINED AT THE HIP WITH THE DEMOCRAT PARTY, APPARENTLY HAS ADOPTED THE FIRST AMENDMENT OF THE CONSTITUTION AS TO BEING THE ONLY CUSTODIAN, TO USE AT THEIR LEISURE, AND OTHER NATIONALLY IS FORBIDDEN TO PARTAKE, THIS DEMORALIZING ACTION BY SOME AFRICAN AMERICANS IS PROOF OF DYSFUNCTIONAL ATTRIBUTES, WITH SLAVERY BEING ABOLISHED OVER A HUNDRED AND FORTY ONE YEARS AGO.

WITH CIVIL AND VOTING RIGHTS BEING RATIFIED TO THE CONSTITUTION FOR AFRICAN AMERICANS OVER FORTY ONE YEARS, HOWEVER SOME ASININE SELF APPOINTED LIBERAL LEADERS, ARE USING SLAVERY TO JUSTIFY THE DISPOSITION OF SOME BLACKS INABILITY TO FUNCTION PROPERLY IN A DIVERSE CIVIL SOCIETY, AND WILL ADHERE TO THIS NONSENSICAL AGENDA ARGUABLY ON NATIONAL TELEVISION, ONE SUCH INCIDENT OCCURED ON MARCH 23, 2006, IN THE LIKES OF A LAUREN LAKE, LEGAL ANALYS AND AND DEFENSE ATTORNEY DEFENDING AGAINST VERBAGE USED BY ANIMAL RIGHTS ACTIVIST, RELATING TO (SLAVERY) SHE AGGRESSIVELY DEFENDED THE USE OF THAT WORD, AND HER DEMONSTRATIVE OPENION WAS THESE THINGS SHOULD NOT HAPPEN BECAUSE IT DEMORALIZES THE ASPECTS OF ALL AFRICAN AMERICANS, AND SHE CHOOSE TO DEFEND IN THAT MANNER, WITH STATEMENTS OF WE, WE, WE, MEANING ALL AND INSISTED THAT WHITES HAD

NOT ALLOWED SLAVES TO BE EDUCATED DURING SLAVERY, WHICH IS TRUE BUT THERE IS A DISTINCTION, APPARENTLY HISTORY IS NOT ONE OF HER STRONG POINTS, BECAUSE DURING AND AFTER THE CIVIL WAR AFRICAN AMERICANS FOUND TRUE ALLIES AMONG NORTHERN REPUBLICANS WHITES THAT FLOODED THE SOUTERN STATES THE MAJORITY WAS TEACHERS AND NURSES, IN AN EFFORT TO EDUCATE FORMER SLAVES, UNFORTUNATELY THE SOUTHERN DEMOCRATS FOUNDED THE KU-KLUX-KLAN IN 1866, AND VIOLENTLY DROVE THEM AWAY AND SHE IS SITTING ON HER PANTS BELLOWING OUT INSINUATIONS THAT ALL WHITES HAMPERED THE EDUCATION OF AFRICAN AMERICANS, WHICH IS POLITICAL DEMAGOGUERY, IF YOU ARE GOING TO TRASH PEOPLE FOR THIS DEBACLE, BEING AN ATTORNEY CLAIRIFICATION IS WARRANTED TO SINGLE OUT THE RESPONSIBLE VILLAINS, HISTORY HAS LAID THESE THESE TRAGEDIES AT THE DOOR STEP OF THE SOUTHERN DEMOCRATS, AND THEIR FOUNDED KU-KLUX-KLAN, WHICH I SUSPECT IS HER PARTY, SHE BEING AN ATTORNEY AND LATELY IS ON NATIONAL TELEVISION, WHINING ABOUT JUSTICE AND INJUSTICE SHE EMPHATICALLY VIOLATED THE FIRST AMENDMENT OF THE CONSTITUTION PERTAINING TO FREE SPEECH, AND CHOOSE TO EXTEND HER AUTHORITY TO REPRESENT APPROXIMATELY THIRTY FIVE MILLION AFRICAN AMERICANS WITH HER SCURRILOUS LIBERAL BUFOONISH IDEOLOGY, I NOTICED THE HOST SEEMED TO LET HER RATTLE ON MOST LIKELY TO AVERT BEING CALLED A RACIST, NOTHING PERSONAL AGAINST ATTORNEY LAKE, BUT SHE BEING AN ATTORNEY MORE CLARITY IS EXPECTED CONCERNING SUSPECTED CONTRIVED RACIAL ISSURES, PIRATICALLY WHEN THE CINSTITUTION GRANT ALL PEOPLE THE RIGHT TO FREE SPEECH. MANY AFRICAN AMERICANS TEND TO HERD TOGATHER BEHIND SELF APPOINTIED LEADERS THROUGHOUT THE COUNTRY AND ENDORSE AN IDEOLOGY THAT IS INCONSISTENT WITH OUR FORM OF GOVERNMENT, THESE SELF APPOINTED LADERS AFTER 1964 AND 1965, HAS CAUSED REPREHENSIBLE HARM MENTALLY AND PHYSICALLY TO THEIR FOLLOWERS BECAUSE OF THEIR INABILITY TO EXCEPT HUMAN DIVERSITY, IT IS

UTTERLY IMPOSSIBLE TO ALIENATE ONE NATIONALLY OF PEOPLE FROM A DIVERSE SOCIETY, PIRATICALLY WHEN IT IS RATIFIED BY THE CONSTITUTION AS BEING UNLAWFUL,NOT TO MENTION AFRICAN AMERICANS ARE LOWEST IN THE POPULATION COUNT ACCORDING TO THE CENSUS STATISTICS BEHIND HISPANICS, SO THESE DYSFUNCTIONAL BRAIN SELF APPOINTED DEMOCRATIC LIBERAL LEADERS, INSTEAD OF BELLOWING ABOUT WHAT GENEROSITIES SHOULD BE EXTENDED TO BLACKS, THEIR EFFORTS SHOULD BE PREDICATED TO ADVISE WHAT AGGRESSIVE INGENUITY SOME AFRICAN AMERICANS NEED TO BESTOW UPON THEM SELVES.

THERE ARE AFRICAN AMERICANS DEMOCRATS IN THE CONGRESS, AND THERE DEMOCRAT STRATEGIST, WHICH OFTEN AVAIL THEM SELVES TO NATIONAL TELEVISION TO DEFEND BLUNDERS MADE BY THEIR POLITICAL DEMOCRATIC WHITE MASTERS, ALSO TO SUGAR COAT DEROGATORY REMARKS MADE BY FOOLISH BLACKS CONCERNING ELECTED PUBLIC OFFICIALS,AND COLLECTIVELY ATTEMPT TO JUSTIFY REMARKS MADE BY DYSFUNCTIONAL MINDED BLACKS.

FOR INSTANCE U.S. SENATOR BORAC OBAMA FROM ILLINOIS WAS ON MEET THE PRESS JANUARY 22, 2006, WHEN ASKED ABOUT HARRY BELAFONTE COMMENTS ABOUT PRESIDENT BUSH BEING A TERROIST, HE EVADED THE QUESTION BY SAYING EVERY ONE IS ENTILED TO FREE SPEECH, AND BASICALLY DEFENDED SENATOR HILLORY CLINTON REMARKS ABOUT SOUTHERN PLANTATION HE HAS BECAME THE POLITICAL POSTER BOY FOR THE DEMOCRATIC PARTY, EVE RAISING TONS OF MONEY FOR SENATOR ROBERT BYRD, A KNOWN FORMER KU-KLUX-KLANSMAN, DURING THE INTERVIEW TIM RUSSERT SPICIFICALLY PURGED HIS POLITICAL AMBITIONS PERTAINING TO ELECTIVE OFFICE AND PIGEON HOLED HIM TO VICE PRESIDENT SELECTION, AND HE NEVER CHALLENGED THIS SELECTIVE DENOUCING, AND SHOULD HAVE EMPHATICALLY STATED IF HE CHOOSE TO RUN FOR A HIGHER POLITICAL POSITION IT WOULD BE FOR THE PRESIDENCY, RUSSERT WAS ONLY FORECASTING THE DEMOCRATIC FAT CATS SUMMATION OF

BLACK POLITICANS, BECAUSE I SUSPECT IF A DEMOCRATIC FRONT RUNNER CHOSE HIM AS A RUNNING MATE THOSE OLD PLANTATION SLAVE MASTERS WOULD TURN OVER IN THEIR GRAVES, HOWEVER SENATOR OBAMA DESERVE NO CRITICISM WHAT SO EVER REGARDS TO HIS EVASIVE ANSWERS PERTAINING TO HARRY BELAFONTA, BECAUSE THE CONSTITUTION GRANT HIM THAT RIGHT TO REMIND PEOPLE OF FREE SPEECH, AND I WOULD SUGGEST ATTORNEY LAUREN LAKE GIVE HIM A CALL CONCERNING FREE SPEECH.

WHAT A MAJORITY OF THIN SKINNED AFRICAN AMERICANS NEED TO UNDERSTAND IS THAT THE CONSTITUTION IS THE GUIDELINE FOR EVERY CITIZEN IN THE UNITED STATES OF AMERICA, AND THESE SELF APPOINTED \.. BLACK DEMOCRATIC SLAVE DRIVING LEADERS HAS SPENT YEARS TRYING TO ESTABLISH AN INDPENDANT CHARTER OUT SIDE OF THE CONSTITUTION FOR AFRICAN AMERICANS ONLY, FOR THEIR OWN PERSONAL GAIN, WHICH WILL NEVER, NEVER, HAPPEN, UNFORTUNATELY THEY MAKE HUNDREDS OF THOUSANDS AND MILLIONS OF DOLLARS OFF CORPORATE INDUSTRIES WITH RACIAL INTERMEDATION AND FOOLISH BLACKS THAT FOLLOW THEIR UNCONSTUTIONAL IDEOLOGY OF ETHICS, THESE PEOPLE ARE WORSE THAN THE PLANTATION SLAVE OWNERS, AT LEAST THEY WOULD FURNISH FOOD AND CLOTHING, AND ALL YOU GET FROM THESE PARASITES IS LIP SERVICE, THERE IS SOME REDUNDANCIES IN THESE WRITINGS, HOWEVER IT IS NECESSARY BECAUSE CHARACTERISTICALLY SOME POLITICAL NOTORIETY AFRICAN AMERICANS USE THE SAME OLD TACTICS BUT IS METHODISED IN A DIFFERENT MANNER TO FRUSTRATE SOCIETY, IN ORDER TO GET THEIR LIBERALIZED IDEOLOGY ACCEPTED, AND THERE ARE A WAVE OF THESE SCOUNDRELS, ON TELEVISION, INTERNET, RADIO, NATION WIDE THAT FEROCIOUSLY FORSAKE HUMMITY IN THE NAME OF SELF DEPRIVATION TO LITRALLY EXTORT THE DIGNITY OF HUMANITY, IF THIS INSANITY PREVAIL THROUGHOUT OUR NATION AND LEFT TO NURISH IT COULD PROVE TO BE ONE OF THE WORST DISASTERS IN THE HISTORY OF OUR NATION.

THE EXISTANCE OF THIS LEFT WING IDEOLOGY IS ROOTED DEEP IN TO OUR SOCIETY, FROM CONGRESS TO THE SLUM GETTOS OF NEW YORK, CHICAGO,CALIFORNIA, AND DETROIT, JUST TO NAME A FIEW, PREFERABLE THE NEWS MEDIA, THAT SEEM TO BE DETERMINED TO CHIP AWAY AT VERY FOUNDATION THIS COUNTRY IS SITTING ON WITHOUT RESERVATION, SUSPECTED IN ORDER TO SUSTAIN AN AN IDEOLOGY THAT IS PREHISTORIC AND DEFUNCT. MR. STEPHEN CHEEK, PRESIDENT OF THE OHIO BLACK REPUBLICAN ASSOCATION WAS A GUEST ON C-SPAN, ON MARCH 26, 2006, AND HE WAS SPICIFICALLY ASKED BY THE HOAST WHY SHOULD AFRICAN AMERICANS WANT TO BE A REPUBLICAN, THERE IS NO QUESTION FOR A HOAST TO ASK SUCH A FOOLISH QUESTION DEMONSTRATE HIS FEVERISH MINDED THINKING, BECAUSE IF HE HAD ANY KNODLEDGE OF HISTORY THE QUESTION WAS OUT OF CHARACTER, MAYBE HE IS NOT AWARE THAT THIS COUNTRY CONSIST OF A TWO PARTY SYSTEM REPUBLICAN AND DEMOCRATIC.

HIS RADICAL QUESTION DICTATED THE HERDING PROCESS OF SOME AFRICAN AMERICANS, NOT HAVING THE ABILITY TO THINK FOR THEM SELVES I PERSONALLY FEEL THIS WAS ONE OF THE MOST INSIDIOUS, PROVOCATIVE, INADVERTENTLY DISPLAYS OF CYNICISM FOR A HOSTJ TO BLATANTLY INTERJECT TO A GUEST, PIRATICALLY ON NATIONAL TELEVISION, BECAUSE .. IT TEND TO INSINUATE HIS PARTY AFFILIATIONS AND FORECAST DENOUNCIATION OF A POLITICAL PARTY NOT OF HIS CHOICE, ALL TO OFTEN SOME AFRICAN AMERICANS WILL TRY AND INTIMIDIATE BLACKS IF THEIR CHOICE OF A POLITICAL PARTY IS NOT DEMOCRATIC, THE HOST ON THE WASHINGTON JOURNAL C-SPAN, WANTED THE GUEST MR. CHEEK, TO OFFER AN EXPLANATION AS TO WHY AFRICAN AMERICANS WOULD (WANT) TO JOIN THE REPUBLICAN PARTY, THAT IS WHAT SO GREAT ABOUT THE AMERICAN ENGLISH IF IT IS USED INAPPROPRIATELYIT CAN MAKE YOULOOK RIGHT FOOLISH, THERE ARE MANY WAYS THIS QUESTION SHOULD HAVE BEEN ASKED WITH DIGNITY, SUCH AS IN OUR TWO PARTY SYSTEM HISTORY DICTATE THERE ARE APPROXIMATELY NINETY FIVE PRECENT OF AFRICAN AMERICANS VOTE

DEMOCRATIC, APPOSE TO REPUBLICAN, WOULD YOU MR. CHEEK CARE TO COMMENT ON THIS ABNORMALITY, HOWEVER IT IS SUSPECTED THAT C-SPAN IS NOTHING MORE THAN THE RIGHT AR! OF MOVE ON DOT ORG, WHEN IT COME TO POLITICAL VIEWS, ON THE WASHINGTON JOURNAL DAILY,AND I THINK THE HOST DISPLAYED THAT SUSPICION WITH MR. CHEEK, RELATED TO THE TWO PARTY SYSTEM IN THIS COUNTRY, THEY HAVE HAMMERED THE REPUBLICAN LIKE CRACKING A WALNUT, AND GOES FOR BRIAN LAMB AND HIS ENTIRE ENTOURAGE, BEGINNING AT SIX A.M. SEVEN DAYS A WEEK, AT LEAST FOR ONE HOUR, THE PROGRAM IS CAREFULLY DESIGNED TO DEMONSTRATE TENDENCIES OF A BIAS IDEOLOGY REGARDS TO CONSERVATIVE THINKING THEIR FORMAT BEGIN WITH BUSH, VERSUS DEMOCRATS, AND INDEPENDENTSF AND THEY AND THEY SERCH THE NEWS COLEMS MAINLY FOR DISPARAGING NEWS REGARDS TO THE ADMINISTRATION, AND OPEN THE PHONE LINES FOR COMMENTS PERTAINING TO THE ISSURE, AND IT IS A ESTABLISHED FACT INDEPENTANTS ARE NOTHING MORE THAN A SECOND HAND DEMOCRAT, AND THEIR VOTING ASPECTS IN THE CONGRESS ALONG WITH DEMOCRATS, IS DOCUMENTED ALMOST UNANIMOUS, I AM SURE THERE ARE SOME IN THE GENERAL PUBLIC EVAULATE CANIDATES ON MERIT, BUT THE MAJORITY THAT CALL IN ON C-SPAN ARE PRONE TO ENDORSE DEMOCRAT IDEOLOGY, AND THE PRECEDENT AT C-SPAN IS TO ASSUME THE RESPONSIBILITY OF BEING FAIR AND BALANCE, UNFORTUNATELY THIS IS A HORRIBLE MISCONCEPTION, BECAUSE OF HOW THE SYSTEM IS DESIGNED, WITH TWO CALL IN LINES FOR DEMOCRATS, AND WHEN A REPUBLICAN CALL IN WITH A SOUND FUNDAMENTAL ANSWER TO THEIR QUESTION THEY ARE NORMALLY CUT SHORT PRIOR TO FINISHING THEIR EXPLANATION, THEY SYSTEMATICALLY CHOOSE SUBJECTS FROM THE PRESS THAT IS NEGATIVE TO THE ADMINISTRATION. AND SOME AFRICAN AMERICANS FLOOD THE PHONE LINES WITH DYSFUNCTIONAL IDEOLOGY AGAINST THE ADMINISTRATION, AND THIS POLITICAL STUPIDY IS CARRIED NATIONALLY TO SOME OTHER POLITICAL DERANGED AFRICAN AMERICANS IN AN EFFORT

TO CONTINUE HERDING THEIR VOTES FOR DEMOCRATS, IN FACT DURING THE INTERVIEW WITH MR. CHEEK, SOME FEMALE IDIOT CALLED IN AND LET THE ENTIRE NATION KNOW WHAT A DERRANGED PSYCHEDELIC IDOIT SHE IS BY DENOUNCING THE CREDIBILITY OF PRESIDENT ABRAHAM LINCOLN, AND JUDGING BY HER DIALECT SHE WAS ONE OF THESE BLACK IDIOTS, AND MOST LIKELY HAVE NO CONCEPTION OF WHO DR. MARTIN LUTHER KING WAS LET ALONE PRESIDENT LINCOLN, BECAUSE TO STATE THAT SHE HATED PRESIDENT ABRAHAM LINCOLN, WHEN HE GAVE HIS LIFE TO FREE HER ANCESTORS INDICATE HER POLITICAL ILLITERACY, THE WHITE DEMOCRATIC POLITICAL MASTERS AND THEIR MIMICKING POLITICAL SLAVE DRIVING BLACKS HAS DEHUMANIZED THE MORAL CHARACTER OF MANY AFRICAN AMERICANS RELATED TO POLITICS AND THE REPUBLICAN PARTY.

SO THIS IDIOT THAT CALLED IN ON C-SPAN IS CIRCUMSTANTIAL EVIDENCE THAT FOR SOME IT IS A VERY DISTINCT POSSIBILITY A HEATHEN ILLITERATE BUSHMSN FROM THE JUNGLES OF AFRICA WOULD FORCAST SUCH BRAZEN UNWARRANTED AND BRAIN DEAD DISPARITIES ABOUT A LEGEND, HIS LIFE SNUFFED OUT BY AN ASSASSIN FIGHTING FOR LIBERTY AND FREEDON FOR ALL PEOPLE, AND SOME OF THESE ODIOUSLY INFORMENTS DISBURSE THEIR SICK OPENION TO THE NATION VIA C-SPAN IS BEYOND REPROACH,AND OBVIOUSLY MEANT TO FEROCIOUSLY DISTORT THE THINKING OF SOME DYSFUNCTIONAL BRAIN,OF SOME AFRICAN AMERICANS, WHICH THEIR INTEGRITY HAS BEEN IMPUGNED BY RADICAL WHITE RACIST DEMOCRATS OVER THE YEARS, BUT THEY REMAIN FATEFUL HERDING TO KEEP THEM IN POLITICAL OFFICE WITH THEIR VOTING BLOC, HERDING IS AL ESTABLISHED IDENTITY IN AFRICAN AMERICAN SOCIETY, EXAMPLE DURING THE VOTING IN THE CONGRESS REGARDS TO TROOPS IN IRAQ, WEATHER THEY SHOULD REMAIN, OR RETURN TO THE UNITED STATES, THERE IS APPROXIMATELY FORTY THREE OR FORTY AFRICAN AMERICANS IN CONGRESS REPRESENTIVES FROM DIFFERENT STATES ALL OVER AMERICA, AND AS THE NATION WITNESSED THEY

HERDED TOGATHER WITH A SINGLE SPOKESMAN FOR THE GROUP,THIS NONSENSICAL DISPLAY OF SEPERATE BUT EQUAL BY SUPPOSEDLY EDUCATED CONGRESS MEN AND WOMEN SHOWS OUTRAGOUS CONTEMPT FOR THE CONSTITUTION AND THE OTHER MAJORITY HOUSE MEMBERS, NOT ONLY THAT IT DEMONSTRATE TO THEIR AFRICAN AMERICAN CONSTITUNCEY THAT THEY ARE BORDERING ON A SECTARIAN PHILOSOPHY, WHICH CAUSES A CONDEMNABLE DISPLAY OF FOOLISHNESS TO THE GENERAL PUBLIC AT LARGE, PIRATICALLY RADICAL BLACKS, ALSO IT IS CONTRARY TO THE CONSTITUTION,REGARDS TO THE SEEMINGLY INTENT OF CHARTER, WHICH IS SYMBALICALLY HINTED BY SELF APPOINTED LIBERAL DEMOCRATIC SUPPORTERS, WHEN I SEE THESE CHARADES I AM REMINDED OF PRIOR CENTURIES WITH AFRICAN AMERICANS RUNNING INTO CONGRESS WITH NO SHOES ON.

ON MARCH 29, 2006, MR. MARC MORIAL, NATIONAL URBAN LEAGUE PRESIDENT AND CEO, WAS ON C-SPAN WASHINGTON JOURNAL, ENDORSING A BOOK ENTITLED THE STATE OF BLACK AMERICA. AND BASED ON HIS BRIEF SYNOPSIS THERE ARE PREVAILING STATISTICS THAT DICTATE AFRICAN AMERICAN SUCCESSES AND FAILURES, POST 911, AND HE TOUCHED ON GOVERNMENTAL NEGLECT MONOLITHIC TENSION, AND POVITY IN THE SLUMS, AND HE PREDICTED THERE WILL NOT BE A DOMINATE MANORITY SOCIETY IN AMERICA IN LATER YEARS, ALSO THAT SOCIAL SECURITY ASSISTED SOME OLDER AFRICAN AMERICANS TO SUSTAIN ABOVE THE POVITY LEVEL, AND SUGGESTED HISPANICS AND AFRICAN AMERICANS COULD JOIN FORCES, BUT WAS SOME WHAT RELUCTANT TO DEFINE WHY, THE POLITICAL POSTURING OF MR. MORIAL SEEM TO SUGGEST THAT SAME OLD BELATED WHINING ABOUT POOR AFRICAN AMERICANS, AND THEIR POVITY GROWTH, BUT RESPECTFULLY IN EVERY NATIONALLY OF PEOPLE THERE ARE THE SUCCESSFUL,AND NONE SUCCESSFUL, AND IT IS DETERMINE BY INDIVIDUAL EFFORT REGARDLESS OF YOUR RACE, IF ONE SHOULD FAIL OR SUCCEED TO FINANICAL STABILITY IN LIFE ITS BECAUSE OF THE AVAILABLE OPTIONS IN A DIVERSE SOCIETY OF PEOPLE, AND THESE OPTIONS ARE

AVAILABLE TO EVERY CITIZEN AND NONE CITIZEN THAT ARE IN THE UNITED STATES OF AMERICA, BECAUSE WE LIVE IN A FREE SOCIETY GUARANTEED BY OUR CONSTUTION,AND IF CHOICES ARE MADE ON A INDIVIDUAL OR HERDED BASIS,AND IT DOES NOT CONFORM TO THE STANDARDS OF NECESSITIES FORMULATED BY FEDERAL, STATE AND LOCAL GOVERNMENTS, WITH OUT QUESTION THERE ARE DIRE CONSEQUENCES,OPTION AND DECISIONS ARE CRITICAL TO ANY PEOPLE SURVIVAL STATUS,UNFORTUNATELY AFRICAN AMERICANS TEND TO HERD AND DEVELOP A SINGLE SCENARO OF ONE SIZE FIT ALL, BECAUSE OF THE LIKE OF INDIVIDUAL THINKING FOR SOME,THIS SINGLE PREHISTORIC ANCESTRIAL FANATICISM HAS DEVELOPED INTO A DEMOTION OF MORAL CHARACTER AND ROCKETED SOME AFRICAN AMERICANS SPIRALING INTO POVITY AND EVENTAULLY TO THE GETTO SLUMS ALL AROUND THE COUNTRY, AND THESE SELF APPOINTED DEMOCRATIC STRATEGIST SPOKESMAN FOR THE HERD IS PART OF A POLITICAL CONSPIRACY CONTRIVED TO MAINTAIN BLOC VOTES FROM BLACKS IN THIS COUNTRY, BECAUSE NO MAN OR GOVERNMENT CAN UNDUE A SELF IMPOSED IDEOLOGY OF A GETTO SLUM WAY OF LIFE, AND ABRUPTLY FOLD HUNDRED OF THOUSANDS OF THESE PEOPLE INTO A SELF SUSTAINING AFFLUENT DIVERSE COEXISTING SOCIETY, AND THESE BLACK LIBERAL LYING PARASITES HAVE BEEN MISLEADING THESE PEOPLE ON FALSE PRETENSES FOR YEARS, SO MR. MORIAL YOUR INTENTIONS ARE VERY WELL UNDERSTOOD WHICH IS TO SPIN DEMAGOGUREY AND SELL A BOOK, BECAUSE I AM SURE MOST INTELLIGENT PEOPLE BLACK AND WHITE IN THIS COUNTRY ARE AWARE OF THE APPALLING OVERALL ABRASIVE STATISTICS OF SOME AFRICAN AMERICANS IN THE UNITED STATES OF AMERICA.

I AM TOTALLY MYSTIFIED AT THE VERBAGE USED BY MR. MORIAL, DOMINATING MANORITIES IN THIS COUNTRY AND FUTURE YEARS IT WILL BE NONEXISTENCE, THE PHRASEOLOGY WAS COMPLETELY OUT OF CHARACTER, BECAUSE THIS IS A DIVERSE NATION, WHERE ARE THE ITALIANS, GERMANS, JEWS, FRENCH, THE POLISH, IRISH,

AND ENGLISH, I WILL TELL YOU THEY HAVE DEVERSIFIED INTO SOCIETY AND NOT LOOKING FOR JESSIE JACKSON AND TAVIS SMILEY TO HAVE THEM SCREAMING WITH A CLINCHED FIST,LIKE SOME AFRICAN AMERICANS THAT THEY ARE BLACK AND PROUD, AS IF EVERY ONE CANT SEE, HOWEVER THE COMMENTS BY MR. MORAL,I SUSPEST WAS TO DICTATE HERDING WITH AN ATTEMPT TO SEDUCE HYSPANICS TO THIS IDEOLOGY OF INSANITY, WHICH WILL NEVER HAPPEN BECAUSE THEIR ANCESTRY IS NOT FROM AFRICA, AND NOT ONLY THAT THEIR IDEOLOGY HAS ALREADY FORMULATED INTO SUPERORITY OVER AFRICAN AMERICANS, AND PROBABLY BECAUSE OF THE NONSENSICAL POLITICAL VIEWS, BECAUSE FOR YEARS A MAJORITY OF AFRICAN AMERICANS HAS RELENTLESSLY FORMED A DEVOUT COALITION WITH THE DEMOCRATIC PARTY POLITICAL SLAVE MASTERS WITH REMNANTS OF DISGUISED IDEOLOGY FROM CENTURIES AGO, AND VOTE APPROXIMATELY NINETY EIGHT PRECENT ACROSS THE BOARD FOR THEIR PARTY AS A CUSTOMARY ENDEAVOR TO SUSTAIN THEIR UNRELENTING THIRST FOR POLITICAL POWER, AND RADICAL SEDATING IDEOLOGY.

THIS UNIQUE ILLUSION DISPLAYED BY THE MAJORITY OF AFRICAN AMERICANS ARE THE ONLY ONE OF ITS KIND IN THE WORLD, PERTAINING TO PEOPLE THAT LIVE IN A FREE AND DEMOCRATIC SOCIETY, AND WHAT IS SO ASTONISHING THAT THEY WOULD ENGAGE IN SUCH A PATHETICENDEAVOR, PIRATICALLYWHENTHEDEMOCRATS PARTY AND THEIR VIOLENT RACIST AGGRESSIVE FOUNDED KU-KLUX-KLAN VIOLENTLY IMPEDED THEIR EDUCATION, AND SOCIALS3?RUCTN£E PERTAINING TO EQUAL, CIVIL AND VOTING RIGHTS, AND THE DEMOCRATIC CONGRESSIONAL LEADERS THEY BLOC VOTE FOR AT A STATE LEVEL TO ASSUME FEDERAL RESPONSIBILITY IN WASHINGTON HAS ATTEMPTED TO BLOCK, DISDAIN, OR IMPUGN THE INTERROGATIVE OF ALL MANORITIES, THAT HAS TO APPEAR BEFORE THEM, EVEN WHITES THAT THEY FEEL IS NOT IN AGREEMENT WITH THEIRA DISGUISED LIBERALISM HOWEVER AFRICAN AMERICANS HAS BEEN INDOCTRINATED TO.SUPPORT THEIR IDEOLOLGY WHICH

IS A DOCTRINE THEY HAVE SUCCESSFULLY USED OVER THE YEARS TO PUNISH IGNORANT BLACKS, FOR BEING FREED FROM THEIR RACIST GRASP DURING SLAVERY. ON THE SOUTHERN PLANTATIONS, CONTROLLED BY A SLAVE MASTER AND A SLAVE DRIVER, THE DRIVER BEING BLACK, AND FATEFUL BEYOND REPROACH, AS THEY ARE TODAY. I AM ALMOST CERTAIN THAT MOST SENSIBLE PEOPLE IN THE NATION AND AROUND THE WORLD THAT FOLLOW POLITICS COULD VERY WELL BE PUZZLED OVER THIS LOYAL DYSFUNCTIONAL LAP DOGIN POLITICAL FOOLISHNESS DISPLAYED BY THE MAJORITY OF AFRICAN AMERICANS, HOWEVER THERE WILL BE SOME NIT-WITS WILL TRY AND JUSTIFY BY INSERTIVE IMPLICATIONS OF PEOPLE CAN CHANGE, BUT HISTORICALLY POLITICAL PARTIES ARE ENGULFED BY ANCESTRY IDEOLOGY, THERE IS DEBATE BUT LOYALITY IS ESSENTIAL, AND RARELY DESERTION OCCUR, PRIOR TO 1994, THE DEMOCRATS CONTROLLED THE CONGRESS FOR FORTY YEARS, AND HOW MANY SECURITY ADVISERS, AND TWO SUCCESIVE SECETARY OF STATE, ATTORNEY GENERAL, SECETARY OF EDUCATION, SECETARY OF LABOR, JUST TO NAME A FIEW.

I APPEAL TO THE POLITICAL SLAVE MASTERS, AND THEIR POLITICAL BOOT LICKING SLAVE DRIVERS, TO COMPARE THEIR FORTY YEAR DEMOCRATIC CONGRESSIONAL CONTROL, OF MANIROTY APPOINTEES TO POSITIONS OF THIS MAGNITUDE, TO APPROXIMATELY FIVE TO EIGHT YEARS OF REPUBLICAN CONGRESSIONAL CONTROL,RESPECTFULLY PRESIDENT GEORGE BUSH, 2000-2008 REPUBLICAN PRESIDENT EISENHOWER DRAFTED THE FIRST CIVIL RIGHTS BILL TO A DEMOCRATIC CONTROLLED CONGRESS IN EIGHTY FIVE YEARS, INITIALLY THEY DEEMED IT VOID WITHOUT READING THE SPECIFIED ISSURES AND OF COURSE THE THE GRAND FATHER AND CHAMPION OF ALL TIMES FOR AFRICAN AMERICANS THE ABOLISHMENT OF SLAVERY, PRESIDENT ABRAHAM LINCOLN, AND MAYBE A LOT OF THOSE IGNORANT MUD SLINGING BLACK DEMOCRAT SUPPORTERS ARE SO STUPID UNTIL THEY ARE UNAWARE THAT HE WAS A REPUBLICAN PRESIDENT.

AND THERE ARE SOME BASED ON THEIR MERIT OF STUPIDITY SHOULD BE GVEN AN AWARD, SUCH AS DEMOCRATIC STRATEGIST MR. BROWN, WHICH COMMITTED THE MOST OUTRAGIOUS LIKE OF KNODLEDGE ON NATIONAL TELEVISION THAT EXPOUND HIM INTO THE DUNGEON OF IGNORANCE OF ALL TIMES, HE DESERVE AN OSCAR FOR POLITICAL STUPIDITY, AFTER THE DEMOCRATIC DESECRATION OF OF THE HONORABLE MRS. CORETTA SCOTT KING FUNERAL, AND FORMER PRESIDENT JIMMIE CARTER PUBLICALLY ADMITTING THE WIRE TAPPING OF DR. MARTIN LUTHER KING, MR. BROWN CHOOSE TO GO PUBLIC AND DISPUTE THE ACCURACY OF A FORMER DEMOCRAT PRESIDENT, AND EMPHATICALLY STATED IT NEVER HAPPENED, THIS KIND OF IMPUNITY COME UNDER THE HEADING OF DELIRIOUSNESS.

HOWEVER FORMER PRESIDENT JIMMIE CARTER NEVER STATED THE ADMINSTRATION THAT PERFOFMED SUCH A BARBARIC ACT, IT WAS ATTORNEY GENERAL ROBERT KENNEDY AND J. EDGAR HOOVER THE F.B.I. DIRECTOR, UNDER THE DEMOCRATIC ADMINISTRATION, IN ORDER TO IMPEDE. CIVIL RIGHTS FOR AFRICAN AMERICANS IN THE SIXTIES.

THE NEXT ACCOLADE IS AWARDED TO A MEMBER OF CONGRESS IN THE HOUSE REPRESENTING THE STATE OF GEORGIA, BASED ON SECTIONAL REGIONS WITH IN THE STATE, WHICH MOST LIKELY THE MAJORITY OF HER CONSTITUENCY ARE BLACK, THE DRAGON FROM THE NEW ORLEANS HEARINGS DEBACLE, IN THE HOUSE, WITH SHE BEING ONE OF THE PANELIST TO QUESTION SOME OF THE VICTOMS THAT ENDURED THIS TRAUMATIZING DISASTER AND OFFER THEIR ASSESSMENT OF TRULY WHAT TRANSPIRED.

IT WOULD BE INTERESTING TO KNOW THE CRITERION THES PEOPLE WAS CHOSEN, UNFORTUNATELY IT DID NOT PASS THE SMELL TEST, MOST COMPLAINED ABOUT ATTENTIVE ISSURES AND LAW ENFORCEMENT INTIMADITIONS AND DRESSING PIGS, WHICH IS TIPICAL OF SLUM GETTO AFRICAN AMERICANS, WHICH THEY HAVE ESTABLISHED THROUGHOUT THE NATION OVER THE

YEARS, PIRATICALLY IN LARGE AND SEMI LARGE CITIES SUCH AS AROUND NEW ORLEANS, THE IMPLICATIONS ARE NOT TO ACCUSE ANY OF THESE GROUPS AS BEING SLUM DWELLERS, HOWEVER BASED ON THEIR DEMEANOR SOME WERE SUSPECT OF INACCURACY BUT BLACKS TEND TO BLAME ANY AND EVERY ONE FOR THEIR OWN INABILITY TO CREATIVELY RESOLVE PROBLEMS THAT REQUIRE INDIVIDUAL THINKING, WHICH THEIR CAUSES ARE ASSUMED BY A SPOKESMAN, IN THE LIKES OF CONGRESS WOMAN CYNTHIA MCKINNEY WHICH IS OBSESSED WITH RAW RADICAL IDEOLOGY, THAT ENDORSE THE NEGATIVE LYING APPROACH THAT SOME OF THESE KATRINA VICTOMS APPRAISED.

CONGRESS WOMAN MCKINNEY EXITED HER PERCH FROM THE PODIUM AND EMBRACED ONE OF THE ELDER KATRINA VICTOMS THAT LATER CAUSED CONGRESSMAN CHRISTOPHER SHAYS COLOR TO CHNAGE RED, IN DISBELIEF WHEN SHE INSINUATED THE WATER CONTAINING LEVEE WAS DELIBERATELY BLOWN UP, SPEWING OUT LOUIS FARRAKHAN FOOLISH PROPAGANDER, AND WHEN ASKED TO DESCRIBE THE METHODOLOGY BY CONGRESSMAN SHAYS, SHE RESPONDED WITH SHE HEARD A LOUD BOOMING NOISE, AND WHEN ASKED HOW FAR DID SHE LIVE FROM THE ILOUD . NOISE THERE WAS A SUDDEN MEMORY LAPSE, THAT FADED INTO GIBBERISH SENILITIES, IT IS TERRIBLY SAD THAT A HORRIBLE DISASTER CAUSED BY MOTHFR NATURE, AND SOME DYSFUNCTIONAL MINDED AFRICAN AMERICANS. AGGRESSIVELY SEARCH FOR GUIDANCE FROM T^ HEIR SLLF APPOINTED LEADERS TO ATTACH RAISM TO A GOD SENT HURRICANE OR TORNADO, AND AS A RESULT IT GIVE THEIR TREASURED DEMOCRATS OPENINGS TO BASH THE ADMINISTRATION AND CONTINUE TO CONSOLIDATE THEIR VOTING BLOC, WHICH HAS DRIVEN THEM INTO POVITY, HAVING THEM DEPEND ON PROMISES OF ECONOMIC RELIEF FROM SOCIAL PROGRAMS, WHICH IS LEGENDARY FOR SOME LAZY GOOD FOR NOTHING STUPID AFRICAN AMERICANS, AND THIS ABSURDITY HAS BECAME A SPECTACLE MOTIVATED BY JESSIE JACKSON AND AL SHARPETON, IN AN ATTEMPT TO HERD SLUM

GETTO DWELLERS BACK TO NEW ORLEANS PRIMARILY TO SUPPORT MAYOR NAGEN TO HOLD HIS POST AS MAYOR, THEY COULD CARE LESS IF THEY SLEPT IN THE RUBBLE COMPILED ON THE GROUND, JUST VOTE AND MAINTAIN NAGIN CHOCOLATE CITY, BUT THIS IS NOTHING MORE THAN POLITICAL PROPAGANDER TO PUT THEM IN THE PUBLIC SPOT LIGHT, BECAUSE MOST OF THESE PEOPLE HAVE SETTLED INTO OTHER SLUMS ALL OVER THE COUNTRY, AND MOST WILL NEVER RETURN, BECAUSE IF I KNOW ANY THING ABOUT BLACKS ONE ONE SLUM GETTO IS JUST AS GOOD AS ANOTHER, BECAUSE THE FUNDAMENTALS ARE THE SAME ALL OVER THE COUNTRY, BECAUSE THEY WERE CREATED JUST FOR THAT PURPOSE WITH GOVERNMENTAL ASSISTANCE, AND THESE TWO BUFFOONISH PARASITES ARE IN NEW ORLEANS TRYING TO CONVINCE THE NTION, THAT A CARE TAKER IS NEEDED FOR THESE PEOPLE, AND THEY ARE TRAUMATIZED AND REALLY NOT RESPONSIBLE FOR THEM SELVES, THEY NEED HELP TO REBUILD, SOME INDUSTRIAL GROUP, PREFERABLE THE GOVERNMENT TO REBUILD THEIR SLUM GETTO SWEPT AWAY BY KATRINA, IN THE MEAN TIME WHILE THE REBUILDING IS TAKING PLACE, THEY SHOULD BE ELIGIBLE TO VOTE FROM AROUND THE COUNTRY, CHICAGO, NEW YORK, DETROIT, JUST TO NAME A FIEW, IT SHOULD BE NOTED SOME OF THESE PEOPLE ARE THE SCUM OF THE EARTH, MOST OF THEM DONT KNOW WHERE THEY ARE THEMSELVES THE PROFILE OF DRUG INFESTED SLUMS IS UNIQUE ALL OVER THE COUNTRY THEY WILL BLEND IN IMMEDIATELY UPON ARRIVAL AND IT DOSENT MATTER WHERE BECAUSE OF THEIR SPECIAL CODES RELATED TO DRUGS, SO MR. JACKSON AND MR. SHARPETON YOU ARE BEATING A DEAD HORSE TRYING TO BREATHE AIR INTO A LOST CAUSE THAT THE ENTIRE NATION IS PLAGUED WITH,AND IT IS GETTING WORSE, ALMOST AT EPIDEMIC PROPORTION. IT IS SUSPECTED ONCE THE ELECTIONS ARE OVER IN TWO THOUSAND AND SIX THE EFFORTS TO BLAME EVERY ONE FOR THESE PEOPLE PROBLEMS WILL VANISH THE SAME AS CONGRESS WOMAN CYNTHIA MCKINNEY WITH THE NEW ORLEANS . HEARING DEBACLE IN THE CONGRESS, SOME OF THESE

SUCCESSFUL BLACKS ARE SENSATIONALIZED BY NAME PRESTIGE COLOR AND GENDER, AS CONGRESS WOMAN MCKINNEY EXPLOITED THAT FACT DURING HER LATEST ESCAPADE WITH SECURITY GUARDS IN WASHINGTON, WITH REPORTED DISTURBING TURBULENCE IN HER PASS, THIS PREDICTABLE LABEL HER AS A FASCIST THAT IS SPINNING OUT OF CONTROL, REGARDLESS TO THE OUT COME, AND IS ALLIED WITH SOME OF THE WORST ACTVIST IN THE UNITED STATES OF AMERICA, CASTRO AND CHAVEZ, LOYALIST HARRY BELAFONTA AND DANNIE GLOVER, THESE PEOPLE ARE SECTARIAN AND DEVOTED TO A COMMUNSTIC CAUSE, AND HAVE DISDAIN FOR OUR GOVERNMENT, AND IF GIVEN THE OPPORTUNITY WOULD ATTEMPT TO OVERTHROW, IN FAVOR OF THEIR PRAISED DICTATORS.

SO APPARENTLY SENATOR HARRY REED AND CONGRESS WOMAN NANCY PLOSI HAVE A POTENTIAL OR ALREADY COMMUNISTIC BLACK RACIST FUNGAS AMONG THEM, AND THE ENTIRE CONGRESS SHOULD BE CONCERNED, THIS WOMAN HAS PUT HER SELF ON A PEDESTAL AND INTEND TO PLAY THAT PREHOSTRIC FOOLERY THAT PEOPLE HAVE DISDAIN FOR HER BECAUSE SHE IS BLACK, IF THERE IS DISDAIN IT IS CERTAINLY NOT BECAUSE SHE IS BLACK, SHE IS WALKING WITH THE SAME OLD STICK THAT MANY AFRICAN AMERICANS USE WHEN THEY CANT GET THEIR WAY, OR MAKE A FOOL OF THEMSELVES, THEY HAVE THIS IMAGINARY GRATUITOUS PERPETUAL HABITUAL INSTINCT TO BELLOW IT HAPPEN BECAUSE I AM BLACK, THIS SICK DERANGED EXCUSE HAS SPIROLLED OUT OF CONTROL, NOT ONLY THAT REVERSE DISCRIMINATION IS ON THE RISE, I HAPPEN TO BE IN A PUBLIC PLACE WAITING IN LINE TO CHECK OUT THERE WAS A BLACK WOMAN WITH LITTLE BOY ABOUT SEVEN AHEAD OF ME, THE CASHIER WAS WHITE, SHE SPOKE TO THE LITTLE FELLOW AND ASKED IF HE LIKED SCHOOL, HE STARTED CRYING, SHE INQUIRED WHAT IS WRONG, HE RESPONDED I HATE WHITE FOLKS.

THIS TYPE OF BEHAVIOR FROM A SEVEN YEAR OLD IS EMBEDDED AND TAUGHT BY DYSFUNCTIONAL MINDED AND IDIOSYNCRASY PARENTS, THAT IS ISOLATING THIS

KID FROM SOCIETY, AND OBVIOUSLY EXPANDING GETTO SLUMS BECAUSE IF HE GET AN EDUCATION WHICH I DOUBT, WHO THE HELL IS HE GOING TO WORK FOR, THIS TYPE OF INSANITY HAS TO BE EXPOSED, BECA< USE OVER A PEROID OF TIME IT REPRESENT COLLATERAL DAMAGE TO ALL AFRICAN AMERICANS, AND COLLECTIVELY CREATE AND EXPAND GETTO SLUMS THROUGHOUT THE COUNTRY.

CONGRESS WOMAN CYNTHIA MCKINNEY BEING A AFFLUENT ELECTED LEADER TO REPRESENT THOUSANDS OF PEOPLE FROM GEORGIA, ARE DISPLAYING SIMILAR MANNERISM OF A SEVEN YEAR OLD,ONLY IN REVERSE PRACTICALLY THERE WAS A CALLER TO WASHINGTON JOURANL C-SPAN, APRIL 01, 2006 MADE AN ASSESSMENT OF CONGRESS WOMAN MCKINNEY APPEARANCE, STATING THAT HER HAIR AND DEMEANOR REMINDED HIM OF A CRACK HEAD DRUGGIE LOOKING FOR A SALE, IT IS QUITE PUZZLING THAT WITH THIS WOMAN TRACK RECORD HER CONSTITUENTS KEEP SENDING HER BACK TO WASHINGTON I WILL GIVE TEN TO ONE ODDS THETMAJORITY ARE AFRICAN AMERICAN, THE HERITAGE OF BLACKS DICTATE THEY WILL SUPPORT A ANOTHER BLACK POLITICIAN, AS LONG AS HE OR SHE IS NOT A REPUBLICAN, THEY WILL SUPPORT DEMOCRATS WITH THEIR VOTING BLOC, AND SEND THEM TO OFFICE OVER AND OVER AGAIN EVEN IF THEY ARE CAMPAIGNING WITH A CRACK PIPE IN THEIR HANDS, THIS IS THE MAJORITY OF BLACKS DUBIOUS INTELLECTUAL MISTAKENLY OPENION OF POLITICS.

HOWEVER THE SHARADE IN NEW ORLEANS LED BY JESSIE JACKSON AND AL SHARPETON, BILL COSBY, MOST LIKELY HE WAS KIDNAPPED, OR HE HAD GOTTEN INTO SOME OF CONGRESS WOMAN MCKINNEY KOOLAID, OF COURSE THIS IS NOT TO SUGGEST THAT MR. COSBY IS OR WAS ANY PART OF A ACTVIST GROUP, BECAUSE HE HAS PREVIOUSLY SPOKEN OUT PUBLICALLY OF THE IDIOSYNCRASIES PORTRAYED BY SOME AFRICAN AMERICANS REGARDS TO FAMILY AND INDIVIDUAL PERSONAL RESPONSIBILITYS, AND MADE SOME SUGGESTIONS TO EXTINGUISH SOME OF THEIR RASH INAPPROPIATE BEHAVIOR, AND HE WAS VICIOUSLY ATTACKED BY THE RADICAL LEFT,WING DEMOCRATIC

POLITICAL BLACK SLAVE DRIVERS AND ACCUSED OF MEDDLLING INTO THE AFFAIRS OF THE POOR,WHEN HE IS RICH AND WOULD NOT UNDERSAND AND HIS IDEOLOGY WAS MISLEADING AND WRONG, SO WHEN I WATCHED HIM THERE ON THE PODIUM WITH MR. JACKSON AND MR. SHARPETON, ITHOUGHT MAYBE HE HAD LUNCH WITH CONGRESS WOMAN MCKINNEY, NO OFFENSE INTENDED, HOWEVER THESE TWO GENTLEMEN MR. JACKSON AND MR. SHARPETON ARE THE ENERGY THAT SOME OF THESE MISFITS OF SOCIETY THRIVE ON, AND MANY OTHERS, BECAUSE REGARDLESS TO WHAT, HOW, AND WHEN THEY DESTROY THE AMERICAN ENGLISH, AND CREATE A DRESS CODE TO A LEVEL OF NONE UNDERSTANDING, SCHOOLING AND WORK IS OBSOLETE, JESSIE JACKSON AND AL SHARPETON AND OTHERS ARE SYMPATHIZERS BY THE WAY THERE IS A NEW KID ON THE BLOCK, MR. TAVIS SMILEY THESE PEOPLE WILL CONTINUE TRYING TO CONVINCE THE NATION, THAT THE REASON THESE PEOPLE ARE LIVING IN POVERTY IS REALLY NOT THEIR FAFAULT, THEY ARE SUFFERING FROM DEPRESSION OF SLAVERY, AND THE WHITE MAN IS GOING TO HAVE HIS DAY OF RECKONING FOR THE PROBLEMS THEY ARE CAUSING FOR THESE POOR PEOPLE WHICH HAVE DRIVEN THEM INTO POVERTY AND SLUM GETTO LIVING.

THE IRONY IS THAT EVERY NATIONALLY AROUND THE WORLD WOULD LIKE TO COME AND RESIDE IN THE UNITED STATES OF AMERICA, BECAUSE THERE IS MUCH OPPORTUNITY FOR SUCCESS, THE OVERALL MAJORITY OF AFRICAN AMERICANS ARE BORN CITIZENS OF THIS COUNTRY, BUT SOME REGRETFULLY ARE INEPT TO WHAT THEY HAVE ACCESSIBLE, IN ORDER TO OVERT POVERTY BUT UNFORTUNATELY THEY SPEND THE MAJORITY OF THEIR LIVES PLANNING STRATEGY TO SEDUCE AND FREE LOAD OFF SOME ONE ELSE,INCLUDING THEIR OWN FAMILY MEMBERS.

THE MAJORITY OF AFRICAN AMERICANS TAKE A NEGATIVE APPROACH TO POLITICS, BECAUSE THEY HAVE BEEN LURED INTO THINKING THIS IS SOMETHING MOSTLY WHITE PEOPLE SHOULD BE INVOLVED WITH,AND THEY JUST VOTE THE WAY THEY ARE TOLD,AND BECAUSE THEY

DO NOT HAVE THE TIME TRYING TO FIGURE THIS MESS OUT, SO AS A RESULT OF THIS PREHISTORIC AFRICAN WITCH DOCTOR ANCESTRY THINKING ON A BROAD SCALE NATION WIDE, IT INSERT THE MAJORITY OF AFRICAN AMERICANS INTO POLITICAL BONDAGE, AND DEPRIVE THEM OF THEIR INDIPENDANT POLITICAL RIGHT TO FUNCTION PROPERLY IN A FREE SOCIETY, SO OBVIOUSLY IF ONE DO NOT UNDERSTAND THE BASIC FUNCTIONS OF THEIR GOVERNMENT, IN WHICH THE COUNTRY THEY LIVE IN, THEIR CHANCES OF BECOMING HIGHLY SUCCESSFUL IS REMOTE, BECAUSE IT PUT THEM IN A POSITION OF HAVING TO RELY ON A SELF APPOINTED SPOKESMAN TO CHOOSE THEIR CANIDATE FOR THEM, IN ACCORDANCE WITH AFFILIATION.

FOR INSTANCE IF A MAJOR POLITICAN IS CAMPAIGNING FOR OFFICE AND SURROUND HIM OR HER SELF WITH BLACK NOTORIETY PERSONELL, HISTORY DICTATE THE MAJORITY OF AFRICAN AMERICANS ARE GOING TO VOTE IN UNISON TO SUPPORT THE CANIDATE, AND ALL OF THE SELF APPOINTED LEADERS AND DEMOCRATIC STRATEGIST ARE STRONG SUPPORTERS OF THE DMOCRATIC PARTY, SO AS A RESULT IT IS NOT A MATTER OF CHOICE BETWEEN THE TWO MAJOR PARTIES IN THE COUNTRY IT NINETY EIGHT PRECENT FOR THE DEMOCRATIC PARTY, MOST AFRICAN AMERICANS HAVE BLINDERS ON REGARDS TO A TWO PARTY SYSTEM IN AMERICA, BECAUSE HISTORICALLY THEY WERE BRIBED WITH SOCIAL PROGRAMS, AND BLACK NOTORIETY PERSONNEL IN THE FORTIES BY PRESIDENT FRANKLIN ROOSEVELT, THEY HAVE BEEN SWALLOWED BY POLITICAL STUPIDITY NOT REALIZING THE SOCIAL PROGRAMS THEY BEGAN TO RECEIVE IN 1935, SOCIAL SECURITY AND 1936, THE FARMERS RELIEF EMPLOYMENT, WERE FEDERAL PROGRAMS, HOBEVER AFRICAN AMERICANS REVELED WITH THE FACT THEY WERE GETTING THE SAME AMOUNT OF FUNDS AS WHITES,AND ASSUMED THE PRESIDENT WAS DOING SOMETHING JUST FOR THEM AND THEY WERE ON THR ROAD TO BECOMING EQUAL TO WHITES, AND ALL OVER THE COUNTRY THEY STARTED BLOC VOYING WITH PRAISE.FOR DEMOCRATS, AND INSISTING THEY WERE

ON THEIR WAY TO EQUALITY WITH WHITES, AND THE END TO SEGREGATION AND THIS WAS WHAT PRESIDENT ROOSEVELT GOING TO DO FOR AFRICAN AMERICANS, THIS IS WHY IT IS SO IMPORTANT TO UNDERSTAND HOW YOUR GOVERNMENT FUNCTION, AFRICAN AMERICANS BECAME CONATITUTIONAL CITIZENS IN EIGHTEEN SIXTY SIX, SO IT WOULD HAVE BEEN A VIOLATION OF THE CONSTUTION IF THEY DIDNT RECEIVE AS MUCH MONEY AS WHITES, BECAUSE THESE WERE FEDERAL PROGRAMS, THAT WAS 1935 AND 1936, THIS IS 2006, AND SOME BLACKS ARE JUST AS IGNORANT NOW AS THEY WERE THEN.

WHICH COME UNDER THE HEADDING OF POLITICAL SELF DESTRUCTION FOR AFRICAN AMERICANS, DEMOCRATS HAVE KNOWN OF THIS POLITICAL IGNORANCE OF AFRICAN AMERICANS FOR YEARS, PLANNED ESCAPADES HAS BEEN A TRADITION OVER THE YEARS TO RECRUIT AFFLUENT BLACKS AS SHOW PONIES TO ENTICE HERD VOTING, WHITE DEMOCRATIC AFFLUENT POLITICANS APPEAR IN CHURCHES, AND PUBLIC GATHERINGS , IN AN EFFORT TO SUGGEST WE ARE JUST ONE OF THE REGULAR BROTHERS OF THE HOOD, AND YOU SEE MORE TEETH THAN A JACKASS EATING BRIERS, IF YOU HAVE NEVER SEEN SUCH A CHARMING EVENT THERE ARE PHOTO OPTS OF CONGRESSMAN CHARLIE RANGLE WHEN HE IS AROUND SENATOR HILLARY CLINTON, THIS VARIFY MY SYNOPSIS OF EVENTS, AND IS THE KIND OF ABSURDY THAT THAT PROFILE MOST AFRICAN AMERICANS COLLECTIVELY AROUND THE COUNTRY, IN ESSENCE IF YOU ASSEMBLE A GROUP OF BLACKS AND ADVISE THEM THAT THE REPUBLICAN CONTROLLED CONGRESS PASSED THE CIVIL RIGHTS ACT OF 1866, AND THE FOURTEENTH AMENDMENT TO THE CONSTITUTION WHICH WROTE ITS PROVISIONS GUARANTEEING AFRICAN AMERICANS CITIZENSHIP WITHIN THE CONSTUTION IN THE UNITED STATES OF AMERICA, BUT UNFORTUNATELY IN 1876, THERE WAS A RUN OFF FOR THE PRESIDENCY BETWEEN DEMOCRAT SAMUEL J. TILDEN AND REPUBLICAN RUTHERFORD B. HAYES, EACH CLAIMED VICTORY, SO THE ELECTORIAL COMMISSION RESOLVED THE ISSURE AND AWARDED THE PRESIDENCY TO REPUBLICAN RUTHERFORD

B. HAYES, BUT THE DEMOCRATS IN THE CONGRESS REFUSED TO CERTIFY THE ELECTION, THEY FILIBUSTED UNTIL A DEAL WAS STRUCK, REPUBLICAN HAYES WOULD BECOME PRESIDENT FOR REMOVAL OF FEDERAL TROOPS FROM THE SOUTH, AND THE SOUTHERN STATES WOULD HANDLE THEIR. OWN CIVIL STABILITY AND CIVIL RIGHTS IN THEIR PERSPECTIVE STATES, IN FOLLOWING YEARS SOUTHERN DEMOCRATS RULED THE SUPREME COURT AND WATERED DOWN CIVIL RIGHTS FOR AFRICAN AMERICANS, FROM THE FOURTEENTH AND FIFTEENTH AMENDMENT OF THE CONSTITUTION THAT THE REPUBLICAN CONGRESS HAD RATIFIED,AND AWARDED THEIR FATE TO THE SOUTHERN STATES JURISDICTION UNDER JIM CROW RULE MEANING BACK OF THE BUS AND EVERY THING EQUAL BUT SEPERATE IN PUBLIC FACILITIES, SO WHAT MANY STUPID BLACKS DONT UNDERSTAND OR FAIL TO RECONCILE IS THAT THE REPUBLIC AN CONGRESS RATIFIED THEIR CIVIL RIGHTS TO THE CONSTITUTION IN 1866, AND THE DEMOCRATS WATERED IT DOWN THROUGH THE COURTS UNDER SOUTHERN STATE CONTROL, AND LATER WHEN THEY BECAME THE MAJORITY IN THE CONGRESS, THEY HELD THEIR FOOT ON THE NECK OF AFRICAN AMERICANS PERTAINING TO CIVIL RIGHTS FOR OVER A HUNDRED YEARS, UNTIL 1964 AND1965, (INTERATION) ALL AFRICAN AMERICANS WERE AWARDED THEIR CIVIL RIGHTS IN 1866, BY THE CONTROLED REPUBLICAN CONGRESS, BUT THE DEMOCRATS DENIED YOU THIS CONSTITUTIONAL RIGHT FOR OVER A HUNDRED YEARS,

(CIVIL AND VOTING RIGHTS)

(CIVIL RIGHTS) THESE ACTS OF CONGRESS WAS RATIFIED THE FOURTEENTH AMENDMENT JULY 9, 1866.

(VOTING RIGHTS) FIFTEENTH AMENDMENT, RATIFIED FEBRUARY 3, 1870. SO IF THE MAJORITY OF AFRICAN AMERICANS DONOT REPEAT DONOTTFEEL THIS IS A GRAVE INJUSTICE THAT (ONLY) THE DEMOCRATS AFFLICTED UPON BLACKS, THEN THE MAGNITUDE OF POVITY, SLUMS AND INCARCERATION IS DESERVING.

ONCE THIS BRIEF SYNOPSIS IS EXPLAINED TO A GROUP OF AFRICAN AMERICANS, MOST LIKELY THE MAJORITY WOULD RESPOND IN THIS MANNER,SO WHAT THEY ARE FOR THE RICH AND DO NOTHING FOR US, WE NEED SOME BODY THAT IS GOING TO DO SOMETHING FOR US, THIS DYSFUNCTIONAL BRAIN DEAD IDEA OF SOME ONE DOING SOMETHING FOR YOU,IS PROPAGANDIZED BY SELF APPOINTED RADICAL BLACK LEADERS ALL OVER THE COUNTRY, PIRATICALLY BY MR. JESSIE JACKSON AND MR. AL SHARPETON, JUST LISTEN TO THE CYNICAL ISSURES BEING RAISED IN NEW ORLEANS, BLOWING SMOKE WE NEED TO DO SOMETHING FOR THESE DISPLACED PEOPLE S.0 THEY CAN VOTE. HYPOTHETICALLY SPEAKING LETS USE MR. BILL COSBY AS AN EXAMPLE

AFTER HE GRADUATED FROM TEMPLE OR LONG BEFORE , AND HE WAS LIVING IN NEW ORLEANS AND SUFFERED THE SAME IDENTICAL EXPERIENCE FROM A KATRINA INCIDENT AND WAS DISPLACED AND HE PLANNED TO MOVE BACK AND THE SAME ISSURE AROSE REGARDS TO VOTING, I WILL BET YOU THE RANCH HE WOULD FIND A WAY TO ACCOMPLISH THAT MISSION, BECAUSE IF HE COULD NOT AND WAITED FOR JESSIE JACKSON, I GUARANTEE YOU HE WOULD NOT BE WHERE HE IS TODAY, INDIVIDUAL THINKING IS THE ESSENCE TO LIFE , IF THESE SELF APPOINTED BLACK LEADERS THAT IS BEING URGED ON BY WHITE POLITICAL MASTERS WOULD REVERSE THEIR DEMOCRATIC DEMAGOGUREY AND START TO FORCE THE ISSURE AS WHAT SOME AFRICAN AMERICANS CAN DO FOR THEMSELVES, MOST LIKELY THERE WOULD BE A DRAMATIC CHANGE IN POVERTY OVER A PEROID OF TIME, HOWEVER THIS WILL NEVER HAPPEN BECAUSE THE DEMOCRATIC PARTY WOULD ABANDON THESE PARASITES, AND THEY WOULD BE OUT OF A JOB AS SPOKESMAN FOR BLACKS TO HERD THEIR VOTING BLOC TO THE DEMOCRATIC PARTY, THE ISSURE IS WHEN WILL THE MAJORITY OF AFRICAN AMERICANS WAKE UP AND REALIZE THEY HAVE BEEN HAD BY THE DEMOCRATIC PARTY SENSE PRESIDENT FRANKLIN ROOSEVELT NEW DEAL, WHEN THEY WILLINGLY INDUCTED THEMSELVES INTO THE HALL OF FAME, TO BE A PSYCHOLOGICAL POLITICAL SLAVE FOR THE

DEMOCRATIC PARTY,ORCHESTRATED TO SIPHON BLACKS AWAY FROM THE REPUBLICAN PARTY.

HOWEVER IT IS SUSPECTED MR. COSBY USED TIME OUT OF HIS BUISY SCHEDULE TO GO TO NEW ORLEANS TO ADDRESS OCCURING ISSURES IN THAT CITY PERTAINING TO THE KATRINA DISASTER, IT WAS SOME WHAT PUZZLING WHY HE WAS THERE, BECAUSE HE IS NOT IN THE SAME LEAGUE WITH JESSIE JACKSON AND AL SHARPETON, BECAUSE HE IS NOT A SLUM BUM SYMPATHIZER HOWEVER THE TOPIC OF HIS SPEECH PORTRAYED THE EXACT DISOBEDIENCE OF SOME BLACKS AROUND THE COUNTRY AND IT IS SPIRALLING OUT OF CONTROL, ILLITERACY, BABIES BEING IMPREGNATED FROM 1112 AND UP, AND VIOLENT DISRESPECT FOR ANY ONE DO NOT AGREE WITH THEIR NONSENSICAL IDEOLOGY, CRACK HEADS MULTIPLYING CRACK BABIES, AND ABSOLUTELY NO RESPECT FOR DIGNITY AND SELF INDULGENCE OF ANY KIND, OTHER THAN THE SEDUCTION OF OTHERS, I APPLAUD MR. COSBY FOR DELIVERING STINGING REALITY IN HIS SUMMATION THAT IS CHRONOLOGICALLY SELF DESTRUCTING SOME AFRICAN AMERICANS, AND THERE ARE THE SYMPATHIZERS, WHILE MR. COSBY WAS SPEAKING IT APPEARED JESSIE JACKSON AL SHAPETON, AND OTHERS WAS AT A GRAVE SIDE FUNERAL AND HAD SEEN A GHOST, IT IS APPALLING THAT SOME OF THESE SELF APPOINTED, SELF RIGHTEOUS, AND SOME CLAIM TO BE MEN AND WOMEN OF THE CLOTH, ARE WILLING TO EXPLOIT THE DANGEROUS SINS AND ALOOF PROMISCURITY OF THESE YOUNG AND OLD AFRICAN AMERICANS, IN THE NAME OF AN UN-JUST SYSTEM IN THIS COUNTRY THAT IS PERPETRATED SPECIFICALLYAGAINST BLACKS,BECAUSE OF THEIR COLOR AND IT CAUSES RADICAL IRRATIONAL BEHAVIOR, THIS TYPE OF FOOLERY HAS CREATED AN ALIBI IN THE FORM OF A LEANING POST FOR SELF APPOINTED BLACK LEADERS TO FOCUS ON THE HE OR SHE BLACK ISSURE, AND THERE ARE ALL KINDS OF SUPPOSEDLY EDUCATED AFRICAN AMERICANS SPREADING THIS PLAGUING BUFFOONISH DEMAGOGUERY AROUND THE GLOBE, AND IF ANY AFRICAN AMERICANS PIRATICALLY THOSE THAT ARE TRYING TO ESTABLISH A FUTURE LISTEN AND INGEST THIS

INSIDIOUS BACK WOODS, SELFISH,UNETHICAL, GRAND STANDING, MISLEADING PREHISTORIC RETORIC, MUCKED UP FROM THE HUTS IN AFRICA, AND THE PLANTATIONS OF THE SOUTH, PACK YOUR BAGS FOR THE GETTO SLUMS, BECAUSE THESE ARE THE PEOPLE THAT PAVE THE WAY FOR YOU WITH THEIR STUPID IDEOLOGY SPEWING VENOM ABOUT WHITE PEOPLE ARE YOUR WORST ENEMY BECAUSE THEY ARE ALWAYS PLANNING TO PREVENT YOUR SUCCESS BECAUSE YOU ARE BLACK, AND IF YOU ARE SUCCESSFUL BEING BLACK, WHITE PEOPLE ARE ALWAYS TRYING TO DEMORALIZE YOU AND REFUSE TO RESPECT YOU AS AN EQUAL BECAUSE OF YOUR COLOR, SO AS A RESULT WE NEED TO HERD TOGATHER AND FORM AN INDPENDANT SOCIETY FOR US.

LIKE WE HAVE SUCCEEDED WITH THE BLACK CACUS WITHIN THE GOVERNMENTTHROUGHOUT THE COUNTRY, SOME AFRICAN AMERICANS NEED TO TAKE A COURSE IN HISTORY BECAUSE FOR SOME DERANGED REASON THEY ARE ACTING AS IF THEY ARE SUPERIOR AND ARE THE FOUNDERS OF AMERICA AND BROUGHT EVERY ONE ELSE HERE, AND THIS SICKINING CHARADE WITH CONGRESS WOMAN CYNTHIA MCKINNEY DEMONSTRATE A GROWING PHANTASMOFSTUPIDITYOFSOMEBLACKSINTHECOUNTRY, AND WITH IGNORAMUS AFFLUENT BLACKS EXPOUNDING ON THIS FOOLISHNESS ABOUT THINGS ARE HAPPENING TO THEM BECAUSE THEY ARE BLACK, YOU ARE GOING TO WITNESS ONE OF THE MOST DRAMATIC ESCALATION IN POVERTY FOR AFRICAN AMERICANS IN THIS COUNTRY EVER, AND PREDOMINATLY FOR THOSE IDIOTS THAT FOLLOW THIS NONSENSICAL DEMAGOGUERY,BECAUSE THE PEOPLE THAT ARE FLAUNTING THIS CRAFTY IDEOLOGY HAVE ALREADY GAINED SUCCESS, BASED ON WHITE PEOPLE (PROVISIONS) THESE ARE THE SIMPLE FACTS, YOU DO THE MATH, HOW MANY LARGE INDUSTRIAL CORPORATIONS IN THE UNITED STATES OF AMERICA THAT AFRICAN AMERICANS INDEPENDENTLY OWN, AND MOST SMALL BLACK OWNED BUISNESSES ARE DIVERSE, THE THINKING CAPACITY OF MOST OLDER AFRICAN AMERICANS HAVE BEEN NEGATED AND MAROONED BY

THE POLITICAL GLUTTONS OF THE DEMOCRATIC PARTY, TO CARRY ON THEIR SADIST COVENANT ADJUDICATED ON THEIR BEHALF BY THE SUPREME COURT IN 1896, WHICH WAS IN VIOLATION OF THE CONSTITUTION RATIFIED IN 1868 CONSUMMATED BY THE REPUBLICAN CONGRESS, HOWEVER IN ESSENCE THE SUPREME COURT DECISION WAS COURSED INTO THIS VIOLATION, BY THE LIKES OF A BOOKER T. WASHINGTON, A CARBON COPY OF JESSIE JACKSON OF TODAY, HE WAS A FORMER SLAVE AND THE FOUNDER OF TUSKEEGE INSTTUTE, AND A INFLUENTIAL BLACK,THE SOUTHERN RACIST DEMOCRATS USED HIS CAPTIVATIONS AS A SPOKSEMAN FOR AFRICAN AMERICANS, AND USED HIS IMAGE TO CONVINCE HERDING BLACKS IN HEAVILY POPULATED SOUTHERN STATES TO ACCEPT THE JIM CROW RULE SEPERATE BUT EQUAL WAS JUST FINE, AND THE SUPREME COURT RULED ACCORDINGLY, AND THIS VIOLATION OF THE CONSTITUTION PERTAINING TO AFRICAN AMERICANS AND THIS BETRAYAL GAVE THE SOUTHERN DEMOCRATS CONTROL OVER BLACKS ILLEGALLY UNTIL 1964, BECAUSE OF THEIR OWN INEPTNESS AND HERDING BEHIND A PROMINENT OF THEIR RACE,THIS UNSCRUPULOUS BEHAVIOR HAS BEEN DETRIMENTAL TO THE ENTIRE AFRICAN AMERICAN CULTURE, BECAUSE THE HERDING PROCESS HAS BEEN GLAMORIZED TO AN EXTENT WITHIN THE AFRICAN AMERICAN SOCIETY, UNTIL IT IS ALMOST BIBLICAL, MOST BLACKS WILL EXPRESS THEIR OPENION REGARDS TO POLITICS MY DADDY WAS DEMOCRAT AND HIS DADDY WAS DEMOCRAT SO I WILL BE A DEMOCRAT UNTIL I DIE, FAMILES AND RELATIVES THROUGHOUT THE NATION SYNCHRONIZE TO THIS STUPIDITY WHICH RELINQUISH THEIR INDEPENDENT OBSERVATION TO A TRADITION, THAT NULLIFY THEIR ABILITY TO EVALUATE POLITICAL CANIDATES WHICH SET THE STANDARDS THAT CONTROL THEIR LIVES, IT IS HIGHLY IMPOSSIBLE FOR A PEOPLE TO INSERT A TRIBAL AFRICAN CULTURE INTO A CIVIL DIVERSE SOCIETY, AND EXPECT TO BE INDEPENDENTLY COMPETITIVE, BECAUSE TRIBES HAVE CHIEFS THAT CONTROL THE TRIBESMAN, UNFORTUNATELY HERE IN THE UNITED STATES OF AMERICA,AFRICAN

AMERICANS HAVE SELF APPOINTED LEADERS, THAT THEY LOOK TO FOR POLITICAL GUIDANCE, AND OTHER SELF IMPOSED DILEMMAS, WHICH THE MAJORITY OF THE TIME DO NOT COINCIDE WITH THE CONSTITUTION, FEDERAL OR STATE LAWS, SO AS A RESULT THE ROADS ARE FILLED WITH BLACKS, HEADED INTO POVITY,GETTO SLUMS, AND DRUG ABUSE, AND THE ONLY EXPLANATION THEIR WEALTHY SELF APPOINTED LEADERS HAVE FOR THEM ARE .BECAUSE THEY ARE BLACK THE WHITE MAN HAS DEPRIVED THEM OF THEIR RIGHTS TO SUCCESS, BUT THE MAIN REASON IS THE REPUBLICANS IS IN POWER AND ARE TAKING FROM THE POOR AND GIVING TO THE RICH.

WHICH REMIND ME OF A COMMENT MADE DURING THE SIXTIES BY SOME OF THE KU-KLUX-KLANSMEN IN THE SOUTH, THAT THE AUTHORITES COULD SEND IN THE NATIONAL GUARD AND THE MILITARY TO THE SCHOOLS IN ORDER OR PROTECTION TO LET THEM ENTER, BUT THEY SURE AS HELL COULD NOT TEACH THEM, REFERRING TO SCHOOL DESEGREGATION IN THE SOUTH FOR AFRICAN AMERICANS, IN COMPARISON THE AFFLUENT INDUSTRIAL COOPERATIING ORGANIZATIONS ESTABLISHED IN AMERICA, THAT FURNISH EMPLOYMENT ON A MASS SCALE FOR A DIVERSE SOCIETY, MEANING BLACK AND WHITE, BASED ON QUALIFICATIONS, SO IF YOU CHOOSE NOT TO PREPARE YOUR SELF FOR ONE OF THESE POSITIONS, THEY SURE AS HELL IS NOT GOING TO TRY AND SPLIT YOUR HEAD OPEN AND PACK KNOWLEDGE INSIDE IN ORDER TO DIRECT YOU TO SELF INDEPENDENCE, HOWEVER THERE ARE THE ELITE AFRICAN AMERICANS THAT ARE SYMPATHETIC AND WILL DEFEND THIS EGREGIOUS BEHAVIOR OF SOME BLACKS IN THE UNITED STATES OF AMERICA, AND TRY TO DISGUISE THE FACT THAT SOME AFRICAN AMERICANS ARE THE MOST UNCIVILIZED POLITICALLY ILLITERATE AND GULLIBLE HUMAN BEING ON GODS EARTH, AND THE STATISTICS ENDORSE THIS FACTOR,/THERE ARE APPROXIMATELY THREE HUNDRED MILLION PEOPLE IN THE UNITED STATES OF AMERICA, OF THAT TOTAL AFRICAN AMERICANS ARE ELEVEN PRECENT, APPROXIMATELY THIRTY THREE MILLION, AND THEY ARE GUILTY OF HAVING THE HIGHEST

CRIME RATE, MOST INCARCERATED AND APPROXIMATELY SEVENTY PRECENT OF CHILDREN BORN OUT OF WED LOCK, THERE IS SCUM IN ALL NATIONALLY, BUT BLACKS ARE AT THE TOP OF THE RUNG WHEN IT COME BREEDING IT, AND IT IS SIMPLY BECAUSE OF THEIR CULTURAL MANNERISM TO HERD TOGATHER AND LISTEN TO A SELF APPOINTED LEADER, OR A DEMOCRATIC STRATEGIST, IN THE LIKES OF A MICHAEL BROWN, DEFENDING A RADICAL CONGRESS WOMEN CYNTHIA MCKINNEY, IN HER BUFFOONISH BLACK SUPREMACIST POWER BEHAVIOR, AND ADJUDICATING HER ACTIONS AS DUE TO PLAYING FIELDS (NOT) BEING LEVEL, WHICH REMIND ME HE IS THE POLITICAL IDIOT THAT DEFAMED DR. MARTIN LUTHER KING BY INSISTING HE WAS NEVER WIRE TAPPED, SO THIS LEVEL PLAYING FIELD DEMAGOGUERY IS PSYCHOLOGY AND POLITICALLY LYNCHING BLACKS THAT LISTEN TO THIS KIND OF FOOLISHNESS AND HERDING THEM OFF TO THE SLUM GETTO, RATHER STRANGE HE MUST HAVE A SIX SENSE BECAUSE HE FOUND THE LEVEL PLAYING FIELD AND APPARENTLY HE IS HOLDING OUT ON THE REST OF THE BLACKS, NOT TELLING THEM WHARE IT IS, BY THE WAY HIS INTERRUPTION OF OCCURRENCES AIRED ON FOX APRIL 6, 2006, ALONG WITH MR.LARRY ELDER,WHICH WAS ALMOST IN SHOCK OVER HIS MISLEADING ASSERTIONS.. PIRATICALLY WITH HIS INSTIGATIVE NONSENSICAL MYTHS ABOUT BLACKS BEING EMBROILED IN INEQUALITY IN THIS COUNTRY, IT SEEM TO BE SOME KIND OF A ANCESTRAL AFRICAN CONGO RITUAL WITH SOME OF THESE POLITICAL AND ECONOMICAL DYSFUNCTIONAL MINDED SYMPATHIZERS, TO TAKE IT UPON THEM SELVES TO SPEAK FOR ALL AFRICAN AMERICANS IN THIS COUNTRY, AND COMPLETELY OMIT THE FACT THAT SOME AFRICAN AMERICANS HAS FORMED AN OPENION THAT THEY CAN BY PASS THE SYSTEM, AND OPEN A CAN AND OUT POP SUCCESS, FUNDAMENTALLY THIS NATION SIT ON A FOUNDATION OF A CONSTITUTION, THAT PROVIDE EQUAL RIGHTS FOR EVERYONE, AND UNTIL SOME BLACKS FIGURE OUT WHAT THEY NEED TO DO REGARDS TO THEIR OWN MERITS, THEY CAN LISTEN TO THESE BLACK POLITICAL INSTIGATORS

UNTIL THEY TURN WHITE,THE SENTIMENTS REMAIN THE SAME DOWN A SLIPPERY SLOPE TO POVERTY, THESE BLACK SYMPATHIZERS ARE POPPING UP ALL OVER THE PLACE LIKE GREEN ONIONS, TO HELP PAVE THE ROAD TO POVERTY AND SLUM GETTO FOR SOME AFRICAN AMERICANS, ONE GOBBLING HEN IS AN ATTORNEY LAUREN LAKE, WHICH IS INTRODUCING A CORRUPT CYNICISM THAT SEDUCE SNOBBISH BLACK TRASH, INTO THINKING THAT THEIR THEAVING DOWNTRODDEN WAY OF LIFE IS CAUSED BY THE SYSTEM.

AND WENT PUBLIC ON NATIONAL TELEVISION APRIL 3, 2006, CHIPPING AWAY AT THE INTEGRITY OF MR. BILL COSBY FOR BEING CANDID ABOUT SOME BLACKS IN THIS COUNTRY, AND DEFENDING AND MAKING EXCUSES FOR SLUMMING ACTIVITY, IT IS PEOPLE LIKE THIS WOMAN THAT INFRINGE ON THE CONSTITUTIONAL RIGHTS OF OTHERS,AND TRY AND JUSTIFY WITH CYNICISM FASHION BY HER OWN HOLLOW INTERPRETATIONS.

AND UNDOUBTABLY SEALING THE FATE OF MANY AFRICAN AMERICANS THAT LIVE IN A FREE DIVERSE SOCIETY AND LISTEN,AND CONDONE THIS KIND C OF GIBBERISH, BECAUSE THERE WILL ALWAYS BE ADVERSITIES IN A DIVERSE SOCIETY OF PEOPLE, WEATHER RACIAL OR NOT, IT IS THE INDIVIDUAL STRENGTH AND WISDOM TO DISSECT THESE FUNCTIONS AND MOVE ON AS SHE DID, NOT PUBLICALLY INSTIGATE TO OTHER BLACKS THAT THE SYSTEM IS WORKING AGAINST THEM,THIS PEDESTAL TYPE OF LIES TO LESS FORTUNATE BLACKS,IS THE EPITOME OF DOUSING URINE IN THEIR FACE AND COVINCING THEM THAT IT IS RAINING,MEANING YOU WERE SMART ENOUGH TO BEAT THE SYSTEM AND WHEN YOU LEFT THEY LOCKED THE GATE TO THEM, AND THE ONLY WAY FOR YOU TO GET IN IS TO REACH OUT FOR ASSISTANCE FROM JESSIE JACKSON, AL SHARPETON, TAVIS SMILEY, LAUREN LAKE, AND OTHER SELF APPOINTED LEADERS, JUST TO NAME A FIEW.

THIS KIND OF HOG WASH HAS PLUNGED MILLIONS OF AFRICAN AMERICANS INTO POVITY AND SLUM GETTOS, BECAUSE IT BRAIN WASH SOME OF THEM TO DISRESPECT OUR GOVERNMENT, WHICH SIT ON THE BED ROCK OF THE

CONSTITUTION THAT ELECTED OFFICIALS SUCH AS THE PRESIDENT, AND CONGRESS.ALSO THE SUPREME COURT MUST ABIDE BY, SO TO FANTASIZE AND PASS ON ERRONEOUS PREDICTIONS IS NOTHING MORE THAN A STUNT FOR AFFLUENT BLACKS TO GAIN ASTUTE NOTORIETY, TO ASSIST THE DEMCRATIC PARTY IN MAINTAINING A CHOKE HOLD ON AFRICAN AMERICAN VOTERS, THIS SICK MASSAGING BY THE MAJORITY OF BLACKS, TO SUPPORT DEMOCRATIC IDEOLOGY,HAS LITERALLLY BEHEADED THEIR ASPIRATIONS, AND SANK THEM INTO HYSTERIA, REGARDS TO RHE REPUBLICAN PARTY, AND THIS IS SHEER NONSENSICAL DEMAGOGUERY BASED ON LIES FROM SLICK DEMOCRATIC POLITICIANS, SENATOR TED KENNEDY ON THE SENATE FLOOR RELEGATING HIS SENTIMENTS TO IMMIGRATION, ON APRIL 7, 2006 AND FOCUSED ON CIVIL RIGHTS, IF I AM NOT MISTAKEN HE IS A MEMBER OF THE DEMOCRATIC PARTY THAT DEPRIVED AFRICAN AMERICANS OF THEIR CIVIL RIGHTS FOR NINETY. EIGHT YEARS.

SOME AFRICAN AMERICANS HAS ADOPTED A FALSITY TO PROTECT OTHER BLACKS REGARDLESS TO THE HEINOUSNESS OF THE OCCURED INCIDENT, THEIR INCLINATION IS TO MANUFACTURE SPECULATIONS AS TO WHAT HAPPENED AND INCRIMINATE THE OPPOSING PARTIES, THERE WAS A FORMER L.A.P.D. DETECTIVE TIM WILLIAMS, VOICING HIS SPECULATIONS ON THE MCKINNEY DEBACLE,AND THE STATEMENTS OF BILL COSBY,CONCERNING THE NEW ORLEANS DISPLACED RESIDENCE, ON APRIL 3, 2006, HE CAME IN WITH HIS CURVE BALL EVADING THE ISSURES, AND SITING SOMETHING ABOUT MCKINEY HAIR, AND NIBBLING AROUND THE EDGES IN AN EFFORT TO DISCREDIT THE HONEST AND TRUTHFUL OPENION OF BILL COSBY IN NEW ORLEANS, THESE CYNICAL SYMPATHIZERS NEED TO HERD TOGATHER AND GIVE A SYNOPSIS OF HOW THEY FOUND AWAY AROUND OBSTACLES THAT THEY ARE PUBLICALLY ACCUSING THE SYSTEM OF CONSPIRING TO PROHIBIT AFRICAN AMERICANS FROM SUCCEEDING IN A DIVERSE SOCIETY, IF THESE CLAIMS ARE TRUE THEN THE GOVERNMENT CAN BE HELD RESPONSIBLE BECAUSE THEY ARE IN VIOLATION OF THE CONSTUTION, AND TO

PROVE THEIR CASE THEY NEED TO SPEND SOME QUALITY TIME IN THE SLUMS, LIKE NIGHTS AND LEAVE THEIR AUTOMOBILES PARKED ON THE LOT AT THE PROJECT, AS WE ALL KNOW THERE ARE MANY SLUMS THROUGHOUT THE COUNTRY BUT ONE COME TO MIND WHICH WAS ARE STILL IS APPROXIMATELY 1012 BLOCKS FROM JESSIE JACKSON RAINBOW PUSH ESTABLISHMENT ON THE SOUTH SIDE OF CHICAGO ON DREXEL BULAVARD AT 51TH ST. AND THE SLUMS ARE ON OR WAS AT 39TH ST. IT IS VERY INTERESTING HE HAS NOT REFORMED THEIR LIVING CONDITONS.

AND IF THE ARRANGED LOCATIONS STILL EXIST IN CHICAGO, WHICH HAS BEEN OVER THIRTY YEARS AGO, LET ME BE PERFECTLY CLEAR HE NEVER LIVED IN THAT AERA, JUST CAME TO HOLD MEETINGS AND COLLECT POOR PEOPLE DONATIONS FROM THE SLUM DWELLERS, WITH PROMISES OF OF LIFTING THEM OUT OF THEIR OWN CREATED PIG STY OF DRUGS, RAPE, INCEST ROBBERY, CHILD MOLESTATION, AND MOST OF ALL A OUT OF CONTROL IMPREGNATION OF YOUNG WOMEN AND CHILDREN, THE CERTAINTY OF A YOUNG WOMAN APPEARED ON TELEVISION DURING THE KATRINA ERUPTION IMPLICATION WERE SHE WAS ABOUT THIRTY FIVE AND HAD SEVEN CHILDREN, THE OLDEST CARRYING THE YOUNGEST, THAT IS WHAT MR. BILL COSBY WAS ELABORATING ON DURING HIS OUT BURST IN NEW ORLEANS, PERTAINING TO SELF DESTRUCTION OF BLACKS, I AM SURE HE HAD AMPLE BODY GUARD PRTECTION, NOT FROM THE CROWD BUT FROM JESSIE JACKSON AND AL SHARPETON, BECAUSE MOST LIKELY MR. JACKSON ARE NEGOTIATING OR PLANNING TO SET UP SHOP TO ACCEPT DONATIONS TO GET THEM OUT OF STATE SATELLITE VOTING RIGHTS, WITH HIS ASSISTANT AL SHARPETON, IN RUNNING THE CITY OF NEW ORLEANS FOR THE POOR DISFRANCHISED BLACK THUGS AND CRACK HEADS OF NEW ORLEANS, BECAUSE MOST BLACKS WITH DIGNETY AND SELFASTEEM HAVE SETTLED SOME PLACE ELSE, OR IS MAKING PREPARATIONS TO REBUILD THERE AND HAVE STARTED A NEW LIFE REGARDS TO PROSPERITY, IT IS TERRIBLY SAD THAT THERE ARE BLACK LIBERAL ACVIST THAT CONDONE THE SICK AND PATHETIC ALSO VIOLENT

BEHAVIOR DIPLAYED BY GETTO SLUM SCUM AND WOULD HAVE THEM THINK THEY ARE RIGHT AND THE REST OF THE NATION WRONG, AND WHITES HAVE PLOTTED TO DEPRIVE THEM OF BEING SUCCESSFUL BECAUSE THEY ARE BLACK, THESE PEOPLE ARE WORSE THAN THE SOUTHERN WHITE JIM CROW ACVTIST DURING THE FIFTIES AND SIXTIES, BECAUSE THEY ARE DIPLOMATICALLY DESTROYING A DYSFUNCTIONAL MIND OF SOME OF THESE PEOPLE AND EVENTUALLY IT WILL EGRESS INTO AN ERUPTION WHICH IS COMPATABLE TO LYNCHING, AND JUST TO THINK A PROMINENT CITIZEN FOUND HER WAY AROUND OBSTACLES OF INJUSTICE FOR BLACKS TO BECOME A U.S. CONGRESS WOMAN CYNTHIA MCKINNEY AND HERDED A COMPULSIVE GROUP TOGATHER IN ATLANTA TO IMPLODE COERCIVE ISSURES RELATED TO RACE, TO DISTRACT THE SUSPECTED ATTENTION FROM HER ERRATIC BEHAVIOR REGARDS TO THE SECURITY GUARD SITUATION IN WASHINGTON, AND WHAT MORE SUTIABLE SURROUNDING WITH PEOPLE THAT ARE LIKE SCHOOLS OF CATFISH ALL MOUTH AND NO BRAINS, SO THEY WILL KEEP SENDING HER TO WASHINGTON AND SHE IS PLAYING THEM LIKE A FIDDLE, BECAUSE THE MAJORITY OF AFRICAN AMERICANS VOTE FOR NAME RECOGNITION AND CELEBRITY STATUS,EVEN IF THE CRACK PIPE IS TUCKED IN HIS OR HER BELT, IT APPEAR THAT MOST OF HER CONSTITUENCES ARE BLACK AS EXPECTED, SO SHORT OF SOME KIND OF MENTAL DEFICIENCY THE DEMOCRATIC PARTY IS STUCK WITH A LOOSE CANNON.

IN CONTRAST THE REV. JOSEPH LOWERY APPEARED ON NATIONAL TELEVISION AFTER A DEBACLE DISPLAYED AT THE FUNERAL OF MRS. CORETTA SCOTT KING, APPARENTLY IN AN ATTEMPT TO JUSTIFY THE INSIDIOUS DEMOCRATIC BEHAVIOR, INCLUDING HIS PERFORMANCE RELEGATED TO A SANCTIMONIOUS SUPPORT FOR DEMOCRATS, HOWEVER PUBLICALLY FALSIFIED HIS POLIICAL AFFILIATIONS WHICH IS NOTHING MOORE THAN BLATANT HYPOCRISY, BECAUSE THE ATLANTA JOURNALCONSTITUTION DATED JUNE 27, 2004, HAS DOCUMENTS TO DISPUTE HIS CLAIM, SOURCE JIM THORPE,HE PUBLICLY CRITICIZED PRESIDENT GEORGE BUSH, OF ALL PLACES AT MRS. CORETTA SCOTT

KING FUNERAL, AND TO USE A SACRED SETTING OF THIS MAGNITUDE IN AN ATTEMPT TO IMPUGN IS SELFISH AND APPALLING, BECAUSE OF THE DISRESPECT FOR THE DECEASED, PIRATICALLY THE WIDOW OF A CIVIL RIGHTS ICON, THIS WAS REPREHENSIBLE AND FOOLISH, COMING FROM A PERSON OF THE CLOTH, ALSO DISPLAY DISTRUST AND PRECEPTS OF BEING OUT OF CONTROL, IN AN EFFORT TO SEDUCE THE CROWD ON BEHALF OF THE DEMOCRATIC PARTY, AND TO DENY HIS AFFILIATIONS OR CLAIM TO BE NEUTRAL BECAUSE IT IS WORLD RENOWN THAT THE OVERWHELMINGLY MAJORITY OF AFRICAN AMERICANS ARE DEMOCRATIC, SO IN ANY FORM OF RENUCIATION IS QUESTIONABLE, TO THE AFFECT THAT IF YOU ARE CAUGHT DELIBERATELY MISLEADING THE GENERAL PUBLIC IN REGARDS TO ANY MANNER, YOUR SINCERITY OF PAST YEARS IS QUESTIONABLE HAVING TO DO WITH WITH INTEGRITY, THE MERE FACT THAT A CIVIL RIGHTS ACTICIST WITH STRONG CREDENTIALS KNOWINGLY ATTEMPT TO ALLEVIATE THE SADIST CRUELITY IMPOSED ON AFRICAN AMERICANS BY DEMOCRATS CONDONE WITH APPEASEMENT IF YOU ARE A DEMOCRAT SAY IT OUT LOUD AND LET THE GENERAL PUBLIC DETERMINE YOUR STANDING, AND I AM SPICIFICALLY REFERRING TO THOSE SELF APPOINTED BLACK LEADERS, THAT DICTATE INSANITY OVERTLY TO APPEASE THEIR POLITICAL SLAVE MASTERS, ONCE AGAIN I REFER TO REDUNDANCY BUT THE ACCASION IS PROFOUND,BECAUSE SOME AFRICAN AMERICANS ARE FASHIONED TO A WHIRLWIND AFFECT PRIMARILY BASED ON THEIR INABILITY TO THINK FOR THEM SELVES DOMINATED BY ANCESTRIAL TRAITS WHICH MOST NATIONS THROUGHOUT THE WORLD ARE AWARE OF THIS DEFICIENCY AND THE TONE IS BY ALL THESE SELF APPOINTED SPOKESMAN AND LEADERS THAT CHARACTERIZE THEIR FAILED FUTURE POTENTIALLY IN THE UNITED STATES OF AMERICA, AND HAVE FOR YEARS BEEN LEGISLATED BY DEMOCRATIC PARTY, WITH CARROTS ON A STICK, ONE PRIME EXAMPLE MRS. CORETTA SCOTT KING FUNERAL AND THE IMPLOSION OF DEMOCRATS THAT DEFACED THE RESPECTED VALUE

WITH THEIR OWN AGENDA PERTAINING TO POLITICAL POWER, JOSEPH LOWERY ATTACKING A SITTING PRESIDENT WITH BUFFOONISH DEMAGOGUERY, FORMER PRESIDENT JIMMIE CARTER EXTRAPOLATING ON HISTORICAL ISSURES SUCH WIRE TAPPING ON DR. MARTIN LUTHER KING AND MAYBE SENILITY AFFECTED HIS MEMORY BUT IT WAS THE DEMOCRATS AND (ONLY) THE DEMOCRATS PERPETRATED THIS UNLAWFUL ACT, IN ORDER TO IMPEDE CIVIL RIGHTS FOR AFRICAN AMERICANS, WHICH IS SUSPECTED EVENTUALLY COST HIM HIS LIFE, AND IRONICALLY FORMER PRESIDENT WILLIAM JEFFERSON CLINTON AND SENATOR HILLORY SEIZED THE OPPORTUNITY TO FURTHER OPTIMIZE HIS THIRD TERM AS PRESIDENT, WHICH IS IN VIOLATION OF THE CONSTUTION, HOWEVER HE IS USING HIS SIDE KICK WIFE,AS PRESIDENT ROOSEVELT DID WITH FIRST LADY ELEANOR, WHEN HE HAD SERIOUS PROBLEMS OR NEEDED TO ACCOMPLISH A VERY IMPTANT MISSION, AND HE BROUGHT THE HOUSE DOWN OF GULLIBLE BLACKS, WHEN HE ELECTED HER PRESIDENT, THIS WAS ONE OF THE MOST AGREGIOUS OFFENSIVE DEMONSTRATIONS CAST UPON THE DIGNITY OF A DIVERSE SOCIETY OF PEOPLE EVER,BECAUSE HE USED THE BACKDROP OF THIS ELEGANT AND MORAL WOMAN CORETTA SCOTT KING FUNERAL, TO HYPNOTIZE A CROWD OF POLITICALLY IGNORANT AFRICAN AMERICANS IN AN EFFORT TO SOLICIT THEIR BLOC VOTES FOR SENATOR HILLARY CLINTON HIS WIFE,THIS DUO IS JOINED AT THE HIP TO DEFRAUD THEIR AND MOSTLY HIS WAY BACK INTO WHITE HOUSE, BECAUSE IF SHE IS ELECTED TO THE PRESIDENCY HE WILL HAVE A SPECIAL LIMO BUILT WITH AN EXTENDED STERRING WHEEL TO THE BACK SEAT ESPECIALLY FOR HER, REMEMBER THE VAST RIGHT WING CONSPIRACY, AND THE INTERIM HE WAS HAVING BOXES OF CIGARS DELIVERED TO THE WHITE HOUSE, I HAVE NO INTENTIONS TO PERSUADE OR DICTATE HOW CITIZENS SHOULD VOTE, I ONLY STATING MY PERSONAL OPINION AND THE AUTHENTICATED FACTS YOU DECIDE, BECAUSE THIS NATION SIT ON THE FOUNDATION OF A CONSTITUTION THAT ENDORSE FREE SPEECH, AND CIVIL LIBERTIES FOR ALL IT CITIZENS, HOWEVER IF THIS NATION

ALLOW FORMER PRESIDENT CLINTON TO BE ELECTED TO THIRD TERM THROUGH HIS WIFE STATUS, THIS COUNTRY WILL SUFFER ONE OF THE MOST TRAUMATIC TRAGEDIES OF ALL TIMES, BECAUSE REGARDLESS TO THE PERSON ELECTED DEMOCRAT OR REPUBLICAN MUST BE A STRONG LEADER, IN ALL PHASES,NOT SOME GAME PLAYING PLAGIARIZERS OF EACH OTHER AND MIMICKING THE ROOSEVELTS, WITH SHOW OFF GRAND STANDING THAT WAS A DISGRACE AT MRS. CORETTA SCOTT HOWEVER IN THE NEAR FUTURE YOU CAN LOOK FOR SAXOPHONE (BLOWING) AND HOLDING BLACK BABIES, ALSO VISITS TO THE MOURNERS BENCH IN AFRICAN AMERICANS CHURCHES, AND LITERALLY MAKING PROMISES THAT ONLY THE CONGRESS CAN RATIFY BASED ON THE CONSTITUTION, PIRATICALLY HAVING TO DO WITH THE CITIZENS OF THIS NATION, BECAUSE EVERY ONE IS ENTILED TO THE SAME TREATMENT, AND COMPENSATION, FROM THE FEDERAL AND ST. TE GOVERNMENTS REGARDS TO CIVIL LIBERTIES,I HAVE NEVER UNDERSTOOD SOME AFRICAN AMERICANS BEING INDOCTRINATED BY DEMOCRATS HAVING THEM BELIEVE THEY ARE SPECIAL, AND SHOULD BE IN A SPECIAL CLASS OF THEIR OWN,RELATED TO GOVERNMENTAL AFFAIRS, THERE IS NOTHING IN THE CONSTITUTION ENDORSE SEPERATE BUT EQUAL. AND NEVER WILL BE, THIS POLITICAL DEMAGOGUERY DEPLOYED BY THE DEMOCRATIC POLITICAL SLAVE MASTERS HAS HERDED BLACK VOTES FOR YEARS, ON FALSE PRETENCES, AND IT IS NO ONE FAULT BUT STUPID BLACKS WHO LISTEN TO THESE SELF APPOINTED POLITICAL SLAVE DRIVERS, HERDING THEIR BLOC VOTES, FOR THEIR DEMOCRATIC POLITICAL MASTERS, BECAUSE IF THEY WOULD TAKE JUST A FIEW MOMENTS OF THEIR BUISY SCHEDULE AND READ THE CONSTITUTION THEY WOULD UNDER STAND IT (FORBID) PARTIALITY,SO WHAT EVER DIVIDENDS ARE AWARDED THROUGH THECONGRES SS IS FOR EVERY CITIZEN IN THE UNITED STATES OF AMERICA, AND HOW THE MAJORITY OF AFRICAN AMERICANS CAN JUSTIFY THAT THE DEMOCRATS HAS BEEN THEIR PARTY OF PROSPERITY IS BEYOND COMPREHENSION, IT IS AN ALLUSION ADOPTED TO DECEIVE BASED ON THEIR

INABILITY TO UNDERSTAND THE FUNDAMENTALS OF THE GOVERNMENT AND RELYING ON OTHERS . TO CHOOSE FOR THEM,SOME AFRICAN AMERICANS HAVE CREATED A HERDING PROCESS AMONG THEM SELVES THAT IS DETRIMENTAL TO THEIR WELL BEING, AND IS TO STUPID TO REALIZE THE REPRECUSSIONS,IF YOU ARE AN AFRICAN AMERICAN YOU HAVE WORKED ALL OF YOUR LIFE RAISED A FAMILY,MADE IT POSSIBLE FOR YOUR CHILDREN TO GET AN EDUCATION, THEY ARE INDEPENDANT IN THEIR OWN RIGHT, OTHER DYSFUNCTIONAL MINDED HERDING BLACKS WILL LABEL YOU AS TRYING TO BE WHITE, BECAUSE THEY ARE TO IGNORANT TO UNDERSTAND THE BASICS OF WHAT THIS COUNTRY HAVE TO OFFER, AND MOST OF THESE TRASHY MIS-FITS WILL LABEL ALL WHITE PEOPLE AS RACIST, AND THIS PROPAGANDA HAVE MOVE UP THE LADDER TO SOME AFFLUENT EDUCATED BLACKS, AND A SYNDROME WAS HATCHED TO THE AFFECT THAT WHITE FOLKS DONT LIKE ME BECAUSE I GOT SOMETHING AND IS BLACK, OR JUST PLAIN WHITES DONT LIKE ME BECAUSE I AM BLACK, THIS OUTRAGEOUS CHARACTERIZATION IS NOTHING MORE THAN A STUPEFIED MYTH BRAUGHT ON BY A ANCESTRAL CULTURE THAT WISHES TO BE IN CHARGE OF OTHERS, TO DOMINATE WITH STUPIDITY.

THERE IS NO DENYING RACISM EXIST IN THIS COUNTRY AND AROUND THE WORLD ALWAYS HAVE AND WILL BE FOREVER, UNFORTUNATELY BLACKS USE RACE TO CULTIVATE THEIR IMAGE, IN ORDER TO ESTABLISH A HERDING PROCESS FOR THEIR OWN PERSONAL GAIN,IN ORDER TO ACCESS PROSPERITY FROM THEIR OWN RACE OF PEOPLE,BECAUSE THEIR IDEOLOGY OF MOVING YOU OUT OF POVITY BY BLASTING THE WHITE MAN WITH RACIST TACTICS OF HINDRANCE, HAS BEEN POUNDED INTO THE SAND BY THE CONSTITUTION AND CONGRESS, SO THEIR DICTATED PROMISES IS NOTHING MORE THAN NONSENSICAL RUBBISH, AND MOST WHITES DO NOT DESPISE AFRICAN AMERICANS BECAUSE OF THEIR COLOR, IT IS BECAUSE OF THEIR IGNORANCE, AND CUNNING DECEPTIVE LACKADAISICAL BEHAVIOR.

OVER THE YEARS I HAVE QUESTION MANY, MANY,BLACKS ABOUT THE RISE OF AFRICANS AMERICANS TO POLITICAL POWER, PIRATICALLY MAIN STREAM SUCH AS FORMER JOINT CHIEF OF STAFF AND SECRETARY OF STATE COLEN POWELL, AND CONDOLEEZZA RICE, FORMER SECURITY ADVISER TO THE PRESIDENT AND NOW SECRETARY OF STATE, THESE AFRICAN AMERICANS ARE PIONEERS IN THEIR APPOINTED POSITIONS BY A REPUBLICAN PRESID ENT, NEVER IN THE HISTORY OF THIS COUNTRY HAS AN AFRICAN AMERICAN HELD THOSE POSITIONS.

AND FOR SOME AFRICAN AMERICANS IT MEAN ABSOUTELY NOTHING BECAUSE OF THEIR PARTY AFFILIATIONS, IT IS ALL TO OFTEN BLACKS FORM AN OPINION BASED ON HEARSAY, THERE ARE RENOWN FOR CHILD DID YOU HEAR OR I WAS TOLD, THIS DISINGENUOUS PRACTICE HAS DRIVEN AFRICAN AMERICANS TO THE BACK SEAT OF THE BUS OVER THE YEARS, MEANING THE MAJORITY OF THE TIME THEIR ASSESSMENT OF OCCURRENCES IS FAR FETCHED AND REMOTE, AND THIS DISGUSTING TRAIT IS RESPONSIBLE FOR THEIR INABILITY TO FOCUS ON REALITY, OVER THE YEARS I HAVE QUESTION MANY, MANY, AFRICAN AMERICANS ABOUT THE RISE OF POLITICAL ADVANCEMENT AVAILABLE TO BLACKS, MEANING POSITIONING TO BECOME PRESIDENT ONE DAY, AND MOST WILL INSTINCTIVELY REFER TO SOME WARMED OVER BELLIGRENT SELF APPOINTED BLACK LEADER WHICH KNOWS AS MUCH ABOUT POLITICS AS I DO ABOUT FLYING A JUMBO JET, THEIR INABILITY TO SCRUTINIZE POLICITIANS ON THEIR MERIT HAS BEEN A TERRIBLE DISADVANTAGE AND CAUSED ONE PARTY TO MONOPOLIZE THEIR BLOC VOTING, BASED ON LIES AND DECEIT, IN QUESTIONING MANY BLACKS ABOUT THEIR PARTY AFFILIATIONS THAT HAS BEEN ON THEIR JOB FOR FORTY YEARS AND HAS MONEY STUFFED UNDER THE MATTRESS TO CHOKE A HORSE, AND THE FIRST THING COME TO THEIR MIND IF WE DONT GET GEORGE BUSH OUT OF OFFICE WE ARE GOING TO STARVE TO DEATH, AND THE NEXT QUESTION IS HOW ABOUT COLEN POWELL AND CONDOLEEZZA RICE, THEY ARE POLITICAL SMART AND INTELLECTUALLY CAPABLE OF BEING PRESIDENT, AND THEIR GROWTH TOWARD THAT

ACCOMPLISHMENT IS ACCREDITED TO PRESIDENT GEORGE BUSH, AND THIS IS SOME OF THE RESPONSES YOU GET, THEY ARE OK BUT THEY ARE WITH THE WRONG PARTY, OR THEY ARE NOTHING MORE THAN PUPPETS, AND THEY ARE WHITE FOLKS NIGGERS, THIS EMPHATICALLY IS A DYSFUNCTIONAL SICKNESS WITH SOME BLACKS THAT IS INCURABLE, WHICH CAST THEM IN A DUNCE SITUATION AROUND THE WORLD.

AND TO ADD TO INSULT THEY WILL INSINUATE THEY ARE UP THERE IN THE WHITE HOUSE BUT THEY ARE NOT ONE OF (US) AND IS NOT GOING TO DO ANYTHING FOR US, THIS KIND OF GUTLESS PUKE SCOOPED FROM THE DUNG PILES OF AFRICA IN ORDER TO IMPUGN THE INTEGRITY OF THESE FINE POPLE, GIVE YOU A DEFINABLE UNDERSTANDING OF WHY THE DEMOCRATS IMPEDED PROGRESS FOR SOME AFRICAN AMERICANS FOR SO LONG. AND THE IMPLICATION ARE SUCH THAT THE ONES ARE SUFFERING IN THE SLUM GETTO THROUGOUT THE NATION DUG THIS PIT FOR THEM SELVES, BCAUSE OF A SELF CONCEITED STUPID IDEOLOGY OF BANNING TOGATHER AS ONE AND DEGRADING OTHER BLACKS THAT IS SMART ENOUGH NOT TO ACCEPT THEIR FOOLISH WAY OF THINKING, THESE PEOPLE ANIMALISTIC AND HAVE NO APPRECIATION FOR THEIR BIRTH RIGHT IN THE UNITED STATES OF AMERICA, AND HYPOTHETICALLY SPEAKING IF IT WAS POSSIBLE THEY SHOULD BE BANNED FROM THIS COUNTRY AND RETURNED TO THE DUNG PITS OF AFRICA AND SOME WOULD NOT BLEND THERE, BECAUSE SOME PARTS OF AFRICA IS CIVILIZE.

AS A CHILD GROWING UP IN WESTERN ALABAMA, I HAD THE OCCASION TO EXPERIENCE ONE OF THE MOST TELLING TRUTHS ABOUT SOME BLACKS FROM A WHITE MAN DURING THE LATE FORTIES, HE WAS CONSIDERED TO BE ONE OF THE MOST RACIST AND HATRED OF BLACKS EVER, THE TERMINOLOGY AWARDED TO HIM BY BLACKS, A PROMINENT FAMILY OF AFRICAN AMERICANS OWNED HUNDREDS ACRES OF LAND, THE ONE THAT HAD SCHOOLING AND THE STABILITY TO SUSTAIN PASSED AWAY, AFTER HIS DEMISE THE OTHERS BORROWED MONEY ON THE LAND AS COLLATERAL, THEY DID NOT FULFILL THE THE

FINACIAL OBLIGATION SO FORECLOSURE PREVALIED, AND HE PURCHASED THE LAND MOVED INTO THE AREA, AND BUILT A MERCANTILE STORE AND BEHIND THE COUNTER HE STORED A BULL WHIP TO WHIP BLACKS, IF YOU MENTION HIS NAME IT RANG OUT LIKE A BELL AMONG BLACKS, HE IS MEAN AND HE HATE NIGGERS, MY PARENTS INSISTED I NOT GO TO THAT STORE, HOWEVER BEING THE TYPE OF PERSON THAT I AM INDIPENDANT AND INVESTIGATIVE MINDED I DISOBEYED THEIR INSTRUCTIONS, AND ENTERED THE STORE.

WE SPOKE AND HE ASKED MY NAME, I TOLD HIM AND HE ASK IF I LIVED IN THE AREA, I DID HIS NEXT QUESTION WAS HOW MAY I HELP YOU, I RESPONDED I AM JUST LOOKING AROUND, REALLY JUST BEING NOSEY BECAUSE I DIDNT HAVE ANY MONEY, HOWEVER I DID ADD JOBS AFTER SCHOOL AND EARNED FUNDS, SO HE ASKED DO SEE ANY THING YOU LIKE I SAID YES SIR, BUT I CANT PAY TODAY, HE SAID GET WHAT YOU NEED AND PAY ME LATER THAT WAS TEMPTING , SO I PICKED OUT SOME THINGS MOSTLY CANDY AND COOKIES ECT. AND DEPARTED, NOW THERE WERE ONE OTHER STORE APPROXIMATELY THREE HONDRED YARDS FROM HIS BUT THEY NEVER LET BLACKS HAVE CREDIT ESPECIALLY KIDS, SO I MET WITH MY FRIENDS AND WE HAD A SNAK PARTY AND FINALLY SOME ONE ASKED WHERE DID YOU GET THE SNAKS, I TOLD THEM I BOUGHT THEM AT THE OTHER STORE, BECAUSE IF WORD REACHED BACK TO MY PARENTS THAT I HAD BEEN SHOPPING IN THAT STORE I WOULD HAVE BEEN GROUND INTO SAUSAGE, SO THE NEXT COUPLE DAYS I RODE MY BIKE BACK TO THE STORE AND TOLD MR. COOPER I DID NOT HAVE HIS MONEY TODAY BUT SATURDAY I WOULD PAY, HE RESPONDED BY SAYING THATS OK IF YOU SEE ANY THING ELSE YOU WANT GET IT AND I WILL SEE YOU SATURDAY, I PICKED SOME MORE THINGS AND ASKED HOW MUCH WAS MY TOTAL BILL, HE TOLD ME AND I LEFT, THAT SATURDAY I RETURNED WITH HIS MONEY, HE CAME FROM BEHIND THE COUNTER AND PUT HIS HAND ON MY SHOULDER AND STATED YOU ARE JUST A KID AND YOU ARE DIFFERENT THAN THE OTHERS INCLUDING THE ADULTS, NOW THE THINGS YOU OWE ME

FOR IS ON THE HOUSE FOR YOU BEING TO YOUR WORD, SO FROM THAT DAY ON WE BECAME THE BEST OF FRIENDS, IF HE HAD SOMETHING NEEDED I CHOOSE IT AND PAID HIM FOR IT MOSTLY ON TIME, HOWEVER I LOST A LOT OF MY ASSOCIATES BECAUSE THEY BEGAN TO LABEL ME AS A WHITE FOLKS NIGGER.

MANY TIMES MY PARENTS WOULD ASK ME IF I HAD HEARD OF A WHIPPING IN THE STORE I KNEW BUT I COLD NOT TELL THEM, FINALLY ONE AFTER NOON I STOPED IN THE STORE, HE SAID TO ME THAT HE WANTED TO SHOW ME SOMETHING TO COME LOOK OUT THE BACK DOOR, I DID AND HE ASKED ME IF I NEW THE FELLOW SNEAKING THROUGH THE WOODS I SAID YES HE SAID TO ME WHEN YOU SEE HIM TELL I SAID BRING ME MY MONEY OR LET ME KNOW WHEN HE WILL PAY, THE SAME AFTERNOON I SAW THE PERSON AND GAVE HIM THE MESSAGE, I CANT REPEAT WHAT HE SAID, (*******) I DIDNT TELL HIM TO LET ME HAVE IT ANYWAY, THE NEXT AFTERNOON I DID NOT TELL WHAT HE SAID BUT I LET HIM KNOW I TOLD THE FELLOW, HE ASKED ME TO HAVE A SEAT BECAUSE HE WANTED TO TALK TO ME, HE SAID ERNEST YOU ARE JUST A KID YOU HAVE A LONG WAY TO GO IN LIFE, BUT WHAT EVER YOU DO OR WHERE YOU GO, DO YOUR BEST TO MEET THE WORLD HEAD ON, IF YOU MAKE A TRANSACTION TRY LIKE HELL TO KEEP YOUR END OF THE BARGIN, HE BECAME A LITTLE EMOTIONAL, AND STATED THAT I HAVE NO RIGHT TO WHIP ANY ONE IT IS WRONG, BUT WHAT EVER IS IN THIS STORE IT BELONG TO ME, BLACKS WILL COME IN AND GET CREDIT AND WHEN THEY GET MONEY THEY WILL SNEAK THROUGH THE WOODS AND GO TO THE NEXT STORE, AND PAY CASH FOR THEIR GOODS, BECAUSE THEY WILL NOT LET BLACKS HAVE CREDIT, SO THEY SPEND THEIR CASH THERE AND WHEN THEY ARE BROKE AGAIN, THEN HERE THEY COME ASKING FOR MORE CREDIT FROM ME, SO THAT IS WHY I WANTED YOU TO SEE THE FELLOW SNEAKING THROUGH THE WOODS, AND ALL THEY HAVE TO DO IS COME IN AND PAY SOME ON THEIR ACCOUNT AND GET MORE ITEMS, HE PAUSED AND STATED , WHITE PEOPLE DO NOT HATE BLACKS BECAUSE OF COLOR, THEY DISLIKE THEM BECAUSE

THEIR STUPID IDEOLOGY, THEY FEEL WHAT IS THEIRS IS THEIRS AND WHAT IS YOURS IS IS THEIRS ALSO, AND IF YOU DONT LET THEM USE YOU THEN YOU ARE A RACIST, AND YOU HATE THEM BECAUSE THEY ARE BLACK, HE ALSO STIPULATED WITH NO OFFENSE, BLACKS ARE TO STUPID AND ARROGANT TO REALIZE THAT THEIR PROBLEMS ARE SELF IMPOSED.

HE ALSO STATED IF YOU STAY OUT OF TROUBLE GET AN EDUCATION, AND MOST OF ALL FIGURE OUT HOW TO EARN YOUR WAY THROUGH LIFE, AND NEVER LET WHAT SOME ONE ELSE HAVE BOTHER YOU, BECAUSE IT IS THEIRS PREPARE YOUR SELF TO GET YOUR OWN, AND FOR GOD SAKE DO NOT LISTEN TO SOME ONE TELL YOU HOW TO LIVE YOUR LIFE, PIRATICALLY YOUR OWN PEOPLE, BECAUSE MOST OF THEM WANT WHAT SOME ONE ELSE HAVE BECAUSE OF THEIR INABILITY TO GET THEIR OWN, AND THIS HAS BECAME A WAY WAY OF LIFE FOR THEM, AND HE SAID AS YOU GET OLDER YOU WILL UNDERSTAND, HE ALSO MENTION ONE OTHER THING I THOUGHT WAS VERY INTERESTING REGARDS TO THE LAND HE BOUGHT, IT WAS IN FORECLOSURE SO HE PURCHASED THE LAND FROM THE LEAN HOLDER, I KNEW HE WASNT LYING BECAUSE WE HAD HEARD OF THEIR FINANCIAL PROBLEMS, HOWEVER OTHER BLACKS CAST A NET OVER HIS HEAD AND IMPUGN HIS INTEGRITY AND SAID HE STOLE THE LAND FROM BLACKS BECAUSE HE HATED NIGGERS AND THAT IS THE WAY WHITE FOLKS DO YOU WHEN YOU HAVE SOMETHING THEY WANT THEY CHEAT YOU OUT OF IT, SO BECAUSE OF THEIR LYING STEALING, CHEATING HIM OUT OF HIS GOODS BY NOT PAYING, HE KEPT A SHOT GUN AND BULL WHIP BEHIND THE COUNTER, AND HAD NO RESERVATION ABOUT USING EITHER ONE.

SOME AFRICAN AMERICANS HAS BECAME OBSESS WITH CHEATING STEALING AND LYING PIRATICALLY ABOUT RACE, AND THEY THINK IF THEY USE THE RACE CARD ENOUGH WHITES WILL BACK OFF AND LET THEM TURN THE UNITED STATES INTO A THIRD WORLD COUNTRY, HOWEVER THIS WILL NEVER HAPPEN BUT SOME ARE FOOLISH ENOUGH TO BELIEVE THAT IT WILL HAPPEN,

AND ONE SUCH PERSON IS CITY COUNCILMAN CHARLES BARRON DEMOCRAT FROM NEW YORK, ON APRIL 11, 2006, HE PROPOSED PEOPLE OF COLOR WILL DRIVE THE WHITE MAN INTO A STATE OF OBLIVION, AND RULE THE COUNTRY AND THIS IS NOTHING MORE THAN STUPID DEMOCRATIC POLITICAL SLAVE DRIVING RHETORIC TO HERD BLACKS AND HISPANICS TOGATHER FOR THEIR VOTING BLOC.

BECAUSE SENATOR HILLARY CLINTON HAVE ALREADY ADDRESS THE FACT HOW STUPID SHE THINK HISPANICS ARE, SHE WENT NATIONAL TO TELL THE WORLD THAT HISPANICS ARE GOOD FOR NOTHING BUT TO SCRUB YOUR FLOORS, WAITE YOUR TABLES, MAKE YOUR BEDS, AND A VARIETY OF DEGRADING GESTURES, AND TO INSINUATE THATS ALL THESE PEOPLE ARE CAPABLE OF DOING IS ABSURD AND NONSENSICAL, HOWEVER THAT HAS BEEN THE IDEOLOGY ABOUT AFRICAN AMERICANS FROM DEMOCRATS FOR ALMOST FOUR HUNDRED YEARS, AND SOME BLACKS ARE TO STUPID TO DETECT THIS SICKNESS, SO NOW THEIR INTENTIONS ARE TO RECRUIT HISPANICS INTO THIS SAME CATEGORY, AND THEY HAVE THEIR BLACK POLITICAL BOOT LICKERS LEADING THE CHARGE SUCH AS CHARLES BARRON, AND A TON OF OTHERS.

SHE VERY WELL LET HER AMBITIONS BE KNOWN BY RELATING TO PLANTATION. WHICH IS NOTHING MORE THAN A WORD BUT ITS THE INTENT BEHIND THE WORD, UNFORTUNATELY SOME BLACKS ARE DOOMED TO THIS OBSESSION BUT I THINK HISPANICS ARE NOT GOING TO BE REALED IN BY THIS TRICKERY FROM DEMOCRATS,SENATOR TED KEENEDY AND SENATOR CLINTON, ARE BEATING THE STUMP IN AN EFFORT TO HERD HISPANICS IN THE SAME MESMERIZED POLITICAL SITUATION ALONG WITH AFRICAN AMERICANS, THEN THEY WILL HAVE TWO NATIONALLY OF PEOPLE UNDER THEIR POLITICAL SPELL FOR VOTES, IF THEY WERE SO EQUALITY MINDED WHY DID THEY TRY TO BLOCK THE NOMINATION OF ROBERTO GONZALES TO BEING ATTORNEY GENERAL, NOT TO MENTION SECTARY OF STATE CONDOLEEZZA RICE, SENATOR BARBARA BOXER IS STILL HEMORRHAGING AND FOAMING AT THE MOUTH, REGARDS TO HER NOMINATION, I THINK EVERY TIME

SENATOR BOXED SEE THIS WOMAN SHE DEVELOP SOME KIND OF ABNORMALITY, NOW THIS IS A FINE EXAMPLE OF RACISM THAT IS CAMOUFLAGED AND OFTEN ERUPT SIMPLY BECAUSE SHE IS ONE ASTUTE INTELLECTUAL ACADEMIC AFRICAN AMERICAN WOMAN, THAT IS IN CONTROL.

AND UNDER STAND THE POLITICAL SYSTEM IN THE UNITED STATES OF AMERICA AND AROUND THE WORLD WITH AFFLUENT AUTHORITY, AND HAS STRUCK FEAR IN ALL DEMOCRATS, SHE HAS THEM BACK ON THEIR HEELS SNORTING LIKE A RAGING BULL FEAR SHE MIGHT RUN FOR THE PRESIDENCY, AND ALL DUE RESPECT THESE DEMOCRATIC PICKING. AND HAMMERING PRESIDENT BUSH WITH WHOPPERS ON A CONSISTENT DAILY BASIS, IT IS NOT ABOUT HIM, THEY HAVE NOTHING ON SECRETARY OF STATE RICE, SO THEY KEEP SLINGING MUD HOPING TO MUDDY MS. RICE POLITICAL FUTURE, THERE ARE SOME IN THE DEMOCRAT PARTY WOULD RATHER SEE OUR GOVERNMENT OVER THROWN THAN SEE AN AFRICAN AMERICAN BECOME PRESIDENT, AND THIS IS THE MAIN REASON THEY DESPISE PRESIDENT GEORGE BUSH BECAUSE HE HAS MADE THIS POSSIBLE, NEVER IN THEIR WILDEST DREAMS AS FAR AS THEY ARE CONCERNED NO AFRICAN AMERICAN COULD BE THIS SMART, BECAUSE MOST OF THEIR DEALINGS HAS BEEN WITH DYSFUNCTIONAL MINDED AND BARBARIC BOOT LICKING BLACKS CONCERINIG POLITICS, DURING THE TIME SHE WAS THE PRESIDENT SECURITY ADVISOR THE DEMOCRATS KNEW VERY LITTLE ABOUT HER, SO THEY WERE FOAMING AT THE MOUTH LIKE A MALE HOG AROUND A SOW IN HEAT, FOR HER TO TESTIFY ABOUT THE BEGINNING OF THE IRAQI CONFLICT AND WEPONS OF MASS DISTRUCTION AND WHAT SHE KNEW, FINALLY SHE DID AND I SUSPECT MOST OF THE DEMOCRATS LEFT THINKING SHE WAS WEARING A DISGUISE, BECAUSE OCCASIONALLY THEY WOULD RATTLE FORMER SECTARY OF STATE CQLEN POWELL, BUT MS. RICE RANG THEIR BELL WITH TENACITY, SUPERIOR DIALECT, COUNTERED THEIR ATTACKS WITH BLISTERING SUMMATIONS, AND NEVER FALTERED ALSO LEFT THE DEMOCRATS IN SHAMBLES, AND THEY HAD ANOTHER GO AT IT WHEN SHE WAS CHOSEN

FOR SECTARY OF STATE, DURING HER CONFORMATION, THE DEMOCRATS LEFT IN A STATE SHOCK WITH TAILS TUCKED NEEDING A RABIES SHOT AND THEY BEEN MAD DOGGING EVERY SENSE, BECAUSE NO AFRICAN AMERICAN IN THEIR BELIEF IS SUPPOSED TO BE THAT INTELLECTUAL WITH POLITICAL DIPLOMACY, AND KICK SAND IN THEIR FACE.

SO KNOW THE DEMOCRATS ARE DOGGING PRESIDENT GEORGE BUSH FOR BRINGING HER ON BOARD, AND KEEP BLOWING HOT AIR ABOUT HIS LEGACY NO WONDER SOME BLACKS ARE SO STUPID BECAUSE THEY LEARNED FROM THE DEMOCRATS, SO IF HE NEVER DO ANY THING FOR THE REST OF HIS TERM BUT HIDE THE SHOT GUNS FROM VICE PRESIDENT DICK CHANEY, THEIR LEGACY IS CARVED IN STONE, WITH THE TRADITIONAL ASPIRATIONS OF THE REPUBLICAN PARTY, PIRATICALLY FOR AFRICAN AMERICANS, PRESIDENT ABRAHAM LINCOLN FREED THEM FROM BONDAGE, AND PRESIDENT GEORGE BUSH GAVE THEM THE OPPORTUNITY TO EXERCISE THEIR ABILITY TO PERFORM AT THE HIGHEST LEVEL IN THE POLITICAL ARENA EVER, THIS IS A MILESTONE THAT NO PRESIDENT HAS EVER ATTEMPTED IN THE HISTORY OF THE UNITED STATES OF AMERICA.

AND THIS IS WHAT HAS CAST A SPELL ON DEMOCRATS, WHILE THEY BEAT ON THEIR BLACK PORCH MONKEYS IN AN ATTEMPT TO WATER THIS HISTORICAL EVENT DOWN, BY NAME CALLING AND SHOWING NO RESPECT FOR THEIR ABILITY TO PERFORM, WHILE THE WORLD OF NATIONS HAS GIVEN THEM 0VERWHELMING SUPPORT REGARDS TO DIPLOMACY, AND THE ASTUTE ABILITY TO PERFORM, HOWEVER THESE BLACK POLITICAL DEMOCRATIC BOOT LICKING CRITICS SHOULD STILL BE ON THE PLANTATION SLOPPING HOGS, AND I DOUBT COULD GET THE JOB DONE WHEN THERE IS AN ARROW POINTING WITH THE WORD TILT WRITTEN ALL OVER THE BUCKET, PRESIDENT GEORGE BUSH HAS DEALT THE DEMOCRATS ANOTHER ANXIETY REPRECUSSION, WHICH COULD BE A THORN IN THEIR SIDE FOR DECADES, HAVING TO DO WITH THE SUPREME COURT WHICH HE APPOINTED TWO VERY KEY JUSTICES,

IN JUSTICE ROBERTS AND JUSTICE OLITO, HISTORICALLY THE DEMOCRATS HAS RULED WITH THEIR RADICAL LIBERAL IDEOLOGY THROUGH THE COURTS, PIRATICALLY THE SUPREME COURT, BECAUSE OF THEIR STRONG TIES TO THE SUPREME COURT IN 1896,THE COURT RULED IN FAVOR OF THE DEMOCRATS SYSTEM OF JIM CROW DOCTRINE SEPERATE BUT EQUAL AND THE DENIAL OF AFRICAN AMERICANS VOTING RIGHTS, AND DEFINED SOUTHERN RACE RELATIONS THROUGOUT THE FIRST HALF OF THE NINETEENTH CENTURY, AND PRESIDENT FRANKLIN ROOSEVELT OWNED THE SUPREME COURT UNTIL HIS DEMISE, THIS TRADITION OF SEPARATE BUT EQUAL FELICIATED BY THE DEMOCRATS IN 1896 LASTED UNTIL 1954, WITH A REVISIT BY THE SUPREME COURT IN BROWN V. BOARD OF EDUCATION, STRUCK DOWN THIS SOUTHERN DEMOCRATIC IDEOLOGY OF SEPERATE BUT EQUAL PERTAINING TO WHITE AND BLACK FACILITIES, HOWEVER IT APPEAR THAT SOME AFRICAN AMERICANS ARE OF THE OPENION THAT THIS CRITERION SHOULD BE REINSTITUTED IN THE SCHOOL SYSTEM, BECAUSE NEBRASKA HAS ARE IN THE PROCESS OF LEGISLATING THIS DEBACLE, BECAUSE IT IS THOUGHT BY SOME BLACKS THAT THEY ARE BETTER SUTTED TO INSTRUCT THEIR OWN NATIONALLY, SO ACCORDING TO THE MEDIA WHITES, HISPANICS, AND BLACKS HAVE BEEN DEVIDED ACCORDINGLY PER. THE SCHOOL SYSTEM, I SUSPECT BLACKS ARE CELEBRATING, AND I AM CERTAIN WHITES ARE EVEN MORE REJOICED, BECAUSE IT IS THE AFRICAN AMERICANS THATS GOING TO LOOSE A GENERATION OF YOUNG PEOOPLE TO STUPIDITY AND POVITY, AND I AM CERTAIN THE DEMOCRATS ARE ELATED, BECAUSE WITH 98% OF BLACKS BELINGING TO THEIR OBSESSION FOR POLITICAL POWER AND BLACK ON BLACK IN THE CLASS ROOM, THEIR INCENTIVE WILL BE REINFORCED FOR BLOC VOTING SUPPORT FROM BLACKS BUT TRUST ME THERE IS A SEVERE HEAVY PRICE TO PAY FOR AFRICAN AMERICANS LIKE NEVER BEFORE, BECAUSE IF THIS INSANITY TAKE HOLD THROUGOUT THE NATION WITH ONLY BLACKS TEACHING BLACKS, WHICH MOST ARE NOT QUALIFIED TO TEACH FUNDAMENTAL

DIVERSITY, IN ORDER FOR A CHILD TO ADJUST REGARDS TO A VERNACULAR WHICH IS ABSOLUTELY NECESSARY TO PREPARE YOUNG CAPABLE PEOPLE OF SUSTAINING AN OPEN MIND TO COMMUNICATE ON A SOPHISTICATED LEVEL WITH ALL PEOPLE, BECAUSE THE MAJORITY OF BLACKS HAVE A INFERIORITY COMPLEX REGARDS TO WHITES, SO AS A RESULT WITH PREDOMINANTLY BLACK INSTRUCTORS THIS RESENTMENT WILL ESCULATE INTO MORE POVITY AND GETTO SLUMS, BECAUSE SOME STUPID AFRICAN AMERICANS SEEM NOT TO RECOGNIZE THAT THE INDUSTRIALIZATION REST ON THE SHOULDERS OF THE DOMINATING CAUCASIANS WHICH FOR CENTURIES HAS DEVELOPED A CIVIL DIVERSE SOCIETY, THAT IS DIFFICULT FOR SOME AFRICAN AMERICANS TO UNDERSTAND, SO THEY ARE CONSTANTLY TRYING TO INSTITUTE THEIR OWN FOOLISH BONE IN THE NOSE IDEOLOGY, AND FORGETTING THE CONSTITUTION AND THE PEOPLE THAT ARE THE FINANCIERS AND CONTROL ALL THE ADVANTAGES AND RESOURCES, THE MOST IMPORTANT ATTRIBUTES SOME BLACKS NEGLECT TO REALIZE AND THAT IS (CULTURE) GENES DICTATE THE PERSON YOU SHOULD BECOME IN LIFE, CAUCASIAN ARE A CULTURED SOCIETY OF PEOPLE, PIRATICALLY IN THE UNITED STATES OF AMERICA, THEY SET THE STANDARD FOR THE ENTIRE WORLD BASED ON DIVERSITY,AND OUR CONSTITUTION IS GEARED TO THAT AFFECT, THE MAJORITY OF AFRICAN AMERICANS ARE MINAS THAT REFINED ANCESTRAL CULTURE, BECAUSE OF WHERE THEY CAME FROM AND THE CONDITIONS EXISTED IN THE UNITED STATES OF AMERICA, PERTAINING TO THEIR SURVIVAL, SO INSTEAD OF TRYING TO LEARN FROM THE PEOPLE THAT ORIGNATED CULTURE AND INCORPORATE THEM SELVES INTO A DIVERSE SOCIETY,THEY TEND TO HERD BEHIND A IDIOTIC SELF APPOINTED LEADER AND ARE CONVINCED THAT THEY HAVE THE QUALIFICATIONS EQUAL TO SUSTAIN IN A CULTURED DIPLOMATIC SOCIETY WITHOUT HAVING ALL THE VALUED NECESSITIES, AND TO BECOME ENGULFED IN THIS FOOLISHNESS CAN PROVE TO BE DETRIMENTAL IN MANY WAYS, PIRATICALLY REGARDS TO COMPETITIVE SUCCESS, THESE SYSTEMATIC MYTHS HAS

NEVER WORKED FOR AFRICAN AMERICANS, SO THEIR SELF APPOINTED BLACK CREEPS FORMULATE A STRATEGY TO BLAME EVERY ONE BUT THEMSELVES FOR THE FAILURE OF BLACKS, AND THIS MISGUIDED MISSION HAS DEVELOPED INTO EPIDEMIC PROPORTIONS FOR AFRICAN AMERICANS IN THIS COUNTRY, AND THERE IS NO END IN SIGHT,BECAUSE OF THE REPRODUCTIVE FUNCTIONS OF SELF APPOINTED DYSFUNCTIONAL MINDED LEADERS AND SPOKESMAN.

SOME AFRICAN AMERICANS ARE SO STUPID UNTIL THEY HAVENT THE ABILITY TO DISTINGUISH BETWEEN CULTURAL IDENTITY,AND THE ACT OF IMITATING, BECAUSE THE TERM MOST COMMONLY USED WHEN YOU DISAGREE WITH THEIR ASSESSMENT OF VALUES, IS THAT HE, SHE, OR THEY ARE TRYING TO BE WHITE, THIS KIND OF INSANITY DEMOTE THE FEASIBILITY OF SOME BLACKS EVER BEING LURED AWAY FROM THIS SEPERATE BUT EQUAL MENTALITY, WHICH GENERATE HOSTILITY TOWARD WHITES AND SUCCESSFUL BLACKS AND IT IS ALL DUE TO THEIR FAILURE TO UNDERSTAND THE AFFLUENT MECHANISM OF A WELL ORGANIZED DIVERSE SOCIETY OF PEOPLE IN THE UNITED STATES OF AMERICA, AND THE MAJORITY OF THIS IGNORANCE CAN BE TRACED AND ACCREDITED TO FAMILY TRADITION, AND MOST OF ALL SELF APPOINTED LEADERS THAT HAS TAPPED INTO THIS INSANITY, THAT IS TAKING ADVANTAGE FOR THEIR OWN PERSONAL NOTORIETY AND FINANCIAL STABILITY, AND I SUSPECT SOME OF THESE BLACK IDEOLOGUES ARE SO DYSFUNCTIONAL MINDED UNTIL THEY DO NOT REALIZE WHAT ECONOMICAL HINDRANCE THEY ARE CAUSING THE PEOPLE THAT FOLLOW THIS LIBERAL RACIST MINDED SICKNESS, THAT IS CONSTANTLY PAVING THE ROAD TO THE GETTO SLUMS, BECAUSE THAT IS YOUR DESTINATION WHEN YOU ATTEMPT TO ISOLATE YOUR SELF FROM A WELL ORGANIZED DIVERSE SOCIETY WITH ZILLIONS OF FINANCIAL CAPABILITIES TO REFUTE THIS NONSENSICAL IDEOLOGY, ALONG WITH THE CONSTUTION AND THE CONGRESS OF THE UNITED STATES IN AMERICA, IF YOU ARE A NATIONALLY OF PEOPLE THAT RESIDE IN THE UNITED STATES OF AMERICA AS A CITIZEN, AND SOME ALLOW THEM SELVES TO CHOOSE AS FAMILIES,

OR INDEPENDENTLY TO BECOME INVOLVED IN POLITICAL FADDISH DEVOTIONS, WILL WITHOUT QUESTION PROHIBIT YOUR ADVANCING INTO A BROAD SCALE DIMENSION TO SUSTAIN ADEQUATELY IN A SYSTEM THAT WAS DESIGNED BY THE FORE FATHERS TO ERADICATE THESE NONSENSICAL FUNCTIONS FROM ERODING THE LEGITIMACY OF THE GOVERNMENT, BY INSTUTING A CONSTITUTION THAT IS INFORCED BY GROUPS OF ELECTED POLITICAL OFFICIALS, SUCH AS A PRESIDENT, SENATE, CONGRESSMAN, SUPREME COURT, AND STATES RIGHTS ADJUDICATED THROUGH THEIR COURTS, IT IS WELL DOCUEMENTED IN HISTORY THAT AFRICAN AMERICANS HAS HAD SERIOUS PROBLEMS REGARDS TO DISCRIMINATION, HOWEVER A LOT OF IT WAS BECAUSE OF THEIR OWN INEPTNESS TO BE SELECTIVE,. SUBORDINATE, AND ANALYTICALSQNTA /INDIVIDUAL BASIS, ALSO THEIR PSYCHOSIS DEFIANCE FOR EXISTING CONTROLLING GOVERNMENTS, IN ORDER TO BE TOLD WHAT THEY WERETO HEAR FROM AGGRESSIVE WHITE DEMOCRATIC POLITICAL MASTERS AND THEIR BLACK POLITICAL COUNTER PART SLAVE DRIVERS, WHICH LEAD TO ASTUTE OPPRESSION, BECAUSE THEIR PROMISES ARE OUT SIDE OF THE SYSTEM THAT IS CONTROLLED BY THE CONSTITUTION,AND WILL NEVER MATERIALIZE, SO THESE ANTICS ARE CONSIDERED TO BE MASS DECPTION ON A NATION WIDE BASIS.

APPROXIMATELY NINETY FIVE PRECENT OF BLACK OWNED BUISNESSES IN THE UNITED STATES OF AMERICA, ARE RAN INDEPENDENTLY BY THEM AND THEIR FAMILY MEMBERS, SO WITH THE EMERGING POPULATION OF HISPANICS IN THE COUNTRY THAT IS WILLING TO ACCEPT DIVERSITY, AND GOBBLING UP EVERY AVAILABLE POSITION JOB WISE, SOME AFRICAN AMERICANS ARE HEADED FOR A SLIPPERY SLOPE WORSE THAN SLAVERY ON THE PLANTATIONS IN THE SOUTHERN STATES DURING THE EIGHTEENTH CENTURY, AND IT IS BECAUSE OF THEIR REBELLIOUS DISPOSITION AND THEIR INEPTNESS TO RLATE,PRIMARILY BASED ON POLITICAL IGONORANCE, MEANING THE SYSTEM IS LIKE NIGHT AND DAY IT WAIT FOR NO ONE, SOME BLACKS HAVE HAD FRTY TWO YEARS

TO ADJUST TO THE CUSTOMS OF THIS NATION, BUT THEY HAVE BEEN TO BUISY TRYING TO CULTIVATE THEIR OWN, BEHIND BLACK POLITICAL DECEPTIVE LEADERS,THE FINAL NAIL IN THE COFFIN IS BEING DRIVEN BY THE STATE OF NEBRASKA AND THEIR LEGISLATORS.

ALONG WITH STATE SENATOR ERNIE CHAMBERS, EMPHATICALLY ENDORSING THIS ABSURDITY WITH CAMPASSION, HIS ASSESSMENT WAS THAT BLACKS ARE NOT COMPATIBLE TO WHITES EDUCATIONALLY BECAUSE THE SYSTEM IS ESTRANGE TO THEIR LEARNING CAPABILITIES, AND CLAIM TO RECTIFY WHAT WRONG WITH HIS PEOPLE BY ENDORSING SEPRATE BUT EQUAL LEGISLATION ON THE BASIS OF BLACKS BEING EDUCATED IN THEIR OWN ENVIRONMENT, WHEN QUESTIONED ABOUT SEPRATE BUT EQUAL HE SPUN THAT WITH THAT NOT THE CASE, THE LEGISLATION IS DISTORTED BECAUSE EVERY ONE MAY ATTEND THE SCHOOL OF THEIR CHOICE, HOWEVER HE ARRESTED THE RESPONSIBILITY COMPLETELY AWAY FROM PARENTS, AND DECIDED THAT HE KNOWS BEST WHAT IS GOOD FOR HIS PEOPLE, AND LEANED HEAVILY ON RACIST AMBIGUITY, WHICH CONFIRMS SUSPISIONS OF SOME BLACK POLITICAL SO CALL LEADERS HAVE INSERTED THEM SELVES INTO A MODERATORS ROLE FOR ALL AFRICAN AMERICANS, AND PERSUE EFFORTS TO SUGAR COAT THEIR INTENTIONS, AND HE WITH THE IMPLICATIONS CHILDREN CAN ATTEND ANY SCHOOL OF THEIR CHOICE WHICH IS TRUE, HOWEVER BLACKS TEND TO HERD AND THIS COME UNDER THE HEADING OF SEGREGATION BY CHOICE, AND ESSENTIALLY THERE WILL BE A MAJORITY OF BLACK INSTRUCTORS, HE ALSO INFERRED THAT WHITES ARE AHEAD OF BLACKS REGARDS TO SCHOOLING, I WONDER WHERE THIS STATE SENATOR HAS BEEN ALL OF HIS LIFE, AND WHAT THE HELL DID HE EXPECT, BLACKS WERE IN THE COTTON FIELDS KNOCING COTTON STALKS WHILE WHITES WERE IN SCHOOL, AND THIS IS NOT TO SAY AFRICAN AMERICANS CAN NOT EXCELL IN EDUCATION BECAUSE IT HAS BEEN PROVEN, BUT IT HAS TO BE IN AN ENVIROMENTAL SETTING THAT INCLUDE PARENTS THAT UNDERSTAND THE IMPORTANCE OF THEIR CHILDREN BEING EDUCATED ON

A DIVERSE LEVEL, BECAUSE THAT IS THE WAY THE NATION IS FORMATTED, IN EIGHTEEN HUNDRED AND NINETY FIVE BOOKER T. WASHINGTON PRESIDENT AND FOUNDER OF TUSKEGEE INSTITUTE,A BLACK COLLEGE IN ALABAMA AND ONE OF THE MOST INFLUENTIAL BLACK LEADERS OF THOSE TIMES, HE GAVE A SPEECH AT THE COTTON STATES EXPOSITION IN ATLANTA GEORGIA, AND FROM ALL INDICATIONS BASED ON HIS SPEECH HE ACCEPTED RACIAL SEGREGATION AND SECOND CLASS CITIZEN SHIP FOR ALL BLACKS IN THE SOUTH AS INEVITIBLE, AND THE SUPREME COURT ENDORSED HIS THINKING, AND THE JIM CROW RULE WAS BORN SCHOOL SEGREGATION AND IT LASTED FOR SIXTY NINE YEARS IN THE SOUTH, BY THE WAY AFTER BOOKER T. WASHINGTON GAVE HIS SPEECH AND BLACKS SEEN TO ADOPT IS IDEA WHITES WAS DANCING IN THE STREETS, AND I AM ALMOST CERTAIN THEY ARE TUNING THEIR FIDDLE IN NEBRASKA NOW, HOWEVER THIS IS NOT A CONDEMNATION OF STATE SENATOR ERNIE CHAMBERS, HE IS ENTITLED TO HIS OBSERVATION AND SUGGEST THAT HE KNOWS WHAT IS BEST FOR HIS PEOPLE, APPARENTLY HE IS (NOT) WELL VERSED ON THE PLIGHT OF HIS PEOPLE EGOISTIC ABILITY TO BE EDUCATED, IT COME UNDER THE HEADING OF LIKE HERDING CATS, I BASE MY ASSESSMENT ON BEING THERE IN THE SOUTH ATTENDING SCHOOL DURING THE EARLY FORTIES, ALSO ATTENDING INTEGRATED SCHOOLS IN THE NORTHERN STATES, SO AS A EYE WITNESS I AM QUITE CERTAIN SEPERATE BUT EQUAL IS (NOT) IN THE BEST INTEREST FOR AFRICAN AMERICANS, BECAUSE MOST BLACKS ARE SELF CONCEITED AND TEND TO REBEL FROM INSTRUCTIONS, I CAN RECALL VERY VIVIDLY DURING MY SCHOOL YEARS IN ALABAMA, KIDS WOULD BE ABSENT FROM SCHOOL FOR WEEKS AT A TIME AND WHEN THET DID REPORT THE TEACHER WOULD INQUIRE ABOUT THEIR ABSENTEEISM AND THE MAJORITY OF THEIR RESPONSES WOULD BE THAT THEIR PARENTS DIDNT SEE THE NEED TO LEARN WHITE FOLKS MESS, BECAUSE IT WASNT GOING TO DO THEM ANY GOOD ANY WAY, BECAUSE WHITE FOLKS OWNED EVERY THING, THIS NONSENSICAL IDEOLOGY TRANSENDS FROM A NONE

CULTURED CONTINENT OF DESCENDANTS DERIVED FROM AFRICA THAT IS EMBEDDED IN GENIC HEREDITY THAT HAUNT AFRICAN AMERICANS TODAY WHICH CAUSE SOME TO BE CIVILLY DISOBEDIENT, DURING THE SEVENTEENTH AND EIGHTEENTH CENTURIES, THE VAST MAJORITY OF AFRICAN AMERICANS PEOPLE IN AMERICA MAINTAINED AND PRACTICED THEIR TRADITIONAL AFRICAN BELIEFS.

WHICH HAVE NOT AND WILL NOT COINCIDE WITH A DIVERSE CIVIL SOCIETY SO STATE SENATOR CHAMBERS BEFORE YOU CAN EXTERMINATE A BLADE OF GRASS YOU MUST DISLODGE THE ROOT, SO INTEGRATED SCHOOLS HAVE ASSISTED IN REMOVING THE STIGMATIZATION FROM MANY BLACKS, BASED ON. THEIR AFFILIATIONS WITH WHITES, BECAUSE ON A ACADEMIC FRIENDLY ENDEAVOR THEY LEARN FROM EACH OTHER,AND AS A RESULT BLACKS LEARN THE BASICS OF DIVERSITY AND REFINEMENT, BECAUSE MOST WHITES TEACH THEIR CHILDREN CULTURE FROM BIRTH, IT IS RECORDED IN HISTORY THAT MOST SLAVES THAT COULD READ AND WRITE LEARNED FROM WHITE CHILDERN AFTER SCHOOL, IT WAS A TRADE OF THEY WOULD LEARN TO READ AND WRITE, AND THE WHITE KIDS WOULD BE TAUGHT THEIR AFRICAN TRADITIONS, THIS WAS CONSIDERED TO BE RESTRICTED DIVERSITY, HOWEVER IT CHARACTERIZED PROSPERITY UNDER INHUMANE CONDITIONS.

THERE IS A SEGMENT OF BLACKS ON THE HORIZON SEEMED TO HAVE BEEN DISORIENTED ABOUT THE DISCOVERY OF AMERICA, THEY ARE PROFILING TEIR INSINUATIONS AS IF AFRICAN AMERICAN DID, BY EXPLOITING VERBIAGE LIKE I, WE, US, AND MY PEOPLE, WITH THIS INSIDIOUS DEMAGOGUERY ONE WOULD THINK BLACKS DISCOVERED THIS COUNTRY AND THE WHITES STOLE IT AND THEY WANT IT BACK, BECAUSE THEY SET THE GUIDE LINES FOR HUMANITY, ORGANIZED THE PROCEDUAL INFASTRUCTURE, AND ARE THE ORDAINING BENEFACTORS OF CULTURE, ALL TO OFTEN BLACKS USE RACE TO TO COVER FOR THEIR MISCHIEVOUS IGNORANCE, AND I CANT THINK OF A BETTER EXAMPLE THAN CONGRESS WOMAN CYNTHIA MCKINNEY, HER CULTURAL DISCIPLINE

DISSIPATED INTO A DEPREDATED STATE OF MIND AND THE ONLY EXCUSE SHE COULD THINK OF FOR THIS KIND OF BEHAVIOR WAS THAT THE SECURITY GUARD TUCHED A BLACK WOMAN SIMPLY BECAUSE SHE IS BLACK AND A CONGRESS WOMAN, THESE TYPE OF ANXIETIES INVENTED BY SOME BLACKS IS DESPICABLE AND APPALLING, AND YOU HAVE THE BLACK BOOT LICKING HERDING,SYMPATHIZERS DEFENDING HER BARBARIC ACTIONS, WITH NO CONCERN FOR THE RESPONSIBILITES OF THE GUARD, AND THE SECURITY FOR THE PEOPLE THAT HE IS DEDICATED TO PROTECT, MOST BLACKS WHEN THEY CONNECT WITH THE ASPECTS OF POLITICAL AMBITIONS,THEY TEND TO ABUSE THEIR AUTHORITY REGARDS TO RACE, IN AN ASSERTED EFFORT TO ASSURE OTHER BLACKS THAT THEY ARE GOING TO JUSTIFY THE REASON FOR THEIR FAILURE IN LIFE, AND MOST OF THE TIME THEY FOCUS ON POVITY AND BLACKS OWNING THINGS, AS NEBRASKA STATE SENATOR ERNIE CHAMBERS, DECLARED ON FOX NEWS, APRIL 21, 2006, AS IF TO SAY ALL BLACKS ARE STILL IN BONDAGE, AS REPORTED HE CHAMBERS IS THE ONLY SPONSER OF THIS BILL ENDORSED BY THE SENATE, AND OF COURSE HE IS THE ONLY BLACK IN THE SENATE OF NEBRASKA, JESSIE JACKSON, AL SHARPETON, TAVIS SMILEY, BLACK CAUCUS, WHERE ARE YOU OF COURSE WE KNOW WHERE MR. JACKSON IS HE IS HIDING UNDERNEATH THE SKIRT OF THE SUPPOSEDLY RAPE VICTOM IN THE DUKE UNIVERSITY FIASCO, THIS SHOULD BE A WAKE UP CALL FOR ALL AFRICAN AMERICANS THAT THESE WORTHLESS CIVIL RIGHTS ADVDCATES THAT ARE POTENTIALLY STANDING BY FOOLISHLY LETTING ONE CLOWN ATTEMPT TO REVERSE HISTORY THAT TOOK ALMOST ONE HUNDRED YEARS AND MOST LIKELY THE LIFE OF DR. MARTIN LUTHER KING TO ACCOMPLISH.

AND THIS RADICAL POLITICAL MIS-FIT OF A POLITICIAN ERNIE CHAMBERS PUBICALLY TRYING TO ADOPT HIAPANICS AND CHARACTERIZE THEM AS BEING EQUIVALENT TO THE STRUGGLE OF BLACKS, APPARENTLY THIS IDIOT HAS NEVER HEARD OF MEXICO, THEY HAVE THEIR OWN COUNTRY TO RESIDE IN, THEY MIGRATE TO THE UNITED STATES ON THEIR FREE WILL, (NOT) HELD IN BIND AGE, THIS IS A BLATANT

ATTEMPT TO HERD BLACKS AND HISPANICS TOGATHER AS ONE TO CAPITALIZE ON THEIR VOTING ASPECTS, AND HE IS NOT ALONE IN SEEMINGLY POLITICAL GRATUITOUSLY ACT OF TREASON AGAINST AFRICAN AMERICANS, THE WHITE DEMOCRATIC POLITICAL SLAVE MASTERS ARE BOARDING THIS TRAIN, AND IT IS SUGGESTED THAT ALL AFRICAN AMERICANS BE AWARE OF THIS TREACHERY BECAUSE IT REVOLVE AROUND QUICK SAND FOR THE FUTURE OF YOUR CHILDREN BECOMING IINVOLVED IN AN OPPORTUNISTIC DIVERSE SOCIETY.

TO GRAVITATE INDIVIDUAL UNDERSTANDING AND THE REQUIREMENTS TO ASCERTAIN THEIR CHOOSING OF EQUALITY AND SUCCESSES, BECAUSE BASED ON THE FOOLISH IDEOLOGY OF NEBRASKA STATE SENATOR ERNIE CHAMBERS, PUBICALLY FLAUNTING HIS EUPHEMISTIC AND CYNICAL DEMAGOGUERY REFERRING TO POLLUTED VERBIAGE, AS WHEN A (BLACK) MAN INTRODUCE A PLAN THAT WORKS, MEANING HIS INSTIGATED AND SUPPORT FOR SCHOOL SEGREGATION IN NEBRASKA, CONTINUITY RELATED TO EDUCATIONAL SUCCESS BASED ON DIVERSITY IS THREATENED TO THE CORE FOR AFRICAN AMERICANS, IF THIS INSIDIOUS LAW REMAIN INTACT INTRODUCED BY CHAMBERS, THE COHESIVENESS OF DIVERSITY IS THE CORNER STONE FOR STABILITY, AND THIS IS WHY SOME BLACKS ARE FOREVER SCREAMING IRREGULARITIES AND PANDERING FOR CHANGE IN LAWS TO LOWER THE STANDARDS OF EXCELLENCE TO COMPLY WITH THEIR OWN RELUCTANCE OF CONFORMANCE, SO APPARENTLY STATE SENATOR CHAMBERS FEEL IF THEY ARE IN CHARGE OF THEIR EDUCATIONAL BUDGET THEY WILL OWN SOMETHING, AND THEY WILL, ILLITERACY, POVITY, A DATE WITH THE JUSTICE SYSTEM, AND EVENTUALLY GETTO SLUMS, THERE IS A GREAT DEAL OF PREPARATION FORTITUDE AND DISCIPLINE REQUIRED FROM PARENTS, OR SOME ONE THAT HAS A GENERAL PRECEPTION OF STABILITY TO INHERENTLY CAUSE A CHILD TO FOCUS ON PROGRESS,AND MAINTAIN THE CHARACTERISTICS THROUGH A COMPULSIVE SOCIETY, THESE CREDENTIALS ARE TAUGHT FROM A STRONG FAMILY BACK GROUND THAT

THEORETICALLY HAS BATTLE SCARS OF THEIR OWN TO SHOW HOW THEY SUCCESSFULLY MAINTAINED,MATURE STABILITY IS EARNED NOT (GIVEN) AND THERE ARE SOME PEOPLE BLACK AND WHITE THAT ARE (NOT) WILLING TO SACRIFICE TO WORK WITHIN A COMPLEX SYSTEM IN ORDER TO ATTAIN TREASURES THAT IS THERE FOR EVERY ONE, TRADITIONALLY SOME AFRICAN AMERICANS WOULD RATHER STAND ON THE SIDE LINE AND WAIT FOR SOMETHING TO HAPPEN, RATHER THAN MAKE THINGS HAPPEN FOR THEM SELVES,TO PENETRATE THIS WAITING PROCESS IS A DAUNTING TASK, BECAUSE IT IS FORMULATED THROUGH A HERDING PROCESS WITH IDEAS ON HOW TO SHORT CIRCUIT THE FOREVER PRESENT CONTROLLING SYSTEM, AND WHEN THEIR FOOLISH INGENIOUS IDEAS FAIL, THERE ARE THE ERRATIC SYMPATHIZERS JUST TO NAME A FIEW, JESSIE JACKSON, AL SHARPETON, TAVIS SMILEY, AND NEW COMER STATE SENATOR ERNIE CHAMBERS, TRYING TO CONJURE UP SOME KIND OF THEORY FOR THEIR FAILURE, AND RATHER THAN PIN THE TAIL ON THE DONKEY, AND ADMIT YOU CAN (NOT) TAKE A JACKASS AND MAKE A RACE HORSE OUT OF HIM, UNFORTUNATELY THEY ENGAGE IN SCANDALIZING THE SYSTEM FOR THESE MIS-FITS FAILURE, WEATHER IT BE THE GOVERNMENT OR THE EDUCATIONAL SYSTEM, ON APRIL 17, 2006, JESSIE JACKSON THE ASSISTANT DISTRICT ATTORNEY,WAS ON MSNBC, TRYING TO OFFER AN EXPLANATION FOR HIS INEPT DECISION REGARDS TO THE RAPE VICTOM EDUCATION GRATUITY FROM HIM, IT IS SUSPECTED IF YOU HIDE A TELEVISION CAMERA IN A HONEY BUCKET HE WOULD LOCATE IT, IF IT SUIT HIS OCCASION FOR NOTORIETY, AND THIS RADICAL ESCAPADE IS ALL ABOUT HIM BABBLING SUGGESTIVE RACIAL OVERTONES WITH NO CIRCUMSTANTIAL EVIDENCE OTHER THAN HIS SUMMATION OF WHITES ATTACKED A BLACK WOMAN, AND THE ASSUMPTION OF THEIR GUILT.

PEOPLE OF THIS KIND ARE SOME OF THE MOST OUTRAGEOUS AND BEFUDDLING IN OUR CIVIL SOCIETY TODAY. BECAUSE OF THEIR INTUITIVENESS TO HYPOTHETICALLY ACCESS ANY SITUATION HAVING TO DO WITH BLACK AND WHITE PEOPLE PERTAINING

TO ALTERCATIONS, AND IMMEDIATELY WITHOUT ANY RECOURSE PLAY THE RACE CARD, AS IF SOME AFRICAN AMERICANS ARE STILL IN DIAPERS AND (DO NOT) HAVE THE CAPABILITY TO ACERTAIN DESCRIPTIVE INVOLVEMENTS ON THEIR OWN, AND REGARDLESS TO WHAT TRANSPIRED THEY ARE GOING TO SUPPORT THE BLACK ISSURE WHICH IS TERRIBLY CYNICAL AND APPALLING, THAT DEMONSTRATE HORRIFIC ANTI-SOCIALISM.

BECAUSE YOU CAN REST ASSURE THAT THERE ARE GOING TO BE CONSTANT ALTERCATIONS AND SKIRMISHES AMONG A DIVERSE SOCIETY OF PEOPLE, UNFORTUNATELY SOME POLITICAL BLACK DEMOCRATIC BOOT LICKER SLAVE DRIVERS FOR THE DEMOCRATIC PARTY, PERSUE THESE ALTERCATIONS AS A TACTIC TO INCITE,IN AN EFFORT TO BOOST THEIR NOTORIETY AND TACTFULLY REINFORCE THEIR RADICAL FOLLOWERS, WHICH HAS NO MERIT WHAT SO EVER OTHER THAN HERD BLACKS INTO A STUPENDOUS VOTING APPARATUS FOR DEMOCRATS BEHIND THEIR SILLY UNETHICAL EXPLOTATIONS, EXAMPLE JESSIE JACKSON HAS BEEN CAMPED OUT IN NEW ORLEANS, IN AN EFFORT TO PERSUADE SATELLITE VOTING FROM AROUND THE NATION, IN THE MAYORAL ELECTION FOR HIS HOMIE, CHOCOLATE CITY HOOD BROTHER, IT DID NOT HAPPEN, NOW HE IS FLAUNTING THIS SILLY NOTION OF CONSTUTUTION VIOLATIONS, TO IMPRESS HIS STUPID FOLLOWERS THAT HE IS ON TO SOMETHING, THE PROBLEM WITH MOST AFRICAN AMERICANS THEY ALLOW THESE BUFFOONISH HIJACKERS TO DICTATE POLITICAL POLICY THAT IS ERRONEOUS.

(THE FIFTEENTH AMENDMENT WAS RATIFIED TO THE CONSTITUTION)

FEBRUARY 3, 1870

(SECTION ONE)

THE RIGHT OF CITIZENS OF THE UNITED STATES TO (VOTE) SHALL (NOT) BE (DENIED) OR ABRIDGED BY THE UNITED STATES OR BY ANY (STATE) ON ACCOUNT OF RACE, COLOR, OR PREVIOUS CONDITIONS OF SERVITUDE. THERE

IS (NOTHING) IN THIS SEGMENT OF THE CONSTITUTION WITH IMPLICATIONS OF FAVORITISM REGARDS TO SHUTTLE OR SATELLITE FOR VOTERS TO REACH THEIR REQUIRED DESTINATION TO VOTE, SECTION ONE EMPHATICALLY DEAL WITH DENIAL, (NOT) CONCESSIONS TO ENHANCE BLACK GOOD BUDDIES TO MAINTAIN POLITICAL POWER, THESE BELLIGERENT MIS-FIT DEMOCRATIC PARASITES ARE PERUSING EFFORTS TO LEGISLATE LAWS THAT IS SUTIABLE ACCOMMODATIONS FOR SOME INEPT BLACKS, AND FORTUNATELY THERE ARE ELECTED LEGISLATED BODIES TO OFFICIALLY DEPRIVE THESE MORONS OF THIS BLOATED CYNICISM, IT IS INCUMBENT UPON THE CITIZENS OF THIS NATION BLACK AND WHITE THAT TAKE PRIDE IN MORAL VALUES, AND UNDERSTAND COHESIVE DIVERSITY, TO PUT FORTH THEIR BEST EFFORT IN ORDER TO ALIENATE THESE HYPERCRITICAL BLACK POLITICANS, AND SELF APPOINTED RADICAL LEADERS, SOME ARE PURSUING RADIFICATION OF A MALICIOUS SOUTHERN JIM CROW RULE OF THE SIXTIES FOR YOUR CHILDREN REGARDS TO EDUCATION IN THE SCHOOL SYSTEM, PERTAINING TO SEPRATE BUT EQUAL, AND THEY ARE SO STUPEFIED WITH OBSESSIONS RELATED TO ELEMENTS OF DIVISION, AND HAVENT THE SLIGHTEST COMPREHENSION THAT THEIR RADICAL BELIEFS WILL IMPOSE ON THE CITIZENS OF THIS COUNTRY, PIRATICALLY AFRICAN AMERICANS, OUR NATION IS BEING TESTED ALMOST TO THE LIMIT INTERNALLY BY DEMOCRATIC IDEOLOGUES, BLACK AND WHITE IN AN EFFORT TO SATISFY THEIR THIRST FOR POLITICAL POWER, WHILE THE TERRORIST ARE WAITING PAITENTLY TO ADVANCE THEIR. CAUSE IN AN EFFORT TO DESTROY OUR LEGENDARY, MORAL, CIVILLY AND INDUSTRIOUS WAY OF LIFE, AND SOME DISPLAY AN ATTITUDE AS IF THEY REALLY DONT CARE, AND I AM CERTAIN THIS KIND OF NONSENSICAL BEHAVIOR SEND A MESSAGE TO THE TERRORIST THAT WE ARE IN A STATE OF DENIAL, WHICH LEAVE THEM NO OTHER CHOICE BUT THINK OUR NATION IS VIRTUALLY INSECURE FOR ATTACK, SEPTEMBER 11, IDENTIFIED THEIR AMBITIONS, AND I SUSPECT THERE ARE A LOT OF AMERICAN CITIZENS FEEL THEY ARE IMMUNE. TO SUCH CATASTROPHIC

ORDEALS, BUT I AM HERE TO ALERT YOU THAT EVERY AMERICAN BLACK AND WHITE CAN BE AFFECTED AND HERDED INTO THIS PSYCHOPATHIC DELIVERANCE IF ONE SHOULD OCCUR AGAIN, SO IN ORDER TO AVERT THESE KIND OF DISASTROUS HAPPENINGS, THE IN FIGHTING FOR POLITICAL PRECEDENCE BASED ON LIES AND FRIVOLOUS DEMAGOGUERY MUST CEASE, IF WE ARE TO SURVIVE UNMOLESTED BY TERRORISM AS A NATION OF CIVILIZED PEOPLE.

THIS IS A ATTENTIVE DEMANDING NECESSITY WITH OUT ANY RECOURSE, BECAUSE WE ARE INVOLVED IN A CULTURAL BATTLE LIKE NEVER BEFORE, THAT WE MUST WIN IF CIVILIZATION IS TO SURVIVE IN THIS COUNTRY, I AM OF THE OPENION THAT BASED ON DEMOCRATS IDEOLOGY THEY HAVE A SCRAMBLED DISSIPATED MISCONCEPTION OF WHAT IS LOOMING,AND THE BARBARIC NATURE OF THESE FANTICIZED KILLERS, THE DEMOCEATS HAVE HAVE LIED THEIR WAY INTO POLITICAL POWER SENSE THE EARLY FORTIES, AND SEDUCED THE MAJORITY OF AFRICAN AMERICANS IN A WAY THAT IS NONE COMPATABLE ANY OTHER PLACE IN THE WORLD , AND MOST LIKELY THE SOLE DESTRUCTIVE FORCE BEHIND THEIR ECONOMICAL FAILURE, BECAUSE BLACKS MIMIC THEIR IDEOLOGY OF SEDUCTIVE BRAIN WASH AND EXTORTION,AND NEVER DO ANY WRONG IT IS ALWAYS SOME ONE ELSE FAULT, AND THEY ARE BEING TAKEN ADVANTAGE OF BECAUSE THEY ARE BLACK,IT IS A RESOUNDING COMPARISION REGARDS TO IMPUGNING HONORABLE PEOPLE INTERROGATIVE FOR PERSONAL OR POLITICAL GAIN, SO THIS CRISIS WE ARE INVOLVED IN REGARDS TO TERRORISM, WHICH IS DETRIMENTAL TO OUR NATION, SOME DEMOCRATS HONESTLY THINK THEY CAN CON AND LIE THEIR WAY OUT OF THIS THREATENING REALITY, SO THEY HAVE PUT ON A ROBUST CACULATED PACK OF LIES TO WIN BACK THE HOUSE OF REPRESENTATIVES AND THE SENATE, AND IF THEY DO WE ALL ARE GOING TO PAY A PRICE LIKE NEVER BEFORE IN THE HISTORY OF THIS COUNTRY, BECAUSE WHILE THEY ARE WALLOWING IN MUCK TRYING TO IMPECH PRESIDENT BUSH HOPING SOMETHING WILL RUB OFF ON THE NEXT PRESIDENTAL

CANIDATE. FOR REPUBLICANS, THE TERRORIST ARE GOING TO BE BLOWING UP OUR COUNTRY, AND THEN THEY WILL START LYING ABOUT IF BUSH HAD NEVER GONE INTO IRAQ THIS WOULD NOT HAVE HAPPENED, BECAUSE THERE WERE NO WEPONS OF MASS DESTRUCTION, AND THAT IRAQ WAS NO THREAT TO THE UNITED STATES AND INSPECTION WAS WORKING, THE MAJORITY OF THE DEMOCRATIC PARTY ARE A ORGANIZATION OF OPPORTUNIST, THAT SEIZE EVERY MOMENT TO CRITICIZE THEIR OPPONETS WITH VICIOUS LIES REGARDLESS TO THE CONSEQUENCES, AND THIS HYPERCRITICAL TENACIOUS DEPLOYMENT OF STUPID FOOLISH LIES HAS IMMENSELY DAMAGED THE CREDIBILITY OF MANY OPPONENTS OVER THE YEARS,ALSO THE INTEGRITY OF THE COUNTRY.

WHICHHASTRANSCENDEDINTOAMOCKERY,SENSETHEY LOST POLITICAL POWER, JUST AS THEIR COUNTERPARTS, MOST BLACKS ARE INCAPABLE OF DEVISING A MEANINGFUL PLAN WITH SUBSTANCE, PERTAINING TO THEIR OWN PERSONAL AFFAIRS, SO AS A RESULT THEY ARE JOINED AT HIP WITH THE DEMOCRATS TO DEGRADE SUBSTANTIATIVE POLICIES THAT IS GOOD FOR THE NATION, THESE NONSENSICAL VAIN ASSESSMENT OF POLITICAL POLICY INTERNALLY,HAS TELEGRAPHED A MESSAGE AROUND THE WORLD THAT WE ARE A DEVIDED NATION THAT IS TRIPPING OVER OUR FEET, THERE IS AN OLD SAYING TOGATHER YOU STAND DEVIDED YOU FALL, AND IT IS SO SAD THAT THE DEMOCRATS HAS MANUFACTURED THIS TRAGEDY FOR OUR COUNTRY WITH NO REMORSE, ALL BECAUSE THEY WERE DEPRIVED OF THEIR TRADITIONAL POLITICAL POWER STRUCTURE,THROUGH CONSTITUTIONAL GUIDE LINES THAT THEY REFUSE TO ACCEPT, THEY ARE SO OBSESSED WITH FOOLERY FOR POLITICAL CONTROL UNTIL THEY NEGLECT TO REALIZE THAT THEY ARE PLAYIING INTO THE SKILLS AND THE HANDS OF THE TERRORIST, AND IT IS A DAMN SHAME TO SACRIFICE YOUR COUNTRY BECAUSE YOU HAVE BENN VOTED OUT OF POLITICAL POWER BY A LEGISLATED DEMOCRATIZED SYSTEM. THEY ARE SO ANGRY AND HOSTILE THEY HAVE PASSED OVER THE FACT THAT TERRORIST DO (NOT) KILL BY COLOR

OR PARTY AFFILIATIONS, INDOCTRINATION IS A DISEASE THAT PLAGUE MAN KIND, AND IT FLURISH MOSTLY FROM IGNORANCE AND THERE IS (NO) SAFE GUARD TO PROTECT ONE FROM BEING SUCCUMBED OTHER THAN ONE SELF, THERE ARE BORN LEADERS ALSO FOLLOWERS, THESE QUALITIES ARE DETERMINE THROUGH MANY ASPECTS OF LIFE,PREDOMINATELY HAVING TO DO WITH CULTURE BACK GROUND, GENIC HEREDITY, AND EDUCATION.

MANY TIMES CULTURE AND GENETICS HEREDITY ALTER THE CHOICES SHOULD BE MADE IN LIFE, AND SPEND PEOPLE INTO A FRENZY TO GIVE UP THEIR LIFE FOR A CAUSE, BECAUSE THEY HAVE ADOPTED A SELFISH MENTALITY THAT OTHERS SHOULD BE UNDER THEIR CONTROL, THERE IS A GROSS MISJUDGMENT WITH SOME DEMOCRATS PLAYING THE BLAME GAME IN POLITICS, THERE ARE TIMES SOME SEEMINGLY MAKE GESTURES THAT FAVOR TERRORIST ACTIVIES, NAMELY DEMOCRATIC VICE PRESIDENT AL GORE, ERRONEOUSLY CASTING DISPERSIONS THAT IS TRULY UNFOUNDED, FOR A FORMER VICE PRESIDENT TO DEMINISH THE INTEGRITY OF HIS COUNTRY, PIRATICALLY ON FOREGIN SOIL IS A MISTERY AND TREASONOUS APPALLING, NOT TO MENTION HARRY BELAFONTA AND DANNY GLOVER, BUT THERE ARE SOME CONCESSIONS ON THEIR BEHALF,THEY ARE TO STUPID TO KNOW ANY BETTER, AND ALL THREE ALONG WITH CYNTHIA MCKINNEY, SHOULD BE CHAINED BY THE ANKLES ALONG WITH THE FORMER HUSBAND OF THE SUSPECTED RAPE VICTIM THAT OCCURED AT DUKE UNIVERSITY, ON APRIL 22, FOX NEWS HOST HAD TO TAKE A SPECIAL COURSE IN IBIBIO, IN ORDER TO OBTAIN INFORMATION THAT PRIOR TO MEETING HIS FORMER WIFE THE SUSPECTED VICTIM, THAT HE WAS TOTALLY ILLITERATE, IN THE APPROXIMATE RANGE OF THIRTY TO FORTY YEARS OLD, THERE IS NO EXCUSE FOR THIS DISGUSTING POLARIZATION THAT PLAGUE MANY BLACKS, AND TO TOP IT OFF LEE PAIGE D.E. A. AGENT ON APRIL 17, 2006, ADMITTED THAT HE WAS TUTORING YOUNG CHILDREN ON SAFETY PRECAUTIONARY MEASURES ON HOW TO MANTLE AND DISMANTLE WEAPONS REGARDS TO SAFETY, AND SHOT HIMSELF IN THE FOOT, THIS GROUP

OF PEOPLE SHOULD BE CHARACTERIZED AS A UNIT, THAT REPRESENT HORROR TO THEM SELVES AND OTHERS IN THIS NATION. THE PULVERIZING COMPULSION RELATED TO POLITICS IN THE UNITED STATES OF AMERICA IS VERY COMPLEX, AND MOST PEOPLE LIVE HERE ALL THEIR LIVES AND NEVER UNDERSTAND THE DETERMINING FACTOR ON WHICH IT EXIST, SO IT IS HIGHLY UNLIKELY THAT TERRORIST WILL ASCERTAIN PROPAGANDA FOR POLITICAL GAIN FROM POWER HUNGRY POLITICIANS, AND MOST LIKELY JUDGE DEMOCRATIC INTERNAL CRITICISM, WITH BASHING COMMENTARY RELATING TO THE IRAQ WAR,WITH IMPLICATIONS IT WAS NOT NECESSARY, COULD VERY WELL BE TAKEN OUT OF CONTEX BY THE TERRORIST AS A SYMPATHETIC GESTURE FOR THEIR CAUSE, PIRATICALLY WHEN THE DEMOCRATS GENERATE A CONCEPT OF THERE WERE NO WEAPONS OF MASS DISTRUCTION, WHICH IS A TROUBLING MISCONCEPTION BECAUSE THEY WERE USED TO EXTERMINATE PEOPLE IN THE PAST,IT IS SUSPECTED DURING THE TIME INSPECTION WAS BEING CARRIED OUT PRIOR TO THE WAR, IN ORDER FOR THE INSPECTORS NOT TO LOCATE THEM THEY WERE HIDDEN SOME PLACE EVENTUALLY THEY WILL TURN UP, AND WATCH SOME OF THE BRIER EATING DEMOCRATS INSTIGATE THEY WERE PLANTED, MOST AFRICAN AMERICANS ARE NOT AWARE OF HOW DESTRUCTIVE AND DANGEROUS CHEMICAL WEAPONS CAN BE, SOME MIGHT ASSUME IT ONLY AFFECT WHITE PEOPLE, DURING THE MOTH OF APRIL 2006,TWO OF THE MOST NOTORIOUS TERRORIST ON THE PLANET SENT A MESSAGE TO OUR NATION, EACH WAS JUBILIANT WITH THEIR PSYCHOTIC DELIVERANCE OF RHETORIC, IT IS SUSPECTED THEY ARE AWARE THAT THIS IS AN ELECTION YEAR . AND ARE ASSUMING THAT THE DEMOCRATS ARE GOING TO DEFEAT THE REPUBLICANS IN THE HOUSE AND SENATE, SO THEY CAN RIP OUR COUNTRY APART WITH TERRORIST ACTIVITY, IT IS POSSIBLE THAT THERE ARE SOME HOME GROWN SPROUTING FROM THE ROOT TO TAKE A RIDE ON THE MOTHER SHIP, THE FEMALE DEMOCRATIC ELITIST THAT SUPPOSEDLY LEAKED PERTINENT INFORMATION TO THE NEWS MEDIA, AND

LOST HER POSITION FOR THIS UNSAVORY ACT, IF (TRUE) COULD HAVE DIRE CONSEQUENCES ON OUR DEALING WITH TERRORIST TO OBTAIN VALUABLE INFORMATION REGARDS TO THE SAFETY OF AMERICAN CITIZENS, THIS A ACT OF COMPULSIVE VINDCTIVENESS IN AN EFFORT TO SABOTAGE THE NATION SECURITY SYSTEM WITH MALICE.

AND AS YOU MIGHT EXPECT ON FOX NEWS APRIL 25, 2006, ONE OF THE DEMOCRATIC BLACK ASININE POLITICAL CARGO CARRIERS OF DISDAINING OBJECTIVES JUAN WILLIAMS, GAVE THE HOST A MILD CASE OF HYSTERIA,IN AN ATTEMPT TO JUSTIFY (IF TRUE) THE MARY MCCARTHY DEBACLE, OF.LEAKING CLASSIFIED INFORMATION, HE DICTATED POLICY AS TO WHERE TERRORIST SHOULD BE INTERROGATED, AND DEMANDED THAT AMERICAN CITIZENS SHOULD BE TOLD OF THESE OPERATIONS, SOUND LIKE CIVIL RIGHTS FOR TERROIST THAT FLY PLANES INTO BUILDINGS AND TAKE THEIR OWN LIVES ALONG WITH THOUSANDS OF INNOCENT PEOPLE, AND MARY MCCARTHY ACTIONS WAS JUST BECAUSE SHE LET THE PEOPLE KNOW BASED ON THE ASSESSMENT OF THE FORE FATHERS RELATED TO FREEDOM OF SPEECH, I HAVE WATCHED THIS GUY CARRY DEMOCRAT WATER, BUT THIS IS COMMON WITH PEOPLE LIKE HIM BECAUSE HE IS DISORIENTED, AND APPEAR TO BE HAVING A PROBLEM IDENTIFYING TERRORIST FROM AMERICAN CIRIZENS, DURING THE EARLY EIGHTEEN HUNDREDS PRIOR TO THE ABOLISHMENT OF SLAVERY HIS KIND,THE DEMOCRATIC PLANTATIONS MASTERS WOULD ISSURE HIM HIGH BOOTS AND A WHIP, AND THEIR TITLE WAS SLAVE DRIVERS, HE IS HONORING THAT SAME TITLE TODAY, ONLY ONE DIFFERANCE HE TRADED HIS WHIP AND HIGH BOOTS FOR A SUIT AND TIE,THERE ARE HUNDREDS OF THOUSANDS OF THESE JUAN WILLIAMS MIS-FITS SCATTERED ALL OVER THE NATION, THAT HAVE TUNNEL VISION REGARDS TO DEMOCRATIC IDEOLOGY, AND ARE THE SPITOONS THAT HOLD DEMOCRATIC WASTE OF POLITICAL IN-JUSTICE, THAT IS SPINNING OUT OF CONTROL IN AN EFFORT TO REINSTATE DEMOCRATIC POLITICAL CONTROL,HOWEVER IF THEY HERD TOGATHER AND CONVINCE THE AMERICAN PEOPLE TO RESTORE

THEM TO POWER, WITH THEIR INTEGRITY IMPUGNING, HORRIFIC LIES, AND TERRORIST SYMPATHIZING, IT IS THE PEOPLE FAULT THAT ARE CITIZENS OF THIS COUNTRY.

UNFORTUNATELY SEPTEMBER 11, HAVE (NOT) REGISTERED WITH THE DEMOCRATS AT ALL AND HOW BRUTALLY IT WAS CARRIED OUT, FANATICS GLOATING AND COMMITTING SUICIDE,IN ORDER TO DESTRUCTIVELY KILL INNOCENT AMERICAN CITIZENS, BY FLYING JET AIR PLANES INTO BUILDINGS LOADED WITH PASSENGERS PRAYING TO GOD, AND TAKING THEIR LAST BREATH ON THIS EARTH, THESE PEOPLE AND OTHERS DID NOT DESERVE TO DIE THIS WAY, APPARENTLY THESE BARBARIC ACTS OF HUMAN SLAUGHTER HAS NOT FAZED THE DEMOCRATS IN ANY WAY, BECAUSE THEY ARE STILL ENGAGED IN DECETIFUL TACTICS THAT ENHANCE THE TERROIST AGENDA,AND ARROGANTLY SHOWING NO COMPASSION FOR THE SAFETY OF THE COUNTRY AND THE PEOPLE THAT LIVE HERE, SIMPLY BECAUSE OF THEIR SICK OBSESSION FOR POLITICAL POWER AND CONTROL, WITH ABSOLUTELY NO IDEA OR AGENDA ON HOW TO COMBAT AND DEFEAT TERRORISM.

THE DEMOCRATS ARE THOROUGHLY SKILLED AT MANIPULATING AND TAKING ISSURES OUT OF CONTEXT, IN AN EFFORT TO IMPUGN THEIR OPPONENTS, AND NEVER HAVE A PLAN OF THEIR OWN TO RESOLVE ANY THING, EXAMPLE DEMOCRATIC CONGRESS WOMAN NITA LOWEY, WAS ON FOX NEWS APRIL 25, 2006, AND WAS SPECIFICALLY ASKED, WHAT IS THE PLAN THE DEMOCRATS HAVE TO SOLVE THE SKY ROCKETING PRICE OF GASOLINE, AND I THOUGHT IT WAS A REPLAY OF THE OLDER LADY ON THE NEW ORLEANS DEBACLE, HELD IN THE CONGRESS THAT CYNTHIA MCKINNEY EMBRACED, CONGRESS WOMAN LOWEY WENT GIBBERISH AND NEVER ANSWERED THE DIRECT QUESTION, WHICH IS TYPICAL DEMOCRATIC STRATEGY TO NIT PICK AND MIMIC WHAT SOME ONE IS ALREADY DOING, AND LAY CLAIM TO THEY COULD DO IT BETER, NOT TO MENTION THEIR STRONG EFFORT TO PREVENT OIL EXPLORATION OFF SHORE AND AROUND THE NATION, SCREAMING OIL SPILLAGE AND ENVIRONMENTAL SAFETY, NOW THE CHINESE ARE IN THE PROCESS OF

EXPLORING FOR OIL OFF THE COAST OF FLORDIA JUST OUT SIDE OF U.S. TERRITORY ON A CLEAR DAY YOU MOST LIKELY COULD SEE THEM AT WORK, WE NEED THE DEMOCRATS LOGIC TO EXPLAIN THIS DEBACLE REGARDS TO OIL SPILLAGE AND ENVIRONMENTAL SAFETY, LET ME GUESS IF PRESIDENT BUSH HAD NEVER GONE TO IRAQ LOOKING FOR WEAPONS OF MASS DESTRUCTION, THIS NEVER WOULD HAVE HAPPEN, AND NOW HE HAS THIS COUNTRY IN A MESS.

A FINE EXAMPLE OF DEMOCRATIC TREACHERY PERTAINING TO CHARACTER ASSASSINATION REGARDS TO THEIR POLITICAL OPPONENTS, REPUBLICAN MICHAEL STEELE, LIEUTENANT GOVERNOR OF MARYLAND HAS SET HIS SITES ON A SENATE SEAT,WHICH IS HIGHLY RESPECTED AS A INDIVIDUAL THINKER SELF MOTIVATED,AND CONDUCTS HIM SELF WITH INTELLECTUAL ABILITIES, AND OFTEN MENTION HIS FAMILY TIES AS A STRONG MOMENTUS,WHICH IS THE FOUNDATIONAL CONGLOMERATINGAUTARCHIC FOR ALL AMERICANS,TIS GENTLEMAN IS A TRUE RED BLOODIED AMERICAN THAT LOVES HIS COUNTRY, AND UNDERSTAND THE FABRIC ON WHICH IT WAS FOUNDED, AND HAS USED THE FORMULA APPROPIATELY TO SUCCEEDE, WHICH IS ACCESSIBLE TO (ALL) AMERICANS AND FOREIGNERS THAT CHOOSE TO ENGAGE THEM SELVES IN THE FUNDAMENTALISM OFFERINGS OF THE UNITED STATES OF AMERICA. AND FOR DOING THIS MR. STEELE IS BEING POLITICALLY ABUSED BY THE DEMOCRATS SIMPLY BECAUSE HE REFUSE TO FOLLOW A SELF APPOINTED STRAINED DEMOCRATIC PORCH MONKEY, THAT HAS BEEN SEDATED WITH A POITICAL PSYCHOLOGICAL ENTRENCHMENT THAT IF ONE DOSENT HERD AND SPPORT THEIR AGENDA OF STUPENDOUS ALLIED AFRICAN AMERICAN, THEN THEY SEND OUT THE BLACK ATTACK SLAVE DRIVERS TO VERBALLY ABUSE, AND THE WHITE POLITICAL SLAVE MASTERS OF SOME BLACKS, DIG INTO YOUR PERSONAL AFFAIRS IN ORDER TO LOCATE SOMETHING THAT WOULD IMPUGN INTEGRITY IN SUCH AWAY IT WOULD DENY ONES EFFORTS TO BE ELECTED TO PUBLIC OFFICE.

ON APRIL 26, 2006, ON FOX NEWS BLACK ACVIST TED HAYES, GAVE HIS EVALUATION OF A BLACK ISSURE HE DEEM THAT IS BREWING IN THIS COUNTRY REGARDS TO AFRICAN AMERICANS, HE ELABORATED ON BLACKS RETURN TO SLAVERY BASED ON THE EMERGENCE CREATED BY HISPANICS INTO THE UNITED STATES OF AMERICA,PERHAPS MR. HAYES IS NOT AWARE BUT MANY BLACKS HAS NEVER LEFT THE PLANTATION OF IGNORANCE PERPETRATED BY THE DEMOCRATIC PARTY, AND THE MAJORITY WILL CONTINUE TO SUPPORT THEIR OWN IMPOSED . LYNCHING, BECAUSE OF PREHISTORIC INDOCTRINATION THAT DEVELOPED INTO A TRADITION REGARDS TO POLITICAL SUPPORT FOR DEMOCRATS, WHICH HAS CAPITALIZED ON THEIR IGNORANCE OF POLITICS TO REMAIN IN POWER FOR YEARS, HOWEVER WHEN MR. HAYES WAS ASKED TO CLARIFY HIS STATEMENTS HE RESPONDED BY SAYING HISPANICS ARE TAKING JOBS THAT BLACKS DO NOT WANT BECAUSE OF LOW WAGES, SO THEY NEED TO RETURN TO THEIR OWN COUNTRY, SO BLACKS CAN GET A HIGHER WAGE FOR THEIR SERVICES, WHEN ASKED TO EXPLAIN HIS CHRONOLOGY OF EVENTS REGARDS TO SLAVERY, HE TUCHED ON THERE IS NO COMPARISON TO HISPANICS PLIGHT AND SLAVERY, MR. HAYES OPENION IS THAT DR. MARTIN KUTHER KING ENDEAVORS ARE BEING SABOTAGED BY HISPANICS RELATED TO EMIGRATION, AND HE IS ABSOLUTELY RIGHT BECAUSE THEY ARE NOT BEING HANGED, BLOWN UP IN CHURCHES, AND DRAGGED BEHIND AUTOMOBILES BY DEMOCRATS AND THEIR KU-KLUX-KLAN, ALSO DEPRIVED OF THEIR CIVIL RIGHTS FOR NINETY NINE YEARS BY A DEMOCRATIC CONTROL CONGRESS, THE SPECIFICS OF HIS TOPIC WERE SPORADIC, WHICH IS FT FINE EXAMPLE OF EXPLOITING DEMOCRATIC TAUGHT DEMAGOGUERY WITH OUT MERIT, MR. HAYES IS ON TO SOMETHING REFERENCE SLAVERY FOR SOME BLACKS, BUT HE LIKE THE ABILITY TO GIVE A SYNOPSIS ON WHAT IS CAUSING THIS REVELATION TODAY AND ALSO PAST YEARS, IT IS EASY TO REVEL AND PLAY THE BLAME GAME, BUT MOST AFRICAN AMERICANS ARE RESPONSIBLE FOR THEIR OWN INSIPID HALLUCINATING FAILURES, BECAUSE OF THEIR NEGATIVE ABILITY TO PROFILE

THEIR CHARACTER AND UTILIZE THEIR CHARACTERISTICS ACCORDINGLY,THEY WOULD RATHER HERD TOGATHER AND BE TOLD AND MOTIVATED BY WHAT THEY WANT TO HEAR, FROM THEIR SELF APPOINTED LEADERS THAT THEIR HOPES AND DREAMS ARE BEING DENIED REGARDS TO SUCCESS BECAUSE OF A UNLEVEL PLAYING FIELD PERPETRATED BY THE WHITE MAN BECAUSE OF THEIR COLOR, AND AFTER DEPARTURE FROM THE GATHERING THEY ARE UNABLE TO READ THE ROAD SIGNS ON THE WAY HOME.

THERE ARE TWO KINDS OF ILLITERATES IN THIS WORLD, ONE IS BEING UABLE TO READ AND WRITE, AND THE OTHER IS POLITICAL ILLITERACY WITH FORMAL EDUCATION AND THIS IS THE WORST KIND PIRATICALLY FOR AFRICAN AMERICANS, BECAUSE THE MOMENT THEY GRADUATE FROM COLLEGE THEY HAVE THIS SENSE OF URGENCY THAT THEY ARE THE CARE TAKERS OF OTHER LESS FORTUNATE AFRICAN AMERICANS, AND HAVE ALL THE ANSWERS TO RESOLVE THEIR PROBLEMS RELATED TO POVITY, AND THE MAJORITY OF THE TIME THEY IMMEDIATELY START TO SPREAD NONSENSICAL DEMOCRATIC DEMAGOGUERY WHICH HAS BEEN PASSED ON TO THEM THROUGH CULTURAL TRADITIONS, EITHER FROM THEIR PARENTS, OR SELF APPOINTED LEADERS OR BOTH, THAT YOUR POVITY PROBLEMS EXIST BECAUSE YOU ARE BLACK,AND WHITE PEOPLE ARE RESPONSIBLE BECAUSE THEY REFUSE TO LEVEL THE PLAYING FIELD, AND BECAUSE OF THIS THEIR FUTURE IS PUT ON HOLD REGARDS TO SUCCESS, THIS KIND OF REBELLIOUS AMBIGUITY OFTEN ARTICULATE INTO THEIR THINKING THEY ARE SUPERIOR, AND TO BE SUBORDINATE TO A WHITE PERSON AS A SUPERVISOR REGARDS TO EMPLOYMENT, THEY WOULD RATHER NOT SEEK EMPLOYMENT UNDER THESE CONDITIONS, AND MOST AFRICAN AMERICANS THAT HALLUCINATE IN THAT MANNER ARE ILLITERATE, ILLITERACY HAS PLAGUED SOME BLACKS IN AMERICA SENSE SIXTEEN NINETEEN, AND WHAT MR. HAYES NEGLECT TO REALIZE AND MANY MANY OTHER BLACKS, IS THAT AFTER OVER THREE HUNDRED AND EIGHTY SEVEN YEARS IT HAS FNALLY CAUGHT UP TO THEM,

AND IT IS CALLED DEMOCRATIC PREVENTIVE MEASURES REGARDS TO EDUCATION, PERPETRATED BEFORE AND AFTER SLAVERY BY SOUTHERN DEMOCRATIC PLANTATION SLAVE OWNERS,AND WHITE SEGREGATIONIST SEPERATE BUT EQUAL LAWS IN THE SOUTHERN STATES, WHICH ENABLED THEM TO MAINTAIN CONTROL OVER AFRICAN AMERICANS THROUGH SHARE CROPPING, AND MOST BLACKS THAT CHOOSE TO BE EMBEZZLED BY THAT SYSTEM DID NOT ALLOW THEIR CHILDREN TO ATTEND SCHOOL REGULARLY BECAUSE OF TRYING TO PAY ACCUMULATED INDEBTEDNESS, AND CONSTANTLY BEING SEDUCED BY THEIR PLANTATION MASTERS THAT EDUCATION WAS NOT FOR THEM ANYWAY, THAT FARMING WAS MORE IMPORTANT.

ANDTHEOTHERFINALNAILINTHECOFFINISMIGRATION OF HISPANICS TO AMERICA. THAT IS CHARACTERIZED AS BEING EQUIVALENT TO SOME BLACKS REGARDS TO ILLITERACY, UNFORTUNATELY THERE IS ILLITERACY IN ALL NATIONALLY OF PEOPLE, BUT STATISTICS DICTATE THAT AFRICAN AMERICANS AND HISPANICS HAVE A RESERVED SEAT ON THE FIRST ROW, IN THE UNITED STATES OF AMERICA, THIS IS NOT MEANT TO CRITICIZE, OR OFFER AN EXPLANATION TO WHAT YOU WANT TO HEAR, BUT IT DEALS WITH REALITY AND THE FACTS OF LIFE PERTAINING TO ALL PEOPLE, THAT RESIDE IN A DIVERSE AND COMPLEX SOCIETY, IN THE UNITED STATES OF AMERICA AS CITIZENS, HOWEVER THERE IS A VAST DIFFERENCE BETWEEN AFRICAN AMERICANS AND HISPANICS, HAVING NOTHING TO DO WITH RACE BUT THE ABILITY TO QUALIFY IN AN EFFORT TO SUSTAIN, HISPANICS REALIZE THEIR DISADVANTAGES REGARDS TO EDUCATION AND ACCEPT THE FACT THAT THEY ARE ILLITERATE, AND WILL ACCEPT EMPLOYMENT THEY ARE CAPABLE AND SUITED FOR.

HOWEVER AFRICAN AMERICANS THAT ARE IN THE SAME CAPACITY REGARDS. TO ILLITERACY HAVE BEEB SUBJECTED TO AN ALLUSION BY THEIR SELF APPOINTED DEMOCRATIC SPOKESMAN THAT THEIR BOUT WITH ILLITERACY IS DUE TO WHITE PEOPLE PREVENTION, SO IN ORDER TO LEVEL THE PLAYING FIELD THEY SHOULD BE

GIVEN SPECIAL PRIVLEDGES, AND BASED ON THAT THEORY SOME WILL (NOT) ACCEPT EMPLOYMENT BASED ON THEIR QUALIFICATION AS HISPANICS WILL, UNLESS HE OR SHE IS OFFERED A SUPERVISION ROLE AND CANT READ OR WRITE, SO MR. HAYES YOU ARE ABSOLUTELY RIGHT THE MAJORITY OF AFRICAN AMERICANS UNDER THESE PRETENCES HAVE ISOLATED THEM SELVES FROM A COMPETIVE JOB MARKET OF UNSKILLED LABOR, BY HALLUCINATING AND LISTENING TO SELF APPOINTED LEADERS THAT HAS COAXED SOME INTO BELIEVING THAT THE PLAYING FIELD MUST BE LEVEL IN ORDER FOR THEM TO BECOME EFFECTIVE REGARDS TO THE JOB MARKET.

SO AS A RESULT OF THEIR WAITING FOR THE LEVELING OF THE PLAYING FIELD, THE HISPANICS HAS BEEN ALLOWED TO MIGRATE TO THIS COUNTRY AND MOVE THE PLAYING FIELD INTO THEIR SOLE POSSESSION, BY PLAYING ON IT WITH COMING TO WORK EVERY DAY, DOING WHAT THEIR SUPERVISORS INSTRUCT THEM TO DO, AND NOT COMPLAINING ABOUT THEY ARE WORTH MORE THAN WHAT THEY ARE BEING PAID, ALSO (NOT) POUTING ABOUT BEING IN CHARGE, SENATOR HILLARY CLINTON SENT A STRONG MESSAGE TO BLACKS WHEN SHE ADDRESSED THE HISPANIC ISSURE, BUY SAYING (WHOSE) GOING TO MAKE BEDS, SCRUBB FLOORS, WAITE TABLES, TAKE CARE OF THE SENIOR CITIZENS, AND PERFORM MANUAL CONSTRUCTION LABOR, THIS MESSAGE WAS MENT FOR FOR SELF APPOINTED BLACK LEADERS AND THEIR FOLLOWERS, THAT HISPANICS HAVE LEVELED THE PLAYING FIELD AND THE SERVICES OF SOME AFRICAN AMERICANS ARE REALLY NOT NECESSARY,SO AS A RESULT THE MAJORITY OF THESE INDOCTRINATED BLACK FOLLOWERS THAT BELIEVED THIS INSANE DEMOCRATIC TRICKERY, CAN PACK THEIR BAGS AND HEAD DOWN THAT ROAD TO POVITY AND GETTO SLUMS,BECAUSE OF THEIR HERDING PROCESS TO BE SEDUCED BY IGNORANCE.

MOST LEGISLATED BODIES THROUGHOUT THE NATION, PIRATICALLY THE STATES ARE AWARE OF THIS HORRIFIC SELF IMPOSED DILEMMA THAT SOME BLACKS HAVE ENGAGED IN FOR YEARS, UNFORTUNATELY HAS BECAME

MORE PRONOUNCED THAN EVER,AND WILL BE DEALT WITH ACCORDINGLY, BECAUSE PRACTICALLY EVERY STATE IN THE UNION IS IN THE PROCESS OF BUILDING OR ADDING ON TO INCARCERATION FACILITIES.

IN SIXTEEN SEVENTY SIX, A WHITE VIRGINIAN FARMER NATHANIEL BACON, SELF APPOINTED LEADER FORMED A REBELLIOUS GROUP OF WHITE FARMERS, WHITE SERVANTS, BLACK SLAVES,AND LED IHEM IN AN EFFORT TO APPROPRIATE NATIVE LANDS IN WESTERN VIRGINIA, BACON LOST HIS LIFE TO DYSENTERY, HOWEVER HIS FOLLOWERS WERE CRUSHED BY VIRGINIA MILITIA, ALONG WITH THE REMAINDING BALANCE CONSISTING OF EIGHTY BLACKS AND TWENTY WHITES.

IN SEVENTEEN THIRTY NINE,MANY SLAVES STAGED A REBELLION IN SOUTH CAROILNA FOLLOWING A SELF APPOINTED LEADER JEMMY, IN AN EFFORT TO OVER THROW THE GOVERNMENT, THE SOUTH CAROLINA COLONIAL MILITIA CRUSHED THEM, AND THIS REBELLION BROUGHT ABOUT SEVERE RESTRICTIONS ON ALL SLAVES, THAT WAS ALMOST UNBEARABLE SUCH AS HARASH LAWS PROHIBITING SLAVES FROM TESTIFYING EVEN UNDER OATH, ALSO FOR A WHITE PERSON TO MURDER A SLAVE WAS CONSIDERED A MISDEMEANOR, AND A SLAVE WAS TO BE EXECUTED FOR PARTICIPATING IN A REVOLT, CONSPIRING TO ESCAPE, COMMITING ARSON AND TEACHING OTHERS RADICAL MISDEEDS.

IN THE EIGHTEEN HUNDREDS,THERE WERE SELF APPOINTED LEADERS REGARDS TO BROTHERS, GABRIEL, SOLOMON AND MARTIN, CONTRIVED TO CAPTURE RICHMOND IN VIRGINIA, THEIR PLANNING CONSIST OF TO TAKE THE GOVERNOR HOSTAGE AND KILL ALL THE WHITES IN THE CITY, AND SET UP A NEW VIRGINIA GOVERNMENT, FORTUNATELY THEIR PLOT WAS REVEALED, GABRIEL HIS BROTHERS AND TWENTY FOUR OTHERS WERE TRIED AND CONVICTED REGARDS TO CONSPIRACY AND HANGED.

OF COURSE THERE IS THE NAT TURNER REBELLION OF EIGHTEEN THIRTY ONE WHICH CAUSED INNOCENT AFRICANAMERICANSTOLOOSETHEIRLIVES,SLAUGHTERED WITH GUN FIRE BULLETS BECAUSE THOUGHT TO HAVE

HAD SOMETHING WITH NAT TURNER MURDERING ACT, HE WAS CAPTURED AND FOUND GUILTY HANGED AND SURGEONS DISECTED HIS BODY AND MADE HEIRLOOMS OF FROM THE PARTS.

AND IN RECENT YEARS UNDER THE PRESIDENT CLINTON ADMINISTRATION, AND THE ATTORNEY GENERAL JANET RENO DEBACLE IN WACO TEXAS,THE LEADER AND HIS FOLLOWERS WERE BLOWN AWAY.

AFTER LISTENING AND WATCHING THE LEADERS OF THE NEW BLACK PANTHER PARTY, ON FOX NEWS LATELY IN APRIL 2006, THAT THEY ARE AT DUKE UNIVERSITY TO GATHER INFORMATION FROM THE STUDENT BODY IN AN INVESTIGATIVE MODE FOR ASSURANCE OF A CONVICTION, BECAUSE IT HAS BEEN DECIDED BY THEM THAT THE VICTOM WAS VIOLATED, AND THEY PLAN TO ORGANIZE THE COMMUNITY TO THAT AFFECT FOR A CONVICTION, AND IT HAS BEEN DECIDED THAT THEY ARE THE PROTECTORS OF THEIR BLACK BROTHERS AND SISTERS AROUND THE NATION AGAINST WHITE MAN LAWS, TO ASSURE THAT JUSTICE IS CARRIED OUT.

THERE HAVE BEEN NUMEROUS OF ORGANIZATIONS THAT HAS BEEN LED BY SELF APPOINTED LEADERS OVER HUNDREDS OF YEARS, I THOUGHT IT WOULD INTERESTING TO OFFER A BRIEF SYNOPSIS ON JUST A FIEW IN ORDER TO REVEAL THEIR SUCCESSES. REGARDS TO THEIR REBELLIOUS ACTIVITIES, AND AS YOU HAVE READ IT WOULD BE COMPLETELY FOOLISH TO ATTEMPT REPLACING INNOCENT UNTIL PROVEN GUILTY, WITH INSENSITIVE GESTURES THAT IS PARALLEL WITH VINDICTIVENESS BASED ON GENERALITY.

THE GENERAL THEORY IS THAT SOME AFRICAN AMERICANS BURN BRIDGES BEHIND THEM SO OTHERS CANT CROSS WITH REBELLIOUS ACTIVITIES, TRYING TO BE CROUSADERS FOR NOTORIETY, AND AS HISTORY HAS PROVEN IT IS THE INNOCENT THAT IS BEFALL WITH SUFFERANCE, FOR INSTANCE THE NAT TURNER CRUSADE AFTER IT WAS ALL OVER, WHITES RESTRICTED THE MOVEMENT OF ALL AFRICAN AMERICANS IN VIRGINIA FEAR OF ANOTHER REBELLION, THE GOVERNOR IN

EIGHTEEN THIRTY ONE ANNOUNCED THAT THERE WOULD BE STRICTER CONTROL ON ALL BLACKS, AND THAT BLACK MINISTERS WOULD BE SILENCED, THE LEGISLATION PASSED A NUMBER OF RESTRAINTS BLACKS WERE BARRED FROM HOLDING RELIGIOUS SERVICES OR NIGHT MEETINGS WITHOUT WRITTEN PERMISSION, THE VIRGINIA LEGISLATURE CONSIDERDED THEY SHOULD REMOVE ALL FREE AFRICAN AMERICANS FROM THE STATE, BUT POSPONED IT IN EIGHTEEN THIRTY FOUR, HOW EVER THEY DID PROHIBIT FREE BLACKS FROM ENTERING THE STATE, ALSO THE TEACHING OF READING AND WRITING WAS STRICTLY PROHIBITED, AND TO THINK THE MAJORITY OF AFRICAN AMERICANS HAD NOTHING TO DO WITH THE NAT TURNER REBELLION.

MANY PLANTATION SLAVE OWNERS AND WHITES THROUGHOUT THE SOUTHERN STATES IN GENERAL, BEGAN TO THINK BASED ON THE SAVAGERY THAT SOME BLACKS DISPLAYED,IT WOULD BE NECESSARY TO BRUTALIZE AND EXTERMINATE THEM, AND LAWS WAS PASSED TO PERMIT JUST THAT GENERALITY, MEANING FOR A WHITE TO MURDER A BLACK WAS ONLY A MISDEMEANOR.

IT IS FAIR TO INSINUATE THAT MOST AFRICAN AMERICANS LIKE THE PERCEPTION OF DEPTH THINKING, BECAUSE AFTER THE SURGEONS SKINNED AND DISSECTED THE BODY OF NAT TURNER AND PARCELED OUT PORTIONS AS SOUVENIRS MADE TROPHIES OF HIS BONES , AND FASHIONED PURSES FROM HIS SKIN, TO SOME AFRICAN AMERICANS TURNER IN THEIR OPENION BECAME A LEGENDARY HERO, BECAUSE HE SYMBOLIZED SLAVES BREAKING THEIR CHAINS AND AVENGING CRUELITY SUFFERED AT THE HANDS OF SLAVE HOLDERS THIS DEMONSTRATE THE CLUSTER OF INSANITY THAT IS SMOLDERING TODAY (NOT) BEING ABLE TO EVALUATE CONSEQUENCES THAT COULD ALTER THE LIVES OF MANY MANY INNOCENT AFRICAN AMERICANS, RLLEGATED TO HARSH REPRISAL THAT CAN AND WILL BE LEGISLATED THROUGH FEDERAL AND STATE LAWS, REGARDS TO HEINOUS ACTIONS OF A FIEW.

NAT TURNER WAS A SLAVE ON THE TRAVIS PLANTATION IN SOUTHHAMPETON COUNTY VIRGINIA, THAT HAD

PREMONITIONS OF DIRECT CONTACT WITH GOD AND WAS NOT A MAN OF THE CLOTH IN ANY FORMAL SENSE, BUT WAS DEEPEU RELIGIOUS HE SAW VISIONS AND INTERPRETED SIGNS OF BLOOD ON CORF N, AND HUMAN FIGURES IN THE AIR, AND DREAMS THAT HE HAD BEEN CHOSEN TO BE A PROPHET, AND WAS TO DELIVER (HIS) PEOPLE, HE SURMISED TO SEE WHITE SPRITS AND BLACK SPRITS IN BATTLE, AND THE SUN DARKEN THE THUNDER ROLLED IN THE HEAVENS, AND BLOOD FLOWED IN THE STREAMS, AND GOD HAD SIGNALED HIM TO REBEL AND PLAN A REVOLUTION. ONCE AGAIN THROUGHOUT HISTORY SOME AFRICAN AMERICANS TAKE A HORRIBLE PLANNED DISASTER AND DECIDE WHAT THEY (THINK) THE REBELLION WAS ABOUT, AND (NOT) REALISTICALLY UNDERSTANDING (WHAT) IT WAS ABOUT, AND DEVISE THEIR OWN INTERPRETATION OF EVENTS WHICH IS ERRONEOUS FROM THE INITIAL INTENT.

NAT TURNER SOLE AMBITIONS WAS TO OVER THROW THE GOVERNMENT BECAUSE OF HIS RADICAL VIEWS AND HATRED FOR PLANTATION SLAVE OWNERS, IN ORDER TO ENHANCE HIS OWN PROPHECY OF CONTROL OVER OTHERS, WHICH THEY FOLLOWED HIM TO THEIR DEMISE, AND CASTED A FOR EVERLASTN ING DRAMATIZING DESPICABLE SCANDAL THAT HINDERED THE PROGRESS OF AFRICAN AMERICANS FOR YEARS, AND MOST LIKELY CAUSED REPRISAL FROM WHITES ON INNOCENT BLACKS THROUGHOUT THE SOUTHERN STATES FOR MANY MANY DECADES, I CHOOSE TO ELABORATE ON SOME OF THE REBELLIOUS LEADERS AND THEIR FOLLOWERS IN PAST HISTORY, IN A EFFORT TO ENLIGHTEN ON THEIR SUCCESSES AND FAILURES.

BECAUSE IT APPEAR THAT THERE ARE SOME RADICAL LEADERS AND THEIR FOLLOWERS ARE FOSTERING IDEAS OF SUCH INSANITY, THESE SELF APPOINTED LEADERS HATCH IDEAS OF THIS NATURE IN ORDER TO GAIN NOTORIETY IN AN EFFORT TO INCREASE THEIR FOLLOWING, PANDERING VISIONS OF INTIMIDATION TO SEEK POLITICAL POWER OVER OTHERS IN THEIR OWN RANKING, AND THEY HAVE MYTHICAL ASSUMPTIONS THAT IT COULD DEVELOP INTO SOMETHING THAT IS REALLY CATCHING THROUGHOUT THE NATION, WITH THE INTENT TO FORMULATE A

REBELLION, UNFORTUNATELY THESE FANTASIZING POOR EXCUSE FOR A HUMAN BEING, IS TOTALLY UNAWARE OF HOW THE AUTHORITIES OF JUSTICE IS PREPARED TO DEAL WITH THESE KIND OF PLOTTED BARBARIC ACTS, AND THIS IS DUE TO (NOT) UNDERSTANDING THE POWERFUL POLITICAL STRUCTURE OF THIS NATION, WHICH STAND ALONE AS THE ONLY SUPER POWER IN THE WORLD, AND THERE IS NO ROOM FOR A RADICAL FOOL AT THE TOP, HOWEVER I WOULD SUGGEST THEY GET A SEAT ON THE FRONT ROW TO WATCH THE WRANGLING WITH LEADERS OF IRAN.

THERE ARE A LOT OF TRADITIONAL VALUES OVER THE YEARS. HAVE DISSIPATED FROM AFRICAN AMERICAN CULTURE, THAT HAD FUNDAMENTAL MERIT PERTAINING TO SELF ACCLAIM AND DIGNITY, WITHOUT THOSE ATTRIBUTES YOU ARE MARRED IN A QUAGMIRE OF DISDAIN WITH VISIONS OF ANY WAY THE WIND BLOW IS COOL WITH YOU, WHICH PRIMARILY REVOLVE AROUND DRUG ABUSE, AND ARE MILLIONS OF YOUNG AND OLD BLACKS CAUGHT IN THIS DISASTER,WHICH SHOULD BE CHARACTERIZED AS BEING SIMILAR TO A SELF IMPOSED PLAGUE, AND BASED ON CULTURAL MANNERISM OF HERDING AND WANTING TO BE LIKE OTHERS, SOME AFRICAN AMERICANS HAVE SOLD THEIR SOUL TO THE DEVIL WHICH IS AT EPIDEMIC PROPORTIONS, AND THERE IS NO LOGICAL REMEDY, WHITES WILL NOT DISCUSS THESE PROBLEMS FEAR OF BEING CALLED A RACIST, AND WHEN SOME BLACKS RAISE THE ISSURE THERE IS AN ATTEMPT TO JUSTIFY WITH PARALLEL INSINUATIONS TO WHITES FROM INFLUENTIAL BLACKS WITH A SYMPATHETIC DEMEANOR,AS IF TO SAY IT IS OK WHAT YOU ARE DOING BECAUSE WHITES ARE DOING THE SAME THINGS.

ON C-SPAN (2) BOOK TV. APRIL 3, 2006, MR. JOHN MC WHORTER GAVE .A BRIEF SYNOPSIS OF CULTURAL ISSURES THAT SOME BLACKS ARE BEING INUNDATED WITH PERTAINING TO THEIR CHOICE OF RADICAL, VIOLENCE, DRUG ABUSE AND JOBLESSNESS,AND WAS REFLECTING ON BROKEN HOMES, AND OUT

OF WEDLOCK BABIES, ALSO FREE LOADING FATHERS AND WELFARE REFORM, AND HIS IMPLICATIONS WERE THAT THESE ARE BLACK CREATED PROBLEMS, AND THEY ARE THE SOUL CURATORS THAT CAN RECTIFY THESE ISSURES BY SEEKING EMPLOYMENT COMPARABLE TO THEIR QUALIFICATIONS, WHICH HE POINTED OUT A FIEW THAT DID NOT REQUIRE FORMAL EDUCATION. AS I MENTION EARLIER IN THE BOOK SOME HIGHLY EDUCATED BLACKS LIKE THE ABILITY TO THINK IN DEPTH, BECAUSE AT MR. MC WORTER SESSION THERE WAS A BLACK FEMALE PROFESSOR IN THE AUDIENCE FROM HOWARD UNIVERSITY THAT VOICED HER OPENION RELATED TO THE PROBLEMS THAT BLACKS HAVE, AND AS EXPECTED SHE JOINED THE SYMPATHETIC CLUB, THE MAJORITY OF BLACKS WILL (NOT) BE CRITICAL OF A DETRIMENTAL REALITY THAT HAS ENGULFED THEIR OWN KIND.

ALMOST TO THE BRINK OF CIVIL EXTINCTION, INSTEAD THEY WOULD RATH ER OFFER FOOLISH EXCUSES, AND HERS WAS THAT SHE LIVE IN A AFFLUENT PREDOMINATELY WHITE NEIGHBOR HOOD AND WHITES DO THE SAME THINGS,THEY HERD AND BEHAVE IN THE SAME MANNER AS BLACKS IN CHOSEN AERAS, AND SEEMED TO TAKE OFFENSE AND BLURTED OUT THAT IT IS A AMERICAN CULTURAL PROBLEM,THESE LUDICRUS SCENARIOS DISPLAYED BY SOME AFFLUENT BLACKS CAUSE ALENATING FACTURES PERTAINING TO SOME AFRICAN AMERICANS MAKING THE NECESSARY ADJUSTMENTS TO REFRAIN FROM A RADICAL, DISRUPTIVE, AND INHUMANE DESPICABLE OFFENCES, IT IS AMAZINGLY SHOCKING AND A MYSTERY, HOW THE MAJORITY OF EDUICATED INFLUENTIAL BLACKS CAN CONTINUE OVER THE YEARS ATTEMPT TO DISRUPT THE LIVES OF THEIR OWN RACE OF PEOPLE, THAT HAS CONSISTE NTLY LED THEM INTO POVERTY BY (NOT) CONDEMING THEIR RADICAL BEHAVIOR

AND WHEN THERE ARE ASTUTE INTELLECTUAL AFRICAN AMERICANS, THAT H AVE THE CAPABILITIES TO CHRONOLOGY ADDRESS THE REVELATIONS OF BLACKS IN GENERAL,WITH OUT CYNICISM OR INDIGNATIONS.THAT PROFILE T HE REALITY OF SOME BLACKS AS IT EXIST,AND

THE CONSEQUENCES REGAR DS TO THEIR FATE, IF NOT RESTRICTED BASED ON THEIR OWN ACCORD, IS AND WILL BE DETRIMENTAL TO THEIR FUTURE REGARDS TO ECONOMICAL GROWTH.

HOWEVER THERE ARE THE FOR EVER PRESENT LIBERATORS, WITH THEIR FOOLISH ASSUMPTIONS SADISTCALLY OBSCURING WITH THEIR DISDAINING RHETORIC, TO EXALT ISSURES THAT ARE DETRIMENTAL TO THE SOCIETY OF AFRICAN AMERICANS, AS THE FEMALE BLACK PROFESSOR FROM HOWARD UNIVERSITY ASSERTED WITH AUDACIOUSNESS, APPARENTLY INEPT TO THE AWFUL ATROCITIES THAT SOME BLACKS PARTICIPATE IN ALL OVER THIS COUNTRY, AND TO ADDRESS THIS KIND OF BEHAVIOR AS SIMPLISTIC AND A AMERICAN CULTURE PROBLEM, THIS MYTHICAL CONDEMNATION HAS CAST THE MAJORITY OF AFRICAN AMERICANS INTO OBSCURITY, BECAUSE THIS IS (NOT) A WHITE AMERICA PROBLEM, THAT HAS RENOUNCED THEIR OVERALL OBJECTIVES, IT IS THE LIKE OF PERSEVERANCE RELATED TO OVERALL TRAITS PERTAINING TO JUDGMENTAL FANTASIES THAT IS INHERITED, AND EXPOUNDED ON BY RADICAL SELF PROCLAIMED BLACK BIGOTS, THAT IS OBSESSED WITH RETALIATORY CONVICTIONS TOWARD WHITE SUPERIORITY, AND ARE SO STUPID WITH VENGEANCE THEY ARE UNABLE TO REALIZE THAT WHITE PEOPLE ARE THE FOUNDERS OF CULTURAL BEHAVIOR THAT LEAD TO SUCCESS, SO THE COMPREHENSIVENESS TO THE OBJECTIVES IS PROFOUND, AND IS COLLECTIVELY MODERATED THROUGHOUT HISTORY, BECAUSE BEHIND EVERY SUCCESSFUL BLACK THERE IS A WHITE STANDING IN THE SHADOW. SO THIS PATERNALISTIC SYSTEMIC DEBACLE CREATED BY SOME BLACKS,IS VALIDATED TO THEIR OWN ACCORD, AND THEY STAND ALONE WITH THE MOST OUT OF WEDLOCK BIRTH RATE, COMMITED CRIMES, AND INCARCERATIONS, AND FOR THIS TO BE OBJECTIVELY REFERRED TO AS BEING SIMPLISTIC, IS A GROSS FOOLISH UNDERSTATEMENT, HOWEVER THESE CLOUDED MINDED EDUCATED BLACKS ARE THEORETICALLY JUST AS GUILTY AS THE CRIME COMMITTERS, BECAUSE OF THEIR INSTIGATING

CLARIFICATION THAT IS THE OPPOSITE OF THE REALITY, AND TO SUMMARIZE THIS AFRICAN AMERICAN TRAGEDY IN THIS MANNER IS PROBABLY ONE OF THE MOST ASININE AND OUT OF TUCH WITH REALITY AS ONE CAN BE, AND THIS IS A MAJOR FACTOR AS TO WHY THE NEBRASKA STATE SENATOR ERNIE CHAMBERS SPONSORED SEGREGATED SCHOOL BILL IS DOOMED TO FAILURE,BECAUSE SOME AFRICAN AMERICANS WILL SELF DISTRUCT INTO IGNORANCE, BECAUSE IF THE GENERAL CONSENSUS IS TO HAVE THE MAJORITY OF BLACK ON BLACK INSTRUCTORS IN THE SCHOOL SYSTEM IT WILL EVENTUALLY REVERSE THE COURSE OF HISTORY FOR MOST AFRICAN AMERICANS IN THAT STATE.

BECAUSE THE MAJORITY OF BLACKS EDUCATORS ARE MARRED IN A CRITERION THAT IS ADVERSE TO THE CREDENTIALS THAT THE NATION HAS PROVIDED FOR THE REFINEMENT OF INTELLECTUAL PERVASIVENESS, AND THEIR 0DIOUSNESS TO CHANGE FROM VULGARITY BASED ON STUPIDITY, AS THE PROFESSOR FROM HOWARD UNIVERSITY SPUN HER RENDITION OF OPPOSITION TO BLACK SELF CONTROL AND OBEDIENCE TO SUSTAIN A DEFINITIVE CONTRITE INITATIVE,AND DEEMED IT TO BE A OVERALL CULTURAL PROBLEM WITH ALL PEOPLE IN AMERICA,AFTER YEARS OF DEMOCRATIC POLITICAL INDOCTRINATING, THE MAJORITY OF AFRICAN AMERICANS ARE STALLED WITH SYMBOLIC LOGIC, THAT HAS DEVELOPED INTO A HORRENDOUS MELT DOWN RGARDS TO ACHIEVEMENT, THAT IS UNIVERSAL FOR SOME BASED ON THEIR ISOLATING THEM SELVES FROM A DIVERSE SOCIETY IN AN EFFORT TO ATTAIN A CULTURAL IDENTITY,WHICH IS NONSENSICAL AND ADVERSE TO ANY CIVILIZED COHESIVENESS, WHICH ERADICATE THEIR ABILITY TO FUNCTION APPROPRIATELY AND PRODUCTIVELY IN A DIVERSE SOCIETY.ON THEIR OWN MERIT.

INSTEAD THEY ARE TRYING TO IMPOSE THEIR INEPT DIVISIBLE LACK-LUSTER, DYSFUNCTIONAL,WAY OF LIFE ON THE REST OF THE NATION,AND THE CONVENTIONAL WISDOM IS THAT THEY WILL BE DEVOURED BY SELF DESTRUCTION BASED ON THEIR OWN IGNORANCE.

BLACKS WERE SQUANDERING THEIR OPPORTUNITIES AS FAR BACK AS NINETEEN HUNDRED AND ONE, THE YEAR HARRY TRUMAN GRADUATED FRON HIGH SCHOOL,SOME WERE HANGING ON CORNERS IN INDEPENDENCE MISSOURI, LOITERING AND LOOTING,WHILE OTHER PEOPLE WERE GAINFULLY EMPLOYED TO MAINTAIN FINANCIAL STABILITY, EVEN DURING SLAVERY THERE WERE THE HAND PICKED BLACK SLAVE DRIVERS, BY THEIR MASTERS TO PREVENT OTHERS FROM SLEEPING ON THEIR COTTON SACKS ALL DAY AFTER SWILLING THEIR GUT WITH SOUR CORN MASH, SO THIS KIND OF RADICAL DYSFUNCTIONAL BEHAVIOR DISPLAYED BY SOME BLACK IS A PART OF THEIR HISTORY FORMULATED AS A CUSTOM FROM AFRICA, AND THAT WAS MAINLY WHY WHITE PLANTATIONS SLAVE MASTERS PICKED MULATTOS TO INTRUST BECAUSE OF THEIR ABILITY TO REASON WITH,REGARDS TO CULTIVATING THEIR SKILLS, GENETIC CONTROLABILITY IS THE DOMINATING FACTOR PERTAINING TO MOST AFRICAN AMERICANS ALSO WHITES, AND HAS VERY LITTLE TO DO WITH EDUCATIONAL BACK GROUND, BECAUSE HISTORY HAS PROVEN THAT PEOPLE CAN BE SUCCESSFUL AND ARE TOTALLY ILLITERATE, IT IS THE GENESIS ORIGIN THAT CONTROLS YOUR DESTINY WITH OUT YOUR AWARENESS, HOWEVER IT IS VERY IMPORTANT TO HAVE SOME EDUCATIONAL BACK GROUND BECAUSE IT ENABLE YOU TO UNDERSTAND REALITY BASED ON YOUR CHOICE, UNFORTUNATELY IT IS A DOUBLE EDGE SWORD, THAT SPLIT REALITY BASED ON YOUR GENETIC CONTROLABILITY, AND THAT IS WHY THERE ARE SO MANY OBSTACLES IN LIFE THAT PEOPLE DO (NOT) UNDERSTAND ABOUT OTHERS ALSO THEM SELVES, BECAUSE GENETIC CONTROLABILITY DICTATE THE MAJORITY OF PEOPLE CHOICES THAT ARE MADE IN LIFE, AND NOT ONLY DOES IT HAVE TO DO WITH PEOPLE, IT PERTAIN TO EVERY CREATURE ON GODS EARTH, TO SHARE A PROUFOUND EXPERIENCE THAT I OBSERVED AS A KID GROWING UP IN ALABAMA ON THE FAMILY FARM WE HAD DOGS TO USE FOR HUNTING, AND THIS FEMALE DOG WAS A MONGREL MIX WITH HOUND THE NEIGHBOR HAD A MONGREL MIX WITH GERMAN SHEPHERD WHICH HAD A BOBBED TAIL,

THAT WAS ATROCIOUS AND WHIPPED EVERY DOG IN THE NEIGHBORHOOD, HE MATED WITH OUR FEMALE DOG AND SHE HAD ONE PUPPY THAT WAS BERTHED WITH A BOBBED TAIL, SO MY PARENTS GAVE ME THE PUPPY WHICH WAS A MALE FOR A PET, IN ORDER TO TEACH ME HOW TO CARE FOR ANIMALS, I NURTURED HIM AND HE GREW UP TO BE A WONDERFUL PET, AND HE COULD WHIP EVERY OTHER DOG EXCEPT HIS FATHER, AFTER A FIEW YEARS THE NEIGHBORS DOG WHICH WAS MY DOG FATHER WAS STRUCK BY AN AUTOMOBILE CROSSING THE HIGHWAY AND LOST HIS LIFE, AND MY DOG BECAME THE KING OF THE HILL FOR MANY YEARS, HOWEVER THIS BOOK IS NOT ABOUT DOGS WITH BOBBED TAILS, IT IS TO DEMONSTRATE THAT PEOPLE SHARE THE SAME PARALLEL DISTINCTION RELATED TO GENETIC CONTROLLABILITY, WHICH HAS NOTHING TO DO WITH BOBBED DOG TAILS, BUT THE HMAN BRAIN, WHERE GENETICS LINKED WITH POLITICS CAN COUSE IT TO BE DYSFUNCTIONAL OR PERSONIFY GREATNESS,HOWEVER MOST AFRICAN AMERICANS ARE ELUSIVE TO THE FUNDAMENTAL ASPECTS OF POLITICS IN THIS COUNTRY, THEY TEND TO DISTORT REALITY FOR SELF INITIATIVE, SEEKING ADVANTAGES FROM PREHISTORIC ACCOLADES TO BOOST THEIR IMAGE. AMONG OTHER BLACKS BY FOCUSING ON TOLERANT AND MORE JUSTICE IN AMERICA, AND REFERRING TO THE CIVIL RIGHTS MOVEMENT OF THE SIXTIES BY DR. MARTIN LUTHER KING, AS THE SENATOR FROM ILLINOIS BARACK OBAMA DID ON C-SPAN, MAY 11, 2006,AS HE ADDRESSED A AUDIENCE AT EMILYS LUNCHEON, LETS JUST ANALYTICALLY DISSECT SENATOR OBAMA COMMENTS AT THIS GATHERING, NOW HE IS AN ACCOMPLISHED ATTORNEY, AND A MEMBER OF THE ONE HUNDRED SENATORS IN THE UNITED STATES OF AMERICA, AND FOR SOME STRANGE POLITICAL FOOLISH REASON HE WOULD ADDRESS A GATHERING OF PEOPLE AND SEEM TO SUGGEST THAT JUSTICE IN THIS COUNTRY IS (NOT) UP TO PAR REGARDS TO HIS SATISFACTION, AND HOPED HIS CHILDREN WOULD SEE A BETTER DAY, AFFLUENT DEMOCRATIC BLACKS SEEM TO THINK THEY CAN SAY ANY THING ABOUT JUSTICE IN THIS COUNTRY AND AS LONG

AS THEY MENTION DR. MARTIN LUTHER KING MARCHING FOR FREEDOM PERTAINING TO EQUALITY,IT IS OK AND THEY WILL NEVER BE CHALLENGED AND THE MAJORITY OF THE TIME THEY ARE NOT, BECAUSE NINETY FIVE PRECENT OF BLACK POLITICAL CRONIES ARE IN THE BUCKET WITH THE REST OF THE CRABS, AND WHITES WANT FEAR OF BEING CALLED A RACIST, SO THEY HAVE A FREE REIGN TO LIE THROUGH THEIR TEETH ABOUT JUSTICE IN AMERICA IN AN EFFORT TO CONTROL OTHER BLACKS FOR THEIR VOTING BLOC.

AND IT IS THESE KIND OF PEOPLE THAT IS CAUSING THE MAJORITY OF AFRICAN AMERICANS TO DISINTEGRATE INTO A DERANGED POLITICAL SELF DESTRUCTION WITH DISDAIN FOR THEIR COUNTRY, BECAUSE OF BLATANT LIES BEING TOLD TO THEM BY SENATOR OBAMA AND OTHER AFFLUENT BLACK DEMOCRATIC PERSONNEL, AND YES OBAMA IS LYING BECAUSE HE IS THE PROOF OF WHAT AMERICA HAS TO OFFER IF YOU CHOOSE TO APPLY YOUR SELF, BECAUSE HE IS A (BLACK) EDUCATED ATTORNEY AND U.S. SENATOR IN AMERICA, AND HE HAVE THE APPALING INSOLENCE TO EPITOMIZE AMERICA AS NEEDING MORE TOLERENCE AND JUSTICE, I ASSUME HE WAS SPEAKING ON BEHALF OF THE ILLEGAL HISPANICS IN THIS COUNTRY, BECAUSE CERTAINLY (NOT) AFRICAN AMERICANS BECAUSE (HE) IS LIVING PROOF THAT THE DOORS ARE WIDE OPEN FOR BLACKS AND OPPORTUNITY IN THIS COUNTRY THE UNITED STATES OF AMERICA, AND ALL YOU HAVE TO DO IS APPLY YOUR SELF IN A DIPLOMATIC DIVERSIFIED MANNER TO ATTAIN PROSPERITY BECAUSE I WILL GUARANTEE YOU THAT IS WHAT SENATOR BARACK OBAMA CHOOSE TO DO, WITH STRONG CULTURALLY MORAL MOTIVATING FROM HIS PARENTS OR SOME ONE INSTRUMENTAL IN HIS ACADEMIC GROWTH, AND BEING A PUBLIC POLITICAL AFFUENT AFRICAN AMERICAN, HE EVADE THE ISSURE OF REALITY BY INSTIGATING NONSENSICAL TOPICS OF TOLERANT AND MORE JUSTICE AND RELATING TO DR. MARTIN LUTHER KING MARCHING IN SELMA ALABAMA DURING THE SIXTIES, OVER FORTY FIVE YEARS AGO.

IT IS TRULY ASTONISHING THAT BLACK DEMOCRATIC SO CALL LEADERS ARE INEPT TO THE TRAVISTY THAT HAS PLAGUED SOME AFRICAN AMERICANS FOR CENTURIES REGARDS TO THEIR INABILITY TO ADAPT TO A PROFOUND CULTURED SYSTEM, THAT THEY HAVE FULL ACCESSIBILITY TO SENSE NINETEEN SIXTY FOUR AND SIXTY FIVE, WHICH IS APPROXIMATELY FORTY ONE YEARS AGO, THERE ARE MILLIONS OF AFRICAN AMERICANS THAT ARE PROSPEROUS AND FINANCIALLY STABLE, BECAUSE THEY CHOOSE TO ALIENATE THEM SELVES FROM THIS CONTEMPTIBLE POLICY OF SEPERATE BUT EQUAL, THAT SOME BLACKS SEEM TO CHERISH, AND IS PURSUING EFFORTS TO REESTABLISH THIS DREADFUL FOOLISH DOCTRINE.

WHEN THEY SHOULD BE FOCUSING ON HOW TO BECOME ACADEMICALLY COMPETITIVE AS OTHER AFRICAN AMERICAN HAS CAPITULATED TO THE CULTIVATED MORALS OF THE NATION, AND ARE PLAYING ON THE FIELD THAT WAS LEVELED IN NINETEEN SIXTY FOUR AND FIVE.

HOWEVER THERE ARE THE BLACK DEMOCRATIC SELF APPOINTED LEADERS, EDUCATORS, LAW PROFESSORS, AND SENATOR, THAT SEEM TO BE DENOUNCING THIS THEORY, WHICH THEY CAPITALIZED ON TO BECOME AFFLUENT, BUT WILL SPREAD OUT ALL OVER THE NATIONS NET WORKS WITH DEMOCRATIC DEMAGOGUERY AND BUFFOONISH LIES, IN AN EFFORT TO POLITICALLY HOLD AFRICAN AMERICANS IN BONDAGE FOR THE DEMOCRAT PARTY REGARDS TO THEIR VOTING BLOC, THE MENDACITY OF THESE DEMOCRATIC POLITICIANS IS APPALLING.

AND WHEN SOME AFRICAN AMERICANS TRY TO SET THE RECORD STRAIGHT ON THIS BLACK SELF INFLICTED DILEMMA AND DIRECT ATTENTION TO THE SOURCE, AND OFFER A SOLUTION FOR CORRECTION, WHICH HAS TO DO WITH TEIR OWN INITIATIVE.

THERE IS THE ALWAYS BLACK DEMOCRATIC OPPONENTS TO WATER DOWN THEIR EFFORTS AND CONSTANTLY BLAME THE NATION GOVERNMENT FOR NOT BEING JUST, OR IT IS AN ALL AMERICAN PROBLEM REGARDS TO THE RADICAL BEHAVIOR OF BLACKS, AND (NEVER) ELABORATE ON HOW AMERICA IMPEDED THEIR ACCOMPLISHMENTS

RELATED TO THEIR FINANCIAL STABILITY. IT IS ONE OF THE DUBIOUS BETRAYED TRAVESTY KNOWN TO MAN KIND, PERPETRATED AGAINST YOUNG AND OLD BLACKS OVER THE YEARS BY INFLUENTIAL BLACK DEMOCRATIC STRATEGIST, EDUCATORS, AND SELF APPOINTED LEADERS, BECAUSE OF THEIR COMPASSION TO EMULATE PRESISTORIC REVELATIONS AND INSINUATE THAT BLACKS ARE MARRED IN THIS DEBACLE TODAY WHICH CAUSE SOME BLACKS TO BECOME REBELLIOUS, AND THINK WHITES ARE IMPEDING THEIR PROGRESS, WHICH COULD NOT BE FURTHER FROM THE TRUTH, NEEDLESS TO SAY THE DEMOCRATIC PARTY AND THEIR SOCIAL PROGRAMS ALONG WITH THEIR COCONSPIRATORS BLACK DEMOCRATIC SELF APPOINTED RADICAL LEADERS, HAS CULTURALLY, MORALLY, AND POLITICALLY DECIMATED AT LEAST FOUR GENERATIONS OF AFRICAN AMERICANS, TO A DEGREE OF HOPEFULNESS AS OF TO DATE WITH THEIR CYNICAL PREHISTORIC MOTIVATIONS THAT HINGE ON THEIR INEPTNESS TO POLITICS, AND TO SECURE THEIR VOTING BLOC FOR THE DEMOCRATIC PARTY.

TO EXAMINE THE PORTRAYAL OF PSYCHOANALYSIS PERTAINING TO AFRICAN AMERICANS EXHIBITED BY THE DEMOCRATIC PARTY, STARTING WITH THE BEGINNING, AFRICANS WERE IN SLAVED ON THE PLANTATIONS IN THE SOUTHERN STATES, AND BRED LIKE ANIMALS FOR QUALITY STOCK, WHILE SOME OF THE AFRICAN WOMEN WERE SEXUALLY MISUSED AT THE LEISURE OF THE SLAVE MASTERS AND OTHER MEMBERS OF THEIR FAMILES, AFRICAN MEN AND WOMEN WERE SOLD AND TRADED LIKE LIVE STOCK, IN EIGHTEEN SIXTY FIVE A REPUBLICAN PRESIDENT ABRAHAM LINCOLN, BROUGHT THIS HORRIBLE DISGRACEFUL ESCAPADE TO A HALT, AND GAVE AFRICAN AMERICANS THEIR FREEDOM, AND FORMATTED LEGISLATION TO GIVE EACH AFRICAN AMERICAN FAMILY FORTY ACRES OF LAND AND A MULE, TO BE TAKEN FROM THE PLANTATION OWNERS, UNFORTUNATELY PRESIDENT ABRAHAM LINCOLN LOST HIS LIFE DUE TO ASSASSINATION BY A DEMOCRATIC RACIST FOR FREEING THE SLAVES, VICE PRESIDENT ANDREW JOHNSON, A DEMOCRAT FROM

TENNESSEE ASSUMED THE PRESIDENCY, AND RECINDED THE LEGISLATION AND GAVE THE LAND BACK TO THE PLANTATION OWNERS, AS A RESULT AFRICAN AMERICANS BEING ILLITERATE AND HAD NO OTHER SKILLS BUT FARMING, THEIR ONLY HOPE WAS RETURNING TO THE PLANTATION MASTERS WITH AGREEMENTS OF SHARE CROPPING.

BLACK AND WHITE REPUBLICANS EDUCATORS FLOODED INTO THE SOUTHERN STATES TO TEACH FORMER SLAVES HOW TO READ AND WRITE, IN EIGHTEEN SIXTY SIX THE DEMOCRATS ORGANIZED THE KU-KLUX-KLAN AND VIOLENTLY DROVE THEM AWAY AND TERRORIZED AFRICAN AMERICANS FOR YEARS.

IT IS TRULY AMAZING AND ASTOUNDING WHY THE MAJORITY OF AFRICAN AMERICANS POLITICALLY SUPPORT THE DEMOCRATIC PARTY, WHEN THEY ARE THE CULPRIT OF (EVERY) MISFORTUNE AND CYNICAL ACT OF IMPEDANCES TO THEIR EDUCATION AND CIVIL LIBERTIES IN THIS NATION, NOT TO MENTION THE EGREGIOUS LYNCHINGS CARRIED OUT BY THE DEMOCRATIC FOUNDED KU-KLUX-KLAN, IN ORDER TO ENHANCE THEIR SUPERIORITY TO MAINTAIN CONTROL OVER AFRICAN AMERICANS THROUGH VIOLENCE, LYNCHINGS ARE NO LONGER IN EXISTENCE, HOWEVER THEIR HOSTILE POLITICAL TECHNICALITIES IS STILL EMBEDDED IN THEIR ROOTS FROM ANCESTORY, WHICH WAS DISPLAYED AT THE CONFORMATION HEARINGS FOR CONDOLEEZZA RICE TO BECOME SECRETARY OF STATE, AND ALBERTO GONZALES TO BE ATTORNEY GENERAL, YOU JUST CAN IMAGINE WHAT THE DEMOCRATIC ELDERS WAS LIKE BY WATCHING THE PERFORMANCE DISPLAYED BY SENATOR BARBARA BOXER, RELATED TO MS. RICE, SENATOR BOXER WAS SIMPLY TERRIFIED TO WITNESS THIS HISTORIC EVENT, AND MOST LIKELY WAS THINKING WOULD. SOME, ONE PLEASE .SAY ITS NOT TRUE.

BECAUSE THE SOUTHERN DEMOCRATS CONNIVED AND FORMULATED THE SEPERATE BUT EQUAL DOCTRINE IN EIGHTEEN NINETY SIX, WHICH THE SUPREME COURT ENDORSED AS BEING CONSTUTIONAL FOR THE SOUTHERN STATES, UNDER THIS SYSTEM BLACKS WERE VICTIMIZED,

AND SOME TIME LYNCHED FOR DRINKING FROM A FOUNTAIN LABELED WHITE ONLY, OR FOR NOT SAYING YES MAM AND YES SIR TO WHITE TEENAGERS, THE DEMOCRATS WERE ELECTED TO THE MAJORITY IN THE SENATE AND THE HOUSE OF REPRESENTATIVES, AND VIRULENTLY PUT FORTH THEIR BEST EFFORT TO IMPEDE CIVIL RIGHTS FOR AFRICAN AMERICANS UNTIL NINETEEN SIXTY FOUR AND FIVE, BUT PRIOR TO THAT TIME DEMOCRATS AND THEIR KU-KLUX-KLAN SLAUGHTERED BLACKS ALMOST AT WILL BY ANY MEANS THEY CHOOSE BUT MOSTLY BY LYNCHINGS, AND HELD POLITICAL CONGRESSIONAL AND MOSTLY PRESIDENTAL POWER FOR FORTY YEARS AND (NEVER) ELEVATED BLACKS TO ANY SUBSTANTIAL POSITION OF POLITICAL AUTHORITY, BECAUSE LEOPARDS DO NOT CHANGE THEIR SPOTS.

THIS IS THE YEAR OF TWO THOUSAND AND SIX, AND THE DEMOCRATS ARE TRYING TO MINIPULATE THE HISPANICS INTO THE SAME STUPOR THEY HAVE HELD THE MAJORITY OF AFRICAN AMERICANS IN FOR OVER SIXTY TEARS, WITH LIES AND DECITFUL DEMAGOGUERY, AND NOW THEY ARE STRATEGICALLY IN A PANIC TO CAST HISPANICS INTO THE SAME POLITICAL DILEMMA ALONG WITH BLACKS, WHICH IS A SUPERFICIAL AGENDA TO PERSUADE THEIR VOTING SUPPORT, BUT IT IS GOING TO BE SOME WHAT DIFFICULT AND A UP HILL POLITICAL BATTLE, BECAUSE OF THE GENETIC CULTURAL BACKGROUND, TRADITIONALLY HISPANICS THINK INDEPENDENTLY AND DO NOT FOLLOW THE GUIDANCE OF A SELF APPOINTED DEMOCRATIC LEADER, AND THIS IS GIVING THE DEMOCRATS SPASMODIC BRAIN DAMAGE, AND THERE ARE SOME REPUBLICANS STRADDLE THE FENCE ON THIS IMMIGRATION ISSURE, BUT THE FACT IS THEY ARE HERE AND THEIR POPULATION HAS EXCEEDED AFRICAN AMERICANS, WHICH HAS BEEN THE LEANING POST FOR DEMOCRATS MAIN STAY IN POLITICAL POWER FOR YEARS, AND THIS IS WHY THE DEMOCRATS ARE ASTATIC AND TRYING TO APPEASE BOTH.AFRICAN AMERICANS AND HISPANICS IN AN EFFORT TO CONSOLIDATE THEIR POLITICAL SUPPORT, AND MAKING THEM SELVES LOOK AWFUL FOOLISH ON MAY 19, 2006 THERE WAS A VOTE

IN THE SENATE TO DETERMINE IF ENGLISH SHOULD BE THE NATIONAL LANGUAGE, THERE ARE ONE HUNDRED SENATORS WITH REPUBLICANS HOLDING A FIFTY FIVE SEAT ADVANTAGE, APPROXIMATELY THIRTY THREE DEMOCRATS VOTED TO DENOUNCE THE AMERICAN ENGLISH IN AN EFFORT TO BRIBE HISPANIC VOTERS TO THINK THEY ARE FOR THEIR CAUSE, PRESIDENT FRANKLIN ROOSEVELT INITIATED THE SAME PRINCIPLES IN THE EARLY FORTIES TO HYPERCRITICALLY DESTROY THE PARTY THAT LINCILN BUILT WITH DECITFUL POLITICAL TACTICS RELATED TO SOCIAL PROGRAMS, AND UTILIZING AFFLUENT BLACKS TO SPEAR HEAD HIS AGENDA, WHICH CAST THE MAJORITY OF AFRICAN AMERICANS INTO POLITICAL BONDAGE BY DEMOCRATS FOR EVER, TO SUPPORT THEIR RADICAL AGENDA FOR NOTHING MORE THAN A FIEW CRUMBS OF SOCIAL PROGRAMS, THAT IS AVAILABLE TO EVERY CITIZEN IN THE UNITED STATES OF AMERICA,IF THEY CHOOSE NOT TO SEEK EMPLOYMENT AND PERSUE A LIFE LONG CAREER IN HAVING BABIES, AND NOT EDUCATING THEM SELVES, THEN YOU ARE A PRIME CANDIDATE TO BE CONSUMED BY THE DEMOCRATIC BUREAUCRACY TO ENHANCE THEIR POLITICAL AGENDA, WHICH THROUGH THEIR BLACK DEMOCRATIC STRATEGIST AND SELF APPOINTED LEADERS, THAT KEEP YOU THINKING THE COUNTRY IS UN-JUST, AND THE PLAYING FIELD SHOULD BROUGHT TO YOUR LEVEL, SO AS A RESULT YOU ARE CHASING A RAIN-BOW RIGHT INTO THE HANDS OF THE JUSTICE SYSTEM OR A UNWARRANTED DEMISE, IT IS FAIR TO SAY THAT THE DEMOCRATS ARE THE CULPRIT AND ARCHITECTS OF THESE MALIGNED STUPENDOUS SELF IMPOSITION CHARACTERIZATION DISPLAYED BY SOME AFRICAN AMERICANS MOSTLY ADOLESCENCE AND YOUNG ADULTS, JUST RECENTLY SENATOR HARRY REID THE DEMOCRATIC MINORITY LEADER, PUBLICLY DENOUNCED ENGLISH AS BEING STANDARD LANGUAGE FOR THE NATION, AND INSINUATED THAT HE THOGHT IT WOULD BE DISCRIMINATORY TO DO SO, A FIEW MONTHS AGO SENATOR HILLARY CLINTON MADE DISPARAGING REMARKS ABOUT HISPANICS WITH NO DISTINCTION,AND PIGEONHOLE THEIR QUALIFICATIONS

TO WATING TABLES, MAKING BEDS, MOWING LAWNS, AND CLEANING HOMES, AND A FIEW OTHER STIGMATIZING INSULTS.

BUT TO DENOUNCE THE AMERICAN ENGLISH IS A TOTAL SELL OUT WITH HYPOCRISY, AND A PATHETIC NONSENSICAL POLITICAL PLOY JUST TO ALIGN THE HISPANIC VOTE IN THEIR FAVOR, THESE CUNNING POLITICAL DECEPTIONS DISPLAYED BY DEMOCRATS HAS LITERALLY SPEAR HEADED THE MORAL SELF DESTRUCTIONS AND CYNICISM RELATED TO THE MAJORITY OF AFRICAN AMERICANS IN THIS COUNTRY, AND THE AFFECTS OF THIS FOOLERY IS BEING FELT IN BLACK COMMUNITIES AROUND THE NATION, THE DEMOCRATS HAS CAUSED A CRUSADE RELEGATED TO BLACK SUPREMACY BY (NOT) BEING REALISTICALLY CANDID REGARDS TO THEIR INTENTIONS, AND THE BACKLASH IS HORRIFIC AND WILL PROGRESSIVELY GET WORSE AROUND THE NATION, BECAUSE THE DEMOCRATIC TRAINED DYSFUNCTIONAL BRAIN INSTIGATORS WILL SOON BE ENTRAPPED WITH THE REALITY THAT LAW ENFORCEMENT THROUGHOUT THE STATES AROUND THE NATION IS FEED UP, AND IS UNITING IN AN EFFORT TO QUELL THIS INSANITY THAT THE DEMOCRATS GAVE LEGS TO YEARS AGO, THROUGH THEIR SUPERFICIAL PLUNDERING FOR POLITICAL POWER, AND SOME AFRICAN AMERICANS ARE CAUGHT IN A CAROUSAL SEEKING A EQUALITY MIRAGE THAT NEVER EXISTED, THAT HAS DESECRATED THEM INTO A WORLD OF SELF DESTRUCTION, CITIES AROUND THE NATION HAVE AND ARE STRENGTHENING LAWS AND ROUNDING UP YOUNG BLACK CRIMINALS AS YOUNG AS THIRTEEN AND PROSECUTING . AS ADULTS, WHILE THEIR MOTHERS ARE CRYING AND MAKING STATEMENTS THAT HE IS JUST A BABY WHICH IS TRUE, HOWEVER THEY ARE COMMITTING HEINOUS CRIMES AND THIS IS A RESULT OF YEARS OF SEDUCTIVE INDOCTRINATING THAT HAD (NO) INTEREST IN THEIR PRODUCTIVE MORAL VALUES FOR MANY BLACKS TO STEER THEM IN A DIRECTION OF WHAT IS IN THEIR BEST INTEREST SO THEY ARE BEING TOLD WHAT THEY WANT TO HEAR, BASED ON THEIR HERDING BEHIND SELF APPOINTED BLACK LEADERS AND

BEING ADVISED THAT THEIR PROBLEMS ARE STIMULATED BY WHITES BECAUSE OF THEIR COLOR, WHICH MAKE THE SYSTEM UN-JUST HAVING TO DO WITH A SYSTEMIC PROBLEM PREPETRATED AGAINST AFRICAN AMERICANS.

THERE WAS A SENIC CHARADE DISPLAYED ON CNN MAY 27, 2006, WITH THE DISCUSSION TO THE USE OF THE WORD (NIGGER) JILL MERRITT ELABORATED ON THE SOUTH AND SOUTHERN DEMOCRATIC PLANTATION SLAVE OWNERS AND THEIR EXCLUSIVE USE OF THE WORD (NIGGER) WHILE COMMITTING HIDEOUS CRIMES AGAINST BLACKS SUCH AS LYNCHINGS, AND SHE FEEL THE WORD SHOULD BE ABOLISHED FROM THE ENGLISH DOCTRINE, THIS IS CONSIDERED TO BE FOOLISH DEMAGOGUERY FOR PUBLIC ATTENTION AND NOTHING MORE, OTHER THAN TO MOBILIZE RADICAL BLACK RACISM.

AND AS I HAVE INDICATED SOME AFRICAN AMERICANS LIKE THE PRECEPTION OF THINKING IN DEPTH, BECAUSE THE SOUTHERN DEMOCRATIC PLANTATION OWNERS ARE RESPONSIBLE FOR ALL THOSE BARBARIC ACTS EXERCISED AGAINST BLACKS INCLUDING THE WORD (NIGGER), HOWEVER AFRICAN AMERICANS STILL SUPPORT DEMOCRATIC IDEOLOGY BY NINETY FIVE PRECENT WITH THEIR POLITICAL VOTING BLOC, AND THIS IS WHY THE TITLE OF THE BOOK IS LABELED POLITICAL SELF DESTRUCTION FOR SOME AFRICAN AMERICANS, BECAUSE MOST BLACKS LIKE THE ABILITY TO CONNECT CORRESPONDING POLITICAL ISSURES THAT HAS AFFECTED THEM FOR HUNDREDS OF YEARS RELATED TO SELF INITATIVE AND MORAL RESPONSIBILITIES, APPARENTLY ITS OK FOR SOME BLACKS TO CALL OUR SITTING PRESIDENT A TERRORIST, AND WHEN SENATOR BARACK OBAMA WAS ASKED ABOUT THE CHOICE WORD, HIS RESPONSE WAS THAT THE FIRST AMENDMENT OF THE CONSTUTION GAVE THEM THAT RIGHT,WHICH IS CORRECT, IT IS PERPLEXING, SICKENING AND APPALLING, TO SEE SOME AFRICAN AMERICANS ALLOW THEM SELVES TO BE BROADCAST TO THE NATION AND THE WORLD THAT DEMONSTRATE THEIR IGNORANCE TO SOCIETY,REGARDS TO HUMAN RIGHTS RATIFIED TO THE CONSTUTION,WITH STUPID

NONSENSICAL INSINUATIONS THAT THE WORD (NIGGER) SHOULD BE ABOLISHED PERTAINING TO BLACKS, AS IF THEY ARE THE ONLY NATIONALLY THAT IS PLAGUED BY DEROGATORY CYNICISM, THE IMPLICATIONS OF STUPIDITY IS STAMPED ON THEIR FOREHEAD, BECAUSE OF THEIR OVERWHELMING SUPPORT FOR THE DEMOCRATIC PARTY THAT GAVE THEM THOSE NAMES, SUCH AS NIGGER, COON, DARKIE, OLD UNCLE TOM,AND SAM BOA, WHICH MEANT ABSOLUTELY (NOTHING) THEN AND CERTAINLY NOT NOW, IT IS THE INDIVIDUAL EFFORT TO PERSUE INTELLECTUAL CREDITABILITY IN A DIVERSE SOCIETY, AND THE ADVERSE SYNONYMS WILL DISSIPATE INTO A AFTERMATH, UNFORTUNATELY THERE WILL ALWAYS BE SOME IDIOT ATTEMPTING TO RAISE PREHISTORIC ISSURES SUCH AS THESE FOR PERSONAL NOTORIETY, WHICH IS SHAMELESS, NONSENSICAL, AND REBELLIOUS BUFFOONERY, THAT IS CONSISTENTLY EXPLOITED BY SOME BLACKS TO (NO) AVAIL, OTHER THAN POLITICAL IGNORANCE TO INCITE OTHERS, BECAUSE TO BAN ANY VERBIAGE FROM THE AMERICAN ENGLISH AND PROHIBIT THE USAGE, IS A GROSS VIOLATION OF FREE SPEECH, THAT IS RATIFIED BY THE CONSTUTION.

THERE ARE SOME AFRICAN AMERICANS HAVE THIS MYTHICAL DOMINEERING CONCEPTION THAT SLAVERY IS RESPONSIBLE FOR THEIR UNFORTUNATE MISGIVINGS TODAY, AND CONTINUE TO TRY AND INFLATE THOSE PREHISTORIC OCCURRENCES IN ORDER FOR WHITES TO FEEL GUILTY AND RELENT TO THEIR STUPID ABSURDITY, AND TO SEDUCE OTHER BLACKS TO REINFORCE THEIR THEORY FOR PURPOSES OF DECEIT WHICH HAS NO MERIT.

SLAVERY WAS A REALITY FOR MANY PEOPLE BLACK AND WHITE, UNFORTUNATELY AFRICAN AMERICANS SUFFERANCE WAS THE SEVEREST, AND MOSTLY BECAUSE OF THEIR GENETIC CONTROLLABILITY THAT STIMULATE HERDING AND THE URGE TO FOLLOW SELF APPOINTED LEADERS, AND THESE TRAITS HAS CAUSED SOME AFRICAN AMERICANS IMMENSELY REPREHENSIBLE HARM, AND IT IS A CULTURAL TRADITION THAT IS EVERLASTING THAT TRANSEND TODAY, BUT IN PAST HISTORY IT COULD BE

DEADLY, BECAUSE OF THE EXISTING CIRCUMSTANCES THAT MOST AFRICAN AMERICANS REFUSED TO ACKNOWLEDGE BASED ON IGNORANCE, AND FORMED EVIL REBELLIOUS TACTICS AGAINST SOCIETY THAT CAUSED STRICT FORMABLE GUIDE LINES BY AUTHORITIES TO PREVENT FURTHER ATROCITIES, AND ONCE THEY STEPPED OUT OF BOUNDS OR DISOBEYED THE RULES THEY MOST LIKELY WOULD BE LYNCHED, THE SAME SELF IMPOSED RENDITION IS OCCURING TODAY, HOWEVER THE METHODOLOGY IS DIFFERENT, SOME ARE SELECTING SELF DESTRUCTIVE INCARCERATION OR AIMLESSLY A VIOLENT DEMISE, AND THIS IS(ALL) RELATED TO THE INABILITY TO CONFORM AND MAKE THE NECESSARY ADJUSTMENTS THAT IS REQUIRED TO FULFILL THE BOUNTY OF A PREDICATED MORAL DIVERSE SOCIETY AND THROUGH INTOLERANCE DEVELOPE SCHIZOPHRENIC BEHAVIORAL PATTERNS THAT LEAD TO CRIMINALITY, THAT IS CAUSING THIRTEEN YEAR OLDS TO BE APPREHENDED TRIED CONVICTED AND SENTENCED AS ADULTS, AND THIS IMMORTALITY IS WORSE THAN SLAVERY, SLAVERY WAS ALMOST AN EXCLUSIVE PHENOMENON FORTIFIED BY SOUTHERN DEMOCRATS, AND THERE ARE THOSE AFRICAN AMERICANS THAT IS IN DENIAL REGARDS TO DIFFERENTIATING BETWEEN OUR MAJOR TWO PARTY SYSTEM AND TEND TO LUMP THEM TOGATHER RELATED TO HOSTILITY WHEN DISCUSSING SLAVERY, THE TWO PARTY SYSTEM CONSIST OF THE REPUBLICAN AND THE DEMOCRATS, THEIR IDEOLOGY WAS TOTALLY THE OPPOSITE REGARDS TO SLAVERY, SOUTHERN DEMOCRATS TREASURED IT, REPUBLICANS DESPISED IT AND DID EVERY THING UNDER THEIR POLITICAL POWER TO ABOLISH THIS ANIMALISTIC BARBARIC BEHAVIOR, UNFORTUNATELY TO NO AVAIL UNTIL EIGHTEEN SIXTY FIVE, HWEVER WHEN AFFLUENT BLACKS ADDRESS THESE ISSURES SELF DEGRADATION SEEN TO PREVAIL AND REGRETTABLE THEY CONCLUDE (NO) DISTINCTION, SUCH AS WALTER HILL, NATIONAL ARCHIVES SENIOR ARCHIVIST ASSERTED ON C-SPAN (2) APRIL 28, 2006, HE GAVE A SYSTEMIC STATISTICAL OBSERVATION OF SLAVERY, DIRECTING THE ATTENTION TO THE EIGHTEEN FORTYS AND FIFTIES, WITH OUT QUESTION

THESE WERE TROUBLING TIMES FOR AFRICAN AMERICANS, GIVEN THE REALITY OF SLAVES LIVES AND THE DIRECT VIOLENT CONFRONTATION OF SLAVERY WAS GENERALLY IMPRACTICAL AND MOST LIKELY TO BE SPONTANEOUS OUT-BREAKS RESULTING FROM SPECIFIC SITUATIONS, JOHN QUITMAN A SOUTHERN MISSISSIPPIAN THAT WAS THE MASTER AND OWNER OF FOUR PLANTATIONS WITH MORE THAN FIVE HUNDRED SLAVES, WAS OF THE OPENION THAT TO ABUSE SLAVES MADE THEM STUBBON REBELLIOUS AND DIFFICULT TO HANDLE, HOWEVER HIS GUIDE LINES WAS RATHER STRICT, THERE WERE WHIPPINGS ADMINISTERED FOR A RANGE OF INFRACTIONS, SUCH AS PICKING COTTON FILLED WITH TRASH, OR NOT MEETING THE DAYS COTTON PICKING QUOTA.

POTENTIAL PROFITS CAUSED SLAVEHOLDERS TO TREAT SLAVES LIKE ANIMALS NOT HUMANISTIC, MANY TRAVLERS THROUGHOUT THE SOUTHERN STATES INDICATED THEY WERE. CERTAIN BREEDING WAS A STANDARD PRACTICE FOR SLAVES IN THE DEEP SOUTH RESPECTIVE TO ANIMALS, IN EIGHTEEN THIRTY THREE AN ENGLISH OBSERVER NAMED EDWARD S. ABDY REPORTED THAT VIRGINIA SLAVE HOLDERS BRED SLAVES AS CATTLE FOR THE MARKET BECAUSE IT WAS A LUCRATIVE BUISNESS, A SLAVE BROKER NAMED EDWARD COVEY, BOUGHT A FEMALE SLAVE NAMED CAROLINE BECAUSE SHE WAS ASSUMED TO BE A BREEDER AND WAS HIS ONLY SLAVE, HIS AMBITIONS WAS TO INCREASE HIS HOLDINGS, COVEY RENTED A MALE SLAVE FROM A NEIGHBOR AND TIED HIM TO CAROLINE EACH NIGHT AND SHE GAVE BIRTH TO TWINS, IN THE EIGHTEEN FIFTIES WILLIAM CHAMBERS A SCOTSMAN WAS VISITING IN VIRGINIA, ALSO FREDERICK LAW OMSTED MENTION THE BREEDING PROCESS FOR THE EXPRESS PURPOSE TO SELL PIRATICALLY SLAVE WOMEN, BECAUSE SALE ADVERTISEMENT DESIGNATED YOUNG FEMALES SLAVES AS GOOD BREEDERS, A GEORGIA SLAVEHOLDER NAMED JAMES ROBERTS, WAS SUSPECTED TO HAVE KEPT FIFTY OR SIXTY SLAVE WOMEN SOLEY FOR THE PURPOSE OF BREEDING, AND IT IS CLAIMED THEY PRODUCED APPROXIMATELY TWENTY FIVE CHILDREN ANUALLY FOR HIS PLANTATION.

DURING THE EIGHTEEN TWENTYS NEW ORLEANS BECAME THE MAJOR SEAPORT FOR WORLDWIDE DISTRIBUTION FOR CROPS AND SLAVES, ALTHOUGH SLAVE PRICES FLUCTUATED YOUNG MEN BETWEEN EIGHTEEN AND THIRTY YEARS OLD WERE SOLD FOR FIVE HUNDRED TO SEVEN HUNDRED DOLLARS, IN VIRGINIA THEY BROUGHT AS MUCH AS SIXTEEN HUNDRED DOLLARS, A ILLITERATE HORSE TRADER NAMED NATHAN BEDFORD FORREST FROM MISSISSIPPI WAS STRUGGLING TO MAKE A LIVING, DURING THE EIGHTEEN FIFTIES HE DECIDED TO MOVE TO MEMPHIS TENNESSEE AND THAT IS WHEN HIS FORTUNES CHANGED, BECAUSE HE BECAME INVOLVED IN SLAVE TRADING, AND BECAME ONE OF THE WEALTHIEST MEN IN THE SOUTH.

THERE WERE NUMEROUS OF OCCURRENCES THAT TRANSPIRED DURING SLAVERY MOST WERE NEVER DOCUEMENTED THROUGHOUT THE SOUTHERN STATES, HOWEVER THE ELEMENTS FORECAST FOR AFRICAN AMERICANS WERE RATHER DISMAL, EVEN TODAY THE MAJORITY OF AFRICAN AMERICANS ARE INEPT TO THE TRANSFORMATIONS AND THE RESPONSIBLE POLITICAL PARTY THAT CAUSED THESE TRAUMATIZING EVENTS, BECAUSE MOST BLACKS HAVE FORMED THEIR OWN OPENION THROUGH HERE SAY WHICH IS PRIMARILY BASED ON DEMOCRATIC IDEOLOGY TO DECEIVE, DURING THE LATE EIGHTEEN FIFTIES ILLINOIS REPUBLICAN CANIDATE ABRAHAM LINCOLN CHALLENGED DEMOCRATIC INCUMBENT STEPHEN H. DOUGLAS FOR THE U.S. SENATE SEAT, SLAVERY WAS AT ITS HEIGHT AND A CENTRAL ISSURE OF DEBATE, THE CANIDATES DEBATED ITS TRANSITIONAL PLACE IN THE NATION, THE DEMOCRATIC CANIDATE DOUGLAS ARGUED THAT THE QUESTION OF SLAVERY SHOULD BE CONTROLLED BY LOCAL COMMUNITIES AS THE NATION MOVED FORWARD REGARDS TO EXPANSION AND PROGRESS, AND CONSTANTLY REPEATED HIS BELIEF THAT THE SIGNERS OF THE DECLARATION HAD NO REFERENCE TO NEGROES WHAT SO EVER, AND PANDERED TO THE WHITE SUPREMACIST ILLINOIS CROWD AS HE ARGUED THAT

AMERICA WAS MADE BY WHITE MEN FOR THE BENEFIT OF WHITE MEN AND THEIR (POSTERITY) FOREVER.

WHILE LINCOLN ARGUED AND AFFIRMED HIS BELIEF THAT SLAVERY WAS MORALLY WRONG AND WOULD DO EVERY THING UNDER HIS POLITICAL POWER TO CONTAIN ITS EXPANSION, THUS IN THE EIGHTEEN SIXTY PRESIDENTAL ELCTION (ONLY) THE REPUBLICANS OPPOSED SLAVERY AND REJECTED ANY EXPANSION, WHILE THE SOUTHERN DEMOCRATS TOOK RADICAL POSITIONS THREATENING SECESSIONS UNLESS SLAVERY WAS PROTECTED,BECAUSE THE DEFIANT WHITE SOUTHERN SLAVE HOLDERS SAW LINCOLNS ELECTION AS A ABOLISHMENT FOR SLAVERY, THE MAJORITY OF THE NATION HALF MILLION FREE BLACKS ESPECIALLY? THOSE IN THE NORTHERN STATES SUPPORTED THE REPUBLICANS, THE SOUTHERN DEMOCRATS DREW PROVOCATIVE CONCLUSIONS AT THE THOUGHT OF SLAVERY BEING ABOLISHED, SO THEY SEVERED FROM THE UNITED STATES AND ESTABLISHED THE SOUTHERN CONFEDERATE STATES OF AMERICA, AND ON MARCH EIGHTEEN SIXTY ONE ADOPTED THE CONFEDERATE CONSTITUTION WHICH EMPHASIZED POLITICAL STATE POWER OVER FEDERAL POWER AND EXPLICITLY PROTECTED THE RIGHTS OF SLAVEHOLDERS, ALSO FURTHER PROTECTED THE SLAVEHOLDERS RIGHTS TO MOVE THEIR HUMAN PROPERTY TO ANY AREA UNDER CONFEDERATE JURISDICTION, WHICH THEY CONCLUDED THE U.S. CONSTITUTION DENIED THEM THAT RIGHT.

SENSE THE INCEPTION OF THE REPUBLICAN PARTY IN EIGHTEEN FIFTY FOUR THEY HAVE INVESTED THEIR POLITICAL ENERGY IN HUMAN RIGHTS FOR AFRICAN AMERICANS, WHILE SERVING IN THE ILLINOIS STATE LEGISLATURE DURING THE EIGHTEEN THIRTIES ABRAHAM LINCOLN DENOUNCED SLAVERY AS BEING UN-JUST AND A REPREHENSIBLE GOVERNMENTAL POLICY, DURING A SPEAKING ENGAGEMENT IN PEORIA ILLINOIS THE YEAR OF EIGHTEEN FIFTY FOUR HE QUOTED THE DECLARATION OF INDEPENDENCE AND ARGUED THAT SLAVERY WAS A TOTAL VIOLATION OF PRINCIPLE, BECAUSE THE SLAVEHOLDER NOT ONLY GOVERNS THE SLAVE WITHOUT HIS CONSENT,

BUT HIS APPROACH TO GOVERNING IS OPPOSITE OF GUIDE LINES HE PRESCRIBE FOR HIMSELF.

THROUGHOUT THIS BOOK I HAVE GONE THROUGH A LITANY OF OCCURRENCES THAT LITERALLY EXONERATE THE REPUBLICANS AND THEIR POLITICAL PARTY OF ANY UN-JUST IMPEACHABLE ACTIVITIES PERPETRATED AGAINST AFRICAN AMERICANS, THEIR CRUSADE WAS TO RELIEVE THEM FROM THE BURDEN OF SLAVERY IMPOSED AT THEIR LEISURE BY SOUTHERN DEMOCRATS. YET YOU HAVE AFFLUENT AFRICAN AMERICANS IN ALL PHASES AND WALKS OF LIFE DEMONIZING AND DEMONSTRATING ERRONEOUS LIBERAL DEMOCRATIC PROPAGANDA TO ENHANCE THE IDEOLOGY OF THE CULPRITS, IF SLAVERY IS TO BE ASSESSED AND A SOCIOLOGICAL ANALYSIS DISPLAYED IN EFFIGY AS WALTER HILL DEMONSTRATED ON APRIL 28, 2006, C-SPAN (2) COVERAGE, AT LEAST HAVE THE COURAGE TO DISTINGUISH WHAT POLITICAL PARTY CAUSED THESE ATROCITIES AND NOT LABEL IT AS A SENATORAL AND CONGRESSIONAL DEBACLE, WHICH IT WAS BUT THE DEMOCRATS AND THEIR SOUTHERN STATES BUREAUCRATS WITH THEIR JIM CROW RULE CONTRLLED ALL THE POLITICAL POLICIES DURING THOSE TIMES.

HOWEVER THE MAJORITY OF AFRICAN AMERICANS HAVE SIGNALED OVER THE YEARS THAT (ALL) IS FORGIVEN THROUGH THEIR POLITICAL VOTING BLOC FOR DEMOCRATS, AND THERE CAN BE ONLY TWO REASONS FOR THIS KIND OF COMPULSION, GENETIC CONTROLLABILITY RELATED TO IGNORANCE PERTAINING TO POLITICAL HISTORICAL EVENTS, OR THEIR INTENT TO COVER UP THEIR INABILITY TO DISSECT DEMOCRATIC STRATEGIES THAT HAS MADE WHAT IS UNDER A DONKEY TAIL OUT OF THEM FOR YEARS, YET THEY CONSTANTLY COMPLAIN IN MASSES ON HOW SLAVERY AFFECTED THEIR LIVES,NOT REALIZING IT IS THE DEMOCRATS LYING THAT HAS LURED THEM INTO A STUPOR TO BELIEVE THAT THE REPUBLICANS ARE RESPONSIBLE FOR THEIR FAILURES AND MISFORTUNES, AND THERE ARE THE FOREVER PRESENT AFFLUENT BLACK DEMOCRATIC POLITICAL LUNATIC STRATEGIST THAT ARE CARRYING. THE HONEY BUCKET

AND ENDORSING DEMOCRATIC IDEOLOGY WHEN THEY MEANING DEMOCRATS ARE THE DECEITFUL CULPRITS, WHICH HAS CAUSED MANY AFRICAN AMERICANS TO SELF DESTRUCT, AND CONSTANTLY RELAPSE INTO A CRIMINAL ELEMENT SEARCHING FOR MIRAGES OF SUCCESSES THAT NEVER EXISTED, HOWEVER IT IS SUSPECTED THAT THE DEMOCRATS DECEIT IS FINALLY UNRAVELING AND THEIR CHICKENS ARE COMING HOME TO ROOST WHICH FOR THE VERY FIRST TIME THEY ARE CONFRONTED WITH A DILEMMA THAT THEY ARE TOTALLY ESTRANGED TO, AND THAT IS HERDING BLACKS THAT TRADITIONALLY HERD AROUND THEIR OWN REGARDS TO THE EXTENT OF RADICAL BEHAVIOR OR ASSERTIONS PERTAINING TO HEINOUS CRIMINALITY, THE DEMOCRATIC REPRESENTATIVE HOUSE LEADER NANCY PLOSI, HAS BEEN GREETED WITH THIS PRESISTORIC GENETIC CONTROLLIBILITY RELATED TO BLACK ANALYSIS OF HOW POLITICS SHOULD FUNCTION, AND MOST LIKELY IS HYSTERICALLY STUNNED BY THE BLACK CACUS DEFENDING AND COMING TO THE AIDE OF REPRESENTATIVE WILLIAM JEFFERSON FROM LOUISIANA, AND THE REPUBLICANS CLEVERLY REFRAINED FROM INTERVENING BY CLAIMING FOWEL TO THE RAIDING OF HIS OFFICE BY AUTHORITIES.

SO THE DEMOCRATS ARE STUCK WITH THIS DILEMMA WITH NO ONE TO LIE ON, GRAB YOUR SELVES A RING SIDE SEAT THIS IS EXPECTED TO BE BETTER THAN DESPERATE HOUSEWIVES, BECAUSE THE DEMOCRATS ARE IN UNCHARTED TERRITORY WHICH THEY HAVE ABUSED AND USED OVER THE YEARS, BUT NEVER HAD TO CONFRONT POLITICAL ELECTED HERDING BLACKS WITHIN THEIR OWN PARTY, HOWEVER I MUST ADMIT THE DEMOCRATS ARE THE BEST AT WHAT THE DO RELATED TO DECEIT, DURING THE EIGHTEEN AND EARLY NINETEEN HUNDREDS THEY WOULD HAVE JUST LYNCHED JEFFERSON AND CARRIED ON AS USUAL, BUT TODAY THEY WILL USE SLICK DIPLOMACY AND HAVE THE BLACK CACUS THINKING THAT AFRICANS DISCOVERED AMERICA AND ARE THE FOUNDERS OF CULTURE FOR THE NATION, WHILE THEY SLIP THE WIENER TO JEFFERSON.

THE DEMOCRATS HAS ALWAYS PRIDED THEMSELVES AS BEING THE PARTY FOR THE POOR, AND ADOPTED AFRICAN AMERICANS AS THEIR PRIME GUINEA PIGS, IN ORDER TO MAINTAIN POLITICAL STABILITY REGARDS TO THEIR VOTING BLOC, AND NEVER DREAMED THAT APPROXIMATELY FORTY FORTY THREE DULEY ELECTED BLACK DEMOCRATS WOULD SNEAK IN UNDER THE RADAR AND BECOME HOUSE REPRESENTATIVES AND HERD TOGATHER AND FORM A INEFFECTIVE UNION CALLED BLACK CAUCUS, THAT HAVE THE DEMOCRATIC LEADERS WALKING A POLITICAL TIGHT ROPE, RELATED TO TWO OF THEIR MEMBERS JEFFERSON AND MCKINNEY, ONE SLIP AND POLITICAL DISASTER IS LOOMING, BECAUSE THE MAJORITY OF BLACKS NORMALLY INTERPRET THEIR DISTINCTIONS FROM AFFLUENT BLACK LEADERS AND HERD BEHIND THEIR OPENIONS RIGHT OR WRONGLY AND INTERJECT RACISM INTO EVERY CHALLENGE, SO THE LATE COUNTRY AND WESTERN PERFORMER BUCK OWENS LIVES ON WITH HIS SONG YOU GOT A TIGER BY THE TAIL, AND IT IS GOING TO BE VERY INTERESTING REGARDS TO DEMOCRATIC STRATEGY ON HOW THEY ARE GOING TO DEAL WITH THESE CIRCUMSTANCES ESPECIALLY REP. WILLIAM JEFFERSONS.

IN THE STATE OF TENNESSEE,MEMPHIS CITY, SEVERAL STATE DIGNITARIES SOME ARE STATE SENATORS WERE CAUGHT IN A STING LABELED TENNESSEE WALTZ, ONE SENATOR HAS ALREADY HAD HIS DAY IN COURT AND FOUND GUILTY OF RECEIVING BRIBERY MONEYS, HE IS WAITING SENTENCING, OTHERS ARE WAITING TRIAL, THE MAJORITY CAUGHT IN THE STING WERE AFRICAN AMERICANS ACCORDING TO THE LOCAL NEWS, ONE OF THEIR DEFENSES ARE THEY WERE CHOSEN TO INVESTIGATE BECAUSE THEY ARE BLACK, IN THE INTERIM THE LOCAL TELEVISION NEWS HAS SHOWN THEM ACCEPTING BRIBERY MONEYS FROM GOVERNMENT STING PERSONNEL AND COMMENTING SMETHING TO THE AFFECT ABOUT BIG TIME, I CHOOSE TO ELABORATE ON THESE EPISODES BECAUSE THIS IS A CARBON COPY OF WHAT REP. WILLIAM JEFFERSON IS ACCUSED OF BEING INVOLVED IN DOING.

THERE ARE A LARGE SEGMENT OF BLACKS IN THIS COUNTRY THAT HAS CAME TO THE CONCLUSION BY LISTENING TO LIBERAL DEMOCRATIC DEMAGOGUERY, MOSTLY FROM SELF APPOINTED BLACK LEADERS, THAT THEY HAVE BEEN ABANDONED THROUGH THE PROCESS OF GOVERNMENT IN THIS COUNTRY, AND THEY OFTEN ASSUME THAT THEY CAN SET THEIR OWN PRECEDENCE ON HOW TO SUCCEED REGARDS TO FINANCIAL PARITY IN A UN-JUST MANNER, AND WHEN THEY ARE CAUGHT THERE ARE FLASHBACKS OF LIBERALIZED TEACHINGS AND GULLIBILITY THAT CAUSE THEM TO INSTINCTIVELY INJECT RACE INTO THE ISSURE, AND THIS APPLICATION IS MOST COMMONLY USED BY ILLITERATES ALSO WELL EDUCATED BLACKS, UNFORTUNATELY THIS GENOCIDAL DELUSIONAL RHETORIC HAS BEEN FORECAST OVER THE YEARS BY AFRICAN AMERICANS, IN ORDER TO SWAY PUBLIC OPENION IN AN EFFORT FOR SYMPATHY,TO GET THEIR FOOLISH LIBERAL GENERALITIES ENDORSED THAT THE NATION IS UN-JUST TO AFRICAN AMERICANS, THERE ARE MANY BLACKS ADOPT THIS INSANE THEORY AS A REASON TO COMMIT HEINOUS CRIMES AND EMBEZZLEMENTS THINKING THAT SOCIETY HAS WRONGED THEM AND WILL UNDERSTAND THEIR PERSONAL OBSESSION FOR GREED.

IT IS HOPED THAT FUTURISTIC POLITICAL DOMINATING OF DEMOCRATIC SEDUCTIVE IDEOLOGY OVER THE MAJORITY OF AFRICAN AMERICANS WILL SLOWLY DISSIPATE, BECAUSE THERE ARE SIGNS THAT SOME OF THE YOUNG GENERATION OF BLACKS ARE BEGINNING TO THINK MORE INDEPENDENT MINDED, RATHER THAN HERD BEHIND A SINGLE OPENION THAT LURE THEM INTO JEOPARDIZING THEIR FUTURES REGARDS TO PROGRESS CONCERNING THE ASPECTS OF POLITICAL ISSURES AND GROWTH, THE DEMOCRATS HAS CLEVER^ LY UTILIZED SPECIFIC TACTICS TO DUPE AFRICAN AMERICANS INTO A MONOLITHIC MONOPOLY OF INEPTITUDE FOR OVER A HUNDRED YEARS TO MAINTAIN POLITICAL POWER BASED ON THEIR BLOC VOTING, THERE SEEM TO BE SOME CRACKS DEVELOPING IN THE LIBERAL DEMOCRATIC ARMOUR, BECAUSE IT APPEAR THAT SOME YOUNGER AFRICAN AMERICANS ARE

BEGINNING TO BREAK AWAY FROM THIS DETRIMENTAL INASNITY OF HERDING AND I GOT YOUR BACK SYNDROME TO PROTECT OTHER BLACKS THAT IS ABUSING THEIR AUTHORITATIVE POLITICAL POWER, AND OTHERS ARE ATTEMPTING TO HOLD THE GENERAL PUBLIC HOSTAGE BASED ON VIOLENCE AND CRIMINAL ACTIVITY, HOWEVER IT DOES APPEAR THAT SOME PHASES OF RECKONING IS BEGINNING TO FORMULATE FOR RECTIFICATION TO EXTINGUISH THESE LITANY OF ATROCITIES.

FOR INSTANCE TENNESSEE STATE SENATOR ROSCOE DIXION WAS CONVICTED ON JUNE 8, 2006, FOR BRIBERY AND EXTORTION ON ALL FIVE COUNTS AS ACCUSED, AND SENATOR DIXON WAS A TWENTY TWO YEAR VETERAN OF POLITICAL CREDENTIALS, THE JURORS THAT CONVICTED HIM WAS COMPOSED OF TWELVE PEERS FIVE WERE OF AFRICAN AMERICAN ORIGIN THAT CONSIST OF THREE FEMALES AND TWO MALE, ESTIMATED AGE RANGE LATE TWENTIES TO EARLY SIXTIES, HOWEVER THREE REPORTEDLY TO BE IN THEIR EARLY TWENTIES, THE OTHERS TWO FORTY TO SIXTY, THE COLLECTIVE SIGNIFICANCE OF THIS ANALYSIS PERTAINING TO AFRICAN AMERICAN JURORS IS TO DEMONSTRATE THEORIES AND EXPOUND ON THE EXISTING REVELATIONS,THAT SOME TIME CAUSE HUNG JURIES BASED ON THEIR ASSESSING GUILT OR INNOCENT PRIOR TO TRIAL,IN AN EFFORT TO EXONERATE OTHER BLACKS BASED ON THE HERDING PROCESS OF I GOT YOUR BACK BLACK BROTHER, HOWEVER IT DOES APPEAR THAT SOME INTELLECTUAL YOUNG BLACKS ARE DEFINITIVELY TRYING TO EVALUATE CIRCUMSTANCES BASED ON THE MERITS OF THE PROPOSED EVIDENTIAL FACTUALLY AND VOICE THEIR OPINION ACCORDINGLY.

UNFORTUNATELY SOME OLDER AFRICAN AMERICANS TEND TO DISTORT EVIDENCE AND INSERT RADICAL CONCLUSIONS AS TO WHY A CRIME WAS COMMITTED AND THIS ELUSIVE BEHAVIOR IS PRIMARILY BASED ON GENETIC CONTROLLABILITY AND INDOCTRINATION THAT HAS SPUN THEM INTO A DYSFUNCTIONAL MANNER TO THINK THAT MOST CRIMINAL ACTIVITY DIRECTED OR LODGED AGAINST BLACKS HAS TO DO WITH A CONSPIRACY AGAINST

THEM BECAUSE THEY ARE BLACK, WHICH IS INSANITY AT ITS WORSE, THIS PREPLEXING BACK WOODS MINDED THINKING IS LARGELY RESPONSIBLE FOR THE DEVASTATING CRIMINAL ACTIVITIES PERPETRATED BY SOME BLACKS IN OUR COUNTRY TODAY,BECAUSE FOR YEARS OF BEING SEDUCED WITH INACCURATE CYNICAL INTERPRETATIONS OF DEROGATORY EXPECTATIONS HAS CAUSED REBELLIOUS ASPIRATIONS THAT HAS AND IS CAUSING SOME BLACKS TO SELF DESTRUCT, IN ESSENCE THE ASSESSMENT OF SOME AFRICAN AMERICANS HAVING TO DO WITH THEIR OVERWHELMING INABILITY TO DECIPHER THE AGREGIOUS DECEPTION DISPLAYED ON A NATIONAL LEVEL BY THEM, AND THEY SYSTEMATICALLY OFFER REVELATIONS LEVELED AT THEM AS DISCRIMINATORY AND FICTITIOUS REGARDLESS OF THE CIRCUMSTANCES.

FOR INSTANCE SEVERAL POLITICAL DIGNITARIES IN MEMPHIS TENNESSEE, WERE INDITED FRAUDULENT ACTIVATES EXTORTION AND BRIBERY, FOUR WERE STATE SENATORS, AND IT APPEAR THAT THE ROAD IS LEADING TO WASHINGTON REGARDS TO REPRESENTATIVE WILLIAM J. JEFFERSON FROM THE STATE OF LOUISIANA, A SIXTEEN YEAR VETERAN ELECTED OFFICIAL TO SERVE THE CONSTITUENCY OF HIS STATE, IS BEING ACCUSED OF BASICALLY THE SAME OFFENSES THE ONLY DIFFERENCE IS THAT HE IS A U.S. CONGRESS MEMBER, AND OF COURSE THERE IS THE REP. MCKINNEY DEBACLE WITH SECURITY IN WASHINGTON PUNCHING A SECURITY PROTECTION PERSONNEL, THESE AFRICAN AMERICANS ARE OR WERE IN THE POLITICAL ARENA OF AFFLUENCE AND IT IS THEIR PREGOGATIVE TO MAINTAIN THE DIGNITY THAT CORRELATE THE RESPONSIBILITIES THAT THEY WERE ELECTED TO COMMAND, IF RACE WAS NOT AN ISSURE GOING UP THE LADDER WHY SHOULD IT BE ON THE WAY DOWN, BECAUSE THEY WERE OR ARE IN COMPLETE CONTROL OF THEIR OWN DESTINY AND THE CHOICES THEY MADE WERE OF THEIR OWN FREE WILL, AND TO INSINUATE THAT THEIR CREDULOUS MISBEHAVIOR WAS DUE TO RACIST DISCRIMINATORY TACTICS BROUGHT ON BY MALICE BECAUSE THEY ARE BLACK IS INSIDIOUSLY

APPALLING, BECAUSE THE MAJORITY OF THE NATION MOST LIKELY ARE UNAWARE OF THEIR POLITICAL STATUS AND WHO THESE PEOPLE ARE AND COULD CARE LESS, UNTIL THEY DECIDE TO ATTRACT ATTENTION BY EXPLOITING THEIR FINANCIAL EMPOWERMENT THAT IS BEYOND THEIR INHERENT CAPABILITIES REGARDS TO THEIR ESTABLISHED RULE OF CONDUCT, AND THIS APPLICATION IS ACROSS THE BOARD RELATED TO BLACK AND WHITE, THAT IS STRICTLY A SELF IMPOSITION.

IN ESSENCE TO ELABORATE ON AFRICAN AMERICANS AND THEIR IDIOSYNCRASIES PERTAINING TO HISTORICAL EVENTS AND TO PUT IT IN A DIPLOMATIC PROSPECTIVE THE MAJORITY OF AFRICAN AMERICANS ARE TOTALLY UNAWARE OF GENETIC CONTROLLABILITY THAT DOMINATE SOCIETY, AFRICAN AMERICAN GENETIC HERITAGE BEGAN IN AFRICA AND WAS TRANSPORTED TO AMERICA THROUGH SLAVERY IN SIXTEEN NINETEEN.

AMERICA WAS DISCOVERED IN FOURTEEN NINETY TWO, WHICH SET THE GENERAL CHARACTER FOR A CIVILIZE CULTURE AND A CONTROLLING DEMOCRACY UNCIVILIZED AFRICANS ARRIVED APPROXIMATELY ONE HUNDRED TWENTY SEVEN YEARS LATER, WITH POTENTIALITY BECOMING UNITED INTO A DIVERSE ESTABLISHED CULTURAL SOCIETY, AND IT WOULD BE RATHER FOOLISH NOT TO TRY AND DO YOUR LEVEL BEST TO CONFORM, PIRATICALLY WHEN YOU ARE ILLITERATE AND ARE THE MINORITY, UNFORTUNATELY SOME BLACKS HAS NEVER UNDERSTOOD OR CONCEDED TO THESE REVELATIONS, WHICH IS A DIVERSE AMERICAN TRADITION THAT WILL (NEVER) BE ABOLISHED, SO FOR ANY PEOPLE TO PROTEST AND ATTEMPT TO DEFACE THE INTEGRITY THAT IT LENDS, AND REPLACE WITH A PREHISTORIC SUBSTITUTE IS HEADING OVER A CLIFF BEHIND SELF APPOINTED LEADERS TO A DISASTROUS ENDING, THE VAST MAJORITY OF AFRICAN AMERICANS ARE SO FAR REMOVED FROM HISTORICAL EVENTS AND I HAS ALLOWED THEMSELVES TO BE CAPTIVATED BY POLITICAL FICTION THAT HAS DRAMATICALLY DICTATED THEIR FUTURE AS AMERICAN CITIZENS TO BECOME AFFLUENT, AND HAS DEVISTATED

THEIR COMPREHENSION RELATED TO VIOLENT BARBARIC OCCURANCES PREPETRATED BY SOUTHERN DEMOCRATIC PLANTATION SLAVE OWNERS.

FOR INSTANCE ONE AGERGIOUS PRACTICE WAS HUMAN BREEDING OF SLAVES, AS IF THEY WERE ANIMALS, AND IT HAS TO DO WITH GENETIC CONTROLLABILITY THAT IS PROFOUND WITH EVERY CREATURE THAT IS ON GODS EARTH TO ACCESS THE INCREDIBLE HARM TO A ORIGN OF PEOPLE, YOU MUST REVERT BACKTO THE ORIGINAL TRANSFORMATION OF SLAVE TRADING BETWEEN EUROPE AND AFRICA DURING THE FOURTEENTH CENTURY WHEN THE MAIN COMMODITY WAS AFRICAN SLAVE TRADING. AND THE METHODOLOGY USED TO CAPTURE THEM, THE PROCESS WAS QUITE SIMPLE BLACK AFRICAN KINGS ASSEMBLED HERDS OF WORRIOR SOLDIERS FOR THE SOLE PURPOSE OF RADING VILLAGES TO ABDUCT SAVAGE SLAVES FOR TRADING, THESE RAIDS PRODUCED MANY ETHNIC GROUPS OF AFRICANS WITH DIFFERENT SAVAGE CUSTOMS, BUT MOST BELIEVED IN HAVING SEVERAL WIVES, SO IN ESSENCE THE THE MAJORITY OF CAPTURED AFRICANS WERE RELATED, THE GREAT EMPIRES OF GHANA AND MALI WERE THE INSTITUTIONS FOR SLAVE TRADE FROM THE FOURTH TO THE LATE FIFTEENTH CENTURY, SLAVE FACTORIES ON THE AFRICAN WEST COAST WERE MAINTAINED BY LOCAL BLACK KINGS FOR DISTRIBUTION OF INTERRIOR SLAVE CAPTIVES TO BE SOLD INTO THE ATLANTIC SLAVE TRADE, THE AFRICAN KINGS CONTROLLED THE AFRICAN EUROPEAN TRADE ROUTES, IT WAS CUSTOMARILY TO HOLD SLAVES IN PORTS UNTIL THEY WERE SORTED FOR DISBURSEMENT TO DESTINATIONS ALL OVER THE GLOBE, SO THE INCREDULOUS PREDICTABILITY OF INCESTUOUS GENETIC BALANCE WAS MOST CERTAINLY AT RISK.

IN SIXTEEN NINETEEN AFRICANS ARRIVED ON THE SHORES OF AMERICA, WITH NO IDEA OF THEIR FUTURISTIC CHALLENGE AHEAD,AND COMPLETELY ILLITERATE TO THE FORMALITIES OF AMERICA, LATER THEY CAME FROM DIFFERENT ETHNIC GROUPS AND SPOKE MANY DIFFERENT LANGUAGES,THEVASTMAJORITYOFAFRICANSMAINTAINED THEIR HERITAGE AND TRADITIONAL BELIEFS THROUGH

THE SEVENTEENTH AND EIGHTEEN CENTURIES, WHICH CAUSED SLAVE OWNERS TO BECOME FRUSTRATED AND SORT TO ADOPT MEASURES TO DEAL WITH SAVAGE ANIMALISTIC BEHAVIOR, THAT OCCASIONALLY DEVELOPED INTO HARASH BRUTALITY EVEN DEATH, SO THE DISCONNECT BETWEEN SLAVE AND SLAVE OWNERS WAS LARGELY DUE TO SLAVES DENOUNCING AMERICAN CULTURE AND PUT FORTH THEIR BEST EFFORT TO ESTABLISH THEIR OWN TO NO AVAIL, AND THIS SCENARIO WAS TOTALLY REJECTED BY EXISTING GOVERNMENT, CITIZENS, AND PLANTATION SLAVE OWNERS, WHICH CAUSED SOME SLAVES TO ASPIRE FORMULATION OF REBELLIOUS GROUPS IN AN ATTEMPT TO OVER THROW THE AUTHORITATIVE RULING FACTIONS, AND AS A RESULT STRICT RESTRAINTS WAS IMPOSED TO CONTROL RADICALISM, DURING THE EIGHTEEN TWENTIES COTTON IN THE SOUTHERN STATES WAS BECOMING A GLOBAL COMMODITY, SO THE SOUTHERN PLANTATION OWNERS WERE FACED WITH MANY PROBLEMS REGARDS TO SLAVES, ONE WAS REBELLIOUS SLAVES CLAIMIMG AMERICA TO BE THEIR OWN AND THEIR ZEALOUS ATTEMPT TO EXPEL WHITES, ONE SUCH REBELLIOUS PROBLEM WAS STIMULATED BY A BLACK SHOPKEEPER FROM NORTH CAROLINA NAMED DAVID WALKER, THAT MOVED TO BOSTON AND ADDRESSED CROWDS OF AFRICAN AMERICANS INSTIGATING AND CALLING FOR A SLAVE REBELLION IN EIGHTEEN TWENTY NINE, WHICH EXACERBATED SOUTHERN FEARS, WALKER STATED AND COMMANDED LET SLAVE HOLDERS COME AND BEAT US FROM (OUR) COUNTRY, AMERICA IS MORE OUR COUNTRY THAN IT IS THE WHITES, DURING THESE TIMES COTTON WAS BECOMING SO PROFITABLE UNTIL BY THE LATE EIGHTEEN FIFTIES THE SOUTH WAS STRONGER THAN EVER, ITS ECONOMY POWER HAD BECOME SO GREAT REGARDS TO COTTON, UNTIL IT WAS THE NATIONS MOST VALUABLE EXPORT, MORE VALUABLE THAN EVERY THING ELSE THE NATION EXPORTED AROUND THE WORLD COMBINED, AND OF COURSE THE WORTH OF SLAVES INCREASED EQUALLY, SO WITH THE ACTS OF RUN AWAY SLAVES IT BECAME A BURDEN FOR SOME PLANTATION SLAVE OWNERS TO MAINTAIN, SO THEY RESULTED TO BREEDING

HUMAN AFRICAN SLAVES IN ORDER TO INCREASE THEIR HOLDINGS WHICH COMPLETELY DISSECTED GENETIC VALUES INTO A INCESTUOUS PHENOMENON. AND AS OF TO DATE WE ARE WITNESSING THE DEFECTS FROM THOSE BARBARIC ACTS BEGINNING IN AFRICA AND SHIFTED TO THE SHORES OF AMERICA ALSO COMPOUNDED BY THE PERPETRATION OF SOUTHERN DEMOCRATIC PLANTATION OWNERS, THAT TRANSFORMED MOST AFRICAN AMERICANS GENETIC CONTROLLABILITY INTO A SPORATIC ECLIPSE, THAT THE NATION HAVE AND ARE BEING TROUBLED WITH TODAY BECAUSE OF A SUSPECTED UNBALANCED BLOOD LINE DUE TO INCEST.

THE SUBSTANTIATED ACCUSATION TO THIS HUMAN DEBACLE, HAS TO DO WITH THE SALE AND TRADING OF SLAVES BASED ON BRAWN (NOT) BRAIN MOTHERS, SISTERS, DAUGHTERS,FATHERS, BROTHERS, AND SONS, WERE SEPERATED PIRATICALLY MOTHERS FROM THEIR YOUNG CHILDREN, WERE SOLD AND TRADED AT AUCTIONS NOT KNOWING THEIR DESTINATION THROUGHOUT THE SOUTHERN STATES, UPON ARRIVAL TO THEIR MASTERS PLANTATION THEIR AFRICAN NAMES WERE CHANGED, AND THEIR MASTERS GAVE THEM OTHER IDENTITIES, AND SOME WERE SOLD AND TRADED MULTIPLE TIMES ALL OVER THE SOUTH, SLAVES HAD NO BIRTH RECORD, EVEN TODAY MANY AFRICAN AMERICANS IN THEIR LATE SEVENTYS AND EIGHTIES HAVE NO BIRTH CERTIFICATE, THEY WERE GIVEN SPECIAL PRIVILEGES BY GOVERNMENTAL OFFICIALS TO OBTAIN SOCIAL SECURITY,SO AFTER THE ABOLISHMENT OF SLAVERY IN EIGHTEEN SIXTY FIVE BLACKS WERE FREE TO ROME ALL OVER THE NATION, PIRATICALLY THE SOUTHERN STATES, AND AFTER BEING SEPERATED FOR DECADES WITH PLANTATION MASTERS GIVEN NAMES ITS. NOT LIKELY THAT SISTERS ARE GOING TO IDENTIFY THEIR BROTHERS, AND BROTHERS ARE AWARE THAT THEY ARE HIS SISTERS, ALSO MOTHERS AND FATHERS WERE CAUGHT IN THIS INCESTUOUS DEBACLE WITH THEIR CHILDREN UNKNOWINGLY, BECAUSE GENETIC CONTROLLING SENSITIZING IS PROFOUND. THE PLANTATIONS SLAVE OWNERS KNEW OF THIS TRAGEDY THAT THEY HAD

IMPOSED THROUGH SLAVE SALE AND TRADING,SO THIS IS ONE OF THE MAIN REASONS PLANTATIONS OWNERS DELIBERATELYCHOSEAFRICANAMERICANSFORPERTINENT RESPONSIBILITIES THAT WERE LIGHT COMPLECTED OR HAD SEMI STRAIGHT HAIR, BECAUSE THEY KNEW THAT THE INCESTUOUS BARRIER HAD BEEN BROKEN AND THEIR DISPOSITION WAS MORE SETTLE, AND THEY WERE WILLING TO ACCEPT AMERICAN CULTURE AS THEIR DOMAIN TO BE TAUGHT POLITICAL DIPLOMACY.

THE MAJORITY OF AFRICAN AMERICANS REALLY (NEVER) UNDERSTOOD SOUTHERN PLANTATION SLAVE OWNERS STRATEGICALLY, BECAUSE OF THEIR REFRAINING FROM SOCIALISTIC COMPREHENSION PERTAINING TO EXISTING CUTURE, IN AN EFFORT TO ESTABLISH AFRICAN TRADITIONAL CULTURE WITH WITCH DOCTORS DICTATING AND CONTROLLING THEIR LIVES, WHICH WILL (NEVER) BE ACCEPTABLE IN A CIVIL DIVERSE SOCIETY, SO UNFORTUNATELY FOR THOSE WHO PARTICIPATED IN THESE RADICAL ENDEAVORS WERE DETRIMENTALLLY PERSECUTED WITH REPRISAL IN MANY WAYS INCLUDING DEATH, NOT BECAUSE THEY WERE BLACK BUT BECAUSE OF THEIR INSISTENCE ON CHANGING A WELL ESTABLISHED AMERICAN CULTURE INTO BEING COMPATIBLE WITH A SAVAGE ILLITERATE AFRICAN TRADITIONAL BEHAVIORAL IDEOLOGY, AND THESE CHARACTERISTIC ENDEAVORS COST AFRICAN AMERICANS DEARLY THEN AND IS STILL PROFOUND TODAY, AND IT IS LARGELY DUE TO HIBERNATION OF PREHISTORIC INCESTUOUS GENETIC CONTROLLABILITY THAT RALLY AROUND REBELLIOUS ACTIVITIES FOR CONTROL, BASED ON INSIIOUS HERDING IDEOLOGY THAT WAS DISTRUCTIVE FOR THEIR PROGRESS HUNDREDS OF YEARS AGO AND IS EVEN MORE DEVASTATING IN SOCIETY TODAY THEIR EFFORTS ARE FORTIFIED AROUND THEORIES OF IDIOSYNCRASIES TO SEDUCE A SOCIETY THAT IS CULTURALLY DIVERSIFIED , TO ENDORSE THEIR AGENDA OF INEPTITUDE WAY OF THINKING THAT THE STANDARDS EXIST IN THE COUNTRY OF BEING EMPLOYED TO SUFFICIENTLY SURVIVE IS INADEQUATE AND SHOULD BE OBSOLETED AND THEY SHOULD BE SUPPORTED BY

SOCIAL PROGRAMS THAT IS INSTIGATED BY DEMOCRATS, THE MAJORITY OF AFRICAN AMERICANS WILL NORMALLY EVALUATE STANDARDIZE PROCEDURES ENFORCED BY LAWS AND THE CONSTITUTION, AND IF IT DOSENT CORELATE WITH THEIR ASSESSED WAY OF THINKING THEY WILL TEND TO EXAGGERATE AND DISTORT ANY RELEVANT DEMANDING SITUATION INTO HOW THEY THINK IT SHOULD HAVE BEEN ORGANIZED TO SUIT THEIR CRITERION, AND WILL BECOME BELLIGERENT EVEN IF THE RATIFICATION OF A STATUS HAS BEEN ON THE BOOKS FOR DECADES, AND WILL HERD AND MAGNIFY THEIR OPENIONS WHICH IS CONTRARY TO THE CIRCUMSTANCES, THESE TRAITS ARE GENETIC CONTROLLABILITY FROM AFRICAN HERITAGE, BECAUSE THERE WERE CONSTANT TRIBAL DISPUTES IN AFRICA THAT WAS SETTLED BY BRUTE FORCE EVEN TO THE EXTENT OF CANNIBALISM TO EXERT SUPERIORITY TO THEIR WAY OF THINKING, AND THIS WAS AND STILL IS THEIR ACHILLES HEEL AS BEING AMERICANS LIVING IN A DIVERSE SOCIETY THAT IS CONTROLLED BY STATE FEDERAL AND CONSTITUTIONL LAWS, AND TO EXEMPLIFY THE SENTIMENTS OF THE STATEMENTS, MINISTER PAUL SCOTT HIP HOP SEGREGATIONST WAS ON FOX NATIONAL TELEVISION JUNE 26, 2006, OFFERING HIS ASSESSMENTS ABOUT WHITE AMERICANS, AND MAKING ACCRETIONS ABOUT THEM AS BEING WHITE DEVILS, AND SHOULD BE BAN FROM PERFORMING HIP HOP, BECAUSE OF THE FINANCIAL STABILITY, AND WOULD SEEK TO ENGAGE WEALTHY BLACK TOGATHER SUCH AS BILL COSBY, OPRA WINFREY, AND OTHERS TO FINANCIALLY CORNER WHITE INVOLVEMENT, THIS NONSENSICAL DEMAGOGUERY IS LARGELY RESPONSIBLE FOR SOME BLACKS NOT TO EXCEL IN SOCIETY ON THEIR OWN MERIT, BECAUSE OF THE AMPLIFICATION FROM SOME BLACKS THAT SEEK TO DEVIDE THE COUNTRY WITH RACIST INSIGNIFICANT BACK WOODS CONGO IDEOLOGY, AND THOSE THAT LISTEN TO THIS RACIST REBELLIOUS FOOLISHNESS WILL BE POOR FOREVER, AND RESULT TO CRIMINAL ACTIVITIES, DRUG ABUSE, INCARCERATION, AND EVENTUALLY A SELF IMPOSED DEMISE, BECAUSE OF THIS SEDUCTIVE RHETORIC PUKE BEING INSTIGATED BY

BLACKS LIKE REVEREND SCOTT, WHO APPARENTLY HAS NEVER READ THE CONSTITUTION,WHICH SUBSTANTIATE THE CLAIM THAT SOME BLACKS HAVE (NO) REGARD FOR ESTABLISHED LAWS, AND FORM THEIR OWN OPENION ABOUT WHAT OCCURRENCES SHOULD BE CONSTITUTED AND CONSTANTLY VILIFY WHITES AS CULPRITS FOR THEIR OWN MISFORTUNES.

WE ARE ENTRENCHED IN A THREATENING DEBACLE IN OUR NATION, PIRATICALLY CONCERNING SOME AFRICAN AMERICANS THAT HAS INVESTED THEIR ENERGY IN CRIMINAL ACTIVITIES, AND MANY T.V. RADIO PERSONALITY TALK SHOW HOSTS ARE ASKING QUESTIONS FROM MANY MINISTERS AND AFFLLUENT BLACKS AS TO WHY, AND THEY ALL SEEM TO BE LOST FOR AN EXPLANATION OTHER THAN MORE CHURCHES NEED TO GET INVOLVED OR THE NEED FOR MORE FATHERLY PARTICIPATION, THESE ARE STANDARD ISSURES THAT HAS BEEN AVAILABLE FOR HUNDREDS OF YEARS THAT IS BEING UTILIZED TO PACIFY OR EVADE IRRATIONAL BLACK BEHAVIOR, AND THERE ARE SOME SO ASININE THEY REFUSE TO ACKNOWLEDGE THAT THERE IS A PROBLEM, BUT THE SERIOUSNESS OF THIS DEBACLE IS THREATENING AT LEAST FOUR DECADES OF AFRICAN AMERICANS WITH SELF IMPOSED EXTINCTION TO INCARCERATION OR EARLY DEMISE, THIS PATHETIC APPALLING DISASTER RESONATED UNDER THE GUIDE-LINES OF A.D.C. AIDE FOR DEPENDENCE CHILDREN WHICH HAS SPUN OUT OF CONTROL OVER THE YEARS, AWARDING FUNDS TO BABIES FOR HAVING BABIES OUT OF WED-LOCK, WHICH HAVE NO IDEA OF CREDIBILITY OR REFINEMENT OF INTELLECTUAL BEHAVIOR, THEIR FUTURES WERE SHAPED BY SELF APPOINTED LEADERS THE LIKES OF JESSIE JACKSON, AL SHARPETON AND OTHERS EXPLOITING THE FACT THAT WHITE AMERICA WAS AND IS THE VILLIANS THAT IMPEDED THEIR PROGRESS, SO THEY ADOPTED THAT THEORY AND RENOUNCED EDUCATION EMPLOYMENT AND AMERICAN CULTURE FOR A WELFARE CHECK AND DRUG ABUSE, ANY INDIVIDUALS THAT ARE CITIZENS OF THE UNITED STATES OF AMERICA AND CHOOSE TO RELINQUISH THEIR PRIDE AND ALLOW THEMSELVES TO

BE SUCCUMB BY METHODS OF OPPOSITION TO MORAL AND REFINEMENT OF INTELLECTUAL ISSURES ARE COMMITTING A GRAVE INJUSTICE TO THEMSELVES AND IS CARRYING A SET OF KEYS IN THEIR POCKET TO THE PRISON DOORS, DUE TO THE STREAMLINING OF WELFARE PROGRAMS BY FEDERAL AND STATE POLITICAL OFFICIALS MOST GETTO BLACKS AROUND THE NATION HAS RESLUTED TO DRUG ABUSE AND CRIMINAL ACTIVITIES, AND ARE SETTLING THEIR DISPUUTES WITH VIOLENCE INTERNALLY AND EXTERMINATING EACH OTHER.

UNFORTUNATELY YOU (NEVER) HEAR SELF APPOINTED BLACK LEADERS ADDRESS THESE PROFOUND VICIOUS ASSAULTS RELATED TO BLACK ON BLACK CRIMINAL ACTIVITY AND PUBLICLY CONDEMN THESE RADICAL BARBARIC ACTIONS, AND WHEN A FIEW AFFLUENT AFRICAN AMERICANS ATTEMPT DENOUNCE THIS KIND OF BEHAVIOR AND SQUARELY PUT THE BLAME WHERE IT BELONG ON BLACKS THEMSELVES, THESE ISSURES ARE PERIODICALLY ADDRESSED BY SUCH PEOPLE AS BILL COSBY, REV. JESSIE L. PETERSON, JOHN MCWHORTER, ANDREW CLARK SR. THE ENNISIS, AND A FIEW OTHERS, UNFORTUNATELY THE SELF APPOINTED BLACK ROTTWEILERS SPREAD OUT ALL OVER THE NATION AIR WAYS DENOUNCING THEIR THEORIES AND SUGGESTING THAT THEY ARE OUT OF TUCH WITH THE BLACK GETTO BECAUSE OF THEIR WEALTH, AND CASTIGATE THEIR OPINIONS IN AN EFFORT TO IMPUGN THEIR INTEGRITY, WHICH IS PREDICATED TO DISTORTING THE TRUTH AND OFFERING FICTITIOUS EXPLANATIONS TO DIVERT ATTENTION IN ORDER FOR AMPLIFICATIONS THAT THESE PEOPLE HAVE (ALL) THE SPICIFIC ATTRIBUTES REQUIRED TO SUCCEED IN LIFE BUT ITS THE WHITES THAT ARE PLANNING AND CAUSING THEIR DIVERSION FROM PROGRESS, THIS IS ONE OF THE MOST OUTRAGEOUS PATHETIC DAMMING PRACTICES DISPLAYED BY SOME BLACKS KOWN TO MAN KIND, BECAUSE IT DESTROY PEOPLE LIVES AND HAVE FOR GENERATIONS, AND IT APPEAR THERE IS NO END IN SIGHT, BECAUSE THERE ARE SOME LITTLE BOYS AND GIRLS OF ALL AGES WALKING AROUND SHOWING THEIR BEHINDS, AND WHEN ASKED HOW DO THEY LIKE

SCHOOL, AND WHAT WOULD THEY LIKE TO BE WHEN THEY GROW UP,MOST OFTEN RESPOND BY SAYING THEY HATE SCHOOL, BECAUSE WHITE FOLKS WASNT GOING TO LET THEM DO ANY THING ANY.WAY, BECAUSE GEORGE BUSH GOT THIS COUNTRY MESSED UP.

THIS TYPE OF RADICAL DEMAGOGUERY COMING FROM KIDS IS IMPOSED ON THEM BY THEIR FOOLISH PARENTS, IT IS TOTALLY REPREHENSIBLE FOR ANY ONE PIRATICALLY PARENTS TO DESTROY THE MORAL, ETHICAL, VALUES OF A CHILD, BASED ON INSIDIOUS IDEOLOGY THAT BELONG IN THE SAVAGE MUD HUTS OF THE AFRICAN CONGO, AND SOME DYSFUNCTIONAL MINDED BLACK PARENTS ARE ATTEMPTING TO RESURRECT THIS INSANITY THROUGH THEIR CHILDREN WHICH IS UTTERLY APPALLING.

IT IS TOTALLY MYSTIFYING HOW MILLIONS OF AFRICAN AMERICANS CAN TRAVEL ABOUT THE WORLD, TURN ON THEIR TELEVISIONS LISTEN TO RADIO, ACCESS COMPUTER DATA, AND NOT BE AWARE THAT MILLIONS OF AFRICAN AMERICANS ARE INVOLVED IN EVERY QUALIFIED DEMENSION OF POSITIONS AROUND THE UNIVERSE, PIRATICALLY IN THE UNITED STATES OF AMERICA, SUCH AS SECRETARY OF THE UNITED STATES, SECRETARY OF STATES, SENATORS, CONGRESSIONAL HOUSE OF REPRESENTATIVES, CITY MAYORS, CHIEF LAW ENFORCEMENT, DOCTORS, LAWYERS, ASTRONAUTS, PROFESSORS AT COLLEGE UNIVERSITIES, RADIO AND TELEVISION TALK SHOW HOSTS, REAL ESTATE DEALERS, ACTORS, PRIVATE BUISNESS OWNERS, SCIENTIST, HOME OWNER SHIP LIKE NEVER BEFORE, TOP MANAGEMENT AND OWNER SHIP IN SPORTS, JUST TO NAME A FIEW, BUT ALL YOU CAN HEAR FROM THE SPITTOON TOTING BOOT LICKING BLACK DEMOCRATIC PARASITES IS THE WHITE MAN IS KEEPING YOU DOWN, AND THE PLAYING FIELD NEED TO BE LEVELED, TM HEY NEED TO BE REMINDED THAT OF THE THREE HUNDRED MILLION PEOPLE IN THIS COUNTRY , AFRICAN AMERICANS ARE ONLY ELEVEN PRECENT, AND OF THAT ELEVEN PRECENT THERE IS DYSFUNCTIONAL BRAIN DAMAGE TO SOME DUE TO INCESTUOUS GENETIC CONTROLLABILITY, BECAUSE ANY TIME YOU ARE UNABLE TO DETERMINE

THE PROGRESS BLACKS HAVE AND ARE MAKING SIMPLY BECAUSE THEY ARE GOING TO SCHOOL FOOL, THEN YOU ARE A PART OF THAT SEGEMENT SUFFERING FROM DYSFUNCTIONAL GENETIC CONTROL THAT IS TRYING TO JUMP START THE SIXTIES TO NO AVAIL, AND OBVIOUSLY CAUSING CONDESCENDING HYPOCRISY WHICH IS DEVASTATING FOR PARENTS AND THEIR CHILDREN REGARDS TO MORAL VALUES IN AN EFFORT TO ASCERTAIN GUIDANCE FOR THE AMERICAN DREAM, THAT HAS BEEN AVAILABLE TO AFRICAN AMERICANS FOR HUNDREDS OF YEARS, AND WHAT IS SO DISGUSTING THERE ARE MANY DISTINGUISH SUCCESSFUL BLACK EDUCATORS OVER THE YEARS, SELF APPOINTED LEADERS, AFFLUENT POLITICIANS, THROUGHOUT THE NATION AND I HAVE (NEVER) WITNESS A CONCERTED EFFORT TO DENOUNCE BLACK MILITANT BEHAVIOR, AND INSTIGATE THAT EDUCATION MORAL ETHICAL VALUES IS RESPONSIBLE FOR THEM BEING WHERE THEY ARE IN A DIVERSE SOCIETY, IT IS ALWAYS UN-JUST GOVERNMENT, AND WHITE FOLKS BASHING REGARDS TO PROHIBITING THEIR SUCCESSES, WHICH IN REALITY THEY ARE CONTRADICTING THEIR OWN IDEOLOGY, BECAUSE TEY (ARE) THE EXAMPLE THEMSELVES THAT PROGRESS IS ESTABLISHED IN THIS COUNTRY FOR EVERY ONE THAT HAS THE MORAL CULTURE TO OBTAIN, AND NOT ABSTAIN BASED ON RADICAL FOOLISH IDEOLOGY,(THAT IF WERE TRUE) THEN WHY ARENT THE STOOGES THAT IS DICTATING THIS MIS-LEADING PROPAGANDA ARE (NOT) IN THE POVITY STRIKEN GETTOS ALONG WITH THE REST OF UNFORTUNATE BLACKS THAT THEY ARE LYING TO, AND THIS IS PARTIALLY THE BASIS FOR SOME BLACKS TO BE FRUSTRATED AND LOOSING THE BATTLE FOR ECONOMIC STABILITY IN THIS COUNTRY, WHICH IS A SELL OUT BY THEIR OWN RACE OF PEOPLE AS IT OCCURED IN AFRICA HUNDREDS OF YEARS AGO, WHICH REMIND ME OF A CATTLE JOKE, MALE BREEDING BULLS SEEK FEMALES TO DETERMINE THEIR ESTROGEN AVAILABILITY TO CONCEIVE, AND AS A HABIT THEY SMELL THEIR BEHIND, AFTERWARDS THEY TURN THEIR NOSE UP, AND THE REASON FOR THAT IS TO SEDUCE THE YOUNGER BULLS INTO THINKING THAT THIS

IS SOMETHING WOULD NOT BE IN THEIR BEST INTEREST, SO IT APPEAR THAT EDUCATED BLACKS APPEAL TO THE ILLITERATES AND SUGGEST THE DESIRE TO BE EDUCATED IS NOT NECESSARY IN ORDER TO EMULATE THEM, IT IS THE WHITE MAN IMPETUS IMPEDIMENTS THAT IS THE MAJOR PROBLEM FOR THEIR LIKE OF SUCCESS.

OUR NATION IS RESPONDING TO SYSTEMATIC COVERT WARFARE THAT PRODUCE TERROR FOR POLITICAL FORCE CONTROL, IN ORDER TO ABILISH OUR UNIQUE CULTIVATED DISTINCTIVE STYLE AND WAY OF LIFE, AND THERE ARE THOSE INTERNAL AMERICAN CITIZENS THAT ARE POLITICALLY APPEALING AND ASSISTING THE TERRORIST. TO UNDERMINE OUR CIVILIZE CULTURE, AS IF THEY ARE EXEMPTED FROM ATTACK, THERE ARE A SEGEMENT OF U.S. CITIZENS IN THIS COUNTRY THAT IS INEPT TO TERRORISM AND THEIR CAUSE, AND THEY SINCERELY HONESTLY BELIEVE THAT NINE ELEVEN WAS JUST A ISOLATED OCCURRENCE RELATED (ONLY) TO USAMA BIN LADEN, NOT HAVING THE ABILITY TO REALIZE THAT TERRORIST ARE A WELL ORGANIZED KILLING MACHINE THAT IS PLANTED ALL OVER THE WORLD, AND THEIR MAIN GOAL IS TO BRING AMERICA TO ITS KNEES AND CHANGE OUR DEMOCRACY AND CULTURE TO THEIR IDEOLOGY AND THEY WILL FOREVER BE LURKING FOR AN OPEN OPPORTUNITY, AND THOSE THAT THINK THIS IS SOME KIND OF TEMPORARY FLUKE OBSESSION IS OBSCURED WITH INSANITY AND IS IN DIRE NEED OF SEDATING WITH A TRUTH CERIUM FOR REHABILITATION PIRATICALLY THE POLITICAL BUREAUCRATS, BECAUSE OUR NATION IS INVILVED IN A CONFLICT WITH TERRORISM WHICH THERE IS ONLY (ONE) WAY OUT AND THAT IS TO VICTORIOUSLY WIN OVER THEM ANY WAY POSSIBLE, BECAUSE CIVIL LIBERTIES IS NOT WORTH A DAMN IF YOU ARE BLOWN TO BITS, UNFORTUNATELY THERE ARE MANY SYMPATHIZERS IN THIS COUNTRY AND IT APPEAR THAT FORMER PRESIDENT JIMMIE CARTER IS LEADING THE CHARGE, HE AND RAMSEY CLARK IS IN A DEAD HEAT REGARDS TO HATRED FOR THE PRESIDENT AND THIS COUNTRY, AND MANY NEWS PERSONALITIES, ALONG WITH A LARGE SEGEMENT OF AFRICAN AMERICANS, BUT

THEIR OBSERVATIONS ARE UNIQUE TO EMULATING THE DEMOCRATS AND VOTING TO KEEP THEM IN POLITICAL REGARDLESS TO THE CIRCUMSTANCES, BECAUSE OF THEIR INEPT UNDERSTANDING OF POLITICAL DEMAGOGUERY AND BETRAYAL, FOR AN EXAMPLE DURING THE LATE FIFTIES AND EARLY SIXTIES THE DEMOCRATS CONTROLLED THE SENATE AND HOUSE OF REPRESENTATIVES WHICH HAD CONSTANTLY DENIED AFRICAN AMERICANS THEIR CIVIL AND VOTING RIGHTS,ENDORSED BY THE SUPREME COURT, THAT TOOK A ACT OF CONGRESS TO ABOLISH IN NINETTEN SIXTY FOUR. AND FIVE WHICH HAD HELD FOR SIXTY EIGHT YEARS, THIS HIDIOUS UN-JUST RULE OF SEPERATE BUT EQUAL IMPOSED ON AFRICAN AMERICANS ADJUDICATED FOR SOUTHERN STATES (ONLY,) TO ENHANSE DEMOCRATS CONTROL OVER BLACKS, THAT PAVED THE ROAD FOR BRUTAL LYNCHINGS, JAILINGS, WATER HOSING, DOG SICKINGS, ON BLACKS,AND THE SUSPECTED DEMISE OF A PRESIDENT, FINALLY ROSA PARKS ILLUMINATED A SPARK THAT CAUSED THEN PRESIDENT LYNDON JOHNSON TWO WEEKS AFTER PRESIDENT JOHN F. KENNEDY ASSASSINATION TO WARN HIS SENATE MENTOR RICHARD RUSSELL OF GEORGIA, THAT IF HE ATTEMPTED TO BLOCK THE CIVIL RIGHTS BILL HE WOULD RUN HIM OVER, AND THIS WAS MAINLY DUE TO JOHNSON FELT WITH ALL THE TURMOIL ABOUT THE SOUTHERN STATES BLACKS WOULD REVOLT BACK TO THE REPUBLICAN PARTY, AFTER RATIFICATION OF THE CIVIL RIGHTS BILL IN NINETEEN SIXTY FOUR,AFRICAN AMERICANS HERDED TO THE DEMOCRATIC CONVENTION IN ATLANTIC CITY NEW JERSEY AUGUST OF NINETEEN SIXTY FOUR BY THE BUS LOADS IN SUPPORT OF THE DEMOCRATS THAT HAD DENIED THEM THEIR CIVIL RIGHTS FOR SIXTY EIGHT YEARS, IN ORDER THAT THEY MAY MAINTAIN POLITICAL POWER, SO TRUST ME THERE IS (NO) CHANCE WHAT SO EVER OF SOME BLACKS UNDERSTANDING THE COMPLEXITY OF TERRORISM EVER.

HOWEVER IT IS A MAJOR DETRIMENTAL PROBLEM AND THREAT TO OUR NATION WHICH IS ROOTED INTO A SEGEMENT OF SOCIETY ABROAD AND INTERNALLY FOR EVER, AND IF ELECTED POLITICAL OFFICIALS REPUBLICANS

AND DEMOCRATS CAN NOT FORESEE THIS SMOULDERING DISASTROUS THREAT TO OUR NATION, ALL AMERICANS WILL PAY A HEAVY PRICE LIKE NEVER BEFORE, INCLUDING THOSE IDIOTS ADVOCATING AND DEMONSTRATING TO BRING THE TROOPS HOME THAT IS FIGHTING TO PROTECT ALL AMERICANS.

JUST TO ELABORATE FURTHER ON THIS BRING THE TROOPS HOME FOOLISH SYNDROME, LETS ASSUME THE TROOPS WERE ORDERED HOME, WHAT DO YOU THINK THE TERRORIST WOULD DO GO HOME ALSO, (NO) THEY WOULD OVER RUN THE IRAQIS TAKE OVER THE OIL FIELDS, UTILIZE THE PROCEEDS TO TO PURCHASE TECHNOLOGY AND FOLLOW THE TROOPS HOME TO AMERICA, AND RECRUIT HOME GROWN IDIOTS, OUR WAY OF LIFE IN THIS COUNTRY LEAVE US EXTREMELY VALNERABLE IF OUR GUARD IS LET DOWN, FOR INSTANCE THE SUICIDAL TERRORIST FOLLOW OUR TROOPS HOME, WE HAVE MAJOR EVENTS YEAR ROUND WHERE APPROXIMATELY THIRTY, FORTY,FIFTY, TO A HUNDRED THOUSAND PEOPLE GATHER AT ONE TIME, AND I AM CERTAIN SOME OF YOU IDIOTS OUT THERE THAT ARE ADVOCATING BRING THE TROOPS HOME HAVE RELATIVES THAT VISIT THESE PLACES INCLUDING YOURSELVES, GOD FOR BID FIVE OR TEN OF THESE PEOPLE STRAP ON BOMBS AND SNEAK INTO SOME OF THESE PLACES, SO YOU IDIOTS DO THE MATH WHAT IS THE GREATES NUMBER OF CASUALTIES TWENTY FIVE HUNDRED TO THREE THOUSAND IN IRAQ, OR FIFTY THOUSAND AT HOME, NOT ONLY THAT YOU GIVE UP YOUR FREEDOM TO PARTICPATE IN EVENTS THAT YOU CHERISH. UNFORTUNATELY THESE ARE TREACHEROUS TIMES AND NO ONE WANTS TO ENDORSE DEATH, BUT THIS IS THE DREDFUL CHALLENGE AND DECISION THAT WE AS A NATION ARE EMBROILED IN, AND THERE ARE (NO) OTHER CHOICES OTHER THAN DEFEAT, AND MAYBE THATS WHAT CINDY SHEEHAN AND OTHERS ARE WHISHING FOR BECAUSE IF THERE IS AN,ATTACK1 AND THEY SURVIVE? A VEILED BURQA WILL BE WAITING, AND MAYBE THEY CAN RELY ON THEIR FREEDOM OF SPEECH BEFORE THEY TURN THEIR BEHINDS TO THE SKYEY.

FORTUNATELY NONE OF THIS IS EXPECTED TO OCCUR, BECAUSE WE HAVE THE KIND OF LEADERSHIP IN PLACE THAT IS VERY WELL AWARE OF THE CONSEQUENCES TO DATE, AND IS UTILIZING EVERY MEANS POSSIBLE TO DETER ANOTHER TERRORIST ATTACK ON THE PEOPLE OF THIS NATION, AND THE MOST IMPORTANT RESPONSIBILITY OF VOTING CITIZENS TODAY IS TO BE ARTICULATE ABOUT THEIR POLITICAL SELECTIONS, BECAUSE THE COUNTRY AND OUR WAY OF LIFE IS AT STEAK.

THERE ARE THOSE IN THIS COUNTRY THAT CONSISTENTLY DEFEND SADDAM HUSSEIN, THAT HE HAD NO WEAPONS OF MASS DESTRUCTION AND NO INVOLVEMENT IN NINE ELEVEN, THOSE ARE PEOPLE THAT HAS A DYSFUNCTIONAL MIND AND SHOULD (NEVER) BE ELECTED TO POLITICAL OFFICE,BECAUSE IT IS EXTREMELY INEPT NOT TO REALIZE THAT SADDAM HAD A MASTER PLAN IN STORE TO HANDICAP ISRAEL AND AMERICA, FORTUNATELY IT WAS FOILED WHEN HE CHOOSE TO INVADE KUWAIT. AND WAS TURNED AWAY BY THE FIRST PRESIDENT BUSH,SADDAM WAS A BRUTAL DICTATOR THAT HAD AMBITIONS AND PLANS TO CRUSH HIS NEIGHBORS AND POSSESS THEIR RICH OIL FIELDS, WHICH WOULD HAVE GIVEN HIM BARGAINING POWER TO PROCURE A ARSENAL OF SOPHISTICATED WEAPONRY, BUT IN ORDER TO ACCOMPLISH HIS MISSION HE NEEDED TO COMBINE KUWAIT AND SAUDI ARABIA OIL, IF HE HAD NOT BEEN EXPELLED FROM KUWAIT HIS DEFENSES WOULD HAVE STRENGTHEN OVER A PEROID OF TIME, IT DOSENT TAKE A ROCKET SCIENTIST TO DETERMINE THAT HIS INVASION OF KUWAIT WAS BECAUSE HE HAD NOTHING ELSE TO DO, IF THERE HAD BEEN (NO) INTERVENTION HE WOULD HAVE MONOPOLIZED ALL OF THE OIL PRODUCING NATIONS IN THAT PROVINCES, AND ONCE UNDER HIS CONTROL HE WOULD HAVE TURNED HIS ATTENTION TO THE MOST FEARED COUNTRY IN THAT AREA THE ISRAELIS, BY THIS TIME WITH ALL THE FUNDING FROM OIL HE HAS SEDUCED AND BRIBED THE RUSSIANS CHINEESE AND MOST OF EUROPEAN NATIONS OUT OF TECHNOLOGY AND HAS A INSURMOUNTABLE STOCK PILE OF WEAPONRY INCLUDING

MASS DESTRUCTION WHICH HE ALREADY HAD, THE FINAL STAGES WOULD BE TO OVER RUN ISRAEL WHICH IS THE ONLY TRUE ALLY TO THE UNITED STATES IN THAT AREA, BY THE WAY HE WAS ALREADY SOLICITING SUICIDAL PERSONNEL BY OFFERING TWENTY FIVE THOUSAND EACH MOST LIKELY TO PLANT IN ISREAL AND THE UNITED STATES, TO COMBAT A TYRANT OF THIS MAGNITUDE YOU NEED LOYAL ALLIES, BUT HE HAS MADE CERTAIN TO HAVE SILENCED MOST OF EUROPE, CHINA AND RUSSIA, WITH OIL AND FINANCES FOR THE SUPPLY OF TECHNOLOGY.

AND ALTHOUGH BEEING FORCED OUT OF KUWAIT AND CHECKED BY INSPECTORS, HE STILL RESUMED ON COURSE TO IMPLEMENT HIS CONQUERING PLAN, REMEMBER THE OIL FOR FOOD DEBACLE AND THE NATIONS THAT WAS INVOLVED, SO IF NOT CHECKED AND LEFT ALONE ISREAL AND THE UNITED STATES WOULD BE EXPERIENCING MANY DESTRUCTIVE MISSIONS BY SUICIDAL MANIACS, SO ALL THE LEFT WING DEMOCRATIC RADICALS ACTING LIKE SCHOOLS OF CAT FISH ALL MOUTH AND NO BRAINS, SOME OF THESE BUFFOONISH CLOWNS ARE ACTING AND SURMISING THAT IF SADDAM WASNT FLYING ONE OF THE JET PLANES ON NINE ELEVEN THERE IS NO WAY HE COULD HAVE BEEN INVOLVED, AND THAT IS EXACTLY WHAT HE WANTED SOME STUPID AMERICANS TO BROADCAST BECAUSE THE INTENT WAS TO SEDUCE ASIA AND EUROPE TO THINK THAT HE DIDNT HAVE DIRTY HANDS, (NO) TYRANT THE RULER OF A NATION WITH POLITICAL CLOUT BASED ON THE RICHES OF OIL, SUCH AS SADDAM HUSSEIN WOULD NEVER LET IT BE KNOWN THAT HE WAS A STAUNCH SUPPORTER OF TERRORISM, BECAUSE TERRORISM IS TRANSFIXED AROUND THE GLOBE AND IT WOULD DENOUNCE HIS CREDIBILITY TO SUCCEED IN LONG RANGE PLANNING FOR CONTROL.

HOWEVER TO FINANCE TERRORISM IS AN ACCOMPLICE AND JUST AS GUILTY IF HE HAD STRAPPED ON A BELT OR FLOWN ONE OF THOSE PLANES HIMSELF, SADDAM HUSSEIN WAS ONE OF THE MOST CUNNING DANGEROUS BARBARIC TYRANTS SENSE ADOLPH HITLER, BECAUSE HE UNDERSTOOD AMERICAN POLITICS AND IMPLEMENTED STRATEGIC PLANS TO DISTORT SOME OF THEIR DERANGED

MINDS WHILE HE WAS PLANNING THEIR DEMISE, IT IS VERY POSSIBLE IF HE HAD MOVED TO THE UNITED STATES AND GAINED CITIZENRY THE DEMOCRATS WOULD HAVE NOMINATED HIM TO BE THEIR PRESIDENTIAL CNIDATE, BECAUSE THEY ARE STILL ENDORSING A IDEOLOGY HE NEVER HAD WEAPONS OF MASS DESTRUCTION AND WAS NO THREAT TO THE UNITED STATES THIS KIND OF POLITICAL INEPTNESS COMING FROM DEMOCRATS AND BLACK SELF APPOINTED LEADERS TO INSINUATE THAT SADDAM WAS NOT A THREAT, IS CONDESCENDING IMMORAL AND DISLOYAL TO THE UNITED STATES OF AMERICA, HOWEVER SOME ARE ENGAGING THEIR OPENIONS FOR POLITICAL ASPIRATIONS AND OTHERS ARE JUST PLAIN STUPID, BUT TO THE CONTRARY OF THE POLITICAL IDEOLOGICAL PREPONDERATES THE INVASION OF IRAQ TO REMOVE A BRUTAL DICTATOR AND TERRORIST FINACIER WAS ONE OF THE MOST BRILLIANT MOVES EVER PERPETRATED BY THIS ADMINISTRATION,IN AN EFFORT TO WARD OFF PLANS TO ATTACK ISRAEL, AND INUNDATE THE UNITED STATES WITH SUICIDAL TERRORIST, I AM A FIRM BELIEVER THAT SADDAM HUSSEIN WAS ONE OF THE PRIME INSTIGATORS OF NINE ELEVEN AND A LOYAL UNDERCOVER FINANCIER,THAT HAD WEAPONS OF MASS DESTRUCTIONS WHICH WILL BE FOUND IN INSURMOUNTABLE PROPORTIONS, BECAUSE THEY WERE A IMPORTANT PART OF HIS ARSENAL IF HE HAD SUCCEEDED WITH HIS MASTER PLAN TO USE ON HIS NEIGHBORS, ESPECIALLY THE ISRAELIS, WHILE SUICIDAL RADICALS WERE RIPPING AMERICA APART WITH BOMBS, SO ONE OF PRESIDENT GEORGE BUSH MOST PRESTIGIOUS LEGACIES WILL BE THE REMOVAL OF A BRUTAL DICTATOR SADDAM HUSSEIN, TO SPARE OUR NATION A HORRIFIC DISASTROUS FATE INCLUDING ISRAEL REGARDLESS TO THE DEMOCRATIC CRITICS.

BECAUSE BRUTAL DICTATORS HAVE NO CONSCIOUSNESS RELATED TO DIPLOMACY THEIR GOALS ARE TO DOMINATE AT ANY COST AND THE LIVES OF PEOPLE IS (NOT) AN OPTION, TERRORIST ARE A SKILFUL NET WORK OF PEOPLE EMBEDDED AROUND THE UNIVERSE FUNDED BY BRUTAL DICTATORS SEEKING TO OVERTHROW ANY ONE THAT

DISAGREE WITH THEIR RADICAL IDEOLOGY, AND THEIR MAIN STRATEGY IS TO SOLICIT LOWER LEVELS ILLITERATES TO DEDICATE THEIR LIVES TO THE CAUSE, BUT REMEMBER THIS TAKE TONS OF FINANCES AND ISOLATED AREAS TO TRAIN, WHICH PRIOR TO NINE ELEVEN THEY WERE UTILIZING AFGHANISTAN AND BEING FINANCED BY SOME ASIAN HEADS OF STATE DICTATORS AND SYMPATHIZERS FROM AMERICA.

AFTER THE INVASION OF AFGHANISTAN IT WAS LIKE KICKING A ANT HILL THEY WERE IN SERCH OF ANOTHER DOMAIN, AND THANK GOD WE HAD A ADMINISTRATION THAT TAPPED INTO THEIR STRATEGIES AND WAS AHEAD OF THEM TO IRAQ AND REMOVED ONE OF THEIR DOMINATE MENTORS IN SADDAM HUSSEIN, AND THE GRATIFYING AFFECTS OF THAT MISSION WAS IS THAT APPROXIMATELY TWENTY FIVE MILLION PEOPLE WERE LIBERATED FROM THE GRASP OF A BRUTAL DICTATOR, AND DEPLOYED OUR FORCES RIGHT IN THE MIDDLE OF SIX OTHER JOINING COUNTRIES, WHICH SOME FINANCE AND SPONSER TERRORISM PIRATICALLY IRAN AND SYRIA, OUR FORCES ARE DEPLOYED WITH THE ABILITY TO ADVANCE IN ANY DIRECTION TO DIARUPT THE WHOLESALE TRAINING OF TERROIST, AND TO PREVENT THEIR CAPITALIZING ON OIL REVENUE WHICH WOULD HAVE BEEN SUPPLIED BY SADDAM IF HE WAS STILL IN COMMAND, ONCE IRAQ HAVE A STABLE GOVERNMENT, AND OUR ALLIANCE WITH THE ISRAELIS, TERRORISM CAN BE DISSIPATED TO AN EXTENT WHERE IT WILL BECOME SOME WHAT DOCILE, BUT UNFORTUNATELY ITS GOING TO BE WITH US FOREVER, BECAUSE THEY ARE ENTICING HOME GROWN PARTICIPANTS.

THERE IS A MAJOR SCENARIO DEVELOPING IN THIS COUNTRY AND IT IS RATHER DISTURBING, THAT COULD PROVE DEVASTATING FOR THE CITIZENS OF THIS NATION, AND THAT IS THE DEMOCRATIC LIBERAL SYMPATHETIC PROPAGANDA TO TERRORIST AND THE NEWS MEDIA ENDORSING THEIR IDEOLOGY IN AN EFFORT TO GAIN POLITICAL POWER, THIS IS EQUIVALENT TO A ONE YEAR OLD BEING HOME ALONE WITH A BOX OF MATCHES, SOME OF THE DEMOCRATS AND THE LIBERAL BIAS NEWS

MEDIA IS ACTING AS IF THEY ARE NOT CITIZENS OF THE UNITED STATES OF AMERICA, AND COULD CARE LESS ABOUT THE SERIOUSNESS OF TERRORISM, WHEN AS A NATION WE ARE DEADLOCKED IN ONE OF THE MOST DISASTROUS CHALLENGES THIS COUNTRY HAS (EVER) BEEN INVOLVED WITH, TO DISLIKE A PRESIDENT AND HIS CHOICE OF CABINET MEMBERS IS ONE THING, BUT TO AIDE THE TERROIST THAT IS TRYING TO EXTERMINATE AMERICANS BY LEAKING PERTINENT INFORMATION AND RANTING ABOUT BRING THE TROOPS HOME, WHICH ALERT THE TERRORIST THAT SOME IN THIS COUNTRY IS STUPID AS HELL, AND I AM CERTAIN SADDAM HUSSEIN IS ELATED LOCKED AWAY IN HIS PLACE OF CONFINEMENT IN IRAQ, BECAUSE THE DEMOCRATS ARE ASSISTING IN CARRYING OUT HIS INITIAL LONG RANGE PLANNING, BY DENOUNCING THAT SADDAM HUSSEIN HAD WEAPONS OF MASS DESTRUCTION AND HE WAS NOT A THREAT TO AMERICA, AND ADVOCATING BRING THE TROOPS HOME.

FORTUNATELY PRESIDENT GEORGE BUSH AND HIS ADMINISTRATION ALONG WITH THE ISRAELIS WERE AWARE OF HIS DECEITFUL PLANNING, AND THE ROAD LEAD THROUGH SYRIA AS THE FINAL STRONG HOLD TO DISRUPT TERRORISM ESTABLISHED IN IRAQ, BECAUSE THE SUICIDAL BODY OF PERSONS ARE CROSSING NEIGHBORING SYRIA BORDERS TO ENTER IRAQ,AND THEY HAVE AMNESIA TO THAT EFFECT,ONCE THE BORDER CROSSINGS IS BROUGHT UNDER CONTROL THERE WILL BE A REDUCTION IN CASUALTIES REGARDS TO SUICIDAL BOMBINGS, AND THE IRAQIS CAN CONTINUE TO PROCEEDE WITH ESTABLISHING A BONAFIDE GOVERNMENT, I NEVER WOULD HAVE CONCEIVED ENTERTAINING THE IDEA THAT DEMOCRATIC ELECTED OFFICIALS CONSIDERED TO BE THEIR PARTY LEADERS, WOULD BE SO OUT OF TUCH WITH REALITY TO SET THIS NATION UP FOR ITS CITIZENS TO BE SLAUGHTED BY TERRORIST, BECAUSE IF OUR TROOPS ARE REMOVED FROM IRAQ THAT WILL BE OUR FATE, EVEN WHEN THERE IS AN ESTABLISHED GOVERNMENT IN IRAQ,, DUE C TO.THE ISRAELIS RESTORING THE SYRIANS MEMORY ABOUT BORDER CROSSINGS, AND THE LOCATION OF MASS

DESTRUCTIVE WEAPONS, A U.S. MILITARY (STABILIZING) RECONNAISSANCE FORCE SHOULD REMAIN IN IRAQ FOR AN ETERNITY IF WE INTEND TO SALVAGE OUR CULTURE.

AND IT IS QUITE INTERESTING WHEN YOU LISTEN TO PRIVATE CITIZENS GO PUBLIC WITH DEMEANING RHETORIC ABOUT THE IRAQ CONFLICT AND DITCATE POLICY AS IF THEY ARE EXPERTS ON MILITARY AFFAIRS, AND CRITICIZE THE PRESIDENT OF THE UNITED STATES, WHEN MOST DO (NOT) UNDERSTAND THE CULTURE THAT HAS BEEN GRANTED TO THEM BY THIS COUNTRY RELATED TO A FREE DIVERSE SOCIETY, THERE ARE THOSE THAT ACCUMULATE RESOURCES BY BOUNCING A BASKET BALL, WHICH DOES (NOT) REQUIRE EDUCATION OR POLITICAL SKILLS, YET ETAN THOMAS WAS ON NATIONAL TELEVISION C-SPAN (2) JUNE 12, 2006, FLAUNTING WITH DEMAGOGUERY FORMULATED BY THE DEMOCRATS TO EXPLOIT HIS NOTORIETY IN AN EFFORT TO IMPUGN THE PRESIDENT INTEGRITY REGARDS TO THE CONFLICT IN IRAQ, WHICH SUGGEST THAT HE IS A AFFLUENT POSTER WATER BOY THAT IS SUPPORTING AND (COMPLEMENTING) THE DEMOCRATS IDEOLOGY FOR FOR THEIR EFFORTS IN LYNCHING, WATER HOSING, DYNAMITING CHURCHES WITH LITTLE CHILDREN INSIDE, AND SICKING DOGS ON AFRICAN AMERICANS DURING THE LATE FIFTIES AND EARLY SIXTIES, AND THEIR CONTROLLED CONGRESS DENIED BLACKS THEIR CIVIL AND VOTING RIGHTS FOR OVER SEVENTY YEARS, HOWEVER THAT IS HIS RIGHT AS A AMERICAN CITIZEN, BUT HE SURE AS HELL DO (NOT) HAVE THE RIGHT TO SET POLICY FOR THE NATION IN IRAQ, BECAUSE THERE HAS BEEN SPECULATION ABOUT SOME SPORTS PERSONALITIES OVER THE YEARS NOT BEING CAPABLE OF DECIPHERING AND WRITING AMERICAN ENGLISH, SO MR THOMAS SHOULD GET ON HIS KNEES AND TURN HIS BEHIND TO THE SKIES AND EXPRESS GRATITUDE FOR PRESIDENT GEORGE BUSH AND HIS ADMINSTRATION, BECAUSE IF NOT FOR THEIR EXPULSION OF SADDAM HUSSEIN FROM IRAQ, IT IS VERY POSSIBLE HE WOULD HAVE BEEN BLOWN TO BITS ON THE BASKET BALL COURT LONG AGO BY A SUICIDAL MANIAC PLANTED IN THIS COUNTRY BY NONE OTHER THAN THE SCHEMING OF SADDAM HUSSEIN.

HOWEVER THERE IS ONE OTHER IMPORTANT NOTE AND GESTURE, IF THE MAJORITY OF AFRICAN AMERICANS ARE UNABLE TO DETERMINE THE SCHEMING OF THE DEMOCRATIC PARTY FOR OVER SEVENTY YEARS IN AN EFFORT TO UTILIZE THEM FOR THEIR VOTING BLOC TO SUSTAIN POLITICAL POWER, THERE IS (NO) WAY ON GODS EARTH THEY COULD CONNECT THE DOTS RELATED TO SCHEMERS AND SPONSERS OF TERRORISM THAT IS DETERMINE TO DESTROY OUR WAY OF LIFE.

AND IT CAN (NOT) BE ENTREATED ENOUGH THAT SOME IN THE DEMOCRATIC PARTY HAS LOST (ALL) INTEGRITY AND MORAL RESPONSIBILITY TO THE UNITED STATES OF AMERICA, IT IS UNBELIEVABLE THAT SOME DEMOCRATIC ELECTED OFFICIALS ARE SO STUPIDLY INCOHERENT REGARDS TO THE SAFETY OF AMERICAN CITIZENS THAT ELECTED THEM TO OFFICE, AS I PREVIOUSLY STATED THE TERRORIST ARE OUT TO DESTROY AMERICA, WHICH WAS THE HIDDEN AGENDA OF SADDAM HUSSEIN, BUT DUE TO HIS EXPULSION FROM POWER THE IRANIAN AND SYRIAN LEADERS HAS ASSUMED HIS INTENTIONS OF DESTROYING ISRAEL AND AMERICA, AND ALL YOU CAN HEAR FROM THE LIBERAL MEDIA AND LEFT WING RADICALS DEMOCRATS,IS THE WAR WAS A MISTAKE, AND BRING THE TROOPS HOME, THIS IS ONE OF THE MOST DESPICABLE BETRAYAL FROM A MAJOR POLITICAL PARTY THAT HAS EVER EXISTED IN THE HISTORY OF AMERICA, AND THE AXES OF THIS EVIL PERPETRATED BY DEMOCRATS IS PLAYING WITH FIRE, BECAUSE TERRORIST ARE A UNIQUE ORGANIZATION WHICH CONSIST OF TOP, MIDDLE AND BOTTOM, THE TOP ARE THE DICTATORS THAT ARE HEADS OF STATE AND FINANICERS WHICH PRODUCE POLICY AND DICTATE STRATEGY, THE MIDDLE ARE ORGANIZERS THAT SOLICIT THE BOTTOM TO CARRY OUT DESTRUCTIVE MISSIONS, AND IT SOLELY DEPEND ON THE GULLIBILITY OF PARTICIPANTS THAT DETERMINE IF THEY BECOME SUCIDAL BOMBERS OR REGULAR WORRIERS ARE A COMBINATION OF BOTH, AND THEIR RESPONSIBILITIES COME FROM THE MASTER PLANNERS AT THE TOP, AND TO BOLSTER THIS CLAIM ISRAELS AMBASSADOR TO THE U.N. AMB. DAN GILLERMAN

ADDRESSED THE ASSEMBLY ON FOX NEWS JULY 14, 2006, AND DIRECTED HIS ASSESSMENTS DIRECTLY TO HIS COUNTERPART FROM LEBANON, AND GAVE A BRIEF SYNOPSIS TO THE AFFECTS OF TOP TERRORIST FINANCIERS AND CONTROLLERS, WHICH THEORETICALLY ENDORSE MY CALCULATED REVELATIONS, THE CHRONOLOGY OF THESE SYSTEMATICALLY EVENTS HAS BEEN DEVELOPING FOR DECADES, AND IT APPEAR THAT THE DEMOCRATS ARE THE ONLY PEOPLE ON THE PLANET THAT IS INEPT TO THEIR DETAIL FUNCTIONS, AND CONTINUALLY DEMAGOGUE WITH INSINUATIONS AS IF WE ARE NOT THREATEN WITH TERRORISM, AND AT TIMES USE VERBIAGE THAT IS ACROSS THE LINE, WHICH COULD LEAVE ONE TO ASSUME THEY ARE ALIGNING WITH PEOPLE THAT IS INTENT ON SABOTAGING THE UNITES STATES OF AMERICA, AND THEIR INTENTIONS ARE QUITE NOTICABLE REGARDS TO LOYALTY, MORAL AND ETHICAL STANDARDS, BECAUSE ANY POLITICAL PARTY UTILIZE THE DRAPED AMERICAN FLAG OVER THE REMAINS OF DEMOCRATIC AND REPUBLICAN SOLDIERS THAT HAS GIVEN THEIR LIVES TO PROTECT THIS NATION FROM TERRORISM FOR POLITICAL GAIN, IS INSENSITIVE AND EQUIVALENT TO THE RADICAL SPONSERS OF TERRORISM THAT LABEL THE CITIZENS OF THIS NATION INFIDELS, THE TOP LEADERS AND SPONSERS OF TERROR ARE NOT STUPID, THEY ARE SMART ENOUGH TO REALIZE THAT THERE IS A DIVISION IN THIS COUNTRY REGARDS TO THE CONFLICT IN IRAQ, AND THE DEMOCRATS ARE ASSISTING THEIR CAUSE, BY BEING (CLUELESS) TO THEIR CUNNING ASPIRATIONS TO DISPOSE OF OUR REFINED INTELLECTUAL SOCIETY, AND ONLY THE VOTERS OF THIS NATION CAN HOPEFULLY PROHIBIT THIS DISASTER FROM OCCURRING ON THE SOIL IN THE UNITED STATES OF AMERICA.

THE CURRENT TIMES ARE THE MOST CRUCIAL IN OUR NATION HISTORY, WHERE MANY INNOCENT CITIZENS LIVES ARE THREATENED BECAUSE OF WHO WE ARE AND OUR WAY OF LIFE, THESE UNIQUELY DECEPTIVE TERRORIST ARE CUNNING AND WILL USE ANY METHOD AT THEIR DISPOSAL TO ACCOMPLISH THEIR MISSION IN DESTROYING ISRAEL AND AMERICA, SO THE POLITICANS THAT IS ELECTED TO

REPRESENT THE CITIZENS OF THIS COUNTRY (MUST) FULLY UNDERSTAND THEIR OBSESSIVE INTENTIONS, BECAUSE THERE IS NO POLITICAL DIPLOMATIC COMPROMISE, AND IF ANY POLITICIAN ELECTED TO OFFICE ENTERTAIN THE IDEA THAT THIS IS A POSSIBILITY IS BADLY MISTAKEN AND IS JEOPARDIZING OUR NATION AND ITS CITIZENS TO COMPROMISE THEIR FREEDOM AND LIVES, BECAUSE POTENTIAL TERRORIST ARE LURKING AMONG OUR MIDST AND THEY ARE COLOR BLIND, SO IT IS ABSOLUTELY OBLOGATORY THAT THE POLITICIANS YOU VOTE FOR TO SERVE THIS COUNTRY IS SCRUTNIZED TO THE FULLEST EXTENT REGARDS TO PROTECTING OUR NATION FROM TERRORISM AT ANY METHOD AVAILABLE, THERE ARE THOSE MAINLY IN THE DEMOCRATIC PARTY HAVE SOME FOOLISH IDEA THAT TERRORISM WAS ESCALATED WHEN PRESIDENT GEORGE BUSH INVADED IRAQ AND EXPELLED SADDAM HUSSEIN FROM POWER, TO THE CONTRARY SADDAM HUSSEIN WAS THE MAIN CULPRIT STRATEGIST AND SPONSER OF TERRORISM THROUGHOUT ASIA, AND IF (ANY) PEOPLE HAVE ASPIRATIONS OF TERRORISM GOING AWAY AFTER PRESIDENT BUSH LEAVE OFFICE, IS SUFFERING FROM A SERIOUS CASE OF DEMENTIA THAT WILL EVENTUALLY CAUSE THEM TO VIOLENTLY BE EXPLODED ALONG WITH A LOT OF OTHER INNOCENT PEOPLE THAT DO NOT SHARE THEIR IDEOLOGY.

AS I SIT ON THIS DAY JULY 16, 2006, AND TRY TO PUT WORDS IN A PROSPECTIVE IN AN EFFORT TO ANALYTICALLY CONTRADICT STATEMENTS AND BELIEFS THAT PRESIDENT GEORGE BUSH LIED THE NATION INTO WAR WITH FALSE INTUITIONS, THERE ARE TWO KINDS OF CRITICS THAT DENOUNCE THE CONFLICT IN IRAQ, AND ONE IS DECITFUL DEMOCRATIC POLITICANS UTILIZING THIS TRAGEDY TO ENHANCE THEIR PLIGHT TO DISLODGE REPUBLICANS FROM THE MAJORITY OF POLITICAL POWER IN CONGRESS, THE OTHER IS BEING SO INEPT TO THE FUNDAMENTALS OF TERRORISM AND THEIR CAUSE THEY ARE WILLING TO ASSIST IN CARRYING OUT THEIR DERANGED IDEOLOGY, HOWEVER PRIOR TO NINE ELEVEN A TERRORIST GROUP CONTROLLED AFGHANISTAN AND UTILIZED THEIR COUNTRY FOR THE

PURPOSE OF TRAINING TERRORIST AND HATCHED THE BOLD SENSLESS SUICIDAL PLOT THAT CAUSED THE DEMISE OF APPROXIMATELY THREE THOUSAND INNOCENT LIVES ON AMERICAN SOIL.

WHICH THE NATION COULD NOT BELIEVE WHAT THEY WERE WITNESSING, ONE THING CERTAIN THERE ARE TWO MAIN INGREDIENTS THAT FORM TERRORIST AND THAT IS FINANCING AND A PLACE FOR TRAINING, BECAUSE IT TAKE TIME TO INDOCTRINATE PEOPLE TO DEDICATE THEIR LIFE FOR A RELIGIOUS FANATIC CAUSE, PRESIDENT GEORGE BUSH WILL BE SALUTED IN HISTORY AS ONE OF THE GREATEST LEADERS OF THIS NATION IN MORDEN TIMES, BECAUSE OF THE UNCHARACTERISTIC CIRCUMSTANCES DEALING WITH UNETHICAL LYING DEMOCRATS THAT DENOUNCE HIS ABILITY TO PROTECT THIS NATION, WHEN HE IS DOING JUST THAT, HE REMOVED A BRUTAL DICTATOR AND FINANCIER OF TERRORISM SADDAM HUSSEIN FROM POWER IN IRAQ, AND DEPRIVED THE TERRORIST FROM A TRAINING SITE AFTER THEIR EXPULSION FROM CONTROL OF AFGHANISTAN, SO THEY HERDED INTO SOUTHERN LEBANON AND SET UP THEIR TRAINING FINANCED BY IRAN AND SYRIA AS REPORTED, ONCE AGAIN PRESIDENT GEORGE BUSH IS TO IS TO BE COMMENDED FOR HIS OVERALL STRATEGY IN ASIA, BECAUSE IT IS REPORTED THAT THE ARAB LEAGUE ON JULY 17,2006, HAS CONDEMNED HEZBOLLAH FOR THE INSURGENCY AGAINST ISRAEL, PERHAPS SOMEONE SHOULD PASS THIS BIT OF INFORMATION TO THE LEADING DEMOCRATS, AND INFORM THEM THAT THIS WAS (NOT NEGOTIATED) IT IS SIMPLY BECAUSE THERE IS APPROXIMATELY ONE HUNDRED AND FIFTY THOUSAND AMERICAN TROOPS SITTING ON THEIR DOOR STEP THAT DEMOCRATS WANT TO BRING HOME AND JEOPARDIZE ALL AMERICAN LIVES, REGARDLESS TO WHAT TERRORIST IDENTIFY THEMSELVES AS BY NAME THEY ARE (ALL) TUNED INTO THE SAME NETWORK GLOBALLY, WITH THE INTENT TO FORCE THEIR RELIGIOUS IDEOLOGY AS BEING STANDARD FOR ALL PEOPLE, HOWEVER WHEN THEY OCCUPIED SOUTHERN LEBANON AND SET UP TRAINING FINANCED BY IRAN AND SYRIA AS

REPORTED, WHICH HAS SUPPLIED SUICIDAL PERSONNEL INTO IRAQ THROUGH SYRIA TO MURDER OUR SOLDIERS AND INNOCENT IRAQIS, FORTUNATELY THE ISRAELIS ARE ON THE PROWL TO ROOT OUT TERROR STARTING WITH THEIR BASE TRAINING SITE IN LEBANON AND THE ROAD LEAD THROUGH SYRIA, AND IF IRAN SHOULD GETSOME STRANGE IDEA THAT THEY ARE GOING TO TAKE REPRISAL AGAINST ISRAEL FOR PROTECTING THEIR HOME LAND, THE BIG DOG IS SITTING ON THEIR FRONT AND BACK DOOR STEP, MEANING AMERICAN TROOPS IN IRAQ AND AFGHANISTAN, AND WILL SERVE NOTICE TO IRAN TO STAY PUT AND LET ISRAEL DEAL WITH THESE EXECUTIONERS,AND TRUST ME THEY ARE SECOND TO NONE.

AND THANK GOD FOR OUR BRILLANT STRATEGICALLY PLANNING PRESIDENT GEORGE BUSH, TO TAKE UP RESIDENCES RIGHT IN THE MIDDLE OF SOME TERRORIST FUNDING AND WEAPON SUPPLIERS TO CREATE TERROR NATIONS, AND IT IS SO GRATIFYING TO KNOW THAT WE DO (NOT) NEED AUTHORIZATION TO TRESPASS FROM ANY SURROUNDING COUNTRY BECAUSE WE ARE ALREADY THERE, AND THIS DEPLOYMENT WAS (NOT) NEGOTIATED FROM SADDAM HUSSEIN.

IT IS PATHETICALLY DISGUSTING WHEN A MAJOR POLITICAL PARTY IN THIS COUNTRY THE DEMOCRATS AND SOME OF THEIR ELECTED LEADERS GO PUBLIC AND INDULGE IN SUCH STUPID DEMAGOGUREY RELATED TO TERRORISM, SEN. CHRIS DODD, REP. JANE HARMON, AND OTHERS INSINUATING THAT THAT THE PRESIDENT AND HIS ADMINISTRATION HAVE NOT NEGOTIATED ENOUGH CONCERNING FOREIGN AFFAIRS IN THE PAST FIVE YEARS TO QUELL TERRORISM, THE ABSURDITY OF THOSE STATEMENTS IS APPALLING AND NONSENSICAL TO TRY AND COURSE THE GENERAL PUBLIC IN THIS MANNER, BECAUSE THEY GET AMNESIA REGARDS TO A PRESIDENT NAMED WILLIAM JEFFERSON CLINTON THAT HELD OFFICE FOR EIGHT YEARS, AND BASICALLY THATS (ALL) HE DID WAS NEGOTIATE TO NO AVAIL, DURING HIS PRESIDENCY SECRETARY OF STATE MADELEINE ALBRIGHT WAS DISPATCHED TO NORTH KOREA AND CLINKED CHAMPAGNE GLASSES WITH KIM JONGIL,

(NEGOTIATING) AND THE ONLY PROGRESS DEVLOPED FROM THAT NEGOTATING WAS MAYBE SHE GOT SOUSED, BECAUSE AS OF TODATE HE REPRESENT A MAJOR PROBLEM FOR THE PENINSULA OF ASIA AND THE ENTIRE CONTINENT.

FORMER PRESIDENT WILLIAM JEFFERSON CLINTON NEGOIATED WITH YASSER ARAFAT DURING HIS ENTIRE REIGN AS PRESIDENT FOR EIGHT YEARS, AND AS OF TO DATE YOU BE THE JUDGE OF WHAT WAS ACCOMPLISHED (ZERO) REGARDS TO PEACE, DEMOCRATIC (NEGOTIATING) IS LARGELY RESPONSIBLE FOR THE SERIOUS PROBLEMS WE ARE EXPERIENCING TODAY WITH THE PALESTINIANS, NORTH KOREA, AND IRAN, TERRORIST ARE A GROUP OF INDIVIDUALS THAT HAS CHOSEN TO FOLLOW A RELIGIOUS DOCTRINE THAT THEY CHERISH TO THE EXTENT OF DEDICATED DEMISE, WHICH IS FORMULATED OF PEOPLE WITH DIFFERENT ETHNIC BACKGROUNDS BUT IS STIMULATED BY THE SAME IDEOLOGY, THAT HAVE THE ABILITY TO CONGREGATE WITH IN A FREE SOCIETY WITH THIS HIDDEN AGENDA AND WOULD STOP A NOTHING TO SUCCEED WITH THEIR FANATICISM OF SLAUGHTERING INNOCENT PEOPLE, AND LEAVE (NO) CHANCE FOR NEGOTIATING BECAUSE THEIR IDENTITIES ARE UNKKNOWN, ALSO THEIR FINANCES ARE SUPPLIED BY SUPPORTERS THAT IS JUST AS CAMOUFLAGED AS THEY ARE,THE NEGOTIATING DEMOCRATS HAVE A IMPAIRED OR ABNORMAL BRAIN THAT IS STUCK ON STUPID BECAUSE YOU CAN (NOT) NEGOTIATE WITH TERRORIST, OR ANY NATION THAT HAS CHOSEN TO SUPPORT AND FINANCE TERRORISM, BECAUSE THEY HAVE ALREADY DECIDED YOUR FATE,EITHER YOU ARE TO BE EXTERMINATED OR CONVERT TO THEIR IDEOLOGY, THE ONLY WAY TO NEGOTIATE WITH TERRORIST IS TO INVEST IN COVERT INTELLIGENCE, AND A BLAST FROM CANNONS, SO THE DEMCRATS HAD BETTER SEEK SOME KIND OF TREATMENT FOR THIS OBSESSION WITH NEGOATING, AND FOR GOD SAKE QUIT PLAYING POLITICAL CHESS GAMES WITH AMERICAN LIVES.

IN AN EFFORT TO SUBSTANTIATE THE CLAIM ABOUT SOME DEMOCRATS THINKING REGARDS TO TRRRORISM AND THEIR DEFINITIVE OBSESSION WITH (NEGOTATING),

CONGRESSMAN REP. NICK RAHALL WAS ON C-SPAN JULY 19, 2006, IMPLYING THAT THERE IS NOT ENOUGH NEGOTIATING OCCURING AND SUGGESTING THAT PRESIDENT BUSH SHOULD FOLLOW THE RONALD REAGAN EAMPLE AND SUGGEST THAT ISRAEL ABANDON THE IDEA OF PROTECTING THEIR HOME LAND AND CITIZENS, AND EXPECTED C-SPAN ALLOWED THE PHONE LINES TO BE FLOODED WITH DEMOCRATS, HOWEVER ONE OR TWO SENSIBLE CALLERS WAS PERMITTED TO RESPOND, AND THIS ONE INDIVIDUAL SUMMED IT BEST WHEN HE STATED THAT FOR FORTY YEARS THE DEMOCRATS WAS HIS PARTY, AND ONCE HE HAD TAKEN AN I.Q. TEST AND TESTED ONE HUNDRED AND THIRTY ONE, BUT EMPHATICALLY SUGGESTED THAT SOME OF THOSE PEOPLE CALLING IN ON THE DEMOCRAT LINE WITH THEIR SUGGESTIONS ABOUT ISRAEL WOULD TEST EIGHTY, AND I CLASSIFY REP. NICK RAHALL AS BEING A PART OF THAT GROUP, BECAUSE HIS ASSESSMENT OF WHAT CAUSED ISRAEL TO INVADE LEBANON WAS EXTREMELY NEGATIVE AND DENOUNCED ISRAEL FOR ITS ACTIONS AND SEEMINGLY HAD RESERVATIONS ABOUT THE VALIDITY ALSO MADE CHASTISING ACCUSATIONS ABOUT PRESIDENT BUSH (NOT) MEETING WITH YASSER ARAFAT TO NEGOTIATE, AND FOR SOME STRANGE INEPT REASON HE LITERALLY ACCUSED SECRETARY OF STATE RICE OF BEING PART OF A CONSPIRACY TO DELAY A TRIP TO ASIA IN ORDER THAT ISRAEL COULD INFLICT MORE DAMAGE TO LEBANON, AND BECAME A TACTICAL MILITARY EXPERT AND SCOLD THE ISRAELIS FOR BOMBING THE AIR PORT IN LEBANON TWICE BUT THE MOST IDIOTIC , NONSENSICAL STATEMENT MADE BY THIS U.S. CONGRESSMAN NICK RAHALL, WAS THAT NEGOTIATING SHOULD BEGIN WITH HEZBOLLAH IN AN EFFORT TO INCORPORATE THEM AS A LEGITIMATE GOVERNING BODY IN LEBANON, C-SPAN SHOULD IMPLEMENT SOME KIND OF TESTING FOR CRACK BEFORE THEY LET THESE BUFFOONS ON AIR, BECAUSE REP. RAHALL IS UNAWARE THAT HEZBOLLAH IS ALREADY IN CONTROL OF LEBANON AND IS TRYING TO DESTROY ISREAL FROM THEIR BORDERS WITH SCUD MISSILE BOMBS.

THE APPERANCE OF REP. RAHALL COMMENTS SUGGEST THAT SECRETARY RICE FLY IN AMONG THE BOMBS AND NEGOIATE WITH HEZBOLLAH, THIS IS TIPICAL PREHISTORIC DEMOCRATIC RHETORIC THAT HAS SEDUCED MILLIONS OF AMERICANS OVER THE YEARS TO GET YOU TO FOCUS ON A MIRAGE AND ONCE THEY ARE ELECTED TO OFFICE IT DISAPPEAR, AND THIS IS A FALLACY THAT IS EMBEDDED IN THEIR HISTORY, WHICH DICTATE WHY IT IS SO DIFFICULT FOR THEM TO GRASP THE DEADLY THREAT OF TERRORISM, BECAUSE FOR HUNDREDS OF YEARS THEY HAVE ALWAYS RESOLVED ISSURES THROUGH VIOLENCE, LIES, DECIET, AND NEGOTIATIONS, WITHOUT UNDERSTANDING THE REALITY OR CARING ABOUT EXISTING CIRCUMSTANCES, AND VERY SELDOM SUFFERED THE CONSEQUENCES OF REPRISAL, SO THROUGH GENETIC CONTROLLABILITY THEY FIRMLY BELIEVE THEY CAN DISSUADE THE TERROIST AWAY THROUGH NEGOTIATING, AND APPARENTLY JULY 19, 2006, WAS NATIONAL BUFFOONS DAY TO ENGAGE IN NEGOTIATING RHETORIC, BECAUSE DEMOCRATIC STRATEGIST MICHAEL BROWN, A BLACK POLITICAL SLAVE DRIVER FOR THE DEMOCRAT PARTY, WAS ON FOX NEWS SCREAMING AT THE TOP OF HIS LUNGS ABOUT THE ADMINSTRATION DO NOT NEGOTIATE ENOUGH THEY JUST GO TO WAR, AND THEY SHOULD USE THE CLINTON PLAN BECAUSE PEOPLE ARE GETTING KILLED THEY SHOULD PUT THE GUNS DOWN AND NEGOTIATE, AND ATTEMPTED TO TALK OVER THE HOST, FINALLY WHEN ASKED WHAT WOULD HIS SUGGESTIONS BE AT THIS STAGE, AND IF HE WOULD NEGOTIATE WITH HEZBOLLAH, HE PONDERED AND SAID NO, BUT NEVER OFFERED A SOLUTION TO THE HOST INQUIRY, IT WOULD BE INTERESTING TO EVALUATE MR BROWN THOUGHTS ABOUT NINE ELEVEN, THESE INNOCENT PEOPLE WERE SLAUGHTERED BY SUICIDAL TERRORIST, WHERE THERE WERE NO GUNS TO PUT DOWN, UNFORTUNATELY MR. BROWN HAS DECIDED TO DICTATE POLITICAL PLICY FOR THE NATION, AND IS INEPT TO THE WIRE TAPPING OF DR. MARTIN LUTHER KING BY THE DEMOCRATS, HOWEVER THIS AN ALL OUT EFFORT BY THE DEMOCRATIC LEADERS AND THEIR FOOLISH INDOCTRINATED EMULATORS TO

USE TERRORISM IN AN ATTEMPT TO DISCREDIT THE ADMINISTRATION, HOPING THIS WILL CATCH ON WITH THE AMERICAN PEOPLE AND GET TEM ELECTED FOR A MAJORITY CONTROL IN CONGRESS, BUT TRUST ME THIS IS THE MOST DANGEROUS GAME IN TOWN, BECAUSE THIS IS A CRUCIAL PEROID IN OUR NATION HISTORY, AND IF THE APPROPIATE LEADERS ARE NOT IN CHARGE THAT UNDERSTAND THE FUNDAMENTAL NET WORKINGS OF TERRORISM, AND HOW THEY UTILIZE NEGOTIATING AS A STALLING TACTIC WHILE THEY SET THEIR PLANS IN PLACE WITH THE INTENT OF DESTROYING AMERICA, AND WHEN AND IF WE GET HIT AGAIN GOD FORBID,IF YOU ARE AROUND ALL YOU ARE GOING TO HEAR FROM DEMOCRATIC POLITICAL MASTERS AND THEIR MIMICING BLACK STOOGES IS THAT PRESIDENT BUSH SHOULD HAVE NEVER EXPELLED SADDAM FROM IRAQ AND MORE NEGOTIATING WOULD HAVE BEEN APPROPRIATE, IT IS SUSPECTED THAT THE FIRST BOMBING SESSION BY ISRAEL ON TERRORIST INSTILLATIONS IN SOUTHERN LEBANON, THERE ARE SOME DEMOCRATS WOULD HAVE LIKED FOR SECRETARY OF STATE CONDOLEEZZA RICE TO HAVE IMMEDIATELY GONE AND NEGOTIATED WITH HEZBOLLAH, AND MOST LIKELY SENATOR BARBARA BOXER WOULD HAVE SPONSERED HER TRIP AND LODGINGS.

ON JULY 20, 2006, THERE WAS A CEREMONIAL ESCAPADE ON FOX NEWS BY THE CHAMPAGNE GLASS CLINKING FORMER SECRETARY OF STATE MADELEINE ALBRIGHT FROM THE CLINTON AREA WITH KIM JONGIL OF NORTH KOREA,TRYING TO OFFER A SYNOPSIS ON THE PERSUIT OF ISRAEL DEFENDING THEIR HOME LAND FROM ATTACKING TERRORIST THAT HAS ANNOUNCED THEIR EXTERMINATION, MS ALBRIGHT CHOSE TO ELABORATE AND TAKE THE DIPLOMATIC APPROACH WHICH NO DOUBT HAS SET THE EMULATING STANDARDS FOR TERRORIST AND THEIR LEADERS, THEIR CONVOLUTED DEMAGOGUERY IS TIPICAL MIMICKING OF DEMOCRATIC DECIET IN AMERICA, FOR AN EXAMPLE FOUAD SINIORA PRIME MINISTER OF LEBONON WAS ON CNN LARRY KING LIVE JULY 20, 2006, AND HE COULD VERY EASY BE A STAND

IN FOR SENATOR JOHN CAREY REGARDS TO DECITFUL, MISLEADING, FLIP FLOPPING DEMAGOGUERY, AT FIRST HE CHOOSE TO INSINUATE IN THE NEWS MEDIA THAT IF ISREAL DEPLOYED GROUND TROOPS IN SOUTHERN LEBONON HE WOULD DEFEND WITH HEZBOLLAH, ON LARRY KING HIS AMBITIONS WAS TO ORGANIZE BASED ON A CEASE FIRE TO GOVERN HIS COUNTRY INDEPENDENTLY OF HEZBOLLAH, WHICH IS NOTHING MORE THAN TWISTED GIBBERISH THAT MIMIC DEMOCRAT IDEOLOGY, WHICH IS MOST COMMONLY EXPLOITED BY THE LEFT, AS FORMER SECRETARY OF STATE MADELEINE ALBRIGHT DUG HER HEELS IN AND SUGGESTED FOR MORE DIPLOMATIC DIPLOMACY, WHILE THE ISRALIS ARE BEING ASSULTED WITH MISSALS FROM HEZBOLLAH WHICH INITIATED THE CONFLICT AND THERE ARE THOSE INEPT LEFT WING SYMPATHIZERS DENOUNCING ISRAEL AND SCREAMING BACK OFF BECAUSE OF MOUNTING CIVILIAN CASUALTIES THESE ARE PEOPLE THAT IS TOTALLY INSENSITIVE ALSO INEPT TO THE REALITY OF WHAT HAS TRANSPIRED IN SOUTHERN LEBONON, OVER THE YEARS HEZBOLLAH IDEOLOGY HAS EXCLUSIVELY OCCUPIED SOUTHERN LEBONON, THEY HERDED TOGATHER AND GENERATED A PEOPLE THROUGH GENETIC CONTROLLABILITY, MEANING FATHERS, MOTHERS, SISTERS, BROTHERS, COUSINS AND FRIENDS, WHICH IS A INDEPENDENT SOCIETY OF PEOPLE THAT IS LINKED TO THE SAME AMBITIONS THAT IS DETERMINE TO DESTROY ISREAL AND THE UNITES STATES OF AMERICA, AND CONTROL (ALL) OF THE OIL RICH COUNTRIES ON THE CONTINENT OF THE EASTERN HEMISPHERE AND SPREAD THEIR IDEOLOGY GLOBAL, WE ARE A MORAL, HUMANE AND INTELLECTUAL SOCIETY OF PEOPLE, AND MURDERING FOR RELIGIOUS BELIEFS IS (NOT) ONE OF OUR CUSTOMS, UNFORTUNATELY THIS IS THE DREADFUL HORRIFIC DILEMMA OUR NATION IS CONFRONTED WITH REGARDS TO TERRORISM, AND WE ARE LEFT WITH (ONLY) TWO CHOICES IN DEFENSE OF OUR FREEDOM, ONE IS TO SUBMIT TO THEIR RADICAL RELIGIOUS IDEOLOGY AND CATER TO THEIR DEMANDS AS THE SLAVES DID FOR OVER TWO HUNDRED YEARS, AND THE OTHER IS

TO REALIZE WHAT PROFOUND CONSEQUENCES THAT IS LURKING AND POOL (ALL) OUR EFFORTS TOGATHER AS A NATION TO DEFEAT TERRORISM THAT IS FORCED UPON OUR COUNTRY BY RELIGIOUS FANATICS, AND IN THE INTERIM BE AWARE THAT MILLIONS OF PEOPLE ARE GOING TO PAY THE ULTIMATE PRICE WITH THEIR LIVES, AND MANY ARE GOING TO BE INNOCENT ESPECIALLY CHILDREN, BUT THIS IS OUR (ONLY) RECOURSE TO RMAIN A FREE SOCIETY AND SET THE TONE FOR THE FUTURE.

IN REALITY THERE ARE A SEGEMENT OF PEOPLE PIRATICALLY IN AMERICA THAT IS INEPT TO THE STRATEGIES OF TERRORIST AND AND SEEM TO BECOME EMOTIONAL WHEN THEY ARE SUCCUMBED TO THE ACT OF REPRISAL, THE TERRORIST ARE SMART ENOUGH CAPITALIZE ON THE CULTURAL SENSITIVITY REGARDS TO MASS DEATH, AND PROPAGANDIZE THIS INTO SYMPATHETIC ISSURES IN AN EFFORT TO SUPPORT THEIR CAUSES RELATED TO TERRORISM, AND TO CONGREGATE AMONG PEOPLE THAT IS THOUGHT TO BE INNOCENT IS ONE OF THE MAIN INGREDIENTS TO THEIR TERRORIZING STRATEGY, BECAUSE THE OPPOSITION IS HESITANT TO ATTACK FEARFUL OF HARMING INNOCENT PEOPLE, SO AS A RESULT MANY TIMES USING THESE TACTICS THEY ARE LEFT ALONE TO CONTINUE BEHEADINGS, SOLICITING AND TRAINING SUICIDAL PERSONNEL TO CARRY OUT MISSIONS OF TERROR, SUCH AS FLYING JET PLANES INTO BUILDINGS, BLOWING UP TRAIN TUNNELS, PLANTING DEADLY EXPLOSIVES ON MOBILE TRAINS, INVADING SCHOOLS AND HOLDING LTTLE CHILDREN HOSTAGE AND DESTROYING THEIR LIVES, KIDNAPPING SOLDIERS AND FIRING RANDOM MISSILES INTO THEIR COUNTRY IN AN EFFORT TO SLAUGHTER THEIR INNOCENT CITIZENS,IT IS OBLIGATORY FOR POLITICAL ELECTED OFFICIALS TO PROTECT THEIR CITIZENS FROM HARM, PURSUANT TO PRESIDENTS, PRIME MINESTERS TO THE POLICE OFFICER THAT WALK THE BEAT, UNFORTUNATELY THERE ARE SOME DYSFUNCTIONAL MINDED BRAIN DEAD CRITICS IN THIS COUNTRY FEEL THAT THE ISRAELIS SHOULD RELINQUISH THAT RIGHT AND NEGOTIATE FOR THEIR VERYEXISTENCE TO SURVIVE,

BECAUSE INNOCENT PEOPLE ARE GETTING KILLED, AS IF THE TERRORIST ARE HOLDING A PICNIC FOR PRAYER MEETING, AND SOME VENT THEIR FRUSTRATION BY GOING NATIONAL IN THE NEWS MEDIA, AS JUAN WILLIAMS DID ON FOX NEWS JULY 21, 2006, HIS DISPLAY OF GIBBERISH WAS APPALLING AND DEMONSTRATED DECITFUL BOORISHNESS TO THE HOST, THE MAGNITUDE OF HIS DISCONTENT WAS AIRED THROUGH HIS FORCEFUL COMMENTS, AS IF HE WAS FILLING IN FOR ORILEY, AND IT IS AMAZING HOW THESE CONVOLUTED PORTERS FOR DEMOCRATIC DEMAGOGUERY,CONSTANTLY USE THE NATIONAL MEDIA FOR THEIR POMPOUS DISPLAY OF DECITFUL RHETORIC, WITH NO SENSE OF DEPTH FOR REALITY.

AND OF COURSE FROM THE GOOD OLD BOY NETWORK FORMER SECRETARY OF STATE LAWRENCE EAGLEBURGER, CHIMED IN ON A NATIONAL T.V. NETWORK JULY 21, 2006, DENOUNCING THE CREDIBILITY OF SECRETARY OF STATE CONDOLEEZZA RICE TO SUCCEEDE WITH A DIPLOMATIC APPROACH TO QUELL THE VIOLENCE CAUSED BY HEZBOLLAH, WITHOUT QUESTION IT IS AGREED THAT MS RICE HAVE A EXTREMELY DIFFICULT TASK AHEAD, HOWEVER MR EAGLEBURGER HAS TO REMEMBER THAT MS RICE IS (NOT) ONE OF THOSE AFRICAN AMERICANS THAT DIRECTOR OF THE F.B.I. J. EDGAR HOOVER ACCUSED OF HAVING A SMALLER BRAIN THAN WHITES, SHE IS ONE OF THE MOST EOQUENT DIPLOMATIC POLITICIANS OF MORDERN TIMES SECOND TO NONE, AND TRUST ME ITS NOT OFTEN THAT I GO OUT ON A LIMB, BUT IF THERE IS ANY ONE CAN PENETRATE THIS STAND OFF DREADFUL DILEMMA IT IS MS RICE, IF POSSIBLE NOT ONLY WILL SHE BRING HOME THE BACON, SHE HAS THE INTELLECTUAL ABILITY TO SHOW UP WITH THE WHOLE HOG, AND SENATOR BOXER WILL TESTIFY TO THAT.

SECRETARY OF STATE CONDOLEEZZA RICE IS A SELF PROCLAIMED INDIVIDUAL THAT HAS BEEN TAUGHT AND UNDERSTAND THE CHRONOLOGICAL RECORDS OF HISTORY, WHICH SHE HAS ANALYTICALLY REFINED AND EXCEPTED AS A GUIDANCE WHICH DEMONSTRATE HER TENACITY TO SUCCEED, AND IS RECOGNIZED GLOBALLY AS A PERSON

WITH DISTINCT REFINED INTELLECTUAL CHARACTER, WHICH WAS PASSED ON TO HER THROUGH GENETIC CONTROLLABILITY AND SHOULD BE CHARACTERIZED AS A ROLL MODEL FOR ALL PEOPLE PIRATICALLY AFRICAN AMERICANS,BUT THERE IS A LARGE SEGEMENT OF BLACKS WILL ARGUE THAT POINT, BECAUSE OF THE FATTY TISSURE THAT HAS SURROUNDER THEIR BRAIN AND MADE IT DYSFUNCTIONAL WITH 0DIOUS BELIEFS, THAT SHE IS UNWORTHYOFHERPOSITIONBECAUSEOFQUALIFICATIONS, AND THERE ARE SOME INDICATE SHE IS QUALIFIED BUT IS AFFILIATED WITH THE WRONG POLITICAL PARTY, AND SHE IS NOT FOR THEM, HOWEVER IT IS DOCUMENTED IN HISTORY THAT THE SOUTHERN DEMOCRATS ORGANIZED THE KU-KLUX-KLAN, DEFAMED, LYNCHED, DENIED CIVIL AND VOTING RIGHTS, AND TURNED AFRICAN AMERICANS GENETIC CONTROLLABILITY INSIDE OUT THROUGH A BREEDING PROCESS THAT IS MOST LIKELY RESPONSIBLE FOR THEIR IGNORANCE TODAY, WHEN I FIRST LEARNED OF THE COMMENT OF, THE LATE F.B.I. DIRECTOR J. EDGAR HOOVER YEARS AGO I DEEMED IT TO BE RACIST, DEGRADING, AND TRULY UNCALLED FOR TO IMPLY THAT BLACKS HAD SMALLERBRAINS THAN WHITES,AND LABELED IT AS FOOLISH INNUENDO WITHOUT SCIENTIFIC PROOF, HOWEVER OVER A PEROID OF TIME DEROGATORY REMARKS TEND TO HIBERNATE, UNLESS SOMETHING OCCUR AS A REMINDER TO CAUSE CONCERN, AND THERE ARE MANY MITIGATING FACTORS PERTAINING TO SOME AFRICAN AMERICANS IS REASON TO THINK OF J. EDGAR HOOVER FRUSTRATION RELATED TO THE AFRICAN AMERICAN SMALL BRAIN FACTOR, OBVIOUSLY HE WAS WRONG, BUT THERE ARE OTHER FACETS OF SOME AFRICAN AMERICANS BEHAVIORAL PATTERNS TO SUPPORT HIS THEORY OF BEING LESS CAPABLE THAN OTHERS REGARDS TO WITS, AND ONE OF THE MOST CYNICAL IDIOTIC GESTURES WAS TO DENOUNCE THE SECRETARY OF STATE CONDOLEEZZA RICE, WHICH IS THEIR WAY OF REPRESENTING PREHISTORIC OBSOLETE IDEOLOGY THAT WAS DESCENDED FROM THE MUD HUTS OF AFRICA RELATED TO HERDING TOGATHER IN

AN EFFORT TO GENERATE FOLLOW THE LEADER GUIDANCE WITH SPECULATIVE FOOLISH CONCEPTS.

FOR INSTANCE C-SPAN WASHINGTON JOURNAL HAD OPEN LINES BEGINNING ON JULY 24, 2006, RELATED TO SECRETARY OF STATE RICE, AND THE ISRAELIS CONFUTATION WITH HEZBOLLAH IN SOUTHERN LEBANON, AND A SEGMENT OF AFRICAN AMERICAN CALLERS PROCEEDED WITH UNFOUNDED ACCUSATIONS FROM CLAIMS OF MS RICE NOT HAVING THE ABILITY TO BE SECRETARY OF STATE, DENOUNCING ISRAEL RIGHT TO PROTECT THEIR HOME LAND ACCUSING PRESIDENT BUSH OF ENDORSING ATROCITIES, AND SOME APPLAUDED HEZBOLLAH, THIS DISPLAY OF DYSFUNCTIONAL IDIOSYNCRASIES HAS DEVELOPED OVER THE YEARS DUE TO THE INABILITY TO THINK INDEPENDENTLY, AND SEEK ADVICE FROM OTHERS THROUGH A HERDING PROCESS, AND MOST OF THEIR ADVISERS ARE JUST AS STUPID AS THEY ARE PERTAINING TO THE ASPECTS OF AMERICAN POLITICS, BECAUSE THE MAJORITY OF BLACKS ALWAYS REVERT BACK TO ISSURES OF SLAVERY, WHICH HAS GENETICALLY DAMAGED THEIR BRAIN AND CAUSED MALFUNCTION REGARDS TO AMERICAN CULTURE PARTICIPATION, AND THEY SPEND AN INORDINATE AMOUNT OF TIME BEGRUDGING SUCCESSFUL BLACKS, AND BLAMING WHITES FOR THEIR FAILURES, AND HERD TOGATHER WITH ASPIRATIONS TO DENOUNCE AND INFILTRATE AMERICAN CULTURE WITH A IDEOLOGY THAT IS SUTIABLE TO THEIR OWN LIBERAL DEMOCRATIC EMULATING DISEASE, THAT THE MAJORITY OF AFRICAN AMERICANS HAVE AND WILL BE SUCCUMB TO FOR GENERATIONS, BECAUSE OF THEIR INEPTNESS TO THE MORAL CULTURAL CHARACTERISTICS OBLIGATIONS TO THIS NATION BASED ON DIVERSITY.

AS I HAVE BEEN CRITICAL OF SOME AFRICAN AMERICANS AND ALLUDED TO THEIR DEFICIENCIES REGARDS TO POLITICAL AFFAIRS, IT IS NECESSARY TO ADDRESS THEIR CAUCASIAN COUNTERPART, IT IS EXTREMELY DIFFICULT TO CRITIQUE SOME PEOPLE IDEOLOGY PERTAINING TO POLITICS, BUT WHEN IT HAS TO DO STUPIDITY IT IS LESS COMPLICATED, BECAUSE WHEN SOME POLITICIANS TEND TO

ACCESS VALUES PERTAINING TO CRITICAL ISSURES EITHER THEY ARE SPEAKING FROM THE HEART OR CATERING TO THE ASSUMPTION OF THEIR CONSTITUENTS, EITHER WAY THE HOUSE OF REPRESENTATION JIM MCDERMOTT, WAS ON C-SPAN WASHINGTON JOURNAL JULY 27, 2006 AND GAVE HIS EVALUATION OF THE ISRAELIS AND HEZBOLLAH CONFLICT AND THE APPROCH SHOULD BE TAKEN REGARDS TO PEACE, AND IT WAS PRIMARILY BASED ON NEGOTIATING WITH TERRORIST TO GET THEM TO LAY DOWN THEIR ARMS, NOW THIS IS A ELECTED OFFICIAL TO THE UNITED STATES CONGRESS THAT IS INVOLVED IN DECISION MAKING FOR THE NATION, AND CHOOSE TO NATIONALIZE HIS FRUSTRATION WITH INSINUATIONS THAT WE MEANING THE ADMINISTRATION (DONT) LIKE HEZBOLLAH AND SHOULD CONSIDER NEGOTIATING WITH THEM, AND SUGGESTED THIS COULD BRING ABOUT PEACE, THE LATE F.B.I. DIRECTOR J. EDGAR HOOVER DEDICATED AND ASSOCIATED SMALL BRAINS EXCLUSICELY WITH BLACKS, UNFORTUNATELY HIS ANALYSIS FOR (IGNORANCE) WAS INAPPROPRIATE , BECAUSE THERE ARE MANY CAUCASIANS SUFFERING FROM THE SAME DISEASE, WHICH SHOULD HAVE BEEN DIAGNOSED AS A FATTY TISSURE GROWTH AROUND THE BRAIN, THAT CAUSE IT TO MALFUNCTION WITH DYSFUNCTIONAL SENILITY WHICH IS APPLICABLE TO ALL PEOPLE, BECAUSE THERE ARE EIGHT IN THE U.S. CONGRESS THAT HAVE A SEVERE CASE OF IT, DINGELL, STARK, PAUL, CONYERS, RAYHALL, ABERCROMBIE, KILPATRICK AND JIM MCDERMOTT, IT IS DIFFICULT TO DETERMINE THE SEVERENESS OF SEVERAL AND WHAT STAGE OF STUPIDITY THEY ARE IN REGARDS TO HEZBILLAH, HOWEVER REP. JIM MCDERMOTT WENT PUBLIC WITH HIS NONSENSICAL AFFLICTION AND PROPOSED NEGOTIATING WITH TERRORIST.

THERE IS A EXTREME SINCERE DISCONNECT WITH MANY AMERICANS REGARDS TO TERRORISM LARGELY BECAUSE OF COMPLACENCY, MOST GET ON WITH THEIR LIVES IN A COMFORT ZONE BECAUSE THE GENEROSITY OF THIS FREE NATION OFFER THAT CHOICE, SO THEY NEGLECT TO REALIZE THE DEADLY PROBLEMS THAT TERRORIST

REPRESENT AND FEEL THAT IT WAS A CALCULATED ERROR INITIATED BY PRESIDENT GEORGE BUSH, AND CONSTANTLY INSINUATE THAT HE IS RESPONSIBLE FOR THEIR INSURGENCY UPRISING BY NOT NEGOTATING ENOUGH, AND THE REMOVAL OF SADDAM HUSSEIN WAS UNNECESSARY, AND PERSUE EFFORTS TO PROHIBIT THE INFILTRATION OF TERROR CELLS BY HOLDING TO RATIFIED PREHISTORIC STANDARDS CLAIMING INFRINGEMENT ON HUMAN RIGHTS, AND ARE TOTALLY INEPT TO THE DIFFERENCE BETWEEN (BARBARIANS) AND CIVILIZATION, TERRORIST HAVE ALREADY SERVED AND DEMONSTRATED NOTICE ON NINE ELEVEN OF THEIR INTENTIONS OF GENOCIDE, AND IS PLOTTING PERPETRATIONS AROUND THE GLOBE PIRATICALLY AGAINST ISRAEL AND AMERICA, AND THERE ARE THOSE THAT ARE CITIZENS OF THIS COUNTRY BORN HERE, AND HAVE AS MUCH DISDAIN AS FOREGIN TERRORIST FOR THEIR OWN COUNTRY, SIMPLY BECAUSE THEY ARE INCAPABLE OF COMPREHENDING THE REFINEMENT OF INTELLECTUAL MORAL CHARACTERIZATION OF A DIVERSE NATION, HOWEVER TERRORIST GROUPS ARE LIKE LINKS IN A CHAIN, THEY HAVE DIFFERENT IDENTITIES BUT ARE LINKED TOGATHER WITH THE SAME IDEOLOGY, AND THAT IS TO DESPISE ANY ONE THAT DISAGREE WITH THEIR RELIGIOUS FANATICISM PIRATICALLY THE JEWISH STATE AND AMERICA. AND IS GRAVITATING TO DESTROY THE INTELLECTUAL DIGNITY OF A CIVILIZED SOCIETY AND CONSTANTLY GENERATING AND PLOTTING PHANTASIES OF DEATH TO MILLIONS OF PEOPLE AROUND THE UNIVERSE.

UNFORTUNATELY THERE ARE TALKING HEADS SPREAD OUT ALL OVER THE NETWORKS PREDICTING, DENOUNCING, PLANNING STRATEGY, AND ASSUMING AS TO WHAT ISRAEL SHOULD DO IN SOUTHERN LEBANON TO RESOLVE A CRISIS, (ALL) OF THIS AMBIGUOUS RHETORIC IS WORTHLESS AS TITS ON A BULL, THERE SHOULD BE ONLY (ONE) MAIN OBJECTIVE AND THAT IS FOR ALLIES TO BE SUPPORTIVE OF ISREAL IN THEIR QUEST TO DIMINISH THE THREAT OF HEZBOLLAH IN SOUTHERN LEBONAN AT (ANY) COST, BECAUSE THIS IS (NOT) JUST A BATTLE FOR ISRAEL, IT IS THE ENDOWED INSTITUTION TO MAINTAIN CIVILIZATION,

AND A CONQUEST FOR ALL PEOPLE THAT TAKE PLEASURE IN LIBERTY AND THE RIGHT TO CONTROL THEIR OWN DESTINY REGARDS TO THEIR INDIVIDUAL LIVES, BECAUSE IF THERE IS ANY COMPROMISE TO TERRORIST INDICATING THEIR ABILIRY TO SUCCEEDE THEIR INITATIVE (WILL) BE STRENGTHEN TO RECRUIT AND SEDUCE OTHERS TO JOIN THEIR FORCES OF TERROR, BECAUSE THEY WOULD HAVE CONVINCE THEIR FOLLOWERS THAT THEY ARE A CONTROLLING FORCE TO BE RECKON WITH IN ORDER THAT THEY MAY CONTINUE TO SLAUGHTER INNOCENT PEOPLE, THIS COULD BE A PIVOTAL SCENARIO IN DILUTING TERRORISM, BECAUSE TERRORIST LEADERS ARE GOING TO MAKE FOOLISH BLUNDERS BASED ON THE CONFLICT IN LEBANON, BECAUSE THERE ARE NONE BETTER AT CONFUSING THE ENEMY THAN THE ISRAELIS, AND WE (MUST) BE READY TO CAPITALIZE, BECAUSE THE ISRAELIS HAVE OPEN THE DOOR BY KICKING THAT TERRORIST ANT HILL IN SOUTHERN LEBANON, NOW THEY (MUST) REGROUP AND LOCATE OTHER AREAS TO TRAIN, ISRAEL CREATED ONE OF THE MOST IMPORTANT INTRUSIONS ON TERRORISM SENSE THE INVASION OF AFGHANISTAN, AND THIS IS WHY HEZBOLLAH ARE SO DELIBERATELY TO SUSTAIN IN SOUTHERN LEBANON, BECAUSE IT IS A LAST MELT DOWN TO THEIR STRONG HOLD TO CONJURE TERRORISM AS A HERD TO PLOT AND TRAIN WITHOUT INTERRUPTION SO THEIR FINANCIERS AND WEAPON SUPPLIERS IRAN AND SYRIA ARE CAUGHT BETWEEN A ROCK AND A HARD PLACE, BECAUSE IF KNOWN TERRORIST ARE LEARENED TO BE CONGREGATING ON THEIR SOIL AND PERPETRATING ACTS OF PLANNING TERROR, THE MAJORITY OF LIBERALS IN THIS COUNTRY WILL GET AMNESIA ACCORDING TO WHAT PRESIDENT GEORGE W. BUSH STATEMENT WAS TO COUNTRYS HARBORING TERRORIST, IT WASNT MEANT TO BE BRAG JUST FACT THERE WOULD BE CONSEQUENCES, TO ANALYTICALLY DESCRIBE THE FUNDAMENTAL FUNCTIONS THAT HAS DEVELOPED IN SOUTHERN LEBANON BETWEEN ISRAEL AND HEZBOLLAH, THERE ARE SPECULATIONS BY MOST LIBERALS THAT A CEASE FIRE FROM ISRAEL IS THE APPROPRIATE GUIDE LINE TO FOLLOW, NEGATING

THE FACT THAT IRAN AND HEZBOLLAH HAS PUBICALLY STATED THAT ISRAEL DOSENT HAVE THE RIGHT TO EXIST AND THBLSTATE OF ISAREL WILL BE DESTROYED, I MUST ADMIT THIS IS A RATHER UNUSUAL REQUEST FROM ONE NATION TO ANOTHER , UNFORTUNATELY THERE IS A BIAS IN SOME OF THE NEWS MEDIA REPORTING, THEY SEEM TO CONSTANTLY FOCUS ON CASULTIES AND EXPLICITYLY DIAGNOSE THEIR WOUNDS AND DEMISE IN LEBANON AS IF IT WAS DELIBERATE PIRATICALLY WOMEN AND CHILDREN, IF THIS KIND OF REPORTING WAS ALLOWED DURING WORLD WAR TWO, TODAY WE WOULD BE HONORING A SWASTIKAS BASED ON PUBLIC OPENION, WARS AND CONFLICTS ARE FAUGHT AND WON BY STRATEGICALLY PLANNING OF COMMANDERS IN CHARGE (NOT) BY PUBLIC OPENION, AND IF ISRAEL RELENT TO THIS DELIBERATE INGENUITY BY HEZBOLLAH TO ATTRACT PUBLIC ATTENTION THROUGH THE NEWS MEDIA EXPLOITING DEATH, THIS COULD BE ONE OF THE WORST MISCALCULATIONS IN THE HISTORY OF THEIR NATION THAT WILL CAUSE GRAVE CONSEQUENCES AROUND THE GLOBE,THESE ARE COLD BLOODIED KILLERS THAT IS INDOCTRINATED FROM CHILD HOOD AND HAVE (NO) COMPASSION FOR THEIR OWN LIVES LESS OTHERS MEANING WOMEN AND CHILDREN, APPARENTLY THESE INHERENT TRAITS HAS NEVER OCCURED TO SOME OF THOSE SURROGATES FOR HEZBOLLAH LIKE JUAN WILLIAMS, ON FOX NEWS JULY 30, 2006, THAT WAS RANTING ABOUT RESTRAINT, STOP THE FIGHTING NOW, PEOPLE ARE GETTING KILLED AMERICA AUTHORITY HAS BEEN DESECRATED GLOBALLY, BECAUSE THE FAR RIGHT HAS GOTTEN IT ALL WRONG, APPARENTLY THE FATTY TISSURE THAT HAS SURROUNDED HIS BRAIN AND CAUSED IT TO DYSFUNCTION INTO AMNESIA REGARDS TO NINE ELEVEN, THOSE WERE THREE THOUSAND INNOCENT PEOPLE WOMEN AND CHILDREN ALSO, AND NO ONE DROPPED LEAFLETS TO WARN THEM OF AN ATTACK AND THEY WERE (NOT) INFILTRATED WITH TERRORIST, SO IF THERE IS ANY DOUBT ABOUT THE STRATEGISTS THAT ARE PLANNING FOR ISRAEL NEED TO REASSESS THEIR ASSUMPTIONS, BECAUSE SYRIA IS ON THE DISTANT OBJECTIVES ALSO IRAN, AND

TIME IS THE ESSENCE, BECAUSE THE TOP GRASS HAVE BEEN SPRAYED WITH HERBICIDE AND EVENTUALLY THE ROOTS (WILL) BE SUCCUMBED.

FOX NEWS THE ORILEY FACTOR JULY 31, 2006, RAN A CARTOON ILLUSTRATION SUBMITTED FROM THE ARAB NEWS MEDIA, DEPICTING OUR HONORABLE SECRETARY OF STATE CONDOLEEZZA RICE IMPREGNATED WITH A MONKEY, THIS CARTOON WAS IN VERY POOR TASTE AND DEMONSTRATED ARAB THOUGHTS OF BLACKS, BECAUSE MS RICE IS ONE OF THE POLITICAL INTELLECTUAL INDIVIDUAL OF MORDEN TIMES, AND ALL OF THE ARAB LEADERS IN THE ASIAN CONTINENT EASTERN HEMISPHERE ARE AWARE OF HER TALENTS AND RESPECT HER AS A ASTUTE INDIVIDUAL, HOWEVER IT IS SUSPECTED THIS CARTOON WAS AN EFFORT TO ILLUSTRATE THE ARAB CONCEPT OF AFRICAN AMERICANS IN AMERICA, BECAUSE SOME BLACKS CONSTANTLY ATTEMPT TO DEMORALIZE MS RICE WITH DEROGATORY REMARKS THROUGH ALL OF THE NEWS MEDIA, AND IT DEMONSTRATE DYSFUNCTIONAL BRAIN IGNORANCE ACTING LIKE MONKEYS, AND SOME WILL VIEW THATCARTOON. AS AMUSING AND ARE TO DAMN STUPID TO REALIZE THAT IT IS A DEPICTION OF THEM ALSO FORTUNATELY MS RICE AND MILLIONS OF OTHER MORAL DIPLOMATIC AFRICAN AMERICANS HAVE UTILIZED THE ESTABLISHED SYSTEM IN AMERICA THAT IS AVAILABLE TO EVERY ONE, AND THE REQUIREMENTS ARE RATHER SIMPLE DEVELOPE MORAL INITIATIVES THAT IS IN ACCORDANCE WITH THE STANDARDS OF THE SYSTEM, MEANING EDUCATION AND EMPLOYMENT, AND WHAT MAKE THE STANDARDS SO UNIQUE THE INSTITUTION OF HIGHER LEARNING IS (NOT) ABSOLUTELY NECESSARY, BUT COMMON SENSE AND THE MORAL OBJECTIVE TO ENGAGE IN THE PAID OCCUPATION OF A DIVERSE SOCIETY (IS), WHICH A LARGE SEGEMENT OF AFRICAN AMERICANS HAVE REJECTED AND DENOUNCED WHICH WITH OUT QUESTION REPRESENT DRAMATIC FAILURE, AND FOR THESE OBSERVED MISCALCULATIONS BY PREDOMINATEY BLACKS, THE STIGMATIZATION IS IDIOTS AND MONKEYS AROUND THE GLOBE, ADOLF HITLER MADE SUCH

DISPARAGING DEROGATORY REMARKS ABOUT THE LATE TRACK AND FIELD STAR JESSIE OWENS DURING THE OLYMPICS OF NINETEEN THIRTY SIX AS BEING A MONKEY, THESE DEMEANING ACCUSATIONS ARE LABEL AGAINST BLACKS NOT BECAUSE OF THEIR (COLOR) BUT UNFORTUNATELY BECAUSE OF THEIR IDIOSYNCRASIES RELATED TO DISPLAYED IGNORANCE BY OTHERS, FOR INSTANCE A SEGEMENT OF BLACKS HAVE DISDAIN FOR THE SECRETARY OF STATE CONDOLEEZZA RICE FOR BEING A REPUBLICAN AND REPRESENTING CONSERVATIVE VIEWS, WHEN THE MAJORITY OF AFRICAN AMERICANS ARE INEPT TO THE DEMOCRATS BEING LARGELY RESPONSIBLE FOR THEIR ILLADVISED AND ALIENATING THEM SELVES FROM MORAL OBLIGATIONS PERTAINING TO INTELLECTUAL CAPABILITIES,AND THESE FACETS ARE DOMINATING, THE GENETIC CONTROLLABILITY IS EMBEDDED WITHOUT (ANY) HOPE FOR SOME EVER RELENTING TO FUNDAMENTAL VALUES, INSTEAD IT IS GETTING WORSE WHICH COULD BE RELEGATED TO A DEMINISHED LESS VIOLENT HEZBOLLAH, BECAUSE THERE IS A SEGEMENT OF BLACKS DENOUNCING AND DECLINING TO ACCEPT THE TRADITIONAL GUIDING PRINCIPLES OF AMERICA, BECAUSE IT IS REPORTED THAT THEY SUDDENLY DEEM THE GAME OF BASE BALL IS FOR CAUCASIANS, EDUCATION, DIPLOMACY, AND ETIQUETTE ALSO, SO MOST AFFLUENT AFRICAN AMERICANS THAT HAS EXCEPTED AMERICAN CULTURE INCLDING MS RICE WHICH IS AT THE TOP OF THE POLITICAL ACCOMPLISHMENTS REFERENCING AFRICAN AMERICANS IS STIGMATIZED BY THE IGNORANCE OF (OTHER) BLACKS, BECAUSE IT IS (NOT) APPLICABLE TO MONKEYS TO GET AN EDUCATION, PLAY BASE BALL, INVEST IN ETIQUETTE OR PARTICIPATE IN ANY OTHER MORAL ADVENTURES, THE ONLY NECESSITY REQUIRED IS A CAGE AND SOME FOOD, WHICH MANY BLACKS ARE EMULATING THAT STANDARD BY COMMITTING HIDEOUS CRIMINAL ACTIVITY BEING CONVICTED AND SHIPPED TO PLACES OF CRIMINAL INSTITUTIONS FOR CAGED INCARCERATION AROUND THE NATION.

THE CONDESENDING REVELATIONS FOR MANY AFRICAN AMERICANS IN THE UNITED STATES OF AMERICA

IS CAUSE FOR CONCERN, BECAUSE IT APPEAR THAT THEIR MORAL INTELLECTUAL ABILITY HAS DISSIPATED INTO ARROGANT REBELLIOUS STUPIDITY,WITHOUT QUESTION ARE AND WILL CONTINUE TO DECLINE INTO OBVIOUS SELF DESTRUCTION, BECAUSE IT IS UTTERLY IMPOSSIBLE TO INTEGRATE A PATHETIC NONSENSICAL IDEOLOGY INTO A STANDARD EXISTING CONTROLLING SYSTEM IN OUR GOVERNMENT TO SUPPORT THEIR IMMORAL BEHAVIOR OF GENOCIDE.

IT APPEAR THAT MANY BLACKS HAVE VESTED THEIR CONCERNS IN A HOPELESS AGENDA OF IRREGULAR FUNCTIONS THAT HAS BEEN FORMATTED BY A GROUP OF WORTHLESS SELF MOTIVATED APPOINTED LEADERS AND BLACK INVITED T.V. AND RADIO INDIVIDUALS, THAT EACH EXPLOIT A GENERAL CONSENSUS OF WHAT THE AMERICAN GOVERNMENT SHOULD DO FOR AFRICAN AMERICANS TO APPEASE THEIR CLAIM OF INJUSTICE, BUT ALMOST (NEVER) RLATE TO THE FORMULATED TRADITIONS THAT AMERICA HAVE AVAILABLE FOR (ALL) INDIVIDUALS TO DO FOR THEMSELVES, HOWEVER A LARGE SEGEMENT OF BLACKS ARE OPPOSE TO THIS DOCTRINE, THAT THE MAJORITY OF THE NATION BLACK AND WHITE IS UTILIZING TO THEIR ADVANTAGE TO SUCCEED AND ALWAYS HAVE FOR HUNDREDS OF YEARS AND WILL (NEVER) BE ABANDON FOR SOME PREHISTORIC SLAVERY AFRICAN CONGO IDEOLOGY, SO THE PEOPLE THAT ENDORSE AND FOLLOW THESE SELF APPOINTED LEADERS MOSTLY BLACKS, THAT ARE INSTIGATING WHAT AMERICA SHOULD DO FOR YOU, THEY ARE NOTHING MORE THAN A WORTHLESS PARASITE THAT IS SEDUCING THEIR FOLLOWERS OUT OF WHAT FUNDS THEY CAN SUPPLY AND PAVING THE ROAD TO A EARLY DEMISE OR LIFE TO MANY YEARS OF INCARCERATION. THERE IS A VAST SIGNIFICANT DIFFERENCE RELATED TO REPUBLICAN CONSERVATISM AND DEMOCRATIC LIBERALISM, CONSERVATIVES STAKE THEIR LOYALTY ON PRINCIPAL AND MORAL VALUES THAT IS IN ACCORDANCE WITH TRADITIONS OF WHAT THE FOUNDING FATHERS RATIFIED FOR THIS NATION, WHICH CONSIST OF EDUCATION, PRUDENCE, AND INDIVIDUAL

THINKING THAT ACCUMULATE WEALTH AND STABILITY, LIBERALS STAKE THEIR OBJECTIVES ON DISTORTING MORAL VALUES TO ALLOW MISCHIEVOUS BEHAVIOR, SUCH AS GAY MARRIAGE, AND TO PROMOTE SOCIAL PROGRAMS AS A SUBSTITUTE FOR EDUCATION AND PRUDENCE, THEN LIE ON THE REPUBLICANS AS BEING THE PARTY FOR THE WEALTHY AND HAVING NO COMPASSION FOR THE POOR, BECAUSE OF THEIR RELUCTANCE TO SUPPORT THEIR BLUNDERS REGARDS TO SOCIAL PROGRAMS THAT THEY DEEM SHOULD BE THE RESPONSIBILITY OF THE LOCAL AND FEDERAL GOVERNMENT TO DICTATE THE PLIGHT OF PEOPLE FOR STABILITY AND SUCCESS, AND THE MAJORITY OF AFRICAN AMERICANS HAS FALLEN INTO THIS DECEITFUL MIRAGE FOUNDED BY DEMOCRATS IN NINETEEN THIRTY FIVE, AND AS OF TO DATE THIS TRICKERY HAS DEVELOPED INTO AN OBSESSION FOR FAR TO MANY AFRICAN AMERICANS WHICH IS NOT QUALIFIED AND WILL (NEVER) BE CAPABLE OF DECIPHERING DEMOCRATIC STRATEGY TO HERD THEM TOGATHER FOR THEIR BLOC VOTING IN AN EFFORT TO PURSUE POLITICAL POWER IN THIS COUNTRY AND CHIP AWAY AT DISSECTING THE MORAL VALUES OF NATION.

ON AUGUST 3, 2006, I AGREED TO PERFORM A CIVIC DUTY AT ONE OF THE LOCAL POLLING STATIONS IN THE STATE WHICH I RESIDE AS A REGISTER FOR VOTERS IN THE PRIMARY, I WAS THERE FOR APPROXIMATELY FOURTEEN HOURS AND REGISTERED HUNDREDS OF VOTERS, AND DURING INTERVALS I GATHERED MY THOUGHTS REGARDS TO AFRICAN AMERICANS VOTING BLOC FOR DEMOCRATS, BECAUSE DURING THE ENTIRE DAY THERE WERE ONLY TWO BLACKS VOTED OTHER, AND AS I MEDITATED OVER THIS UNIQUE DILEMMA TWO KEY POLITICAL INDIVIDUALS CAME TO MIND, THE LATE F.B.I. DIRECTOR J. EDGAR HOOVER AND PRESIDENT ABRAHAM LINCOLN, J. EDGAR HOOVER WAS FRUSTRATED WITH THE IGNORANCE OF BLACKS AND ASSESSED IT AS A (SMALL) BRAIN FACTOR, ABARAHAM LINCOLN KNEW THE MAJORITY WAS STUPID AT THAT TIME, AND ATTEMPTED TO MAKE RESTITUTION ON THEIR BEHALF PRIOR TO HIS ASSASSINATION IN EIGHTEEN SIXTY FIVE, BY GIVING THEM FORTY ACRES OF SOUTHERN

LAND AND A GOVERNMENT MULE TO EACH FAMILY, UNFORTUNATELY AFTER HIS DEMISE VICE PRESIDENT ANDREW JOHNSON RESCINDED HIS PROCLAMATION AND RETURNED THE LAND TO THE SOUTHERN CONFEDERATE DEMOCRATS, WHICH FOR OVER A HUNDRED AND FORTY YEARS THE MAJORITY OF AFRICAN AMERICANS HAVE BEEN ABUSED AND USED AS A STABILIZING FACTOR TO PURSUE CONTROLLING POLITICAL DEMOCRATIC POWER.

HOWEVER THE REPUBLICAN PARTY IS OF COMPASSION AND TOLERATE STUPIDITY AS A GENETIC DYSFUNCTION IN SOME BLACKS, AND (DO NOT) PLAN REPRISAL FOR IGNORANCE, BUT DEMOCRATS ARE LESS SYMPATHETIC AND WILL NOT TOLERATE STUPIDITY WHAT SO EVER, BECAUSE HISTORY HAS PROVEN THIS FACTOR DURING THE NINETEEN CENTURY SOUTHERN DEMOCRATS LNCHED BLACKS FOR WHISTLING AT CAUCASIAN WOMEN, SO WHEN AND IF BLACKS PLAY AN INSTRUMENTAL ROLL IN VOTING THEM BACK INTO POLITICAL POWER REFERENCE CONGRESS AND THE SENATE, HISTORY HAS PROVEN THAT THERE IS A DRAMATIC PRICE FOR SOME BLACKS TO PAY FOR THEIR IDIOSYNCRASIES, THEY ARE GOING TO BE CRUSHED LIKE A BUG NATION WIDE, IT IS PROFOUNDLY ASTONISHING AND DIFFICULT TO REALISTICALLY DETERMINE THIS MAGNETIZING ATTRACTION THAT THE MAJORITY OF AFRICAN AMERICANS HAVE FOR THE DEMOCRATIC PARTY, AND THERE IS (NO) EXPLAINABLE REASON OTHER THAN HISTORICAL POLITICAL GENETIC CONTROLLABILITY IMPOSITION BY DEMOCRATIC IDEOLOGY ON BLACKS FOR THEIR SLAVE LABOR AND LATER FOR THEIR VOTING BLOC,AND REMORSE HAS NEVER BEEN A FACTUAL IN ANY OF THEIR ATROCITIES PERPETRATED AGAINST AFRICAN AMERICANS, SO IT IS QUITE OBVIOUS WHY SOME BLACKS ARE CONSTANTLY COMPLAINING ABOUT EQUALITY, BECAUSE THEIR I.Q. IS (.FAR) BELOW THE REQUIRED STANDARDS TO COMPREHEND THE MEANING OR MAKE THE NECESSARY ADJUSTMENTS TO FACILITATE, SO THEIR ONLY RECOURSE IS SOME KIND OF CHARITY TO SUSTAIN EITHER FROM FAMILY MEMBERS OR THE FEDERAL GOVERNMENT, MANY OF THESE PEOPLE ARE EDUCATED

BUT LIKE THE ABILITY TO GRASP THE MORAL VALUES THAT IS REQUIRED TO SUSTAIN ADEQUATELY, SO THEY RETREAT TO AN OLD DEMOCRATIC TAUGHT BRAINWASH TACTIC USE ANYTHING THAT YOU THINK WILL COMPENASTE FOR RADICAL BIGOTRY AND LAZY IGNORANCE, AND THE MAJORITY OF THE TIME FOR BLACKS ITS WHITE PEOPLE THAT IS CAUSING THEIR FAILURE IN LIFE BY NOT GVING THEM A CHANCE TO SUCCEED BASED ON RACISM BECAUSE THEY ARE BLACK, UNFORTUNATELY THEIR BRAIN IS SO DYSFUNCTIONL WITH IRONIC STUPIDITY THEY ARE (NOT) AWARE THAT MILLIONS OF AFRICAN AMERICANS ARE SELF SUPPORTING SUCCESSFUL AND FINANCIALLY STABLE, IT IS INCUMBENT UPON ANY INDIVIDUAL BLACK OR WHITE TO SYSTEMATICALLY UNDERSTAND THE POLITICAL BAROMETERS THAT SET PRECEDENTS ADJUDICATED TO SUPPORT MORAL VALUES, HOWEVER IF YOU ARE INEPT OR CHOOSE NOT TO EXCEPT THESE STANDARDS THAT CHRONOLOGY CONTROL CULTIVATED CONCEPTS AS GUIDE-LINES TO A INDIVIDUAL DIPLOMATIC SUCCESS PERTAINING TO A DIVERSE SOCIETY, AND IF THESE ATTRIBUTES ARE NOT ADHERED TO OBVIOUSLY YOU ARE A PRIME CANIDATE TO BE TRODDEN ON WITHOUT ANY RECOURSE OTHER THAN CONSTANTLY COMPLAIN TO NO AVAIL, WHICH THE MAJORITY OF AFRICAN AMERICANS HAVE ADOPTED THIS SICK COMMONALITY AS A PLOTTED REALITY THAT HAS PLUNGED SOME OF THEM INTO DESTITUTION FOR OVER ONE HUNDRED AND FORTY YEARS, WHICH CAN BE ACCREDITED TO THEIR (OWN) GENETIC CONTROLLABILITY. OF IGNORANCE THAT DICTATE HERDING BEHIND SELF APPOINTED LEADERS WHICH!IS CONSISTENT WITH POLITICAL SELF DESTRUCTION ON THE BASIS OF REBELLIOUS DEMAGOGUERY. ON AUGUST 8, 2006, NED LAMONT WAS THE DEMOCRATIC PRIMARY WINNER FOR THR SENATE OVER INCUMBENT SENATOR JOSEPH LIBERMAN, AND GAVE AN INCEPTION SPEECH AFTERWARDS, AND WAS SURROUNDED BY THE GOOD 0LD BOY WEALTHY NET WORK, THAT HAD DIRTY HANDS TOWARDS BLACKS DURING EIGHTEEN SIXTY SIX AND NINETEEN SIXTY FOUR AND FIVE, WITH DEMOCRATIC CYNICISM RELATED TO

(HIDDEN) AGENDAS THAT THEY WOULD SLASH THEIR WRIST TO CONTROL CONGRESS AND THE SENATE AGAIN, BECAUSE THE CONGRESS IS THE CONTROLLING FACTOR HAVING TO DO WITH THE NATION GUIDE-LINES REPRESENTATION FOR ALL AMERICAN CITIZENS APPROVING OR DENYING SUBSTANTIVE ISSURES.

FOR INSTANCE THE REPUBLICAN CONTROLLED CONGRESS OF EIGHTEEN SIXTY SIX PASSED THE CIVIL RIGHTS ACT THAT WAS RATIFIED TO THE FOURTEEN AMENDMENT GUARANTEEING AFRICAN AMERICANS CITIZENSHIP REGARDS TO THE CONSTITUTION, ALSO THE RATIFICATION IN EIGHTEEN SEVENTY TO THE FIFTEENTH U.S. CONSTITUTION AMENDMENT OUTLAWING THE USE OF RACE TO DISENFRANCHISE VOTERS, HIRMAN RHODES WAS THE FIRST REPUBLICAN AFRICAN AMERICAN U.S. SENATOR IN EIGHTEEN SEVENTY THAT REPRESENTED MISSISSIPPI FOR ONE YEAR, BLANCHE K. BRUCE A REPUBLICAN ELECTED TO THE SENATE IN EIGHTEEN SEVENTY FOUR WAS THE FIRST BLACK TO SERVE A FULL TERM IN THE SENATE FROM LOUISIANA.

AFRICAN AMERICAN POLITICAL POWER WAS SIGNIFICANT IN THE REPUBLICAN ARENA DURING RECONSTRUCTION, BASED ON APPROXIMATELY TWENTY PERCENT OF WHITE MALES BEING BAN FROM VOTING DUE TO THEIR REBELLING AGAINST THE UNITED STATES AFTER THE CIVIL WAR, AFRICAN AMERICANS WERE A MAJORITY OF THE ELECTORATE IN FIVE SOUTHERN STATES, THEIR VOTES PROVIDED THE FOUNDATION FOR THE REPUBLICAN PARTY IN THE SOUTH, WHICH HAD (NOT) EXISTED BEFORE THE CIVIL WAR, THIS WAS THE VERY BEGINNING OF AFRICAN AMERICANS BEING UNITED IN ASPIRATIONS REGARDS TO AMERICAN CULTURE AND MORAL POLITICAL INTELLECTUAL CHARACTER, WHICH WAS SOON TO BE ABOLISHED BY THE SOUTHERN DEMOCRATS, THEY BECAME HIGHLY ENRAGED THAT BLACKS WERE AFFILIATED WITH THE REPUBLICAN PARTY AND MAKING POLITICAL ENRODES TO ACCESS MORAL VALUES TO BECOME INTELLECTUAL CITIZENS OF AMERICA, THE SOUTHERN DEMOCRATS ACCUSED BLACKS OF BEING IGNORANT INCOMPETENT AND

ATTEMPTING TO RISE ABOVE THEIR SUBSERVIENT PLACE IN SOCIETY, THE SOUTHERN DEMOCRATS PLOTTED TO QUELL THE POLITICAL PROGRESS OF AFRICAN AMERICANS AND DESTROY THE REPUBLICAN PARTY, WHITE SOUTHERNERS THAT SUPPORTED AND BECAME REPUBLICANS OR ALLIED WITH BLACKS WERE CALLED SCALAWAGS RIDICULED AND WAS SUBJECT TO VIOLENT ATTACK BY VIGILANTE POLITICAL TERRORIST GROUPS, THE KNIGHTS OF THE WHITE CAMILLA , THE PALE FACE BROTHERHOOD, IN AN EFFORT TO INTIMIDATE AND FRUSTRATE REPUBLICAN RULE TO FORCE BLACKS BACK TO SERVITUDE IN SOUTHERN SOCIETY, BUT THE MOST FEARED BRUTAL AND LONG LASTING WAS A SOCIAL CLUB FORMED IN TENNESSEE IN EIGHTEEN SIXTY SIX, LATER BECAME KNOWN AS THE KU-KLUX-KLAN LED BY FORMER SLAVE TRADER NATHAN BEDFORD FORREST AND VIOLENTLY FORCED BLACK AND WHITE REPUBLICANS FROM POLITICAL POWER, AND FORMED THEIR OWN DEMOCRATIC ALLIANCE OF CONTROL IN THE SENATE AND CONGRESS AND RUINED THE POLITICAL PROGRESS FOR AFRICAN AMERICANS FOR AN ETERNITY, AND PROHIBITED THEIR CIVIL AND VOTING FOR NINETY NINE YEARS.

THE OBSERVATION OF NED LEMONT AND SENATOR JOSEPH LIBERMAN SCHARADE PIRATICALLY THE WINNER NED LEMONT,IS AN ATTEMPTED REPLAY OF EIGHTEEN SIXTY SIX ALL OVER AGAIN IN THIS FALL GENERAL ELECTION IN 2006, THE REPUBLICANS ARE IN CONTROL OF THE CONGRESS AS THEY WERE IN EIGHTEEN SIXTY SIX, AND PRESIDENT GEORGE BUSH HAS INFURATED SOME DEMOCRATS BY CHOOSING QUALIFIED CONSERVATIVE AFRICAN AMERICANS TO SERVE IN HIS CABINET THAT MADE HISTORY REGARDS TO POLITICAL ASPIRATIONS IN AMERICA FOR AFRICAN AMERICANS, AND THEY HAVE PROVEN THEIR ABILITY TO FUNCTION UNDER EXTREME PRESSURE AND MAINTAIN MORAL VALUES EQUAL OR ABOVE ANY CAUCASIAN REPRESENTING A DIVERSE SOCIETY AND HAVE POTENTIAL OF BECOMING PRESIDENT OF AMERICA, AND ONCE AGAIN THE DEMOCRATS ARE OVERWHELMED AND PLOTTING TO DERAIL THE COLOR BLINDNESS OF THE REPUBLICAN PARTY AND HALT THE POLITICAL PROGRESS OF

CONSERVATIVE AFRICAN AMERICANS, FORTUNATELY THEY (DO NOT) HAVE THE ASSISTANCE OF THE KU-KLUX-KLAN TO INTIMIDATE MURDER AND MAIM WITH VIOLENCE, HOWEVER THEIR EPILOGUE IS REMINISCENT TO EIGHTEEN SIXTY SIX THAT (ALL) BLACKS ARE STUPID AND SHOULD BE RELEGATED TO SUBSERVIENCY,UNFORTUNATELY TO RATIFY THIS INSANE IDEOLOGY THEY NEED ASSISTANCE, SO THEY CREATED A NEW STRATEGY OVER THE YEARS AND ITS CALLED SELFSERVING POLITICAL IGNORANT BOOT LICKING, SPITTOON CARRYING BLACKS, WHICH THERE WERE THREE STAGED AS POSTER BOYS BEHIND NED LEMONT DURING HIS ACCEPTANCE SPEECH AFTER THE DEMOCRATIC PRIMARY DEFEAT OF SENATOR LIBERMAN, STARRING AT EACH OTHER AS IF THEY HAD FOUND A HENS NEST AND COULDNT COUNT THE EGGS, ALSO ACTING AS IF THEIR SUITS WERE TWO TIGHT.

IF THE DEMOCRATS ARE SUCCESSFUL IN OUSTING THE REPUBLICANS FROM CONGRESS IT WILL BE A SET BACK FOR CONSERVATIVE AFRICAN AMERICANS AGAIN, BUT NOT AS DEVASTATING DURING EIGHTEEN SIXTY SIX, IT IS THE REPUBLICAN CONSERVATIVE AFRICAN AMERICANS THAT DEMOCRATS FEAR THE MOST, (NOT) THE SEDATED LIBERAL DEMOCRATIC BLACKS, BECAUSE THEY ARE LED AROUND LIKE A RING NOSE BULL AND TO STUPID TO REALIZE THAT THE DEMOCRATS HAS MAIMED AND DEMORALIZED THEM FOR HUNDREDS OF YEARS, BECAUSE DURING THE EIGHTEEN HUNDREDS THEY EMPHATICALLY ASSERTED THAT BLACKS WERE TO STUPID AND SHOULD NEVER HOLD POLITICAL OFFICE AND SHOULD REMAIN AS SERVITUDE PERSONNEL, AND WITH THE MAJORITY OF BLACKS BEING LIBERAL THAT AFFILATION ALONE LEND SUPPORT TO THE THEORY, WHICH TEND TO ISOLATE CONSERVATIVE MORAL VALUE AFRICAN AMERICANS AS BEING ODD BECAUSE THEY REJECT HERDING, AND LEND CREDENCE TO THE DEMOCRATIC REFERENDUM THAT BLACKS ARE INEPT FOR POLITICAL ASPIRATIONS, SO AS A RESULT WITH THIS UNIQUE FOOLISHNESS OF APPROXIMATELY NINETY EIGHT PERCENT OF AFRICAN AMERICANS SUPPORTING DEMOCRATS IT SERVE THE SAME PURPOSE AS THE KU-

KLUX-KLAN MINUS THE VIOLENCE, BECAUSE IT ALIENATE BLACKS FROM MAKING THE NECESSARY ADJUSTMENTS TO INTEGRATE INTO A MORAL VALUES DIVERSE SOCIETY THAT COEXIST WITH THE GUIDE-LINES OF OUR NATION, TEAT CHARACTERIZE ASK NOT WHAT YOUR COUNTRY CAN DO FOR YOU BUT WHAT YOU CAN DO FOR YOUR SELF AS A CITIZEN OF THIS COUNTRY, WHICH DEMOCRATS HAVE INDOCTRINATED BLACKS INTO THINKING ITS THE CONSERVATIVE IDEOLOGY THAT IS RESPONSIBLE FOR THEIR FAILURE, BECAUSE OF THE NATION RELUCTANCE TO ENDORSE WHOLE SALE SOCIALISM THAT IS REJECTED BY CONSERVATIVE MORAL VALUES, HOWEVER THE VAST MAJORITY OF BLACKS HAVE ADHERED TO THIS NOTION FAR BACK AS THE PRESIDENT FRANKLIN ROOSEVELT ERA OF THE EARLY FORTIES, THAT GOVERNMENT SHOULD BE A LEANING POST, AND EDUCATION INTELLECTUAL MORAL VALUES IS SOMETHING FOR WHITE FOLKS, AND AS A RESULT DEMOCRATS HAVE MOBILIZED BEHIND THIS STUPIDITY AND CONSTANTLY UTILIZE IT TO THEIR POLITICAL ADVANTAGE, AND THEY HAVE SUFFICIENTLY SUCCEEDED WITH THIS PATHETIC REFERENDUM FOR OVER SEVENTY YEARS, AND THE MAJORITY OF AFRICAN AMERICANS ARE MESMERIZED BY THEIR SKILFUL DECEITFUL WELL ORGANIZED POLITICAL TACTICS AND MANY CAUCASIANS, THEY HAVENT THE SLIGHTEST IDEA OF HOW TO DETER TERRORISM NOR DO THEY UNDERSTAND THE REPERCUSSIONS, YET THEY ARE UTILIZING THE IRAQ CONFLICT TO BOLSTER THEIR IMAGE REGARDS TO DISCREDITING THE PRESIDENT BUSH ADMINISTRATION SEEKING TO UNSEAT REPUBLICANS IN AN EFFORT TO CONTROL CONGRESS, AND IT APPEAR THAT THEIR LEADERSHIP AND THEIR TRAINED BLACK PORCH MONKEYS ARE COMPLETELY OBLIVIOUS TO THE MOTIVATIONS OF TERRORIST, THEIR MAIN OBJECTIVE IS TO DETER THE POLITICAL ASPIRATIONS OF CONSERVATIVE AFRICAN AMERICANSAS THEY DID IN EIGHTEEN SIXTY SIX WITH THE AID OF THE KU-KLUX-KLAN, BUT TODAY THEY UTILIZE BLACK BOOT LICKERS SUCH AS DEMOCRAT CONGRESSMAN ALBERT WYNN ON FOX NEWS ORILEY FACTOR AUGUST 9, 2006, DENOUNCING THE IRAQ

CONFLICT, THE HOST SUBJECTED HIM TO QUESTIONS THAT TURNED HIS ERRONEOUS VERBIAGE TO GIBBERISH, AND YOU COULD VERY WELL UNDERSTAND WHY F.B.I. DIRECTOR J. EDGAR HOOVER SUGGESTED THAT BLACKS HAVE SMALLER BRAINS THAN WHITES, YET OTHER BLACKS WILL NOTICE THIS BUFFOON ON NATIONAL TELEVISION AS A DEMOCRATIC U.S. CONGRESSMAN AND HERD BEHIND DEMOCRATIC IDEOLOGY AND THEIR HIDDEN AGENDA TO KEEP CONSERVATIVE INTELLECTUAL MORAL VALUED AFRICAN AMERICANS POLITICALLY SITTING AT THE BACK OF THE BUS, DEMOCRATS CONSTANTLY RELEASE THIS MIRAGE OF LIES THAT THEY ARE FOR THE POOR, YES THEY ARE BUT (ONLY) IF YOU ARE SUBSERVIENT AND ADHERE TO THEIR POLITICAL OBEDIENCE BY (NOT) HAVING MORAL CONSERVATIVE INDEPENDENT POLITICAL VIEWS, AND SUPPORT THEIR IDEOLOGY OF SOCIAL PROGRAMS THAT SUSTAIN ILLITERACY AND IGNORANCE WHICH IS CAUSING BLACKS TO SLAUGHTER EACH OTHER THROUGH OUT THE NATION, THAT MAKE THE LOSS OF AMERICAN TROOPS IN IRAQ MORE LIKE ACCIDENTAL DEATH.ON A DAILY BASIS, THERE ARE APPROXIMATELY FORTY THREE BLACK U.S. CONGRESS MEN AND WOMEN,ALSO ONE SENATOR AND SCORES OF SELF APPOINTED LEADERS, ALONG WITH BLACK DEMOCRATIC STRATEGIST, AND MOST OR ALL CONDEMN THE CONFLICT IN IRAQ, CLAIMIMG THE PRESIDENT AND HIS ADMINISTRATION LIED ABOUT REASONS FOR THE REMOVAL OF SADDAM HUSSEIN, BECAUSE THERE WERE NO WEAPONS OF MASS DESTRUCTION AND THE AMERICAN TROOPS SHOULD BE BROUGHT HOME BECAUSE OF THE TROOP LOSS OF LIFE, BUT (NEVER) ADDRESS THE LOSS OF LIFE IN THE UNITED STATES OF AMERICA PERPETRATED BY BLACK ON BLACK CRIME WHICH TRAGICALLY EXCEED AMERICAN TROOP LIFE IN IRAQ ON A DAILY BASISNATION WIDE, AND ONE HAS TO WONDER WHY THE SO CALLED AFRICAN AMERICAN LEADERS ARE NOT ENRAGED ABOUT THE LOSS OF LIFE ON THE HOME FRONT AS THEY ARE IN IRAQ, IT IS FAIRLY SIMPLE IT HAS (NOTHING) TO DO WITH BEING ELECTED TO UNSEAT REPUBLICANS, BECAUSE THE MAJORITY OF AFRICAN AMERICANS ARE SURROGATES

IN THE DEMOCRATIC PARTY THAT STUPIDLY ENDORSE DEMOCRATIC IDEOLOGY OF BLACK SERVITUDE WHICH INITIATED THE DISBANDING OF THEIREPUBLICAN PARTY IN EIGHTEEN SIXTY SIX, THAT HAD ASPIRATIONS OF (ALL) AFRICAN AMERICANS BECOMING EDUCATED INTELLECTUALLY AND INTRODUCED TO MORAL VALUES WHICH COINCIDE WITH THE FUNDAMENTALS OF A DIVERSE SOCIETY,THAT IS IN CONJUNCTION WITH THE FOUNDATION OF OUR NATION.

I WATCHED JUAN WILLIAMS AND MICHAEL ERIC DYSON DEBATE A BOOK REVIEW AUGUST 13, 2006, ON C-SPAN (2) AS THEY PUT FORTH THEIR BEST EFFORT TO CHRONOLOGICALLY EVALUATE MR JUAN WILLIAMS BOOK TITLED ENOUGH, WHICH WAS A ENTHUSIASTIC DEBATE BETWEEN TWO LIBERALS REFERENCING COMMENTS EXPOSED IN MR WILLIAMS BOOK, I DETERMINED THE DEBATE TO BE RATHER INTERESTING TWO BLACK LIBERALS ONE EXTREME RADICAL, THE OTHER UTILIZING CONSERVATIVE IDEOLOGY TO DENOUNCE BLACK BEHAVIOR WRITTEN IS HIS BOOK, AND BEING HARASSED BY THE OTHER WITH UNINTELLIGIBLE NONSENSICAL FLOWERY SPEECH DEMONSTRATING SADISTIC BEHAVIOR, HOWEVER I AM NOT A FAN OF JUAN WILLIAMS BUT I GIVE CREDIT WHEN DUE, HIS PSYCHOANALYSIS WHEN ALLWED TO SPEAK IS A REALITY PERTAINING TO SOME AFRICAN AMERICANS NOT HAVING AN AGENDA OF SELF CONTROL AND INDEPENDENT MORAL RESPONSIBILITY, UNFORTUNATELY IT IS TO LATE FOR SOME THE DEMOCRATS DERAILED THAT TRAIN ONE HUNDRED AND FORTY YEARS AGO, WHEN THEY VIOLENTLY EXPELLED THE REPUBLICANS EDUCATORS FROM THE SOUTHERN STATES VIA KU-KLUX-KLAN WHICH THEIR (ONLY) AGENDA WAS TO EDUCATE FORMER SLAVES, AND PERPETUATED THIS DISASTROUS DILEMMA WITH CUNNING DECEITFUL TACTICS SUCH AS SHARE CROPPING TO SEDUCE BLACKS INTO THINKING THAT THEY WERE BOUND TO SERVITUDE, THAT EDUCATION WAS (NOT) NECESSARY FOR THEM AND THEIR FAMILIES FARMING WAS MORE IMPORTANT, AND DISALLOWED SCHOOLING FOR THE MAJORITY OF BLACK CHILDREN, SO THROUGH GENETIC CONTROLLIBILITY SOME

AFRICAN AMERICANS LIVES WERE ALTERED FOREVER DUE TO ANCESTRY ILLITERACY, AND THE EXISTING PROBLEMS OF TODAY IS A CARRY OVER THAT IS STIMULATED BY THE SAME DEMOCRATIC PARTY IDEOLOGY THAT INITIATED THIS DEBACLE FOR BLACKS,THEN IT WAS FOR SLAVE LABOR TODAY ITS FOR BLOC VOTING, AND THE ASTONISHING FACTOR JUAN WILLIAMS CHOOSE TO INTERVIEW AND DEBATE WITH AN ECCENTRIC THAT IS INEPT TO BLACK REALITY,AND CHASTIZED JUAN WILLIAMS FORAPPLAUDING BILL COSBY AND SUGGESTED THAT MR COSBY IS NARROW MINDED, FOR NOT JOINING THE J. EDGAR HOOVER CLUB OF SMALL DYSFUNCTIONAL BRAIN BLACKS THAT IS STILL PERSUING REPARATION FOR SLAVERY, SO THIS BOOK REVIEW DEBATE TURNED INTO QUITE A FIASCO WITH MICHAEL ERIC DYSON GIVING JUAN WILLIAMS A TONGUE LASHING,BLATANTLY DEFENDING HISTORIC STUPIDITY OVER BLACKS REJECTING MORAL VALUES BY REFUSING TO PARTICIPATE IN INSTITUTIONS FOR LEARNING, JUAN WILLIAMS WAS ONLY TRYING TO PROMOTE HIS BOOK TITLED ENOUGH, AND ELABORATE ON THE SUBSTANCE OF BLACK ISSURES PERTAINING TO DENIGRATION OF SELF IMPOSED DYSFUNCTIONS, AND MICHAEL ERIC DYSON WAS TRYING TO WATER DOWN HIS THEORY WITH GIBBERISH OF MALICE PERPETRATED BY OTHERS AGAINST BLACKS, AND HE IS ABSOLUTELY (CORRECT) AND IT IS CALLED THE DEMOCRATIC PARTY WHICH THEY (ALL) ARE AFFILIATED WITH, AND IS AN ACCESSORY TO THE INAPPROPIATE INCOMPETENCE DISPLAYED BY SOME AFRICAN AMERICANS TODAY IN AMERICA, UNFORTUNATELY AS OF TODATE THINGS HAVE REALLY GOTTEN OUT OF HAND WHEN A LIBERAL DEMOCRAT ATTEMPT TO STIPULATE THE AGREGIOUS BARBARIC IMMORAL BEHAVIOR OF SOME BLACKS WRITTEN IN A BOOK AS BEING INSIDIOUS, APPARENTLY HE UNDERSTAND THAT DOOMSDAY FOR MANY BLACKS IS LURKING AROUND THE CORNER, JUAN WILLIAMS BOOK SHOULD HAVE BEEN TITLED ENOUGH STUPIDITY, THERE ARE APPROXIMATELY NINETY SEVEN PERCENT OF AFRICAN AMERICANS SUPPORT THE DEMOCRATIC PARTY, THIS IRREGULARITY HAS CAUSED A LARGE SEGEMENT OF BLACKS

TO SELF DISTRUCT, SIMPLY BECAUSE OF THIS RIDICULOUS HERDING THEY ELIMINATE POLITICAL BALANCE IN AFRICAN AMERICAN SOCIETY WHICH DISALLOW INTEGRATED DIVERSITY WITHIN, WHICH CAUSE THE DEMOCRATIC PARTY COMPLACENCY AND THEY CONSTANTLY LIE TO THE NATION ABOUT HOW BLACKS ARE NOT (GIVEN) THEIR FAIR SHARE, AND BLAME THIS KINDERGARTEN FOOLISHNESS ON THE OPPOSING REPUBLICAN PARTY IN AN EFFORT TO MAINTAIN THE STATUSQUO OF AFRICAN AMERICANS BLOC VOTES, THIS ONE SIDED UNIQUE DISASTER CONSIST OF NUMEROUS DENOMINATED AFRICAN AMERICANS PEOPLE, ILLITERATE, EDUCATED, POOR, MIDDLE CLASS WEALTHY, AND EXTREMELY WEALTHY, WITH THE MAJORITY THEORETICALLY SUPPORTING THE DEMOCRATIC PARTY FOR WHAT THEY DEEM IS IN THEIR BEST INTEREST, AND IN THAT VICIOUS CIRCLE THE AFFLUENT DOMINATE AND DICTATE DEMOCRATIC VAIN STRATEGY OF IDEOLOGY TO APPROXIMATELY THIRTY THREE MILLION AFRICAN AMERICANS, AND THIS KIND OF BEHAVIOR SUGGEST THE EMULATING OF AFRICAN HERITAGE, THROUGH GENETIC CONTROLLABILITY FOR OVER EIGHT HUNDRED YEARS AGO, RELATED TO THE TRIBAL CHIEFS AND WITCH DOCTORS WHERE THEY HERDED TOGATHER FOR SAFETY COMPANIONSHIP AND SHARED ALL NECESSITIES, ALSO VIOLENTLY ASSULTED AND SWINDLED EACH OTHER, THE TRIBAL CHIEF WAS THE SOLE ARBITRATOR AND ALL THE TRIBESMEN AND WOMEN WERE SUBMISSIVE TO HIS DOCTRINE, THAT RENDITION OF TRAITS EXIST IN BLACK SOCIETY TODAY IN THE UNITED STATES OF AMERICA, UNFORTUNATELY ON A UNIVERSAL SCALE AMONG AFRICAN AMERICANS, FOR INSTANCE APPROXIMATELY NINETY FIVE PERCENT HAVE BEEN SEDUCED AND INDOCTRINATED BY THE DEMOCRAT PARTY, DUE TO BLACK SURROGATES CONGLOMERATES WITHIN THE PARTY THAT IS EMULATING THROUGH ANCESTRAL GENETIC CONTROLLABILITY THE CONTROLLING DOCTRINE UTILIZED BY AFRICAN TRIBAL CHIEFS HUNDREDS OF YEARS AGO, BECAUSE THE AGUMENTATION OF BLACKS CHOOSE TO ADHERE RESPECTFULLY DUE TO A GENETIC

CONTROLLING FACTOR THAT ABOLISH INDIVIDUAL THINKING AND SUBSTITUTE HERDING BEHIND BLACK DEMOCRATIC POLITICAL DICTATORS, HERDING HAS BEEN THE SOLE DESTRUCTIVE FACTOR RELATED TO AFRICAN AMERICAN SOCIETY, PROVEN IN ACCORDANCE TO HISTORY, THE MOST NOTABLY AND DAMMING WAS IN EIGHTEEN NINETY FIVE PERPETRATED BY BOOKER T. WASHINGTON PRESIDENT AND FOUNDER OF TUSKEGEE INSTITUTE, THE MOST INFLUENTIAL BLACK LEADER IN THE SOUTH AT THAT TIME, WHICH HE GAVE SPEECHES IN DOMINATED AREAS OF AFRICAN AMERICANS AND APPEARED TO HAVE INSTIGATED RACIAL SEGREGATION AND SECOND CLASS CITIZENSHIP BY CLAIMING IT WAS INEVITABLE, SOUTHERN BLACKS HERDED BEHIND HIS DOCTRINE, WHICH PLACATED SOUTHERN WHITES AND THE SUPREME COURT,THAT MOST LIKELY CAUSED THE SUPREME TO BE INSTRUMENTAL IN BYPASSING THE REPUBLICAN CONTROLLED CONGRESS RATIFIED CONSTITUTION AMENDMENT FOURTEEN IN EIGHTEEN SIXTY EIGHT, ALSO THE FIFTEENTH IN EIGHTEEN SEVENTY, AND VOTED TO IMPOSE THE JIM CROW RULE SEPERATE BUT EQUAL IN FAVOR FOR THE SOUTHERN STATES, WHICH LASTED FOR SEVENTY YEARS, BUT THE ONE THAT COMPLETELY CHANGED THE COURSE IN HISTORY FOR AFRICAN AMERICANS REGARDS TO MORAL AND INTELLECTUAL VALUES OCCURRED DURING THE PRESIDENT FRANKLIN ROOSEVELT ERA, HE ENGAGED IN A SPECIAL INQUIRY CONCERNING AFRICAN AMERICANS TO ELICIT THEIR VOTING TRADITIONS,AND DISPATCHED A SPECIAL DELEGATION THROUGHT THE NORTHERN STATES TO REPORT BACK, AND THEY REPOTED BACK WITH A DISCOVERY THAT THEY VOTED IN HERDED BLOC FASHION, AND THAT IS WHEN HE DEVISED A PLAN TO DISMANTLE THE BLACK REPUBLICAN INFRASTRUCTURE THAT PRESIDENT ABRAHAM LINCOLN WAS RESPONSIBLE FOR THAT CONSISTED OF MORAL VALUES AND INTELLECTUAL PROMISE FOR (ALL) AFRICAN AMERICANS, TRADITIONALLY AFRICAN AMERICANS ARE RELIGIOUS PEOPLE AND FROM GOING TO CHURCH BEING TAUGHT FROM THE BIBLE, TREAT PEOPLE AS YOU WISH TO BE TREATED, HONOR YOUR

MOTHER AND FATHER, REFRAIN FROM STEELING,EARN YOUR LIVING.IBY THE SWEAT OF YOUR BROW, SPARE THE ROD AND SPOIL THE CHILD, THESE BIBLICAL REVELATIONS ARE THE MORAL FOUNDATION OF OUR SOCIETY, WHICH BLACKS REVERED AND ADHERED TO THESE PRINCIPLES AS A GUIDANCE THROUGH OUT HISTORY IN AMERICA,THAT COINCIDE WITH STANDARDS OF MORAL VALUES, WHICH IS THE BEDROCK OF CONSERVATISM AND THE REPUBLICAN PARTY.

HOWEVER DURING THE LATE THIRTIES AND EARLY FORTIES IT WAS REPORTED TO PRESIDENT ROOSEVELT BY HIS SPECIAL ENVOY THAT MANY AFRICAN AMERICANS HAD MIGRATED TO THE NORTHERN STATES AND MOSTLY BLOC VOTED ALONG CONSERVATIVE LINES OUT OF LOYALTY TO PRESIDENT LINCOLN FOR THEIR FREEDOM. FROM BONDAGE, THERE WERE APPROXIMATELY TWELVE MILLION AFRICAN AMERICAN CITIZENS IN AMERICA WHICH ACCOUNTED FOR ALMOST FIVE PERCENT OF TOTAL VOTES, AND BASED ON THEIR BLOC VOTING COULD BE A DETERMINING FACTOR IN THEIR STATES REGARD TO ELECTORIAL VOTES, SO TO REASSURE AFRICAN AMERICAN CONSTITUENCY AND LURE THEM FROM THE REPUBLICAN PARTY, THE NEW DEAL OF (WELFARE) AND WORKFARE BENEFITS PROGRAMS HAD BEEN IMPLEMENTED, WHICH CAUSED A SEGEMENT OF BLACKS TO ABANDON THE REPUBLICAN PARTY THAT PRESIDENT LINCOLN HAD ESTABLISHED HAVING TO DO WITH EDUCATION AND MORAL VALUES WHICH COULD HAVE ENHANCED AFRICAN AMERICANS STABILITY INTO THE INTELLECTUAL POLITICAL ARENA FOR THE BETTERMENT OF BLACKS AND THE ENTIRE NATION, UNFORTUNATELY PRESIDENT ROOSEVELT HAD ASSESSED BLACKS IDIOSYNCRASIES OF BLOC VOTING,AND HERDING BEHING AFFLUENT BLACKS . THINKING THIS WOULD HELP THEIR CAUSE REGARDS TO DESEGREGATION, SO HE FURTHER UTILIZED CONTRIVED METHODS TO COMPLETELY DISSOLVE BLACKS SUPPORT FOR THE REPUBLICAN PARTY, BY ELEVATING COLONEL BENJAMIN C. DAVIS TO GENERAL THE HIGHEST RANKING BLACK OFFICER IN THE ARM FORCES, AND APPOINTED

WILLIAM HASTIE ANOTHER BLACK TO STAFF OF WAR SECRETARY, STINSON AND THE VAST MAJORITY OF AFRICAN AMERICANS THROUGHT THE NATION APPLAUDED THESE (TWO) PROMOTIONS AND ASSUMED THAT SEGREGATION WAS BEING RESOLVED AND DISBANDED THEIR ALLEGIANCE TO THE REPUBLICAN PARTY, LEAVING BEHIND EDUCATION, AND MORAL INTELLECTUAL VALUES FOR WELFARE, WHICH PRESIDENT ROOSEVELT WAS VERY WELL AWARE THAT THE JIM CROW RULE WAS IN AFFECT AND COULD NOT BE REMOVED WITHOUT A ACT OF CONGRESS, WHICH LASTED FOR APPROXIMATELY TWENTY FIVE YEARS LATER, AND WITHIN THOSE YEARS BLACKS CAUGHT HELL WITH LYNCHINGS, WATER HOSING, DENIED ACCESS TO PUBLIC COMMUNITY PLACES, AND MANY JALING ALL DUE TO SOUTHERN DEMOCRATIC CONTROL IN THE SOUTH.

FINALLY IN NINETEEN SIXTY FOUR AND FIVE AFRICAN AMERICANS WAS GRANTED EQUALITY CIVIL AND VOTING RIGHTS, DUE TO THE OVERWHELMING PRESISTENCE AND SUPPORT FROM THE REPUBLICAN CONGRESS, IT HAS BEEN APPROXIMATELY FORTY ONE YEARS PASS, AND MILLIONS OF AFRICAN AMERICANS ARE STILL HOLDING ON TO RELIGIOUS VALUES THAT IS GUIDING THEM INTO MORAL INTELLECTUAL FINANCIAL STABILITY IN ACCORDANCE WITH THE INFRASTRUCTURE OF THE SYSTEM, AND THEY ARE LIBERAL UNAWARE THEY ARE USING CONSERVATIVE GUIDE-LINES TO SUCCEED, AND THE MAJORITY VOTE DEMOCRATIC BECAUSE OF A GENETIC ROLL OVER FROM PAST YEARS CONSIDERED TO BE A FAMILY TRADITION RENDITION FROM THE ROOSEVELT ERA, WHICH THE CURRENT DEMOCRATS CONSTANTLY DEVISE SCHEMES TO EXALT THIS DEMORALIZING DOCTRINE BESTOWED ON BLACKS HISTORICALLY

IT IS EXTREMELY DIFFICULT TO ANALYTICALLY DESCRIBE THE HISTORY OF AFRICAN AMERICANS CONCEPTS BECAUSE OF THE REPETITIOUS REDUNDANCY WITHIN THE SOCIETY, THEY ALL HAVE A AMBIGUOUS PHILOSOPHY THAT IS ESTRANGE TO DECIPHER, BECAUSE THERE ARE MILLIONS CONSTANTLY COMPLAINING AND TRYING TO MODIFY OR ABOLISH MORAL VALUES WITH IN THE SYSTEM, AND THERE

OTHERS THAT HAVE AFFECTIVELY USED MORAL VALUES TO BECOME FINANCIALLY STABLE WITHIN THE STANDARDS OF THE SYSTEM, BUT THE MAJORITY WILL PUBLICLY HERD AND DENOUNCE THE CRITERION OF MORAL VALUES AS (NOT) BEING RELEVANT TO SOME AFRICAN AMERICANS HIGH SCHOOL DROP OUT AND INSIDIOUS CRIMINAL ACTIVITY, AND CLAIM THE SYSTEM HAS FAILED THEM.

IT APPEAR THAT THERE IS A CONSPIRACY WITHIN TO JUSTIFY THE INADEQUACY OF MORAL VALUES THAT SHOULD BE THE SOLE RESPONSIBILITY OF THE IMMEDIATE FAMILY, AND ALL REQUIRED IS THE. HOLY BIBLE THAT HAS ALL THE ATTRIBUTES RELATED TO MORAL VALUES, UNFORTUNATELY THERE ARE AFFLUENT BLACKS THAT ATTEMPT TO DICTATE EXCUSES FOR THIS INEPT MADNESS AND BLAME EVERYONE BUT THE REAL CULPRITS BLACKS THEM SELVES.

IN AN ATTEMPT TO SORT OUT THESE AMBIGUOUS MALICIOUS RENDITIONS WHICH IS DEEM TO BE DYSFUNCTIONAL AND SELF IMPOSED BASED ON LEGENDARY PHENOMENONS INDUCED IN AN ATTEMPT TO DISSUADE FROM BLACKS IABILITY TO CONFORM OR ACCEPT MORAL VALUES, AND THESE ARE THE PEOPLE THAT CONSTANTLY COMPLAIN ABOUT HENDRANCE AND ACCUSE CAUCASIANS AS BEING RACIST TOWARD THEM BECAUSE THEY ARE BLACK, AND IF ANY AFRICAN AMERICAN DENOUNCE THEIR RADICAL BEHAVIOR THEY ARE TO STU TO UNDERSTAND BLACK CULTURE, AND ONLY RAISING ISSURES BECAUSE THEY SUCK UP TO WHITE FOLKS, AND THATS HOW THEY GOT THEIR MONEY, UNFORTUNATELY THERE ARE HIGHLY EDUCATED AFFLUENT BLACKS THAT ARE COMBATANTS TO DISTORT THESE FOOLISH OFFENSIVE REALITIES IN THEIR FAVOR, ONE OF THE MOST UNIQUE DISASTROUS PHENOMENON PERTAINING TO AFRICAN AMERICANS SOCIETY IS THEIR ALLIANCE TO ADHERE AND LISTEN TO JERKS THAT IS DISTORTING REALITY ON THEIR BEHALF, WHICH CAUSE REBELLIOUS CRAVINGS THAT INITIATE LOW ECONOMIC ACTIVITY, BECAUSE THE BLACKS THAT IS OBSESSED WITH THIS KIND OF VOODOO MANDATING IS OUT SIDE THE RANGE OF INFLUENCE REGARDS TO

MORAL VALUES, AND IS CONSTANTLY TRYING TO MODIFY THE SYSTEM TO THEIR AGENDA, WHICH IS TO APPOSE INTELLECTUAL IDEOLOGY, AND WHEN A FIEW AFFLUENT AFRICAN AMERICANS ATTEMPT TO ILLUSTRATE THESE DEFICIENCIES AS BEING AN ERRONEOUS PRECEPTION THAT IS RESPONSIBLE FOR THEIR SELF DESTRUCTION BASED ON POVITY AND CRIMINAL ACTIVITY, ITS LIKE KICKING A ANTHILL WITH AFFLUENT BLACK LIBERALS TAKING TO THE AIR WAYS DENOUNCING THE SIGNIFICANCE OF THEIR THEORY, AND INSINUATING THAT AFRICAN AMERICANS LIKE BILL COSBY, JESSIE LEE PETERSON, JOHN WHORTER, LARRY ELDER, ANDRED CLARK SR. AND NOW JUAN WILLIAMS, THERE ARE A FIEW OTHERS THAT IS AFRAID TO ADDRESS THESE PSYCHEDELIC ISSURES FEAR OF BEING LABELED INSENSITIVE TO BLACK CULTURE FOOLISH AND TAKING SIDES WITH THE WHITE MAN, FORTUNATELY THE DEVASTATION OF BLACK CRIME IS BECOMING SO INTENSE AT A SYMMETRY DISPARITY MALICIOUS AND BARBARIC RATE, FINALLY SOME BLACK LIBERALS ARE FEELING THE URGENCY TO REMOVE THE BLINDERS AND DENOUNCE THIS SOLELY AS A INSURGENCY OF BLACKS WITHOUT CAUSE, OTHER THAN BEING MINUS EDUCATION MORAL VALUES AND RESPECT FOR OTHERS.

I CAN RECALL VERY VIVIDLY GROWING UP WHILE MY BEHIND WAS BEING STRAPPED FOR MIS DEEDS, MY PARENT WOULD BE SPEAKING INDISTINCTLY CHARITY BEGINS AT HOME AND SPREAD ABROAD, MEANING MORAL VALUES, I AM OF THE OPENION ABSOLUTELY (NOTHING) CAN CONTAIN THIS RADICAL UPSURGE IN BLACK BEHAVIOR, BECAUSE MORAL VALUES HAS NEVER EXISTED IN THEIR LIVES, WHICH HAS TO BE TAUGHT AT A VERY EARLY AGE AND OBSERVED FOR QUALITY, UNFORTUNATELY MORAL VALUES HAS BEEN NEGLECTED FOR DECADES BECAUSE OF BABIES HAVING BABIES, AND THE LUCRATIVE SOCIAL FALLOUT FROM THE DEMOCRATIC PARTY, ALONG WITH SELF APPOINTED BLACK LEADERS PATRONIZING AND JUSTIFYING BLACK RADICAL BEHAVIOR FOR YEARS AND INSTIGATING BLAME ON THE SYSTEM BEING UN-JUST PIRATICALLY CONSERVATISM, IF THE DEMOCRATS WERE SO

INSTRUMENTAL IN THE WELL BEING OF BLACKS THEY HAD FORTY YEARS TO RATIFY AND IMPROVE THEIR CONDITIONS ALONG WITH THEIR CRUSADING BLACK EMULATORS (I WONDER WHAT HAPPEN) OH I KNOW THERE MUST HAVE BEEN A REPUBLICAN CONSPIRACY GLITCH AGAINST BLACKS TO KEEP THEM DOWN, ACCREDITED TO DEMOCRATIC PHILOSOPHIES.

SELF APPOINTED BLACK LEADERS HAVE CORRUPTED A LARGE SEGEMENT OF AFRICAN AMERICANS FOR MANY DECADES,BECAUSE OF ERRONEIOUSLY PUBLICLY INDITING (ALL) CAUCASIANS FOR THE CHOICES BLACKS HAVE MADE WITH THEIR PERSONAL LIVES, SO BASED ON THE HERDING FACTOR THE MAJORITY OF BLACKS BECAME OBSESSED WITH THIS DOCTRINE, AND OVER THE YEARS HAVE REBELLED AGAINST WHITE SOCIETY SOCIALLY, AND AS OF TO DATE IT HAS ESCULATED INTO A SNEERING FOOLISH EPIDEMIC, WITH BLACKS THAT ARE UNABLE TO ADJUST OR ACCEPT MORAL INTELLECTUAL DIVERSITY IN THE UNITED STATES OF AMERICA, AND AS A RESULT THEY ARE ADOPTING A CONGO STYLE IMAGE THAT REJECT THE FUNDAMENTALS OF THE NATION THAT IS REQUIRED TO SUCCEED, SUCH AS EDUCATION AND INTELLECTUAL MORAL VALUES, AND THROUGHOUT THE NATION IN MOSTLY PREDOMINATLY BLACK AREAS , THERE IS A FORCE OF INTIMIDATING OCCURING AGAINST PEOPLE THAT ARE PERSUING ACADEMIC SUCCESS, THEY ARE BEING IDENTIFIED AS TRYING TO BE WHITE, THE MAJORITY OF AFFLUENT EDUCATED LIBERAL BLACKS HAS WORN ROSE COLORED GLASSES TO THESE INSIDIOUS REVELATIONS THAT THEY INSTIGATED FOR YEARS, PERSUING AND DICTATING DOCTRINES THAT THE FEDERAL, STATE, AND LOCAL GOVERNMENTS SHOULD BE THE CARE TAKERS OF DESTITUTE BLACKS AND PAMPER THEM TO SEEK INDULGE IN LEARNING, FOR INTELLECTUAL DIPLOMACY WHICH IS FOR THEIR BENEFIT, UNFORTUNATELY THERE ARE MANY AFFLUENT BLACKS ARE SLOW TO COMPREHEND SUCH AS THE MAYOR OF NEW ORLEANS RAY NAGIN STILL FLAUNTING KATRINA AS A RACIST NEGLECT TOWARDS BLACKS, WHEN HE SHOULD BE THE NEGLECTING CULPRIT, HOWEVER

THE FAULT RELY WITH THE WEAKNESS IN CHARACTER OF THE VICTOMS, THERE ARE THREE MAJOR REASONS FOR THE MAJORITY OF LOST LIFE, BLACKS TEND TO RELY ON SPIRITUAL INSTINCTS THAT GOD WILL TAKE CARE, NOT REALIZING THATS WHY GOD GAVE THEM FIVE TSENSES, ALSO REMAIN IN THE EYE OF THE STORM TO PROTECT THEIR BELONGINGS FROM VANDALS, AND THE THEIVES ARE LURKING IN THE EYE OF THE STORM FOR THEM TO LEAVE, AND AS A RESULT THEY ALL GET DROWNED AND BLOWN AWAY.

THERE ARE FICTITIOUS DEMOCRATIC LIBERAL BLACKS HERDING TOGATHER IN MEETINGS, WRITING BOOKS, AND MAKING SUGGESTIONS OVER THE NET WORKS, IN AN EFFORT TO APPEASE AND TRY TO ATONE FOR THEIR IGNORANCE IN MISCALCULATING THE SURGE IN BLACK CRIMINAL ACTIVITY, NOW THESE HYPOCRITICAL SELF SERVING PARASITES ARE BACK PEDDLING AND NOT ACKNOWLEDGING THAT THEY PLAYED AN INTRIGUING PART IN DISTORTING THE TRANSIENT PRECEPTION OF BLACKS RELATED TO CAUCASIANS BY CONSTANTLY OSTENTATIOUSLY REBUKING WHITES FOR THEIR FAILURES, AND DEMANDING REPARATION FOR SLAVERY, WHICH INFLUENCED AND EMBOLDEN THEIR INCENTIVE TO COMMIT HIDEOUS CRIMES BECAUSE THEY ARE MADE TO FEEL FORSAKEN DUE TO FASLE DECEPTION PORTRAYED BY SELF APPOINTED LEADERS AND PEOPLE THE LIKES OF PROFESSOR CHARLES OGLETREE.

NOW THAT A SEGMENT OF REBELLIOUS BLACKS ARE OPENLY SHOWING DISREGARD FOR MORAL VALUES AND INTELLECTUAL STANDARDS THAT IS REQUIRED TO ADEQUATELY SHUN DESTITUTION, AND ARE CLAIMING THESE INHERENT CHARACTERISTICS ARE RELEGATED FOR CAUCASIANS, AND THEY WANT (NOTHING) TO DO WITH IT BECAUSE IT REPRESENT BEING WHITE, AND IT IS QUITE INTRIGUINGLY ALSO VERY INTERESTING THAT AFFLUENT AFRICAN AMERICANS ARE DISCUSSING AND SHARING OPENIONS OF THEIR PAST, REGARDS TO DATA FROM THEIR ERA,AND HOW THEIR PERSISTENCY PREVAILED RREGARDLESS TO THE CIRCUMSTANCES, BECAUSE AT

TIMES THERE WERE FRUSTRATING BARRIERS PIRATICALLY IN THE SOUTHERN STATES PRIOR TO THE EARLY SIXTIES, HOWEVER THEY ARE THE PREVAILING PROOF THAT BLACKS CAN BE A SUCCESS IN THIS COUNTRY ALWAYS HAVE, AND ALWAYS WILL BECAUSE APPROXIMATELY SEVENTY PRECENT OF THIRTY SIX MILLION HAVE ALREADY PROVEN THAT FACTOR, AND IF THEY HAD BEEN HERDING TOGATHER THREE OR FOUR DECADES AND ALLUDING TO THEIR PRESISTENT REVELATIONS REGARDS TO MORAL VALUES AND THE PERSUIT OF INTELLECTUAL COMPREHENSION, INSTEAD OF STICKING THEIR HEADS IN THE SAND ENDORSING AND INSTIGATING THAT WHITE AMERICA WAS AND IS RESPONSIBLE FOR THE FAILURE OF SOME BLACKS, IT IS A VERY DISTINCT POSSIBILITY THERE WOULD (NOT) BE TWENTY FIVE TO THIRTY PERCENT WHICH CONSIST OF APPROXIMATELY TEN AND THREE QUARTERS MILLION OF AFRICAN AMERICANS CHARACTERIZED AS BEING DESTITUTE COMMITTING HEINOUS CRIMES, AND SLAUGHTERING EACH OTHER LIKE CHICKENS ON A DAILY BASIS, THE STATISTICAL CALCULATIONS REGARDS TO AFRICAN AMERICANS REFERENCING CHILD BIRTH OUT OF WED LOCK, HIGH SCHOOL DROP OUT, AND CRIMINAL ACTIVITY IS RATHER ALARMING BUT CERTAINTLY A REALITY, AND IT HAS BLACK AFFLUENT LIBERAL LEADER STRATEGIST SCRAMBLING FOR ANSWERS, HOLDING THEIR FINGERS TO THE WIND AND PLAYING THE BLAME GAME ON EACH OTHER, WITH (NO) LOGICAL EXPLANATION FOR THIS ELICIT DEBACLE FOR SOME RADICAL BLACKS INSTIGATING THAT THEIR INTENTIONS ARE TO AVOID EDUCATION, MORAL VALUES, AND INTELLECTUAL PARTICIPATION BASED ON THESE INHERENT CHARACTERSTICS BEING RELEGATED FOR WHITES, AND WHEN I REFER TO SCRAMBLING FOR ANSWERS JUAN WILLIAMS,AND AL SHARPTON, ON FOX NEWS ORILEY FACTOR AUGUST 21, 2006, WRANGLING OVER ACCUSATIONS WRITTEN IN JUAN WILLIAMS BOOK THAT AL SHARPTON IS A SELF-SERVING OPPORTUNIST THAT NEVER DELIVER MESSAGES TO BLACK AMERICA DENOUNCING INSIDIOUS AND BARBARIC BEHAVIOR, SHARPTON HAD A SCOWL ON

HIS FACE AS IF SOME ONE HAD STOLEN HIS HAIR SOLUTION, HOWEVER IT WAS UTTERLY APPALLING TO WATCH TWO LIBERAL BLACKS ATTEMPT TO INTIMIDATE EACH OTHER BASED ON (NOT) INFORMING AND CHASTISING BLACKS ABOUT MORAL INTELLECTUAL VALUES THAT IS THE ESCAPE FROM DESTITUTION, AND THE REASON I DEEM THIS TO BE AN INHERENT PATHETIC MISCHIEVOUS ADVENTURE THEY EACH ARE STAUNCH SUPPORTERS OF THE LIBERAL LEFT PARTY THAT INITIATED AND IS INDIRECTLY RESPONSIBLE FOR THE ENTIRE DEBACLE, THE SOUTHERN DEMOCRATS OFTEN TREATED AFRICAN AMERICANS AS IF THEY WERE CATTLE THROUGHOUT HISTORY SIMPLY BECAUSE OF THEIR GENETIC HERDING INSTINCTS, CATTLE INSTINCTIVELY FOLLOW A LEADER WHICH IS CALLED A MATRIARCH, YOU CAN HAVE HUNDREDS OF CATTLE AND IF THEY SHOULD BOLT FROM THEIR PLACE OF CONFINEMENT, ALL IS NECESSARY TO LOCATE THE LEADING MATRIARCH AND THE REST WILL FOLLOW, SLAVE MASTERS ALSO USED ANIMALIZE TECHNIQUES FOR BREEDING BLACKS SUCH AS HALTERING MALE AND FEMALE TOGATHER OVER NIGHT, SO BASICALLY THIS IS WHY SOUTHERN DEMOCRAT PLANTATION SLAVE OWNERS REFERRED TO BLACKS AS THE HERD BECAUSE OF THEIR NATURAL APTITUDE TO FOLLOW A LEADER AND HERD TOGATHER, SO JUAN WILLIAMS IS ON TO SOMETHING ABOUT THESE SELF APPOINTED LEADERS WHICH HAS ADOPTED THE LIBERAL DEMCRATIC IDEOLOGY THAT AFRICAN AMERICANS SHOULD BE TREATED LIKE CATTLE CONFINE THEM TO PUBLIC HOUSING, GIVE THEM JUST ENOUGH WELFARE SOCIAL INCOME TO FEED THEM SELVES AND LET THE SELF APPOINTED LEADERS DO THEIR THINKING, AND WHEN THEY BOLT HE IS ALWAYS THERE FOR THEM TO HERD BEHIND BACK TO DISPARITY, THERE IS A PATHETIC REALITY THAT HAS BEEN UTILIZED TO CONTROL AFRICAN AMERICANS FOR HUNDREDS OF YEARS, UNFORTUNATELY PRESIDENT FRANKLIN DELANO ROOSEVELT WAS A MASTER AT THESE TECHNIQUES DURING THE EARLY FORTIES, HE CONTROLLED APPROXIMATELY THIRTEEN MILLION AFRICAN AMERICANS NATION WIDE FOR THEIR VOTING BLOC, WITH THREE AFFLUENT BLACK

LEADERS A. PHILIP RANDOLPH, ARNOLD HILL AND WALTER WHITE, AND THESE RELENTLESS TACTICS HAVE BEEN PERPETRATED BY AMBITIOUS DEMOCRATIC KINDRED AGREEABLENESS BLACKS FOR APPROXIMATELY SEVENTY YEARS, AND NOW IT HAS CATAPULT OUT OF CONTROL FROM THE BABY HAVING BABY GENERATION WHERE THEY HAVE FORMED THEIR OWN OPENION ABOUT LEADERS TO FOLLOW, BECAUSE THE MAJORITY OF MATRIARCH GRAND FATHERS AND MOTHERS OF THE THIRTIES AND FORTIES THAT TAUGHT DISCIPLINE AND LARGELY RAISED THEIR GRAND CHILDREN, ARE EITHER MENTALLY DEFICIENT THROUGH OLD AGE, DECEASED OR LABELED WHITE FOLKS LOVERS, THE ISSURE AND REALITY OF THIS THIRTY PERCENT OF BLACK MIS-FITS, POVITY STRIKEN, NON EDUCATED, DRUG SEDATED, SQUANDERS, ARE GENERALLY INCOMPETENT AND WILL (NOT) ELICIT ASSISTANCE THAT EXERCISE TACT AND INTELLECTUAL MORAL VALUES, THE MORAL REVERENCE OF APPROXIMATELY SEVENTY PERCENT OF AFRICAN AMERICANS THAT HAS CHOSEN TO AVOID HIDEOUS DOCTRINES INSTIGATED BY SELF APPOINTED LEADERS HAS SOUNDLY PROVEN THAT ADEQUATE JUSTICE IN AMERICA PREVAIL AND IS APPROPRIATE FOR (ALL) CITIZENS,THAT CHOOSE TO EXTEND THEM SELVES BEYOND DOCTRINES OF DICTATORIAL ASSUMPTIONS OF HENDERANCE FOR SELF SERVING GAIN,THERE ARE MANY FACETS TO DESTITUTION FOR SOME AFRICAN AMERICANS, AND MOST HAVE TO DO WITH A (HERDING) ADOPTIVE IDEOLOGY THAT HAS BEEN HASTEN BY A THEORY OF REBELLIOUS DEMAGOGUERY THAT SHUNS DIDACTIC, WITH ASPIRATIONS OF THRIVING ON CONGO INHERENT CHARACTERISTICS, THIS LEGENDARY NARRATIVE OF PHENOMENON THAT SELF APPOINTED BLACKS USE IS A TACTICAL PROVOCATIVE TO MOTIVATE IDIOSYNCRASIES SUCH AS THERE IS A WHITE CONSPIRACY DEVELOPED AGAINST THEM BECAUSE THEY ARE BLACK, AND THATS WHY THEY ARE UNABLE TO RISE ABOVE DESTITUTION, THIS INSENSITIVE PATHETIC NONSENSICAL RHETORIC IS SENSATIONALIZED BY THE MAYOR OF NEW ORLEANS RAY NAGIN, AND MANY OTHER AFFLUENT BLACKS THAT

CONSTANTLY CORRELATE THIS INSANITY WITH RACISM, WHEN APPROXIMATELY SEVENTY PERCENT OF AFRICAN AMERICANS IN THIS COUNTRY HAVE TRIUMPH IN EVERY SPHERE OF ACTIVITY ACCESSIBLE, BECAUSE THEY CHOOSE AND ARE CHOOSING TO UTILIZE THE STANDARDS OF OUR NATION THAT DICTATE EDUCATION AND INTELLECTUAL MORAL VALUES, AND (NOT) VOODOO ECONOMICS FROM THE CONGO THAT HAS PRODUCED A THIRTY PERCENT OF BLACK DESTITUTION, THAT IS INCREASING ON A DAILY BASIS AND FURTHER ALIENATING THEM FROM NATIONAL INTELLECTUAL DIVERSITY, THE HARD CORE THIRTY PERCENT OF POVERTY STRIKEN BLACKS, ARE OF THE OPENION THAT TO LIVE AN AFFLUENT LIFE THE REQUIREMENTS CONSIST OF ENCROACHMENT OF OTHERS WITH THE INTENT TO INVADE, STRONG ARM ROBBBERY, THE USE AND DEALING OF DRUGS,AND TO CASTIGATE CAUCASIANS FOR THEIR VILLAINOUS BEHAVIORS, ALSO REMAIN IN READINESS FOR THEIR ABNORMAL FUNCTIONING WELFARE CHECKS TO ARRIVE, C-SPAN WASHINGTON JOURNAL ACKNOWLEDGED HURRICANE KATRINA A FIEW DAYS IN AUGUST 2006, AND ILLUSTRATED THE CATASTROPHICS CAUSED BY THIS HURRICANE AND RESPECTFULLY ACCEPTED CALLS.. IN AN EFFORT TO MONITOR OPENIONS A YEAR LATER, THERE WERE VARYING ASSESSMENTS, THE PRIMARY CONCERNS SOME BLACKS WERE IF ANY ADDITIONAL CHECKS WOULD BE (GIVEN) OUT TO FORMER RESIDENTS OF NEW ORLEANS RESIDING IN OTHER STATES, IT IS EXCEEDINGLY APPALLING THAT SOME AFFLUENT BLACKS WILL CONTIUALLY CHARADE ON NATIONAL TELEVISION AND CONVINCINGLY ESTABLISH F.B.I. DIRECTOR J. EDGAR HOOVER THEORY THAT THE BRAINS OF BLACKS WERE TWENTY PERCENT SMALLER THAN WHITES, SUCH AS (LEGAL AGENT) LAUREN LAKE AND DEMOCRATIC STRATEGIST MICHAEL BROWN, ON AUGUST 24, 2006, THEY EACH WERE ON FOX NEWS SEPERATE PROGRAMS, LAUREN LAKE ON THE ORILEY FACTOR MAKING NONSENSICAL CONTRADICTABLE STATEMENTS ABOUT RACE, FIRST SHE IS SYMPATHETIC TO THE BILL COSBY ASSESSMENT OF BLACKS BEING OUT OF CONTROL ON THEIR

OWN ACCORD DUE TO IMMORAL BEHAVIOR, AND THEN SHE DOES AN ABOUT FACE AND START MAKING INSINUATIVE COMMENTS THAT THERE IS A COVERT CONSPIRACY GEARED IN FAVOR OF CAUCASIANS TO CREATE RACIAL OPRESSION FOR BLACKS, AND RACISM IS INSTITUTIONALIZED IN THE UNITED STATES OF AMERICA AGAINST AFRICAN AMERICANS BASED ON COVERT PRIVILEGES TO HENDER, AND THAT ORILEY IS AN EXAMPLE OF HER OPENION BECAUSE HE WOULD NEVER BE ON A RAFT SEEKING ASSISTANCE, I SIMPLISTICALLY GRANT YOU SHE (WOULD NOT) BE EITHER.

IT IS TERRIBLY PATHETIC AND CYNICAL FOR AN ACCOMPLISHED BLACK ATTORNEY TO COMPLETELY IGNORE THE FACT THAT SHE IS A PART OF THAT SEVENTY PERCENT OF AFRICAN AMERICANS THAT IS EQUIVALENT TO ORILEY REGARDS TO PRIVILEGES, I THINK SHE IS INEPT TO THE FACT THAT PRIVILEGE IS A BASIC CIVIL RIGHT GRANTED AND GUARANTEED BY THE CONSTUTION FOR (ALL) AMERICAN CITIZENS, AND YOUR SUCCESS SOLELY DEPEND AND IS BASED ON YOUR INTELLECTUAL ABILITIES TO SUCCEED AS SHE (DID) TO BECOME AN ATTORNEY, SO SHE AND MANY OTHER BLACKS ARE PRODIGIES THAT CONTRADICT HER FOOLISH THEORY THAT THERE IS A UNDER COVER COVERT TACTIC TO ENHANCE WHITE PRIVILEGES OVER BLACKS, WHICH CAUSE RACIAL OPPRESSION AND HINDER AFRICAN AMERICANS, AND ON THE NEXT SEGMENT OF FOX NEWS HANNITY AND COLMES CAME MY FAVORITE STOOGE MICHAEL BROWN, AFFLUENT DIPLOMATIC BLACK DEMOCRATIC STRATEGIST DRAGGING THE COTTON SACK FOR HIS LIBERAL MASTERS, SHARING HIS SENTIMENTS ABOUT THE IRAQ CONFLICT AND TERRORIST ACTIVITY,WHEN ASKED BY HANNITY WHAT IS THE DEMOCRATS SOLUTION TO THE PROBLEM AND BE SPECIFIC, HE LIT UP WITH A SHINE OF A FRESH FRIED PORK CHOP, AND ELUDED THE QUESTION WITH GIBBERISH WHICH IS A FORMALITY WITH MOST LIBERAL DEMOCRATS, (NEVER) HAVE A SPECIFIC PLAN FOR ANY THING, BUT CONSTANTLY IMPUGN AND DISTORT QUESTIONS WITH PALLUTED ASSESSMENTS OF SOMETHING THAT IS TO THE CONTRARY, FOR INSTANCE

HE CHOOSE TO EVADE HANNITY QUESTION BY RELATING TO HOME GROWN TERRORIST , REFERENCING TIMMOTHY MCVEY AND THE OKLAHOMA ACT OF YEARS PAST, WHICH WAS A HOME GROWN WHITE TERRORIST, BUT FOR SOME STRANGE REASON HE HAD A MEMORY LAPSE WITH AMNESIA ABOUT THE CURRENT BLACKS ACCUSED OF PLANNING TO BLOW UP THE SEARS TOWER IN CHICAGO, THERE IS A CONGLOMERATE OF AFFLUENT AFRICAN AMERICANS IN THE UNITED STATES OF AMERICA FROM ALL OPEN DECLARATIONS OF BELIEFS,MANY TEND TO HERD AND SYNCHRONIZE IMAGINARY CONDEMNATION TREATMENT OF BLACKS, AND THE BASIS FOR THIS INJECTION HAS TO DO WITH A MENTALITY THAT IS OBSESSED WITH HERDING WHICH IS DOMINATED AND DRIVEN BY GENETIC CONTROLLABILITY FROM HERITAGE THAT LEAVE (NO) ROOM FOR CHANGE OF COURSE, FROM THEIR ADOPTED CONCEPTS RELATED TO STANDARDS IN THE UNITED STATES OF AMERICA,WHICH IS A DOCTRINE THAT THE MAJORITY OF AFRICAN AMERICANS SHARE AND ADHERE TO, AND THE HABITUAL DEMAGOGUERY IS PRESISTENT IN AN EFFORT TO OBTAIN DEPRIVED RESTITUTION WHEN BLACKS THEM SELVES ARE THE REAL CULPRITS OF IGNORANCE, TO THE CIRCUMSTANCES THAT EXIST,THE CYNICAL SIMULTANEOUS ATTRACTION TO BE REPUGNANT, IS DUE TO THE INABILITY TO GRASP FUNDAMENTAL ISSURES THAT IS STANDARD MORAL VALUES OF AMERICA, CAN BE ATTRIBUTED TO A DOCILE EXPERIENCE MANY YEARS AGO, FROM SOUTHERN PLANTATION SLAVE OWNERS, WHICH THROUGH ILLITERACY BLACKS WERE FORCED TO BECOME BEHOLDEN DUE TO A SOPHISTICATED REALIGNMENT OF BONDAGE CALLED SHARE CROPPING,AFTER BEING EMANCIPATED FROM SLAVERY DURING EIGHTEEN SIXTY FIVE, IN ORDER TO CREATE SOLUTIONS IN AN EFFORT FOR RESOLVING PROBLEMS AND DISPUTES, YOU MUST EVALUATE AND DECIPHER ALSO UNDERSTAND WHY AND HOW IT WAS ORIGINATED, AFRICAN AMERICANS WAS CREATED WHEN PRESIDENT ANDREW JOHNSON RESCINDED THE ASSASSINATED PRESIDENT LINCOLN PLAN TO GIVE EACH AFRICAN AMERICAN FAMILY FORTY ACRES

OF SOUTHERN LAND AND A GOVERNMENT MULE, AND BLACKS WAS FORCED TO RETURN TO THEIR SLAVE MASTERS BASED ON ILLITERACY, THAT WAS AN OPPRESSION EQUAL TO BONDAGE, WHICH THE SOUTHERN DEMOCRATIC PLANTATION OWNERS CONTROLLED THEIR LIVES AND DICTATED GUIDE LINES TO DISCOURAGE LITERACY, ALSO DEPRIVED AFRICAN AMERICANS FROM ATTAINING ANY DEGREE OF KNOWLEDGE ABOUT ANYTHING OTHER THAN FARMING, SO AS A RESULT OF THAT AGENDA THEY CREATED A VAST GENETIC UNBALANCE IN SOCIETY THAT IS DEPENDABLE, BECAUSE (WITH OUT) THE REFINEMENT OF INTELLECTUAL SUFFICIENT SKILLS TO ADJUST MRAL VALUES BECOME OBSOLESCENCE, AND TO COMPOUND THE ISSURE WAS THE JIM CROW RULE OF SEPERATE BUT EQUAL, WHICH DENIED BLACKS PRIVILEGE OF INTRODUCTION TO HOSPITABLE TREATMENT OF DISPOSITION TO RECEPTION, SO MOST HERDED TOGATHER ISOLATED THEM SELVES AND CONFORMED TO MADE UP VALUES OF DECEIT MINIPULATING AND DISDAIN FOR LIKE OF EQUALITY, DURING THE FORTIES BLACKS WERE OFTEN TAUNTED BY SOUTHERN WHITES REGARDS TO THEIR IGNORANCE AND HUMILATED WITH INSULTING REMARKS THAT SCHOOLING WAS FOR WHITE FOLKS ONLY, BECAUSE IT WOULD NOT THEM ANY WAY WHERE WOULD THEY USE IT, SO SOME BLACKS BEGAN TO ACCEPT THIS DOCTRINE AND MANY WOULD NOT INSIST THAT THEIR CHILDREN ATTEND SCHOOL, AND CONSTANTLY STIPULATED THE DOCTRINE THAT EDUCATION WAS FOR WHITE FOLKS, THIS INEPTNESS CREATED A AIR OF FRUSTRATION WHICH WHEN THEY HAD FREE TIME THEY HERDED TOGATHER IN PLACES ON SATURDAY NIGHTS THAT WAS CALLED HOE DOWN JUKING, AND THESE PLACES WERE RESPONSIBLE FOR MANY VIOLENT ACTS CUTTINGS, STABBINGS, AND OCCASIONAL DEATH BY STABBING, MOSTLY DUE TO THEIR BECOMING INEBRIATED FROM MOON SHINE LIQUOR, IF THE COUNTY SHERIFF HAD TO BE CALLED AND A ARREST WAS MADE, THEY WOULD BE SET FREE IN A MATTER OF HOURS, BECAUSE THE SHERIFF WOULD CALL THE PLANTATION OWNER WHERE THE BLACK LIVED AND WORKED, AND INFORM THAT HE HAD

ARRESTED ONE OF HIS NIGGERS FOR STABBING ANOTHER NIGGER AND WHAT SHOULD HE DO, THE PLANTATION OWNER WOULD ADVISE LET THAT NIGGER GO HE WOULD SETTLE UP LATER, BECAUSE HE NEEDED HIM FOR WORK MONDAY MORNING, AND OCCASIONALLY BLACK ON BLACK MURDERS WERE SETTLED THAT WAY, BECAUSE THE VICTOM FAMILY AND WITNESSES REFUSED TO COMMENT ON THE ACT, FEAR OF REPRISAL FROM THE KU-KLUX-KLAN.

AFRICAN AMERICANS LIVED AND SURVIVED UNDER THESE EXTORTIONATELY CONDITIONS MOST MINAS EDUCATION AND MORAL VALUES FOR A HUNDRED YEARS, IN THE INTERIM THEY WERE PRODUCING AND RAISING FAMILIES AND SOME WERE INDOCTRINATING THEIR CHILDREN TO STANDARDS OF NONE EDUCATION, AND FOR DECADES THESE CHILDRENS GREW INTO ADULTS AND MIGRATED ALL OVER THE UNITED STATES OF AMERICA, AND STARTED FAMILIES OF THEIR OWN, UNFORTUNATELY GENETIC HERITAGE CONTROL DICTATE YOUR MOTIVATIONS THAT DETERMINE YOUR SUCCESSES AND FAILURES IN LIFE, AND THE MAJORITY OF ALL PEOPLE ARE UNAWARE OF THESE MAGNETIZING KINDRED DISTINGUISHED QUALITIES, AND FOR CERTAIN GENETIC CONTROLLABILITY AUTOMATICALLY WITH OUT YOUR AWARENESS ADJUST YOUR EMULATION TO YOUR PARENTS, AND THE MAJORITY OF THE TIME YOU ARE HELPLESS TO MODIFY SOME OF THE CHARACTERISTICS, SO THIS IS WHY NTELLECTUAL CAPABILITIES AND MORAL VALUES ARE EXTREMELY IMPORTANT AND ABSOLUTELY NECESSARY BECAUSE IT TEND TO MINIMIZE GENETIC REBELLIOUS RADICAL BEHAVIOR, THERE ARE THOSE THAT WILL ARGUE SCHOOLS WERE AVAILABLE TO BLACKS IN THE SOUTH FOR LEARNING WHICH IS TRUE, SOME WERE TAUGHT AND LEARNED, AND MANY DIDNT BECAUSE OF OBSTINACY RELATED TO HOME ENVIRONMENT, ALSO THE MAJORITY OF EDUCATORS WERE BLACK, THAT HAD BEEN INTIMIDATED BY JIM CROW RULE, SO MANY OF THEIR TEACHINGS WERE DIVISIVE AND INSTIGATED REBELLIOUS IDEALS AGAINST WHITES, THAT WAS CAUSED BY SOUTHERN DEMOCRAT PLANTATION OWNERS DENUNCIATION AND DENIAL OF

THEIR EQUAL RIGHTS, AS A RESULT THEY FELT COMPELLED TO HOLD (ALL) CAUCASIANS ACCOUNTABLE, AND THE MAJORITY IF NOT ALL DID NOT HAVE THE INTELLECTUAL ABILITY OF INTELLIGENCE TO DIFFERENTIATE BETWEEN CONSERVATIVE AND LIBERAL IDEOLOGY THEN,AND ONE HUNDRED FORTY ONE YEARS LATER STILL (DONT), AND THE REASON WHY THEY CHERISH AND SUPPORT LIBERALISM IS BECAUSE IT COINCIDE WITH THEIR MAKESHIFT GENETIC DEMEANOR OF CHRONOLOGICAL SIGNIFICANT EVENTS YEARS AGO, THAT SUBSTITUTED MORAL INTELLECTUAL VALUES FOR IMMORAL DEPENDENT COMPLACENCY, AND THAT GENETIC CONTROLLED IDEOLOGY HAS AGGRESSIVELY ESCALATED AND EVOLVED INTO CRIMINAL ACTIVITY NATION WIDE, AND GENERATED A THIRTY PERCENT DESTITUTION FOR AFRICAN AMERICANS,

THERE ARE MANY ILLADVISED AFFLUENT BLACK DEMOCRATIC LIBERALS THAT ARE INEPT TO THE CHRONOLOGICAL EVENTS OF THE PAST, AND IF THEY ARE THEIR ASSERTED EFFORTS TO SYSTEMATICALLY CONTINUALLY DEFEND AND DISTORT THE IMPACT THAT SOME BLACKS EGREGIOUSLY PORTRAYED IN INDUCING THEIR (OWN) DESTITUTION IS APPALLING AND STUPIDLY HYPERCRITICAL.

THERE IS (NO) DENYING THAT THE KU-KLUX-KLAN CONTROLLED THE SOUTHERN STATES, BECAUSE THEY INFILTRATED POLICE DEPARTMENTS THROUGH OUT SOUTHERN CITIES THAT GAVE THEM LEGAL PERMISSION TO ENGAGE IN ANY BARBARIC ACT OF THEIR CHOOSING, AND IF THEY WERE BROUGHT TO TRIAL FOR HIDEOUS CRIMES AGAINST BLACKS ALL WHITE JURORS WOULD NOT CONVICT, AND THE SAME WAS FOR ANY WHITE THAT SYMPATHIZED WITH CAUSES FOR BLACKS, THE FEDERAL INSTITUTION HAD TO DO THE HEAVY LIFTING THAT WEAKEN THE KU-KLUX-KLAN POWER STRUCTURE IN THE SOUTHERN STATES, BECAUSE VICIOUS UNLAWFUL KILLINGS BECAME SUCH A AGREGIOUS AND SADISTIC EVENT AGAINST BLACKS AND SOME WHITES WITH REGULARITY, REGARDS TO ASSASSINATING BLACK MILITARY SERVICE MEN ALONG PUBLIC ROADS, HUNTING DOWN INNOCENT

BLACKS SLASHING THEIR THROATS AND HANGING THEM, KIDNAPPING BLACK AND WHITES SHOOTING THEM POINT BLANK AND BURYING THEM IN SECRECY, SHOOTING WHITE WOMEN THAT WAS SYMPATHETIC TO BLACK CAUSES, DYNAMITING LITTLE GIRLS IN CHURCH, THESE ATROCITIES BECAME SO MAGNIFIED UNTIL IT ATTRACTED THE ATTENTION OF THE NATION, ALSO THE CONCERNS OF PRESIDENT LYNDON JOHNSON DURING THE SIXTIES, WHICH F.B.I. DIRECTOR J. EDGAR HOOVER WAS THE DRIVING FORCE IN INFILTRATING THE KU-KLUX-KLAN THAT CAUSED A REDUCTION IN THEIR EFFORTS TO MAIM AFRICAN AMERICANS, AND ALONG WITH THIS EFFORT TO QUELL VIOLENCE,AND THE FEAR OF LOOSING AFRICAN AMERICAN VOTERS BACK TO THE REPUBLICAN PARTY, GAVE PRESIDENT JOHNSON LEVERAGE TO THERATEN THE DEMOCRATIC CONTROLLED CONGRESS ALONG WITH SOLIDARITY FROM THE REPUBLICANS INCENTIVE TO GET THE CIVIL AND VOTING RIGHTS ACTS RATIFIED TO THE CONSTUTION FOR AFRICAN AMERICANS IN NINETEEN SIXTY FOUR AND SIXTY FIVE, AS YOU ARE AWARE THAT WAS OVER FORTY ONE YEARS AGO, IT IS ESSENTIAL THAT AFRICAN AMERICANS UNDERSTAND THAT NINETEEN SIXTY FOUR AND SIXTY FIVE WAS THE YEARS OF RECKONING FOR (ALL) AFRICAN AMERICANS TO SEIGE THEIR PRIVILEGES THROUGH EDUCATION AND MORAL INTELLECTUAL VALUES, BUT UNFORTUNATELY SOME REVERTED OR NEVER REFRAIN FROM SUBSIDES THAT THEY RELIED ON PRIOR TO THE RATIFYING OF THEIR EQUALITY, AND THEY CONSISTENTLY CARRY THE WATER FOR THOSE THAT WERE RESPONSIBLE FOR (ALL) THE ATROCITIES THAT OCCURRED TO THEM, WHICH WERE THE SOUTHERN DEMOCRAT PLANTATION OWNERS, AND THERE ARE THOSE SELF APPOINTED BLACK JUDAS HORNED RUMINANTS CONSTANTLY SPREADING NONSENSICAL DEMAGOGUERY AS IF THE RATIFICATION FOR BLACK EQUALITY (NEVER) HAPPENED, AND THE KU-KLUX-KLAN IS STILL IN POWER INTIMIDATING AND VIOLATING THE RIGHTS OF AFRICAN AMERICANS TO PROHIBIT THEIR PRIVILEGES, AND ALL THIS FOOLISH ERRONEOUS DECEIT IS TO SUSTAIN VOTES FROM

BLACKS FOR THE DEMOCRATIC PARTY, THAT SERVE AS A TWOFOLD PURPOSE BLACKS REMAIN LOYAL TO THE PARTY, ALSO INCREASE THAT THIRTY PERCENT OF DESTITUTION FOR BLACKS THAT SWALLOW THEIR INAPPROPIATE PUKE OF INSANITY, BECAUSE IF SEVENTY PERCENT OF AFRICAN AMERICANS CAN PAVE THEIR WAY TO SUCCESS DUE TO GRANTED EQUAL PRIVILEGES, IT DOES NOT TAKE A BRANCH OF SYSTEMATIC STUDY TO DETERMINE THE PROBLEMS WITH THE OTHER THIRTY PERCENT, THAT BLACK POLITICAL PARASITES ADVOCATES ARE CLAIMING SOME ONE NEED TO LEVEL THE PLAYING FIELD FOR, THESE THIRTY PERCENT OF MIS-FITS HAVE A CONTAGIOUS DYSFUNCTIONAL MINDED DISEASE, THAT IS CALLED SPORADIC DEMENTIA THAT IS RELATED TO REBELLING FROM EDUCATION INTELLECTUAL MORAL VALUES, AND THE AVOIDANCE OF A PAID OCCUPATION, THESE GENETIC DIDTINGUISHED QUALITIES ARE HISTORICALLY FORMULATED THROUGH ANCESTRY, AND TO CURE IS EXTREMELY REMOTE, BECAUSE THERE IS NO COLLECTIVE SENSE OF DIGNITY AND SELF CONTROLLED RESPONSIBILITY REGARDS TO MORAL VALUES, IT IS A FAR GONE CONCLUSION THAT THE AMERICAN HISTORY OF AFRICAN AMERICANS BEGAN IN THE SOUTHERN STATES, TOTALLY INCOMPETENT TO THE FUNDAMENTALS OF A CIVILIZE SOCIETY THAT TAKE PRIDE IN INTELLECTUAL MORAL VALUES, UNFORTUNATELY DEMOCRATIC SOUTHERN PLANTATION SLAVE OWNERS USED THIS INEPTNESS OF AFRICANS AS AN ADVANTAGE FOR RESOURCES TO CONTROL, AND THAT POLITICAL DIPLOMACY STILL EXIST TODAY WITH APPROXIMATELY NINETY FIVE PERCENT OF BLACKS SUPPORTING DEMOCRATIC IDEOLOGY OF TYRANNY PERPETRATED AGAINST THEM DURING THE SIXTIES, WHICH DENIED THEM PRIVILEGES TO BE TAUGHT AND ADVISED OF THEIR RIGHTS UNDER THE CONSTITUTION, BECAUSE THROUGHOUT THE SOUTHERN KU-KLUX-KLAN CONTROLLED STATES, LEARNING INSTITUTIONS FOR BLACKS WAS RELUCTANT OR NEVER TAUGHT CONSTITUTIONAL RIGHTS AT ALL, BECAUSE THE SOUTHERN PLANTATION OWNERS AND THEIR FOLLOWERS UNDER DEMOCRATIC SUPERVISION

RESCINDED THOSE RIGHTS UNDER THE SEPERATE BUT EQUAL JIM CROW RULE DOCTRINE WHICH HELD FOR SEVENTY YEARS, SO AS A RESULT OF THIS DISPARAGEMENT OF OSTRACISM,THE MAJORITY OF AFRICAN AMERICANS TO INCLUDE THE AFFLUENT EDUCATED, ARE INEPT TO THE DIPLOMATIC SOPHISTICATED ESSENCE OF PERSUASIVE DEMAGOGUERY EXECUTED BY THE POLITICAL POWER HUNGRY DEMOCRATS, THAT HAS SEDUCED THE MAJORITY OF AFRICAN AMERICANS TO POLITICALLY SUPPORT THEIR CAUSE.OF HIDDEN DECEIT, THIS IS THE YEAR TWO THOUSAND SIX AND THE MAJORITY OF OLDER BLACKS WILL INSIST THAT POLITICS ARE FOR WHITE FOLKS, AND IF THEY VOTE ITS BECAUSE OTHER BLACKS SAID THE POLITICAN IN QUESTION WAS FOR THEM, AND ONLY IF THEY ARE A DEMOCRAT, THIS DERANGED OBSESSION OF BLACKS FOR DEMOCRATIC POLITICIANS IS A LEGENDARY GENETIC SYSTEMATIC POLITICAL HERDING DISTRUCTION, BECAUSE THE MAJORITY WILL (NEVER) UNDERSTAND THE FUNDAMENTAL CONJUNCTION IMPACTED BY POLITICAL ASPIRATIONS, THAT HAS CAUSED A THIRTY PERCENT DESTITUTION IN AFRICAN AMERICAN.SOCIETY, SIMPLY BECAUSE THEY ARE STILL WAITING FOR PROMISED POLITICAL COMPENSATION FROM THEIR.SELF APPOINTED LEADERS REGARDS TO EQUALITY, AND IS INEPT TO THE FACT THAT IT WAS CONSUMMATED RATIFIED TO THE CONSTITUTION BY THE CONGRESS OVER FORTY ONE YEARS AGO, THESE F.B.I. DIRECTOR J. EDGAR HOOVER DYSFUNCTIONAL SMALL BRAIN INSIDIOUS LUNATICS, THAT HERD AND ADHERE TO THESE ERRONEOUS COERCED LIES OF BEING TOLD WHAT THEY WANT TO HEAR, WHICH IS COMPOSED BY LIBERAL DEMOCRATIC DOCTRINES IN AN EFFORT TO KEEP BLACKS VOTING BLOC CONSOLIDATED, WHILE A SEGEMENT OF BLACKS CONSTANTLY HEAD OF TO THE SLUMS AND IMMORAL DESTITUTION.

IT IS ENORENORMOUSLY DEPRESSING AND DISCOURAGING TO WATCH THE INFLUX EXHIBITED BY SOME AFFLUENT BLACKS FOR THE EGOISTIC CRIMINAL BEHAVIOR THAT EXACERBATE THE CAUSE OF OTHER REBELLIOUS BLACKS, CNN HEADLINE NEWS 09/12/2006, EXHIBITED

THAT THERE ARE APPROXIMATELY ONE HUNDRED FIFTY THOUSAND EVACUEES RELOCATED FROM NEW ORLEAANS TO HOUSTON TEXAS TO ESCAPE THE HAVOCS OF KATRINA, AND THE MAJORITY WERE PREDOMINATELY AFRICAN AMERICANS, IT IS REPORTED ACCORDING TO THEIR STSTISTICS CRIMINAL AND MURDER ACTIVITY HAS RISEN APPROXIMATELY TWENTY FIVE PERCENT, WITH TWO HUNDRED SIXTY TWO KILLINGS, FIFTY NINE COMMITTED BY BLACKS AND THEIR POPULATION IS LESS THAN SEVEN PERCENT, THE CITIZENS OF HOUSTON HAVE BECAME ALARMING DISCOURAGED AND ARE PUBLICLY REQUESTING RELIEF TO DISPEL NEW ORLEANS MIGRATED INHABITANTS, THE MAYOR OF HOUSTON BILL WHITE STRONGLY INFORMED THE AUDIENCE THAT SWIFT ACTION IS AND WILL BE TAKEN TO CURVE VIOLENCE, AND MANY WILL HAVE RESIDENTS IN THEIR JAILS INSTEAD OF BACK HOME TO NEW ORLEANS, THE MAYOR OF NEW ORLEANS RAY NAGEN CHIMED IN WITH A RESPONSE,AND HIS COMMENTS WERE THAT HOUSTON JUSTICE SYSTEM IS MUCH TOUGHER THAN WHAT THE NEW ORLEANS INHABITANTS ARE ACCUSTOM TO DURING THE PAST, HIS INSINUATIONS ARE DIFFICULT TO DECIPHER FOR CLARITY, BECAUSE HE SEEM TO IMPLY THAT LAW ENFORCEMENT IN NEW ORLEANS WHICH CONSIST OF A POLICE FORCE AND JUDGES, ARE (NOT) COMPETETIVE TO ARREST AND PROSECUTE AS OTHER CITIES FOR HEINOUS CRIMES SUCH AS MURDER, RAPE AND ROBBERY AS IT IS OCCURING IN HOUSTON, IT APPEAR THAT HE GAVE THE LAW ENFORCEMEMENT IN HIS CITY THAT HE IS THE MAYOR OF A SHOT BELOW THE BELT, OF COURSE THIS IS NOTHING UNUSAL MAY BE THIS IS HOW IT WORK IN A ALL CHOCOLATE CITY WHICH HE PREDICTED IF HE WAS RELECTED, TO REINFORCE MY SUSPICIONS ABOUT BLACKS IN THE SOPHISTICATED POLITICAL ARENA, THE MAJORITY ARE INEPT TO THE INTRICATE FUNDAMENTALS, MAYOR RAY NAGIN OF NEW ORLEANS IS A FINE SPECIMEN FOR THAT CANDIDACY FIRST HE SPEAKS HIS TRUE HERDING INSTINCTS ABOUT A ALL CHOCOLATE CITY BEING IN NEW ORLEANS WHICH CONSIST OF A MAJORITY OF BLACKS THAT IS HOBBLING WITH DESTITUTION, THEN HE ALLOW

HIM SELF TO BE INTERVIEWED BY THE NEWS MEDIA AND MAKE USE OF THE TIME TO BESMIRCH THE INTEGRITY OF A SACRED AREA IN NEW YORK CITY, WHERE THREE THOUSAND INNOCENT PEOPLE LOST THEIR LIVES TO TERRORIST ATTACKS, BY INEXPLICABLE DECLARING IT TO BE JUST A HOLE IN THE GROUND, SOME BLACKS TEND TO THINK BECAUSE THEY ARE FORTUNATE ENOUGH TO BE ELECTED TO OFFICE WITH A CLUSTERED AREA OF AFRICAN AMERICAN CONSTITUENTS THAT THEY ARE CHAMPIONS OF THE POLITICAL ARENA, AND OFTEN GO ON A HABITUALLY COURSE OF DOCTRINES THAT IS INEFFECTIVE AND DEMORALIZING TO THE TRAITS AND DISTINCTIONS OF OTHERS, AND ONCE THEY ARE ALERTED TO THEIR ECCENTRIC BEHAVIOR THEY TEND TO TRY AND EXPLAIN IT AWAY WITH FOOLISH INNUENDO, WHICH ESTABLISH THE FACT THAT SOME ARE NOT QUALIFIED TO FUNCTION APPROPRIATELY WITH IN THE CONFINES OF A WELL ESTABLISHED SOPHISTICATED POLITICAL ARENA, FOR INSTANCE NEW ORLEANS MAYOR RAY NAGIN GOES TO NEW YORK CITY IN AN ATTEMPT TO SOLICIT CAUCASIANS FUNDS TO REESTABLISH HIS CHOCOLATE CITY OF HURRICANE KATRINA RUBBLE, AFTER REFERRING TO THEIR CITY TERRORIST DISASTER AS A HOLE IN THE GROUND, AND WHAT REALLY DESTABILIZE HIS CREDIBILITY AS BEING INADEQUATE TO LEAD, WHEN HE CHOSE TO RESPOND ABOUT THE CRIMINAL ELEMENTS THAT IS OCCURRING IN HOUSTON FROM NEW ORLEAN INHABITANTS, AND SUGGESTED THAT HOUSTON JUSTICE SYSTEM IS TOUGH ON CRIME, AND NEW ORLEANS RESIDENTS ARE NOT ACCUSTOM TO THIS IN THE PAST, STATEMENTS OF THIS NATURE COMING FROM A CITY MAYOR SEEM TO IMPUGN THE INTEGRITY OF LAW ENFORCEMENT IN THE CITY RAN BY HIM AS BEING SOFT ON CRIMINALS, DUE TO THE FUNDAMENTAL BASIC QUALITY OF THESE EPISODES, OUT BURST OF THIS NATURE IS CONSIDERED TO BE POLITICAL SELF DESTRUCTION, HOWEVER NOT LIKELY FOR THE PUBLIC FIGURE, BUT MOST LIKELY FOR HIS SUPPORTING CONSTITUENCY, THIS IS JUST ONE EXAMPLE THAT DEMONSTRATE THE LIKE OF FORTITUDE TO UNDER-STAND THE FUNDAMENTAL

REPRECUSSIONS OF POLITICAL BLUNDERS THAT CAN BE A DISASTROUS FATE, UNFORTUNATELY MANY BLACKS THAT CLIMB THE POLITICAL LADDER NEVER REACH THE TOP RUNG BECAUSE OF THEIR INEPTNESS TO REALIZE POLITICAL CONSEQUENCES, AND THIS IS DUE TO THE LIKE OF INDEPTH THINKING, AND SOME WILL ARGUE THAT WHITES DO THE SAME IDENTICAL THING, WHICH IS TRUE, BUT THERE IS A FUNDAMENTAL DIFFERENCE IN CAUCASIANS ASPIRATIONS AND APPROACH RELATED TO POLITICAL AFFAIRS THAT IS GENERATED FROM GENETIC CONTROL WITH-IN THE POLITICAL STRUCTURE, THEY UNDERSTAND AND ARE ACCUSTOM TO THE HIDDEN DANGERS THAT EXIST, BUT WILL CHALLENGE THE EVIDENCE OF QUALIFICATION ON A DARE IN AN ATTEMPT TO OUT WIT THE SYSTEM BASED ON INTELLECTUAL DIPLOMACY,BECAUSE OF THEIR BEING HISTORICALLY UNITED WITH IN THE POLITICAL ARENA WITH A HIDDEN AGENDA THE MAJORITY OF THE TIME, AND IF FAILURE SHOULD OCCUR BASED ON BLUNDERS THEY WILL RELY ON THEIR PREVIOUS EXPERIENCES AND ASSOCIATED CONTACTS, IN AN EFFORT TO RECTIFY, BUT IF NOT THEY WILL REGRETFULLY ACCEPT THE CONSEQUENCES AS A SEVERELY TRYING EXPERIENCE PACK THEIR BAGS AND MOVE ON.

THE PRACTICAL POLITICAL ASPIRATIONS OF AFRICAN AMERICANS,ISANATTEMPTTOEMULATEANDHISTORICALLY BEING OUT SIDE OF THE POLITCAL ARENA, THEIR OBJECTIVES ARE CONCEITED IN AN EFFORT TO SOLIDIFY ADVERSITY AS SOME KIND OF A CRUSADE FOR ANARCHISM THAT THEY ASSUME TO BE POLITICALLY PERPETRATED AGAINST OTHER BLACKS,WHICH DILUTE DIVERSITY THAT IS THE RECIPE TO FUNDAMENTAL COHESION FOR. THE CONCEPTS OF OUR NATION, AND AS A RESULT THE CONSTITUENCY THAT SUPPORT AND BELIEVE IN THESE PEOPLE ARE THE LOOSERS, BECAUSE WHEN POLITICAL EROSION BECOMES A FACTOR REGARDS TO CREDIBILITY OR FINANCIAL APPREHENSIVE DISDAIN TO SUPPORT THEIR CAUSE FROM OTHERS, THEIR POLITICAL RECOURSES ARE LIMITED DUE TO HISTORICAL DEPRIVATIONS FROM THE POLITICAL ARENA UNTIL NINETEEN SIXTY FOUR AND

SIXTY FIVE IN THE SOUTHERN STATES, WHENCE THE MAJORITY OF AFRICAN AMERICANS DERIVED FROM, SO THERE IS (NO) CHRONOLOGICAL ANCESTRIAL GENETIC AWARENESS OF LATITUDE TO SUSTAIN, OTHER THAN NONSENSICAL INNUENDOS OF IT HAPPEN BECAUSE WE ARE BLACK, AND AS A RESULT OF HERDING AND I GOT YOUR BACK BROTHER TYPE OF SYNDROME,THIS IS HIGH PROFILE POLITICAL SELF DESTRUCTION, ALSO ENDORSE A ILLEGITIMATE CONTENTION TO DISTORT FOR THE LIKE OF HAVING INGENUITY RELATED TO MORAL VALUES THAT HAS CREATED A THIRTY PERCENT POVERTY STRIKEN RLENTLESS DESTITUTION FOR BLACKS IN AMERICA.

AND THIS RADIO ACTIVE AGENDA IS STIMULATED BY DECEPTIVE ELECTED BLACK POLITICANS AND SELF APPOINTED LEADERS THAT UNITE IN AN EFFORT TO DISTORT ISSURES FOR PERSONAL NOTORIETY, AND THIS HERDING PROCESS IS DEVASTATING TO MILLIONS OF BLACKS THAT FOLLOW AND BELIEVE THIS CONTAMINATED DEMAGOGUERY PROPOSED BY THESE SELF MADE BIGOT PARASITES, THAT IS RESPONSIBLE FOR THE MALIGNANT TUMOR OF IGNORANCE THAT IS EATING AWAY AT A THIRD OF AFRICAN AMERICAN SOCIETY, THAT PROHIBIT THEIR INTELLECTUAL AND ECONOMIC SUSTAINING SKILLS OF EFFICIENCY FROM INTEGRATING INTO A DIVERSE SOCIETY THAT THEY THEM SELVES HAVE UTILIZED TO SUSTAIN AND BECOME FINANCIALLY FIRMLY ESTABLISHED, YET THEY FORMULATE BACK WOODS CONGO DYSFUNCTIONAL THEORIES OF ASSUMPTIONS TO CREATE GENERAL COLLECTIVE OPENIONS THAT DESECRATE THEIR FOLLOWERS INTO A LETHARGIC STUPENDOUS DISGRACE THAT LEAD TO INSURMOUNTABLE CRIME AND DESTITUTION,LETS JUST ANALYTICALLY FOCUS ON HURRICANE KATRINA ONE OF THE WORST CATASTROPHE DISASTERS IN AMERICAN HISTORY,TO DESTRUCTIVELY INVADE THE COAST OF LOUISIANS AND MISSISSIPPI, WITH THE CITY OF NEW ORLEANS BEING ENGULFED WITH FLOODING WATERS, AND BASED ON FUNDAMENTAL NEGLECT NONE CORPORATION OF SOCIETY WITH IN THE CHARACTERISTICS NATURAL ENVIRONMENT OF THE CITY,

WHICH HAD ELECTED A MAYOR RAY N. AGIN THAT WAS INCOMPETENT AND LACKING A SENSE OF RESPONSIBILITY, FOR THEIR CAUSES, THAT CHOOSE TO EXEMPLIFY THIS CRISIS AS A STRUCTUAL DESIGN CONSPIRACY TO DELAY ASSISTANCE BECAUSE THE MAJORITY OF THE PEOPLE WERE BLACK, AND ACCORDING TO HISTORIAN DOUGLAS BRINKLEY, FOX NEWS SEPTEMBER 4, 2006,THE MAYOR WAS CUTTLED AWAY IN A COZY CONFORTABLE HOTEL SUITE,DICTATING MONOLOGUES OF DEROGATORY PROFANITY, AND AFRAID TO EMERGE DUE TO HIS CITY BEING INUNDATED WITH THIEVING CRIMINALS, AND NEGLECTED TO INTERCEDE REGARDS TO GUIDANCE AND COMPASSION WHICH IS DEPLORABLE, AND DENOUNCE EVERY ONE ELSE FOR NOT DOING ENOUGH, UNFORTUNATELY THESE SENTIMENTS ARE BESTOWED ON SOME BLACK POLITICANS THAT FORFEIT THEIR ADHERENCE TO A CODE OF INTELLECTUAL MORAL VALUES, AND ATTEMPT TO SEDUCE THE GENERAL PUBLIC WITH AMBIGUOUS INNUENDO OF RACISM, THAT IS ENDORSED BY DEMOCRATIC LIBERALS BLACK AND WHITE NATION WIDE, IN AN EFFORT TO MAINTAIN THE HERDING PROCESS OF BLACK VOTERS, MAYOR RAY NAGIN IS A TYPICAL EXAMPLE OF BLACK ELECTED LEADERS IN POLITICAL POSITIONS THAT ARE SUPPOSE TO MAKE CRUCIAL DECISIONS, BUT THE MAJORITY OF THE TIME THEY GET ELECTED BASE ON A HEAVY POPULATED AREA OF BLACK CONSTITUENCY THAT VOTE FOR THEM BECAUSE THEY ARE BLACK, WHICH IS A GENETIC HERDING FORMALITY THAT PLAGUE THE MAJORITY OF AFRICAN AMERICANS THROUGHOUT THEIR HISTORY, AND BEING DEPRIVED OF THE FUNDAMENTAL INTRICACIES OF POLITICS THROUGHOUT THE SOUTHERN STATES UNTIL NINETEEN SIXTY FOUR AND SIXTY FIVE DID NOT HELP THEIR ASPIRATIONS FOR POLITICAL ADVENTURES, AND YOU ARE (NOT) GOING TO BECOME A POLITICAL GURU IN FORTY SOME YEARS, PIRATIALLY WHEN WHEN YOUR GENETIC ANCESTRY WAS NOT CLOSELY ACQUAINTED WITH THE FUNDAMENTAL ASPECTS OF THE POLITICAL ARENA, MOST WHITES POLITICAL SKILLS ARE DEVELOPED FROM LONG LINES OF ANCESTRY, OR DEALING

WITH HUGE FINANCIAL EMPIRES THAT THEY OWN, OR AFFILIATIONS INTERNALLY AS CHIEF EXECUTIVE OFFICER WHERE POLITICS ARE PREVALENT, AND MOST LIKELY WILL PRODUCE SELF MADE MILLION AIRS THAT IS ACCESSIBLE TO NOTORIETY AND THEY CHOOSE TO PERSUE POLITICS IN AN EFFORT TO CONTRIBUTE TO THEIR AGENDA, MOST AFRICAN AMERICANS ENTER POLITCS FROM POOR OR MIDDLE CLASS FAMILES, WITH NO LONGEVITY ANCESTRIAL GUIDANCE OR NO DEVELOPED LEARNING ABILITIES ORGANIZING CORPORATE EMPIRES, AND MILLION AIRS ARE GENERATED THROUGH SPORTS OR HIP HOP AND MOST CAN BARELY READ, SO IF THEY ARE ECECTED TO SERVE CONSTITUENCIES THEY HAVENT THE ABILITY TO ORCHESTRATE FOR SUFFICIENT COLLABORATIONS, ALSO THE VAST MAJORITY OF AFRICAN AMERICAN VOTING CONSTITUENCY TEND TO SUPPORT A CANIDATE BASED ON SELFISH MOTIVES, EITHER BLACK OR WHITE BECAUSE MOST HAVE THIS MYTHICAL PRECONCEIVED NOTION THAT THEY ARE THE ONLY PEOPLE ON THE PLANET EARTH THAT NEEDS TO BE ADJUDICATED WITH PERSONAL ASSISTANCE, OTHER THAN WHAT HAS ALREADY BEEN ESTABLISHED BY CONGRESS, BLACKS HAVE A PREDICTABLE SAYING REFERRING TO POLITICIANS, AND THAT IS WHAT IS HE GOING TO DO FOR (US). AND LIBERAL POLITICAL PREPONDERATES ARE MAGNETIZED TO THIS CONVOLUTED PRECEPTION, AND FLOCK TO TAKE ADVANTAGE OF THIS INEPTNESS RELATED TO POLITICS,AND TELL THEM WHAT THEY WANT TO HEAR, CAUCASIANS POLITICIANS TELL THEM THEY SHARE THEIR FEELINGS AND IF THEY ARE ELECTED THEY ARE GOING TO ADOPT A POLICY FOR (THEM) TO THAT AFFECT, THE POLITICAL ASPIRATIONS OF AFRICAN AMERICANS ARE TWOFOLD THEY UTILIZE AND REFER TO WHITES AS BEING CONTROLLING MERCHANTS AND HAS CONSPIRED TO HENDER THEIR SUCCESS BECAUSE THEY ARE BLACK, AND IF HE IS ELECTED HE WILL CHANGE THE COURSE ON THEIR BEHALF,IN ORDER TO LEVEL THE PLAYING FIELD, AS MAYOR RAY NAGIN ASSERTED WITH HIS ALL CHOCOLATE CITY AND AS A RESULT THEY ARE SCATTERED ALL OVER THE NATION LOOKING FOR CONSESSIONS, AND THE REST

ARE SITTING ON A PILE OF HURRICANE KATRINA RUBBLE SOURROUNDED BY THUGGISH DRUG DEALING CRIMINALS IN NEW ORLEANS,WHICH RAY NAGIN IS THE MAYOR AND ARE OVERSEEING, BECAUSE THEY WANTED SOME ONE IN OFFICE TO DO SOMETHING ESPECIALLY FOF THEM,THAT IS ONE OF THEM.

THERE ARE TORTUOUS VACUUMS THAT MOST AFRICAN AMERICANS ARE CONSTANTLY SUCCUMB TO IN POLITICS, BECAUSE OF THEIR INEPTNESS TO THE FUNDAMENTALS, BLACKPOLITICIANSINALIENABLEFORTITUDEISTOSECLUDE THEM SELVES AND THEIR CONSTITUENCY FROM MAIN STREAM AMERICA, WHICH CONSIST OF CONGLOMERATE PYRAMIDS OF FINANCIALLY STABLE TYCONS THAT CONTROL THE UNIVERSE, AND RESORT TO PANDERING BLACK BUISNESS OWNERS AS A SHOW OF CREATIVE DISSENSION WITH IMPLICATIONS THAT THEY CAN RECONSTRUCT NEW ORLEANS, AS REPRESENTATIVE MAXINE WATERS AND MEL WATT FROM THE BLACK CAUCUS DEMONSTRATED ON C-SPAN SEPTEMBER 8, 2006, AND THIS IS MOST LIKELY WHY DURING HIS LIFE TIME J. EDGAR HOOVER F.B.I. DIRECTOR SUGGESTED BLACKS HAVE TWENTY PERCENT SMALLER BRAINS THAN WHITES, UNFORTUNATELY THIS IS NOTHING MORE THAN A POLITICAL STUNT TO CONSOLIDATE THEIR BLACK CONSTITUENCY IN THEIR PROSPECTIVE STATES FOR NOTORIETY ACQUIESCES BLACK CAUCUS,WHICH IS DIVISIVE IN CONGENIALITY TO OTHERS THAT OPPOSE THEIR VIEWS MOST POLITICAL BLACK ELECTED LEADERS AND THEIR CAST OF SELF APPOINTEES, ARE PREOCCUPIED INTENSELY WITH A DYFUNCTIONAL IDEOLOGY THAT THE MAJORITY OF THE DIVERSIFIED NATION SHOULD ADOPT THEIR THEORY OF EQUAL BUT SEPERATE, AND SUBSIDIZE THEIR INALIENABLE QUEST FOR BLACK INDEPENDENCE IN AMERICA, AFTER THE REPUBLICAN CONGRESS OF EIGHTEEN SIXTY SIX PASSED THE CIVIL RIGHTS ACT AND THE FOURTEENTH AMENDMENT TO THE CONSTITUTION WITH PROVISIONS GUARANTEEING AFRICAN AMERICANS CITIZENSHIP EQUAL TO ALL, AND IT IS QUITE APPARENT THAT SOME BLACK POLITICIANS ARE TOTALLY UNAWARE OF THE RATIFYING, ALSO INEPT TO THE FACT THAT THERE

ARE (NO) FINANCIAL INSTITUTIONS OR INDUSTRIAL ASSEMBLIES BLACK OWNED WILL ATTEMPT TO RESURRECT NEW ORLEANS FROM THE KATRINA DISASTER, AND MOST INTELLECTUAL POLITICIANS WOULD BE AWARE AND NOT HAVE TO BE TOLD, SUCH AS REP. MAXINE WATERS WAS,FROM SOME OF THEIR ASSEMBLY OF BLACK BUISNESS OPERATIVES, ANY POLITICIAN BLACK OR WHITE CAN NOT ASTUTELY DECIPHER THE CONTRACTUAL SERVICE OBLIGATIONS AND THEIR FINANCIAL STATUS TO SUPPLY AND CARRY OUT PERFORMANCE, IS OBSESSED WITH IGNORANCE AND INAPPROPIATE TO BE A LEADER, BIG BUISNESS IS A CONGLOMERATE FORMED BY MERGERS AND AQUISITIONS OF OTHER COMPANIES UNRELATED AND GLOBALLY DIVERSIFIED THAT CONSIST OF CONTRACTORS AND SUB CONTRACTORS THAT HAVE (NO) COLOR BARRIERS PENDING LEGITMACY AND ADHERENCE TO A COMPETITIVE BIDDING PROCESS, WHICH APPARENTLY MAXINE WATERS NEVER HEARD OF, HUGE LUCRATIVE CONTRACTS ARE PREDOMINATELY ALWAYS AWARDED TO CAUCASIANS CONTRACTERS, BECAUSE OF THEIR FINANCIAL STABILITY AND THEIR EXPERTEES IN THE ABILITY TO HANDLE PRAGMATIC SITUATIONS REGARDS TO COST CUTTING PRACTICES AS LOWEST BIDDER, WHICH IS DUE TO THEIR ABUNDANT RESOURCES,THERE IS AN ORDINARY AMOUNT OF SUCCESSFUL AFRICAN AMERICAN BUISNESS OWNERS IN AMERICA, BUT TO EMBLEMATICALLY SUGGEST THAT THEY ARE EQUIPT AND EQUIVALENT IN RECOURSE STATUS AND HAVE THE POLITICAL INGENUITY TO REBUILD NEW ORLEANS, IS NOTHING MORE THAN A DECITFUL DEMOCRATS IC PROPAGANDA MYTH, WHICH IS A POTENTIAL PRELIMINARY OUT LINE OF AN AGENDA BEING DRAFTED TO DEMAGOGUE THE OPPOSING POLITICAL PARTY WITH DILUTED ALTERING DISDAINING INNUENDOS REGARDS TO THEIR PROHIBITING BLACKS FROM GETTING THE BIG CONTRACTS BASED ON RACE, HOWEVER IT DOES APPEAR THAT SOME AFRICAN AMERICANS ARE BEGINNING TO WEIGH THE PROSPERITY OF INFLUENCE COMING FROM THESE BLACK HYPERCRITICAL POLITICAL BOOT LICKING SLAVE DRIVERS FOR THE DEMOCRATIC PARTY,

DEMOCRATS HAVE BEEN AWARE OF GENETIC HERDING AFRICAN AMERICANS FOR HUNDREDS OF YEARS, AND HAVE SUFFICIENTLY USED BLACK INFLUENTIAL LEADERS TO HERD OTHER AFRICAN AMERICANS TOGATHER IN AN EFFORT TO SUPPORT THEIR IDEOLOGY AND MAINTAIN POLITICAL POWER, BGINNING IN EIGHTEEN NINETY FIVE WITH BOOKER T. WASHINGTON, WHICH WAS ONE OF THE WORST HE SUPPOSABLY COAXED BLACKS TO ADHERE TO THE JIM CROW RULE IN THE SOUTHERN STATES, BY IMPLYING THAT IT WAS IN EVITABLE AND REALLY WASNT A BAD DEAL, AND BLACKS LOST THEIR CIVIL AND VOTING RIGHTS FOR SEVENTY YEARS DUE TO THE SEPARATE BUT EQUAL RULING BY THE SUPREME COURT, AND THE SECOND MOST TRAGEDY TO OCCUR WITH AFRICAN AMERICANS THAT STILL EXIST TODAY, PRESIDENT FRANKLIN DELANO ROOSEVELT MADE USE OF, A. PHILIP RANDOLPH, ARNOLD HILL, WAALTER WHITE, BENJAMIN C. DAVIS, WILLIAM HASTIE,AND THE NEW WELFARE DEAL, DURING THE EARLY FORTIES TO LURE AFRICAN AMERICANS AWAY FROM THE REPUBLICAN PARTY, AND THE JUDAS GOATS THEY ARE HERDING BEHIND TODAY CONSIST OF JESSIE JACKSON, AL SHARPTON, TAVIS SMILEY MAXINE WATERS, AND MANY OTHERS THAT IS RESPONSIBLE FOR (NOT) ADVOCATING INTELLECTUAL MORAL VALUES RELATED TO EDUCATION, WHICH HAS CREATED A INFLUX OF CONGO IDEOLOGY SUBSTITUTION, THAT HAS CAUSED A THIRTY PERCENT DESTITUTION,CRIMINAL BEHAVIOR, AND DAILY EXTERMINATION OF EACH OTHER, AND THESE BLACK POLITICAL DEMOCRATIC BUFFOONISH PARASITES ARE BLAMING CAUCASIANS FOR NOT LEVELING THE PLAYING FIELD IN ORDER FOR THEM TO SECURE THEIR FINANCIAL EQUALITY.

THE DEMOCRATS HAVE ALWAYS KNOWN OF THIS UNIQUE GENETIC HERDING INSTINCT DEMONSTRATED BY MOST AFRICAN AMERICANS, AND HAS EFFECTIVELY UTILIZED TO THEIR ADVANTAGE FOR HUNDREDS OF YEARS,DURING AND AFTER SLAVERY, EVEN TODAY THE MAJORITY OF BLACKS GIVE DEMOCRATS CARTE BLANCHE TITLE TO THEIR VOTING RIGHTS IN ORDER TO SECURE AND MAINTAIN

POLITICAL POWER AS A COURTESY TO PROLIFERATE THEIR EXPULSION INTO IMMORAL VALUES AND RADICAL DESTITUTION, FORTUNATELY THEIR MESMERIZED CHOKE HOLD SEEM TO BE LOOSENING BASED ON HISPANIC MIGRATION AND A FIEW BLACKS BEGINNING TO WONDER FROM THE PLANTATION AND EXPLORE DEMOCRATIC IDEOLOGICALLY DOCTRINES OF DECEITFUL COVERT DELUSIONAL AGENDA,TO INSTRUCT BLACKS WITH ILLICIT FUNDAMENTAL PROPAGANDA ABOUT THE NATION THAT DOSENT EXIST, AND WHEN IT DID THEY ARE THE CULPRITS THAT INITIATED SUCH TRAUMATIZING OCCURANCES, HOWEVER AT THE PRESENT TIME DEMOCRATS SEEM TO BE IN A PANIC MODE, ALL OVER THE PLACE LIKE KIDS AT A FROG LEAP WITH DERANGE INSINUATIONS, THAT LEAVE MANY THINKING AND WONDERING IF THEY ARE NOT IN CAHOOTS WITH THE TERRORIST TO DESTROY OUR WAY OF LIFE FOR POLITICAL GAIN, AND MOST CITIZENS IN THIS COUNTRY PIRATICALLY BLACKS HAVE NO IDEA WHY THE DEMOCRATS LEADERS ARE IN SUCH RAGE, THEY ARE USING IRAQ TO VENT THEIR FRUSTRATION REGARDS TO THEIR OWN SUSPECTED CRISIS, THEIR PARTY HAVE WONDERED SO FAR TO THE LEFT BHIND REBELLIOUS RADICALS CLAIMING NINE ELEVEN WAS A INSIDE CONSPIRACY, AND NOT CAUSED BY TERRORIST, ALSO THE LEVEE IN NEW ORLEANS WAS BLOWEN UP AND NOT CAUSED BY HURRICANE KATRINA, AND MANY OTHER FATUOUS REMARKS MADE BY THEIR LEADERS DISDAINING THE CURRENT ADMINSTRATION, UNTIL SOME OF THE CITIZENS IN THIS COUNTRY ARE BECOMING UNEASY, BECAUSE IN ESSENCE THE DEMOCRATIC PARTY CHRONOLOGICAL RECORD IS RACIST BY NATURE AGAINST AFRICAN AMERICANS PIRATICALLY IF THEY ARE INTELLECTUAL, THIS IS A TRADE MARK EMBEDED IN THE HISTORY OF DEMOCRATS, ANY ONE THAT THREATEN OR INVADE THEIR IDEOLOGY OF SUPREME POWER AND AUTHORITY USUALLY HAVE AN APPOINTMENT WITH DEATH, LETS GO BACK IN HOSTORY PRESIDENT ABRAHAM LINCOLN FREED THE SLAVES ASSASSINATED, PRESIDENT JOHN F. KENNEDY WAS IN THE PROCESS OF GETTING THE DEMOCRATS HOLD ON CIVIL AND VOTING RIGHTS FOR

AFRICAN AMERICANS ABOLISHED ASSASSINATED, DR. MARTIN LUTHER KING JR. WAS INSTRUMENTAL AND DID THE HEAVY LIFTING TO GET IT PASSSED, ASSASSINATED, AND NOW THE LEFT WING DEMOCRATIC SUPREMACIST HATE RADICALS FOR THE ADVANCING OF AFRICAN AMERICANS IN THE CONSSERVATIVE POLITICAL ARENA ARE TERRIFIED, AND TO THINK THAT THERE ARE (NO) BIGOTS IN THE REPUBLICAN PARTY IS A UNDERSTATEMENT, THEY HAVE BEEN THERE THROUGHOUT HISTORY, BUT MORE PREVALENT IN THE DEMOCRATIC PARTY, THE ONLY DIFFERENCE BETWEEN A REPUBLICAN BIGOT AND A DEMOCRAT, IS THE REPUBLICAN IS A SILENT FOE THAT HIDE BEHIND DEMOCRATS AND LET THEM CASTIGATE POLITICAL DEMAGOGUERY THAT HINDER A SEGMENT OF AFRICAN AMERICANS FROM SUSTAINING ECONOMICALLY BASED ON REPUDIATING FUNDAMENTAL STANDARDS THAT EXIST IN AMERICA TO SUCCEED RELATED TO MORAL VALUES HISTORICALLY.

PRESIDENT GEORGE W. BUSH HAS CREATED THE MOST HORRIFYING DEVIATING DIGRESSION FOR THE DEMOCRATIC PARTY IN MODERN HISTORY, BY CLASSIFYING CONSERVATIVE INTELLECTUAL MORAL VALUE AFRICAN AMERICANS AND ASSIGNING THEM TO POSITIONS IN HIS CABINET THAT IS HISTORICAL FOR THE HIGHEST AFRICAN AMERICAN POLITICAL AUTHORITY EVER, AND THE DEMOCRATSHAVEMAGNIFIEDTHEIRACTOFPERFORMANCE IN THE POLITICAL ARENA, AND THIS HAS TURNED THEIR LEADERSHIP INTO BABBLING IDIOTS, BECAUSE THEY SENSE THIS COULD JEOPARDIZE THEIR POLITICAL POWERFUL INFLUENCE OVER AFRICAN AMERICANS, BECAUSE SOME BLACKS ARE BEGINNING TO VENTURE AWAY FROM THE HERDING PLANTATION AND TEST CONSERVATIVE MORAL VALUES WHICH HISTORICALLY STABILIZES DIGNITY, AND THIS HAS SENT SHIVERS DOWN DEMOCRATS SPINES, WHICH HAS CAUSED A TIGHT ROPE PERFORMING ACT, THEY ARE RELUCTANT TO ATTACK POLITICALLY ASTUTE AFRICAN AMERICANS VERBALLY FEAR OF AILENATING OTHER BLACKS, AND IF ANY ONE IS AWARE OF GENETIC HERDING AMONG THE RACE THEY ARE, BECAUSE THEY

HAVE PERSEVERED ON THIS UNIQUE FORMALITY TO POLITICALLY CONTROL BLACKS FOR HUNDREDS OF YEARS, AND NOW IT COULD PLUNGE THEIR PARTY INTO POLITICAL CHAOTIC DEVASTATION IF SOME BLACKS BEGAN TO DEFECT THEIR EGREGIOUS SELFSERVING PROPAGANDA TO DISSUADE OTHERS TO SUPPORT THEIR IDEOLOGY OF GOVERNMENTAL DEPENDENCY, SO THIS IS WHY THEY ARE VIGOROUSLY TRYING TO DESTROY THE CREDIBILITY OF PRESIDENT GEORGE W. BUSH, HOPING TO DISTRACT ATTENTION FROM THE REAL ISSURE, PRESIDENT BUSH CHOOSE ONE OF THE MOST ASTUTE INTELLECTUAL STEADY AT THE HELM POLITICAL ARTFUL AFRICAN AMERICANS OF ALL TIMES BE IT BLACK OR WHITE AS HIS SECRETARY OF STATE IN CONDOLEEZZA RICE, THE DEMOCRATS ROUNDED UP THEIR BLACK BOOT LICKING SMALL DYSFUNCTIONAL BRAIN ROTTWEILERS, IN AN EFFORT TO BESMIRCH HER DISTINGUISH QUALITY WITH DEROGATORY INSINUATIONS, BUT THESE NONSENSICAL TACTICS ROLLED OFF AS WATER DOES FROM A DUCK BACK, THAT NEGATED THEIR TACTICAL MANEUVERING OF RACIST EXPLOITATIONS TO DEMEAN, THE DEMOCRATS WERENT QUITE SURE OF WHY SECRETARY RICE WAS CHOSEN TO THE PRESIDENT CABINET AS SECURITY ADVISOR THEY (ASSUMED) TOKENISM, SO THEY DEMANDED HER APPERANCE REGARDS TO REVELATIONS LEADING TO THE REMOVAL OF SADDAM HUSSEIN FROM IRAQ, SHE COMPLIED AND LEFT THEM SPUTTERING LIKE A MODEL T, OR A FORD, THEY HAD ANOTHER GO AT IT DURING HER CONFORMATION TO BECOME SECRETARY OF STATE, LEADING DEMOCRATS ARE STILL EMOTIONAL DISTURBED BY HER SKILLS AND POLITICAL INTELECTUAL UNCANNY ABILITY TO FOIL THEIR PERCEPTION FORECAST BY OTHER SMALL DYSFUNCTIONAL BRAIN BLACKS LABELING HER AS A BUSH LACKEY AND INCOMPETENT TO THE FUNDAMENTALS OF POLITICS, UNLIKE FORMER SECRETARY OF STATE COLEN POWELL, HE IS A FINE GENTLEMAN BUT SEEM TO HAVE HAD LIMITED CONDITIONS RELATED TO HIS RESPONSIBILITES AS (CHOSEN) SECRETARY OF STATE OR AN ELECTED OFFICIAL, HOWEVER SECRETARY OF STATE RICE HAS BLAZED A CONSERVATIVE TRAIL THROUGH

LIBERAL DEMOCRAT FORTIFIED TERRITORY AND IT IS SLOWELY CAUSING SOME BLACKS TO GET OFF THEIR KNEES AND STOP SETTLING FOR THE CHITLINS FROM THE HOG, AND G ROW THEIR OWN PIGS FOR HAMS, THERE SEEM TO AN OSTENTATIOUSLY CONSERVATIVE INTEREST THAT IS FORMULATING FROM SOME BELATED AFRICAN AMERICANS, THERE ARE THREE CONSERVATIVE AFRICAN AMERICANS CANIDATES SEEKING MAJOR POLITICAL OFFICES IN TWO THOUSAND SIX, MICHAEL STEELE LIEUTENANT GOVERNOR OF MARYLAND CAMPAIGNING FOR A SEAT IN THE U.S. SENATE, KEN BLACKWELL SECRETARY OF STATE FROM OHIO HAS POLITICAL AMBITIONS TO BECOME GOVERNOR, LYNN SWANN AFFLUENT SPORT FIGURE HAS HIS ARMS OUT REACHED TO SNAG THE GOVERNING OF PENNSYLVANIA, AND IF ANY OF THESE CANDIDATES SHOULD BE ELECTED OR ALL IT WILL EMULATE THE HISTORICAL EVENTS OF EIGHTEEN SIXTY EIGHT, WHEN FORMER GENERAL ULYSSES S. GRANT REPLACED LIBERAL PRESIDENT ANDREW JOHNSON, THE REPUBLICAN PARTY IS ONE OF THE TWO MAJOR PARTIES IN THE UNITED STATES OF AMERICA ORGANIZED IN EIGHTEEN FIFTY FOUR TO (OPPOSE) THE EXTENSION OF SLAVERY, AND THROUGH OUT HISTORY HAS EMBRACED LEGISLATION TO ACCOMMODATE AFRICAN AMERICANS, DURING THE EIGHTEEN SIXTIES REPUBLICAN AFRICAN AMERICANS BEGAN THEIR QUEST FOR POLITICAL RECOGNITION, OSCAR J. DUNN WERE SELF EDUCATED AND BECAME LIEUTENANT GOVERNOR OF LOUISIANS, HIRMAN RHODES REVELS BECAME AMERICA FIRST BLACK U.S. SENATOR REPRESENTING MISSISSIPPI, BLANCHE K. BRUCE THE FIRST AFRICAN AMERICAM TO SERVE A FULL TERM AS A U.S. SENATOR ELECTED FROM LOUISIANA, EGBERT SAMMIS WAS ELECTED TO THE FLORDIA STATE SENATE, FRANCIS LOUIS CARDOZO SERVED AS SOUTH CAROLINAS SECRETARY OF STATE, AND RECEIVED AN APPOINTMENT TO THE TREASURY DEPARTMENT IN WASHINGTON, D.C. PICKNEY BENTON STEWART PINCHBACK BECAME THE NATIONS FIRST AFRICAN AMERICAN GOVERNOR TO SERVE IN LOUISIANA.

DURING THE YEARS BETWEEN THE END OF THE CIVIL WAR AND THE FIRST DECADE OF THE TWENTIETH CENTURY MORE THAN SIX HUNDRED REPUBLICAN AFRICAN AMERICANS SERVED THEIR COUNTRY AS STATE LEGISLATURES, TWENTY WERE ELECTED TO THE U.S. HOUSE OF REPRESENTATIVES, AND TWO WAS ELECTED TO THE U.S. SENATE, DURING THIS ERA OF RECONSTRUCTION MANY FACETS OF FEDERAL AND STATE OFFERED CONCEPTS OF IMPROVING THE LIVES OF PEOPLE BLACK AND WHITE IN THE SOUTH, IN EIGHTEEN SIXTY EIGHT MANY PROGRESSIVE MEASURES WERE ADOPTED TO ENHANCE DIVERSITY, SUCH AS ABOLISHING RACIAL DISCRIMINATION REGARDS TO VOTING, MORE THAN FOUR THOUSAND SCHOOLS WERE OPEN TO BLACK AND WHITE BY EIGHTEEN SEVENTY SEVEN,MORE THAN SIX HUNDRED THOUSAND AFRICAN AMERICANS WERE ENROLLED IN ELEMENTARY SCHOOLS, BECAUSE REPUBLICANS KNEW IT WOULD ENHANCE THEIR HOPES FOR A BETTER FUTURE, SINCE MANY FORMER SLAVES WERE PROHIBITED FROM LEARNING TO READ AND WRITE BY SOUTHERN DEMOCRATIC PLANTATION OWNERS, BLACKS FLOCKED TO SCHOOLS IMMEDIATELY AFTER THE CIVIL WAR AND INSISTED ON SCHOOLS TO PROVIDE STRONG EDUCATIONAL PROGRAMS AND THE BLACK POLITICANS RESPONDED TO THE PEOPLES DESIRES, BY ESTABLISHING THE FIRST FREE PUBLIC SCHOOL SYSTEM, LAWS WERE ENACTED TO ABOLISH DUELING, CONSUMMATED DIVORCE LAW, ALSO RATIFIED LAWS TO ELECT JUDGES RATHER THAN APPOINT, ROBERT SMALLS A FORMER SLAVE AND NATIVE SOUTH CAROLINIAN ALSO CIVIL WAR HEROWAS ENTHUSIASTIC AND ESPICALLY INTERESTED IN DEVELOPING THE EDUCATION SYSTEM IN A STATE OFFERED VERY LITTLE EDUCATION TO ITS CITIZENS BLACK OR WHITE, HE WAS A DELEGATE ON THE EIGHTEEN SIXTY EIGHT STATE CONSTITUTIONAL CONVENTION WHERE HE SPONSERED A RESOLUTION FOR PUBLIC SCHOOLS, AND SERVED IN THE SOUTH CAROLINA HOUSE OF REPRESENTATIVES WHICH EDUCATION WAS ONE OF HIS PRIMARY CONCERNS, UNFORTUNATELY THIS DIVERSE CONSERVATIVE PLITICAL AGENDA TO UNITE THE

SOUTH IN HARMONY WITH INTELLECTUAL MORAL VALUES BETWEEN BLACK AND WHITE WHICH WAS INSTITUTED BY THE REPUBLICAN PARTY WAS SHORT LIVED, BECAUSE THE SOUTHERN DEMOCRATS WERE DETERMIND TO REINSTATE RACIAL CONTROL OF WHITE SUPREMACY, THEY HAD ALREADY ORGANIZED THE KU-KLUX-KLAN IN EIGHTEEN SIXTY SIX AND OTHER TERRORIZING GROUPS WERE ESTABLISHED CALLING THEM SELVES RED SHIRTS, THE WHITE LEAGUE, AND RIFLE CLUBS, THE WHITE LEAGUE MARCHED ON THE STATE HOUSE IN NEW ORLEANS TO INTIMIDATE BLACK AND WHITE REPUBLICANS AND OPENLY DECLARED THEY WERE GOING TO OVER THROW THE REPUBLICAN STATE GOVERNMENT IN LOUISIANA, IN VICKSBURG MISSISSIPPI WHITE DEMOCRATIC TERRORIST SLAUGHTED THREE HUNDRED BLACKS AS A CAMPAIGN TO DENY THEIR SUPPORT FOR THE REPUBLICAN PARTY THE VIOLENCE BECAME SO INTENSE UNTIL A SEGMENT OF POLITICAL AFFLUENT AFRICAN AMERICANS AND BASICALLY ALL THE REPUBLICAN WHITES DEPARTED THE SOUTH, BUT THE MAJORITY OF BLACKS HAD NO OTHER CHOICE BUT REMAIN DUE TO INDEBTED TIES TO SHARE CROPPING WITH PLANTATION OWNERS AND ILLITERACY,ALSO WAS FORCED THROUGH INTIMIDATION AND VIOLENCE TO SUPPORT THE DEMOCRATS IN THEIR QUEST FOR SEGREGATED WHITE SUPREMACY CONTROL,ABANDONING THEIR CONSERVATIVE POLITICAL ASPIRATIONS FOR SERVITUDE TO THE SOUTHERN DEMOCRATS, AND THAT FUNDAMENTAL DEMORALIZATION PERPETRATED BY DEMOCRATS HAS DESTABILIZED AFRICAN AMERICANS INITIATIVE TO PERSUE ASPIRATIONS IN THE REPUBLICAN PARTY WHICH WAS FOUNDED IN AN EFFORT TO CIRCUMVENT THE DESPARITY IMPOSED ON AFRICAN,AMERICANS BY SOUTHERN DEMOCRATS,DEMCRATS HAS SUCCESSFULLY UTILIZED COVERT FASCISM TO CUNNINGLY INFLUENCE AFRICAN AMERICANS FOR THEIR INEPT ACQUIESCENCE TO PROMOTE THEIR AGENDA FOR POLITICAL POWER, WHICH THROUGH THESE SKILLFUL TACTICS THEY HAVE DENIED THE MAJORITY OF AFRICAN AMERICANS THEIR POLITICAL CONSERVATIVE LEGACY WHICH BEGAN IN EIGHTEEN

SIXTY EIGHT WHEN REPUBLICAN FORMER GENERAL ULYSSES S. GRANT REPLACED LIBERAL PRESIDENT ANDREW JOHNSON

AFTER THE DEMOCRATS VIOLENTLY DISRUPTED THE REPUBLICAN PARTY AND CAUSED THEIR DEPARTURE FROM THE SOUTH, THE FOLLOWING YEARS THEY GAINED SUPREMACY THROUGH THE SUPREME COURT FOR STATE AUTHORITY OVER CONSTITUTIONAL RIGHTS, WHICH REMOVED FEDERAL PROTECTION FOR AFRICAN AMERICAN RIGHTS IN THE SOUTHERN STATES AND EMPLEMENTED THE JIM CROW RULE SEPARATE BUT EQUAL THAT PROHIBITED SOUTHERN BLACKS FROM PARTICIPATING IN (ANY) POLITICAL AFFAIRS UNTIL NINETEEN SIXTY FOUR AND FIVE, MEANING AFRICAN AMERICANS WERE NEGATED FROM THE PROCESS OF POLITICAL ASPIRATIONS FOR APPROXIMATELY NINETY YEARS IN THE SOUTHERN STATES (ALL) DUE TO DEMOCRAT OBJECTIONS AND THE FAILURE OF A DEMOCRATIC CONTROLLED CONGRESS TO INTERCEDE. HOWEVER IT DOES APPEAR THAT THE YEAR OF TWO THOUSAND SIX CONSERVATIVE AFRICAN AMERICANS ARE BEGINNING TO VENTURE INTO THE REPUBLICAN POLITICAL ARENA ONCE AGAIN, UNFORTUNATELY THE DEMOCRATS HAVE CONTROLLED AFRICAN AMERICANS FOR HUNDREDS OF YEARS EITHER THROUGH VIOLENCE OR RELYING ON THEIR POLITICAL INEPTNESS TO THE UTMOST DEGREE OF THEIR INTELLIGENCE TO DECIPHER THE CENTRAL IMPORTANCE OF THEIR DELIRIOUS QUEST FOR POLITICAL POWER THROUGH COVERT DECITFUL TACTICAL IMPUGNING DEMAGOGUERY, FORTUNATELY THIS DEVASTATING SOVEREIGN AUTHORITY OVER BLACKS SEEM TO BE TENDING TO CHANGE SOME WHAT, WITH THE POWERFUL STRUCTURED INTELLECTUAL POLITICAL LEADERSSHIP OF CONSERVATIVE SECRETARY OF STATE CONDOLEEZZA RICE, AND AT LEAST THREE AFRICAN AMERICANS SEEKING TOP POLITICAL POSITIONS UNDER THE CONSERVATIVE BANNER, ALONG WITH REPUBLICAN STRATEGIST ANGELA MCGLOWAN AND RON CHRISTIE DISPUTING DEMOCRATIC DECITFUL IDEOLOGY, THIS COULD BE THE ACHILLES HEEL FOR DEMOCRATS IN THE

FUTURE YEARS AND THEY ARE MORE CONCERN ABOUT THIS LURKING INSURGENCY FROM CONSERVATIVE INTELLECTUAL AFRICAN AMERICANS THAN THEY ARE ABOUT TERRORISM, THE DEMOCRATS ARE IN A DEFENSIVE MODE AND IT IS GEARED TO SUPPRESS AFRICAN AMERICANS INTEREST IN CONSERVATISM AND WITH OUT THE ASSISTANCE OF THE KU-KLUX-KLAN THEY ARE HAVING TO APPEAL TO BLACK POLITICAL IGNORANCE OF THEIR HISTORICAL IDEOLOGY, WHEN IN THE EIGHTEEN SEVENTYS SEEING AFRICAN AMERICANS HOLD POLITICAL OFFICE INCENSED SOUTHERN DEMOCRATS, THEIR ASSESSMENT OF ALL BLACKS WERE THAT THEY ARE TO IGNORANT,AND INCOMPETENT TO HOLD PUBLIC OFFICE AND MOST OF ALL THEY WERE ATTEMPTING TO RISE ABOVE THEIR NATURAL PLACE OF SUBSERVIENT IN WHITE SOCIETY, IT IS PATHETICALLY APPALLING AND DEMONSTRATE IMMORAL HYPOCRISY TO OBSERVE POLITICAL INEPT BLACKS BEING CODDLE BY DEMOCRATS PLAYING THE RACE CARD FOR THEIR VOTING BLAC, AND THE SOUTHERN DEMOCRAT PARTY WAS EQUIVALENT TO THE TALIBAN AGAINST BLACKS IN THE SOUTH FROM THE MID EIGHTEEN HUNDREDS TO THE EARLY NINETEEN SIXTIES WHICH THEY TERRORIZED AFRICAN AMERICANS FOR APPROXIMATELY NINETY FIVE YEARS, SIMPLY BECAUSE THEY WANTED CIVIL AND VOTING RIGHTS THE SAME AS EVERY OTHER CITIZEN IN AMERICA THAT THE REPUBLICAN CONGRESS HAD AMENDED TO THE CONSTUTION IN EIGHTEEN SIXTY SIX.

THIS IS THE YEAR OF TWO THOUSAND SIX AN ELECTION YEAR IN NOVEMBER IT IS REGARDED WITH SUSPICION THAT THE DEMOCRATS SENSE THAT THERE ARE SOME AFRICAN AMERICANS FLIRTING WITH DEFECTION, AND THEY WOULD RATHER ENDORSE THE TALIBAN THAN WITNESS AFRICAN AMERICANS RETURN TO THE CONSERVATIVE ROOTS OF THE REPUBLICAN PARTY, THE DEMOCRAT PARTY LEADERS CONCERNS ARE (NOT) ABOUT THE EXTREME AGITATED CONDITIONS IN IRAQ, THE CYNICISM OF IRAN AND NORTH KOREA, TERRORISM OR IMMIGRATION, THEIR ALLUMINATED MAIN OBJECTIVES ARE TO DENOUNCE AND DEMORALIZE THE REPUBLICAN PARTY IN AN EFFORT

TO SYSTEMATICALLY DESTRUCT AS THEY DID IN THE MID EIGHTEEN HUNDREDS, AND ALIENATE AFRICAN AMERICANS FOR THEIR OWN POLITICAL SERVITUDE TO CONTROLL CONGRESS,IN AN EFFORT TO STALL THE POLITICAL ASPIRATIONS OF BLACKS FOR CONSERVATIVE INTELLECTUAL MORAL VALUES WHICH IS CONSISTENT WITH DEMOCRATIC IDEOLOGY.

THIS IS TWO THOUSAND SIX, AN ELECTION YEAR FOR CONTROL OF THE SENATE, ALSO THE HOUSE OF REPRESENTATIVES, WHICH IS VITALLY IMPORTANT FOR DEMOCRATS, BECAUSE THIS IS THE FIRST TIME SENSE THE MIDDLE AND LATE EIGHTEEN HUNDREDS, THAT THEY ARE BEING THREATEN WITH DEFECTION FROM SOME AFRICAN AMERICANS FROM THEIR PARTY, TO INTELLECTUAL CONSEVATIVE MORAL VALUES, AND THEY ARE KU-KLUX-KLAN VIOLENTLY ANGRY WITH PRESIDENT GEORGE BUSH, FOR SEEMINGLY CAUSING THIS CATASTROPHIC POLITICAL DILEMMA BY CHOOSING MINORITIES ESRITCULARLY AFRICAN AMERICANS TO SERVE THIS NATION IN HIS CABINET, AND THAT MY FRIENDS IS A HISTORICAL EVENT, AND IS NOTE WORTHY OF SINCERE ACCOLADES.

THE DEMOCRATS ARE HYSTERICAL BECAUSE THEY ARE PROVING TO THE WORLD THAT THERE SOME AFRICAN AMERICANS QUALIFIED INTELLECTUALLY TO PERFORM ACTS OF ANSWERABLE DECISIONS, OTHER THAN SERVITUDE FOR DEMOCRATIC POLITICAL CONTROL.

IN ESSENCES THE DEMOCRATS ARE DOING WHAT THEY DO BEST, UTILIZING POLITICAL INEPT AFFLUENT LIBERAL BLACKS AS THEY DID IN EIGHTEEN NINETY FIVE, WITH BOOKER T. WASHINGTON TO DENY AFRICAN AMERICANS THEIR CIVIL RIGHTS, WITH THE IMPLEMENTATION OF THE SEPERATE BUT EQUAL JIM CROW RULE.

TO EXPAND FURTHER ON DEMOCRATIC DELIVERANCE OF REPRISAL AGAINST CONSERVATIVE AFRICAN AMERICANS IN A MORE REPRESSIVE MODE, THEIR AMBITIONS ARE FORMULATED BASED ON POLITICAL IGNORANCE OF BLACKS, AND IT IS PROFOUNDLY AMAZING TO UNDERSTAND THE DEMEANING OF BLACKS BY DEMOCRATS, AND HELPLESSLY OBSERVE THEM BEING MADE DYSFUNCTIONAL POLITICAL

IDIOTS, BASED ON GRATUITOUS RELIEF, AND THEIR GENETIC CONGO TRIBAL HERDING INSTINCTS TO FOLLOW AFFLUENT SELF APPOINTED LEADERS, ILLITERATE OR EDUCATED.

AND TO FULLY ALLUMINATE POLITICAL DEMORALIZATION OF BLACKS, PERTAINING TO THEIR INEPTNESS OF DEMOCRATIC DECEIT.

ON OCTOBER 22, 2006, SENATOR BARACK OBAMA WAS ON MEET THE PRESS WITH TIM RUSSERT AS MODERATOR, AND WAS LURED INTO GIBBERISH ACCLAIMS BASHING THE CURRENT ADMINISTRATION WITH REMARKS OF BUFFOONISH DEMAGOGUERY, AND IS INEPT TO THE FACT THAT HE IS BEING USED AS A POLITICAL DEMOCRATIC BLACK VOTE HERDING FOR THE DEMOCRAT PARTY. THE DEMOCRAT PARTY AND AFRICAN AMERICANS HAVE ONE OF THE MOST UNIQUE POLITICAL ARRANGEMENTS KNOWN TO MAN KIND, THE MAJORITY OF AFRICAN AMERICANS ARE UNABLE TO DISTINGUISH BETWEEN PROPAGANDER AND REALITY PERPETRATED BY DEMOCRATS, APPARENTLY THIS IS WHY FORMER F.B.I. DIRECTOR J. EDGAR HOOVER SURMISED THAT BLACKS BRAINS WAS TWENTY PRECENT SMALLER THAN WHITES, BECAUSE OF FRUSTRATION OVER THEIR POLITICAL BEHAVIOR, PRESIDENT DWIGHT D. EISENHOWER A REPUBLICAN PRESIDENT ORDERED HOOVER TO RELENTLESSLY PERSUE THE DEMOCRATIC FOUNDED KU-KLUX-KLAN, TO PREVENT AFRICAN AMERICANS FROM BEING SLAUGHTERED, IN THE SOUTHERN STATES, WHICH HE DID INFILTRATED THEIR TACTICS AND CRUSHED THEIR REGIME.

PRESIDENT EISENHOWER WROTE THE FIRST CIVIL RIGHTS BILL IN EIGHTY FIVE YEARS, DEMOCRATS CONTROLLED CONGRESS AND RIPPED IT TO BITS AND PIECES, AND DISALLOWED CIVIL AND VOTING RIGHTS.

AND ABOUT THAT TIME IS WHEN HOOVER, MADE THE SMALL BRAIN STATEMENT, BECAUSE THE MAJORITY OF AFRICAN AMERICAN DEMOCRATS WAS IN PHILADELPHIA, PENNSYLVANIA AT THE DEMOCRAT CONVENTION (VOTING) THEM BACK IN OFFICE.

THE HYPOCRISY AND FIENDISH DECEIT PERPETRATED AGAINST SOME AFRICAN AMERICANS IS ASTOUNDING REGARDS TO POLITICAL AFFAIRS BY DEMOCRATS, AND HAS BEEN FOR OVER ONE HUNDRED THIRTY YEARS, YOU WOULD HAVE TO BE A SMALL DYSFUNCTIONAL BRAIN IDIOT (NOT) TO ASSESS DEMOCRATIC STRATEGY MOTIVATING SENATOR BARACK OBAMA ACCLAIM TO PERSUE THE PRESIDENCY IN TWO THOUSAND EIGHT, THIS IS ONE OF THE MOST DECEITFUL CONTRIVED PRANKS BY DEMOCRATS OF THE CENTURY INTENDED (ONLY) TO LURE AFRICAN AMERICAN VOTERS TO THE POLLS TO SUPPORT DEMOCRATS AMBITIONS FOR CONTROL OF THE TWO THOUSAND SIX ELECTIONS TO CONGRES AND THE SENATE, AND THEY HAVE SADDLED UP POLITICAL PLANTATION POSTER BOY SENATOR BARACK OBAMA TO RIDE FOR TWO YEARS FOR BLACKS TO HERD BEHIND THINKING HE COULD BECOME PRESIDENT, THIS IS (NOT) INTENDED TO BE DISRESPECTFUL TO SENATOR OBAMA CREDENTIAIALS UNFORTUNATELY HE IS A DEMOCRAT PARTY MEMBER AND THE STUDY OF PAST EVENTS DICTATE DEMOCRATS REJECTION OF AFRICAN AMERICANS CONTAINING (ANY) POLITICAL OFFICE OF AUTHORITY,

BECAUSE THE CHRONOLOGICAL HISTORICAL EVENTS DEMONSTRATE THAT AFRICAN AMERICANS IN THEIR PARTY IS SUBJECTED TO POLITICAL (VOTING) SERVITUDE, AND IS INEPT TO THE DEMOCRATIC POLITICAL STRATEGY TO HERD THEIR VOTING BLOC, AN EXAMPLE OF THIS DEVIOUS EXPLOITATION, THERE ARE APPROXIMATELY FORTY FOUR AFRICAN AMERICANS IN THE DEMOCRATIC CONGRESS, THAT LABEL THEMSELVES THE BLACK CAUCUS, CHECK THE NEWS MEDIA INCLUDING THE INTERNET NATION WIDE TO DETERMINE HOW MANY HAVE STRAYED FROM THE DEMOCRAT PLANTATION IDEOLOGY OF POLITICAL SERVITUDE, AND VOICED THEIR OPPOSITION AGAINST THEIR POLITICAL DEMOCRATIC SLAVE MASTERS.

IN ORDER TO BE CONTRADICTABLE ONE (MUST) BE CAPABLE OF (INDIVIDUAL) COMPREHENSION, (NOT) A PREDICTABLE GENETIC HERDING PHENOMENON. APPROXIMATELY EIGHTY EIGHT PRECENT OF AFRICAN

AMERICANS ARE LOYAL TO THE DEMOCRAT PARTY, WITHIN THAT EIGHTY EIGHT PRECENT THERE ARE THREE SEGEMENTS OF POLITICAL BELIEFS, I VOTE FOR DEMOCRATS BECAUSE IT IS A FAMILY TRADITION, MY PARENTS VOTED THAT WAY ALSO THEIR PARENTS.

I DO-NOT VOTE BECAUSE THIS IS SOMETHING ORGANIZED BY WHITE FOLKS AND I AM (NOT) CONCERNED ABOUT IT, BECAUSE ITS NOT GOING TO HELP ME, FINALLY YES WE VOTE BUT NOT UNTIL WE KNOW (WHO) OUR BLACK LEADERS ARE GOING TO VOTE FOR.

THIS IS MOSTLY DUE TO A GENETIC CONTROLLABILITY DERIVED FROM AFRICAN CULTURE WHERE AFRICAN VILLIAGES ARE CONTROLLED BY A CHIEF OR WITCH DOCTOR, THIS IS A GENETIC TRAIT THAT WILL FOREVER DICTATE MOST AFRICAN AMERICANS POLITICAL BEHAVIOR, AND THEIR EVERY DAY LIVES, AND MOST ARE NOT AWARE OF THIS INEVITABILITY THAT IS A GENETIC TRAIT.

TODAY IS NOVEMBER 26, 2007. THERE IS AN ELECTION IN 2008 FOR THE PRESIDENTAL ELECTION, THAT OCCUR EVERY FOUR YEARS TO DETERMINE THE LEADER FOR OUR NATION, REPUBLICANS AND DEMOCRAT CANIDATES ARE MANEUVERING IN THEIR PROSPECTIVE PARTIES IN ORDER TO BE ELECTED, BY A CONSTITUENCY OF VOTERS IN THEIR PRELIMINARY ELECTION TO ELECT A ELIGIBLE CANIDATE FOR THE GENERAL ELECTION TO BECOME PRESIDENT OF THE UNITED STATES OF AMERICA.

THE DEMOCRATS ARE OFFERING A PIONEERING UNIQUENESS REGARDS TO TWO OF THEIR LEADING CANIDATES, A FEMALE SENATOR FROM NEW YORK, HILLARY CLINTON, AND SENATOR BARACK OBAMA FROM ILLINOIS, AN AFRICAN AMERICAN.

LETS FOCUS ON CANIDATE BARACK OBAMA, HE IS GETTING THE SUPPORT OF BLACK SELF APPOINTED LEADERS THROUGH-OUT THE NATION, MANY BLACK ACTOR CELEBRITIES, BUISNESS OWNERS, TO INCLUDE TALK SHOW HOAST OPRA WINFERY, THESE ARE GREAT ACCOLADES FOR BARACK OBAMA, HOWEVER THERE IS AN INEPTNESS REGARDS TO MOST AFRICAN AMERICANS PERTAINING TO MOST DEMOCRATS IDEOLOGY.

IN 1852 WHEN ILLINOIS REPUBLICAN ABRAHAM LINCOLN, CHALLENGED INCUMBENT DEMOCRAT STEPHEN H. DOUGLAS, FOR THE U.S. SENATE, SLAVERY WAS A CENTRAL ISSURE, THE CANIDATES DEBATED ITS PLACE IN THE NATION, LINCOLN DENOUNCED SLAVERY AND REFERENCED THE DECLARATION OF INDEPENDENCE, WHERE IT DECLARE (ALL) MEN TO BE CREATED EQUAL, STEPHEN A. DOUGLAS, THE DEMOCRATIC CANIDATE MOCKED AT LINCOLN STATEMENT THAT AFRICAN AMERICANS WERE (NOT) INCLUDED IN THE DECLARATION AND PANDERED TO THE WHITE SUPREMACIST CROWD IN ILLINOIS THAT AMERICA WAS MADE BY WHITE MEN FOR THE BENEFIT OF WHITE MEN AND THEIR POSTERITY (FOREVER).

THAT WAS IN 1858, THAT IDEOLOGY WITH MOST POLITICAL DEMOCRATS STILL EXIST TODAY. THE ODDS OF A AFRICAN AMERICAN WINNING THE PRESIDENCY IN THE DEMOCRAT PARTY WITH FIFTY OPRA WINFRIES, HAS MUCH CHANCE AS SOME ONE CALLING ME TO FLY A JUMBO JET LOADED WITH PASSENGERS.

THE MAJORITY OF AFRICAN AMERICANS THAT ARE CITIZENS IN THE UNITED STATES OF AMERICA, EVEN THOSE ELECTED TO HOLD POLITICAL OFFICE ARE INEPT TO THE FUNDAMENTALS OF A GRUESOME POLITICAL IDEOLOGY THAT IS UTILIZED BY UNIFIED AUTHORITY POLITICIANS IN THE TWO MAJOR PARTIES IN THE NATION, PIRATICALLY DEMOCRATS, BECAUSE THEY HAVE MONOPOLIZED AFRICAN AMERICANS VOTERS BASED ON POLITICAL INTELLECTUAL CYNICISM, BY UTILIZING THEIR GENETIC CONTROLLED IDIOSYNCRASIES TO HERD BEHIND AFFLUENT AND SELF APPOINTED BLACK LEADERS. I DO (NOT) MAKE STATEMENTS WITH OUT RELIANCE ON CHRONOLOGICAL RECORD OF SIGNIFICANT EVENTS.

IN 1895 THE SOUTHERN DEMOCRATS USED THE INFLUENCE OF BOOKER T. WASHINGTON TO DECEIVE THE MAJORITY OF SOUTHERN AFRICAN AMERICANS THAT SEPERATE BUT EQUAL WAS INEVITABLE, AND SEEMED TO ACCEPT RACIAL SEGREGATION, AND SECOND CLASS CITIZEN-SHIP.

IN 1936 FOR THE FIRST TIME PRESIDENT ROOSEVELT ARRANGED FOR AN AFRICAN AMERICAN CONGRESSMAN ARTHUR MITCHELL FROM ILLINOIS TO ADDRESS THE DEMOCRATIC CONVENTION, HE PRAISED THE PRESIDENT FOR HIS PROGRAMS BENEFITS FOR BLACK PEOPLE RECEIVING RELIEF EMPLOYMENT AT THE SAME RATES AS WHITES, AND THE NEW DEAL WELFARE BENEFITS, NOT AWARE IT WAS A FEDERAL PROGRAM THE PRESIDENT WAS BOUND BY THE CONSTUTION.

AND THEN CAME THE ADVANCE RANK OF BENJAMIN C. DAVIS, TO GENERAL IN THE ARMY, AND APPOINTED WILLIAM HASTIE, TO STAFF WAR SECETARY, THE INTENT WAS TO DISMANTLE THE CONSERVATIVE AFRICAN AMERICANS LOYAL TO THE PARTY THAT PRESIDENT ABRAHAM LINCOLN HAD BUILT. IT (WORKED) AND DEMOCRATS HELD CONGRESS FOR FORTY YEARS, WHILE BLACKS WERE RELEGATED TO SECOND CLASS CITIZENS, DRINKING FROM DIFFERENT WATER FOUNTAINS IN PUBLIC PLACES, AND SITTING AT THE BACK OF THE BUS, AND RECEVING THEIR RELIEF BENEFITS.

OVER ONEHUNDRED YEARS HAS PASSED, AND THE REPULSIVE POLITICAL STRATEGY IS STILL FUNDAMENTALLY ALIVE AND DOING VERY WELL. SENATOR HILLARY CLINTON,THE DEMOCRAT FRONT RUNNER IS ADVOCATING IF SHE BECOME PRESIDENT, SHE IS GOING TO GIVE EACH CHILD BORN IN AMERICA $5,000.00 DOLLARS AT BIRTH, WHILE BARACK OBAMA HERD AFRICAN AMERICAN VOTES FOR THE DEMOCRAT PARTY, MOST BLACKS ARE SO INEPT TO AMERICAN POLITICS, THEY WILL (NEVER) UNDERSTAND HOW THE DEMOCRATS HAVE POLITICALLY DESECRATED THEIR VOTING RIGHTS THROUGH THEIR GENETIC HERDING PROCESS.

IT IS AN ESTABLISHED FACT THAT MOST AFRICAN AMERICANS IDEOLOGY IS FUNDAMENTALLY FLAWED PERTAINING TO POLITICAL INTELLECT, BECAUSE OF NOT BEING CAPABLE OF DISTINGUISHING OPERATIVES RELATED THE MAJOR PARTIES IN THE UNITED STATES OF AMERICA, WHICH CONSIST OF TWO DEMOCRAT AND REPUBLICAN, UNFORTUNATELY THEIR POLITICAL ASSESSMENT IS

THAT (ALL) WHITE FOLKS ARE HERDING TOGATHER AND CONSPIRING TO DEPRIVE THEM OF THEIR RIGHT TO SUCCEED IN THE UNITED STATES. THIS INCENDIARY COMPLEXITY IS BUFFOONISH AND BRAIN DYSFUNCTIONAL, TO ILLUSTRATE MY THEORY OF BACK WOODS INEPTNESS OF BLACK POLITICAL PROTEGES FOR THE DEMOCRAT PARTY.

TO DATE IS DECEMBER 89, 2007, AND THE NEWS MEDIA IS FLAUNTING OPRAH WINFREY STRUTTING ON STAGE IN SUPPORT OF BARACK OBAMA FOR PRESIDENT, WHICH REMINDED ME OF THE EARLY FORTIES WHEN BLACK WOMEN WOULD STRUT TO THEIR SHARE CROPPING PLANTATION MASTERS HOUSE TO DO THE CLEANING AND COOKING, AND LATER DAWN THE COTTON SACK FOR PICKING, THIS INGENIOUS LOYALTY HAS TRANSLATED INTO BLACK (VOTE) HERDING FOR THEIR DEMOCRATIC PARTY MASTERS.

AND THIS INSIDIOUS DILEMMA IS PORTRAYED, IF YOU VOTE FOR BARACK OBAMA YOU VOTE FOR CHANGE, AND SHE IS INEPT TO THE FACT THAT HE IS NOTHING MORE THAN A DEMOCRATIC POLITICAL SERVITUDE TO HERD BLACK VOTERS FOR THE DEMOCRATIC PARTY.

OH I MIGHT MENTION ON THE SAME DATE, FORMER (BLACK) PRESIDENT WILLIAM CLINTON WAS PORTRAYED CAMPAINING FOR HIS THIRD TERM TO BE PRESIDENT, SURROUNDED BY (ALL) HERDING BLACK WOMEN.

AND THIS MY FRIENDS IS CALLED MOST AFRICAN AMERICANS POLITICAL SELF DESTRUCTION BY (CHOICE), BY THE WAY IF YOU SHOULD CHOOSE TO READ THIS BOOK THE VALIDITY OF MOST DEMOCRATIC LIBERAL PARTY ELITES AND THEIR CHRONOLOGICAL IDEOLOGY IS DOCUMENTED PERTAINING TO AFRICAN AMERICANS AND THEIR THOUGHTS OF PERSUING A POLITICAL ENDEAVOR OF AUTHORITY, IT IS INSANITY TO CONCLUDE THAT (ALL) WHITE PEOPLE IS IMPEDING YOUR FUTURE, IT IS THE DEMOCRATIC LIBERAL ASSESSMENT OF MOST AFRICAN AMERICANS GENETIC CONTROLLABILITY, THROUGH HERDING BEHIND INFLUENTIAL ELITE DEMOCRATIC ORIENTATED BLACKS, AND THEY HAVE UTILIZED THIS DYSFUNCTIONAL INSANITY TO FURTHER THEIR POLITICAL

AGENDA ON SOLIDIFYING BLACK VOTERS TO PREDOMINATE POLITICAL CONTROL.

AND ONCE YOU HAVE EXTENDED GRATITUDE AND GOTTEN THEM ELECTED YOUR MAIN RESPONSIBLE ACT IN PROOVING THAT YOU HAVE INTELLECTUAL MORAL VALUES, IS SWEEP THE BACK OF THE BUS WITH YOUR RELIEF CHECK. AND TRUST ME THE YEAR 2008 ELECTION IS A BANNER YEAR FOR DEMOCRATS, HERDING BLACK VOTERS, BECAUSE SENATOR BARACK OBAMA AND OPRAH WINFREY, SUPERSEDE BOOKET T. WASHINGTON BETRAYAL OF 1895. IN UNISON WITH LUNACY, THIS IS THE AFTER NOON OF DECEMBER 9, 2007 I CHOOSE TO LISTEN TO RADIO PROGRAM, A.M. WREC 600, ANDREW CLARK SR. MODERATOR HOSTS, THE MAJORITY OF CALLERS WERE AFRICAN AMERICAN, THAT PARTICIPATED IN THE DIALOGUE.

I AM FIRMLY CONVINCED THIS IS WHY FORMER DIRECTOR OF THE F.B.I. J. EDGAR HOOVER, WAS LURED INTO ASSESSING THAT AFRICAN AMERICANS HAD 20% SMALLER BRAINS THAN WHITES, THIS RADIO PROGRAM SHOULD BE PRESERVED FOR VALIDITY OF VARIFICATION, AND IS A FINE EXAMPLE OF WHY DEMOCRATS ENGAGE IN DISTORTED CYNICISM TO DEPRIVE THEM OF THEIR INTEGRITY, TO EXPLOIT THEIR INSISTENCIES OF RADICAL HISTORICAL EVENTS RACISM FOR POLITICAL GAIN, BECAUSE MOST BLACKS ARE INDOCTRINATED BY DEMOCRATS TO THINK THAT REPUBLICANS HAVE DESTROYED THEIR AMERICAN DREAM FOR SUPERIORITY, WHICH IS DETRIMENTAL TO (ALL) OF CONSERVATIVE MORAL VALUED SOCIETY, REGARDS TO HERDING DEMAGOGUERY, WHICH IS FILL WITH HORROR AND DISMAY THAT GENERATE MOTIVES OF DISDAIN THAT IS LOYAL TO SEPARATISM WHICH EVENTUALLY WILL CAUSE SELF DESTRUCTION, BASED ON THEIR FAILED INEPTNESS TO UNITE WITH THE FUNDAMENTALS OF THE NATION THAT OUR ANCESTORS WERE BROUGHT.

THE GENETIC TRAITS OF TRIBAL HERDING ALSO APPLIES TO THE AMERICAN INDIANS, THERE WERE TRIBES THAT REBELLED AGAINST CIVILIZATION BEING INTRODUCED TO THEIR CULTURE IN THEIR (OWN) COUNTRY. WHICH WE LIVE IN TODAY THAT IS CALLED THE UNITED STATES OF

AMERICA, THERE WERE BRAVE CULTURED INDIVIDUALS THAT WAS INSTRUMENTAL IN EXECUTING THE CAUSE FOR (OUR) CIVILIZE LIBERTY OF INDEPENDENCE, FOR INSTANCE MANY AMERICANS ARE TATALLY UNAWARE OF WHY ANDREW JACKSON IS PICTURED ON THE CURRENCY OF A TWENTY DOLLAR BILL.

HE BECAME OUR SEVENTH PRESIDENT, THAT WAS RUTHLESS IN HIS IDEOLOGY PRIOR TO HIS PRESIDENCY, A DISPUTE OCCURED BETWEEN HE AN OPPONENT, WHICH RESULTED IN A CHALLENGE FOR A PISTOL DUEL, HE KNEW THAT HIS CHALLENGER WAS AN EXPERT SHOOTER, HOWEVER HE ALLOWED HIM TO FIRE FIRST HE WAS HIT IN THE CHEST MISSED HIS HEART BY INCHES, HIS WIT COURAGE AND STAMINA ENABLED HIM TO FIRE AND KILL THE CHALLENGER, AFTER HIS RECOVERY FROM THE GUN SHOT WOUND, HE WAS INSTRUMENTAL IN DEFEATING THE TRIBAL INDIANS, BY INSTIGATING DISSENT AMONG THE TRIBES WHERE THEY OVER POWERED EACH OTHER IN HIS FAVOR, THEN CAME THE WAR OF EIGHTEEN TWELVE, FOR OUR INDEPENDENCE FROM BRITISH CONTROL, DURING THE YEAR 1814, ANDREW JACKSON SPEAR HEADED THE PLANNING TO DEFEAT A SEGMENT OF THE MOST POWERFUL ARMY ON THE CONTINENT,AT THAT TIME IN AND AROUND THE NEW ORLEANS AERA HE DEVISED A PLAN TO BUILD A TRENCHED WALL, UTILIZING WHITES AND SLAVES WORKING TOGATHER, THAT WOULD SUSTAIN BRITISH ATTACK, THE BRITISH WERE DEFEATED AND SUFFERD MANY CASUALTIES, LOOSING APPROXIMATELY SEVERAL THOUSAND SOLDIERS, TO JACKSON TWO THOUSAND. SOON AFTER THE WAR OF EIGHTEEN TWELVE WAS ENDED, AMERICA DECLARED ITS INDEPENDENCE FROM BRITISH RULE OF INDENTURED SERVITUDE. A FIEW YEARS LATER ANDREW JACKSON RAN FOR PRESIDENT,AND WAS ELECTED YEAR EIGHTEEN TWENTY NINE.

UNDER HIS ADMINISTRATION HE WAS ACCUSED OF BETRAYING INDIANS THAT WAS LOYAL AND INSTRUMENTAL DURING THE INDIAN UP-RISING AND OPPOSITION .TO CIVILIZATION.

HIS ORDERS WERE TO REMOVE THEM FROM (THEIR) HOME LAND IN THE SOUTH, AND MARCH THEM WEST TO THE RESERVATIONS, OVER EIGHTY THOUSAND IT WAS CALLED THE TRAIL OF TEARS.

THOUSANDS LOST THEIR LIVES ON THE WAY, DUE TO ACCIDENTS, STARVAATION, AND CONTAGIOUS DISEASES PASSED ON FROM THE SETTLERS, DURING ANDREW JACKSON PRESIDENCY, AN ASSASSIN ATTEMPTED TO TAKE LIFE,WITH TWO PISTOLS, THEY EACH MIS-FIRED.

PRESIDENT ANDREW JACKSON EXPIRED IN EIGHTEEN FORTY FIVE, DUE TO OLD DUELLING WOUNDS, AND ILL HEALTH FROM NATURAL CAUSES, WITH HIS TRUSTED ATTENDANTS BY HIS SIDE INCLUDING SLAVES.

THE FUNDAMENTAL DELIVERANCE THAT IS TRANSCRIBED TO UNITE A NATION THE STATUS OF THE UNITED STATES OF AMERICA IS ASTOUNDING ALSO OVERWHELMING, (YET) THERE PARASITIC BUFFOONISH IDEOLOGUES THAT SHOULD BE CLASSIFIED AS MIS-FITS TO RESIDE HERE.

FORTUNATELY WE ARE A NATION OF LAWS, THAT IS BOUND BY A CONSTITUTION AND DECLARATION OF INDEPENDENCE, THAT GIVE THEM THE RIGHT TO CRITIQUE HUMANITY BASED ON INEPT CYNICISM, GRANTED IT IS AN EXCEPTED FUNDAMENTAL IN AMERICA AT THE PRESENT TIME WITH (NO) REMORSE AND IS EXPLOITED BY LIBERALISM TO ACCESS POLITICAL POWER. WHICH WILL EVENTUALLY DEMINISH AND SACRIFICE OUR INTEGRITY.

THAT COULD BE REPRESENTATIVE TO THIRD WORLD STATUS. IT APPEAR THAT SOME LEFT WING ELITIST ARE TESTING THE AUTHENTICITY OF THE RIGHT TO PROTECT OUR COUNTRY AND ITS CITIZENS, ALSO THEY ARE CHALLEGING THE AUGMENTATION TO CHRISTANITY. NOTABILITY LAW PROFESSOR JONATHAN TURLEY, WHEN ASKED ON NATIONAL TELEVISION IF A CAPTURED TERRORIST WAS UNDER HIS JURISDICTION, AND WAS SUSPECTED OF HAVING PERTINENT INFORMATION CONTAINING TO THE DESTRUCTION OF MANY INNOCENT AMERICAN LIVES, WOULD HE USE SOPHISTICATED METHODS TO OBTAIN THE PLOT.

HE LEFT THE HOAST WITH THE ANALYSIS THAT IF DIALOGUE WAS (NOT) SUFFICIENT HE WOULD WALK AWAY, NOW THIS GENTLEMAN JONATHAN TURLEY IS A PRIME CANIDATE TO BE DISROBED SMEARED WITH HUMAN DUNG, AND SHIPPED OFF TO AFRICA THROWN INTO A PACK OF HYENAS. AND OF COURSE THERE IS LORI LIPMAN BROWN, THE BIBLE IS OUR (ONLY) DECLARATION TO INTWLLECTUAL CHRISTIANITY AND IT EMPHATICALLY STIPULATE THAT MAN IS MADE IN GODS IMAGE, IT IS NOT NECESSARY THAT YOU BE A ROCKET SCIENTIST TO STAND IN A MIRROR AND EVALUATE YOUR GOD CREATED BODY FOR EFFICIENCY, AND HAVE INTELLECT TO THE FUNCTIONING ORGANS, HEART, LUNGS, KIDNEYS, LIVER, VESSELS, INTESTINES, HEARING, SMELL, TASTE, EYE SIGHT, AND MOST OF ALL BRAINS, WHICH GOD MISTAKENLY LEFT LORI LIPMAN BROWNS OUT.

SERIOUSLY QUESTION YOUR SELF HOW DID ALL THIS MAGNIFICENT ARTICULATION OCCUR WITH OUT SUPREME AUTHORITY.

AND COLLECTIVELY THESE ORGANS ARE OPERATING IN UNISON TWENTY FOUR HOURS DAILY FOR A LIFETIME, MAYBE MRS. BROWN KNOW SOMETHING WE DONT.

THIS KIND OF RHETORIC FORM THESE TWO IDEOLOGS REPRESENT EGOISTIC FASCISM, THAT IS DETRIMENTAL TO OUR NATION, AND THREATEN OUR LIBERTY TO SUSTAIN AS A (FREE) DIVERSE SOCIETY, BECAUSE INTELLECTUAL MORAL VALUES REPRESENT OUR STANDARDS, AND IF YOU (NEVER) ACQUIRED IT THROUGH TEACHING, OR FOR SOME REASON YOU LOST IT, THEN YOU BECOME A DESTRUCTIVE LIABILITY TO OTHERS, BECAUSE MORAL VALUES IS IMMORTAL TO MAN KIND IN HIS QUEST FOR ECONOMIC DEVINE SURVIVAL.

RECENTLY SUPREME COURT JUSTICE CLARENCE THOMAS WAS BEING INTERVIEWD V.I.A. RADIO,PERTAINING TO HIS BOOK RELEASE, AND WAS ASKED TO ELABORATE ON THE AFFIXING OF SOME AFRICAN AMERICANS, REGARDS TO THE ELEMENT OF CRIMINAL BEHAVIOR.

I UNDERSTOOD HIM TO SAY HE DID (NOT) KNOW, HOWEVER I WILL ATTEMPT TO CLARIFY THAT QUESTION FOR JUSTICE THOMAS, YOU HAVE TO RELATE TO TWO

AUTHENTIC CULTURE OF PEOPLE, INDIANS AND AFRICANS, THE INDIANS WERE ALREADY HERE, AFRICANS WERE BROUGHT HERE APPROXIMATELY FOUR HUNDRED YEARS AGO, EACH CULTURE WITH GENETIC TRAITS OF BEING UNCIVILIZED THAT HERDED BEHIND CHIEFS FOR THEIR GUIDANCE, THE INDIANS REBELLED AGAINST CIVILIZATION AND LOST THEIR LIVES,ALSO THEIR LAND. THE INTRODUCTION OF AFRICANS TO A CIVILIZE SOCIETY WAS VERY TESTY, THEIR REBELLIOUS BEHAVIOR BECAME AN OBSTACLE TO SUCCEED, SOME WENT TO THE EXTREME AND ORGANIZED REBELLIOUS MILITANT GROUPS TO TAKE OVER THE COUNTRY AND CALL IT THEIR OWN.

IT BECAME SO HOSTILE UNTIL DURING THE EIGHTEENTH CENTURY COLONIES ADDED REGULATIONS PROHIBITING INTERRACIAL MARRIGE, IN SEVENTEEN HUNDRED AND EIGHT RHODE ISLAND DECLARED THAT A FREE PERSON COULD NOT ENTERTAIN A SLAVE UNLESS THE SLAVE MASTER WAS PRESENT, SOUTH CAROLINA LAW MADE IT A MISDEMEANOR FOR A WHITE PERSON TO KILL A SLAVE. THEIR PRESISTENCE TO REBUFF CIVILIZATION CAUSED DETRIMENT TO MANY BLACKS, AND SEVERED THEIR PROGRESS TO ATTAIN CIVILITY, AND MARRED THEIR HOPES OF EQUALITY INTO SERVITUDE.

CULTURAL GENETIC CONTROLLABILITY INITIATE AN ABUNDANCE OF MIS-FITS IN (ALL) NATIONALITY OF PEOPLE UNFORTUNATELY THERE IS A LARGE SEGEMENT OF AFRICAN AMERICANS (STILL) RELYING ON THE WITCH DOCTOR FOR THEIR GUIDANCE, IN THE LIKES OF SELF APPOINTED PARASITIC BLACK LEADERS THAT MOLEST THEIR CHARACTER BY ELICITING AND PROPAGANDIZING DEMAGOGUERY FROM THE PAST, TO ENHANCE THEIR DIPLOMATIC NOTORIETY AS SPOKESMAN FOR ALL BLACKS AT THE EXPENSE OF MANY UNSTABLE AFRICAN AMERICANS, THAT IS MINAS MORAL VALUES, AND IS INEPT TO THE CONSTUTION AND DECLARATION OF INDEPENDANCE, THAT GIVE EVERY CITIZEN THE RIGHT TO PURSUE A SUCCESSFUL CAREER BASED ON INDIVIDUAL MERIT (IF) THEY CHOOSE TO DO SO HOWEVER AS REPORTED APPROXIMATELY 70% OF AFRICAN AMERICAN MOTHERS ARE

YOUNG AND UNEDUCATED AND HAVING BABIES OUT OF WEDLOCK, AND THEY ARE SARDINE INTO WELFARE LIVING FACILITIES ALL OVER THE NATION, AND MANY OF THESE FACILITIES HAVE LIVING CONDITIONS THAT IS PARALLEL TO THE TRIBES IN AFRICA WITH TRAITS OF DISDAIN FOR CIVILITY, SO AS A RESULT IT GENERATE HOSTILITY AND CRIMINAL ACTIVITY THAT IS INEVITABLE.

BECAUSE THE MAJORITY OF AFRICAN AMERICANS THAT ARE CITIZENS OF THE UNITED STATES OF AMERICA, CHOOSE TO ALTER THEIR RIGHTS UNDER THE CONSTITUTION AND RELENTLESSLY PURSUE RADICAL INDOCTRINATION THAT TEND TO REBELL AGAINST THE DOCTRINE PROVIDED THROUGH THE CHAIN OF LAWS THAT GOVERN THIS NATION.

(EXAMPLE) AN UNFORTUNATE TRAGEDY OCCURRED IN WEST MEMPHIS, ARKANSAS, A YOUNG BLACK MALE WAS SHOT AND KILLED BY A WHITE UNDER COVER POLICE LAW OFFICER.

THERE WAS A FULL BLOWN INVESTIGATION TO DETERMINE THE VALIDITY OF THE INCIDENT. BY THE FEDERAL JUSTICE DEPARTMENT WASHINGTON, D.C. THE STATE OF ARKANSAS JUSTICE DEPARTMENT, ARKANSAS ATTORNEY GENERAL OF THE STATE, AND THE CITY OF WEST MEMPHIS, ARKANSAS INTERNAL AFFAIRS. (ALL) THEIR DECISIONS WAS (UNANIMOUS); JUSTIFIABLE HOMICIDE BASED ON THE EVIDENCE.

APPARENTLY THEIR DECISION IRRITATED AL SHARPTON, HE CHOSE TO ORGANIZE., AND MARCH ON THE JUSTICE DEPARTMENT IN WASHINGTON TO PROTEST THEIR FINDINGS, AND CONDEMN THEIR DECISION, WE ARE A NATION OF LAWS THAT IS NOT PERFECT, BUT THAT IS (ALL) OUR FORE FATHERS GAVE US TO ADHERE TO. AND ONCE YOU BEGIN TO CHALLENGE ITS INTEGRITY BASED ON HEDGING ALONG RADICAL RACIAL ETHNICITY, YOU ARE DENOUNCING THE INTENT OF JUSTICE, WHICH WILL AUGMENT RETALIATIVE REBELLIOUS DISASTERS IN MANY WAYS FOR AFRICAN AMERICANS, BECAUSE MOST INTELLECT CITIZENS THAT RESIDE IN THE UNITED STATES OF AMERICA SHOULD BE AWARE OF WHAT TRANSPIRED

WHEN THE INDIANS AND AFRICANS REBELLED AGAINST ACCEPTING CIVILIZATION.

SO THIS ATTEMPT BY AL SHARPTON TO SABOTAGE THE JUSTICE SYSTEM, FEDERAL AND LOCAL IS OUT RAGIOUS, AND I DO NOT RECALL ANY OF THE NEWS MEDIA RELATING TO THIS DYSFUNCTIONAL DEBACLE, SIMPLY BECAUSE HE IS BLACK, AND ARE ATTEMPTING TO INTIMIDATE THE JUSTICE SYSTEM BASED ON HIS OWN PRIVATE FORM OF SOCIALISTIC FOLLOWING, THAT LURE YOUNG AND OLD AFRICAN AMERICANS INTO DESTITUTION AND CRIMINAL ACTIVITY, THINKING THE GOVERNMENT AND THE LAWS OF THIS NATION IS RACIST AGAINST BLACKS, AND IS RESPONSIBLE FOR THEIR FAILURES, ALSO FOREVER PLOTTING TO THAT REPULSION.

HOWEVER THERE IS ONE THING FOR CERTAIN, WHEN YOU CROSS THE LINE WITH RACIST DYSFUNCTIONAL IDIOSYNCRASY, YOU ARE SUBJECT TO BE PENALIZED ONE WAY OR ANOTHER REGARDLESS OF YOUR ETHNIC.

SO SUPREME COURT JUSTICE CLARENCE THOMAS, WHEN YOU WERE QUESTIONED ON OCTOBER 2, 2007. RADIO 600, ABOUT THE IMPROPRIETY OF SOME AFRICAN AMERICANS RELATED TO DYSFUNCTIONAL UNLAWFUL ACTIVITY, AND YOUR RESPONSE WAS AS I RECALL (I DO NOT UNDERSTAND THIS) I RESPECT YOUR STATUS AS BEING A SUPREME COURT JUSTICE, HOWEVER I AM A LITTLE DISAPPOINTED IN YOUR DO NOT UNDERSTAND RELATED TO SOME AFRICAN AMERICANS DRUG AND CRIMINAL BEHAVIOR.

I HAVE CAME TO YOUR AID IN THIS MATTER WITH EXPLICIT REVELATION TO THE CRITERIA THAT EXIST AND WHY.

BY THE WAY IF YOU ARE EVER IN CHICAGO, NEW YORK, DETROIT, AND THERE OTHER CITIES AROUND THE NATION, AND VISIT THE HIGH RISE FOURTEEN STORY LOW INCOME HOUSING THEY WILL JOG YOUR MEMORY PERTAINING TO MOTIVATED UNLAWFUL DISSEMINATION.

IN AN EFFORT TO CRITIQUE THE CRITERION FOR SOME AFRICAN AMERICANS MANY MANUFACTURES AND FAST FOOD OPERATIONS HAVE STRUCTURED THEIR POLICY REGARDS TO BAGGY PANTS BELOW THE RUMP.

IF YOU ARE TO REMAIN EMPLOYED, OR GET EMPLOYMENT, YOUR ATTIRE MUST BE APPROPRIATE TO THEIR CODE MINAS BAGGY PANTS EXPOSING RUMP. MANY BLACKS WILL REFUSE TO APPLY FOR EMPLOYMENT, OR QUIT THEIR JOB IN PROTEST, AND THERE IS AN OLD SAYING IF YOU DO NOT WORK YOU ARE GOING TO STEAL, AND IF YOU STEAL YOU ARE GOING TO PRISON. AND THEY ARE SEDUCED AND INDOCTRINATED BY PARASITIC SELF APPOINTED BLACK BIGOTS THAT INCITE THEIR MOTIVATIONS TO THINK THAT THE JUSTICE SYSTEM IN OUR NATION IS BIAS, AND UN-JUST TO (ALL) AFRICAN AMERICANS.

SO JUSTICE CLARENCE THOMAS,I HOPE THIS REVELATION WILL GIVE YOU A CLEAR (UNDERSTANDING) OF THIS DISASTROUS DILEMMA PREMEDITATED AT THE END OF A GUN BARREL.

HOWEVER HISTORICAL EVENTS DICTATE THAT FEDERAL, STATE,AND CITY LAWS ARE BEING IMPLEMENTED TO RATIONALLY DEMINISH THIS IRRATIONAL VIOLENT BEHAVIOR, BASED ON LOITERING AND VINDICTIVENESS IN AN EFFORT TO DIMINISH CHARACTER FOR IMMORAL APPEASEMENT. RECENTLY C-SPAN AIRED A PATHETIC CHARADE OF SENATOR BARACK OBAMA IN WATERLOO, IOWA, PEACOCKISH IN DEMEANOR ON STAGE FLAUNTING AND INSTIGATING ARISTOCRATIC DEMOCRATIC POLITICAL PROPAGANDA, SUSPECTED OF RESPONDING TO CONGRUENT QUESTIONS THAT ONE COULD SURMISE PLANTING.

HE CHOOSE TO ELABORATE ON AN APPOINTMENT WITH A HOUSE AID REGARDS TO HOUSE CARE, AND HOW HE TRAVEL TO WORK WITH HER AT FIVE OCLOCK IN THE MORNING, AND CAUTION HIS AUDIENCE WITH DEMANDING SINCERITY THAT THESE (TYPE) PEOPLE ARE (NOT) BEING PAID ENOUGH.

APPARENTLY HE BEING AN ATTORNEY IS DENOUNCING EXTRA CORRICULA DERIVED FROM INTELLECTUAL MORAL VALUES, THAT ENHANCE INDIVIDUALS REGARDLESS OF THEIR ETHNICS,TO OBTAIN EMPLOYMENT BASED ON THEIR EDUCATIONAL EXTRAORDINARY.

SENATOR BARACK OBAMA IS EXPLOITING LIBERAL DEMOCRATIC IDEOLOGY THAT IS RENOWN, AND MANY

AFRICAN AMERICANS HAVE ADOPTED AS THEIR AGENDA TO EXCLUDE EDUCATION AND EXTRA CURRICULUM CLAIMING IT IS FOR WHITE FOLKS.

(YET) THEY WANT HOUSE CARE, AND FAST FOOD INSTITUTIONS, TO PAY THEM $75,000.00 ANUALLY, AND SENATOR BARACK OBAMA WAS UP AT FIVE A.M. LATER WITH HIS FIRED UP SPEECH, SYMPATHETICALLY ENDORSING AND ATTEMPTING TO ESTABLISH THAT FACT.

THIS IS NOT INTENDED TO DEMEAN SENATOR BARACK OBAMA CHARACTER R BUT HE IS A DEMOCRAT PARTY POLITICIAN, AND THERE ISAN ELECTION IN THE YEAR 2008. AND HE IS PURSUING THE PRESIDENCY WITH IN THE DEMOCRATIC PARTY.

WHICH IS ELECTRIFYING SIMPLY BECAUSE OF THE CHRONOLOGICAL RECORD OF DEMOCRATS PERTAINING TO AFRICAN AMERICANS, THAT THE MAJORITY OF (ALL) SOCIETY IS INEPT TO BLACK AND WHITE.

AND I AM SIMPLY UTILIZING HIS POPULARITY TO EXPOSE DEMOCRATIC SEDUCTIVE HYPOCRISY TO (HERD) AFRICAN AMERICAN VOTERS TO THE POLLS, AND HE IS ONE OF THE MOST POLARIZING AFRICAN AMERICANS FOR DEMOCRATS SINCE BOOKER T. WASHINGTON IN 1895, WITH THE INTENT TO DISTORT AND DECEIVE AFRICAN AMERICANS PERTAINING TO THEIR HISTORICAL IDEOLOGY REGARDS TO BLACKS.

ELITE DEMOCRATS ARE EXPLOITING HIS POPULARITY ALONG WITH OTHER BLACK DIGNITARIES SUCH OPRAH WINFREY AND ERVIN MAGIC JOHNSON, TO ENHANCE THEIR CHANCES IN HOPES OF WINNING THE WHITE HOUSE AS PRESIDENT, AND THEIR INTENT IS TO SEDUCE THE INFLUX OF HERDING BLACK VOTERS FOR THE DEMOCRAT PARTY, (NOT FOR SENATOR BARACK OBAMA) BECAUSE THEY KNOW HE (CANNOT WIN).

BECAUSE FUNDAMENTALLY IT IS THE REGISTERED VOTERS IN THIS NATION DECIDE PRESIDENCIES, HOWEVER IF THE MAJORITY OF AFRICAN AMERICANS HAD THEIR WAY BARACK OBAMA WOULD BE CHOSEN FOR PRESIDENT. BUT UNFORTUNATELY BLACKS ARE ONLY TEN AND ONE HALF

PERCENT OF THREE HUNDRED MILLION PEOPLE IN THIS NATION.

SO IT IS THE CAUCASIAN SOCIETY THAT HOLD THE TRUMP.CARD, AND WILL USE IT AT THEIR LEISURE WHEN NECESSARY,ASTHEYDIDINTHEEARLYFORTIES,DEMOCRATS IN THE SOUTHERN STATES BECAME IRRITATED WHEN PRESIDENT FRANKLIN DELANO ROOSEVELT, INITIATED SOCIAL RELIEF PROGRAMS AND AFRICAN AMERICANS WERE INCLUDED, SO IN AN EFFORT TO VENT THEIR ANGER MOST SWITCHED TO THE REPUBLICAN PARTY, AND THAT IS WHY OUR SOUTHERN STATES IS CONSERVATIVE TODAY.

THERE ARE MANY FACTORS SORTED OUT TO BECOME PRESIDENT, AND MOST HAVE TO DO WITH CHARACTER, BELIEFS, AND AFFILIATION. SO HYPOTHETICALLY IF BY SOME MIRACLE SENATOR BARACK OBAMA WON THE PRIMARY, AND BECAME THE THE DEMOCRATIC NOMINATION OF CHOICE TO RUN FOR PRESIDENT.

THE NATIONAL CONSTITUENCIES ARE GOING TO BE REMINDED OF HOW MOST OF THE AMERICAN CITIES ARE RAN BY BLACK MAYORS, TURN OUT TO BE A DUMP FOR CRIMINAL ACTIVITY, AND HOW JESSIE JACKSON AND AL SHARPTON ARE ATTEMPTING TO SABOTAGE THE JUSTICE SYSTEMALONG RACIAL LINES CATERING TO BLACKS.

TRUST ME IT WOULD (NOT) BE THE REPUBLICANS CUT HIM OFF AT THE ANKLES, IT WOULD BE THE DEMOCRATS SWITCHING PARTY, AND VOTING REPUBLICAN BECAUSE THEIR IDEOLOGY DICTATE THEY WOULD RATHER SEE A WHITE REPUBLICAN AS PRESIDENT, OPPOSE TO A BLACK DEMOCRAT YOU MUST UNDERSTAND THE FUNDAMENTALS OF HISTORIC CONSISTENCY OF THE COUNTRY THAT YOU LIVE IN. ALSO THE SYSTEMATIC LAWS THAT GOVERN OUR SOCIETY, FEDERAL, STATE, CITY, AND TOWN.

WHEN OFFICIALS IMPLEMENT LAWS THEY DOING SO WITH REASON, NOT BECAUSE THEY HAVE IDLE TIME.

AND THESE LAWS ARE INTENDED TO PROTECT INNOCENT CITIZENS FROM MALICIOUS BAD BEHAVIA FROM OTHERS, BASED ON JUSTICE THROUGH THE COURT SYSTEM, UNFORTUNATELY THERE IS A SEGEMENT OF SMALL DYSFUNCTIONAL BRAIN AFRICAN AMERICANS

ATTEMPTING TO DISTORT THE GUIDE-LINES OF THE JUSTICE SYSTEM.

WITH AFRICAN CONGO IDEOLOGY WHERE THE BONE IN THE NOSE CHIEF RULE THE TRIBE, FOR ANY PERSON OR GROUP OF PEOPLE ATTEMPT TO INFILTRATE AND DISMANTLE LAWS PERTAINING TO FEDERAL, STATE, AND CITY, FOR THEIR OWN RADICAL RACIST IDIOSYNCRASIES.

IS APPALLING AND SHOULD BE LABELED GOVERNMENTAL TREASONABLE, CNN HEADLINE NEWS REPORTED ON DECEMBER 22, 2007.

THAT THE CONGRESSIONAL BLACK CAUCUS (JACK ASSES) DEMANDED THAT THE GOVERNOR OF LOUISIANA, COMMUTE PARDON AND RELEASE THE JENA SIX IMMEDIATELY.

IF THIS IS TRUE,FOR ANY PERSON OR GROUP OF PEOPLE ATTEMPTING TO INFILTRATE AND DISMANTLE FEDERAL, STATE, AND CITY LAWS, BECAUSE OF THEIR RACE IDIOSYNCRASIES RAISE QUESTIONS ABOUT THEIR FITNESS TO SERVE IN THE CONGRESS.

THIS BLACK THING IS OUT OF CONTROL IN THIS NATION, JUST WHOM AUTHORIZED THESE (NIT-WITS) TO DICTATE POLICY T,Q. SITTING STATE GOVERNORS, IT SEND CHILLS UP MY SPINE TO THINK BARACK OBAMA COULD BECOME PRESIDENT, CAN YOU IMAGINE HIM HERDING WITH THESE BLACK CAUCUS POLITICAL SUGGESTIVE LAW BREAKING MIS-FIT SOCIALISTIC RADICALS IN THE CONGRESS.

WE ALL SHOULD CONSIDER PUTTING OUR ORDER IN TO AFRICA FOR THE HEAD DRESS, SPEAR, AND NOSE BONE, BECAUSE I SUSPECT THERE WOULD BE MASS SOLICITATION BY THEBLACK CAUCUS, FOR THE COMMUTATION AND RELEASE OF ALL KIND OF BLACK CRIMINALS AROUND THE NATION THAT HAS COMMITED HIDEOUS CRIMES.

I THINK THE MAJORITY OF INTELLECT CITIZENS IN OUR NATION BLACK AND WHITE ARE DISGUSTED WITH THIS BLACK DOUBLE STANDARD, CONSTANTLY PORTRAYING THEM SELVES AS VICTOMS OF THE FIFTIES DISCRIMINATION, WHEN IT IS NOTHING MORE THAN A SYNDROME OF REVERSE BIGOTRY THAT REPRESENT RACISM PARALLEL TO THE KU-KLUX-KLAN.

THE INTENT IS TO BOOST THEIR SUPERIORITY IN DENOUNCING THE LAWS OF THIS NATION TO THEIR CONGO IDEOLOGY. BECAUSE THEY SUSPECT MOST WHITES ARE RELUCTANT TO CRITICIGE THIS INSANITY.

THAT IS MOTIVATED IN AN EFFORT TO INTIMIDATE THE JUSTICE SYSTEM, AND LAW ENFORCEMENT PERSONNEL THROUGH OUT OUR NATION, TO BE COMPASSIONATE REGARDS TO BLACKS COMMITTING HIDEOUS CRIMES NATION WIDE IT IS ESSENTIAL THAT THIS DIABOLICAL CONDESCENDING PLOY INITIATED BY SOME ELITE BLACKS BE EXPOSED REGARDS TO THE SHAM THAT IT IS. CAN YOU IMAGINE WHAT KIND OF CYNICAL DEBRIEFING WAS PERVADED TO MANY YOUNG AND OLD BLACKS, THAT SUGGEST BASED ON THE CONGRESSIO NAL BLACK CAUCUS AND AL SHARPTON ASSESSMENT THAT LAWS OF OUR NATION IS CORRUPT AND BIAS AGAINST ALL AFRICAN AMERICANS. YOU CANT EXPECT ANY MORE FROM SHARPTON, BECAUSE HE IS INEPT TO THE FUNCTIONS OF THE JUSTICE DEPARTMENT, SENATE AND CONGRESS. AND HE LET THE ENTIRE NATION KNOW OF HIS IGNORANCE BY ORGANIZING AND STAGING A MARCH ON THE JUSTICE DEPARTMENT IN WASHINGTON, AS IF THE JUSTICE DEPARTMENT SHOULD HAVE CONSULTED WITH HIM PRIOR TO THEIR DECISION, ALSO SOME WHERE SCREAMING WITH THAT DUCK ON HIS HEAD, THAT THE TWENTY FIRST CENTURY IS FOR CIVIL RIGHTS. I WONDER WHAT ROCK HE HAS BEEN HIDING UNDER SENSE 1964 AND 1965 ALSO SOME ONE NEED TO ADVISE THIS SELF APPOINTED DICTATOR THAT 70% OF AFRICAN AMERICANS ARE FAR ABOVE THE POVITY LEVEL IN THE UNITED STATES OF AMERICA.

WITH INTELLECTUAL POSITIONS THAT CONSIST OF SECRETARY OF STATE, SENATORS FEDERAL AND STATE, MAYORS, JUDGES, LAW PROFESSORS, CONGRESS (@) REPRESENTATIVES, MOVIE STARS, BUISNESS OWNERS, YOU NAME IT ASTRONAUTS, AND WEALTHY SELF APPOINTED DICTATORS LIKE HE AND JESSIE JACKSON, DOCTORS, LAWYERS, I COULD GO ON AND ON. SO IT´A WAS A NONSENSICAL BUFFOONISH REMARK FOR AL SHARPTON TO STIPULATE THAT THE TWENTY FIRST CENTURY IS

REGULATED TO PURSUING AND MANDATING CIVIL RIGHTS FOR AFRICAN AMERICANS.

THIS IS ONE OF THE MOST ASININE PERVERTED REMARKS OF MORDERN TIMES, ON OUR FARM IN THE SOUTH IS WHERE I PARTIALLY GREW UP UNTIL I WAS APPROXIMATELY FIFTEEN, I OWE A GREAT DEAL OF GRATITUDE TO MY PARENTS ESPECIALLY MY GRAND MOTHER, SHE HAD A HEART OF GOLD BUT IF YOU WERE DOING SOMETHING MISCHIEVIOUS HER LOOK WOULD ALMOST CAUSE YOU TO SELF DISTRUCT, HOWEVER SHE WAS LIKE THE ROCK OF GIBRALTER WHEN IT CAME TO COMMON SENSE, HERE IS JUST A FIEW OF HER MORAL VALUE INSTRUCTIONS.

IF YOU WANT A (FREE) RIDE GO TO THE BARN AND GET YOU A MULE, AND THERE WAS NOT A DAY GO BY THAT SHE DID NOT QUOTE SOME PARTS OF THE TEN COMMANDMENTS, BUT SHE PRIMARILY VOICED HER OPINION ON INDIVIDUAL THINKING LEARNABLE ISSURES PERTAINING TO (ALL) PEOPLE PIRATICALLY BLACKS, IN HER PASS TIME SHE MADE QUILTS MOSTLY AT W NIGHT, AND WE WOULD BE SITTING AT THE FIRE PLACE AND ALL OF A SUDDEN AT DARK SHE WOULD CALL ME TO THE BACK DOOR OF THE HOUSE AND SHOW ME A LIGHT FAR IN THE WOODS LIT WITH A KEROSENE BOTTLE STUFFED WITH A RAG.

AND THEN SHE WOULD SAY I WANTED TO SHOW YOU THAT LIGHT BECAUSE I AM GOING TO TELL YOU THE STORY BEHIND IT, THERE IS A BUNCH OF MEN OUT GAMBLING INCLUDING SOME OF YOUR UNCLES, SHOOTING DICE BECAUSE THEY HAVE LAID BY THEIR CROPS AND HAVE MONEY, NOW WHEN SOME OF THEM LOOSE THEIR MONEY WHICH IT TOOK THEM A YEAR TO EARN, THE LOOSERS ARE GOING HOME TO THEIR WIVES AND PICK A FIGHT AND TELL A LIE ON WHITE FOLKS, THAT THEY WERE CHEATED AT THE COTTON GIN, BECAUSE THE GIN OWNER IS RACIST AND HATE BLACKS.

NOW IF ONE OF YOUR UNCLES LOOSE HE IS GOING TO COME BY HERE AND TELL ME THE SAME LIE AND TRY AND BORROW MONEY, WHICH I AM NOT GOING TO LET HIM HAVE, THEN HE IS GOING TO GO RIGHT BACK TO THE

WHITE MAN THAT HE ACCUSED OF BEING A RACIST AND CHEATING HIM, TO BORROW MONEY HE MIGHT LET HIM HAVE IT OR NOT, BUT IF HE DONT HE IS GOING TO HERD HIS GAMBLING BUDDIES TOGATHER AND TRY TO CONVINCE THEM THAT THE COTTON GIN OWNER IS A RACIST AND HATE BLACKS AND THEY SHOULD NOT GI HERE AND THEN MY GRAND MOTHER WOULD PAUSE AND TELL ME TO BRING HER SNUFF BOX, SHE WOULD TAKE A BIG WAD AND TELL ME I WANT YOU TO LISTEN TO ME CAREFULLY NO BODY LIKE TO BE LIED ON, ESPECIALLY WHITE FOLKS, BECAUSE THE OTHER NIGGERS ARE GOING BACK AND TELL WHO LIED FOR A SLAB OF FAT BACK, AND THEN SHE WOULD SAY THE MAIN REASON WHY NIGGERS GET HURT THROUGH OUT THE SOUTH BY WHITE FOLKS BECAUSE OF LIES AND MESSING WITH THEIR STUFF, WHEN IT DONT BELONG TO THEM, AND THEY WILL HAVE NOTHING TO SHOW FOR A LIFETIME OF WORK BUT THEY WILL TRY AND TELL YOU HOW TO RUN YOUR BUISNESS AND CANT EVEN READ.

SO WHAT EVER YOU DO WHEN YOU GROW UP THINK FOR YOUR SELF, AND FOR GOD SAKE STAY AWAY FROM HERDING NIGGERS, BECAUSE THEY ARE TEN TIMES AS RACIST AS WHITES, ALSO TEN TIMES AS STUPID, SOME HAVE THE BRAINS MUCH LIKE AN OPOSSUM, A PACK OF HOUND DOGS WILL BE CHASING HIM AND THERE IS A FIFTY FOOT OAK TREE NEAR A CORN STALK, AND HE WILL CHOOSE TO CLIMB THE CORN STALK.

SO IF YOU CANT ADJUST TO THE STANDARS OF NATION AND FOLLOW THE TEN COMMANDMENTS YOU ARE GOING TO HAVE MANY PROBLEMS, BECAUSE SOME DAY DURING YOUR LIFE TIME YOU ARE GOING TO GET EQUAL RIGHTS, AND WHEN YOU DO IF YOU CHOOSE TO FOLLOW HERDING NIGGERS YOU MIGHT AS WELL TAKE YOUR ASS TO AFRICA JOIN A TRIBE WHERE THE CHIEF OR WITCH DOCTOR DO YOUR THINKING FOR YOU, BECAUSE WHITE FOLKS COULD CARE LESS ABOUT WHAT YOU THINK, BECAUSE THEY ARE SMART ENOUGH TO KNOW THAT AS LONG AS YOU ARE A NIGGER YOU ARE GOING TO COME TO THEM FOR SOMETHING, BECAUSE THEY HAVE ALL THE MONEY AND EVERY THING YOU NEED TO SURVIVE.

AND (ALWAYS) REMEMBER OUR ANCESTORS WERE BROUGHT HERE NOTHING MORE THAN SAVAGES,NOT CUSTOM TO THIS LAND, HOWEVER NOW WE ARE HERE WE SHOULD TRY AND UNDERSTAND WHAT THEY ARE ALL ABOUT, AND HEED TRUST IN GOD AND MOVE ON BECAUSE HATE WILL GET YOU NOTHING BUT A HOLE IN THE GROUND, EXCEPT YOUR FATE WITH GRACE AND GOD WILL SHOW YOU THE ROAD TO HAPPINESS ON YOUR OWN SENSES.

AND WHAT EVER YOU DO (NEVER) PASS ON TALK FROM WHAT SOME BODY ELSE SAID, BECAUSE IT COULD BE A LIE, AND IF IT IS A LIE AND YOU GO BACK TO THE PERSON TOLD IT TO YOU FOR PROOF, HE OR SHE IS GOING TO LIE AND SAY THEY DIDNT SAY IT, SO YOU ARE STUCK WITH SOME BODY ELSE LIE, AND FOLKS IS GOING TO CALL YOU A LIAR.

AND ALWAYS REMEMBER THAT ABOUT THE OPOSSUM BRAIN WHEN IT COME TO (SOME) NIGGERS, BECAUSE A BUNCH OF THEM CARRIED ON LIES ABOUT THE COTTON GIN OWNER, AND THEY WERE LIES BECAUSE WHEN YOU TAKE YOUR COTTON TO THE GIN YOU DRIVE ON A WEIGHING SCALE, EVERY THING IS WEIGHED TOGATHER, DRIVER, WAGON, MULES, AND COTTON, THEN YOU DRIVE AROUND TO ANOTHER SCALE, THE DRIVER SIT ON THE WAGON TO HOLD THE MULES UNTIL THE COTTON IS GINNED, THERE IS A SCALE THAT YOU CAN SEE IN EACH WINDOW WHEN YOU COME IN AND WHEN YOU LEAVE THE GIN HOUSE.

BUT YOU DONT LEAVE UNTIL YOU, MULES AND WAGON HAVE BEEN WEIGHED, WITH OUT THE COTTON, AND YOU ARE SITTING THERE WATCHING THE SCALE ALL THE TIME, WHITE FOLKS AND NIGGERS USE THE SAME GIN, AND ALL OF THE CHORES AROUND THE GIN IS RUN BY NIGGERS, THE GINNING AND SOME TIME WEIGHING.

BECAUSE THE OWNER IS HARDLY EVER THERE, NOT ONLY THAT I HAVE GIN MY COTTON THERE FOR YEARS AND NEVER HAD A PROBLEM, THERE IS A PRICE TO PAY FOR LYING ON PEOPLE, BECAUSE THE ONES THAT CARRIED THE LIES COULD NOT GET CREDIT ANY WHERE TO BUY SUGAR, FLOWER, AND LARD TO FEED THEIR FAMILIES, ALSO SEEDS

AND FERTILIZER TO GROW THEIR CROPS FOR THE NEXT YEAR.

IN SOME SOUTHERN STATES THE KU-KLUX-KLAN HUNG NIGGERS FOR THEIR MADE UP LIES AND STEALING THAT DIDNTBELONGTOTHEM.MYGRANDMOTHERANDPARENTS HAS SINCE PASSED ON, BUT THESE CHRONOLOGICAL QUOTATION IS PRICELESS FOR ME, BECAUSE IT TRANSCENDS INTO (SOME) AFRICAN AMERICANS AGENDA TODAY.

WELL THAT WAS OVER SIXTY YEARS AGO, AFRICAN AMERICANS DO NOT HAVE TO WORRY ABOUT ACCESSIBILITY TO SUGAR, FLOWER, LARD, PLOWS, LARD, COTTON SEED,OOR THE KU-KLUX-KLAN.

HOWEVER MY FORE PARENTS MUST HAVE BEEN ON TO SOMETHING ABOUT (SOME) AFRICAN AMERICANS PERTAINING TO LIES AND CRIMINAL ACTIVITY. BECAUSE THERE ARE APPROXIMATELY THREE HUNDRED (MILLION) PEOPLE IN THE UNITED STATES OF AMERICA, BLACKS ARE ONLY APPROXIMATELY 12% OF THAT THREE HUNDRED MILLION,WHICH CONSIST OF THIRTY SIX MILLION PEOPLE, AND THAT IS ON THE HIGH SIDE.

ACCORDING TO THE 2007, 126 ADDITION OF THE SATISTICAL ABSTRACT OF THE UNITED STATES OF AMERICA, THERE ARE APPROXIMATELY (713.990) (TOTAL) INMATES INCARCERATED IN THE UNITED STATES OF AMERICA, FOR VARIOUS CRIMINAL ACTIVITIES THAT CONSIST OF (ALL) NATIONALITIES OF PEOPLE INCLUDING BLACKS.

OF THAT (713.990) TOTAL OF ALL INMATES, BLACKS IS COMPRISED OF A STUNNING (275.400). THE AFFIRMATION OF THIS TRAGEDY IS APPALLING SO CONGRESSIONAL (BLACK CAUCUS), AL SHARPTON, JESSIE JACKSON, AND OTHERS, I WOULD ASSUME THAT YOUR PRESUMPTUOUS ASSESSMENT THESE HIDIOUS TREACHEROUS REVELATIONS PERTAINING TO CRIMINAL ACTIVITY REGARDS TO BLACKS, IS DUE TO RACIST BIGOTRY BY CAUCASIANS THAT CAUSE THIS INFLUX IN CRIME BY (SOME) AFRICAN AMERICANS. NOTABILITY THE STATISTICS OF MILITANT BLACK CRIMINAL BEHAVIOR IN OUR NATION IS EGREGIOUS AND APPALLING.

HOWEVER IT APPEAR THAT THERE SOME HERDING DYSFUNCTIONAL SMALL BRAIN BLACKS IN OUR NATION

THAT IS ENDORSING THEIR BEHAVIOR, REQUESTING THEIR COMMUTATION PARDON AND RELEASED BACK INTO THE GENERAL PUBLIC PRIOR TO SERVING THEIR TIME JUDGED BY THE COURTS. WE WE ARE A NATION OF LAWS THAT IS EMBEDDED IN OUR CONSTITUTION AND DECLARATION OF INDEPENDENCE, WHICH IS FOR GUIDANCE PERTAINING TO GOVERNMENTAL LAWS FOR OUR NATION.

AND THESE LAWS ARE ADHERED TO BY GOVERNING BODYS THAT CONSIST OF A SUPREME COURT THAT HAVE NINE JUSTICES THAT ARE APPOINTEES, A. CONGRESS THAT CONSIST OF FOUR HUNDRED AND THIRTY FIVE ELECTED OFFFICIALS, A SENATE OF ONE HUNDERD ELECTED OFFICIALS, AND OF COURSE AN ELECTED PRESIDENT.

OUR FIFTY STATES ARE SEQUENCED IN THE SAME MANNER BUT HAVE LESS PERSONNEL, AND A GOVERNOR THAT IS ELECTED TO SERVE AS THEIR TOP OFFICIAL INSTEAD OF A PRESIDENT.

THESE GOVERNING BODIES ARE BOUND BY A MAJORITY RULE, (NO) LAWS WILL BE PASSED PERTAINING TO THE GENERAL PUBLIC UNLESS THERE IS A VOTE BY THE MAJORITY, WITHIN THEIR PROSPECTIVE BODIES. I LIST THESE CHRONOLOGICAL PARITIES OF OUR GOVERNMENTAL STRUCTURES AND FUNDAMENTAL STANDARDS, BECAUSE IF ONE OR SOME SHOULD CHOOSE TO IGNORE OR VIOLATE, HISTORICALLY THIS REPRESENT DOOM FOR THE PERPETRATORS, ALSO TRAGEDY FOR MANY INNOCENT CITIZENS OF THIS NATIONPIRATICALLY AFRICAN AMERICANS.

BECAUSE HISTORY DICTATE RETALIATION FOR BIGOTRY, HOSTILITY, LYING STEALING, AND IGNORANCE.

LETS JUST ANALYTICALLY ACCESS AFRICAN AMERICANS CHOSEN OR ELECTED TO ANY OF THE (MAJOR) GOVERNING POLITICAL BODYS THAT DICTATE OUR LAWS, FEDERAL AND STATE THAT HAVE THE POWER TO (OVER-RIDE) OR SORT OUT AND RULE ACCORDING TO THE STANDARDS OF LAW.

THE FEDERAL SUPREME COURT CONSIST OF (NINE) JUSTICES (ONE) BLACK, THE SENATE CONSIST OF (ONE HUNDRED) ELECTED OFFICIALS (ONE) BLACK THE

CONGRESS CONSIST OF (FOUR HUNDRED THIRTY FIVE) ELECTED OFFICIALS (FORTY TWO) BLACK.

THERE ARE APPROXIMATELY (THREE HUNDRED FORTY) STATE SUPREME COURT JUSTICES NATION WIDE DEVIDED ACCORDINGLY IN FIFTY STATES, (TWENTY FOUR) BLACK, YOU DO THE MATH THERE ARE SOME STATES DO NOT HAVE (ANY) BLACK STATE SUPREME COURT JUSTICES.

SO IN RETROSPECT THIS (BLACK CACUS) CONGO HERDING IS NOTHING MORE THAN A MYTH, THAT REPRESENT A RACIST IDEOLOGY, THAT IS DYSFUNCTIONAL AND UNFIT FOR A INTELLECT DIVERSE SOCIETY.

BECAUSE THERE ARE MANY BLACK AND WHITES THAT ARE (NOT) FAMILIAR WITH THE COMPLEX UNIQUE FUNCTIONS OF OUR GOVERNMENTAL PROCEDURES, AND WHEN THE NATIONAL NEWS AIRED THAT THE CONGRESSIONAL (BLACK CAUCUS) HAD CONTACTED GOVERNOR KATHLINE BLANCOOF LOUISIANA, AND DEMANDED THE COMMUTAION PARDON AND RELEASE THE JENA SIX, MANY BLACKS WOULD ASSUME THAT THEY CONTROL THE CONGRESS, AND THE GOVERNOR SHOULD HAVE ORDERED THEIR RELEASE.

AND MOST HERDING BLACKS ARE GOING TO MISINTERPRET THIS AS AN APPEAL FROM THE CONGRESS FOR INJUSTICE RELATED TO BLACK CAUSES. INHERENTLY (NOT) REALIZING THESE (FORTY TWO) OUT LAW EXEBITIONIST HAVE (NO) AUTHORITY TO CHESTISE A SITTING STATE GOVERNOR, AND DEMAND THE RELEASE OF (ANY) CONVICTED FELONS BLACK OR WHITE REGARDLESS OF THE JUDICIAL VERDIC.

THIS WAS ONE OF THE MOST OUTRAGEOUS RACIST DIVISIVE DECEITFUL DYSFUNCTIONAL SMALL BRAIN ENDEAVOR TO INTIMIDATE OF MORDEN TIMES, PIRATICALLY WHEN THEY ARE ELECTED TO REPRESENT IN A POLITICAL BODY OF GOVERNMENT THAT SET THE LAWFUL AGENDA FOR OUR NATION, PERTAINING TO (ALL) CITIZENS THAT LIVE IN OUR DIVERSE SOCIETY. THIS KIND OF ASININE BEHAVIOR BY THESE LONE (FORTY TWO) CONGRESS PEOPLE THAT LABEL THEM SELVES THE BLACK CAUCUS IS AN DELIBERATE ATTEMPT TO INCITE DISBELIEF BY MANY BLACKS THAT

HAVE NO REGARD FOR THE COMPREHENSION OF THE JUSTICE SYSTEM, AND REBELL BASED ON THE ABSURDITY OF THESE FORTY TWO CONGRESS BLACKS, THINKING THAT THE JUSTICE SYSTEM IS OUT TO IMPEDE THEIR PROGRESS BASED ON RACIST TACTICS BECAUSE THEY ARE BLACK.

AND AS A RESULT MANY HAS CHOSEN TO VENT THEIR FRUSTRATION BASED ON A EGOISTIC AGENDA, THAT REPRESENT HOSTILITY, MOSTLY DUE TO HERDING BEHIND FASCIST BLACK PROTEGEES THAT IS INEPT TO THE FUNDAMENTAL FUNCTIONS OF THE LAWS THAT GOVERN THIS NATION. IT IS APPAULING ON HOW THE ELITE BLACK EXEBITIONIST USE DEMAGOGIC ORENTATION IN AN EFFORT TO SEDUCE OTHER HERDING BLACKS INTO THINKING THAT THE INSTITUTION OF CAUCASIANS,NATION WIDE IS OUT TO DEPRIVE THEM OF THEIR CIVIL RIGHTS, AND REVERT BACK TO SERVITUDE, WHICH REMIND ME OF MY GRAND MOTHER STATEMENT OVER SIXTY YEARS AGO,ABOUT THE OPOSSUM WHICH DOSENT HAVE THE THINKING CAPACITY TO DETERMINE WHICH IS SAFER FROM CHASING HOUNDS A FIFTY FOOT TALL OAK TREE OR A CORN STALK.

HOWEVER AS WE MOVE INTO THE YEAR TWO THOUSAND EIGHT, WHICH IS AN ELECTION YEAR FOR THE PRESIDENCY OF THE UNITED STATES OF AMERICA IF A DEMOCRAT SHOULD WIN THE WHITE HOUSE, HOSTILE AFRICAN AMERICANS (BE AWARE) BECAUSE THEY ARE THE PARTY THAT FOUNDED THE (KU-KLUX-KLAN) THAT MAIMED, HUNG, AND ASSAULTED BLACKS IN THE SOUTHERN STATES, FOR FAR LESS THAN WHAT IS GOING ON TODAY. AL SHARPTON IS SCREAMING TO THE TOP OF HIS LUNGS, THAT THE TWENTY FIRST CENTURY IS FOR CIVIL RIGHTS, AND IS INEPT TO THE FACK THAT IT WAS THE SOUTHERN DEMOCRATS, THE PARTY THAT HE SUPPORTS DEPRIVED BLACKS OF THEIR CIVIL RIGHTS IN SOUTHERN STATES FOR THREE HUNDRED AND FORTY SIX YEARS.

AND FOR CERTAIN THEY WILL (NOT) TOLERATE ERRATIC BEHAVIOR FROM HOSTILE BLACKS, EXAMPLE DURING HURRICANE KATRINA IN NEW ORLEANS GOVERNOR KATHLINE BLANCO GAVE THE ORDER (SHOOT TO KILL) FOR LOOTERS, SO IF THE DEMOCRATS MAINTAIN THE MAJORITY

IN THE SENATE AND CONGRESS AND A DEMOCRAT PRESIDENT IS ELECTED IN TWO THOUSAND AND EIGHT, ARROGANT BLACKS ARE IN (SERIOUS) TROUBLE.

THIS IS (NOT) MEANT TO INSINUATE THAT CAUCASIAN DEMOCRATS ARE OUT TO GET BLACKS (NOT TRUE) BUT THEIR GENETIC HERITAGE DICTATE THAT BLACK OR WHITE IF YOU CANT MEASURE UP TO EXPECTED DIGNETY THEN THERE ARE SEVERE CONSEQUENCES PIRATICALLY AFRICAN AMERICANS, SOME MIGHT WONDER WHAT WILL THEY DO.

WELL LISTEN UP IF THEY CONTROL THE PRESIDENCY, SENATE, AND CONGRESS THERE IS (NO) ·VETO POWER, AND THEY WILL PASS CONSTRAINT LAWS THAT WILL TRICKLE DOWN TO THE STATES THAT WILL HAMMER ARROGANT BLACKS INTO THE GROUND LIKE A TENT STAKE, HISTORICALLY EVEN DURING SLAVERY IN THE SOUTH THE DEMOCRATS AT TIMES WERE RELUCTANT AND MOST OF THE TIME (NEVER) WAS DELIGHTED IN MAIMING BLACKS, BECAUSE THEY WERE NEEDED TO WORK THE PLANTATIONS, UNFORTUNATELY THEY HAVE A SHORT FUSE WHEN IT COME TO ARROGANCE, STEALING, MURDER, AND RAPE, ALSO IGNORANCE PIRATICALLY FROM BLACKS.

I GREW UP IN THE SOUTH DURING THE EARLY FORTIES, AND HAVE FIRST HAND UNDERSTANDING AS TO WHY SOME BLACKS WERE VICTOMS OF BARBARIC TORTURE, FOR INSTANCE IN SOME SOUTHERN STATES IT WAS REPORTED SOME BLACKS WOULD SNEAK INTO WHITE CEMETERIES AND DISLODGE THEIR LOVE ONES AND REMOVE THEIR JEWELRY, STEALING COTTON, ALSO ANIMALS AND SOME TIME USING ANIMALS FOR SEX, AND THERE MANY OTHER DEVIOUS TACTICS THAT SOME BLACKS WERE INVOLVED IN, MY ENTIRE ANCESTRY RESIDED IN THE SOUTH, THERE IS A PHOTO OF MY GREAT GRAND FATHER ALONG WITH HIS LAND DEED DURING THE EIGHTEEN CENTURY.

I WAS (NEVER) ADVISED NOR DO I REMEMBER HAVING PROBLEMS FROM WHITES IN THE SOUTH, AND WE TRAVELED EXTENSIVELY TO LOUISIAN, TEXAS ALABAMA, TENNESSEE, MISSISSIPPI, GEORGIA, AND ARKANSAS. SO TO THOSE THAT ARE INEPT REGARDS TO FORMALITIES THAT TRANSPIRED

IN THE SOUTHERN STATES, AND DELIBERATELY LIE ABOUT WHAT HAPPEN AND (NEVER) HAVE AN EXPLANATION AS TO WHY.

SUCH AS AL SHARPTON, JESSIE JACKSON, AND THE EXEBITIONIST HERDING (UNREADABLE TEXT) AROUND THE NATION.

MY ANCESTORS INCLUDING MY SELF EARN THE RIGHT TO BE RESPECTED BY (NOT) BEING ARROGANT LYING AND STEALING, BUT MOST OF ALL BY UNDERSTANDING THE MEANING OF MORAL VALUES, THAT OFFER YOU THE CREDENTIALS TO COMMUNICATE WITH (ALL) PEOPLE, AND BECOME INVOLVED IN THIS INTRICATE DIVERSE SOCIETY THAT EXIST BASED ON MERIT. I AM COMPELLED TO DETAIL THE SHOWING ON THE TRAVEL CHANNEL SUNDAY DECEMBER 30, 2007, TITLED TRIBAL LIFE MEET THE NAMAL, THESE WERE PEOPLE ADVERSE TO CIVILIZATION WITH TRADITIONAL HERDING INSTINCTS BEHIND A CHIEF SPOKESMAN, WITH HEAD DRESS AND NUMEROUS AFRICAN TRIBAL TRADITIONAL ATTIRES.

THIS WAS AN AMAZING PHENOMENON, THEY WERE CAPABLE OF RESOLVING A DISPUTE BETWEEN TRIBAL DIFFERENCES PERTAINING TO VIOLENCE AND AGREE ON A PEACEFUL SALUTION.

AS I SAT AND OBSERVED THIS HOSTILE DIABOLIC EPISODE OF TRIBAL MANNERISM, IT REMINDED ME OF THE (UNREADABLE TEXT) PROUFOUND CHARACTERISTICS OF OUR GENETIC DERIVED CULTURAL TRAITS.

HOWEVER THEY HAD THE UNCANNY ABILITY TO QUELL TRIBAL VIOLENCE AMONG THEM SELVES, HAVING (NO) SENSE OF DIGNITY, CHARACTER CIVILITY CLOTHES, ELECTRICITY, AND CURRICULAR.

AND WE ARE THE DESENDANTS OF THIS CULTURE OF PEOPLE, THREE HUNDRRED AND EIGHTY NINE YEARS LATER, THAT RESIDE IN THE UNITED STATES OF AMERICA LABELED AS AFRICAN AMERICANS, WHERE EDUCATE, CIVILITY, AND EXTRA CURRICULAR IS PROFOUND AND AT OUR DISPOSITION,(YET) SOME BLACKS CAN (NOT) DISPOSE OF THE ACT TO SLAUGHTERING EACH OTHER,

THESE HOSTILE AFRICAN TRIBESMEN WERE CAPABLE OF RESOLVING THEIR TRIBAL ALTERCATIONS.

SIMPLY BECAUSE THERE ARE (NO) WHITE TRIBES IN THE AFRICAN BUSH, AND MOST OF ALL THERE IS (NO) AL SHARPTON, JESSIE JACKSON, AND BLACK CAUCUS TO DEMAGOGUE AND BLAME THEIR TRIBAL DISPUTES ON (WHITES). HOWEVER REPUBLICANS HAVE ALWAYS BEEN SENSITIVE AND HAD COMPASSION FOR MOST AFRICAN AMERICANS IGNORANCE, THAT IS WHY PRESIDENT ABRAHAM LINCOLN PRIOR TO HIS BEING ASSASSINATED HE HAD DRAFTED A DIRECTIVE TO (GIVE) EVERY AFRICAN AMERICAN FAMILY, FORTY ACRES OF SOUTHERN LAND AND A GOVERNMENT MULE, IN HOPES OF THEIR ATTAINING INTELLECTUAL MORAL VALUES AND INDEPENDANCE. ALSO LEARNING THE STRUCTURE OF NEGOTIATING FROM WHITES AND BECOMING INTEGRATED INTO AMERICAN CULTURE.

UNFORTUNATELY THIS DID NOT HAPPEN BECAUSE PRESIDENT LINCOLN WAS ASSASSINATED, HIS VICE PRESIDENT ANDREW JOHNSON FROM TENNESSEE A DEMOCRAT, BECAME PRESIDENT AND GAVE THE LAND BACK TO THE SOUTHERN PLANTATION OWNERS.

AND AL SHARPTON IS STILL WONDERING WHAT HAPPEN TO THE FORTY ACRES AND THE MULE, AND LYING ON REPUBLICANS.

HE SHOULD CONTACT HIS FIRST BLACK PRESIDENT WILLIAM JEFFERSON CLINTON, ONE OF THE MOST DEVIOUS SEDUCTIVE HYPOCRITE OF MODERN TIMES, PERTAINING TO AFRICAN AMERICANS, BILL CLINTON WAS IN LITTLE ROCK AT THE HIGH SCHOOL CELEBRATING THE FIFTY YEAR ADMITTANCE TO NINE BLACKS, WHEN IT WAS HIS SEGREGATIVE DEMOCRATIC PARTY THAT DENIED THEM ACCESS TO PUBLIC EDUCATION.

AND IT WAS A COMPASSIONATE REPUBLICAN PRESIDENT, DWIGHT DAVID EISENHOWER, THAT REJECTED THE GOVERNOR OF ARKANSAS REFUSAL OF ADMITTANCE, FEDERALIZED THE NATIONAL GUARD AND THE NINE BLACK STUDENTS ENTERED THE SCHOOL WITH OUT PROVOCATION.

(YET) BILL CLINTON IS THERE ON THE FIFTIETH ANNIVERSARY CELEBRATING LYING, AND SEDUCING BLACKS TO THINK THAT THE DEMOCRATS WAS INSTRUMENTAL IN THEIR STRUGGLE FOR EDUCATION IN THE SOUTH, IN AN EFFORT TO DECEIVE THEM FOR THEIR (VOTES) FOR HE AND SENATOR HILLARY CLINTON FOR PRESIDENT.

MOST SOUTHERN DEMOCRATS KNOW MORE ABOUT BLACKS THAN THEY KNOW ABOUT THEM SELVES, THEY HAVE STUDIED THEIR DEMEANOR ALSO THEIR THEIR ANCESTRY TRAITS FROM AFRICA, AND CALCULATED THEIR INTELLECT PIRATICALLY HAVING TO DO WITH THE POLITICAL ARENA, AND DEMOCRATICALLY DECIDED THAT MOST ARE UNFIT TO CHOOSE DIVERSE OFFICIAL CANDIDATES BASED ON THEIR INDIVIDUAL MERIT.

AND THAT IS WHY DEMOCRATS UTILIZE OTHER CELEBRITY TYPE BLACKS TO SOLIDIFY THEIR HERDING VOTE BLOC.

THE EPISODE SHOWN ON THE TRAVEL CHANNEL DECEMBER 30, 2007, LEND CREDENCE TO THEIR THEORY, BECAUSE IT ILLUSTRATE HERDING BEHIND A CHIEF FOR THEIR GUIDANCE, AND THIS IS PROFOUND IN AFRICAN AMERICAN SOCIETY BASED ON GENETIC CONTROLLABILITY FROM AFRICA. THIS STIGMA (WILL) BE EMBEDDED IN BLACK CULTURE AS LONG AS WE ARE ON GODS EARTH, AND THE MAJORITY OF BLACKS ARE TOTALLY UNAWARE OF THIS GENETIC TRAIT, BUT THE DEMOCRATS ARE.

HOWEVER DURING THIS ELECTION YEAR TWO THOUSAND EIGHT, IS QUITEUNIQUE BECAUSE IT IS THE FIRST TIME IN DEMOCRATIC HISTORY THAT A AFRICAN AMERICAN IS AN ELITIST AND POLLING PARALLEL TO CAUCASIANS REGARDS TO THE CAUCUS.

THE DEMOCRATS OR REPUBLICANS HAS (NEVER).IN THE HISTORY OF OUR NATION ENCOUNTERED ANY THING OF THIS POLITICAL MAGNITUDE WITH AN AFRICAN AMERICAN PERSUING THE MOST POWERFUL OFFICE IN THE WORLD, AND GETTING ATTENTION EQUAL TO WHITES.

THIS COULD VERY WELL BE AN ACHILLES HEEL FOR DEMOCRATS, BECAUSE THE REASON THIS BOOK IS TITLE POLITICAL SELF DESTRUCTION OF MOST AFRICAN

AMERICANS, IT IS THEIR INEPTNESS RELATED TO THE AMERICAN POLITICAL FUNDAMENTALS TO POLITICS, GENETIC CONTROLLABILITY IS INEVITABLE IN MAN AND ANIMALS.ETERNALLY, IF IT WASNT HORSE RACERS WOULD (NOT) PAY MILLIONS TO BREED A CONSISTENT CHAMPION WINNER. BUT IN ORDER TO DEVELOP A CHAMPION IT TAKE TIME, PATIENCE, COMPASSION, BUT MOST OF ALL THE HORSE MUST BE WILLING TO COOPERATE WITH A GOOD TRAINER.AND HAVE SPEED.

THE SAME CRITERION APPLY TO PEOPLE, THE ONLY DIFFERENCE IS THAT GOD GAVE EACH A BRAIN MAN AND ANIMAL, MAN HAS A SUPERIOR BRAIN TO THINKAND SORT OUT ISSURES BASED ON INTELLECT, ANIMALS DO (NOT) HAVE THIS ABILITY.

UNFORTUNATELY THE MAJORITY OF AFRICAN AMERICANS (DO NOT) USE THEIR BRAIN TO THINK AND SORT OUT ISSURES PERTAINING TO THE POLITICAL GENERALIZATION OF THIS NATION.ON AN INDIVIDUAL BASIS SO.

THE MAJORITY OF AFRICAN AMERICANS HAVE A PROBLEM WITH THINKING IN DEPTH, MEANING THEY WILL LISTEN TO SOMETHING OR SOME ONE AND (ASSUME) IT OR THEY ARE RIGHT, AS LONG AS IT IS APPEASABLE TO THEM, PIRATICALLY IF IT INVOLVE A BLACK OR BLACKS, THROUGH OUT THIS BOOOK THERE ARE DOCUEMENTED DIALOGUES WITH BLACKS. STRESSING THEIR VIEWS ON TELEVISION AND RADIO, AND THEIR IDEOLOGY IS WHEN ADDRESSING ISSURES PERTAINING TO OTHER BLACKS IS ALWAYS (US) AND (WE) WHICH INDICATE HERDING.

SENATOR BARACK OBAMA AND OPRAH WINFREY ON THE CAMPAIGN TRAIL, STIPOLATING WE NEED A CHANGE, AND SHE KNOW IN HER HEART THAT BARACK OBAMA IS THE RIGHT PERSON FOR CHANGE, TRANSLATE THAT VERBIAGE AND RELATE IT TO BLACKS IDEOLOGY THEMMEANING IS ITS TIME FOR ONE OF (US) TO BE PRESIDENT.

I REFERENCED ACHILLES HEEL REGARDS TO THE DEMOCRATSPARTYI SUSPECT IT COULD VERY WELL BE SENATOR BARACK OBAMA AND OPRAH WINFREY BECAUSE THESE ARE TWO SOPHISTICATED ELITES IN AFRICAN

AMERICAN SOCIETY AND BASED ON THEIR CHARISMA, ALSO SENATOR OBAMA IS BEING CASTS AS A POSSIBLE WINNER IN THE IOWA AND NEW HAMPSHIRE CAUCUS, AND THE MAJORITY OF AFRICAN AMERICANS NATION WIDE ARE GOING TO (ASSUME) HE IS GOING TO BE OUR NEXT PRESIDENT, I CAN ALMOST HEAR THE CHATTER INCLUDING TALK SHOW HOSTS OPRAH WINFREY, HONEY ONE OF (US) IS GOING TO BE PRESIDENT.

AND (WE) DESERVE THIS BECAUSE OF WHAT WHITES DID AND IS DOING TO (US) ITS ABOUT TIME FOR A (CHANGE), AND WHERE HAVE YOU HEARD THAT BARACK OBAMA AND OPERAH WINFREY.

IN ORDER TO CLARIFY MY STATEMENT ABOUT MOST BLACKS LIKE THE ABILITY TO THINK IN DEPTH, I SUSPECT BASED ON SENATOR OBAMA BEING COMPETITIVE IN IOWA AND NEW HAMPSHIRE, AND THE POLLS PREDICT THAT HE COULD PERHAPS WIN ONE OR BOTH CAUCUSES.

MOST BLACKS ARE SO OBSESSED WITH THIS SURGE, THEY MOST LIKELY HAVE FORGOTTEN ABOUT THE OTHER FORTY EIGHT STATES, PIRATICALLY THE SOUTH, AND GENETIC TRAITS PREVAIL IN PEOPLE AND ANIMALS ANCESTRY THAT IS LIFE SUSTAINING.

GENETIC TRAITS CAN BE ALTERED AT TIMES IF YOU ARE AWARE OF WHAT THEY ARE.THROUGH INTELLECT AND EXTRA CORRICULA, BUT WHEN INDIVIDUALS OR ANIMALS ARE ANTAGONIZED IT MAY CAUSE REVERSIONS, AND THIS COULD BE RELATED TO SOUTHERN DEMOCRATIC CONSTITUENCIES, BECAUSE IN EIGHTEEN SIXTY EIGHT THE SOUTHERN DEMOCRATS AND THEIR KU-KLUX-KLAN INTIMIDATORS, WERE INCENSED TO SEE BLACKS HOLD POLITICAL OFFICE, AND BLATANTLY ACCUSED THEM OF BEING IGNORENT, INCOMPETENT AND WAS TRYING TO RISE ABOVE THEIR NATURALLY SUBSERVIENT PLACE IN SOCIETY.

THESE GENETIC TRAITS ARE EMBEDDED IN SOME CAUCASIANS, AS AFRICAN AMERICANS HAVE THEIRS, HOWEVER IT IS DOCUMENTED THAT DURING THE EIGHTEEN SEVENTYS, THERE WERE MANY. EDUCATED BLACKS, (ALE) CONSERVATIVE REPUBLICANS JUST TO

NAME A FIEW, AND THEIR INTELLECT WAS EQUIVALENT TO WHITES, HIRMAN RHODES REVELS,FIRST BLACK U.S. SENATOR, OSCAR J. DUNN LIEUTENANT GOVERNOR OF LOUISIANS, BLANCHE K. BRUCE, FIRST BLACK TO SERVE A FULL TERM IN THE SENATE, JONATHAN GIBBS, SECRETARY OF STATE FOR FLORDIA, EGBERT SAMMIS ELECTED TO THE FLORDIA STATE SENATE, FRANCIS LOUIS CARDOZA SERVED AS SOUTH CAROLINA SECRETARY OF STATE, BENTON STEWART PINCHBACK BECAME THE NATION FIRST BLACK GOVERNOR OF LOUISIANA, (ALL) OF THESE BLACK DIGNITARIES AND OTHERS WORKED WITHIN THE STRUCTURE OF THE REPUBLICAN PARTY, ALONG(WITH) WHITE CONSERVATIVES.

MORE THAN SIX HUNDRED SERVED IN STATES LEGISLATURE, TWENTY WERE ELECTED TO THE U.S. HOUSE OF REPRESENTATIVES, TWO WERE ELECTED TO THE U.S. SENATE.

UNFORTUNATELY THE SOUTHERN DEMOCRATS SORT TO IMPEDE THE AFRICAN AMERICAN POLITICAL PROGRESS THROUGH VIOLENT TACTICS, THE SOUTHERN DEMOCRATIC PARTY MADE A COMMITMENT TO WHITE SUPREMACY IN VICKSBURG, MISSISSIPPI WHITE TERRORIST SLAUGHTERED THREE HUNDRED BLACKS AS AN ON SLAUGHT TO DETER, PROHIBIT, AND DRIVE AFRICAN AMERICANS FROM THE REPUBLICAN PARTY, AND INSTALL DEMOCRATIC SUPREMACY WHITE POLITICAL POWER.

AND THEY WERE SUCCESSFUL, BY FOUNDING AND FORMING TERRORIST GROUPS , SUCH AS THE RED SHIRTS, THE RIFLE CLUBS, AND THE KU-KLUX-KLAN WHICH WAS THE MOST MONSTROUS AND INTIMIDATING OF ALL, AND AS A RESULT WHITE AND BLACK REPUBLICANS DEPARTED THE SOUTHERN STATES, BUT THE MAJORITY OF BLACKS REMAIN AND WAS FORCED TO ABANDON THEIR MORAL CONSERVATIVE BELIEFS, AND ADOPT DEMOCRATIC LIBERAL IDEOLOGY OF (NONE) INTELLECT SERVITUDE AS A WAY OF LIFE FOR BLACKS, WHICH WAS DEVASTATING TO AFRICAN AMERICANS POLITICAL AGENDA IN THE SOUTHERN STATES FOR EIGHTY NINE YEARS.

SO IT IS QUITE OBVIOUS WHY MOST AFRICAN AMERICANS DISASSOCIATE THEM SELVES WITH THE FUNDAMENTALS OF POLITICS, AND IS INEPT TO THE IMPORTANCE OF ITS. FUNCTIONS, WHICH IS THE CONTROLLING FACTOR IN (ALL) PEOPLE LIVES THAT RESIDE IN THE UNITED STATES OF AMERICA HOWEVER THE DEMOCRATS HAVE CREATED A POLITICAL MONSTER IN BARACK OBAMA, HE HAS THEM AND THE NEWS MEDIA REELING, THE NEWS MEDIA IS SKEPTICAL AND RELUCTANT TO DICTATE HIS OMINOUS ACCOLADES, THEY ARE GRAMMATICALLY CENSORING THEIR CRITICAL VERBAGE OF HIM, FEAR OF BEING CALLED A RACIST, AND DEMEANING HIM JUST BECAUSE HE IS BLACK AND THIS AGENDA ALSO APPLIES TO TELEVISION ANCHORS, TALKING HEADS ON TELEVISION, RADIO TALK SHOW HOST, AND PIRATICALLY REPUBLICANS THEY ARE AS QUIET AS A CHURCH MOUSE.

AND HOPEFULLY THEY WILL REMAIN THAT WAY, AND LET THE DEMOCRATS BAIL THEM-SELVES OUT OF THIS VOTE OBSESSION WITH BLACKS, WHICH TEY HAVE HAD POSSESSION OF FOR OVER SEVENTY YEARS, BECAUSE THERE HAS BEEN (NO) OTHER POLITICAL BLACK CANIDATE RISE TO THE STATUS OF SENATOR BARACK OBAMA IN THE HISTORY OF EITHER PARTY. AND THE MAJORITY OF AFRICAN AMERICANS ARE (ASSUMING) AND FILLED WITH DESIRE OF EXPECTATION, THAT SENATOR BARACK OBAMA IS GOING TO BE PRESIDENT, UNFORTUNATELY I SUSPECT THAT THIS IS A MYTHICAL PERCEPTION, THAT IS GOING TO BE AN ACHILLES HEEL FOR THE DEMOCRATS, BECAUSE OVER THE DECADES THEY HAVE SOLIDIFIED HERDING AFRICAN AMERICAN VOTES THROUGH OTHER CELEBRITY BLACKS.

BY LYING ON REPUBLICANS AND SEDUCING POLITICAL INEPT BLACKS LIKE BILL CLINTON WAS DOING IN ARKANSAS, AT THE CELEBRATED FIFTIETH YEAR OF THE NINE STUDENTS THAT WAS ADMITTED.

ALSO HE AND SENATOR HILLARY CLINTON AT THE LATE MRS CORETTA KING FUNERAL SERVICES, AND DEMORALIZED HER SERVICES WITH POLITICAL PROPAGANDA, IN A EFFORT

TO INSINUATE AT MOSTLY A BLACK AUDIENCE THAT THEY ARE THE PARTY FOR BLACKS.

HOWEVER I SUSPECT THAT THIS TRICKERY IS ABOUT TO COME TO AN END ON SOME BLACKS, SIMPLY BECAUSE OF THEIR INHERITANCE OF SENATOR BARACK OBAMA, THAT HAS ASTUTE INTELLECT,FEATURES OF A BAT, AND CROWS LIKE A ROOSTER AT DAWN WITH POLITICAL LIBERAL RHETORIC, HOWEVER I SUSPECT HE HAS BAFFLED THE NEWS MEDIA ESPECIALLY TELEVISION, YOU HAVE SEEN SO MANY BLACK TALKING HEADS ON TELEVISION TRYING TO MAKE AN ANALYSIS OF THE CRITERION PERTAINING TO POLITICAL ASPIRATIONS.

AND RELUCTANTLY TRYING TO PREDICT THE FUTURE OF THE WINNERS IN THE IOWA CAUCUS, BUT MOSTLY THEY ARE THERE TO DISCUSS SENATOR BARACK OBAMA SIMPLY BECAUSE OF THE DON IMUS DEBACLE MOST OF THE TELEVISION AND RADIO HOST ARE RELUCTANT TO RIDICULE PROMINENT BLACKS, FEAR OF AL SHARPTON IS TUNED IN, SO PRACTICALLY ALL OF THE MAJOR NET WORK HOST ARE SHADOWING BEHIND SUPPOSEDLY ELITE BLACKS.

IN HOPES THAT THEY ARE GOING TO EXPRESS WORDS THAT THEY WOULD BE CALLED A RACIST FOR SAYING, THIS IS A ONE TIME CHARADE FOR SENATOR BARACK OBAMA,THE ELITE GOOD OLD BOY DEMOCRATS ARE AWARE OF THIS MYTHICAL CHARADE, ALSO THE REPUBLICANS, BUT THE RISK FOR DEMOCRATS IS DIRE, I SUSPECT THE IOWA CAUCUS DELIVERED A BLOW TO THE DEMOCRATS, THAT IS PARALLEL TO PRESIDENT ABARHAM LINCOLN FREEING BLACKS FROM BONDAGE.

AND SOME CONSERVATIVES ARE KICKING SAND IN THE DEMOCRATS FACE, FOR INSTANCE DICK MORRIS EQUATED OBAMA VICTORY SPEECH TO ONE THAT PRESIDENT JOHN F. KENNEDY MADE.

BUT THE REALITY OF THIS WHOLE SCENARIO IS THAT THE MAJORITY OF BLACKS ARE INEPT TO THE GRASS ROOT FUNDAMENTALS OF POLITICS, AND BECAUSE OF SENATOR OBAMA WIN IN IOWA, THERE ARE FIRED UP AND COMING OUT OF THE WOOD WORK TO SUPPORT ONE OF (US).

BUT THERE IS ONE THING THEY DO (NOT) UNDERSTAND, AND THAT HE IS AT THE DISPOSALOF THE VICIOUS DEMOCRATIC POLITICAL WELL OILED MACHINE, AND I HAVE CRITIQUED DEMOCRATIC IDEOLOGY REGARDS TO THEIR CHRONOLOGICAL RECORD PERTAINING TO AFRICAN AMERICANS, PIRATICALLY IN THE SOUTH, HOWEVER THE DEMOCRATS ARE BETWEEN A ROCK AND A HARD PLACE REGARDS TO SENATOR BARACK OBAMA ESCAPADE. EITHER LET HIM KEEP UP HIS ENTHUSIASTIC RHETORIC, EMBARRASSING THE CLINTONS, OR GO AFTER HIM AND TAKE HIS WHILTLE, TRUST ME THEY ARE BEHIND CLOSED DOORS CONTEMPLATING AROUND THE CLOCK ON HOW TO ACCOMPLISH THIS FEAT WITH OUT BLATANT DEMEANING.

BECAUSE IF THEY GO AFTER HIM DEROGATORILY WITH SMUT, THEY RUN THE RISK OF ALIENATING THE BLACK CONSTITUENCY THAT IS HERDING BEHIND HIM, NATION WIDE.

THE MAJORITY OF AFRICAN AMERICANS ARE QUITE UNIQUE IN THEIR ASSESSMENT OF THEIR BEING INVOLVED IN ANY PUBLIC EVENT OR ADVENTURE, THEIR PRECEPTION IS MOSTLY RELEGATED TO EXHIBITIONISM AND IF THEY ARE CALLED TO RECOGNITION BECAUSE OF INANITY, THEY BECOME PROVOKED AND CLAIM EITHER THE EVENT WAS RACIST OR OTHER BLACKS WAS TRYING TO BE WHITE, THIS STIGMATIC REDUNDANCY IS RELENTLESS IN AFRICAN AMERICAN CULTURAL SOCIETY.

AND IT IS SIMPLY BECAUSE MOST ARE RECULSE BASED ON HERDING, AND LIKE THE ABILITY TO MINGLE WITH OTHERS BASED ON INTELLECT, SO AS A RESULT THEY CONSTANTLY PLAY THE RACE CARD, IN AN EFFORT TO PLACATE THEIR EGOTISTICAL DEMEANOR.

THE MAJORITY OF AFRICAN AMERICANS HAVE (NEVER) ACCEPTED DIVERSITY THEIR MAIN PREMEDITATED ASPIRATIONS IS TO DOMINATE IN A DIVERSE SOCIETY OF THREE HUNDRED MILLION PEOPLE, WHEN THEIR PRECENTAGE OF THE POPULATION IS ONLY 12% MAYBE, AND THAT IS WHY I SUSPECT THIS THING WITH SENATOR BARACK OBAMA IS GOING TO CAUSE CHAOTIC DISCORD

WHEN HE LOOSE THE DEMOCRATIC PRIMARY TO BE THEIR CHOICE FOR PRESIDENT, I COULD BE WRONG BUT FOR SOME REASON I SUSPECT THE MAJOR ITY OF AFRICAN AMERICANS ARE GOING TO BE DISAPPOINTED, AND OUT COME THE RACIAL IINNUENDOES BASED ON (ASSUMPTIONS).

SENATOR BARACK 0BAMA. EFFORTS TO BECOME PRESIDENT IS TRULY REMARKABLE, AND SHOULD BE APPLAUDED FOR HIS INTELLECT AND INTUITIONS PERTAINING TO POLITICAL CHARACTERISTICS.

HOWEVER THE FUNDAMENTAL REALITY IS LURKING, AND THE MAJORITY OF AFRICAN AMERICANS DISPLAY TREMENDOUS IDIOSYNCRASIES, AND IS OFTEN ADVERSE TO (REALITY) AND SPONTANEOUSLY RESPOND TO REALITY WITH (ASSUMPTIONS) BASED ON THEIR THEORY, WHICH IS EMBEDDED IN THEIR GENETIC TRAITS. THAT IS CONCENTRATED WITH SELF PROCLAIMED VOODOOISM PERTAINING TO THE FUNDAMENTALS OF IDELISM.

THE AUTHENTICITY OF REALISM IS PROUFOUND HISTORICALLY OR CURRENT EVENTS, AND IF ANY INDIVIDUAL IS INEPT OR IN DENIAL, IT HAS A TENDENCY TO DISTORT FUNDAMENTAL ISSURES IN A DIVISIVE MANNER THAT DICTATE SUSPECTED PSYCHOLOGICAL PROBLEMS.

UNFORTUNATELY THE MAJORITY OF AFRICANS WERE ACCLIMATED TO SLAVERY BECAUSE IT WAS AN ANCIENT INSTUTION THAT HAD BEEN FOUNDED IN NORTH AND WEST AFRICA BY AFRICAN KINGS, LONG BEFORE THE EUROPEANS INVOLVEMENT IN THE FOURTEEN SEVENTYS.

IN THE UNITED STATES OF AMERICA CONGRESS ENDED THE SLAVE TRADE IN EIGHTEEN HUNDRED AND EIGHT, AND ON SEPTEMBER 22, EIGHTEEN SIXTY TWO, REPUBLICAN PRESIDENT ABRAHAM LINCOLN, ISSURED THE PROCLAMATION DECLARING FREEDOM FOR (ALL) BLACKS HELD IN BONDAGE. AND IT WAS RATIFIED TO THE THIRTEENTH AMENDMENT OF THE CONSTITUTION ON DECEMBER 6,EIGHTEEN SIXTY FIVE, AND IN EIGHTEEN SIXTY SIX THE REPUBLICAN CONGRESS PASSED THE CIVIL RIGHTS ACT, GUARANTEEING BLACKS CITIZENSHIP INTO THE FOURTEENTH AMENDMENT OF THE CONSTUTION, AND BLACKS WERE ABLE TO VOTE AND ENTERTAIN THEIR

CIVIL RIGHTS UNTIL EIGHTEEN NINETY FIVE WHEN THE SOUTHERN DEMOCRATS COAXED THE SUPREME COURT, THROUGH SEDUCING BOOKER T.WASHINGTON, THE PRESIDENT TUSKEE INSTITUTE, BY PARADING HIM AROUND THE POPULATED BLACK AREAS IN THE SOUTH, CONVINCING THEM THAT SEPERATE BUT EQUAL WAS (INEVITABLE) AND IT WOULD NOT BE SUCH A BAD DEAL.

SO BASED ON THEIR APPLAUDING AND EXCEPTING HIS ADVICE, THE SOUTHERN DEMOCRATS AIDED BY THE SUPREME COURT RULING TO STRIKE DOWN THE AFRICAN AMERICANS CIVIL RIGHTS FROM THE THIRTEENTH AND FOURTEENTH AMENDMENT TO THE CONSTITUTION, WHICH GAVE THE SOUTHERN STATES SOLE CONTROL OVER THE RIGHTS OF BLACKS IN THE SOUTH. UNTIL NINETEEN SIXTY FOUR AND FIVE, AND ONCE AGAIN THE REPUBLICANS HAD TO COME TO THE AID OF BLACKS, BY VOTING OVERWHELMINGLY IN THE CONGRESS TO OVER TURN THE SUPREME COURT RULING, AND RESTORED AFRICAN AMERICANS CIVIL AND VOTING RIGHTS.

SOME OF THESE DECLARINGS COULD BE SUSPECT OF REDUNDANCY,HOWEVER IT IS COORDINATED TO OFFER DESCERNIABLE CHARACTERIZATION PERTAINING TO PEOPLE,MOST NOTABLE AFRICAN AMERICANS, IN AN EFFORT TO CHALLENGE THEIR CHRONOLOGILAL RECORD OF SIGNIFICANT EVENTS, OUR NATION CONSIST OF A DIVERSE SOCIETY OF PEOPLE, THAT IS GOVERN BY A SOPHISTICATED CODE OF ETHICS, THAT WAS ESTABLISHED PRIOR TO THE INTRODUCTION OF AFRICANS TO THIS LAND IN SIXTEEN NINTEEN. UNFORTUNATELY AFRICAN AMERICANS HONORED AND PRACTICED THEIR AFRICAN CHARACTERISTICS CULTURE AND HERITAGE, THROUGH THE EIGHTEENTH CENTURY, INSTEAD OF FOCUSING ON THE EXISTING CULTURAL GENERALITY THAT IS EMBEDDED IN THE TRAITS OF AMERICAN DIVERSE SOCIETY. AND THIS HAS BEEN AN ACHILLES HEEL FOR THE MAJORITY OF AFRICAN AMERICANS, INEPT TO THE BASIC FUNDAMENTALS AND TRANSFORMATION REQUIRED TO INCORPORATE INTO A INTELLECT MORAL SOCIETY PERTAINING TO THE

POLITICAL ARENA THAT IS INEVITABLE ALSO IMMORTAL IN THE UNITTED STATES OF AMERICA.

THERE IS A VAST MAJORITY OF AFRICAN AMERICANS THAT ARE (ASSUMING) SOME FORM OF DEVIATIONS IS GOING TO OCCUR, RELATING TO THEIR AFRICAN HERITAGE, THAT WILL OFFER CONCILIATORY ADJUSTMENTS TO THEIR GENETIC IDIOSYNCRASIES THAT REPRESENT FASCISM, AND BLATANT ACCUSATIONS OF OTHERS FOR THEIR HERDING STUPIDITY, BASED ON THEIR EXEBITIONIST BEHAVIOR.

IN AN ATTEMPT TO ESTABLISH DOMINANCE IN A SEGMENT OF COMMUNITY LIFE, WHICH IS PREDOMINANTLY THEIR OWN NEIGHBORS.

SO ITS QUITE EVIDENT THAT MANY PEOPLE BLACK AND WHITE, UNFORTUNATELY ARE NOT WELL VERSED ON THE FUNDAMENTAL STANDARDS THAT EXIST IN OUR NATION, THEY ARE (ASSUMING) AND BADLY MISCALCULATING THE DISASTROUS CIRCUMSTANCES THAT CAN BE FATAL, BASED ON THEIR EXTREME AGGRESSIVE RADICAL BEHAVIOR.

IN EIGHTEEN ELEVEN CHARLES DESLONDES AN AFRICAN AMERICAN, WAS THE ORGANIZER OF APPROXIMATELY FOUR HUNDRED MILITANT SLAVE ARMED FORCES, AND MOVED TOWARD NEW ORLEANS MARCHING IN CADENCE BEATING DRUMS AND BURNING PLANTATIONS, THEIR INTENT WAS TO TAKE POSSESSION AT ANY COST FROM WHITES EVEN AT THE EXPENSE OF MURDERING SOME. BUT STATE AND LOCAL MILITIA ROSE TO THE OCCASION AND SUPPRESSED THE UPRISING KILLING OVER SIXTY AFRICANS, AND DISMEMBERING THEIR HEADS FROM THEIR BODYS, PLACING THEM ON POLES ALONG THE MISSISSIPPI RIVER AS A WARNING TO OTHER BLACK VILLIONS.

CHARLESTON, SOUTH CAROLINA EIGHTEEN TWENTY, DENMARK VESEY ..AFRICAN AMERICAN AMERICAN, PLOTTED A MALICIOUS ATTACK AGAINST WHITES, BUT HIS PLOT WAS DISCOVERED AND SUPPRESSED THE UPRISING BEFORE IT BEGAN, ROUNDED UP THE CONSPIRATORS CONVICTED THEM OF PLOTTING A REVOLUTION, THIRTY FIVE WERE HANGED INCLUDING DENMARK VESEY, THEIR BODIES WERE DISSECTED AND DISPLAYED AS A WARNING TO OTHER MILITANT BLACKS.

HOWEVER THE MOST UNFORTUNATE DETRIMENTAL ILLUMINATING SUICIDAL ESCAPADE OCCURED IN EIGHTEEN THIRTY ONE, ARRANGED AND PERPETRATED BY NAT TURNER, THE MAGNITUDE OF THIS REBELLION SURPASSED ANY OTHER, AND WAS THE MOST ATROCIOUS SLAVE REVOLT IN AMERICAN HISTORY, NAT TURNER AND HIS REBELS SLAUGHTERED WHITES AT WILL, LOOTING AND TAKING THEIR POSSESSIONS, SUCH AS GUNS, HORSES, AXES, SWORDS AND AMMUNITION.

THIS NAT TURNER ATROCITY ESCAPADE WAS THE MOST SINGLE INCIDENT THAT SEALED THE FATE FOR BLACKS INL THE SOUTH AND AROUND THE NATION, BECAUSE DURING THIS REVOLT MORE THAN SIXTY WHITES WERE SLAUGHTERED, THE MILITIA AND THE TOWNS PEOPLE JOINED FORCES AND ROUTED TURNERS BRIGADE. AFTER THAT MANY INNOCENT AFRICAN AMERICANS WOULD BE UCCUMBED TO ONE OF THE MOST BRUTAL, HORRIFYING, ATTACKS OF RETALIATIONS EVER, THEY PAID A HEAVY PRICE WITH THEIR LIVES.

WHITES KILLED ONE HUNDRED AND TWENTY BLACKS IN ONE DAY, THEY RAMPAGED THROUGH THE COUNTRY SIDE, SHOOTING AND BURNING TO DEATH AT WILL, WIDE SPREAD BRUTAL ASSAULTS OCCURED ON BLACK MEN, WOMEN AND CHILDREN, MANY WHITES WERE UNDER THE IMPRESSION THAT NAT TURNER SLAVE INVASION WAS RACIAL WARFARE, AND IT INFLAMED WHITES WITH GENERAL HYSTERIA.

AS A RESULT STATE LAWS WERE LEGISLATED TO RESTRICT BLACKS MOBILITY TO A CONFINEMENT THAT WAS PROFOUND THROUGHOUT SLAVERY, AND CARRIED OVER AFTER SLAVERY BY THE KU-KLUX-KLAN, TO MAINTAIN AND DISCIPLINE HERDING AFRICAN AMERICANS, IN AN EFFORT TO QUELL ANOTHER UPRISING.

AND IT APPEAR THAT THIS GENETIC REVELATION IS BEING STIMULUS TODAY BY AL SHARPTON, NAT TURNER WAS A PREACHER ALSO, THAT WAS TRIED HUNG DISSECTED, AND SHOES, PURSES, WERE FABRICATED FROM HIS SKIN, AND MANTLE TROPHIES FROM HIS BONES.

IT IS AN ESTABLISHED (FACT) THAT WHITES ARE THE DOMINATE CONTROLLING POWER IN THE UNITED STATES OF AMERICA, AND MANY BLACKS HAVE CHOSEN TO COORDINATE THEIR EFFORTS IN UNISON, AND DISPELLED (RACE) BATING AND ARE EQUIVALENT TO WHITE SOCIETY,INTELLECTUALLY AND ECONOMICALLY HISTORICALLY, ALSO IN CERTAIN ENDEAVORS HAVE EXCEEDED WHITES IN MANY CAPACITIES THROUGH OUT THE UNITED STATES OF AMERICA, BASED ON INTELLECT AND FUNDAMENTAL MORAL VALUES. APPARENTLY THIS IS A FUNDAMENTAL REASON WHY F.B.I. DIRECTOR J. EDGAR HOOVER JUDGED BLACKS AS HAVING BRAINS 20% SMALLER THAN WHITES, BECAUSE THEY LIKE THE ABILITY TO REASON WITH REALITY, AND PRAY FOR UN-JUST MIRACLES.

THAT HAS TO DO WITH EXEBITIONIST EXTORTION OF OTHERS, AND (NOT) REALIZING THE OBSTRUCTIVE CONSEQUENCES THAT IS INEVITABLE. ALSO AFTER BEING BROUGHT TO AMERICA THREE HUNDRED AND EIGHTY NINE YEARS AGO, THE MAJORITY OF AFRICAN AMERICANS APPARENTLY HAVE (NOT) ACCEPTED THE FACT THAT THEY ARE NOT THE MAJORITY OF THE POPULATION, NOR DO THEY HOLD THE MAJORITY OF (ANY) FEDERAL OR STATE GOVERNING BUREAUCRACY.IN THE NATION.

THE MAJORITY OF AFRICAN AMERICANS HAVE (NOT) FIGURED OUT THAT CAUCASIANS CONTROL (EVERY) FEASIBLE CONGLOMERATE ENTERPRISE IN THIS NATION, INCLUDING (ALL) THE BRANCHES OF GOVERNMENT THAT DICTATE OUR FUTURE BASED ON CHANGING LAWS, AND DETERMINING FATE. THE MOST PREPOSTERIOUS IDEOLOGICAL IDOSYNCRASY, IS THAT MANY MANY AFRICAN AMERICANS (CHOOSE) TO HERD BEHIND AL SHARPETON AND JESSIE JACKSON, AS THEIR SELF APPOINTED CONGO CHIEF,AND PRESIDENT TO RESOLVE THEIR PROPLEMS, BASED ON THEIR INEPTNESS TO THE FUNDAMENTALS OF INTELLECT THAT IS THE SUSTAINING FACTOR EMBEDDED IN COMPREHENSION RELATED TO INDIVIDUAL CORRECTNESS TO AVOID HUMAN PARASITES, THESE PEOPLE AL SHARPTON AND JESSIE JACKSON, ARE NOTHING MORE THAN SURROGATES POSSESSED BY THE

IDEOLOGY OF CHARLES DESCONDES, DENMARK VESEY AND NAT TURNER, INSTIGATING PROPAGANDA THAT IS DIVISIVE TO THE CONTROLLING BUREAUCRACY OF WHITES THAT IS PROFOUND, SIMPLY BECAUSE OF SOMETHING MOST CHILDREN ARE TAUGHT IN GRADE SCHOOL (MAJORITY) RULE.

APPARENTLY AL SHARPTON IS INEPT TO THE WORD MAJORITY, ALSO SOME ONE NEED TO INFORM HIM THAT THE SOUTHERN DEMOCRATS JIM CROW RULE, SEPERATE BUT EQUAL WAS ABOLISHED BY THE CONGRESS IN 1964-1965 AND AFRICAN AMERICANS CIVIL AND VOTING RIGHTS WAS RESTORED, AND THERE (NOTHING) IN THE UNITED STATES OF AMERICA THAT AFRICAN AMERICANS ARE PROHIBITED FROM PARTICIPATING IN, IF THEY CHOOSE TO DO SO. HOWEVER UNFORTUNATELY MANY ARE SYMPATHETIC TO AL SHARPTON AND JESSIE JACKSON, RADICAL REHETORIC DENOUNCING THE CONTROLLING GOVERNING BUREAUCRACY BY WHITES, AND CHOOSE TO BECOME THE (ONLY) MAJORIETY THAT IS ACCREDITED TO BLACKS, WHICH IS INCARCERATION. HOWEVER THERE ARE SOME PROMINENT WHITES, EQUAL TO AL SHARPTON INEPTNESS TO CHRONOLOGICAL RECORDS OF SIGNIFICANT EVENTS, SUCH AS SENATOR HILLARY CLINTON, SHE CHOOSE TO ADDRESS CIVIL RIGHTS DURING THE DR. MARTN LUTHER KING ERA. ON NATIONAL TELEVISION. AND SEEM TO GIVE A WATERED DOWN VERSION OF HIS PARTICIPATION. ON JANUARY 11, 2008, SHE ACCLAIM THAT THERE WAS NO PRESIDENT BEFORE PRESIDENT LYNDON JOHNSON, INITIATED CIVIL AND VOTING RIGHTS FOR AFRICAN AMERICANS, THAT HE WAS THE (FIRST) AND (ONLY) TO DO SO, WHICH WAS A BLATANT (LIE).

IN NINETEEN FIFTY SIX, UNDER REPUBLICAN PRESIDENT DWIGHT D. EISENHOWER ADMINISTRATION, BROWNELL CIVILRIGHTS BILL WAS SENT TO THE DEMOCRAT CONTROLLED CONGRESS, VOTING AND CIVIL RIGHTS WAS EXPELLED FROM THE BILL FOR BLACKS, LATER THE ENTIRE BILL WAS KILLEDIN THE SENATE JUDICARY COMMITEE, WHERE SENATOR JAMES EASTLAND FROM MISSISSIPPI WAS THE CHAIRMAN.

FERTHER MORE PRESIDENT LYNDON JOHNSON, DURING HIS ENTIRE STINT IN THE SENATE (NEVER) SUPPORTED A CIVIL RIGHTS BILL PERTAINING TO AFRICAN AMERICANS.

ALSO DURING HIS PRESIDENCY, THERE WAS A PROTEST MARCH INITIATED BY DR. MARTIN LUTHER KING, ON MARCH OF NINETEEN SIXTY FIVE, TO INSTIGATE REGISTRATION FOR AFRICAN AMERICANS TO VOTE, THE MARCH BEGAN IN SELMA, ALABAMA TO MONTGOMERY.

THE GOVERNOR OF ALABAMA GEORGE WALLACE, APPOSED THE MARCHERS AND ORDERED THE STATE POLICE TO RESTRAIN THE UNARMED BLACK MARCHERS, IT WAS BRUTAL, THEY WERE ATTACKED AND BEATEN WITH BILLY CLUBS. THESE BRUTAL ATTACKS WERE DEPICTED ON NATIONAL TELEVISION, WHICH CAUSED TELEGRAMS, LETTERS AND PICKETS AROUND THE WHITE HOUSE DEMANDING ACTION FROM THEN PRESIDENT LYNDON JOHNSON, TO MOBILIZE THE NATIONAL GUARD, PRESIDENT JOHNSON REFUSED TO (BUDGE) UNTIL HE MET WITH GOVERNOR OF ALABAMA GEORGE WALLACE, FOR APPROXIMATELY THREE HOURS, THE VIOLENCE CONTINUED, HOWEVER WITH CRITICS AND TELEVISION CLIPS PORTRAYING THESE VICIOUS ACTS.

UNTIL IT BECAME AN ACHILLES HEEL FOR PRESIDENT JOHNSON, BECAUSE THE NORTHERN AFRICAN AMERICAN VOTERS WERE BECOMING RESTLESS, AND FEAR OF LOOSING THEIR VOTES FOR THE DEMOCRATIC PARTY. HE HESITANTLY REQUESTED TROOPS TO BE SENT TO ALABAMA, AND LATER SCOLDED THE SENATE AND DEMANDED THEY PASS THE VOTING RIGHTS FOR BLACKS, BECAUSE OF (FEAR) THAT THEIR HERDING BLOC VOTING WOULD RETURN TO THE REPUBLICAN PARTY, OR REFUSE TO VOTE AT ALL. MRS ROSA PARKS, REFUSAL TO VACATE HER SEAT ON A BUS, INSPIRED DR. MARTIN LUTHER KING TO ORGANIZE AND INITIATE PEACEFUL PROTEST THRUGH MARCHING ON AUGUST 6, 1965, PRESIDENT JOHNSON SIGNED THE VOTING RIGHTS ACT, WHICH MANY DEMOCRATS WERE APPOSE AND REFUSE TO SUPPORT, THE REPUBLICANS ARE LARGELY RESPONSIBLE FOR THE PASSING OF THE BILL THAT RESTORED AFRICAN AMERICANS, CIVIL, AND, VOTING RIGHTS, HOWEVER THE

SENTIMENT OF FRUSTRATION PERTAINING TO AFRICAN AMERICANS STILL EXIST TODAY.

BASED ON AFFIRMATION OF THEIR CONVICTIONS, WHICH IS TO ELUDE SELF DEROGATION IN AN EFFORT TO DISTORT SELF IMPOSED REALITY, BASED ON POLITICAL IGNORANCE, THAT IS CONSTITUTED BY GENETIC CONTROLLABILITY, AND THE OVERALL STIGMATIZATION IS INEVITABLE.

BECAUSE HISTORICALLY WHITES HAVE (ALWAYS) BEEN SYMPATHETIC TO BLACKS THAT WOULD THINK HARMONIOUS, AND ENTERTAIN THE PHANTOMS OF INTELLECT REGARDS TO DIVERSITY.

PLANTATION SLAVE OWNERS CATERED TO THOSE THAT THEY COULD COMMUNICATE AND REASON WITH, OTHERS THAT CLUNG TO CONGO VOODOOISM WITH THE INTENT TO ALTER GUIDE-LINES WERE SERVERELY PUNISHED. THE SOME PRINCIPLE IS APPLIED IN TODAYS SOCIETY, SLAVERY WAS ABOLISHED IN EIGHTEEN SIXTY FIVE, CIVIL AND VOTING RIGHTS WAS RESTORED IN NINETEEN SIXTY FOUR AND FIVE.

THERE ARE APPROXIMATELY THREE HUNDRED MILLION PEOPLE IN THE UNITED STATES OF AMERICA, (YET) BLACKS HOLD THE RECORD FOR MOST ETHNIC OF PEOPLE BEING (INCARCERATED) BEHIND BARS.

UNFORTUNATELY THE PRODICTABILITY OF CRITERION DEMINISHING IS VERY REMOTE, BECAUSE OF THEIR MENTAL TELEPATHY PERTAINING TO DISTORTED VALUES, TO HERD BEHIND SELF APPOINTED PARASITIC LEADERS THAT HAS LURED THE MAJORITY INTO THINKING THAT THEY ARE BEING SEDUCED BY WHITES BECAUSE THEY ARE BLACK, AND THEIR CIVIL RIGHTS ARE BEING VIOLATED BY THE GOVERNMENTAL ESTABLISHMENTYWITH OUT CAUSE. THE CONTINUITY OF THIS VILE STIGMATIZATION WITH THE MAJORITY OF AFRICAN AMERICANS IS PROFOUND BASED ON POLITICAL IMMATURITY, AND LACK OF HARMONY WITH OTHERS WHICH IS INEVITABLE, ALSO IMMORTAL.

THE MAJORITY OF AFRICAN AMERICANS HAVE HAD FORTY THREE YEARS SENSE NINETEEN SIXTY FOUE AND FIVE, TO ANALYTICALLY REFINE THEIR POSTERITY WITH

INTELLECT PERTAINING TO THE AMERICAN PHILOSOPHY. BECAUSE THE GRATITUDE OF SUCCESS IS MEASURED AND VALIDATED BY INDIVIDUAL DEVOTION TO MORAL VALUES AND DIGNITY.

UNFORTUNATELY MANY BLACKS DEVOTE THEIR TIME TO RADICAL BEHAVIOR, IN AN EFFORT TO CAPTIVATE AN AUDIENCE, TO MOBILIZE AND DICTATE DEGRADATION,IN ORDER TO EXPLOIT PERSONAL EXHIBITIONISM TO ATTAIN NOTORIETY RELATED TO HATRED, AND RACISM.

THE CHRONOLOGICAL RECORD OF SIGNIFICANT EVENTS DICTATE THAT THE MAJORITY OF AFRICAN AMERICANS HAVE AND ARE SUPPORTIVE OF DEMOCRATIC POLITICAL POLITICIANS, WHETHER BLACK OR WHITE. AND THE POLLUTED ASPIRATION OF THIS UNSAVORY DEBACLE OF REALITY, IS BEGINNING TO BECOME MORE PREVALENT AND MALIGNANT IN THE ELECTION YEAR OF TWO THOUSAND EIGHT PERTAINING TO DEMOCRATS.

INHERENTLY BECAUSE OF AN AFRICAN AMERICAN, SENATOR BARACK OBAMA, ASPIRING TO BECOME PRESIDENT, AND WITH POLITICAL INTELLECT ALONG WITH PEACOCK CHARISMA, IS THE FIRST BLACK (EVER) TO CHALLENGE THE DEMOCRATIC POLITICAL SUPREMACY WITH ANY REGULARITY. AND MANY ARE HYSTERICAL WITH PUZZLING EMOTIONS, ON HOW TO DERAIL HIS FAME, THE DEMOCRATS COULD CARE LESS ABOUT SENATOR OBAMA AS A PERSON, BECAUSE THEY (KNOW) THAT HE COULD (NEVER) BECOME PRESIDENT AS A DEMOCRAT REPRESENTATIVE.

HOWEVER THEIR ULTIMATE CONCERN IS BLACK (VOTERS). BECAUSE THERE ARE MANY BLACKS AROUND THE NATION IS EQUATING SENATOR OBAMA TO DR MARTIN LUTHER KING DREAM, AND HE SHOULD BECOME PRESIDENT BECAUSE HE IS BLACK, AND THIS WOULD JUSTIFY DR. KING DREAM OF EQUALITY. UNFORTUNATELY THIS IS THE SENTIMENT OF INSANITY THAT IS PROFOUND AND EMBEDDED IN THE MAJORITY OF AFRICAN AMERICANS IDEOLOGY HISTORICALLY, THE EGOISTIC VENERABILITY DRIVEN RELATED TO (COLOR). BASED ON RACIST PROPAGANDA, THAT IS INSIDIOUS AND DIABOLIC TO THE CORE ..WITH INEPTNESS.

BECAUSE (EVERY) AFRICAN AMERICAN THAT RESIDE IN THE UNITED STATES OF AMERICA, THEIR PROSPERITY AND SURVIVAL DEPEND ON THE PERVASIVE ATTRIBUTES OF CAUCASIANS WEALTH AND ABILITY TO SUSTAIN, AND THEY IGNORE THE CYNICISM OF BLACKS, BASED ON THEIR ASTUTE INTELLECTUAL FORTITUDE TO ADHERE TO CIVILITY, AND MINIPILATING BLACKS. BECAUSE MOST WHITES ARE AWARE THAT MOST BLACKS WILL EVENTUALLY SELF DESTRUCT FROM BIAS IGNORANCE.

THEMAJORITYOFAFRICANAMERICANSSYSTEMATICALLY DEALING WITH REALITY IS ALOOF AND CHAOTIC.

BECAUSE THEY LIKE THE ABILITY TO DETERMINE WHAT IS TINEVITABLE) YOU CAN (NOT) COMPETE WITH SOME ONE FOR (DOMINANCE) WHEN YOU ARE RELYING ON THEIR SUPPORT FOR PROSPEROUS SURVIVAL, PIRATICALLY WHEN YOU ARE ONLY (12%) OF THE POPULATION.

OVER THREE HUNDRED AND EIGHTY YEARS, MOST BLACKS HAVE NOT DETERMINE THAT THEY ARE NOT THE MAJORITY IN THE UNITED STATES OF AMERICA. AND THE EFFECTS OF THIS IMBECILE MISCONCEPTION STIMULATED THROUGH DECEPTION, BY BLACK PARASITIC SELF APPOINTED LEADERSIS DETRIMENTAL TO (ALL) AFRICAN AMERICANS IN SOME FASHION, BUT MOSTLY POLITICALLY AND ECONOMICALLY.

THERE ARE MANY AFRICAN AMERICANS, THAT IS ADVERSE TO RACIST RADICAL BEHAVIOR, AND REFUSE TO PARTICIPATE IN THIS ABNORMAL RUBBISH, INSTIGATED BY SELF APPOINTED BLACK LEADERS DISCRIMINATIVE DIVIDIING THE NATION ALONG RACIAL LINES, AS THEIR GUIDANCE SPOKESMAN WHICH IS PARALLEL TO A CONGO AFRICAN TRIBAL CHIEF, AND CONTINUALLY INITIATING DEROGATORY SENILITY THAT AFRICAN AMERICANS ARE BEING DENIED THEIR CIVIL EQUALITY BY WHITES.

(YET) THERE IS A BLACK SENATOR BARACK OBAMA, CAMPAIGNING TO BECOME PRESIDENT OF THE MOST POWERFUL COUNTRY IN THE WORLD, THE UNITED STATES OF AMERICA.

SO THIS INSANITY GENERATED BY THESE DERANGED (SEPARAIST) INDIVIDUALS AND BLACK CACUS GROUPS

ARE REPULSIVE AND POLLUTED WITH DEMORALIZING DISCORD, THAT HAS BEEN DISRUPTIVE TO THE PROGRESS OF ALL AFRICAN AMERICAN SOCIETY HISTORICALLY.

UNFORTUNATELY THE REGRETTABLE SIGNIFICANCE OF CHRONOLOGICAL RECORDS OF SIGNIFICANT EVENTS DICTATE THAT SOME AFRICAN AMERICANS HERDING BEHIND SELF APPOINTED RADICAL BLACK LEADERS, WAS INSTRUMENTAL IN ABOLISHING THEIR OWN CIVILITY AND SEMI EQUALITY FOR (ALL) AFRICAN AMERICANS.

BECAUSE DURING THE FALL OF SEVENTEEN THIRTY NINE, A REBELLION WAS INCITED AND PERPETRATED AT THE STINO RIVER IN SOUTH CAROLINA, LED BY A AFRICAN SLAVE NAME JEMMY, RAIDING AND PILLAGING PLANTATIONS, THE CONSEQUENCES FOR THIS UPRISING WAS DEVASTATING FOR BLACKS. BECAUSE STATE LAWS WERE IMPLEMENTED , THAT IF A WHITE MURDERED A BLACK, IT WAS CONSIDERED TO BE A MISDEMEANOR.

ALSO THERE WERE BLACK GUERRILLA GROUPS FORMED FOR FIFTY YEARS, ONE SUCH GROUP WAS IDENTIFIED AS THE KINGS OF ENGLAND SOLDIERS H RAIDING PLANTATIONS MOLESTING AND RECRUTING OTHER SLAVES. IT BECAME SO SEVERE UNTIL COLONY AFTER COLONY IMPLEMENTED HARSH LAWS TO IMPEDE (ALL) BLACKS, EVEN TO THE EXTENT OF PROHIBITING INTERRACIAL MARRIAGE.

THERE WERE OTHER NOTABLE HERDING TERRORIZING GROUPS OF BLACKS, CLAIMING THE NATION BELONG TO THEM.

THESE GUERRILLA REBELLIOUS GROUPS EACH LED BY TREASONOUS INDIVIDUALS, SUCH AS CHARLES DESLONDES, DENMARK VESEY, AND NAT TURNER. THEIR REBELLIOUS CHARADE WAS EQUIVALENT TO THE KU-KLUX-KLAN, RELATED TO VIOLENCE, HOWEVER THEY WERE CRUSHED AND BUTCHERED FOR THEIR MALICIOUS SAVAGE ACTS.

THESE RELENTLESS SAVAGE ACTS PERPETRATED BY THESE MILITANTS GROUPS, THE REPERCUSSIONS RETALIATED AGAINST (ALL) AFRICAN AMERICANS FOR THESE INSANE ACTSWAS ATROCIOUS, THEY WERE CAST INTO WATCHFUL SERVITUDE FOR ONE HUNDRED TWENTY SIX YEARS.

AND AFTER THEIR FREEDOM FROM SLAVERY IN EIGHTEEN SIXTY FIVE, BY PRESIDENT ABRAHAM LINCOLN, THE SOUTHERN DEMOCRATS FOUNDED THE KU-KLUX-KLAN, IN PULASKI, TENNESSEE.

IN AN EFFORT TO COUNTERACT POTENTIAL FREED SLAVES FROMORGANIZING AND REBELLING AGAINST WHITES AGAIN, BECAUSE OF THEIR HISTORICAL POSSESSIVE AGENDA.

THE KU-KLUX-KLAN GREW INTO A MONUMENTAL TERRORIZING FORCE AGAINST AFRICAN AMERICANS, AND DOMINATED THE SOUTH, BY INFILTRATING LOCAL LAW INFORCEMENT WHICH GAVE THEM EXTEREMITY TO MAIM HANG AND DEMORALIZE BLACKS WITH OUT CONSEQUENCES.

THEIR RANGE SPREAD TO THE STATE OF INDIANA, BUT MOSTLY FOR POLITICAL CONTROL RELATED TO (UNREADABLE TEXT)

HOWEVER AFTER A FIEW KEY ARREST THEY REVERTED BACK TO THE SOUTHERN STATES.

HOWEVER THERE IS A FUNDAMENTAL ISSURE THAT MANY WILL CONSIDER DEBATABLE UNDER THE CIRCUMSTANCES, AND THERE IS A VERY DISTINCT POSSIBILITY THAT SLAVERY COULD HAVE BEEN (AVERTED) IF BLACKS HAD (NEVER) INITIATED VIOLENCE FOR DOMINANCE TO CHANGE AMERICA INTO A CONGO IDEOLOGY, HERDING BEHIND SOME SELF APPOINTED REBELLIOUS TREASONOUS PREACHERS FOR A PERSONAL TRIBAL CHIEF REPRESENTATION, INSTEAD OF PLEDGING TO THE EXISTING LAWS OF THE NATION.

HISTORIC EVENTS ARE EXTREMELY CORRELATED RELATED TO PRACTICALITY, AND IT IS CERTAINLY IRONIC THAT THERE ARE STILL SURROGATES LEADING INTO THE TWENTY FIRST CENTURY, ATTEMPTING TO EMULATE THIS STIGMATIC REBELLIOUS FAILURE WITH MALICE, OF PAST CENTURIES THROUGH EXPLOITING EQUAL RIGHTS FOR BLACKS.

BUT IN (REALITY) THEIR ATTEMPT IS TO CREATE DISCORD AGAINST THE CONTROLLING BUREAUCRACIES

RELATED TO BLACKS, IN AN EFFORT TO IMPLEMENT A CHIEF LIKE CONGO AGENDA.

WHERE THEY ARE SELF APPOINTED ABERRANCE CYNICAL SPOKESMAN OF GUIDANCE FOR AFRICAN AMERICANS, NEGATING THE CONSTUTION AND DECLARATION OF INDEPENDANCE.

WHEN THE KU-KLUX-KLAN WAS FOUNDERED BY THE DEMOCRATS THEIR MAIN OBJECTIVE WAS TO DRIVE WHITE AND BLACK REPUBLICANS FROM THE SOUTH IN AN EFFORT TO PREVENT THEM FROM TEACHING FORMER SLAVES TO READ AND WRITE, ALSO TO FORCE BLACKS TO BECOME DEMOCRATS, AND THEY FORMULATED STRATEGIC GUIDE LINES FOR BLACKS, THERE WAS (NO) TOLERANC FOR HERDING BEHIND A SELF APPOINTED BLACK LEADER, OR TAUNTING WHITE WOMEN IN ANY FASHION.

AND BLACKS WERE PROHIBITED FROM SAYING YES OR NO TO (ANY) WHITES, IF ANY OF THESE GUIDE LINES WERE VIOLATED, THERE WERE GRAVE CONSEQUENCES FOR ANY BLACK.

HOWEVER THERE ARE CURRENT DAY BLACK ORBITERS THAT INSIST ON REVIVING AND EMULATING THE PAST, LESS THE VIOLENCE.

AND IT IS QUITE FASCINATING BECAUSE UNDER FALSE PRETENSES THEY DISTORT (REALITY) PERTAINING TO RACE AND EQUALITY FOR BLACKS, AND IT IS INTENDED TO GENERATE HERDING TO THEIR ABERRATION AS SPOKESMAN FOR (ALL) BLACKS, IN ORDER TO ADVANCE THEIR EGOISTIC CYNICAL CONGO HERDING GENETIC IDEOLOGY FOR DOMINANCE.

AND IT IS NOTHING MORE THAN EMULATING SURROGATE HOSTILE VILLAINS OF PAST GENERATIONS WITH INCONGRUOUS DIPLOMACY.

AND THE TWO MAIN INSTIGATORS ARE PREACHERS, AL SHARPTON AND JESSIE JACKSON, THEY HAVE A NEW STRATEGY AND THAT IS TO INTIMIDATE THE INSTITUTIONS OF THE GOVERNMENT, CONGLOMERATE WHITE OWNED BUSINESSES, AND THE AFFLUENT WHITES THAT ARE CONTRACTUALLY EMPLOYED, ESPECIALLY TELEVISION AND RADIO PERSONALITIES, BY MONITORING FREE SPEECH

FOR INCENFIARY REMARKS PERTAINING TO BLACKS. AND MANY WHITES ARE BEING COWARDLY DOCILE BY THIS INSANITY, AND CATERING IN AN EFFORT TO APPEASE, BY DISMISSING ANY WHITE THAT MAKE ANY DISPARAGING REMARK ABOUT BLACKS.

THERE (IS) A DOUBLE STANDARD EFFECTED IN OUR NATION RELATED TO BLACKS, THAT EVENTUALLY IS GOING TO CAUSE MANY MANY INNQCENT BLACKS TO SELF DESTRUCT, SIMPLY BECAUSE THE POWER STRUCTURE IN THE UNITED STATES OF AMERICA CONSIST OF CAUCASIANS POLITAICAL INTELLECT AND WEALTH, CAPITALIZED WITH MORAL VALUES.

WHICH SELF APPOINTED BLACK LEADERS WITH THEIR CONGO CHIEF MENTALITY .IS INEPT TO,AND TRANSLATE TO THEIR HERDING EOLLOWERS AS CIVIL RIGHTS DISCRIMINATION, WHICH IS ASININE AND THOSE THAT FOLLOW THESE IMPERIALISTIC PARASITIC REBEL DICTATORS ARE DOOMED TO POVITY, INCARCERATION, AND THE WORST OF HUMANITY, WHICH IS THE GETTO SLUMS. IT IS INCONCEIVABLE THAT APPROXIMATELY 30% OF AFRICAN AMERICANS ARE CYNICAL AND OUT OF TUCH WITH (REALITY) PERTAINING TO THE CENTRAL IMPORTANCE OF GRASPING THE MONOLITHIC DIVERSITY OF OUR NATION. INSTEAD THEY CHOOSE TO GENETICALLY GRAVITATE BEHIND A SYMBOLISTIC REBEL SEPARATIST WHICH IS WORTHLESS AS TITS ON A BULL AND FOR YEARS HAVE MADE A SUBSTANTIAL FINANCIAL LIVING BY LYING AND DECEIVING OTHERS WITH ENCIVILITY AND BIGOTRY.

AND THE MOST OUTRAGEOUS OBSERVABLE FACT OF EVENTS, IS THAT THEY HAVE APPOINTED THEM SELVES TO CONGO TRIBAL CHIEF FOR (ALL) AFRICAN AMERICANS, THAT RESIDE IN THE UNITED STATES OF AMERICA. AND TO VALIDATE THEIR FASCIST AGENDA, (EXAMPLE) NOTABLY WHOES ASS DID DON IMAS AND FORMER PRESIDENT BILL CLINTON (KISS) FOR BEING ACCUSED OF MAKING SUPPOSEDLY INCENDIARY REMARKS ABOUT BLACKS.

(PREACHER) AL SHARPTON, THEORETICALLY THE INFLAMMATORY PRECEPTION PERTAINING TO THE MENTAL

TELEPATHY OF THE MAJORITY RELATED TO AFRICAN AMERICANS CONSIST OF THEIR PLEDGING TO SACRED ENDEAVORS TO ATTAIN DOMINANCE OVER WHITES.

SOME HAVE ALREADY STAKED THEIR CLAIM TO FAME AND SELECTED SENATOR BARACK OBAMA AS THE NEXT PRESIDENT OF THE UNITED STATES, TO HERD BEHIND STIPULATING THAT IT IS (NOW) TIME FOR BLACKS TO TAKE OVER THE COUNTRY FROM WHITES, REGARDS TO ATONEMENT FOR SLAVERY, AND SENATOR BARACK OBAMA IS GOING TO PURSUE REPARATION FOR SLAVERY, AND IT IS SUSPECTED THAT SENATOR OBAMA IS PLAYING TO THOSE SENTIMENTS, BECAUSE IN SOME OF HIS SPEECHES HE REFERENCE THE VERBIAGE THIS IS (OUR) COUNTRY.

VALIDATED JANUARY 30, 2008. RADIO WREC 600, BEN FERGERSON, AND THE HANNITY SHOW JANUARY 31, 2008.

HOWEVER UNFORTUNATELY THESE SENTIMENTS ARE SHARED WITH A SEGEMENT OF AFRICAN AMERICANS NATION WIDE, WHICH HAS BEEN DETRIMENTAL TO THEIR DIVERSITY SUCCESS,AND HINDERING THEIR EQUALITY FOR CENTURIES, AND JUST AS PREVALENT TO DAY AS EVER.

WITH (NO) FUNDAMENTAL VALIDITY OTHER THAN NONSENSICAL REBELLIOUS HERDING RACISM PERTAINING TO WHITES.

WHICH IS A DOUBLE STANDARD THAT IS A DANGEROUS AGENDA TO (ALL) CIVILIZE SOCIETY IN OUR NATION, BECAUSE IF A WHITE PERSON WOULD HAVE WRITTEN OR EMAILED SUCH FOOLISH VULGARITY, IMPLYING THAT BLACKS CIVIL AND VOTING RIGHTS BE REVOKED.

AL SHARPTON AND JESSIE JACKSON, WOULD BE UNCONTROLLABLE, AND ATTEMPTING TO INTIMIDATE OR EXTORT THE RADIO STATION,AND GET THE HOST FIRED THAT READ THE MEMORANDUM.

IT APPEAR THAT THE FUNDAMENTALS OF OUR CIVILITY PERTAINING TO SOCIETY IS BEING THREATEN BY A IMPETUS OF IMPERIALISTIC IDEOLOGUES THAT IS DESTINE TO IMPEDE MOST AFRICAN AMERICANS INVOLVEMENT IN DIVERSITY, WITH REBELLIOUS SATNIC DEMAGOGUERY, THAT HAS GRAVE CONSEQUENCES IF CONTINUED AT THIS RATE.

PRIMARILY BASED ON CHRONOLOGICAL RECORDS OF SIGNIFICANT REPERCUSSIONS EMULATING EVENTS, IN THE UNITED STATES OF AMERICA. UNFORTUNATELY THERE IS A IMBECILIC SEGEMENT OF AFRICAN AMERICANS, THROUGH GENETIC CONTROLLABILITY THAT IS DETERMINE TO QUANTIFY SUPERIORITY PERTAINING TO OTHERS.

AND THEIR ATTEMPT TO ACCOMPLISH THIS UNSAVORY AGENDA, HAS ALWAYS BEEN PULVERIZING REGARDS TO THEIR INHERENT ETHNIC STABILITY. INCLUDING THE LOSS OF THEIR LIVES, AND THOSE THAT HERD BEHIND THEM, THERE IS A UNDERCURRENT OF IMMORALITY THAT IS FESTERING IN OUR NATION, BASED ON GOVERNMENTAL POLITICAL INEPTNESS, PARTICULARLY SOME AFRICAN AMERICANS, BECAUSE MOST THINGS THEY DO (NOT) UNDERSTAND THEY TEND TO (ASSUME) AND REBEL WITH HOSTILE EXHIBITIONISM, IN AN EFFORT TO RECTIFY THEIR (ASSUMPTIONS) AND THIS IS A GENETIC DEVIATION TRAIT THAT HAS BEEN NURTURED BY MOST BLACKS FOR CENTURIES.

WHICH UNFORTUNATELY IS BECOMING MORE EXCEEDINGLY PREVALENT IN OUR SOCIETY TO DAY MORE THAN EVER. FOR INSTANCE IN THE STATE OF TENNESSEE, A POLICE OFFICER FOR OVER TWENTY FIVE YEARS WAS GUN DOWN IN OWN HOME FOR REASONS UNKNOWN, IN THE STATE OF MISSOURI, APPROXIMATELY SIX INNOCENT INDIVIDUALS WERE GUN DOWN EXECUTION STYLE, BASED ON (ASSUMPTIONS) AS REPORTED AND THE EXECUTIONER BROTHER STIPULATED IT TO BE JUSTIFIABLE POLITICAL (WAR). AND REFUSED TO CLARIFY THE WORD WAR RELATED WHAT THESE HIDEOUS REBELLIOUS NONSENSICAL CRIMES WERE PERPETRATED BY (BLACKS). WHICH COULD INSTIGATE RETALIATION IN SOME MANNER FROM (WHITES) AND IF SO THERE IS GOING TO BE SELF APPOINTED BLACK LEADERS MARCHING AND SCREAMING EQUAL RIGHTS AND RACISM. WHEN BLACKS INITIATED VIOLENCE AS THEY DID IN THE SEVENTEENTH CENTURY, FOR DOMINANCE TO CONTROL THE POLITICAL GOVERNING UNWIELDY ADMINISTRATIVE SYSTEM IN THE UNITED STATES OF AMERICA, TO NO REPREHENSIBLE AVAIL.

IT IS SUSPECTED THAT OUR NATION IS SLOWLY DRIFTING INTO DEVIATING RACISM, PREDICATED ON DEROGATORY VERBIAGE, THAT SOME BLACKS ARE AIMLESSLY PERSUING, IN AN ATTEMPT TO JUSTIFY THEIR REASON TO ATTAIN DOMINANCE FOR PERSONAL ACCOLADES WITHOUT MERIT. FORTUNATELY THIS IS A GENETIC OBSESSION THAT WILL (NEVER) EXIST UNDER ANY CIRCUMSTANCES, BECAUSE IF YOU ARE INEPT TO THE CONSTITUTIONALITY OF THE NATION THAT YOU RESIDE IN.

IT IS QUITE OBVIOUS YOUR AGENDA TO MANY ENTITLEMENTS ARE (NIL). HOWEVER THERE IS A CONSTANT BEFUDDLING TO ATTAIN THAT WHICH IS BEYOND YOUR CAPACITY TO DEVELOP MENTALLY AND MORALLY. SO AS A RESULT YOU ARE ATTRACTED TO SELF APPOINTED BLACK PARASITES THAT DICTATE APPEALING REBELLIOUS ANARCHIES, THAT GRATIFY YOUR INABILITY TO ATTAIN BASED ON INCOMPETENT DEFICIENCY. THE GENERAL CONSENSUS THAT PROFILE GENETIC TRAITS AND HOW IT DOMINATE THE AFFECTS OF (ALL) MAN KIND SOCIETY.

ONCE A CHILD IS CONCEIVED IN THE MOTHERS ANITOMY, IT IS PRONOUNCED THAT THE FIRST ORGAN TO DEVELOPE IS THE HEART, THE NEXT IS THE BRAIN WHICH UNIQUELY TAKE OVER PROFILE AND COORDINATE THE GENETTIC TRAITS FORM EACH PARENT, (THROUGHOUT) THE CHILD BODY WITH PRECISE UNANIMITY PERTAINING TO EACH PARENT.

ONCE THE CHILD IS BROUGHT INTO LIFE, IT BECOME THE (SOLE) OBLIGATION OF THE PARENTS OR PARENT, TO GIVE GUIDANCE PERTAINING TO INTELLECTUAL MORAL VALUES.

WHICH IS THE FOUNDATION TO THE FUNDAMENTALS OF OUR NATION, AS YOU GROW UP AND UTILIZE YOUR PARENT TAUGHT MORAL VALUES, THROUGH EXTRA CURRICULA YOU WILL BEGIN TO ABSOB THAT WE AS A PEOPLE LIVE IN A VERY DIVERSE SOCIETY, THAT IS GOVERN BY LAWS EMBEDED IN THE CONSTITUTION AND DECLARATION OF INDEPENDENCE.

AND (IF) YOU SHOULD ASPIRE TO COMPREHEND AND TAKE ADVANTAGE OF THOSE TAUGHT ATTRIBUTES,THEN

YOU WILL SUDDENLY REALIZE THAT THE UNITED STATES OF AMERICA IS THE (GREATES) COUNTRY ON GODS GLOBE TO RESIDE IN AND (ALWAYS) MAINTAIN THE IDEOLOGY THAT GENETIC TRAITS ARE PASSED ON ETERNALLY.

ALSO ONE MUST UNDERSTAND THE VALIDITY OF GENETIC TRAITS, AND THRROUGH INTELLECT MASTER YOUR (INDIVIDUAL) DOMINANCE PERTAINING TO SUCCESS IN LIFE BASED ON MERIT.

HOWEVER THERE ARE MISGIVINGS IN LIFE TO IMPEDE, THAT ONE SHOULD BE AWARE OF, BUT IF YOU RELY ON THOSE GENETIC TRAITS PASSED ON YOU WILL AVOID MOST BECAUSE GENES DICTATE THE FUNDAMENTALS OF HEHERITAGE AND INTELLECTUAL MORAL VALUES PASSED ON.

THROUGH A PROCESS OF GROWING UP, AND WHEN ONE BECOME THE APPROPRIATE AGE TO ATTAIN COMPANION SHIP BE CERTAIN TO SCREEN THEIR DEMEANOR, BASED ON CULTURE AND THEIR UNDERSTANDING OF THE FUNDAMENTALS THAT EXIST IN OUR NATION PERTAINING TO DIVERSITY, AND THE INHERENT SYSTEMATIC FUNCTIONS OF OUR COMPLEX GOVERNMENT.

THIS SINGLE CRITERIA IS LARGELY RESPONSIBLE FOR MANY AFRICAN AMERICANS ALSO OTHERS, HAVING A DYSFUNCTIONAL ATTITUDE THAT LEAD TO CRIMINAL ACTIVITY.

BECAUSE THEY ARE INEPT TO THE FUNDAMENTALS OF POLITICAL INTELLECT AND MORAL FORTITUDE, PERTAINING TO VALUES.

HOWEVER MOST BLACKS ARE COAXED INTO THINKING BY SELF APPOINTED LEADERS THAT THEY HAVE BEEN DUPED BY CAUCASIANS AND THE FEDERAL GOVERNMENT, AND THEIR COMPENSATION IS LONG PASS DUE. SO IN ESSENCE THEY ALLOW THEM SELVES TO BECOME INVOLVED IN A GENETIC AFRICAN HERDING PROCESS, THAT CONSTITUTE A SELF APPOINTED LEADER GUIDANCE, WHICH IS PARALLEL TO THE CONGO STRAW HUTS IN AFRICA WHERE THE CHIEF AND WITCH DOCTOR CONTROL TRIBAL AFFAIRS. MOST AFRICAN AMERICANS ARE PLAGUED WITH THIS GENETIC STIGMATIZATION (TODAY). THAT WAS BROUGHT ALONG

WITH OUR ANCESTORS IN 1619, AND THIS POLITICAL PREPONDERANCE PREVALENCE OF BLACKS ALIENATING THEM SELVES, BASED ON SEPARATISM IS TRULY SUICIDAL.

THIS IS THE UNITED STATES OF AMERICA,(NOT) AFRICA, APPARENTLY SOME OF THESE IMBECILES THAT ARE ADVOCATING THIS ANARCHY, EITHER THEY ARE INEPT OR IN DENIAL TO THE FACT THAT OUR NATION IS FORMULATED BY GUIDE LINES THAT IS EMBEDDED IN THE CONSTUTION, DECLARATION OF INDEPENDENCE, THAT IS ENFORCED BY A PRESIDENT, SENATE, CONGRESS, AND SUPREME COURT.

AND THIS AFRICAN HERDING HOG PIN MENTALITY IS GOING TO REPRESENT DOOMS DAY FOR MANY AFRICAN AMERICANS THAT HERD BEHIND THIS NONSENSICAL IDEOLOGY, AS IT HAS HISTORICALLY.

OUR NATION IS BEING PLAGUED WITH CONTEMPTIBLE INCENDIARY BLIGHT, THERE ARE MANY VIABLE CITIZENS THAT ARE TRYING TO DETERMINE THE REASON FOR THESE INCENDIARY VIOLENT MOLESTATIONS OF OTHERS, PIRATICALLY WITH FIRE ARMS, IN THE EXTRA CURRICULAR SCHOOL SYSTEM. MANY PEOPLE ARE TRYING TO DETERMINE (WHY) SOME SCHOOL YOUNGSTERS ARE SO ANGRY, THE PREMISE OF THIS FLOUNDERING DEMAGOGUERY IS PRIMARILY BASED ON INEPTNESS , BECAUSE THE DOMINATING FACTOR HAS TO WITH THE INGENUITY RELATED TO POLITICAL SOCLISTIC GRATUITY EOR THE PAST THIRTY FIVE OR FORTY YEARS, THAT HAVE CREATED RELENTLESS DEPENDANT DEFICIENCES, PIRATICALLY PERTAINING TO AFRICAN AMERICANS.

SATISTICALLY THERE ARE APPROXIMATELY SEVENTY PERCENT OF BABIES BORN TO PARENTS THAT ARE BLACK, WHICH HAS INSTITUTIONALIZED THE THE VERBIAGE SINGLE PARENT.

AND EACH PARENT MOTHER AND FATHER ARE PRACTICALLY ILLITERATE, MANY HAVENT THE SLIGHTEST IDEA WHO DR. MARTIN LUTHER KING WAS, OR THE NAME OF THE SITTING PRESIDENT OF THE UNITED STATES OF AMERICA IS, SO AS A RESULT THEIR CHILDREN ARE TUTORED INITIATIVES FROM BIRTH, REALISTICALLY THAT

IS SO OUT OF TUCH WITH MORALITY, UNTIL THEIR LIVES ARE SO FILLED WITH VINDICTIVENESS FOR OTHERS.THAT DO NOT SHARE THEIR REMOTE IDEOLOGY, OF PARENT TAUGHT IDIOSYNCRASIES, THAT CREATE FRUSTRATION, WHICH LEAD TO MAIMING VIOLENCE, BASED ON THEIR HOSTILE ENVIRONMENT OF CYNICISM TAUGHT FROM BIRTH, THAT (ALL) WHITES ARE OUT TO PROHIBIT THEM FROM INGENUITY BECAUSE THEY ARE BLACK.

AND IF A AFRICAN AMERICAN FAMILY SPEAK APPROPIATE ENGLISH AND TEACH THEIR CHILDREN INTELLECT THAT IS CONSISTENT WITH MORALITY, THERE ARE CLANNISH REBELLIOUS BLACKS ATTEMPTING TO DEMORALIZE AND INTIMIDATE WITH ACCUSATIONS OF THEY ARE TRYING TO BE (WHITE), SO AS A RESULT THIS SATANIC REVELATION OF INSANITY IS INFILTRATED INTO PUBLIC PLACES, LEARNING. INSTITUTIONS, OR ANY PLACE WHERE THEY CONGREGATE.

WITH OUT QUESTION THERE IS A VINDICTIVNESS IN OUR NATION AMONG MANY AFRICAN AMERICANS, THAT IS PREMEDITATE WITH PRESISTENCY BY SELF APPOINTED BLACK LEADERS AND WEALTHY RADICAL MINISTERS. ALSO MANY PROFESSIONAL ELITE BLACKS THAT IS ACCESSED WITH DOMINANCE, AND IS TOTALLY INEPT TO THE DECLARATION OF INDEPENDENCE AND THE CONSTITUTION, RELATED TO THE POLITICAL FUNDAMENTALS OF OUR NATION.

THIS EVALUATION IS BASED ON THEIR CONTINUED REPREHENSIBLE DEMAGOGUERY REFERRING TO BLACK (EQUALITY) AND CIVIL RIGHTS. THIS BACK WOODS SMALL BRAIN HOSTILE INSANITY IS ALOOF AND ILLUSTRATE THE ABANDONING OF INTELLECT.

AND THERE ARE DIRE CONSEQUENCES FOR THOSE THAT ADHERE TO THIS HOG PIN MENTALITY, THERE IS AN OLD SAYING IT IS UTTERLY IMPOSSIBLE TO TAKE A JACK ASS AND MAKE A RACE HORSE OUT OF IT.

THIS NATION WAS FOUNDED ON INTELLECTUAL MORAL VALUES, AND MANY MANY AFRICAN AMERICANS HAVE MADE THE NECESSARY ADJUSTMENTS AND ADOPTED THESE PRINCIPLES, AND LAUNCHED INCREDIBLE SUCCESSFUL FINANCIAL INVOLVEMENT IN AMERICAN SOCIETY.

UNFORTUNATELY MANY HAVE THIS DYSFUNCTIONAL SMALL BRAIN HOG PIN MENTALITY TO TECHNICALLY DENOUNCE THEIR (OWN) CREDIBILITY REGARDS TO PROMINENCE, AND SUPPORT A SELF APPOINTED BUFFOONISH BLACK IDEOLOGUE THAT INSTIGATE AFRICAN AMERICANS ARE BEING DENIED THEIR CIVIL RIGHTS, THIS IS A LUDICROUS PHENOMENON THAT CONSIST OF RADICAL DIVERSIONS TO ATTAIN SYMPATHY RELATED TO DOMINANCE MINAS VIOLENCE TO INTIMIDATE SOCIETY, IN AN EFFORT TO GAIN SUPPORT FOR THEIR INEPT RADICAL IDEOLOGY OF A GENETIC CONGO CONCEPT, AND IT WILL (NEVER) DISSIPATE BECAUSE OF A GENETIC INNATENESS TO BE CHIEE.

JUST THINK HOW BLACKS COULD HAVE PROSPERED HISTORICALLY IF THEY HAD (NOT) PRACTICED THEIR AFRICAN HERITAGE, THROUGH THE SEVENTEENTH AND EIGHTEEN CENTURY, INSTEAD OF TRYING TO ADAPT AND ACCEPT THE ESTABLISHED CULTURE.

THAT WAS HERE PRIOR TO THEIR INTRODUCTION TO AMERICA THREE HUNDRED AND EIGHTY NINE YEARS AGO, INSTEAD THEY CHOOSE TO CLING TO THER AFRICAN CULTURE, AND UNITE REBELLIOUS GROUPS AND OUT RITE MURDER SETTLERS AND CLAIM THE COUNTRY TO BE THEIR OWN.

THIS GENETIC INSANE MENTALITY STILL EXIST TODAY, BUT IS DISGUISED WITH RADICAL RACIST INNUENDOES SEEKING DOMINANCE. FORTUNATELY IT WILL (NEVER) EXIST BASED ON THE NATIONS PARITY. HOWEVER THERE ARE MANY BLACKS THAT ARE SO OVER COME WITH FENDISH INEPT OBSESSION UNTIL THEY BLATANTLY REFUSE TO ACKNOWLEDGE THE GENERAL CONSENSUS OF REALISTIC REALITY.

AS I DENOTED EARLIER, MANY AFRICAN AMERICANS ARE TAUGHT BY BLACK SELF APPOINTED.LEADERS AND RADICAL MINISTERS, THAT THEY WILL INHERIT THE EARTH AND DOMINATE.

THIS IDITOTIC DERANGED FETISH CULT DEVOTION, HAVE AND ARE GOING TO CAUSE MANY BLACKS TO SELF DESTRUCT.

TO REALISTICALLY ELABORATE ON THIS FOOLISH SATANIC IDEOLOGY DISPLAYED BY APPROXIMATELY NINETY FIVE PERCENT OF AFRICAN AMERICANS BEGINNING WITH SENATOR BARACKA OBAMA, MANY BLACKS ASSUME THAT HE IS A GOD SENT PRODIGY IN ORDER TO ASSIST IN THEIR INSIDIOUS ACCOMPLISHMENT OF DOMINANCE.

WHEN HE AND HIS WIFE IS (NOTHING) MORE THAN SELF PROCLAIMED INDIVIDUALS THAT SPEAK ENGLISH WITH ELEGANCE, AND HAS FORMULATED A UNIQUE BODY APPEAL IN CONJUNCTION, AND BLACKS ARE ESTATIC WITH THIS DECEITFUL DEMEANOR.

AND MILLIONS OF WHITES ARE BEFUDDLE AND INEPT TO THIS KIND CYNICAL CONGENIALITY EXPLOITED BY A BLACK IN THE DEDEMOCRAT PARTY, OPPOSE TO JESSIE JACKSON AND AL SHARPTON MURDERING THE AMERICAN ENGLISH.

THERE ARE MANY CONSERVATIVE AFRICAN AMERICANS IN THE REPUBLICAN PARTY, THAT ARE POLITICALLY INTELLECTUALLY MORALLY SOPHISTICATED. UNFORTUNATELY THERE ARE ELITE SMALL DYSFUNCTIONAL BRAIN BLACK BOOT LICKS IN THE DEMOCRAT PARTY, THAT IMPUGN THEIR INTEGRITY WITH DISTORTION.

SO AS A RESULT THEIR POLITICAL QUALITIES ARE ALIENATED AND DENOUNCED WITH DEMOCRAT POLITICAL PROPAGANDA.

HOWEVER AS SENATOR BARACK OBAMA PASTER, SO RADICALLY PHRASED CHIICKENS COMING HOME TO (ROOST).

THIS AROUSING RIDICULE SHOULD (NOT) HAVE BEEN REFLECTED ON THE UNITED STATES OF AMERICA, BUT ON THE DEMOCRATIC PARTY. BECAUSE THEY ARE IN A STATE OF DISARRAY, HAVING TO CHOOSE BETWEEN A SOPHISTICATED SLICK TALKING RADICAL AFRICAN AMERICAN, AND A TWO FOR ONE LYING WHITE WOMAN, MEANING SENATORS BARACK OBAMA, AND HILLARY CLINTON, I SUSPECT THE ELITE DEMOCRATS ARE IN THE WOOD WORK LIKE TERMITE CONSPIRING ON HOW TO DESTROY EACH OF THEIR POLITICAL AMBITIONS FOR EVER.

THE DEMOCRAT PARTY IS CONFRONTED WITH A UNIQUE DILEMMA, THAT HAS (NEVER) OCCURRED IN THE HISTORY OF AMERICA, AND THAT IS CHOOSING BETWEEN A WHITE WOMAN, AND A BLACK MAN FOR THEIR PRESIDENTIAL CANIDATE.

AND I THINK ITS FAIR TO SAY, WHEN THE DEMOCRAT PARTY BEGAN THEIR PRIMARYF CAMPAIGN, ALMOST (NONE) POLITICAL STRATEGIST WOULD HAVE DEEM THIS TO BE A REALITY.

HOWEVER THE ISSURE IS NONE ESSENTIAL AT THIS TIME, BUT THE GRAVITY OF HOW THE DEMOCRATS ARE GOING TO RESOLVE THIS UNIQUE CHRISIS, BECAUSE AT THE NERVE CENTER OF THIS DEBACLE, IS HERDING CONSTITUENCY OF BLACK VOTERS FOR SENATOR BARACK OBAMA, WHICH WHITE DEMOCRAT POLITICAL CANIDATES HAVE CAPTIVATED FOR OVER SEVERAL DECADES, AND I SUSPECT THAT THE DEMOCRAT PARTY HAVE (NO) INTENTION OF DISSOLVING THAT INSIDIOUS RELATIONSHIP.

THE SENSITIVITY OF THIS DEMOCRATIC POLITICAL DEBACLE WILL FOREVER BE SCRUTINIZED, BECAUSE THE FUNDAMENTAL ISSURE IS BASED ON THE POLITICAL IGNORANCE OF MOST AFRICAN AMERICANS.

ASSUMING THAT BARACK OBAMA IS GOING TO BE PRESIDENT, BECAUSE OF THEIR HERDING APPROXIMATELY NINETY FIVE PERCENT SUPPORT. AND TO STUPID TO REALIZE THAT BLACKS ARE ONLY TWELVE PERCENT OF THE POPULATIONTHAT CONSIST OF THREE HUNDRED MILLION. THE DEMOCRATS UTILIZE POLITICAL DECEITFUL SEDUCTIVE TACTICS, BECAUSE OF A STABILIZING FACTOR, TO RATIFY THEIR POLITICAL AGENDA OF DOMINANCE.

THE DEMOCRAT PARTY ELITE ELDERS HAVE A INGENIOUS PERSONA WHEN IMPLEMENTING VINDICTIVNESS TO EXECUTE THEIR AGENDA.

PIRATICALLY WHEN SEDUCING AND MANIPULATIND BLACKS, EARLIER I PREDICTED THAT BARACK OBAMA COULD NOT WIN THE DEMOCRATIC PRIMARY, IT APPEAR IT MIGHT BE APPROPIATE TO RECANT, BASED ON A EGOISTIC CHARISMATIC SILK TONGUE BLACK CANIDATE SENATOR BARACK OBAMA AND A PASSIVE WHITE WOMAN SENATOR

HILLARY CLINTON, THAT APPEAR SKEPTICAL TO MAKE EYE CONTACT WITH OBAMA DURING THEIR DEBATES, IT COULD BE BECAUSE OF BITTER ANXIETY.

THERE IS A UNIQUE FUNDAMENTAL SCENARO THAT HAS DEVELOPED (WITHIN) THE DEMOCRATIC PARTY, THAT IS RATHER BEWILDERING.

FOR HUNDREDS OF YEARS THE DEMOCRAT PARTY HAVE OPPRESSED AFRICAN AMERICANS, AND LABEL THEM AS BEING INCOMPETENT. EITHER THERE HAS BEEN A DRAMATIC CHANGE IN THE DEMOCRAT PARTY IDEOLOGY OF SUPREMACY, OR THEY WERE CAUGHT OF GUARD WITH THE POLITICAL NEGATIVES OF THE CLINTONS TO BE ELECTABLE, HOWEVER THE (ONLY) WAY TO DETERMINE THE VALIDITY OF EITHER PARTY IS EXAMINE THEIR CHRONOLOGICAL RECORD OF SIGNIFICANT EVENTS, THE DEMOCRAT PARTY HAS BEEN EXTREMELY STUBBON WHEN ANY ONE, OR THINGS TEND TO ALTER THEIR AGENDA.

I AM AN AFRICAN AMERICAN THAT (LOVE) THIS COUNTRY, GREW UP PART SOUTH, PART NORTH, AND IS OVER SIXTY FIVE YEARS OLD, AND HAS NEVER HAD PROBLEMS WITH ANY NATIONALLY OF PEOPLE OTHER THAN MY OWN. SOME BLACKS ARE THE WORST INSIDIOUS INEPT PEOPLE ON GODS EARTH, BECAUSE MOST ARE IGNORANT TO THE TRADITIONAL POLITICAL PRINCIPLES THAT THIS COUNTRY WAS FOUNDED ON.

FOR ANY DEROGATORY REMARK THAT I ASSERT, I HAVE SUFFICENT EVIDENCE TO VALIDATE THE REASON.

FOR APPROXIMATELY TWENTY YEARS,I WAS A EMPLOYEE FOR GENERAL DYNAMICS LAND SYSTEMS DURING THE EARLY EIGHTIES, MY RESPONSIBILITY WAS A TRAVELING LIAISON,CONDUCTING COMMUNICABLE STANDARDS WITH OTHER COMPANIES,FOR A ECONOMICAL RELIANCE.

I TRAVELED ALL OVER THE UNITED STATES OF AMERICA INCLUDING MEXICO, AND BASED ON MY RESPONSIBILITY IT WAS NECESSARY TO MEET WITH ONLY OWNERS, PRESIDENTS, AND GENERAL MANAGERS, COINCIDENTALLY THEY WERE ALL WHITE.

BY THE WAY AT THAT TIME I WAS THE ONLY AFRICAN AMERICAN CHOSEN BY THE COMPANY TO HOLD THAT

TITLE FOR A NUMBER OF YEARS AND (NEVER) ONCE DID I EXPERIENCE RACIST ANTICS, AND THERE WERE MORNING, AFTERNOON, AND DINNER MEALSTOGATHER WITH COMPANY DIGNITARIES, BECAUSE MY PLATEAU WAS FIRMLY BASED ON INTELLECTUAL MORAL VALUE SENTIMENTS, AND IT WAS ALWAYS RETURNED WITH RESPECT AND MORALITY.

AS I RECALL IT WAS MORE THAN ONCE THAT I WAS CALLED ON TO FLY FROM ONE END OF THE COUNTRY TO ANOTHER, IN ORDER TO APPEASE A MANUFACTURER THAT A WHITE HAD INSULTED, AND WAS ESCORTED OFF THE PREMISES.

OH I MIGHT ADD WHEN I WAS ASKED TO ACCEPT A POSITION IN PROCUREMENT, THE COMPANY PROMOTED ANOTHER (BLACK) TO THAT RESPONSIBILITY AND WITHIN SIX MONTHS HE WAS RELIEVED, FOR CHASING WHORES ON COMPANY TIME, (CASE CLOSED).

HOWEVER THIS IS TWO THOUSAND AND EIGHT, PRESIDENTIAL ELECTION, THE REPUBLICANS HAVE RESOLVE THE ISSURE OF THEIR CANIDATE FOR CHOICE, UNFORTUNATELY THE DEMOCRATS ARE STILL UNDECIDED, AND HAVE A POTENTIAL FIASCO DEVELOPING WITHIN THEIR PARTY PERTAINING TO THEIR PRIMARY CANIDATE.

WHICH CONSIST OF SENATORS HILLARY CLINTON AND BARACK OBAMA, THE INTENSITY COULD BE GRUESOME, BETWEEN A WHITE WOMAN AND BLACK MAN, THEY EACH ARE EMBROILED IN A BATTLE TO SALVAGE THEIR POLITICAL CAREERS.

HOWEVER THERE IS SOMETHING IN THE BACK OF MY MIND, THAT CONSTANTLY REMIND ME AS THIS POLITICAL MOVEMENT FOR CHANGE CONTINUE, AND THAT IS THE POLITICAL RIVALRY BETWEEN INCUMBENT DEMOCRAT STEPHEN A. DOUGLAS, AND ABRAHAM LINCOLN, FOR THE US SENATE IN EIGHTEEN FIFTY EIGHT.

STEPHEN A. DOUGLAS LET HIS IDEOLOGY BE EXPLICITLY WELL KNOWN, BY IMPLYING AMERICA WAS MADE BY WHITE (MEN) FOR THE BENIFIT OF (WHITE) MEN, AND THEIR POSTERITY (FOREVER);

TESE KIND OF DEROGATORY COMMENTS REPRESENT BIGOTRY, HOWEVER IT IS A REALITY THAT STILL EXIST TODAY IN OUR SOCIETY.

I AM AN INDIVIDUAL THAT WILL ALWAYS EXCEPT THE FACTS OF REALITY, TO DISTORT REALITY CAN BE DETRIMENTAL, AND CAUSE SELF DESTRUCTION

HOWEVER TO DISPEL THE UTTERANCE OF DEMOCRAT INCUMBENT STEPHEN A. DOUGLAS, ONE HUNDRED FIFTY YEARS AGO CHALLEGING ABRAHAM LINCOLN FOR THE U.S. SENATE, IS UTTERLY LUDICROUS, BECAUSE THOSE SENTIMENTA ARE STILL PREVALENT PREDOMINANTLY IN THE UNITED STATES OF AMERICA AND WILL (NEVER) CEASE TO EXIST, BECAUSE OF HUMAN GENETIC CONTROLLABILITY.

IN EIGHTEEN SEVENTY, HIRMAN RHODES REVELS, BECAME THE FIRST REPU^BLICAN AFRICAN AMERICAN SENATOR FROM MISSISSIPPI.

AND SEEING BLACKS HOLD POLITICAL OFFICE, SOUTHERN WHITE DEMOCRATS BECAME BELLIGERENT AND ACCUSED BLACKS OF BEING IGNORANT, INCOMPETENT PEOPLE, AND ATTEMPTING TO RISE ABOVE THEIR NATURALLY SUBSERVIENT PLACE IN SOCIETY.

AND THE REASON THAT I AM RAISING THESE ISSURES, ALTHOUGH THIS IS TWO THOUSAND EIGHT, TRUST ME THESE ARE THE SAME IDENTICAL OBSTICLES THAT SENATOR BARACK OBAMA IS GOING TO BE PLAGUED WITH. OH BY THE WAY HIRMAN RHODES REVELS WAS FORMALLY EDUCATED, LETS CONCENTRATE ON THE DEMOCRATIC UNIQUE PRIMARY POLICIES, OVER SEVEN HUNDRED (UNCOMMITTED) SUPER DELIGATES, YOU REALLY DO NOT HAVE TO BE A HARVARD GRADUATE IN ORDER TO DETERMINE THAT STRATEGY. THIS BOOK IS WRITTEN TO EXPOSE SOME OF THE BLATANCY THAT OCCURED RELATED TO POLITICS HISTORICALLY, AND THE COVERT CYNICAL REVELATION OF TODAY, AMERICAN POLITICS ARE THE MOST COMPLEX UNIVERSALLY BECAUSE OF THE DEVIATING FORMULATION COMPOSED BY OUR FOUNDERS. MOST PEOPLE BLACK AND WHITE, LIVE AND DIE OVER A

LIFE TIME AND (NEVER) UNDERSTAND THE INTRICATE FUNCTIONS.

BUT THATS WHAT MAKE THIS COUNTRY SO GREAT, IT OFFER APPROPRIATE OPPORTUNITY FOR EVERY CITIZEN, ALTHOUGH MOST ARE UNABLE TO DECIPHER THE TRUE FUNDAMENTALS OF OUR TWO PARTY SYSTEM, AND HOW THE CORRELATION FUNCTION REGARDS TO THE FACTION.

UNTIL HE OR SHE CHOOSE TO MANIFEST IN POLITICAL ASPIRATION TO SEEK OFFICE, AND YOU HAD BE WELL VERSED AND PREPARED TO CCEPT THE ULTIMATE SCRUTINY.

PRESIDENT FRANKLIN DELANO ROOSEVELT AND ELEANOR, WAS MOST LIKLEY THE CINNINGNESS AND SHREWDEST POLITICIANS THAT EVER EXISTED. THEIR IDEOLOGY HAVE SET THE STANDARDS FOR THE DEMOCRAT PARTY FOR OVER SEVENTY YEARS.

HOWEVER ANY WAY YOU DISSECT IT, AMERICAN POLITICS IS FORMULATED FOR THE PEOPLE TO CHOOSE AN ELECTED OFFICIAL, AND YOU CAN FOOL (SOME) OF THE PEOPLE AT TIMES, BUT TO FOOL ALL THE PEOPLE IS UTTERLY IMPOSSIBLE.

MOST AFRICAN AMERICANS FROM EITHER PARTY INTER INTO THE POLITICAL ARENA SEEKING OFFICE, IS FACED WITH A UP HILL BATTLE, UNLESS IT IS LOCAL WITH A LARGE CONSTITUENCY OF BLACKS, WHICH THE MAJORITY SUPPORT A DEMOCRATIC LIBERAL AGENDA.

THERE ARE THREE MAJOR HISTORICAL REALITIES, THAT DOMINATE THE PROGRESS OF AFRICAN AMERICANS POLITICAL ASPIRATIONS.

(1) QUOTE DEMOCRAT U S. SENATOR STEPHEN A. DOUGLAS, EIGHTEEN FIFTY EIGHT, AMERICA WAS MADE BY WHITE MEN, FOR THE BENIFIT OF WHITE (MEN) AND THEIR POSTERITY (FOREVER).

(2) IN EIGHTEEN SEVENTY ONE,SOUTHERN DEMOCRATS BECAME (OUTRAGED) TO THE FACT THAT SOME BLACKS WERE ELECTED TO HOLD POLITICAL OFFICE, THEY ANGRILY RETALIATED WITH REMARKS THAT BLACKS WERE INCOMPETENT, IGNORENT AND ATTEMPTING TO RISE ABOVE THEIR INITIATIVE STATUS OF SERVITUDE.

(3) DURING THE PRESIDENTAL ELECTION OF EIGHTEEN SEVENTY SIX, BETWEEN DEMOCRAT SAMUEL J. TILDEN, AND REPUBLICAN RUTHERFORD B. HAYES, EACH PARTY CLAIMED VICTORY IN LOUISIANA, SOUTH CAROLINA, AND FLORDIA, THE ELECTORIAL COMMISSION AWARDED THE PRESIDENCY TO HAYES, UNFORTUNATELY THE DEMOCRATS CONTROLLED THE CONGRESS, AND REFUSED TO CERTIFY THE ELECTION.

UNTIL A DEAL WAS COMPROMISED AND CONSUMATED, TO LEAVE THE SOUTHERNERS IN COMPLETE (STATE CONTROL) OF CIVIL OBEDIENCE AND STABILITY REGARDS TO THE RIGHTS FOR BLACKS.

WITH THIS COMPROMISE (ALL) FEDERAL PROTECTION WAS REMOVED FOR AFRICAN AMERICANS IN THE SOUTH, WHICH THEY WERE CASTIGATED, DEMORALIZED AND MAIMED FOR EIGHTY EIGHT YEARS,, BY SOUTHERN DEMOCRATS. IN THE INTERIM THE REPUBLICANS WERE COMPENSATED FOR THIS TRUCULENT TRADE OFF, WITH THE ASSURANCE THAT THE DEMOCRATS WOULD NOT INTERFERE IN THEIR ECONOMIC BENEFITING BUISNESS POLICIES. I CONSTANTLY REFERENCE THESE CHRONOLOGICAL EVENTS BECAUSE THEY ARE EMBEDDED IN THE GENETIC ETHNICS OF SOCIETY TODAY, UNDER COVERT PRETENSE, THAT THE MAJORITY OF AFRICAN AMERICANS ARE INEPT TO. BECAUSE OF THEIR BASELESS TENACITY TO DISTORT REALITY, AND CORRELATE DISCORD DUE TO A HERDING PROCESS.

EACH PASSING DAY THAT THIS POLITICAL SKIRMISH CONTINUE BETWEEN SENATORS CLINTON AND OBAMA, I AM REMINDED OF THE LATE F.B.I. DIRECTOR J. EDGAR HOOVER ASSESSMENT OF BLACKS IN THE MID FIFTIES, THAT THEIR BRAINS WAS TWENTY PERCENT SMALLER THAN WHITES. IT IS TRULY TROUBLING WHEN THERE IS HUNDREDS OF BLACKS SUPPOSEDLY PROFESSIONALS, THAT CONSIST OF ATTORNEYS, LAW PROFESSORS, DEMOCRATIC STRATEGIST, OVER THE MEDIA AIR WAYS LIKE SCHOOLS OF CATFISH ALL MOUTH AND NO BRAINS.

SUPPORTING AND DEFENDING SENATOR BARACK OBAMA, EVADING AND DISTORTING ISSURES RELATED TO

HIS AFFILIATIONS, AND IMPLYING RACIST HYPOTHETICAL GENERALITIES, THERE IS APPROXIMATELY NINETY PERCENT OF AFRICAN AMERICANS THAT SUPPORT SENATOR OBAMA PRIMARY CANDIACY NATION WIDE, AND WHEN THESE ELITE BLACKS IS QUESTIONED ABOUT THIS HERDING PHENOMENON, AND IF THIS COULD INCITE WHITES TO SUPPORT SENATOR CLINTON.

THEIR RESPONSE IS PREDICATED ON RACIST FACTIONS, BASED ON DECEIT AND STUPID DISTORTION REGARDS TO THE REALITY OF BARACK OBAMA ELECTABLE ABILITY,

FOR INSTANCE THERE ARE (NOTED) BLACK CONGRESS PEOPLE CONTENDING THAT FORMER PRESIDENT CLINTON IS RAISING ISSURES ABOUT RACE, THIS IS ABERRATIONAL LUDICROUS.

BLACKS ASSISTED HIM IN MAINTAINING THE PRESIDENCY FOR EIGHT YEARS AND MANY DEFENDED HIS REPULSIVE ACTS AS PRESIDENT, WITHOUT THE SPECULATION OF RACISM.

WHILE DURING HIS REIGN WAS LABELED THE FIRST BLACK PRESIDENT, SO THIS INSUNATION OF RACE AND THE CLINTONS, IS NOTHING MORE THAN AN ATTEMPT TO ALIENATE THEM SELVES FROM THE CLINTONS, WITH A STUPID EXCUSE TO HERD BEHIND BARACK OBAMA, WHICH IS HISTORICALLY TRADITIONAL OF BLACKS.

MANY ELITE BLACKS ARE ENGAGING IN SILLY SCHOOL YARD TACTICS, IN AN EFFORT TO INTIMIDATE AND LULL WHITES TO SLEEP WITH RACIST GUILT, IN ORDER TO SOLICIT THEIR VOTE FOR SLICK PERSONA AFRICAN AMERICAN BARACK OBAMA, THAT INSTIGATE CHANGE WHICH MOSTLY APPEAL TO HIS NINETY PRECENT BLACK CONSTITUENCT, AND POLITICAL STUPID WHITES, THAT IS AMAZED WITH HIS CHARISMA TO ANALYZE GRAMMATICALLY, AND IS NOTHING MORE THAN A BLACK DEMOCRATIC LIBERAL POLITICAL PIMP.

THAT IF ELECTED TO BECOME PRESIDENT, WOULD DEMORALIZE AND INSECURE THE VALOROUS STABILITY OF AMERICA.

THE MAJORITY OF BLACKS COULD CARE LESS WHAT HAPPEN TO THIS NATION BECAUSE MOST ARE INEPT TO

ITS HISTORICAL FORTITUDE, YOU CAN (NOT) CHERISH SOMETHINGIFYOUARENOTFAMILIARWITHTHEPRINCIPLE. THE MAJORITY OF BLACKS ARE GOING TO SUPPORT SENATOR OBAMA, EVEN IF HE WAS CAMPAIGNING WITH A BAG OF CRACK IN HIS SHIRT POCKET, SIMPLY BECAUSE HE IS BLACK, AND MOST AFRICAN AMERICANS ARE PLAGUED WITH THIS GENETIC ANCESTRAL CONTROLLABILITY THAT DICTATE HERDING, AND MOST ARE NOT AWARE OF THIS STIGMATIC ALOOF INHERITED CHARACTERISTIC IGNORANCE, THAT PROLIFERATE RACISM.

HOWEVER THE TALKING HEADS PERTAINING TO POLITICAL STRATEGIES RELATED TO DEMOCRAT PARTY, BLACK AND WHITE, IS OUT OF TUCH WITH REALITY ACCORDING TO CHRONOLOGICAL RECORSD OF SIGNIFICANT EVENTS, BASED ON DEMOCRATIC IDEOLOGY.

I AM NOT A ADVOCATE OF POLITICAL PREDIVTABILITY, BECAUSE OF THE UNCANNY UNCERTAINTY, HOWEVER I RESPECT CHRONOLOGICAL SIGNIFICANT EVENTS, BASED ON THEIR INEVITABILITY OF FORECASTING THE FUTURE, PERTAINING TO THE INDULGENCE OF PEOPLE.

IN ESSENCE THE IDEOLOGICAL SCENARIO WITHIN THE DEMOCRAT PARTY IS TO DICTATE DEPENDENCE REGARDS TO OTHERS.

THEY HAVE EFFECTIVELY USED THIS METHOD OF CONTROL ON AFRICAN AMERICANS FOR OVER SEVENTY YEARS, IT APPEAR THAT THIS FORMALITY COULD BE SEVERED, BASED ON HOW THEY RESOLVE THE CLINTON, OBAMA, POLITICALDEBACLE, THIS IS ONE OF THE MOST UNIQUE CIRCUMSTANCES TOE EVER OCCUR IN THE UNITED STATES OF AMERICA.

AND JUSTIFIABLY IT SHOULD BE THE DEMOCRAT PARTY HELD RESPONSIBLE ,BASED THEIR CONVICTIONS TO DEDUCE AND MANIPULATE BLACKS. BECAUSE THE HIDDEN AGENDA OF BIAS DISCRIMINATORY POLICY RELATED TO POLITICS HAS SPRUNG A LEAK, AND MOST LIKELY THEY ARE GOING TO TRY AND PERSECUTE THE CLINTONS, IN ORDER TO QUELL THIS DILEMMA, THAT THE DEMOCRATIC PARTY CREATED DURING THE PRESIDENTIAL ELECTION

OF EIGHTEEN SEVENTY SIX, REPUBLICAN RUTHERFORD B. HAYES WAS CHOSEN TO BE THE WINNER BY THE ELECTORIAL COMMISSION. HOWEVER THE CONTROLLED DEMOCRAT CONGRESS REFUSED TO CERTIFY HAYES, UNLESS THEY WERE GIVEN COMPLETE SOUTHERN STATE CONTROL, WHICH THEY ELIMINATED (ALL). CIVIL RIGHTS FOR BLACKS, THAT EXISTED FOR EIGHTY NINE YEARS.

IT HAS BEEN FORTY THREE YEARS SENSE THESE REPULSIVE CIVIL RESTRICTIONS IMPOSED BY SOUTHERN DEMOCRATS WERE LIFTED FOR BLACKS. HISTORICALLY THE (PARTY OF THE DEMOCRATS) HAS BEEN THE CULPRITS FOR (EVERY) VILLAINESS ATTEMPT TO PROHIBIT THE INTELLECT AND POLITICAL DISCORD OF AFRICAN AMERICANS FROM AUGMENTING IN AMERICAN SOCIETY, BEGINNING WITH THE CIVIL WAR, IN EIGHTEEN SIXTY ONE TO FREE BLACKS FROM SOUTHERN (DEMOCRAT) BONDAGE.

ALSO THE ADOPTION OF THE SOUTHERN (DEMOCRAT) RULE SEPERATE BUT EQUAL, JIM CROW RULE OF EIGHTEEN NINETY FIVE, WHICH BLACKS LOST TOTAL CIVIL EQUALITY IN THE SOUTHERN STATES.

AND THE RECENT DEBACLE OF THE LATE FIFTYS AND SIXTIES, WHERE THE (SOUTHERN DEMOCRATIC REGIME) MAIMED AND DEMORALIZED BLACKS FOR SIMPLY REFUSING TO GIVE THEIR SEAT UP FRONT ON A BUS AND MOVE TO THE BACK.

SENSE THAT TIME FORTY THREE YEARS LATER, AFRICAN AMERICANS HAVE FLURISHED POLITICALLY, WITHIN THE DEMOCRATIC PARTY, EVEN TO THE PINNACEL OF SENATOR, AND A PRIMARY RUN OFF TO REPRESENT THE PARTT AS THEIR SELECTED CANIDATE TO RUN NATIONALLY FOR PRESIDENT HOWEVER I SUSPECT THEIR LEADING CANIDATE, SENATOR BARACK OBAMA IS SAILING INTO UNCHARTED WATERS, AND (IF) HE SHOULD REACH LAND THERE IS GOING TO BE THE LARGEST ROAD BLOCK OF HIS LIFE, WITH A SIGN THAT IS GOING TO READ POLITICAL SELF DESTRUCTION DUE TO PERSONAL AFFILATION. AND IF HE SHOULD ATTEMPT TO DETOUR, THERE WILL BE ANOTHER THAT IS VERY EXPLICIT, TO DELIVER A MESSAGE

OF DEMOCRATIC POLITICAL GUIDANCE, DELIVER TO AN ENEMY BY TREACHERY.

AND IN ESSENCE THIS SIGN WAS (ENDORSED) BY NONE OTHER THAN SENATOR STEPHEN A. DOUGLAS, ONE HUNDRED AND FIRTY YEARS AGO, DURING A DEBATE IN ILLINOIS FOR THE SENATE, AND HIS OPPONENT WAS ABARHAM LINCOLN, CHRONOLOGICAL RECORDS OF (SIGNIFICANT) EVENTS DICTATE THAT OVER NINETY PRECENT OF BLACKS, AND A SEGEMENT OF POLITICAL INEPT DERANGED WHITES ARE LIVING IN A PHANTASY OF DISARRAY RELATE ED TO THE MIND, IF THEY ARE ADVOCATING FOR SENATORS OBAMA AND CLINTON TO BECOME PRESIDENT OF THE UNITED STATES OF AMERICA. THESE TWO RADICAL ELITE PINICAL DEMOCRATIC PRIMARY CANIDATES SENATORS HILLARY CLINTON AND BARACK OBAMA, ARE POLITICALLY FLAWED, BASED THE REALITY OF SELF IMPOSED AFFILIATION AND IMMATURE LIES. FOR INSTANCE HILLARY IS THE EX FORST LADY AND WIFE OF EX PRESIDENT WILLIAM JEFFERSON CLINTON, THAT LOWERED THE STANDARDS OF THE PRESIDENCY, PHILANDERING WITH A INTERN IN THE WHITE HOUSE. AND SHE HILLARY LIED ABOUT AVOIDING SNIPER FIRE IN A WAR ZONE, ALSO ADVOCATING THAT FORMER PRESIDENT LYNDON JOHNSON WAS THE FIRST PRESIDENT TO APPEAL FOR CIVIL RIGHTS RELATED TO BLACKS IN THE SOUTHERN STATES, IN NINETEEN FIFTY SEVEN REPUBLICAN PRESIDENT EISENHOWER WAS THE FIRST TO INTRODUCE LEGISLATURE TO THE CONGRESS IN EIGHTY FIVE YEARS PERTAINING TO CIVIL RIGHTS FOR BLACKS. LYNDON JOHNSON WAS A SENATOR THAT VOTED TO WATER DOWN THE BILL, AND WARNED PRESIDENT EISENHOWER THAT THE SENATE IS GOING TO FIGHT THIS CIVILRIGHTS BILL ISSURE, TEMPERS ARE FLARING ALREADY. THE REALITY OF DECEPTION RELATED TO POLITICIANS IS ASTOUNDING PARTICULARY IN THE CONTROLLING BODY OF THE CONGRESS AND SENATE, DURING THE DEFEAT OF THE WATERED DOWN VERSION OF THE CIVIL RIGHTS BILL INTRODUCED BY PRESIDENT EISENHOWER, TWELVE OF HIS REPUBLICANS DEFECTED AND VOTED WITH THE DEMOCRATS IN ORDER TO DEFEAT

THE BILL, THAT SUBJECTED BLACKS TO SUCH QUESTIONS AS HOW MANY BUBBLES ARE THERE IN A BAR OF SOAP, IN ORDER TO REGISTER.

SOME POOLING STATIONS CLOSED DOWN WHEN BLACKS CAME TO REGISTER, AND THERE WAS NO PENALITY FOR THIS CONSISTENCY IN THE SOUTHERN SOUTHERN STATES, BASED ON A COHESIVE VOTE IN THE SENATE BETWEEN DEMOCRATS AND REPUBLICANS.

I RAISE THIS VERY IMPORTANT OCCURRENCE OF THE FIFTIES TO ILLUSTRATE THAT THERE ARE DIRE CONSEQUENCES RELATED TO HERDING, BECAUSE THIS INNATE HERDING PROCESS DEMONSTRATED BY DEMOCRATS AND REPUBLICANS, DENIED AFRICAN AMERICANS ONE OF THE MOST IPORTANT RIGHTS A CITIZEN CAN HAVE IN THE UNITED STATES OF AMERICA, AND THAT IS EQUALITY AND THE INDIVIDUAL RIGHT TO CHOOSE.

UNFORTUNATELY THIS IS THE FATEFUL PORTRAYAL OF REALITY IN AMERICA PEOPLE LIVE A LIFE TIME ACCORDING TO THEIR GENETIC CONVICTIONS, RELATED TO DIFFERENT DISTINGUISHING QUALITIES, AND THERE IS ABSOLUTELY (NOTHING) OR NO ONE THAT EXIST CAN DO TO SOLIDIFY A DIVERSE SOCIETY OF THEIR INDIVIDUAL POLITICAL COMMITMENTS. BECAUSE VARIABLES TEND TO DISTORT REALITY FOR REASONS THAT IS PREDICTABLE, BUT MOST ARE NOT BASED ON THE CIRCUMSTANCES, AND POLITICS ARE THE ULTIMATE BECAUSE IT DICTATE THE GRAVIRY OF (ALL) CITIZENS THAT RESIDE IN AMERICA.

BECAUSE OUR NATION IS UNDER THE GUIDANCE OF A PRESIDENT, SENATE, CONGRESS, SUPREME COURT, THAT IS SWORN TO UPHOLD THE GUIDELINES OF THE DECLARATION OF INDEPENDENCE AND THE CONSTITUTION, WHICH GVE (PEOPLE) THE INALIENABLE RATIFIED RIGHT TO CHOOSE A POLITICAL CANIDATE OF THEIR CHOICE, BASED ON A MAJORITY RULE OF VOTES. THERE HAVE BEEN PAST PRESIDENTS ELECTED THAT HAS HAD CONTROVERSIAL ISSURES REGARDS TO THEIR CANDIDNESS, HOWEVER ALL BEING (MEN) FROM THE AUTHENTICITY OF CAUCASIAN SOCIETY, WHICH IS A PRACTICE OF INEVITABILITY IN AMERICA.

AND (NONE) THAT I HAVE WITNESS OR READ ABOUT WERE EVER DISLOYAL TO THE DIPLOMATIC MORALITY OF THIS NATION, OR HAD TO DEFEND THEIR INTEGRITY REGARDS TO PATRIOTISM.

UNFORTUNATELY THAT DUBIOUS DISTINCTION HAS RISEN IN THE LIKES OF A BLACK CHARISMATIC ELEGANT SPEAKING, DISTORTING, DECITFUL, ARISTOCRAT, LYING SENATOR FROM ILLINOIS NAME BARACK OBAMA, TRYING TO CON THE AMERICAN PEOPLE INTO CHOOSING HIM FOR THEIR PRESIDENT. THERE ARE TWO STABILIZING FACTORS EMBEDDED IN LIFE, AND THAT IS GENETIC CONTROLLABILITY RELATED TO REALITY, MEANING YOU CAN NOT ESCAPE FROM BEING WHO YOU ARE, AND REALITY IS INEVITABLE. THERE IS A DEVISIVE POLITICAL CONFLICT WITH IN THE DEMOCRAT PARTY, TO SELECT A VIABLE CANDIDATE BETWEEN SENATORS BARACK OBAMA A BLACK MAN, AND HILLARY CLINTON A WHITE WOMAN, TO DETERMINE A REPRESENTIVE FOR THE DEMOCRAT PARTY IN THE GENERAL ELECTION. THERE IS POLITICAL DECEPTION IN EACH PARTY, DEMOCRAT AND REPUBLICAN PERTAINING TO REALITY, HOWEVER THE DEMOCRATS HAVE INDULGED IN POLITICAL DECEPTION OF AFRICAN AMERICANS FOR OVER SEVENTY YEARS. IN ORDER TO MAINTAIN THEIR HERDING BLOC VOTING.

THE CONSISTENCY OF THIS ELICIT POLITICAL COVERT DECEIT, HAVE LITERALLY BEWILDERED AND CAUSED PANDEMONIUM, REGARDS TO THEIR PRIMARY ELECTION OF TWO THOUSAND EIGHT.

FOR THE FIRST TIME IN OUR NATION HISTORY, PERTAINING TO THE DEMOCRAT PARTY, IT IS PLAGUED WITH A PARTY FORMULATED DISASTER, BY IMPLEMENTING A POLITICAL SAFETY NET, IN ORDER TO SCRUTINIZE INCOMPETENT CANIDATES, WITH A UNCOMMITTED HERD OF JUDGMENTAL SUPER DELIGATES.

IN AN EFFORT TO DETERMINE CANIDATES THAT IS APPROPIATE TO THEIR CHOICE OF IDEOLOGY, MEANING BLACKS NEED NOT DEVOTE THEIR ATTENTION UNLESS HE OR SHE CAN DETERMINE HOW MANY BUBBLES ARE IN A BAR OF (SOAP) AND IF YOU SHOULD THE SUPER DELIGATES

WILL REQUEST A RECOUNT AND DETERMINE YOUR FATE REGARDS TO ANNULMENT. AS THEY DID IN NINETEEN FIRTY SEVEN WHEN THEY DESTROYED THE CIVIL AND VOTING RIGHTS BILL FOR AFRICAN AMERICANS, INTRODUCED BY PRESIDENT DWIGHT D. EISENHOWER.

HOWEVER UNFORTUNATE FOR THE DEMOCRAT PARTY, ALONG CAME A HABITUAL LYING CYNICAL MULATTO FROM ILLINOIS, SENATOR BARACK OBAMA, AND FORMULATED HIS OWN DEFENSE AGAINST THIS PREHISTORIC DEMOCRATIC POLITICAL STRATEGY, THAT WAS FOUNDED IN THE EARLY EIGHTIES TO SECLUDE BLACKS POLITICAL ASPIRATION TO A MINIMUM, BASED ON JESSIE JACKSON RUN FOR PRESIDENT, AND HAD SHOWN SOME SUCCESS, ACCORDING TO FORMER PRESIDENT BILL CLINTON.

UNFORTUNATELY FOR THE DEMOCRAT PARTY, SENATOR BARACK OBAMA IS (NO) COMPARISON TO JESSIE JACKSON, HE IS A DISTINGUISH HYBRID THAT RELY ON HIS GENETIC TEACHINGS FROM WHITE ANCESTRY. WITH A COMBINE OBVIOUSNESS FROM HIS FATHER, THAT ENABLE HIM TO INFILTRATE ELITE BLACK SOCIETY WITH A (WHITE) COVERT METHODOLOGY THAT THEY ARE INEPT AND UNACCUSTOMED TO, INSTIGATED BY ANOTHER BLACK, SO AS A STRATEGIC PLOY HE HAS UTILIZED HIS TRAITS TO MESMERIZE THE MAJORITY OF POLITICALLY IGNORANT BLACKS AND A LARGE SEGEMENT SMALL BRAIN INCOMPETENT WHITES.

THERE ARE TWO SIGNIFICANT MESSAGES CALCULATED BY SENATOR OBAMA ONE IS FOR BLACKS AND THE OTHER FOR WHITES, WHEN HE REFERE TO (CHANGE) BASED ON THE HERDING INSTINCTS OF BLACKS HE (KNOW) THEY ARE GOING TO PRECEIVE THAT TO BE AN ESTABLISHED FACT,THAT HE IS ONE OF (US) AND WE ARE GOING TO SUPPORT HIM BECAUSE HE IS BLACK. AND THE OTHER ELICITATION IS FOR WHITES, WHEN HE STIPULATE WE CAN (ALL) COME (TOGATHER) THAT STATEMENT IS INTENDED GRAMMATICALLY TO SEDUCE (WHITES) INTO THINKING THAT THE DESTITUTION OF (SOME) BLACKS IS THEIR (FAULT) AND COMING TOGATHER IS A FORM OF

ATONEMENT. HOWEVER THIS IS HIS AGENDA OF BRINGING THE COUNTRY TOGATHER, BASED ON RACE RELATION.

THIS KIND OF SLICK ANALYTICAL GRAMMATICAL GIBBERISH IS A INSULT TO THE INTEGRITY OF (ALL) INTELLECT SOCIETY IN AMERICA. WHEN HE BARACK OBAMA SAT AS A MEMBER AND STILL IS FOR APPROXIMATELY TWENTY (YEARS) IN A CONGREGATION THAT EMPHATICALLY TEACHES RADICAL DIVISIVE BLACK (NAT TURNER) IMPERIALISM.

HOWEVER THERE IS A (REALITY) THAT EXIST WITHIN THE FUNDAMENTAL CHRONOLOGICAL EVENTS IN THE UNITED STATES OF AMERICA. AND THAT IS THE MAJORITY OF AFRICAN AMERICANS ARE (INEPT) TO THE TRADITIONS OF EACH POLITICAL PARTY DEMOCRATIC AND REPUBLICAN HISTORICALLY, MOST BLACKS HAVE AND ARE BASING THEIR MOTIVES ON DISTORTED ASSUMPTIONS.

WHILE WHITES ARE STRATEGICALLY DIPLOMATICALLY GOING ABOUT THEIR BUISNESS AND INDORSING BLACK POLITICAL STUPIDITY, AND PRIVATELY RIDICULING BLACK POLITICAL INCOMPETENCY.

THERE IS A COMMON DOMINATOR EXECUTED BY MOST WHITES, RELATED TO THE MAJORITY OF BLACKS, AND THAT IS FOR HUNDREDS OF YEARS BLACKS HAVE NEGLECTED TO UNDERSTAND OR JUST PLAIN INEPT TO (WHITE) GENETIC TRAITS, BECAUSE THE MAJORITY OF BLACKS TEND TO ORIENT TO A PROCESS OF SUPERFICIAL AFRICAN HERDING, BEHIND SELF APPOINTED BLACK LEADERS THAT TEACH A SEDUCTION OF OUR DAY WILL COME. AND ARE TO STUPID TO REALIZE THAT IT HAS BEEN HERE ALL ALONG, IN ORDER FOR ONE OR A GROUP TO INCORPORATE INTO A ORGANIZATION OR SOCIETY THERE ARE STIPULATING FACTORS.

THAT (MUST) BE ADHERED TO, COMMON SENSE IS A GOD GIVEN ABILITY THAT IS GENERATED THROUGH THE BRAIN, TO BE USED IN ACCORDANCE WITH INDIVIDUAL CHOICE, MEANING THAT HERDING IS A INDIVIDUAL CHOICE THAT HAS AND WILL CONTINUE TO BE ONE OF THE MOST DEVASTATING, DETRIMENTAL, SELF IMPOSED SABOTAGING

FACTORS IN THE HISTORY OF AFRICAN AMERICAN SOCIETY IN AMERICA.

BECAUSEITILLUSTRATEATECHNICALFORMOFSEPARATE BUT EQUAL IN A DIVERSE SOCIETY OF APPROXIMATELY THREE HUNDRED MILLION PEOPLE, WITH BLACKS BEING ONLY APPROXIMATELY TWELVE PERCENT. THE REALITY OF THIS PHENOMENON IS BASED ON PREFERENTIAL CONSIDERATION, REGARDLESS TO THEIR ADAPTABILITY AND INTELLECT TO MORALITY SO JUST ADHERE TO THIS KIND OF CONGO IDEOLOGY OF LIVING OFF THE LAND, MEANING GOVERNMENT RELIEF DEPENDENCY, ILLITERACY, AND HAVING BABIES OUT OF WEDLOCK AT THIRTEEN,ALSO BLACK ON BLACK CRIME EXTERMINATING EACH OTHER NATION WIDE AT AN ALARMING RATE. HOWEVER IF THIS IS A PHILOSOPHY YOU DO (NOT) AGREE WITH AND YOU ARE BLACK, YOU ARE DENOUNCED AS TRYING TO BE WHITE, AND NOT FAMILIAR WITH BLACK CULTURE.

AND IF YOU ARE WHITE YOUR LABEL IS BEING A RACIST, TRYING TO IMPEDE EQUALITY AND CIVIL RIGHTS FOR BLACKS.

THIS IS A GENETIC TRAIT THAT HAS BEEN EMBEDDED IN AFRICAN AMERICAN IDEOLOGY FOR APPROXIMATELY FOUR HUNDRED YEARS.

HERDING ALIENATED SELFISH STUPIDITY, THAT HAS MALICIOUSLY CAST A SEGMENT OF BLACKS INTO THE DUNGEONS OF HELL BY THEIR OWN ADMISSION RELATED TO INEPTNESS.

SO THE ESSENCES OF THIS SLICK WIT PORTRAYED BY SENATOR BARACK OBAMA REFERRING TO UNITY RELATED TO BALCK AND WHITE, IS NOTHING MORE THAN A FANTASIZING MIRAGE TO DISTORT REALITY.

BECAUSE THERE IS A LARGE SEGEMENT OF BLACK AND WHITES IN AMERICA THAT IS OBLIVIOUS TO MORALITY AND SEEK TO PERSECUTE OTHERS FOR THEIR OWN INSIDIOUS IDEOLOGY.

THESE ARE TRAITS THAT IS EMBEDDED IN THE FUNDAMENTALS OF A DIVERSE SOCIETY, THAT IS PREDICATED TO A GENETIC CULTURAL DOCTRINE BASED ON INSTINCTS.

THAT IS EQUIVALENT TO A SELF IMPOSED MALIGNANCY, RELEGATED TO MISCONCEPTION ,STIGMATIZED BY STUPIDITY.

AND IT IS A GLOBAL DYSFUNCTION WITH A SEGEMENT OF (ALL) PEOPLE, THERE ARE MULTIPLE PHASES OF ETHNICS PERTAINING TO PEOPLE, AND HOW THEY COMPREHEND GENERALIZATION IN RESOLVING PROBLEMS. UNFORTUNATELY THE MAJORITY OF AFRICAN AMERICANS ARE INDOCTRINATED AT A VERY EARLY AGE, EITHER BY PARENTS, A SEGEMENT OF MINISTERS, AND MOST OF ALL SELF APPOINTED BLACK LEADERS, THAT AMERICA IS UN-JUST TO BLACKS.

AFRICAN AMERICAN (HERDING) IN A DIVERSE SOCIETY IS PARAMOUNT,AND HAS BEEN A DISASTROUS OBSTACLE BASED ON CHRONOLOGICAL RECORDS OF EVENTS, AND IS AS PREVALENT IN BLACK SOCIETY TODAY AS EVER. THE REVELATION TO THIS INSANE GENETIC HERITAGE WAS DISPLAYED ON MSNBC CHRIS MATTHEW HARD BALL, ON MAY 14, 2008.

A (YOUNG) AFRICAN AMERICAN WOMAN WAS HIS GUEST, MICHELLE .BERNARD, AND WHEN QUESTIONED ABOUT THE ENDORSEMENT OF JOHN EDWARDS, FOR FOR BARACK OBAMA, AND THE EFFECTS IT WOULD HAVE REGARDS TO MALE CONSTITUENCY ESPECIALLY WHITES, HER COMMENTS WERE (NOW) THAT JOHN EDWARDS HAVE ENDORSED OBAMA, THE OTHER WHITES (WILL) FOLLOW. AND THIS IS TYPICAL OF THE MAJORITY OF AFRICAN AMERICANS GENETIC IDEOLOGICAL PRELUDE OF IGNORANCE.

THE (ONLY) TIME WHITES WILL HERD IS THROUGH A GENERAL CONSENSUS OF INDIVIDUAL INDEPENDENT DIPLOMACY, RELATED TO INSTRUMENTAL OR R DESTRUCTIVE ISSURES.

FOR INSTANCE THE DEMOCRATIC ENLISTMENT OF HERDING KU-KLUX-KLAN IN THE SOUTHERN STATES, DENYING BLACKS THEIR EQUAL AND CIVIL RIGHTS TO BECOME INTELLECTUALLY MOTIVATED.

AND THE REPUBLICANS HERDED TO RESTORE IT IN NINETEEN SIXTY FOUR AND FIVE.

THE ENIGMA OF BLACKS HERDING BEHIND IDIOTS THAT IS INEPT TO THE FUNDAMENTAL ECONOMICS PERTAINING TO VALUES IN A DIVERSE SOCIETY, IS WHOLE SALE VINDICTIVE SABOTAGE.

AND AFTER ALMOST FOUR HUNDRED YEARS THEY (STILL) HAVE NOT FIGURED IT OUT. AND THIS WAS ONE OF THE MAIN REASONS THAT THE LATE F.B.I. DIRECTOR J. EDGAR HOOVER ACCUSED BLACKS OF HAVING BRAINS TWENTY PERCENT SMALLER THAN WHITES.

BECAUSE MOST DO (NOT) HAVE THE ABILITY TO CHOOSE ON A INDIVIDUAL BASIS AS TO WHAT IS A BEST INTEREST POLITICALLY, ALONG WITH MANY OTHER PERSONAL RECREANTS.

SENATOR BARACK OBAMA ENTERED THE DEMOCRATIC PARTY PRIMARY, WITH A DIALECT OF INTELLECT GRAMMAR, WITH CHARISMATIC BODY DEXTERITY TO ACCOMMODATE, AND LURED OVER NINETY PERCENT OF BLACKS NATION WIDE HERDING TO SUPPORT HIM POLITICALLY WITHIN THE DEMOCRAT PARTY, UNFORTUNATELY FOR SENATOR BARACK OBAMA, UNKNOWINGLY TO HIM THERE IS ANOTHER DIPLOMATIC HERD OF (WHITES) COVERTLY DEVELOPING WITHIN THE DEMOCRAT PARTY PRIMARY RANKS.

THERE ARE (MANY) BUT JUST TO NAME A FEW, BEGINNING WITH SENATORS DICK DERWIN, ROBERT BYRD, JOHN KERRY, TED KENNEDY, JOSEPH BIDEN, CHRIS DODD, JOHN EDWARDS, TOM DASCHEL, AND BILL BRADLEY. IN RETROSPECT I HAVE (NOT) READ, HEARD,OR SEEN, THIS MANY DIPLOMATIC DEMOCRATIC ELITE (WHITES) HERDING BEHIND A BLACK SENSE THE KU-KLUX-KLAN ERA.

AND THAT ILLUSTRATED PHYSICAL AGGRESSION TO DESTROY, THERE IS A UNIQUE POLITICAL EROSION WITHIN THE DEMOCRATIC PARTY. THAT ILLUSTRATE ANARCHY, BASED ON TOTAL FRUSTRATION AND CHAOS DUE HISTORICAL DISTORTED CYNICISM, PERTAINING TO AFRICAN AMERICANS. THE DEMOCRAT PARTY HAVE SEDUCED BLACKS POLITICALLY FOR OVER SEVENTY YEARS, DUE TO THEIR GENETIC HERDING AMERICAN INSTINCTS, AND THIS IS WHAT THE ENTIRE POLITICAL DEBACLE IS

(ALL) ABOUT. THEIITERRIBLE CONVOLUTED DESPICABLE (FALSE) ACCUSATION, WAGED AGAINST MRS. GERALDINE FERRARO, AS BEING A RACIST FOR DESCRIBING (REALITY) REGARDS TO SENATOR BARACK OBAMA.

ONE WOULD HAVE TO BE A SMALL DYSFUNCTIONAL BRAIN IDIOT (NOT) TO REALIZE THAT BARACK OBAMA,IS NOTHING MORE THAN A SOPHISTICATED, RHETORICAL, SPEAKING AFRICAN AMERICAN, THAT HAS REACHED ELITE POLITICAL PINNACLE STATUS SOLELY BECAUSE HE IS (BLACK). THIS RATHER UNUSUAL RENDITION OF ANARCHY IS DUE TO POLITICAL INEPT BLACKS, HERDING WITH A ACCLIMATED VISION TO ELECT ANOTHER BLACK TO BECOME PRESIDENT.

UNFORTUNATELY THE REALITY OF CONSTENCY, BASED ON POLITICAL IRREGULARITY PERTAINING TO MOST AFRICAN AMERICANS, IS ASTOUNDING WIITH INEPTITUDE.

IN ESSENCE THE MAJORITY OF BLACKS WILL (NEVER) BECOME ACCLIMATED TO THE CULTURAL MORALITY OF THE UNITED STATES OF AMERICA, SIMPLY BECAUSE OF STIGMATIC TRAITS THAT AUGMENT REVERENCE, BASED ON A CNGO GENETIC DOCTRINE THAT DICTATE INCOMPETENCY.

AND THAT TREND IS INEVITABLE, BASED ON OBLIGATORY VALIDATED CHRONOLOGICAL RECORDS OF SIGNIFICANT EVENTS, RELATED TO THE GENERAL CONSENSUS OF BLACKS.

HOWEVER AMERICA IS GROSSLY MISUNDERSTOOD, BY A SEGEMENT OF WHITES AND A VAST MAJORITY OF BLACKS, RELATED TO RACE RELATION. UNFORTUNATELY THERE IS A DIVISIVE ORIENTATION THAT IS INEVITABLE EMBEDDED IN HAUGHTY (COMPETENCY). BASED ON MERIT.

WHICH IS A RICH TRADITION OF WHITES, FORTUNATELY MANY BLACKS HAVE ADAPTED TO THOSE PRINCIPLES, AND ARE EQUIVALENT TO THE SAME STATUS OF SUCCESS.

BUT THE AGGRAVATING MISCONCEIVED PRECEPTION, IS WHEN BLACKS REACH THE PINNACLE OF SUCCESS, MANY CHOOSE TO ASSUME THAT THEIR SUCCESS EQUATE TO A

HERDING ADVISORY RELATED TO DOMINACE TO SPEAK FOR OTHER MISFIT BLACKS.

FOR INSTANCE ON JUNE 01, 2008. SENATOR BARACK OBAMA GAVE A RALLY SPEECH IN SOUTH DAKOTA, AND REFERRED TO BRINGING (ALL) THE PEOPLE TOGATHER REGARDS TO RACE.

ON JUNE 03, 2008. REP. JAMES CLYBURN, ENDORSED SENATOR OBAMA ON MSNBC AND ECHOED THAT SAME SENTIMENT, BYINSTIGATING THAT OBAMA (WILL) BRING THE COUNTRY TO A (NEW) HEIGHT, AND ELABORATED ON THE CIVIL RIGHTS MOVEMENT OF THE SIXTIES.

SOME ONE NEED TO ADVISE THESE TWO POLITICAL INEPT ELITES THAT THIS IS AMERICA, (NOT) A CONGO TRIBE IN AFRICA, THAT IS LED BY A CHIEF, OR KING.

APPARENTLY THESE TWO GENTLEMEN BARACK OBAMA, AND REP. CLYBOURN ARE SO STUPEFIED WITH CONGO ETHNICS THEY HAVE FORGOTTEN THEIR ELITE PROMINENCE IN AMERICA.

SENATOR BARACK OBAMA, IS SUSPECTED TO BE THE FIRST BLACK TO BE CHOSEN WITHIN THE DEMOCRAT PARTY, AS THEIR REPRESENTATIVE TO BECOME PRESIDENT, OF THE UNITED STATES OF AMERICA.

REPRESENTATIVEJAMESCLYBURN,ISAELECTEDCORNER STONEINTHECONGRESS,SOITISVERYUNFORTUNATETHAT THEIR DEMAGOGIC, DISTORTING RELENTLESS RHETORIC, IS RELATED TO THE PERSUIT OF ELITE BLACK POWER SUPERIORITY. BECAUSE THEY EPITOMIZE BLACK SUCCESS. OUR COUNTRY AMERICA WAS FOUNDED ON INTELLECT AND MORALITY, THAT IS FORMULATED AND ENDORSED WITH-IN THE DECLARATION OF INDEPENDENCE AND THE CONSTITUTION, BASED ON INDIVIDUAL THINKING THROUGH A DIALOGUE OF DIPLOMACY, IN AN EFFORT TO ATTAIN A DIVERSIFIED SOLUTION FROM INDIVIDUAL OPINIONS TO RESOLVE PROBLEMS.

(NOT) FROM A AFRICAN CONGO IDEOLOGY OF HERDING BEHIND ONE INDIVIDUAL THAT HAVE A SOLUTION TO RESOLVE (ALL) AND EVERY ONE PROBLEMS I HAVE TRAVELED EXTENSIVELY, AND STUDIED RACE RELATION IN AMERICA FOR OVER SIXTY YEARS, PERTAINING TO ETHNICS.

AND THE MOST EXCLUSIVE DOMINATING FACTOR HAVE TO DO WITH BLACK AND WHITE, SIMPLY BECAUSE OF THE NEGATIVE ORIENTATION RELATED TO MOST BLACKS, PERTAINING TO BLACK SUPERIORITY WITH DISDAIN FOR OTHERS, AND THAT IS ANY ONE FAIL TO AGREE WITH THEIR EMBLEMATIC DISTINCTION OF GENETIC HERDING.

AND MOST ARE TOTALLY UNAWARE OF THIS DREADFUL ANCESTRAL DIVISIVE SEGREGATIVE TRAIT, THAT HAVE BEEN A DISASTER FOR BLACKS HISTORICALLY. RELATED TO IGNORANCE POVERTY AND DESTITUTION.

JUNE 04, 2008. THE MORNING AFTER SENATOR BARACK OBAMA, WAS DEEMED TO BE THE NOMINEE WITHIN THE DEMOCRAT PRIMARY, TO REPRESENT THE PARTY IN THE GENERAL ELECTION FOR PRESIDENT.

IT WAS TRULY A MOMENTOUS OCCASION, A HISTORICAL EVENT RELATED TO AFRICAN AMERICAN POLITICAL PROGRESS.

AND HOPEFULLY THIS REMARKABLE EVENT WILL DISPEL THE NOTION THAT THERE IS A CONSPIRED EFFORT BY WHITE AMERICA TO SABOTAGE THE PROGRESS OF BLACKS.

HOWEVER IF SENATOR OBAMA, IS (NOT) ELECTED TO BECOME PRESIDENT, THE SELF APPOINTED BLACK RADICALS, ALONG WITH THEIR HERD IS GOING TO PORTRAY THE COUNTRY AS BEING UNJUST TO BLACKS, AND IS ATTEMPTING TO DEPRIVE THEM OF EQUALITY.

TRUST ME THIS IS A (NEVER) ENDING IDIOSYNCRASY PERPETRATED BY HERDING BLACKS, RELATED TO IGNORANCE,SEEKING. NOTORIETY RELATED TO SUPERIORITY.

WHEN I REFER TO HERDING HAS AND IS DETRIMENTAL TO BLACKS, THIS IS (NOT) MEANT TO BE A DEROGATORY REMARK, BUT A CAREFULLY SCRUTINIZED HISTORICAL (REALIY).

WHICH IS REVEALED THROUGH OUT THE BOOK MANY TIMES, THE ENTIRE NEWS MEDIA OF (ALL) BRANCHES ARE IN A DISORDERLY MASS, TRYING TO DETERMINE THE POLITICAL SKILLS OF SENATOR HILLARY CLINTON. (I AM NOT) IT IS FAIRLY SIMPLE BASED ON (REALITY)

THE CLINTONS ARE CONSIDERED TO BE POLITICAL MONARCHS, OF MODERN DAY POLITICS PARELLEL TO THE ROOSEVELTS.

APPROXIMATELY THIRTY FIVE YEARS OF PUBLIC SERVICE, LOOSING (ONLY) ONE POLITICAL CHALLENGE DURING THAT TIME, THIS DUO WAS GOVERNOR OF ARKANSAS, EIGHT YEARS AS PRESIDENT OF AMERICA, AFTER THAT STINT SHE MOVED TO STATE OF NEW YORK, AND WAS ELECTED SENATOR, THIS IS QUITE A POLITICAL LEGACY.

SHE SENATOR CLINTON, CHOOSE TO RUN FOR PRESIDENT IN TWO THOUSAND EIGHT, PRACTICALLY IGNORING WHITE HOUSE ANTICS DISPLAYED BY PRESIDENT CLINTON, BUT THE GENERAL POBLIC HAVE A LONG MEMORY, THERE ARE A SEGMENT OF WHITES THAT WOULD LIKE NOTHING BETTER THAN PUNISH THE CLINTONS.

SO IN ORDER TO ACCOMPLISH THIS VINDICTIVE FATE, MANY OF THE CLINTONS LOYALIST DESERTED AND HERDED BEHIND HER OPPONENT SENATOR BARACK OBAMA, BUT THE MOST (DAMING) POLITICAL BLUNDER COMMITTED BY SENATOR CLINTON WAS TAKING HERDING BLACKS FOR (GRANTED);

AS THE DEMOCRAT (PARTY) HAS FOR OVER SEVENTY YEARS, UNFORTUNATELY THEY NEGLECTED TO REALIZE THAT SENATOR OBAMA IS BLACK, AND IS EMBEDDED WITHIN THE RANKS OF THE DEMOCRAT PARTY.

SO AS A RESULT IT IS INEVITABLE, GEOGRAPHICALLY THE GENETIC INSTINCTS OF OTHER BLACKS, IS DICTATED THROUGH HERITAGE TO HERD BEHIND OBAMA.

SO BASED ON THE ASPECTS OF POLITICALLY HERDING BLACKS, AND A SEGEMENT OF DISGRUNTLE HERDING (WHITES) THE CLINTON POLITICAL MONARCH OF SUPERIORITY IS SABOTAGED, BY A SLICK TALKING UNKNOWN BLACK MAN, WITH RENOWN INSIDIOUS BIAS CONTEMPTIBLE AVERSIONS. THAT HAS COMPLETELY OBLITERATED THEIR LEGACY OF FORTY YEARS. PERTAINING TO THE POLITICAL RANGE OF ACTION OR (INFLUENCE);

THIS IS TRULY A TRAUMATIC DEBACLE FOR THE CLINTONS, AND WITHOUT QUESTION THEY ARE FRUSTRATED AND MOST LIKELY WILL RESULT TO POLITICAL VENGEANCE.

RELATED TO COVERT DECEPTIONS, I LISTENED TO HER CONCESSION SPEECH ON JUNE 07, 2008. AND I AM FULLY AWARE THAT1 AMERICAN ENGLISH IS THE GREATEST LANGUAGE ON THE UNIVERSE, BECAUSE CONE CAN ADDRESS AN AUDIENCE, BASED ON CERTAIN CIRCUMSTANCES, AND MANY WILL DEPART TRYING TO DETERMINE THE TRUE CONCEPT OF REALITY.

THE GENERAL CONSENSUS OF THE CONSESSION SPEECH GIVEN BY SENATOR HILLARY CLINTON, WAS DELIBERATE, COMPLIMENTARY, CONGENIAL, AMBIGUOUS WITH INGENUITY.

RELATED TO A CONSPIRACY, BASED ON QUOTED SCENARIOS, SUCH AS HER UTMOST (PLEDGE) IS TO EIGHTEEN MILLION PEOPLE FROM (ALL) WALKS OF LIFE. THAT CONSIST OF ALL THOSE WOMEN IN THEIR EIGHTYS AND NINETYS, AND WOULD CONTINUE TO STAND STRONG, FORTY YEARS OF POLITILAL SERVICE, A FIGHT THAT SHE (WILL) CONTINUE, THROUGH BARRIERS AND BIASES. AND THAT SHE WOULD ENDORSE AND STAND BY SENATOR OBAMA. AND THAT HER CAMPAGIN WAS (SUSPENDED); SHE GAVE HER SPEECH TO A CROWD OF NINETY NINE PRECENT WHITES AND SOME HISPANICS, BLACKS WERE ALMOST NONE EXISTENCE. AND (NEVER) UTTERED A WORD ABOUT SENATOR JOHN MCCAIN.

THIS IS A STRONG MESSAGE TO SENATOR BARACK OBAMA, THAT HE IS IN THE MIDDLE OF THE ROAD BLINDED BY POLITICAL HEAD LIGHTS, AND SHE IS THE DRIVER HEADED IN HIS DIRECTION.

REALITY IS INEVITABLE, HOWEVER THERE ARE MANY WILL TRY AND DISTORT THE SANCTIONS OF LIGITMACY. I FIND IT RATHER INSIDIOUS AND REPUGNANT, THAT THE POLITICAL STRATEGIST, NEWS ANCORS, AND COMMENTATORS, ALSO RADIO ANALYST, ARE STILL TRYING TO DETERMINE WHAT HAPPEN TO SENATOR HILLARY CLINTON PRIMARY CAMPAGIN, AGAINST SENATOR BARACK OBAMA, EITHER THEY ARE INEPT TO (REALITY) OR EVADING THE ISSURE, WITH ALL KINDS OF STUPID ASSESSMENTS, AND THE MOST IGNORANT ONE WAS THAT THE MAJORITY OF IOWANS ARE WHITE, AND OBAMA WON BASED ON THEIR

DETERMINING FACTOR, VALIDATING PROOF THAT HE WAS A VIABLE CANIDATE AMONG WHITES.

THESE SMALL DYSFUNCTIONAL BRAIN IDIOTS, ARE COMPLETELY IGNORING FACTS, THAT SENATOR OBAMA IS A (BLACK) MAN WITHIN THE DEMOCRAT PARTY,AND I WOULD LIKE TO CLARIFY ONE THING WHILE I AM ON THE SUJECT, AND THAT IS (MULATTO) THAT IS DESCRIBED BY WEBSTER, IS A FIRST GENERATION OFF SPRING, BETWEEN A BLACK AND WHITE PERSON. AND THE UNITED STATES OF AMERICA CHRONOLOGICAL RECORDS DICTATE HE OR SHE SHALL BE LISTED AS AFRICAN AMERICAN BASED ON SKIN TEXTURE. SO SENATOR BARACK OBAMA, BEING BLACK, OTHER HERDING BLACKS CHOOSE TO ALIENATE THEM SELVES FROM THE CLINTONS.

BY A MARGIN OF OVER NINETY PERCRNT, IN MOST GEOGRAPHIC POPULATED AREAS OF BLACKS IN THE UNITED STATES OF AMERICA.

SO ALONG WITH WHITE HOUSE BAGGAGE OF ANATHEMAS, AND HERDING BLACKS BEHIND OBAMA, IS THE DOMINATING FACTOR FOR SENATOR HILLARY CLINTON DEMOCRATIC PRIMARY (LOST);

AND YOU CAN BET THE RANCH THE CLINTONS ARE AWARE OF THIS BEFALLING POLITICAL DEBACLE, AND MOST LIKELY WILL (NEVER) RELENT TO ADAPTATION. THERE ARE MILLIONS OF POLITICAL INEPT PEOPLE BLACK AND WHITE, THAT ARE ASSUMING AND TERRIBLY DISCONNECTED FROM REALITY. BECAUSE POLITICAL SABOTAGE OF A FORTY YEAR LEGEACY, IS REASON FOR DISMAY WITH MALICE.

AND THE PRESENTATION OF SENATOR HILLARY CLINTON CONCESSION SPEECH ILLUSTRATED VENGEANCE. BASED ON CERTAIN VERBIAGE, WHEN SHE REFERENCED EIGHTEEN MILLION CRACKS IN THE IN THE SEALING. (BARRIERS AND BIASES) ALONG WITH A SOBBING MOTHER, WITHOUT QUESTION SENATOR BARACK OBAMA IS IN A POLITICAL (BOX)

AND THERE IS ABSOLUTELY (NOTHING) HIS PREDOMINATLY CAUCASIAN ADVISORY STAFF, AND OVER NINETY PERCENT OF AFRICAN AMERICAN SUPPORT CAN DO BUT ASSUME, SURMISE AND DISTORT.

BECAUSE (REALITY) WILL PREVAIL, BIAS IS A FUNDAMENTAL WORD THAT IS EMBEDDED IN COMMUNITY LIFE GLOBALLY.

UNFORTUNATELY IT IS MORE PREVALENT IN THE UNITED STATES OF AMERICA, BECAUSE OF THE CULTURAL DIVERSITY, HOWEVER BIAS HAS SEVERAL DIFFERENT MEANINGS, BUT MOST COMMONLY USED TO ESTABLISH ADVANTAGE, PERTAINING TO SINGLE OR PLURAL ISSURES. THE SOUTHERN DEMOCRATS USED A SENARIO OF BIAS TO INTRODUCE BLACKS TO SERVITUDE AGAINST THEIR WILL, BECAUSE WHITES ARE THE MAJORITY.

AND REGARDLESS TO THE CIRCUMSTANCES OUR NATION IS CONTROLLED BY A LEGALITY OF MAJORITY RULE.

AND THE CONSTITUTION OFFER EVERY AMERICAN CITIZEN THE RIGHT TO CHOOSE, BASED ON THEIR COMPREHENSIBLE MORALITY, THAT HAS BEEN THE STANDARD OF AMERICA CULTURE SENSE DISCOVERY.

HOWEVER THERE ARE INEVITABLE CONSEQUENCES RELATED TO CHOICE, BASED ON MAJORITY AND MINORITY, BECAUSE OUR GOVERNMENT IS FORMULATED ON A PRINCIPLE OF MAJORITY RULE.

THERE ARE TWO MAJOR POLITICAL PARTIES IN THE UNITED STATES OF AMERICA, DEMOCRATIC AND REPUBLICAN, AFRICAN AMERICANS HAVE CHOSEN FOR OVER SEVENTY YEARS TO SUPPORT THE DEMOCRAT PARTYI WHICH IS THEIR CHOICE. HOWEVER THE SOUTHERN DEMOCRATS INTRODUCED THEM TO SLAVERY, FOUNDED THE KU-KLUX-KLAN, DENIED THEM CIVIL RIGHTS, ACTHEM OF BEING INCOMPETENT, AND IF THEY WERE EDUCATED THEY WERE ACCUSED OF TRYING TO RISE ABOVE

UNFORTUNATELY THE MAJORITY OF AFRICAN AMERICANS (CHOOSE) TO REMAIN IN POLITICAL SERVITUDE FOR THE DEMOCRATIC PARTY. FINALLY A CHARISMATIC, SOPHISTICATED, EDUCATED, BLACK MAN SENATOR BARACK OBAMA , ROSE TO THE PINNACLE OF POLITICAL SUCCESS, DEDICATED TO ANOTHER BLACK, ALLEN KEYES.

AND ONCE SENATOR OBAMA WAS ELECTED TO THE SENATE, THE ELITE DEMOCRATS SCRUTINIZED HIS ELITE

DEMEANOR, THE PLAN BEGAN INSTANTANEOUSLY TO ABORT HIM WITH DIGNITY.

SO HIS COUNTERPART DICK DERWIN, AND OTHERS ENCOURAGED HIM TO RUN FOR THE PRESIDENCY, BY WAY OF THEIR PRIMARY.

AND THERE WAS ONE THING THEY NEGLECTED TO REALIZE, AND SO DID I, AND THAT WAS HERDING OTHER BLACKS, BEHIND ANOTHER ELITE BLACK BASED ON GENETIC CONTROLLABILITY.

SO WITH HIS CHARISMA AND THE MAJORITY OF HERDING BLACKS, ALONG WITH SOME WHITES, HE STOLE THE THUNDER FROM THE POLITICAL MONARCHS, SENATOR HILLARY AND BILL CLINTON.

AND SET THE DEMOCRATIC PARTY BACK ON ITS HEELS, WITHIN THE PARTY (EVER) RELATED TO A BLACK.

BECAUSE HISTORICALLY THE SOUTHERN DEMOCRATS, HAVE ALWAYS LYNCHED THEM SELVES OUT OF SITUATIONS OF THIS MAGNITUDE.

HOWEVER IN TODAYS WORLD THEY WERE LEFT WITH (ONLY) TWO CHOICES EITHER HERD AROUND SENATOR OBAMA, AND CHOOSE HIM FOR THEIR PRESIDENTAL CANIDATE, OR THROW THE POLITICAL MONARCHS SENATOR HILLARY AND BILL CLINTON UNDER THE POLITICAL BUS.

AND THE ENTIRE GLOBAL CIVIL SOCIETY WITNESSED WHAT TRANSPIRED, THEY (CHOOSE) TO POSSIBLY CONCEDE THE PRESIDENCY TO SENATOR JOHN MCCAIN, RATHER THAN ALIENATE THEIR POLITICAL SEDATED HERDING OBAMA BLACKS, WHICH IS AND HAVE A DOMINATING POLITICAL INTRICY WITHIN THE DEMOCRAT PARTY RELATED TO ELECTORIAL CONSTITUENCY. AND RATHER THAN ALIENATE OR HAVE THEIR DISTORTED IDEOLOGY REVEALED, THEY SUCCEEDED IN MANIPULATING THE MAJORITY OF BLACKS, INTO THINKING THAT SENATOR OBAMA, WAS THE MORE ELECTABLE CANIDATE, THEY THE DEMOCRATS ARE (NOT) THAT SMART, ITS THE MAJORITY OF BLACKS SO DAMN POLITICALLY STUPID.

MANY BLACKS ARE REVELING OVER THE AIR WAYS, TELEVISION, TALK RADIO, WITH SUCH VULGARITY AND STUPID REMARKS,AS WHITEY IS GOING TO UNDERSTAND

WHAT SLAVERY WAS ALL ABOUT,BECAUSE US GOT US A BLACK PRESIDENT, AND THE WHITE HOUSE IS GOING TO BE CHANGED TO BLACK HOUSE, UNFORTUNATELY THESE BELEAGUERED CONCEPTS ARE MOST LIKELY RESPONSIBLE FOR MANY LYNCHINS, PRIOR TO CIVIL RIGHTS FOR BLACKS THAN ANY ONE WILL EVER KNOW.

REALISTICALLY THIS KIND OF HERDING IGNORANT GIBBERISH,IS BIAS OF A CONGO MANNERISM THAT CAUSE BITTER VENGEFUL RETALIATION. THAT TRADITIONALLY IS EMBEDDED IN HUMANITY, WHICH IS CONSISTENT WITH (REALITY) AND CHRONOLOGICAL RECORDS OF SUCH EVENTS. THE MAJORITY OF AFRICAN AMERICANS, ARE RELENTLESSLY UNIQUE IN THEIR QUEST FOR (SUPERIORITY);

WHICH WILL (NEVER) EXIST OR DISSIPATE BASED ON REALITY,BECAUSE OF THEIR VINDICTIVE RENOUNCING OF DIVERSITY, STIMULATED BASED ON (BIAS) HERDING, WHICH HISTORICALLY HAS BEEN THEIR SELF DESTRUCTIVE VULNERABILITY.

AND EVENTUALLY (WILL) SABOTAGE SENATOR BARACK OBAMA,POLITICAL ASPIRATIONS TO BECOME PRESIDENT. ALONG WITH ELITE DEMOCRATIC DUPLICITY, WHICH HAS ALREADY BEGAN.

WITH THE CCONCESSION SPEECH OF SENATOR HILLARY CLINTON, SHE MENTION THREE SIGNIFICANT WORDS, BARRIER, BIASAND EIGHTEEN MILLION CRACKS IN THE CEILING.

THIS WAS A CLEAR VILE MESSAGE TO SENATOR OBAMA, THAT YOU AND YOUR OVER NINETY PERCENT OF HERDING BLACKS, BARRICADED (ME) WITH A BIAS RENDITION, SO I AM ALERTING WHITE AMERICA THAT THEY CAN CRACK YOUR POLITICAL CEILING. (BASED ON BIAS) RELATED TO YOU BEING BLACK, THE FUNDAMENTAL (REALITY) OF AMERICA IS INEVITABLE PERTAINIIG TO A DIVERSE SOCIETY, WHICH EACH AND EVERY INDIVIDUAL IS MOTIVATED BY PERSONAL IDEALS, THAT IS CONSISTENT WITH EITHER MORALITY OR IMMORALITY, AND IT IS PREDICATED ON INDIVIDUAL CHOICE. MORALITY IS THE FOUNDATION TO ESTABLISH CREDIBILITY IN A DIVERSE SOCIETY, IN ORDER TO ATTAIN

PROMINENCE REGARDS TO EQUALITY.AND RACE IS (NOT) AN OBSTACLE, BASED ON INDIVIDUAL INTELLECT, AND VANITY IN ONE SELF.

MORAL AND IMMORAL ARE TWO OF THE MOST IMPORTANT (WORDS) IN GLOBAL SOCIETY PERTAING TO (ALL) ETHNICS OF PEOPLE, BECAUSE THOSE TWO WORDS DETERMINE THE ELIGIBILITY OF FITNESS, AND THE SUSTAINING QUALITY TO COMMUNICATE WITH OTHERS WITHOUT MALICE. AND THAT IS WHY THESE TWO WORDS ARE THE DETERMINING FACTOR IN AMERICAN ELECTIVE POLITICS, RELATED TO SCRUTINY FOR LOYAL FITNESS BASED ON A MAJORITY RULE OF THE PEOPLE.

AND THE FOUNDERS FORMULATED SUCH ARTISTIC METHOD IN AN EFFORT TO PROHIBIT IMMORAL LYING SCOUNDRELS,FROM IMPEDING OR SABOTAGING THE FUNDAMENTAL GUIDING PRINCPLE, THAT IS THE STABILITY OF OUR BELOVED NATION THE UNITED STATES OF AMERICA.

I AM PROUD TO AN AMERICAN, OF AFRICAN HERITAGE, THAT PARTIALLY , GREW UP IN THE SOUTH, AND BEING AN ONLY CHILD, MY DEAR GRAND MOTHER CAPTIVATED, REPROOF AND DEMANDED THAT I ADHERE TO THE TEN COMMANDMENTS WHICH IS (MORALITY);

BECAUSE IT IS THE GUIDING PRINCIPLE IN LIFE, THAT IS ABSOLUTELYINDISPENSABLEPERTAININGTOADAPTABILITY OF HUMANITY. UNFORTUNATELY IT IS INEVITABLE THAT IF A CHILD IS (NOT) TAUGHT MORAL VALUES, HE OR SHE WILL MOST LIKELY JOIN A HERD OF IMMORALIST, THAT WILL ADVOCATE THEIR DESTRUCTIVE FATE.

AND THIS ILL WILL APPLIES TO (ALL) PEOPLE, EDUCATED, ALLITERATE, IGNORANT, BLACK AND WHITE.

BECAUSE ACCORDING TO THE BIBLE, GOD CREATED MAN IN HIS (OWN) IMAGE, MEANING HE GAVE EVERY ONE A (BRAIN) TO USE FOR THEIR OWN THINKING CAPACITY.

AND IF HE HAD (NOT) INTENDED SUCH BENEVOLENCE, THE BRAIN WOULD HAVE BEEN LEFT (OUT).

THE FAITHFUL PORTRAIL OF REALITY IS INEVITABLE, BASED ON INDIVIDUAL THINKING, REFERENCE THE PEOPLE ONE CHOOSE TO PARTICIPATE WITH IN A SOCIAL

GATHERING CONTINUOUSLY, THIS DISTINCTIVE BEHAVIOR ILLUSTRATE ACCEPTANCE OF THEIR IDEOLOGY, THIS IS HUMAN NATURAL INHERITED SUBCONSCIOUS MOTIVATED BEHAVIOR.

AND FOR ANY ONE TO DENY THIS HUMAN CHARACERISTIC OF (REALITY) IS (LYING) THROUGH HIS OR HER TEETH.

SO THE GENERAL CONSENSUS IS THAT MANY CITIZENS OF THIS NATION INCLUDING MY SELF, IS SUSPICIOUS OF SENATOR BARACK OBAMA, OF BEING A HABITUAL LIAR.

RECENTLY HE WAS ON MSNBC MAY 05, 2008,WITH MODERATOR MORNING JOE, AND WAS SPECIFICALLY ASKED (WHY ARE YOU PROUD TO BE AN AMERICAN). THERE WAS A SUDDEN (PAUSE) . AND FINALLY HE BLURTED OUT WITH A GRAMMATICALLY ANALYZING EXPLANATION, RELATED TO HIS ANCESTORS BEING AND COMOMG TO AMERICA, EVADING THE QUESTION PERTAINING TO HIM SELF. SENATOR BARACK OBAMA IS A VINDICTIVE INCOMPETENT POLITICAL CANIDATE, THAT IS OBSESSED WITH (BLACK) SUPERIORITY, A HARVARD EDUCATED (NAT TURNER) IN DECEITFUL DISGUISE.

WE LIVE IN A DIVERSE SOCIETY OF GULLIBILITY, THAT PERTAIN TO ALL (PEOPLE) UNFORTUNATELY THE MAJORITY OF AFRICAN AMERICANS ARE AT THE EMPIRICAL OBSESSION. BECAUSE OF THEIR INEPT TAUGHT IDEOLOGY RELATED TO POLITICS, SENATOR BARACK OBAMA, IS GOING TO BE ONE OF THE MOST PUBLICIZED BLACK INDIVIDUALS OF MODEPN TIMES. BASED ON DEMOCRATIC HISTORICAL IDEOLOGY OF DEVIOUS OPPRESSION OF BLACKS, RELATED TO POLITICAL SLAVE DRIVING INCOMPETENCY. IT IS A ESSENTIAL FACT OF REALITY, THAT THE ELITE DEMOCRATS ARE GOING TO (SABOTAGE) SENATOR BARACK OBAMA, POLITICAL AMBITIONS. AND LAY THE BLAME AT THE DOOR STEP OF THE REPUBLICANS, AS THEY HAVE FOR OVER SEVENTY YEARS, ENGAGING IN SLANDER THAT REPUBLICANS ARE RACIST AGAINST BLACKS.

AND THE MAJORITY OF BLACKS ARE SO POLITICAL INEPT, TO THE REALITY OF CHRONOLOGICAL RECORDS

OF SIGNIFICANT EVENTS, UNTIL THEY ARE MESMERIZED WITH ASSUMING IGNORANCE.

IT IS TERRIBLY SHAMEFUL AND DEPLORABLE TO RESIDE IN A NATION WITH THE GREATNESS OF THE UNITED STATES OF AMERICA, AND (NOT) UNDERSTAND THE REALITY OF THE TWO PARTY SYSTEM, BASED ON IDEOLOGY AND THEIR COMMITMENT.

THE REPUBLICAN PARTY IS RESPONSIBLE FOR (EVERY) MAJOR RACIST OBSTACLE THAT AFRICAN AMERICANS HAD TO OVERCOME.

SUCH AS ABOLISHING SERVITUDE IN EIGHTEEN SIXTY FIVE, AND THEIR OVERWHELMING COMMITMENT OF SUPPORT TO OVER-RIDE A DEMOCRATIC FILIBUSTER IN NINETEEN SIXTY FOUR AND FIVE.

IN ORDER FOR BLACKS TO RID THEM SELVES OF SOUTHERN JIM CROW RULE, ESTABLISHED BY THE SOUTHERN DEMOCRATS.

TO RESTORE CIVIL AND VOTING RIGHTS, AND EQUALITY FOR SOUTHERN BLACKS.

WHILE THE SOUTHERN DEMOCRATS HAD FOUNDERED THE KU-KLUX-KLAN, AND TERRORIZED BLACKS FOR ONE HUNDRED YEARS.

HOWEVER THERE IS A SINCERE HEAVY PRICE TO PAY FOR IGNORANCE, RELATED TO THE SENATOR BARACK OBAMAUNIQUE DEBACLE.

SIMPLY BECAUSE OF HIS LITTLE PEACOCKISH AGENDA OF POLITICAL INEPT ARROGANCE, COMBINED WITH MELIGNED PERSONAL AFFILIATES, WITH MORE BAGGAGE THAN A PASSENGER LOCOMOTIVE TRAIN. AND REPORTS OF A HOLLYWOOD BIAS BUFFOON. SPIKE LEE, IS GOING TO ESTABLISH A (ALL) CHOCOLATE CITY WHEN BARACK OBAMA BECOME PRESIDENT.

SO THE BLACK PHENOMENON OF POLITICAL IGNORANCE HAS BEGUN, APPLAUDING SENATOR OBAMA, AS THEY DID IN EIGHTEEN NINETY FIVE, FOR BOOKER T. WASHINGTON, AND WAS FORCED TO SIT ON THE BACK OF THE BUS, FOR SEVENTY YEARS.

HOWEVER THAT WAS A DIFFERENT ERA, BUT THE RENDITION OF HERDING WILL HAVE THE SAME PARALLEL

AFFECTS, WITH A HIDDEN COVERT AGENDA RELATED TO SENATOR BARACK OBAMA BECOMING PRESIDENT.

AS I HAVE OFTEN REITERATED THROUGH OUT MY BOOK, THAT THIS IS SWEET PROMISING DIPLOMATIC AMERICA, (NOT) AFRICA.

AND WE HAVE A MORALISTIC, PRAGMATIC, UNIVERSAL, DIPLOMATIC TRADITION, TO ENHANCE PROSPERITY.

IF ONE SHOULD (CHOOSE) TO ACCEPT, AND ADAPT TO THE EMBEDDED PRINCIPLE, WITH SYMPATHETIC COMPASSION, FOR AUTHENTIC SYMBOLISM THAT CHARACTERIZE THIS GREAT NATION. (THEN THERE ARE (NO) BARRIERS). HOWEVER IF YOU SHOULD (CHOOSE) TO DEVIATE FROM THESE STANDARD CONCEPTS. IT REPRESENT A FORM OF (BIAS) ANARCHY, THAT AFFECT YOU AND ALL THE PEOPLE THAT ADHERE TO THIS KIND OF IGNORANCE. UNFORTUNATELY THIS IS A MAJOR PREVALENT ACHILLESHEEL FOR SENATOR BARACK OBAMA, AND HIS OVER NINETY PERCENT OF HERDING BLACK SUPPORTERS, BECAUSE OF A PRECARIOUS TRADITION RELATED TO BLACKS. THEY HAVE SUPPORTED THE DEMOCRAT PARTY FOR OVER SEVENTY YEARS, BY THAT SAME NINETY PERCENT MARGIN.

AND THE REPUBLICANS HAVE BEEN WINNING THE GENERAL ELECTION, SO IT IS FAIR TO INDICATE THAT THEIR BLOC VOTING FOR THE DEMOCRAT PARTY IN THE GENERAL ELECTION, IS NULLIFIED RELATED TO THE REPUBLICAN PARTY, BECAUSE OF HISPANIC VOTERS, AND BLACKS ARE (NOT) THEIR MOST FAVORITE PEOPLE.

IT IS ABSOLUTELY ESSENTIAL THAT THE FUNDAMENTAL (REALITY) THAT EXIST IN OUR NATION, BASED ON CHRONOLOGICAL HISTORY, PERTAINING TO (ALL) PEOPLE THAT RESIDE IN THE UNITED STATES OF AMERICA, AND ABROAD.

BE ACCEPTED AS FACTUAL, THAT PEOPLE AND ANIMALS ARE MOTIVATED BY GENETIC TRAITS ETERNALLY.

BECAUSE GENETIC CONTROLLABILITY DICTATE IDEOLOGY, AND THIS IS WHY THE NECESSITY TO IMPLEMENT CONTROLLING LAWS TO DETERMINE THE VALIDITY OF CONTRASTABLE TAUGHT BELIEFS.

OUR SOCIETY CONSIST OF DOCTRINAL IDEOLOGY, THAT IS EMBEDDED IN THE FUNDAMENTALS OF POLITICS.

BECAUSE OF THE MAJORITY RULE, AND WHEN A CANIDATE IS PERSUING PUBLIC OFFICE BASED ON CONSTITUENCY.

HE OR SHE WILL ATTEMPT TO DISTORT (REALITY). AND OUT RIGHT (LIE) FOR PERSONAL FORTITUDE.

AND THE RESPONSIBILITY IS BESTOWED UPON THE GENERAL PUBLIC TO DETERMINE ELECTIVENESS, THIS MONETARY PROCESS IS USUALLY MOTIVATED BASED ON INTELLECT, CHARISMA, ASSOCIATES, FALSE PROMISES, AND OUT RIGHT INCOMPETENT (LIES).

THIS IS THE YEAR OF TWO THOUSAND AND EIGHT, AND THE MOST UNIQUE ELECTION IN THE HISTORY OF OUR NATION. PARTICULARLY FOR THE DEMOCRATIC PARTY, A HISTORIC TRIUMPH FOR AFRICAN AMERICANS, THE COMPLEX DEMOCRATIC PRIMARY SYSTEM CHOOSE A BLACK MAN, SENATOR BARACK OBAMA, AS THEIR PARTY LEADER TO REPRESENT THEM IN THE GENERAL ELECTION, AGAINST REPUBLICAN SENATOR JOHN MCCAIN, THIS ELECTION IS DEEM TO BE ONE OF THE MOST INSPIRING UNIQUE CHALLENGES IN THE HISTORY OF OUR NATION.

THE VAST MAJORITY OF BLACKS, ARE SINGING SWING LOW SWEET CHARIOT MESSIAH BARACK OBAMA IS HERE TO CARRY (US) HOME.

HOWEVER OVER WHELMED DEMOCRATIC WHITES ARE STILL SCRATCHING THEIR HEADS, TRYING TO DETERMINE HIS POLITICAL ABERRATION, RELATED TO HIS CREDIBILITY, PERTAINING TO COUNTRY LOYALTY.

LETS JUST EVALUATE THE FUNDAMENTAL (REALITY) PERTAINING TO SENATOR BARACK OBAMA CHANCES OF BECOMING ELECTED PRESIDENT OF THE UNITED STATES OF AMERICA, AS A DEMOCRATIC CANIDATE.

BECAUSE THERE ARE CONTROVERSIAL INNUENDOES PREVAILING AROUND SENATOR BARACK OBAMA, WITH HIS PERSONAL AFFILIATES.

ALSO HE IS A EGOTISTICAL, TEMPERAMENTAL COVERT RADICAL, WITH OVER NINETY PERCENT OF OTHER BIAS BLACK CONSTITUENCY HERDING BEHIND HIM, AND THERE

ARE MANY INSTIGATING BLACK SUPERIORITY, WHILE HE IS CATERING AND ATTEMPTING TO SEDUCE (WHITES) TO VOTE FOR HIM. SENATOR BARACK OBAMA IS A POLITICAL WEASEL, THAT IS AWARE OF HIS HERDING BLACK BIAS CONSTITUENCY, THAT HAS SOLIDIFIED BEHIND HIM BECAUSE HE IS BLACK, AND HE IS WALKING A THIN LINE TO ENTICE ENOUGH SMALL DYSFUNCTIONAL BRAIN (WHITES) TO JOIN THE BLACK HERD, AND ELECT HIM PRESIDENT.

THIS STRATEGY WORKED DURING THE DEMOCRATIC PRIMARY, AND THREW THE POLITICAL MONARCH CLINTONS UNDER THE BUS.

FORTUNATELY DURING THE GENERAL ELECTION BLACK ELECTIVE POWER IS HELD TO MINIMUM.

PERSONALLY I HAVE (NOTHING) AGAINST SENATOR OBAMA AS A PERSON, HOWEVER HE HAS A ANTIQUATED DELIVERENCE THAT HAS BEEN USED ON BLACKS BY DEMOCRATS FOR OVER SEVENTY YEARS, IMPUGNING THE MORAL INTEGRITY OF THE REPUBLICANS, AND FAULTING THEM FOR BLACKS BEING POLITICALLY STUPID AND INCOMPETENT.

I HAVE GONE THROUGH A LITHNY OF INSIDIOUS ENTOURAGES PERTAINING TO THE FUNDAMENTALS OF (REALITY) RELATED TO DISTORTED POLITICAL IGNORANCE, OUR COUNTRY IS SLOWLY BEING INVADED BY IMMORALITY OF DECEPTION WITHIN.

MEANING THAT THE LOYALTY TO MORALITY, WHICH IS THE STABILITY TO BONDING IS DISSIPATING REGARDS TO FUNDAMENTAL PRINCIPLES, THAT WILL EVENTUALLY INITIATE SELF DESTRUCTION INTERNALLY. AND YOU CAN BE CERTAIN OUR ADVERSARIES ARE AWARE OF THIS FACTOR, AND THEY ARE GLEEFULLY WAITING THE OPPORTUNE TIME TO TAKE ADVANTAGE, MEANING TERRORISM IN AN EFFORT TO CONQUER OUR WAY OF LIFE. WE ARE LIVING IN A AGE OF DIRE VULNERABILITY, AND FOR SMALL DYSFUNCTIONAL BRAIN (WHITES) TO ANTICIPATE ELECTING A PRESIDENT THAT CAN (NOT) DETERMINE THE DISDAINING IDEOLOGY OF PEOPLE THAT HE (CHOOSE) TO PARTICIPATE WITH IN A SOCIAL GATHERING, THAT HAS VAIN BIAS, HOSTILE

MOTIVES TOWARD (WHITES) IN THE UNITED STATES OF AMRICA.

THE UNITED STATES OF AMERICA HAS A LONG EMBEDDED TRADITIONAL HISTORY OF ESSENTIAL MORAL VALUES.

THAT IS INSTITUTIONALIZED GLOBALLY, AND TO REDUCE THE SENTIMENTS OF OUR CHARACTER AND ELECT (ANY) ONE, BASED ON ELECTRIFYING GRAMMATICALLY ANALYTICAL VERBIAGE, WITHOUT SCRUTINIZING THEIR IDEOLOGY, IS FOOLISHLY GULLIBLE, AND COULD SACRIFICE OUR DIGNITY, AND SABOTAGE THE STRUCTURE OF OUR NATION.

BECAUSE IT IS BLATANTLY BIAS AND POLITICAL HYPOCRITICAL, FOR A EITE DIGNITARY SUCH AS SENATOR BARACK OBAMA, TO ADDRESS A AUDIANCE OF HISPANICS, AND DENOUNCE OTHER ETHNIC CITIZENS OF THIS NATION. WHEN HE STIPULATED ON JUNE 28, 2008. THAT (NO) ONE HAS MORE SUFFRAGE RELATED TO CASUALTY THAN THE LATIN COMMUNITY.

REFERRING TO MILITARY ACTIVITY, HE ALSO STATED THAT WHEN HE BECAME PRESIDENT,.AMERICA WILL BECOME MORE (EQUAL) TO HISPANICS AND BLACKS.

THIS IS TYPICAL RADICAL LIBERAL DECITFUL PERSUASION BY PROPAGANDA GIBBERISH, AND TO CONFIRM MY PROUFOUND BELIEF, OF THIS INSIDIOUS CALAMITY.

APPARENTLY THE UNIVERSITY OF HARVARD IS LOCATED IN THE CONGO OF AFRICA, AND AFFORDED HIM THE LUXURY OF AN EDUCATION, AND HE MIGRATED TO AMERICA, AND THE DEMOCRATIC PRIMARY CONSTITUENCY CHOOSE HIM AS THE LEADER OF THEIR PARTY, TO RUN FOR THE PRESIDENCY. SENATOR BARACK OBAMA, IS A POLITICAL SYMBOLIC CONTRADICTABLE MYTH THAT IS UTILIZING HIS CHICAGO, BLACK RADICAL STREET CRAFTIES WITH A EDDIFIED (MIX) OF GRAMMATICALLY ANALYZED SOPHISTICATED GRAMMER, THAT IS ATTRIBUTED TO MOST AMERICAN (WHITES).

WHICH IS MOST EDUCATE AND APPROPIATE. HOWEVER THE INTENDED AGENDA IS QUESTIONABLE, BASED ON HIS ASPIRING POLITICAL IDEOLOGY. MEANING HE OBAMA, IS

SEDUCING AND LYING TO BLACKS, AND HISPANICS, THAT AMERICA IS DENYING THEM THEIR (EQUALITY);

WHEN HE HAS A NATIONAL TELEVISION COMMERCIAL, ILLUSTRATING ON HOW HIS IMMEDIATE FAMILY, TAUGHT HIM MORAL VALUES, AND THE LOVE OF (COUNTRY).

AND THIS EXPOSURE WAS THE LEADING INSTRUMENTAL FACTOR, PERTAINING TO HIS PINNACLE OF UNIQUE POLITICAL LEADING PRODIGY. FORTUNATELY THERE ARE MILLIONS OF WHITES, BLACKS, HISPANICS, AND OTHER CITIZENS THAT RESIDE IN THE UNITED STATES OF AMERICA. HAVE ADHERED TO THE SAME PRINCIPLES THAT SENATOR BARACK OBAMA WAS TAUGHT ACCORDING TO HIS COMMERCIAL.

AND HAVE RISEN TO THE PINNACLE OF PROSPERITY, RELATED TO DIFFERENT FACTIONS EMBEDDED IN THE (LIBERTY) AND INDEPENDENCE, THAT OUR NATION CONSTITUTION GUARANTEE.

AND AS SENATOR BARACK OBAMA SO ELOQUENTLY PHRASED THE VALIDITY OF (REALITY) TO PROSPERITY , IN HIS TELEVISED COMMERICAL. MORAL VALUES, HARD WORK, AND LOVE OF COUNTRY

SENATOR BARACK OBAMA , HAS THE MAJORITY OF HERDING BLACK SUPPORT POLITICALLY SOLIDIFIED.

BASED ON HE BEING (BLACK) AND THEY ARE SO ENTRENCHED WITH HIS ASININE DECITFUL RHETORIC, UNTIL IF THEY WERE GIVEN A CHOICE OF VOTING FOR OBAMA, OR ALLOWING BIN OLADEN MOVE INTO AN APARTMENT IN MANHATTEN, NEW YORK, THEY WOULD AGREE TO PAY BIN LADEN RENT RATHER THAN (NOT) VOTE FOR BARACK OBAMA.

THERE IS A RARE MENTAL DEFICIENCY OF MOST BLACKS, DUE TO GENETIC HERITAGE HERDING, THAT IS IMMORTIAL.

AND MOST ARE (NOT) AWARE OF THIS INHERITED CAUSATION, WHICH IS A IDIOSYNCRASY THAT HAS BEEN DETRIMENTAL TO MOST AFRICAN AMERICANS PROGRESS IN AMERICA FOR OVER THREE HUNDRED YEARS.

THE PARTY OF DEMOCRATS HAS USED THIS MORALLY OFFENAIVE ACT OF BIAS POLITICAL IGNORANCE, ENFORCED

BY (BLACKS) TO SUSTAIN THEIR POLITICAL ASPIRATIONS FOR OVER SEVENTY YEARS.

THE PREDICTABILITY NOW THAT SENATOR BARACK OBAMA IS THE BLACK CHIEF MONARCH WITHIN THE DEMOCRAT PARTY.

THERE IS GOING TO BE A DIRE REPERCUSSION, REGARDS TO BLACK RADICAL SUPERIORITY NATION WIDE.

PARTICULARLY WITH HIGH RISE CITY SLUM DWELLING, SUCH AS CHICAGO WHERE BARACK OBAMA IS STATE SENATOR.

BECAUSE MOST OF THOSE GHETTO DWELLERS ARE ILLETERATE AND HOSTILE, PERTAINING TO SENATOR OBAMA TELEVISED COMMERCIAL, RELATING TO MORAL VALUES, HARD WORK, AND LOVE OF COUNTRY, WHICH IS CONSIDERED TO BE DEROGATORY COMPELLING REMARKS, RELATED TO GHETTO SLUM IDEOLOGY,

UNFORTUNATELYTHERE IS A INORDINATE INACCURACY, PERTAINING TO BLACK INEQUALITY, AS SUGGESTED BY JESSIE JACKSON AND AL SHARPTON. APPARENTLY THIS RADICAL OBAESSION WILL (NEVER) END. BECAUSE THERE IS A DEMOCRATIC NOMINEE CAMPAIGNING TO BE ELECTED PRESIDENT OF THE UNITED STATES OF AMERICA, WITH A COMBINE IDEOLOGY OF NAT TURNER, JESSIE JACKSON, AND AL SHARPTON. WHICH SENATOR BARACK OBAMA, IS.A STAUNCH^ADVOCATE, FOR APPROXIMAS TELY THIRTY PERCENT OF ILLITERATE, BELLIGERENT, MIS-FIT BLACKS, INSINUATING THAT THEIR CHOSEN STYLE OF LIFE IS DUE TO A UN-JUST MEAN AMERICA, ESTABLISHED BY RACIST (WHITES) TO PREVENT BLACKS FROM EQUALITY.

WHEN IN ESSENCE (HE) SENATOR OBAMA, AND HIS TELEVISION COMMERICAL CONTRADICT HIS FOOLISH POLITICAL DEMAGOGUERY.

HE IS INTENTIONALLY UTILIZING HYPOCRISY TO JUSTIFY THE REMOTE INCOMPETENCE OF SOME MIS-FIT BLACKS, IN AN EFFORT TO ESTABLISH CREDITABILITY BASED ON RACIST RADICAL INNUENDO.

THIS BACK WOODS AGENDA IS INTENDED TO DISGUISE THE (REALITY), PERTAINING TO A SEGEMENT OF INEPT

BLACK INDIFFERENT APPROACH TO INTELLECT AND HUMANITY.

GROWING UP IN THE SOUTH DURING THE FORTIES, WE HAD SCHOOLS TO OBTAIN THE VALUE OF EDUCATION, SO DID MY PARENTS AND GRAND PARENTS HOWEVER MANY BLACKS (CHOOSE NOT) TO ATTEND, INFLUENCED BY PARENT GUIDANCE, SUGGESTING THAT EDUCATION WAS FOR WHITE FOLKS, SO AS A RESULT THIS OBLIVIOUS CONCEPT BACK THEN, SERVES AS A GENETIC MALIGNANCY FOR MANY AFRICAN AMERICANS TODAY. REGARDS TO PRINCIPLE AND EQUALITY.

THE DISTORTING HYPOCRISY DISPLAYED, RELATED TO SEGEMENTS OFIMMOR AL, BELLIGERENT (BLACK) ILLITERACY, IS ASTOUNDING, BECAUSE SELF APPOINTED BLACK LEADERS, CIVIL RIGHTS GROUPS, AND MANY CHURCH MINISTERS, AND THEIR CONGREGATIONS, IGNORE THE FACT THAT INEPTITUDE EXIST. AND (NEVER) ADDRESS THE INCOMPATIBILITY OF MIS-FIT BLACKS, AND THEIR CYNICAL, INCONGRUITY IGNORANT BEHAVIOR, AND IF ANY ONE SHOULD ATTEMPT, BLACK OR WHITE, SUCH AS BILL COSBY AND RALPH NADER, INDICATING MORALITY, BASED ON PERSONAL RESPONSIBILITY, ITS LIKE TUCHING A THIRD RAIL, WITH A STEAK DRIVEN THROUGH THEIR HEART.

AND YOU ARE CHARACTERIZED EITHER AS TRYING TO BE A RACIST WHITE ELITIST, OR A BLACK ELITE TRYING TO BE WHITE.

THIS IS A CANTANKEROUS DEVOTION THAT HAS PLAGUED AFRICAN AMERICANS, SYSTEMATICALLY FOR OVER FORTY YEARS.

AND IS MORE PREVALENT IN OUR SOCIETY TODAY THAN EVER, AND WHAT IS SO APPALLING, THE CITIZENS OF THIS NATION IS CONTEMPLATING ON ELECTING SENATOR BARACK OBAMA, AS PRESIDENT.

WHICH IS A STAUNCH ADVOCATE, OF BLACK SUPERIORITY UNDER FALSE PRETENSES TO ATTAIN NOTNRIETY, THAT IS EMBEDDED IN POLITICAL IGNORANCE.

IT HAS BEEN A TRADITIONAL ESCAPADE HISTORICALLY, TO FOCUS ON WHAT SOME ONE IS DOING TO AFRICAN

AMERICANS, AND MANY OF THEIR SELF APPOINTED LEADERS HAVE UTILIZED THIS EGOTISTICAL DISTORTING CRITERIA, TO NEGATE ATTENTION TO THEIR RELENTLESS PURSUIT OF DOMINANCE IN AN EFFORT TO ATTAIN SUPERIORITY EQUAL TO WHITES.

THIS BOOK IS INTENDED TO ELABORATE ON A SEGMENT OF AFRICAN AMERICAN CONCEPT, THAT IS PREDOMINANTLY EMBEDDED ON ASSUMPTIONS, AND TO ACCUSE OTHERS FOR THEIR INABILITY, TO ATTAIN THE FUNDAMENTAL VALUES REQUIRED TO INFILTRATE A MODERATE MORALISTICLDIHERSE.SOCIETY. INSTEAD THEY TEND TO CAMOUFLAGE THEIR IGNORANCE BY STIPULATING STUPIDITY, THAT AMERICA IS UN-JUST, AND WHITES ARE OUT TO GET THEM, BASED ON DENYING THEM THEIR EQUAL RIGHTS.

AFRICAN AMERICANS HAVE (NEVER) BEEN TRULY PROFILED, ACCORDING TO THEIR EMBEDDED GENETIC TRAITS, THAT DICTATE THEIR COMPREHENDABLE INTELLECT, THE REALISTIC REVELATIONS ILLUSTRATED THROUGH OUT THIS BOOK IS BASED ON CHRONOLOGICAL RECORDS OF EVENTS, INTENDED TO REFLECT ON BLACK INTERNAL PRECEPTION, AND THEIR EQUIVALENCY BEING PARELLEL TO (ALL) CIVIL SOCIETY, BASED ON LITANY IDEOLOGY. HOWEVER THERE IS A DISTINCTIVE MYTHOLOGY CREATED BECAUSE OF THEIR HERDING INSTINCTS TO ARBITRARY FOLLOW BLACK LEADERS, AND ASSUME MYTHS.

LET ME BE PERFECTLY CLEAR, THIS PATTERN OF ORIENTATION DOES (NOT) APPLY TO (ALL) BLACKS, BUT ENOUGH TO DISTORT (REALITY) RELATED TO DEROGATION, THAT (SELF) DESTRUCT THEIR AMBITIONS BASED ON UNAWARE INEPTNESS.

MOST AFRICAN AMERICANS ADHERE TO A SYSTEMATIC MYTHICAL IDEALISM, WHICH IS PREMEDITATED TO ATTAIN PREROGATIVES.

AND IF THEY ACCOMPLISH ECONOMICAL OR POLITICAL PINNACLE, THE MAJORITY OF BLACKS AND MANY WHITES ARE (NONE) AWARE OF THE HISTORIC IMMORTAL DECLARATION, THAT COLLECTIVELY STIPULATE A DECREE

FOR THE CONSTITUTION, THAT EXHIBIT EQUALITY AND FREEDOM FOR (ALL);

(WE THE PEOPLE) OF THE UNITED STATES, IN ORDER TO FORM A MORE PERFECT UNION, ESTABLISH JUSTICE, INSURE DOMESTIC TRANQUILITY, PROVIDE FOR THE COMMON DEFENCE, PROMOTE THE GENERAL WELFARE, AND SECURE THE BLESSINGS OF LIBERTY TO OURSELVES AND OUR (POSTERITY) DO ORDAIN AND ESTABLISH THIS CONSTITUTION FOR THE UNITED STATES OF AMERICA.

THE TRANSCRIBED METHODOLOGY, IS ATTRIBUTED TO THE GREATEST COUNTRY ON GODS EARTH (AMERICA);

HOWEVER THERE ARE IMAGINARY IMBECILES, SUCH AS JESSIE JACKSON, AL SHARPTON AND BARACK OBAMA, THAT HAS PROSPERED FROM THE CHARACTERIZATION OF THIS DOCUMENTATION, YET THEY DECEIVE OTHER HERDING, DYSFUNCTIONAL DERANGED BLACKS, THAT IT IS OBSOLETE.

AND (NO) LONGER REPRESENTATIVE OF OUR NATION, AND THAT IS WHY THEY ARE ADVOCATING FOR CHANGE TO RESTORE THE CRITERIA.

THE GENETIC FALLACY THAT HAS BEEN CREATED IN OUR NATION BY SOME BLACKS, AFTER NINETEEN SIXTY FOUR AND FIVE, WHEN OUR CIVIL AND VOTING RIGHTS WAS RESTORED, FROM THE SOUTHERN DEMOCRATS. AFRICAN AMERICANS HAVE HAD AMBITIONS TO BECOME POLITICIANS, AND THEIR DESIRE HAVE IMPROVED IMMENSELY, THEY HAVE BEEN ELECTED AND APPOINTED TO POLITICAL POSITIONS OF AUTHORITY, AT CITY, STATE, AND FEDERAL (LEVEL) NATION WIDE.

HOWEVER HAVING A GENETIC TRAIT OF HERDING AND INSTIGATING THAT WHITES ARE UTILIZING RACIST TACTICS TO IMPEDE THEIR FUNDAMENTAL PROGRESS, IS A MYTH BEYOND REPROCH, THAT IS A POLITICAL HERDING TCTIC TAUGHT, BY SOME PARENTS, MINISTERS, AND SELF APPOINTED LEADERS, DUE TO SOLIDIFIED POLITICAL INEPTNESS.

AND MOST ARE TOTALLY UNAWARE OF THE SUBSTANCE FOR THIS DERANGED, DIATORTED, DECEPTIVE, MYTH.

GROWING UP AS A CHILD IN THE SOUTH, MY DEAR OLD GRAND MOTHER WOULD CONSTANTLY REMIND ME THAT SOME BLACKS, ARE THE MOST RACIST, BELLIGERENT, IGNORANT, PEOPLE ON GODS EARTH.

BECAUSE THEY ARE CONSTANTLY DIGGING HOLES FOR OTHER PEOPLE, AND FALLING INTO THE HOLE THEMSELVES.

HER PSYCHOANALYSIS WAS BASED ON THEIR OBJECTIVE TO ANALYZE EVERY ONE ELSE FOR FAULTS, WHILE AVOIDING THEIR OWN ACKNOWLEDGMENT OF ASSUMING CYNICAL BEHAVIOR.

SO THEY CREATE LIES ON OTHER PEOPLE TO COMPENSATE FOR THEIR OWN IGNORANCE. AND IF YOU FOLLOW THEM, YOUR FATE (WILL) BE EITHER DISAPPOINTMENT, JAIL, OR HELL BOUND.

UNFORTUNATELY MANY BLACKS, NEGLECT TO REALIZE THAT OUR NATION DOES (NOT) CONSIST OF FIFTY PERCENT WHITE, AND FIFTY PERCENT BLACK, THERE ARE APPROXIMATELY THIRTY SIX MILLION AFRICAN AMERICANS, OPPOSE TO TWO HUNDRED AND SIXTY FOUR MILLION OTHER ETHNICS. SO IT IS FAIR TO SAY THAT SENATOR BARACK OBAMA, HAS STIMULATED A MYTHICAL HOPE OF BLACK SUPERIORITY.

BASED ON BLACK MISCONCEIVED POLITICAL IGNORANCE, AND THERE ARE DIRE CONSEQUENCES RELATED TO THIS DIVISIVE CHAOTIC BLACK LIBERAL AGENDA TO ACHIEVE RENOWN DOMINANCE. CATERING TO A HERDING PHILOSOPHY, THE DEMOCRAT PARTY HAVE UTILIZE THE MAJORITY OF AFRICAN AMERICANS POLITICAL IGNORANCE FOR OVER ONE HUNDRED AND FORTY YEARS, TO STABILIZE SERVITUDE, AND WHEN THEY BECAME ELIGIBLE TO VOTE IN THE SOUTH DURING NINETEEN SIXTY FIVE, THEY USED SEDUCTIVE POLITICAL TACTICS, SUCH AS SOCIAL PROGRAMS, AND LYING ON REPUBLICANS, AS BEING RACIST AND IMPEDING BLACK EQUALITY, WHEN THEY ARE THE VILLAINOUS CULPRITS.

THIS POLITICAL AGENDA HAS ENABLED DEMOCRATS TO MAINTAIN AND DOMINATE CONGRESS FOR FORTY YEARS.

UNFORTUNATELY IN TWO THOUSAND EIGHT, THEIR CYNICAL MAGIC, HAS BEEN RUDELY INTERRUPTED BY THE SAME PEOPLE THEY POLITICALLY SCORNED AND CAPTIVATED WITH LIES AND DECITFUL DISTORTION.

GENERATIONAL CHANGING TIMES TEND TO ALTER THE ABILITY TO PRECEIVE PERTAINING TO THE HUMAN RACE, RELATED TO SOME PEOPLE. BASED ON THEIR INDIGNATION OF COMMITMENT, CHRONOLOGICAL RECORDS INDICATE THAT AFRICAN AMERICANS, HAS ALWAYS ASPIRED TO BE CHIEF DICTATOR IN AMERICA.

WITH (NO) CONCEPT OF THE CONSTITUTION, AND WITH CHANGING TIMES THERE ARE MANY POLITICAL INEPT SMALL DYSFUNCTIONAL BRAIN (WHITES) THAT ARE SYMPATHETIC TO THIS BLACK RHETORICAL COVERT RETRIBUTION. AND THE NOTICEABLE APPERANCE IS THAT MANY (WHITES) ARE BEING CONSUMED WITH RADICAL, MYTHICAL, DISTORTED, HAUGHTY EGOISM. THAT IS INTENDED TO PERSUADE THEIR HERDING WITH BLACKS, TO ELECT SENATOR BARACK OBAMA FOR PRESIDENT.

HOWEVER THAT IS TIPICAL POLITICS, (BUT) BARACK OBAMA IS A INDIVIDUAL THAT SAT FOR TWENTY YEARS, IN A CONGREGATION ASSOCIATED WITH GULLIBLE, FIENDISHEXPLOITATIONS DENOUNCING THE UNITED STATES OF AMERICA. AND (DELIBERATELY) LIED ABOUT HIS AWARENESS. WHICH IS AN INSULT TO THE INTELLIGENCE OF UNITED STATES CITIZENS, WITH IMPLICATIONS OF THEIR BEING IGNORANT.

BECAUSE HE KNEW OF THIS IMBECILIC IDEOLOGY PRIOR TO HIS ATTENDING AND IF HE DID (NOT) HIS INCOMPETENCE IS A HINDRANCE TO RESOLVING COMPLEX ISSURES, AS THE DEMOCRATS PREDICTED IN EIGHTEEN SIXTY EIGHT, AND TO ELECT HIM FOR PRESIDENT OF THIS GREAT COUNTRY AMERICA OR ANY OTHER INDIVIDUAL BLACK OR WHITE, WITH PARALLEL DYSFUNCTIONS, THE SOUTHERN DEMOCRATS WERE QUITE FAMILIAR WITH AFRICAN AMERICAN DISPOSITION, RELATED TO POLITICAL AUTHORITY.

IN EIGHTEEN SIXTY EIGHT, BLACKS BEGAN THEIR QUEST FOR POLITICAL OFFICE IN THE SOUTH.

HOWEVER (NOT) WITHOUT CONTROVERSIAL DISAPPROVAL BY WHITE SOUTHERN DEMOCRATS, THEY ACCUSED BLACKS OF (NOT) BEING CAPABLE OF DECIPHERING POLITICAL COMPLEX ISSURES, AND CONCEITED WITH EGOISM. THIS IS A ELECTION YEAR, AND WE ARE AT THE POLITICAL CROSS ROAD, OF A DEAD END.

EITHER YOU GO RIGHT OR LEFT, SENATOR OBAMA ON THE LEFT, AND SENATOR MCCAIN ON RIGHT, SENATOR OBAMA HAS INFILTRATED THE DEMOCRATIC PARTY, AND THROWN THE POLITICAL MONARCH CLINTONS UNDER THE BUS, WITH INTELLECTUAL, BIAS, MYTHICAL, INSPIRING, ARROGANT RHETORIC. WITH THE MAJORITY OF PEOPLE TRYING TO DETERMINE HIS MOTIVES, RELATED TO HIS COUNTRYS LOYALTY.

BASED ON DEMEANING VERBIAGE, AND HIS CHOICE OF AFFILATES. AND SENATOR MCCAIN, HAS BEEN REVERTING BACK TO THE HORSE AND BUGGY AREA TRYING TO INFILTRATE MODERN CALIBRATIONS, HIS TECHNICS ARE BEING POUNDED, BECAUSE OF HIS DOCILE GENETIC APPROACH, WITH A CONCILIATORY DEMEANOR, THAT APPEAL TO MOSTLY (NOSE) HOLDERS, MEANING HE IS OUT OF TUCH WITH (REALITY)

AND HAVE (NO) IDEA ON HOW TO COUNTERACT SENATOR BARACK OBAMA, ARROGANT, SADISTIC RIDICULING.

SO LIKE IT OR NOT THE UNITED STATES OF AMERICA IS IN A POLITICAL DECIDING CRITERIA OF THE UTMOST.

REGARDS TO A PRESIDENTAL NOMINATION OF THE CITIZENS CHOICE, SENATOR BARACK OBAMA, FORTY SIX YEARS OLD A ARROGANT, LYING, CONCEITED ARISTOCRATIC BLACK MAN, THAT THINK AMERICA IS UNJUST TO BLACKS.

SENATOR JOHN MCCAIN, A SEVENTY ONE YEAR OLD, WHITE SENIOR CITIZEN THAT IS A STUDENT OF THE GOOD OLD BOY NET WORK, THAT APPEAR TO BE OVER HIS HEAD RELATING TO CHANGING TIMES, WHICH CREATE PROBLEMS FOR HIM ORGANIZING AN AGENDA WITH SUBSTANCE.

HOWEVER THIS IS OUR CHOSEN CHOICE TO CHOOSE FROM AS OUR PRESIDENT FOR THE NEXT FOUR YEARS.

A BLACK SOPHISTICATED LYING HYPOCRITE. AND A HORSE AND BUGGY WHI1 TE SENIOR CITIZEN, AT INTERVALS ILLUSTRATE SIGNS OF (POOR) JUDGEMENT.

OUR NATION IS CONFRONTED WITH A RARE UNIQUE JUDGEMENT LIKE NEVER BEFORE, THE DECIDING ISSURES WILL BE BASED ON (MANY) PRACTICALITY PERTAINING TO EACH CANIDATE.

I AM GOING TO REFERENCE THE HARD CORE GIST OF (REALITY) SENATOR BARACK OBAMA HAS OVER NINETY PERCENT OF AFRICAN AMERICAN CONSTITUENCY SUPPORTING HIM, AND MANY ARE BEGINNING TO INSTIGATE ARROGANCE OVER THE AIR WAYS, AND SOME IS QUITE INSULTING TO WHITES. REALITY IS PROFOUNDLY INEVITABLE, WHICH MOST BLACKS IS INEPT TO, BECAUSE OF THEIR NEGATIVE INSIGHT.

ON JULY 11, 2008, A YOUNG AFRICAN AMERICAN CALL MY HOME, TO SOLICIT MY VOTE FOR SENATOR OBAMA, AND HE BLATANTLY SUGGESTED THAT I SHOULD GET ON BOARD, BECAUSE BARACK OBAMA WAS GOING TO WIN BY A LAND SLIDE, BECAUSE OF BLACKS.

I BRIEFLY QUESTION HIM REGARDS TO HIS CENSUS INTELLECT, BY ASKING HOW MANY PEOPLE ARE THERE IN THE UNITED STATES OF AMERICA. AND WHAT PERCENTAGE ARE BLACK. (HE DID NOT KNOW).

THIS SENTIMENT IS SHARED BY THE MAJORITY OF BLACKS NATIONALLY, WHICH IS COLLECTIVE POLITICAL BIAS ALIENABLE BEHAVIOR. WHICH HAS BEEN PASSED ON FOR GENERATIONS, EVERY THING IS ALWAYS ABOUT THE BLACK COMMUNITY, AND BLACK LEADERS, AND BLACK SUCCESS IT APPEAR THAT THEY NEGLECT TO REALIZE, THAT WHITES ARE THE DOMINATE FORCE IN CIVILIZATION, WE AS BLACKS WOULD STILL BE IN SLAVERY, IF IT WASNT FOR WHITES. WE WOULD STILL BE DRINKING FROM SEPARATE WATER FOUNTAINS AND SITTING ON THE BACK OF THE BUS, IF IT WASNT FOR WHITES.

DR MARTIN LUTHER KING, WAS THE INITIATOR OF CAUSING WHITES TO BE SYMPATHETIC FOR OUR CAUSE RELATED TO SOUTHERN DEMOCRATIC JIM CROW RULE,

BUT IT WAS WHITE PEOPLE IN THE CONGRESS, RESTORED OUR CIVIL AND VOTING RIGHTS.

EVERY SUCCESSFUL BLACK IN AMERICA IS A SPIN OF FROM WHITE ENDORSEMENT, NOT TO MENTION WE DID (NOT) MIGRATE TO AMERICA, OURANCESTORS WERE BROUGHT HERE BY WHITE PEOPLE.

I MENTION THIS YOUNG BLACK MAN THAT CALLED REGARDS TO VOTING FOR SENATOR OBAMA, BECAUSE HE WAS ONLY TWENTY FIVE YEARS OLD, AND HAS THE (SAME) MYTHICAL PRECEPTION AS A SIXTY YEAR OLD BLACK. TIMES ARE CHANGING, BUT MOST MINDS OF BLACKS ARE STAGNATED, WITH A ADHERENCE TO IDEALS OF BIAS HERDING, WHICH HAS AND ALWAYS WILL BE A SELF DESTRUCTIVE ACHILLES HEEL FOR THE MAJORITY OF AFRICAN AMERICANS, AND IT IS A GENETIC HIDDEN TRAIT THAT MOST ARE TOTALLY UNAWARE OF.

BUT (WHITES) ARE AND THIS IS ONE OF THE MAIN REASONS BLACKS, SUFFERED THE BRUNT OF BRUTALITY DURING BONDAGE, HOWEVER CHANGING TIMES HAS TRANSFORMED PHYSICAL BRUTALITY TO THE BALLOT BOX. (REALITY) IS INEVITABLE, SENATOR JOHN MCCAIN IS (NOT) THE MOST IDEAL PRESIDENTAL CANIDATE, BUT MANY (WHITES) ARE GOING TO SUPPORT HIM BECAUSE SENATOR BARACK OBAMA IS (BLACK) AND PRETENTIOUS. AND MANY OLDER WHITES FEAR ARROGANT REPRECUSSIONS FROM BIAS STUPID HERDING BLACKS IF SENATOR OBAMA WAS ELECTED.

AND AS THE SOUTHERN DEMOCRATIC WHITES, STIPULATED IN EIGHTEEN SIXTY EIGHT, BLACKS SEEKING POLITICAL OFFICE WERE BESIDE THEM SELVES, INCOMPETENT AND TRYING TO RISE ABOVE THEIR NATURAL PLACE OF SERVITUDE.

THIS DISTINGUISHED CHARATERIZATION OF BLACKS STILL EXIST, BUT IS A COVERT HIDDEN AGENDA WITH MANY WHITES.

AND IF ANY ONE DARE DENOUNCE THIS (REALITY) IS INEPT TO THE FUNDMENTALS OF OUR CULTURE, WHICH HAS AND ALWAYS WILL BE IMMORTAL, EVEN IN GLOBAL SOCIETY, IN NINETEEN THIRTY SIX ADOLF HITLER,

CHARACTERIZED OLYMPIC TRACK STAR JESSIE OWENS, AS BEING A MONKEY. RECENTLY THE JAPANESE PORTRAYED BARACK OBAMA AS A PODIUM MONKEY MIMICKING FOR CHANGE.

THE CHANCLLOR OF GERMANY HAS RESERVATIONS ABOUT WHERE SENATOR OBAMA SHOULD SPEAK AS A GUEST OF THEIR COUNTRY.

THIS PRESIDENTAL ELECTION IS QUITE (UNIQUE) THE STAKES ARE EXTREMELY HIGH LIKE (NEVER) BEFORE.

BECAUSE THERE COULD BE GRAVE CONSEQUENCES, BASED ON THE CANIDATE THAT WE ELECT, PERTAINING TO OUR GLOBAL REPUTABLE DIPLOMATIC REPRESENTATION. OUR CHOICE AS A ELECTIVE CONSTITUENCY, COULD SHIFT OUR NATION FROM A SOLID FOUNDATION TO QUICK SAND.

(THE CHOICE IS OURS) ONE THING IS FOR (CERTAIN) SENATOR BARACK OBAMA, WILL HAVE (NO) PROBLEMS IF HE SHOULD LOOSE, BECAUSE ALL HE HAS TO DO IS HEAD FOR HOLLYWOOD, BECAUSE HE IS ONE DAMN GOOD ACTOR. HOWEVER THE ETHNIC AND CUSTOMARY RELIGIOUS STANDARDS, ALSO AFFILIATIONS, HAVE ALWAYS BEEN SCRUTINIZED FOR AMERICAN PRESIDENTS IT APPEAR THAT THE STANDARDS HAVE BEEN (RELAXED) BY DEMOCRATS FOR SENATOR BARACK OBAMA. BECAUSE HE IS BLACK.

MOTIVATED BY OVER NINETY PERCENT OF OTHER BLACKS HERDING TO SUPPORT HIM POLITICALLY. AND THIS IS WHY I ELABORATE SO EXTENSIVELY ON HERDING, BECAUSE IT CAN BE POLITICALLY DEVASTATING AND SELF DESTRUCTIVE.

AS THE CLINTONS EXPERIENCED, THEIR PARTY THROW THEM UNDER THE BUS, FOR A PRETENTIOUS LIBERAL UNKNOWN ARROGANT BLACK MAN. THIS IS UNPRECEDENTED IN OUR SOCIETY, THE REPUBLICANS ELECTED SENATOR MCCAIN, OVER MITT ROMNEY, MOSTLY DUE TO HIS MORMAN ALLEGIANCE.

YET SENATOR BARACK OBAMA, IS A TWENTY YEAR (MEMBER) OF A CONGREGATION, THAT DESPISE AMERICA AND (WHITES);

AND HE IS REWARDED WITH THE DEMOCRATIC NOMINATION FOR PRESIDENT. HOWEVER PAY (VERY) CLOSE ATTENTION TO (WHITE) ELITE DEMOCRATIC STRATEGIST THEIR MOUTHS ARE CHANGING FROM CROSS TO VERTICAL, IN ORDER TO APPROPIATELY FIT THE BLACK ANATOMY.

SENATOR BARACK OBAMA, AND HIS HERDING AFRICAN AMERICAN CONSTITUENCEY, HAVE REORGANIZE THE STRUCTURE OF THE DEMOCRAT PARTY. BASED ON A POLITICAL BLUNDER, LETS DEAL STRICTLY WITH (REALITY) SENATOR BARACK OBAMA IS A (BLACK) MAN, THAT IS DEEMED TO HAVE AFFILIATION WITH RACIST RADICAL INDIVIDUALS;

THERE ARE QUESTIONABLE RESERVATIONS REGARDS TO LOYALTY FOR THE UNITED STATES OF AMERICA.

HE HAS A MALICIOUS TONE OF ELITE DICTATING ARROGANCE, AND THE DEMOCRATS ARE TRYING TO SHOVE THIS MAN DOWN THE THROAT OF THE GENERAL PUBLIC AS SOME KIND OF A PRESIDENT JOHN F. KENNEDY EFFIGY. UNLESS THE DEMOCRAT PARTY (WHITE) ELDER ELITES, HAVE A (MASTER) PLAN TO STABILIZE COHESION, TO RECTIFY THIS POLITICAL BLUNDER. THEIR PARTY HAVE POLITICAL PROBLEMS BEYOND COMPREHENSION, EVEN TO THE POINT OF SELF DESTRUCTION.

THIS IS THE GENERAL ELECTION, FOR THE MOST POWERFUL POSITION IN THE WORLD, AND IF ANY ONE TAKE ON THE ROLL OF TRYING TO BULL SHIT THEIR WAY THERE, IS GOING TO BE SCRUTINIZED TO NO END, AND DISAPPOINTED WITH A POLITICAL (ENDING) CAREER.

SENATOR BARACK OBAMS, WAS GIVEN A MEDIA PASS DURING THE PRIMARY, THE CARTOON SKIT ON THE COVER OF THE NEW YORKER MAGAZINE, IS JUST THE BEGINNING, SO HE HAD BETTER CINCH UP HIS BELTS, BECAUSE THE RIDE IS GOING TO HIT HORRIFYING TURBULENCE.

HOWEVER I WILL ELABORATE ON THE FLAWED DEMOCRATIC PRIMARY PROCEDURE, THAT MOST LIKELY ENABLE SENATOR BARACK OBAMA TO SUCCEED IN WINNING THE PRIMARY, THE AMERICAN CITIZENS ARE NOT STUPID. SENATORS CLINTON AND OBAMA, ACCUMULATED APPROXIMATELY THE SAME AMOUNT OF

POPULAR CONSTITUENCY, BUT THEIR SYSTEM CONSIST OF UNCOMMITTED SUPER DELEGATES, AND THEY (CHOOSE) SENATOR OBAMA, OPPOSE TO SENATOR CLINTON, COULD IT BE BECAUSE SENATOR BARACK OBAMA IS (BLACK). AND HAVE OVER NINETY PERCENT OF BLACKS HERDING AROUND HIM POLITICALLY SUPPORTIVE.

SO REALISTICALLY THIS COULD BE SYMPATHETIC APPEASEMENT TO SEDUCE IN AN EFFORT (NOT) TO ANGER AND ALIENATE BLACK VOTERS. NOW THAT THEY HAVE CHOSEN SENATOR OBAMA, THEY ARE SUCCUMB BY A PROCESS OF HERDING BLACKS.

WHICH IS THE MOST DANGEROUS POLITICAL MOVE SENSE THE NEW DEAL OF PRESIDENT FRANKLIN ROOSEVELT, NEW DEAL OF NINETEEN THIRTY FIVE. INITIATING SOCIAL PROGRAMS TO INCLUDE BLACKS.

SOUTHERN WHITES SHIFTED TO THE REPUBLICAN PARTY, THEY WERE ANGRY BECAUSE BLACKS HAD (NOT) PAID INTO SOCIAL SECURITY IN THE SOUTH, BUT BASED ON IT BEING A FEDERAL PROGRAM, THEY WOULD RECEIVE A EQUAL SHARE.

REALISTICALLY CHRONOLOGICAL RECORDS OF POLITICAL SIGNIFICANT EVENTS, SUBSTANTIATE WHEN YOU (APPEASE) BLACKS, YOU RUN THE RISK OF ALIENATING (WHITES), THAT IS A INEVITABILITY CONSIDERED TO BE IMMORTAL IN A DIVERSE CULTURAL AMERICAN SOCIETY.

AND THE DEMOCRAT PARTY HAS (CHOSEN) THIS STAUNCH ELITE LIBERAL ARROGANT IMPOSTER TO THE CORE.

AND INTEND TO PASS HIM OF AS PRESIDENTAL MATERIAL IS LUDICROUS, WHICH MOST LIKELY IS GOING TO SABOTAGE THEIR PARTY, ONE WAY OR THE OTHER.

AND WHEN I REFER TO ONE WAY OR THE OTHER, THE OVERALL MAJORITY OF ELITE (WHITES), ARE (NOT) WELL VERSED ON AFRICAN AMERICAN GENETIC TRAITS, WHICH HAVE A IDEALISTIC INHERITED TAUGHT PHILOSOPHICAL DERRANGED PRECEPTION OF THE DECLARATION OF INDEPENDANCE AND THE CNSTITUTION, ALSO MOST GOVERMENTAL MORALISTIC PROCEDURES. ALSO THEY ARE EXTREMELY TEMPERAMENTAL REGARDS TO ETHICS,

AND ARE OBSESSED WITH CREATIVE AUTHORITATIVE REPRESENTATION, AND HAVE MINIMUM RESPECT FOR EDUCATIONAL BACK GROUND QUALITY.

HOWEVER ONCE THEY REACH POLITICAL PINNACLE TO BE ELECTED TO A COCONTROLLING POSITION, THEIR (BIAS) INSTINCTS DICTATE TO REPLACE QUALIFIED (WHITES) WITH INFERIOR (BLACKS);

WHICH IS CONSISTENT WITH THE HERDING PROCESS, THE MAJORITY OF BLACKS HAVE (NOT) FIGURED OUT THAT THE CENSUS BUREAU DICTATE THAT THERE ARE THREE HUNDRED MILLION PEOPLE IN THE UNITED STATES OF AMERICA, OF THAT THREE HUNDRED MILLION THERE ARE (ONLY) APPROXIMATELY THIRTY SIX MILLION AFRICAN AMERICANS.

SO BASED ON EFFICIENCY IN (ANY) METHODOLOGY THERE ARE MORE QUALIFIED WHITE THAN BLACKS.

UNFORTUNATELY MOST AFRICAN AMERICANS IGNORE THIS FACTOR, AND THIS IS WHY IN MOST CITIES HEADDED BY BLACK MAYORS, THEY ARE INFESTED WITH CRIMINAL ACTIVITY, BECAUSE ONCE THE MAYOR TAKE OFFICE, HE RELENT TO THE HERDING PROCESS, AND REPLACE WHITES, WITH MOST BLACKS, THAT TEND TO HERD AND SABOTAGE THE JUSTICE SYSTEM. REGARDS TO BLACK HERDING MYTHICAL SUPERIORITY, BASED ON BLACK DEPRAVATION.

SO AS A RESULT MOST MORAL AND AFFLUENT, BLACK AND WHITE, MOVE TO THE SUBUBS. AND THE INNER CITY BECOME A BLACK CRIMINAL MORGUE. THE MAJORITY OF AFRICAN AMERICANS, THAT RESIDE IN AMERICA. IS INEPT TO THE FUNDAMENTALS OF CHRONOLOGICAL MORALISTIC HERITAGE OF VALIDITY, RELATED TO DISTINGUISHED QUALITY HISTORICALLY. SO MOST BLACKS RATIONALIZE REGARDS TO (REALITY); TO JUSTIFY THEIR INCOMPETENCE REGARDS TO INTELLECTUAL (PARITY);

WHICH IS MANIFESTED THAT AMERICA IS UN-JUST, AND WHITES ARE RESPONSIBLE FOR BLACK INEQUALITY.

THE MAJORITY OF AFRICAN AMERICANS ARE ENGROSSED WITH A MYTHICAL THEORY THAT THEY ARE THE SMARTEST PEOPLE ON THE PLANET, ONLY IF SOME ONE WOULD OFFER THEM A CHANCE TO PROVE IT.

YET THEY NEGLECT TO PREPARE THEM SELVES WITH INTELLECT, TO ATTAIN VARIOUS RESPONSIBILITIES.

THERE ARE A VAST MAJORITY OF EDUCATED BLACKS, THAT IS UNABLE TO DECIPHER THE DIFFERENCE BETWEEN MORALITY AND IMMORALITY, PERTAINING TO THE FUNDAMENTALS OF (REALITY), THEY TEND TO IMPROVISE WITH AN ENIGMA DISCOURSE.

AND SENATOR BARACK OBAMA IS THE EPITOME OF THIS UNSAVORY BLACK MYTHICAL GENETIC TRAIT, MALIGNED WITH IMPROVISING ARROGANT IMPLICATIONS THAT HE IS THE MESSIAH OF INTELLECT.

AND EVERY ONE ELSE IS STUPID, AND HE IS TOTALLY UNAWARE THAT THE ELITE (WHITE) DEMOCRATIC ESTABLISHMENT ARE LEADING HIM TO POLITICAL SLAUGHTER ETERNALLY. AND WILL STILL MAINTAIN HERDING BLACK VOTERS WITHIN THE DEMOCRATIC PARTY.

(REALITY) IS INEVITABLE, ALSO IMMORTAL. AND CAN (NOT) BE DISTORTED IF ONE CHOOSE TO ADHERE.

SENATOR BARACK OBAMA WAS APPROXIMATELY THREE YEARS OLD, WHEN AFRICAN AMERICANS, CIVIL AND VOTING RIGHTS WAS RESTORED FORM THE GRASP OF THE SOUTHERN DEMOCRATS.

HOWEVER IF (ANY) INDIVIDUAL BLACK OR WHITE, PARTICIPATE IN A SOCIAL GATHERING THAT HAVE DISDAIN FOR THE UNITED STATES OF AMERICA IS FANTASIZING A FAIRYTALE, AND IT IS QUITE OBVIOUS THEY ARE INEPT TO THE FUNDAMENTALS OF (REALITY) RELATED TO THE MORALITY THAT THIS COUNTRY WAS FOUNDED ON.

SENATOR BARACK OBAMA, MOST DEFINITELY HAVE A DISTINCT OVERSIGHT OF PEOPLE IN GENERAL, THE AUTHENTICITY OF MOST AFRICAN AMERICANS, ARE INHERENTLY SPORADIC, REGARDS TO AMERICAN DIVERSE CULTURE. HOWEVER THEIR PREMISE IS (ALL) ABOUT THEM.

AND THERE ARE SELF APPOINTED VAIN BLACK SYMPATHIZERS, THAT DOMINATE SOCIETY WITH COMPLEX RHETORICAL SPEECHES, RELATED TO DESTITUTION, PERTAINING TO EQUALITY. BASED ON DIVISIVE

CONGLOMERATION WITHOUT A COMMON SOLUTION TO THEIR ENMITY MYTHICAL PROBLEMS. WHICH IS SYSTEMATIC TO THE MAJORITY OF BLACKS IN AMERICA, THAT IS A INBORN TRAIT TO DICTATE AMBIGUITY, RELATED TO SUBSTANCE OF (REALITY) MEANING THAT AMBIGUOUS LYING TO ACCOMPLISH AND SUCCEEDE IS A EMBEDDED GENETIC TRADITION, THAT IS SYSTEMIC TO THE MAJORITY OF BLACKS HISTORICALLY, IN THE UNITED STATES OF AMERICA. THERE IS A VAST SEGEMENT OF BLACKS, THAT ARE HABITUAL LIARS, IN AN EFFORT TO PERSUADE FOR PERSONAL GAIN.

AND THESE ARE BASIC TRAITS, THAT ARE UTILIZED IN A IMPOSTURE FASHION, AS A POSITIVE EFFORT TO SUBSTANTIATE MORAL VALIDITY, WHEN THEY ARE TOTALLY INCOMPETENT TO CERTAIN VANITIES OF TRANSFORMATION, RELATED TO CONSTUTIONAL DOCTRINES OF THE UNITED STATES OF AMERICA. AND WE ARE CONFRONTED WITH THE GRANDFATHER OF (ALL) BLACK IMPOSTERS, WITH SENATOR BARACK OBAMA.

OPITIMIZING HIS INEPT RHETORIC, TO THE FACTION OF GLOBAL DOCTRINE TO DECEIVE FOR PERSONAL STABILITY, IN AN EFFORT TO CONVINCE AND ATTAIN INDIVIDUAL NOTORIETY, IN ORDER TO BE ELECTED PRESIDENT OF THE UNITED STATES OF AMERICA.

THE MORAL FABRIC OF OUR NATION IS BEING DEMORALIZED, AND SEEM TO BE DISSIPATING INTO IMMORALITY.

AND IF SENATOR BARACK OBAMA IS ELECTED PRESIDENT, WE WILL SLOWLY SELF DESTRUCT WITHIN, BECAUSE THE MAJORITY OF (WHITES) ARE INEPT TO THE UNSAVORY MOTIVATED BLACK IDEOLOGY THAT SOME AFRICAN AMERICANS ARE SEDUCED TO HATRED FOR WHITES.

THIS IS A (REALITY) THAT HAS BEEN SUPPRESSED, BUT COVERTLY ACTIVE SENSE THE (NAT TURNER) ERA OF EIGHTEEN THIRTY ONE, ONE HUNDRED AND SEVENTY SEVEN YEARS LATER.

SENATOR BARACK OBAMA, HAS STIMULATED THIS MYTHICAL INSANITY, THAT BLACKS ARE GOING TO BE

(HERDING) BEHIND A CONGO CHIEF, SPEAKING FOR THE CITIZENS OF AMERICA.

MOSTBLACKSWOULDPREFERTHATTHEFUNDAMENTALS OF OUR CONSTUTION BE NEGATED AND EQUATED WITH THEIR (OWN) CONGO RELATIVE DISCIPLINE OF MYTHICAL PRECEPTION, RELATED TO RADICAL TAUGHT MISCONCEPTIONS CONCERNING THE FUNDAMENTAL MORALITY OF AMERICA.

AND A (FULL) BLOWN EXPOSURE OF THIS INEPT ANXIETY, WAS DISPLAYED BY SENATOR BARACK OBAMA, FORMER (EXCEPTED) CHURCH CONGREGATION MINISTER. AND THIS IS A EMBEDDED CYNICISM WITH A LARGE SEGEMENT OF AFRICAN AMERICANS, THROUGH OUT AMERICA.

MEANING WIN OR LOOSE THE ELECTION, SENATOR OBAMA HAS CREATED A REBELLIOUS INSIDIOUS MYTHICAL REVOLUTION, BY BLACKS AGAINST THE (WHITE) CONTROLLED ESTABLISHMENT.

AND THE MAJORITY OF BLACKS ARE SO ENGULFED WITH THIS STUPIDITY, UNTIL THET WILL (NEVER) REALIZE THE GRAVE CONSEQUENCES THAT COULD OCCUR, TO MOSTLY INNOCENT BLACKS, THAT THINK THIS ELITE LYING ERRATIC, SOME TIME GIBBERISH SPEAKONG IMPOSTER, THOUGHT TO BE A BLACK MESSIAH);

MOST AFRICAN AMERICANS, HAVE A DEVIOUS CONCEPT PERTAINING TO REALISM, THEIR GENETIC TRAITS ARE METHODICAL TO CHANGE WHAT EVER IS LEGALLY VALIDATED TRADITIONAL IN AMERICA. TO A WITCH CRAFT DOCTRINE, IN ORDER TO APPEASE THEIR (OWN) SATISFACTION OF INDOCTRINATED IGNORANCE.

BECAUSE MOST BLACKS HAVE A BIOLOGICAL INSIDIOUS VINDICTIVE BEHAVIOR REGARDS TO AMERICAN PRINCIPLES, WHICH MOST DEEM TO BE UN-JUST TO THEIR METHODOLOGY OF CYNICISM.

THIS BOOK IS (NOT) A CONDEMNATION OF BLACKS OR WHITES, NEITHER RACIST INNUENDO.

BUT INTENDED TO REVEAL THE GENERAL CONSENSUS OF CHRONOLOGICAL SIGNIFICANT EVENTS , PERTAINING TO (REALITY); CORRELATED BY GENETIC CONTROLLABILITY,

EMBEDDED IN THE IMMORTALIZATION OF THE HUMAN RACE.

THERE ARE VAGRANTS IN (EVERY) NATIONALLY, BASED ON SELECTIVE IGNORANCE, RELATED TO PRINCIPLES.

HOWEVER UNFORTUNATELY THE MAJORITY OF AFRICAN AMERICANS, CHOOSE TO BE THE RECIPIENTS FOR THE (AWARD) OF THIS UNSAVORY STIGMATIZATION, RELATED TO HERDING.

THE REALITY OF HISTORICAL STATISTICAL DATA IS INEVITABLE, AND BLACKS HAVE (CHOSEN) TO BE THE STANDARD BARRIERS OF POLITICAL IGNORANCE . CLAIMING HERDING INEQUITIES.

MOST AFRICAN AMERICANS ARE THE STANDARD BARRIERS OF SELF DESTRUCTIVE VIRULENCY, AND DEPREDATED SYSTEMATIC STIGMATIZATION. RELATED TO THEIR ERODING SELF DESTRUCTION BY (CHOICE) FOR INSTANCE A SEGEMENT OF BLACKS ARE THE STANDARD BARRIER OF MOST CHILDREN BORN OUT OF WEDLOCK, HIGH SCHOOL DROP OUT, PENAL INCARCERATION, AND THE NUMBER (ONE) RECIPIENT OF SEXUAL CONTAGIOUS AIDS. THESE EGREGIOUS TRAITS REPRESENT ENORMOUS BRAIN DYSFUNCTION THAT HAS A DISTINGUISH QUALITY OF INSANITY.

AND THERE IS (NO) METHODOLOGY OF MORAL COMPREHENSION TO ALLEVIATE. THEIR BELEAGUERED AMBITION IS TO FORTIFY IMMORALITY AS A WAY OF LIFE. WITH A CESSPOOL MENTALITY, AND EXPECT OTHERS TO ENDORSE THEIR CONGO IDEOLOGY.

PERTAINING TO FUNDAMENTAL ALOOF IGNORANCE, THAT IS A CONGLOMERATE ABSURDITY, THAT MOST BLACKS HAVE HAD AN OBSESSION WITH HISTORICALLY, SENSE BEING BROUGHT TO AMERICA IN SIXTEEN NINETEEN. REGRETFULLY IN PRESENT DAY SOCIETY, THERE IS A LARGE SEGMENT OF AFRICAN AMERICANS, THAT ARE JUST AS HOSTILE AND POLITICAL ILLITERATE, AND PRIMITIVE AS THEY WERE DURING SERVITUDE, BASED ON PREDICATED BIOLIGICAL GENETIC HEREDITY, THAT IS SUSTAIN WITH EGOTISTICAL VINDICTIVE HERDING PERSUASION, BY SELF APPOINTED BLACK LEADERS, THAT IS (ERODING) THE

CONFIDENCE OF (MANY) BLACKS IN THE FUNDAMENTAL STRUCTURE OF MORALITY, THAT OUR (AMERICA) WAS FOUNDERED (ON).

THE MAJORITY OF AFRICAN AMERICANS, HAVE SMALL DYSFUNCTIONAL SHALLOW BRAINS, THAT IS EMBEDDED IN PREHISTORIC CONGO ODEOLOGY, TO THINK THAT THEY CAN INFILTRATE AMERICAN TRADITIONAL GOVERNING CUSTOMS, WITH A PRINCPILE OF ASIATIC SOCIALISM.

BECAUSE CHRONOLOGICAL RECORDS OF SIGNIFICANT EVENTS, DICTATE SUCH BEHAVIOR FROM REBELLIOUS SELF APPOINTED BLACK LEADERS, SUCH AS THE GABRIEL BROTHERS,EIGHTEEN HUNDRED. DAVID WALKEREIGHTEEN TWENTY NINE, CHARLES DESLONDES, EIGHTEEN TWELVE, NAT TURNER, EIGHTEEN THIRTY ONE, HENRY HIGHLAND GARNET, EIGHTEEN FORTY THREE, THERE ARE NUMEROUS MYTHICAL PRECEPTIONS PERTAINING TO THE TRANSFORMATION OF AFRICANS TO AMERICA.

HOWEVER (REALITY) IS CONSISTENT IF NOT DISTORTED, AFRICANS WERE UNCIVILIZED, AS THE NATIVE INDIANS WERE, AND HAD TO BE (TAUGHT);

THE REFINEMENT OF AMERICAN CULTURAL INTELLECT BY (WHITES) IN ESSENCE THE CREDIBILITY FOR (ALL) AFRICAN AMERICANS PROGRESSIVE ATTAINMENT IN AMERICA IS DUE TO THE TOLERANCE OF WHITES. AND IF BLACKS HAD BEEN MORE RECEPTIVE TO THE GENERAL PRINCIPLE OF AMERICAN ETHNICS, THERE WOULD HAVE BEEN A DRAMATIC (CONCILIATION) REGARDS TO SERVITUDE.

INSTEAD OF BARBARIC HOSTILITY FOR THE CONTROL OF REBELLIOUS BLACKS. THE PERSECUTION OF SOME AFRICAN AMERICANS FOR ALMOST FOUR HUNDRED YEARS, IS (NOT) BECAUSE OF THEIR ETHNIC COLOR. UNFORTUNATELY IT IS THEIR INABILITY TO CONFORM TO THE VALIDITY OF MORALITY, WHICH IS CONSISTENT WITH THE FUNDAMENTALS OF AMERICAN TRADITIONS, AND THE MAJORITY WILL (NEVER) INTERCEDE FROM THIS INSIDIOUS IMMORTAL IGNORANCE.

CONSERVATIVE AFRICAN AMERICANS ARE SOME OF THE MOST UNDERRATED PEOPLE IN AMERICA INTELLECTUALLY,

BECAUSE THEY QUALIFY TO EVALUATE HOG PIN HERDING BLACK MENTALITY.

AND EAGERLY REFUSE TO BE INTIMIDATED, REGARDS TO ENTERING INTO A SEDUCTIVE ALIENATING ALLIANCE OF BIAS STUPIDITY.

SO AS A RESULT THEY ARE SCORNED BY THE MAJORITY OF POLITICAL LIBERAL INEPT BLACKS, INCLUDING THEIR IMMEDIATE FAMILY MEMBERS. HOWEVER THIS IS A RELENTLESS POLITICAL PERSUIT OF STIGMATIZATION

CREATED BY THE SOUTHERN DEMOCRATS, DURING THE EIGHTEEN SIXTIES, AFTER THE CIVIL WAR.

THE DEMOCRATIC STRONG HOLD IN THE SOUTH, LITERALLY DROVE THE REPUBLICANS OUT OF THE SOUTHERN STATES, WHICH WAS THERE TO TEACH FORMER SLAVES INTELLECT.

IT BECAME SO BRUTAL, UNTIL AFRICAN AMERICANS WERE PHISICALLY FORCED TO BECOME LOYAL DEMOCRATS.

AND DURING THE EARLY THIRTIES PRESIDENT ROOSEVELT, SEALED THE DEAL WITH SOCIALISTIC BRIBERY, AND THE PROMOTION OF TWO BLACKS IN THE MILITARY, THAT ENTICED OTHER HERDING BLACK TO DEMOCRATIC LOYALTY.

AND THIS POLITICAL MENOPOLY IS STILL IN EXISTENCE, PERTAINING TO BLACKS WITHIN THE DEMOCRATIC PARTY TODAY.

THE FUNDAMENTAL ACT OF ASTUTE UNSAVORY AGGRESSION, AND THE SEDUCTION OF HERDING BLACK LOYALTY TO THE DEMOCRATIC PARTY THAT HAS EXISTED FOR APPROXIMATELY ONE HUNDRED AND FORTY THREE YEARS TO DATE.

HOWEVER THE DEMOCRAT PARTY ARE GOING TO (REGRET) TO THEIR SOUL THAT THESE POLITICAL ENTRAPMENTS (EVER) OCCURRED, BECAUSE AS OF TO DATE THE (DEMOCRAT PARTY) IS IN HORRIFIC CHAOS.

DUE TO AFRICAN AMERICAN POLITICAL INVASION FOR SUPERIORITY, AND THEY CAN SEND (ALL) THE LYING DEMOCRATIC TALKING STRATEGIST EVER, BUT THE VALIDITY OF REALITY IS INEVITABLE.

THE POLITICAL SUPERIORITY OF THE CLINTONS, HAS BEEN CAPTIVATED AND BESTOWED TO A BLACK MESSIAH AS THE DEMOCRATIC PARTY LEADER. MEANING SENATOR BARACK OBAMA AND HIS HERD.OF BLACK CONSTITUENCY, WHICH THERE IS CONTEMPTIBLE ANARCHY CONVEYED BY MILLIONS OF (WHITES) THAT COULD LEAVE THE DEMOCRAT PARTY ON THE BRINK OF DIASTER BECAUSE THE MAJORITY OF BLACKS ARE A UNIQUE DIVISIVE, ASIATIC MONOLITHIC EGOISTIC SOCIETY OF PEOPLE.

THAT WANT THE ENTIRE CONTINENT TO KNOW THAT THEY ARE IN (CHARGE) OF THE DEMOCRATIC PARTY, INSTEAD OF THE CLINTONS.

AND SENATOR BARACK OBAMA EXEMPLIFY MY SENTIMENTS, WITH HIS ASIA AND EUROPEAN ESCAPADE.

THE MAJORITY OF BLACKS HAVE (NEVER) UNDERSTOOD THE DIPLOMATIC DIPLOMACY, PERTAINING TO OBJECTIVES OF INTELLECTUAL MORAL VALUES, THAT GUIDED THE UNITED STATES OF AMERICA TO A UNIQUE STANDARD OF FOUNDING PRINCIPLES.

SO IN ESSENCE THEY IMPROVISE WITH A BACK WOODS NINETEEN FIFTIES AGENDA, IN AN EFFORT TO GAIN COMPASSION, IN AN ATTEMPT TO NEGATE THEIR HISTORICAL IGNORANCE, OF AMERICA FORTITUDE TO ENHANCE, BASED ON INDIVIDUAL MORAL INTELLECT, AND THIS IS THE (NONE) INGENUITY THAT IS GOING TO BE DETRIMENTAL FOR THE DEMOCRATIC PARTY. RELATED TO THE OFFICIATING OF SENATOR BARACK OBAMA, NARCISSISTS (NAT TURNER) COVERT DECITFUL INTENT TO SABOTAGE THE CREDIBILITY OF THE UNITED STATES OF AMERICA AROUND THE GLOBE, WITH A BLACK AGENDA OF MARXIST SOCIALISM.

AND THIS REVELATION IS (NOT) INTENDED TO INSINUATE THAT AFRICAN AMERICANS POLITICAL INCOMPETENCY NULLIFY THEIR ABILITY TO GUIDE AN ELECTED OR APPOINTED POLITICAL AGENDA.

BECAUSE THERE WERE AFRICAN AMERICAN (REPUBLICANS) DURING THE EIHTEEN HUNDREDS, SUCH AS OSCAR DUNN, BECAME LIEUTENANT GOVERNOR OF

LOUISIANA, HIRMAN RHODES REVELS, BECAME THE FIRST BLACK U.S. SENATOR IN EIGHTEEN SEVENTY.

BLANCHE K. BRUCE THE FIRST BLACK TO SERVE A FULL TERM IN THE U.S SENATE A REPUBLICAN ELECTED IN LOUISIANA EIGHTEEN SEVENTY FOUR. JONATHAN GIBBS, SERVED AS FLORDIAS SECRETARY OF STATE, FROM EIGHTEEN SIXTY EIGHT TO EIGHTEEN SEVENTY TWO.

LATER HE SERVED AS SUPERINTENDENT OF EDUCATION, EGBERT SAMMIS, WAS ELECTED TO FLORDIA STATE SENATE.

FRANCIS LOUIS CARDOZA, SERVED AS SOUTH CAROLINAS SECRETARY OF STATE, FROM EIGHTEEN SIXTY EIGHT UNTIL EIGHTEEN SEVENTY TWO. ALSO WAS STATE TREASURER FOR FIVE YEARS, BENTON STEWART PINCHBACK BECAME THE NATIONS FIRST BLACK GOVERNOR OF GEORGIA. DURING THE FIRST DECADE OF THE TWENTIETH CENTURY, MORE THAN SIX HUNDRED AFRICAN AMERICANS SERVED AS STATE LEGISLATURES. MORE THAN TWENTY WERE ELECTED TO THE U.S. HOUSE OF REPRESENTATIVES, TWO WERE ELECTED TO THE U.S. SENATE.

UNFORTUNATELY THESE POLITICAL BRAVE PIONEER AFRICAN AMERICANS, POLITICAL ELECTIVE STABILITY OF HOPE, . WERE BRUTALLY AND VIOLENTLY SABOTAGED BY SOUTHERN (DEMOCRATS)

SIMPLY BECAUSE THEY WERE (REPUBLICANS). WITH A MESSAGE OF SELF ESTEEM AND MORAL INTELLECTUAL DELIVERANCE, THAT COINCIDED WITH (AMERICAN) EMBEDDED PRINCIPLES OF DIVERSE INTEGRITY. THEY WERE BLATANTLY ACCUSED BY THE SOUTHERN DEMOCRATS OF BEING INCOMPETENT, AND TRYING TO RISE ABOVE THEIR NATURAL PLACE OF SERVITUDE.

IN ESSENCE IT HAS BEEN OVER ONE HUNDRED AND FORTY YEARS, THAT THE DEMOCRAT PARTY HAVE MAIMED AND SEDUCED AFRICAN AMERICANS, INTO STABILIZING THEIR POLITICAL ASPIRATIONS TO MAINTAIN A LIBERAL FASCIST AGENDA.

IT HAS BEEN OVER A HUNDRED AND FORTY YEARS OF DEMOCRATIC POLITICAL ABUSE OF AFRICAN AMERICANS,

WITH THE MAJORITY BEING SUBJECTED TO SEDUCTIVE OBLITERATED POLITICAL IGNORANCE.

CHRONOLOGICAL RECORDS OF SIGNIFICANT EVENTS, DICTATE THAT THE DEMOCRATS HAVE DEMORALIZED AND SEDUCED MOST AFRICAN AMERICANS POLITICALLY FOR CENTURIES.

AND (ACCUSED) THE REPUBLICANS OF BEING THE CULPRITS, AND THIS ABSURDITY IS RESPONSIBLE FOR OVER NINETY PERCENT OF POLITICAL IGNORANT BLACKS SUPPORTING DEMOCRATS.

HOWEVER THE DEMOCRATS HAVE (NOT) CONFRONTED A POLITICAL DILEMMA LIKE TWO THOUSAND AND EIGHT, SENSE EIGHTEEN SIXTY. WHEN THEIR CONVENTION DELIGATES FROM THE DEEP SOUTH, DURING THE PRESIDENTAL ELECTION, BETWEEN ABRAHAM LINCOLN AND STEPHEN A. DOUGLAS, WALKED OUT AND FORMED THEIR OWN SOUTHERN DEMOCRATIC PARTY,

AND THE REMAINDER OF THE DELIGATES MOVED THE CONVENTION TO BALTIMORE.

THIS WAS DURING THE AFTERMATH OF JOHN BROWNS EXECUTION OF EIGHTEEN FIFTY NINE.

WHERE BLACKS WERE AT THE CENTER OF CONTROVERSY RELATED TO SERVITUDE, WHEN A BLACK ABOLITIONIST NAMED JOHN ROCK, CONTENDED THE BLACK MAN SERVICES WILL BE REQUIRED TO STRIKE A GENUINE BLOW TO WHITES FOR FREEDOM.

ALTHOUGH SLAVERY WAS ABOLISHED IN EIGHTEEN SIXTY FIVE BY PRESIDENT ABRAHAM LINCOLN, THE SOUTHERN DEMOCRATS (STILL) HELD AFRICAN AMERICANS IN BONDAGE, WITH A DESIGN GIMMICK CALLED SHARE CROPPING, LATER IN NINETEEN SIXTY FOUR AND FIVE, WHEN THEY BECAME ELIGIBLE TO VOTE AND THEIR CIVIL RIGHTS WERE RESTORED.

THEY WERE SEDUCED AND INTIMIDATED TO SUPPORT THE DEMOCRAT PARTY BY A MARGIN OF OVER NINETY PERCENT.

HOWEVER AFTER ONE HUNDRED AND FORTY EIGHT YEARS.LATER, AFRICAN AMERICANS HAVE FINALLY

ATTAINED AN OBJECTIVE (END) TO DEMOCRATIC DEMAGOGIC POLITICAL SUPERIORITY.

WITH HERDING BLACKS BEHIND A SLICK INTELLECT RHETORIC TALKING JACK ASS, WITH LARGE EARS AND A BLACK MOUTH, FROM CHICAGO, ILLINOIS AND THE DEMOCRAT PARTY IS TRYING TO DISGUISE HIM AS A RACE HORSE. TO COMPENSATE FOR THEIR COWARDLY ANXIETY OF (CHOOSING) HIM AS THEIR PARTY LEADER.

BASED ON THEIR BEING HELD HOSTAGE BY (HERDING) BLACKS, WHICH WAS A INEPT CALCULATED DYSFUNCTIONAL ERROR, THAT COULD POTENTIALLY BE A DEVASTATING DILEMMA FOR THE DEMOCRATIC PARTY.

SIMPLY BECAUSE THEY HAVE (CHOSEN) TO ALLOW (BLACKS) TO TAKE OVER THEIR PARTY LEADER SHIP.

AND THAT IS A HORRENDOUS LABILITY, BECAUSE I AM AFRICAN AMERICAN AND HAVE A GENERAL CONSENSUS OF BLACK GENETIC IDEOLOGY THROUGH YEARS OF STUDY.

SOME ARE THE MOST ASININE PEOPLE ON GODS EARTH TO RECKON WITH, PERTAINING TO THE VALIDITY OF REALITY.

BECAUSE MOST HAVE A SYNCHRONIZED BELIEF THAT THEY ARE GODS CHOSEN PEOPLE, AND THAT THEIR DAY OF RECKONING HAS ARRIVED.

BASICALLY THE SIGNIFICANCE ARE THE SAME AS IT WAS IN EIGHTEEN THIRTY, WHEN NAT TURNER PLANNED AN INSURRECTION, BASED ON GOD COMM. AND, WHEN HE SAW VISIONS OF BLOOD ON CORN, AND HUMAN FIGURES IN THE AIR, HE WAS CONVINCED THAT HE WAS A CHOSEN PROPHET, BELIEVING IT WAS A SIGN FROM GOD TO EXTERMINATE (ALL) WHITES. HOWEVER THIS IS A TOTALLY DIFFERENT SCENARIO, WHERE OVER SEVENTY YEARS THE DEMOCRATS HAVE CREATED THIS POLITICAL SELF DESTRUCTION, BY SEDUCING AND DISTORTING REALITY TO MOST AFRICAN AMERICANS FOR THEIR PARTY LOYALTY.

AND NOW THEIR CHICKENS HAVE CAME HOME TO ROOST, IN THE FORM OF A SELF PROCLAIMED POLITICAL THUGGISH CON ARTIST, NAME BARACK OBAMA, AND HIS HERDING CONSTITUENCY OF SMALL DYSFUNCTIONAL BRAIN BLACK AND WHITES, BECAUSE HE IS WARNING THOSE

IDIOTS OF HIS INTENT, BASED ON HIS SHORT COMMENTARY AT THE DEMOCRATIC CONVENTION, AUGUST 27, 2008. WHEN HE REVEALED HIS INCENDIARY VISION OF CHANGE, BY STATING CHANGE DOES (NOT) START AT THE TOP.

IT BEGIN FROM THE (BOTTOM) , AND WITH THIS CHANGE (WE) CAN TAKE (BACK) AMERICA.

MOST WHITES ARE INEPT TO THIS KIND OF BIAS RHETORIC, UNFORTUNATELY IT ENERGIZE BLACKS TO HERD BEHIND HIM, WITH THE CONCEPT THAT HE IS FOR (US).

AND THAT IS SPECIFICALLY WHY THE DEMOCRAT PARTY IS GOING TO SUFFER GRAVE CONSEQUENCES FOR THIS CHOSEN POLITICAL BLUNDER. BECAUSE THEIR BUFFOONISH INTIMIDATED CONDESCENDING LEADERS HAVE

CONCEDED THEIR PARTY TO A BIAS BLACK CAUCUS IDEOLOGY, BEING INEPT TO THE FACT THAT CHRONOLOGICAL RECORDS OF SIGNIFICANT EVENTS DICTATE THAT MOST BLACKS FEEL CONTEMPT FOR (WHITES).

HOWEVER I MIGHT ADD THAT THE DEMOCRATS HAVE EARNED THE RIGHT TO THIS DIVISIVE RETINUE FROM BLACKS.

BASED ON THEIR REPULSIVE BRAIN WASH TACTICS OF POLITICAL DISTORTION, AND FOR BLACKS TO POSSESS THE SUPERORITY LEAD OF THEIR PARTY EVENTUALLY IT IS GOING TO BE QUITE APPROPRIATE, THAT THE DEMOCRAT PARTY NAME BE CHANGED TO THE DEMOCRATIC (BLACK) CAUCUS PARTY. IN ESSENCE THE DEMOCRATIC PARTY IS IN POLITICAL JEOPARDY, BASED ON THEIR DUBIOUS DEBACLE OF CHOOSING SENATOR BARACK OBAMA, AS THEIR PRESIDENTAL CANIDATE, OVER SENATOR HILLARY CLINTON. MANY BLACKS ARE BEGINNING TO BECOME AGITATEDLY FRUSTRATED SIMPLY BECAUSE OF THEIR INABILITY TO DEDUCE THE FUNDAMENTAL (REALITY) OF THE COMPLEXITY PERTAINING TO AMERICAN POLITICS.

THIS IS THE FIRST TIME IN AMERICAN HISTORY, THAT A BLACK HAS BEEN (CHOSEN) AS EITHER PARTY PRESIDENTAL NOMINEE.

SO BASED ON BLACKS CUSTOMARILY HERD INTO THE DEMOCRATIC PARTY, THEY ASSUME THAT THE (CHOSEN) NOMINEE SENATOR BARACK OBAMA,IS A SURE GIVEN TO BECOME PRESIDENT.

UNFORTUNATELY THE MAJORITY OF AFRICAN AMERICANS ARE GOING TO BE ENGULFED WITH THE DECEPTIVE SCHEME OF POLITICAL MANEUVERING, AND HOPEFULLY WILL COMPREHEND THAT THE DEMOCRAT PARTY IS (NOT) THE ONLY MAJOR PARTY IN AMERICA.

AND THAT (ALL) WHITE PEOPLE ARE NOT THE SAME, ALSO THEY ARE THE VAST MAJORITY IN AMERICA, AND THAT IF (ANY) MAJOR SUCCESS IS TO ACCOMPLISHED BY A BLACK, IT HAS TO BE ENDORSED BY WHITES PARTICULARLY RELATED TO POLITICS.

SO IN ESSENCE THIS INSIDIOUS CONGLOMERATION OVER SENATOR BARACK OBAMA, BY THE CYNICAL MAJORITY OF BLACKS, IS WORTHLESS AS TITS ON A BULL, UNLESS WHITES CAN BE CONVINCED THAT HE IS WORTHY OF BEING THE PRESIDENT, OF THIS GREAT NATION.

UNFORTUNATELY THERE IS A PREVAILINNG SKEPTICISM PERTAINING TO THE IGNORANCE OF AFRICAN AMERICANS, RELATED TO THE DEMOCRATIC PARTY. WHEN IN EIGHTEEN FIFTY EIGHT, STEPHEN A. DOUGLAS A DEMOCRAT DEBATED ABRAHAM LINCOLN, FOR THE ILLINOIS SENATE, HE EMPHATICALLY STATED THAT THIS COUNTRY WAS FOUNDED BY WHITE MEN, FOR WHITE MEN, AND THEIR POSTERITY FOR EVER.

ALSO IN EIGHTEEN SEVENTY, HIRMAN RHODES REVELS, A REPUBLICAN WHO REPRESENTED MISSISSIPPI, BECAME THE FIRST BLACK TO SERVE AS A U.S. SENATOR.

WHITE SOUTHERN DEMOCRATS BECAME HIGHLY INCENSED, AND ACCUSED BLACKS OF BEING IGNORANT, INCOMPETENT PEOPLE, ATTEMPTING TO RISE ABOVE THEIR NATURALLY SUBSERVIENT PLACE IN SOCIETY.

ALSO NOTED LAW ENFORCEMENT PERSONALITY F.B.I. DIRECTOR J. EDGAR HOOVER, STATED IN THE LATE FIFTIES, THAT HE WAS CONVINCED THAT BLACKS HAD BRAINS TWENTY PERCENT SMALLER THAN WHITES. I TOTALLY DISAGREE WITH HIS ANALYSIS, HOWEVER MOST

BLACKS HAVE A ABNORMAL DYSFUNCTION, RELATED TO THE DEMOCRATIC PARTY AND MORALITY, BASED ON F.B.I. DIRECTOR J. EDGAR HOOVER BEING DISPACHED BY REPUBLICAN PRESIDENT DWIGHT EISENHOWER, DURING THE LATE FIFTIES TO QUELL THE SOUTHERN DEMOCRATIC CLANNISH VIOLENCE AGAINST BLACKS SUCH AS LYNCHINGS, WATER HOSING, DOG ATTACKS, SEGREGATED SCHOOLS, AND WITH THE ASSISTANCE OF THE NATIONAL GUARD HE WAS SUCCESSFUL. UNFORTUNATELY THE DEMOCRATS CONTROLLED CONGRESS, AND PROHIBITED PRESIDENT EISENHOWER CIVIL AND VOTING RIGHTS BILL FROM PASSING, TO RESTORE EQUALITY FOR AFRICAN AMERICANS IN THE SOUTH.

HOWEVER DURING THE NINETEEN FIFTIES TRANSFORMATION ERA FOR BLACKS IN THE SOUTH.

TO ENHANCE AND RESTORE THEIR CONSTITUTION RIGHTS FROM SEPARATE BUT EQUAL, SOUTHERN DEMOCRATIC JIM CROW RULE.

PRESIDENT EISENHOWER AND F.B.I. DIRECTOR J. EDGAR HOOVER, BECAME FRUSTRATED WITH (NORTHERN) AFRICAN AMERICANS THAT COULD (VOTE) BECAUSE THE MAJORITY WERE HERDING TOGATHER (VOTING) FOR THE DEMOCRATS TO MAINTAIN CONTROL OF CONGRESS.

WHILE IN ESSENCE THE SOUTHERN DEMOCRATS, WERE MAIMING AND PROHIBITING EQUAL RIGHTS FOR THEIR SOUTHERN ANCESTORS.

F.B.I. DIRECTOR J. EDGAR HOOVER, BECAME SO INCENSED OVER THIS IGNORANCE, HE ACCUSED BLACKS OF HAVING BRAINS TWENTY PERCENT SMALLER THAN WHITES.

THERE ARE THREE FUNDAMENTAL ASSESSMENTS RELATED TO MOST AFRICAN AMERICANS, AND THAT IS POLITICAL IGNORANCE. AND THE INABILITY TO DECIPHER COMPLEX ISSURES, AND A HERDING PROCESS, THAT DICTATE INEPT DIVERSITY, AS TO WHAT SOMETHING SHOULD BE, OPPOSED TO ACTUALITY, THIS GENETIC INSTICT HAS BEEN TAUGHT AND DUPLICATED FOR HUNDREDS OF YEARS HISTORICALLY, BASED ON MYTHICAL PRECEPTIONS, RELATED TO BIAS (HERDING) IDIOSYNCRACIES.

FOR INSTANCE THE GENETIC HERDING BEHIND BOOKER T. WASHINGTON IN EIGHTEEN NINETY FIVE, THE MAJORITY OF BLACKS WERE CONVINCED BY HIS INFLUENCE, THAT SEPERATE BUT EQUAL WAS INEVITABLE IN THE SOUTH, WHICH CAUSED BLACKS IN THE SOUTHERN STATES, TO BE EXCLUDED FROM SITTING ON PUBLIC LUNCH COUNTERS, DRINKING FOUNTAINS, AND SITTING ON THE BACK OF BUSSES FOR OVER SEVENTY YEARS. UNFORTUNATELY ONE HUNDRED AND THIRTEEN YEARS LATER, MOST BLACKS ARE HERDING BEHIND ANOTHER EDUCATED ASININE LARGE EAR, BLACK MOUTH AFRICAN AMERICAN, THAT HAS BEEN (CHOSEN) AS THE DEMOCRATIC NOMINEE, TO PERSUE THE PRESIDENCY OF THIS GREAT NATION AMERICA. MEANING SENATOR BARACK HUSSIAN OBAMA, AND HE IS JUST AS INEPT TO THE FUNDAMENTALS OF THE DEMOCRATIC PARTY, AS THE MAJORITY OF POLITICAL IGNORANT BLACKS THAT IS HERDING BEHIND HIM, THEIR OBSESSION WITH THIS EGOTISTICAL POLITICAL RADICAL LYING IMPOSTER, IS BEYOND REPROACH.

ALSO THE MAJORITY OF BLACKS ARE (ASSUMING) THAT OBAMA WILL BE ELECTED PRESIDENT, NOT REALIZING THAT .THEIR BIAS IGNORANT APPROACH TO THIS POLITICAL AGENDA, WHICH IS EMPHATICALLY AROUSING POLITICAL VINDICTIVENESS AMONG A LARGE SEGMENT OF WHITES. WHICH WILL AUGMENT POLITICAL SELF DESTRUCTION FOR BARACK OBAMA, AND THE MAJORITY OF BLACKS AND SOME WHITES ARE INEPT TO THE SPECIFIED CONGLOMERATE ETHNICS OF MOST (ELITE) COMBINATION OF WHITES IN AMERICA THAT CHARACTERIZE THE MAJORITY OF AFRICAN AMERICANS, AS BEING POLITICAL (INCOMPETENT) OVERALL

HOWEVER THE DEMOCRAT PARTY HAS (CHOSEN) A SOPHISTICATED LIBERAL BLACK AS THEIR PARTY (LEADER) BASED ON HERDING BLACK SUPERIORITY, WITHIN THEIR PARTY.

INEPT TO THE FACT THAT THE MAJORITY OF AFRICAN AMERICANS ARE LIVING IN A DISTORTED ASSUMING FANTASY, CONGO GENETIC ENIGMATIC CRITERIA IN THE UNITED STATES OF AMERICA.

BECAUSE UNFORTUNATELY MOST BLACKS HAVE THE SAME PARALLEL IDEOLOGY AS PASTER WRIGHT, AND MRS OBAMA, THAT AMERICA IS A MEAN AND EVIL COUNTRY, BECAUSE IT IS CONTROLLED BY WICKID RACIST WHITE FOLKS, THAT CONTINUE TO OPPRESS BLACKS INTO POVITY.

(YET) THE OBAMAS ARE MILLION AIRS, SURROUNDED BY BLACK ASS KISSING ELITE (WHITE) DEMOCRATS.

THAT HAS CHOSEN SENATOR BARACK OBAMA AS THEIR PARTY LEADER, THAT WAS RELUCTANT TO WEAR A PATRIOTIC LAPEL FLAG PIN.

SOME TIME YOU CAN ASS KISS INTO SELF DESTRUCTION, AND THIS IS A CONSEQUENCE THAT (AWAIT) THE DEMOCRATIC PARTY,BASED ON HERDING BLACKS WITHIN THE RANKS OF THEIR PARTY.

WITH IRONIC IGNORANCE PERTAINING TO THE CULTURE OF AMERICA, WHICH MOST INEPTLY ASSUME IS FOR WHITE PEOPLE (ONLY);

AND THIS IS A CREATED IDIOTIC HERDING DISSENSION, THAT HAS CAUSED A EXCEPTIONAL LARGE SEGMENT OF AFRICAN AMERICANS TO PERISH INTO GHETTO POVITY THROUGH OUT AMERICA, WITH (NO) HOPE OF DIVERSE PROSPERITY, WRAPPED IN A COCOON OF IGNORANCE, PERTAINING TO THE FUNDAMENTALS OF AMERICA.

AND THE MAJORITY OF BLACKS ARE HERDING BEHIND SENATOR BARACK OBAMA, (ASSUMING) THAT THEY ARE GOING TO REPRESENT AMERICA WITH CONGO IDEOLOGY.

BUT TRUST ME THE DEMOCRAT PARTY, HAVE MADE A FATAL. BLUNDERING DEASTATING ERROR

THAT IS PARALLEL TO EIGHTEEN SIXTY, WHEN THE PARTY SPLIT, WALKED OUT OF THE CONVENTION, AND FORMED THE SOUTHERN DEMOCRATIC PARTY. OUR BELOVED AMERICA IS BEING BESIEGED, AND SLANDERED WITH IDIOSYNCRASY OF DEMAGOGIC DISSENSION, RELATED TO POLITICAL IGNORANCE. BASED ON ETHNIC OBSESSION, TO ATTAIN POLITICAL SUPERIORITY. THE MAJORITY OF AFRICAN AMERICANS ARE CONSUMED WITH RACIST INNUENDO, IN AN ATTEMPT TO INTIMIDATE AND

SEDUCE WHITES TO VOTE FOR A CHRONOLOGICAL LYING LIBERAL RADICAL, SENATOR BARACK OBAMA. IN ORDER TO VALIDATE THE VALIDITY OF MY SENTIMENTS, A WELL KNOWN SMALL DYSFUNCTIONAL BRAIN MEMBER OF CONGRESS, JOHN LEWIS. ON OCTOBER 11, 2008. COMPARED SENATOR JOHN MCCAIN AND GOVERNOR SARAH PALIN, TO THE LATE (RACIST) GOVERNOR GEORGE C. WALLACE, A DEMOCRAT FROM ALABAMA, DURING THE SIXTIES.

AND I AM CERTAIN THAT THIS OUTRAGIOUS RACIST VENOM, SPEWED BY JOHN LEWIS, BECAUSE HE IS TO IGNORANT TO BE CALLED CONGRESSMAN, WAS THE REASON WHY THE SOUTHERN DEMOCRATS DURING THE EIGHTEEN HUNDREDS DENOUNCED POLITICAL BLACKS AND ACCUSED THEM OF BEING INCOMPETENT AND TRYING TO RISE ABOVE THEIR NATURAL PLACE OF SERVITUDE. ALSO DURING THE FIFTIES THE LATE F.B.I. DIRECTOR J. EDGAR HOOVER, ACCUSED BLACKS OF HAVING BRAINS TWENTY PERCENT SMALLER THAN WHITES, AND WITH CHAOTIC, DEROGATORY DEMORALIZING, AMBIVALENT COMMENTS FROM BIGOT JOHN LEWIS.

ONE HAS TO WONDER IF THE SOUTHERN DEMOCRATS, AND J. EDGAR HOOVER WAS ON TO SOMETHING PERTAINING TO (SOME) BLACKS.

I HAVE A GREAT DEAL OF SIMPLISTIC CONFIDENCE IN THE DIVERSE SOCIETY OF AMERICA.

UNFORTUNATELY THE MAJORITY OF AFRICAN AMERICANS ALIENATE THEM SELVES FROM THE MORAL STANDARDS THAT AMERICA WAS FOUNDERED ON, AND FOR THREE HUNDRED AND EIGHTY NINE YEARS AGO, BASED ON SOUTHREN DEMOCRATIC PARTY, VIOLENT COERCE INTIMIDATION.

THIS TWO THOUSAND EIGHT PRESIDENTAL ELECTION IS BECOMING SO INSIDIOUS, UNTIL I AM HAVING DIFFICULTY MAINTAINING MY COMPOSURE, SIMPLY BECAUSE MOST AFRICAN AMERICANS ELUDE REALITY, BY (NOT) READING, AND A LARGE SEGEMENT (CANT);

SO IN ESSENCE THEIR MOTIVATIONS ARE BASED ON (ASSUMPTIONS) AND A DISTORTED IDEOLOGUE, FROM DECITFUL (DEMOCRATS)

THE MAJORITY OF AFRICAN AMERICANS ARE (TOTALLY) INEPT TO THE FUNDAMENTALS OF THE TWO MAJOR PARTY SYSTEM IN THE UNITED STATES OF AMERICA.

FOR INSTANCE THE BUFFOON ELECTED TO CONGRESS FROM GEORGIA,(JOHN LEWIS) IS DISTORTING THE VALIDITY OF THE MAJORITY OF THE REPUBLICAN PARTY, BASED ON STUPITIDY.

THE REPUBLICAN PARTY WAS FOUNDED IN EIGHTEEN FIFTY FOUR, ABARAHAM

LINCOLN BECAME THEIR FIRST PRESIDENT IN EIGHTEEN SIXTY, IN FIVE YEARS HE ABOLISHED SOUTHERN (DEMOCRATIC) SLAVERY FOR AFRICAN AMRICANS IN THE SOUTH, AT THE EXPENSE OF A CIVIL WAR.

WHICHFULFILLEDHISAGENDAATTHEAGEOFNINETEEN, HE WAS IN LOUIAIANA AND WITTNESSED A BLACK WOMAN BEING AUCTIONED OFF, HE STATED AT THAT TIME IF HE EVER BECAME A POLITICAL AUTHORITY, HE WOULD END THIS ATROCITY, WHICH HE DID SUCCEEDE, IN EIGHTEEN SIXTY FIVE, HE ALSO AUTHORIZED A PROCLAMATION TO GIVE EVERY AFRICAN AMERICAN FAMILY FORTY ACRES OF SOUTHERN (DEMOCRATIC) SLAVE OWNERS LAND, AND A GOVERNMENT MULE, BECAUSE MOST WERE ILLITERATE AND FARMING WAS THEIR (ONLY) MEANS OF SURVIVAL

HE ALSO INSISTED THAT SCHOOLING BE MADE AVALIABLE TO BLACKS, UNFORTUNATELY HE CHOOSE A SOUTHERN (DEMOCRAT) ANDREW JHONSON AS HIS VICE PRESIDENT, AND AFTER HIS ASSASSINATION, THEN PRESIDENT ANDREW JOHNSON, RESCINDED PRESIDENT LINCOLN ORDER, AND RETURNED THE LAND (BACK) TO THE SOUTHERN DEMOCRATIC PLANTATION SLAVE OWNERS, (NOT) REPUBLICANS.

REPUBLICAN PRESIDENT ABRAHAM LINCOLN, CHOOSE TO DISPEL AFRICAN AMERICANS FROM THE GRASP OF SOUTHERN (DEMOCRATIC) PLANTATION SLAVE OWNWRS, IN AN EFFORT FOR THEM TO BECOME INTELLECT IN A DIVERSE SOCIETY.

UNFORTUNATELY HE PAID A HEAVY PRICE WITH HIS LIFE, BASED ON HIS COMPASSION TO INTERGRATE AFRICAN

AMERICANS INTO A MORAL INTELLECT DIVERSE CIVIL SOCIETY.

(REPUBLICAN) PRESIDENT DWIGHT DAVID EISENHOWER, DURING THE FIFTIES, INITIATED THE FIRST CIVIL RIGHTS BILL FOR BLACKS IN THE SOUTHERN STATES, IN EIGHTY FIVE YEARS, HOWEVER IT WAS REJECTED, BY A DEMOCRATIC CONTROLLED SENATE, LED BY NONE OTHER THAN SENATOR LYNDON BAINES JOHNSON.

(REPUBLICAN) PRESIDENT RICHARD M. NIXON, ENDORSED AFFIRMATIVE ACTION, AND SIGNED INTO EXISTENCE DURING HIS PRESIDENCY.

(REPUBLICAN) PRESIDENT GEORGE H. BUSH, APPOINTED JUSTICE CLARENCE THOMAS TO THE U.S. SUPREME COURT, TO THE OPPISITION OF DEMOCRATIC SENATOR JOSEPH BIDEN.

(REPUBLICAN) PRESIDENT GEORGE W. BUSH APPOINTED MORE MINORITIES TO TOP AUTHORITY POLITICAL POSITIONS THAN ANY PRESIDENT IN U.S. HISTORY.

EVEN REACHED ACROSS THE ISLE, AND APPOINTED (DEMOCRAT) COLAN POWELL, TO THE FIRST AFRICAN AMERICAN POSITION AS SECRETARY OF STATE HOWEVER DURING HIS REIGN, HE COULD (NEVER) DECIPHER IF HE WAS APPOINTED OR ELECTED. WHICH IS TYPICAL DEMOCRATIC ANARCHY. DURING THE ADMINISTRATIVE LEADER SHIP, OF (REPUBLICAN) PRESIDENTS GEORGE H. BUSH AND GEORGE W, BUSH, COLEN POWELL BECAME AN INSTITUTION , REGARDS TO PROGRESSIVE ACCOUNTABILITY.

HE WAS PROMOTED TO A FOUR STAR GENERAL, SELECTED TO. GENERAL CHAIRMAN JOINT CHIEF OF STAFF.

ALSO CHOSEN AS THE FIRST AFRICAN AMERICAN TO BECOME SECRETARY OF THE UNITED STATES, THESE WERF HONORABLE POSITIONS BESTOWED UPON AN AFRICAN AMERICAN, BY (REPUBLICANS)

BASEDONINDIVIDUALMERIT, WHICHISAFUNDAMENTAL TRADITION OF THE REPUBLICAN PARTY.

BEGINNING WITH THEIR FIRST PRESIDENT ABRAHAM LINCOLN, UNFORTUNATELY THE (MAJORITY) OF BLACKS HAS (NEVER) UNDERSTOOD THIS (DIDACTIC) OVER A PEROID OF ONE HUNDRED AND FORTY THREE YEARS. AND

APPARENTLY (NEVER) WILL, WHICH LEND CREDENCE TO STATEMENTS INSINUATED BY (REPUBLICAN) PRESIDENT DWIGHT D. EISENHOWER AND F.B.I. DIRECTOR J. EDGAR HOOVER DURING THE LATE FIFTIES.

WHICH PRESIDENT EISENHOWER STATED, THAT (ALL) WE DO TO TRY AND RLIEVE BLACKS FROM THE OPPRESSION OF (DEMOCRATIC) SLAVISH IDEOLOGY. THEY RELENTLESSLY HERD BEHIND DEMOCRATS, THAT HAS ACCUSED THEM OF BEING INCOMPETENT, IGNORANT AND TRYING TO RISE ABOVE THEIR NATURAL ABILITY OF SERVITUDE.

F.B.I. DIRECTOR J. EDGAR HOOVER, MADE ACCUSATIONS THAT AFRICAN AMERICANS HAD BRAINS TWENTY PERCENT SMALLER THAN (WHITES) FIFTY ONE YEARS LATER, COLEN POWELL, AND JOHN LEWIS, ARE LIVING PROOF OF THIS INEVITABLE GENETIC AILENATING PATHETIC INEPT SICKNESS, COLEN POWELL (BETRAYED) THE TRUST THAT THE REPUBLICAN PARTY. INTRUSTED TO HIM.

HIS IMPECCABLE LEGACY, THAT (NO) OTHER AFRICAN AMERICAN IN THE HISTORY OF AMERICA HAS RECEIVED FORM THE (DEMOCRATIC) PARTY THAT HE HAS HIGH REGARD AND VENERATION FOR.

AND OF COURSE THERE IS SMALL DYSFUNCTIONAL BRAIN JOHN LEWIS, THAT DOES (NOT) HAVE THE INTELLECT TO DISTINGUISH THE DIFFERENCE BETWEEN DEMOCRATS, AND REPUBLICANS.

BYCOMPARINGSENATORMCCAINANDGOVERNORPALAN TO (DEMOCRATIC) SEGREGATIONIST, ALABAMA GOVERNOR GEORGE C. WALLACE. CHRONOLOGICAL RECORDS OF SIGNIFICANT EVENTS, DICTATE THAT THERE HAS (NEVER) BEEN A ELITE POLITICAL (REPUBLICAN) DIGNITARY, SUCH A STAUNCH (DEMOCRATIC) SEGREGATIONIST,THE LATE GOVERNOR GEORGE C. WALLACE, THAT STOOD AT THE DOORS OF A UNIVERSITY, IN AN EFFORT TO PROHIBIT BLACKS FROM ATTAINING EQUALITY, PERTAINING TO INTELLECT AND MORAL VALUES.

ALSO BLATANTLY ASSERTED PERTAINING TO BLACKS, SEGREGATION TODAY, SEGREGATION TOMORROW, AND SEGREGATION (FOREVER);

HOWEVER BEFORE I ELABORATE ON (DEMOCRATIC) PROFUNDITY, PERTAINING TO AFRICAN AMERICANS.

I AM GOING TO COMMENT ONCE MORE ON THIS REPUBLICAN IMPOSTER PARASITE COLEN POWELL, HE HAS THROWN HIS LEGACY UNDER NEATH THE CLINTONS , UNDER THE (BUS).

THERE IS ONE TROUBLING UNIQUE SCENARIO PERTAINING TO COLEN POWELL AND IT EVOLVE AROUND A FAMOUS LADY, APPOINTED AS HIS SUCCESSOR. THAT IS LOYAL, INTELLECTUAL, MORAL VALUED, AND IS INSURMOUNTABLE AS SECRETARY OF STATE, AND THAT IS MS. CONDOLEEZZA RICE. WITH THE UNCANNY IMPECCABLE EXTRAORDINARY DIPLOMATIC SKILLFUL ABILITY TO RESOLVE ISSURES AT (ANY) POLITICAL LEVEL IF POSSIBLE, WITH MORALISTIC DIPLOMACY.

WHICH LEFT COLEN POWELL IN A UNIQUE SCENARIO OF HIBERNATING SHAMBLES, REGARDS TO HIS LEGACY AS BEING THE (FIRST) AFRICAN AMERICAN APPOINTED TO THE HIGHEST POLITICAL POSITION EVER.

UNFORTUNATELY FOR HIM, SECETARY OF STATE RICE, BLANKETED HIS EGO. BY OBLITERATING HIS RETENTION AS SECETARY OF STATE.. WHICH IS SUSPECTED THE REASON FOR HIM TO RECOIL LIKE A RATTLER, WAITING TO SPEW VENOM, WHICH HE (DID) BY ENDORSING THE DEMOCRATIC PARTY, IN TWO THOUSAND AND EIGHT.

HOWEVER HE COLEN POWELL, IS INEPT TO THE FACT THAT THIS WAS THE MAIN OBJECTIVE FOR THE LATE F.B.I. DIRECTOR J. EDGAR HOOVER, DECLARING THAT BLACKS BRAINS ARE TWENTY PERCENT SMALLER THAN WHITES. BECAUSE IN NINETEEN FIFTY SEVEN, THE SENATE WAS CONTROLLED BY DEMOCRATS, LED BY (DEMOCRATIC) SENATOR LYNDON BAINES JOHNSON, THAT REJECTED (REPUBLICAN) PRESIDENT EISENHOWER (EQUALITY) CIVIL AND VOTING RIGHTS BILL FOR SOUTHERN BLACKS.

WHILE IN THE INTERIM AFRICAN AMERICANS IN THE NORTHERN STATES, WERE UTILIZING THEIR (HERDING) VOTING CONSTITUENCY WHOOPING IT UP AT THE (DEMOCRATIC) CONVENTION IN ORDER FOR DEMOCRATS

TO (DENY) SOUTHERN BLACKS THEIR EQUAL, AND CIVIL RIGHTS.

AND THAT WAS THE INTERICATE REASON FOR F.B.I. DIRECTOR J. EDGAR HOOVER SUGGESTING THAT BLACKS HAD BRAINS TWENTY PERCENT SMALLER THAN WHITES, FIFTY ONE YEARS AGO.

THE IDIOSYNCRASY RELATED TO THE (MAJORITY) OF AFRICAN AMERICANS, (HERDING) TO THE DEMOCRATIC PARTY, (DOES) INDICATE A BRAIN DYSFUNCTION, LED BY SUCH (DEMOCRATIC) POLITICAL SLAVE DRIVING INDIVIDUALS IN MODERN TIMES, SUCH AS COLEN POWELL AND JOHN LEWIS. LETS JUST EVALUATE CHRONOLOGICAL RECORDS OF SIGNIFICANT EVENTS RELATED TO (DEMOCRATIC) JUSTICE FOR BLACKS.

BEGINNING WITH EIGHTEEN SIXTY FIVE, WHEN ANDREW JOHNSON BECAME PRESIDENT AFTER THE ASSASSINATION OF (REPUBLICAN) PRESIDENT LINCOLN, THEN (DEMOCRATIC) PRESIDENT ANDREW JOHNSON, RESCINDED THE PROCLAMATION OF PRESIDENT LINCOLN, TO GIVE (EVERY) AFRICAN AMERICAN FAMILY FORTY ACRES OF SOUTHERN PLANTATION SLAVE OWNWRS LAND, AND A GOVERNMENT MULE.

AND GAVE THE LAND BACK TO THE SOUTHERN (DEMOCRATIC) SLAVE OWNERS. ALSO DURING HIS ADMINISTRATION IN EIGHTEEN SIXTY SIX, THE SOUTHERN (DEMOCRATS) FOUNDERED THE KU-KLUX-KLAN, IN HIS HOME STATE OF PULASKI, TENNESSEE. THAT TORMENTED , MAIMED AND LYNCHED, AFRICAN AMERICANS FOR APPROXIMATELY ONE HUNDRED YEARS.

UNFORTUNATELY THE MOST DEVASTATING BETRAYEL OF AFRICAN AMERICANS CAME DURING (DEMOCRATIC) PRESIDENT FRANKLIN DELANO ROOSEVELT ADMINSTRATION, WHEN HE SEDUCED BLACKS TO ALIENATE FROM THE (REPUBLIAN) PARTY.

BASED ON PRAGMATIC SOCIALISM, AND THEIR IDEOLOGUE OF GENETIC FUNDAMENTAL TRADITIONAL OBSESSION WITH (HERDING)

AND THE MOST INTRIGUING ELEMENT OF HIS ADMINISTRATION, WAS THAT FOR THE FIRST SEVEN

YEARS OF HIS PRESIDENCY, OVER EIGHTEEN BLACKS WERE LYNCHED ANUALLY, BY SOUTHERN (DEMOCRATIC) KU-KLUX-KLANSMEN, . THAT WAS REINFORCED IN NINETEEN FIFTEEN IN ATLANTA, GEORGIA. AND (DEMOCRATIC) PRESIDENT FRANKLIN DELEANO ROOSEVELT, SAT SILENTLY BY AND DID ABSOLUTELY (NOTHING) TO DETER.

LATER DURING THE FIFTIES, ELITE (DEMOCRATIC) SURROGATES OF RACIST ANARCHY, SUCH AS (DEMOCRATIC) GOVERNOR GEORGE C. WALLACE OF ALABAMA, (DEMOCRATIC) GOVERNOR ORVAL FAUBUS, OF ARKANSAS, MAYOR WOODROW MANN, OF LITTLE ROCK, ARKANSAS, AND WATER HOSING, DOG SICKING BULL CONNER.

JUST TO NAME A FIEW, THAT INSTIGATED ATROCITIES AGAINST AFRICAN AMERICANS IN THE SOUTHERN STATES, INCLUDING THE DESPICABLE ACT OF BOMBING A CHURCH IN BIRMINGHAM, ALABAMA, WITH LITTLE BLACK CHILDREN INSIDE.

THE CONSTITUTION OF (AMERICA) OFFER EVERY CITIZEN THE (RIGHT) TO TO CHOOSE,,BASED ON INDIVIDUAL INTELLECTUAL MORAL VALUES, (NOT) A PRESUPPOSITION RELATIVE TO ASSUMPTIONS, REGARDS TO (HERDING) THIS ENIGMA HAS STIGMATIZED THE (MAJORITY) OF AFRICAN AMERICANS FOR ALMOST FOUR HUNDRED YEARS.

AND THE PERSISTENCE OF THIS AGONIZING (IGNIRANCE) IS BEING SALUTED BY COLEN POWELL, JOHN LEWIS, AND THE MAJORITY OF AFRICAN AMERICANS, WHICH MAKE THE LATE F.B.I. DIRECTOR J. EDGAR HOOVER, A PERSON OF CONSIDERABLE POLITICAL COMPREHENSIBLE PRONUNCIATION. HOWEVER OUR SOCIETY TODAY CONSIST OF ADVANCED CONTEMPTABLE ARROGANCE, THAT MANY POLITICIANS INDULGE IN.

AND A LARGE SEGEMENT DEPLORE, SO IN ESSENCE THERE IS A REPREHENSIBLE ISSURE BASED ON FUNDAMENTAL DEMAGOGUERY, TO ENTICE BASED ON HUMAN IGNORANCE.

THAT TRANSPIRED ON JANUARY 20, 2009 WITH THE ELECTION OF SENATOR BARACK OBAMA FOR PRESIDENT, OF THE UNITED STATES OF AMERICA.

BASED ON HE BEING A REPLICA OF (NAT TURNER) OF THE EIGHTEEN THIRTIES IN DISGUISE, UTILIZING THE AMERICAN ENGLISH, ALONG WITH BODY STATURE AND EYE CONTACT, THAT COMPLEMENT AS A FORMALITY TO INDOCTRINATE POLITICAL INEPT BUFFOONS TO HIS NONSENSICAL IDEOLOGY. THAT COULD VERY WELL CAUSE GREAT MISFORTUNE TO OUR NATION. WHEN REV. WRIGHT INSINUATED THAT AMERICA CHICKENS IS COMING HOME TO ROOST. LITTLE DID HE KNOW HOW POLITICALLY CORRECT HE WAS. IT HAPPENED IN DRAMATIC FASHION ON JANUARY 20, 2009. OUR NATION HAS MOVED CLOSER TO DISCORD SOCIALISM.

THIS IS A ALARMING CIRCUMSTANCE, AN IF NOT CORRECTED OUR SOLVENT CREDITABILITY IS AT STEAK GLOBALLY.

TO BECOME A POLITICAL DOOR MAT FOR THE WORLD. BASED ON A ELECTED PRESIDENT (NOT) HAVING THE MORAL MENTALITY TO APPROPRIATELY GOVERN THIS NATION, BASED ON A IDEOLOGY OF INTELLECTUAL CAPITALISM. THIS GENTLEMAN IS A EXPERT (ACTOR) THAT HAS MASTERED THE CUNNING DIALECT OF ENGLISH WITH A NOTICEABLE SHRILL.

THAT HAS CHARMED THE MAJORITY OF THE POLITICAL INEPT, SMALL DYSFL FUNCTIONAL BRAIN AMERICANS TO ELECT HIM PRESIDENT.

THIS HAS (NOTHING) TO DO WITH RACE, IT HAS TO DO WITH POLITICALLY INEPT (WHITES) THAT WAS (UNABLE) TO DETECT A NAT TURNER LIKE ARROGANT SCOUNDREL, AND WILLINGLY DRANK HIS JIM JONES KOOLAID. WHICH WILL DETERMINE THE (FATE) OF MANY OF OUR LOVE ONES THAT RESIDE IN LARGE CITIES IN THE UNITED STATES OF AMERICA.

NOT (IF) BUT WHEN THIS HAPPEN, YOU SMALL DYSFUNCTIONAL BRAIN POLITICAL INEPT BUFFOONS, THAT SUPPORTED BARACK OBAMA TO BECOME PRESIDENT.

FALL TO YOUR KNEES, TURN YOUR ASS TO THE SKY, IN HONOR OF YOUR ELECTED (LORD) MESSIAH PRESIDENT BARACK OBAMA.

AND LISTEN TO HIM CONSOLE THE NATION, WITH ONE OF HIS WONDERFUL POLITICAL RHETORICAL PROPAGANDA SPEECHES, IN AN EFFORT TO CLARIFY THAT IT IS (NOT) THE TERRORIST FAULT IT IS THE UNITED STATES OF AMERICA.

BECAUSE WE ARE A DAWN RIGHT (MEAN) COUNTRY THIS PRESIDENT IS A SOCIALIST RADICAL SYMPATHIZER, THAT HAS RESERVATIONS PERTAINING TO EXECRATING AND DOMINATING RICH (WHITE) PEOPLE THAT CONTROL AMERICA.

MAY I REMIND YOU SMALL DYSFUNCTIONAL BRAIN (WHITE) POLITICAL IDIOTS, REMEMBER REV. WRIGHT PRESIDENT OBAMA PASTER FOR (TWENTY) YEARS, EMPHATICALLY STATED, THE EVIL (RICH) WHITE PEOPLE THAT CONTROL AMERICA, YOUR CHICKENS ARE COMING HOME TO ROOST THIS PRESIDENT COULD CARE LESS ABOUT THIS COUNTRY, HE IS ON A ELATED EGO, FANTASY MISSION, OF CONTROLLING (WHITE) AMERICA, AND I DEMORALIZING THEIR AGENDA.

OVER NINETY PERCENT OF AFRICAN AMERICANS CAN (NOT) DISTINGUISH RELATIVE ISSURES PERTAINING TO DEMOCRATL AND REPUBLICANS, THE ONLY THING THEY ADHERE TO IS THAT YOU ARE (WHITE)

AND THIS HAS BEEN A COVERT GENETIC TAUGHT TRADITION FOR HUNDREDS OF YEARS. HOWEVER THEY HAVE (NO) OTHER CHOICE BUT BE HYPERCRITICAL LYING IMPOSTERS.

BECAUSE IT IS INEVITABLE THAT THE MAJORITY OF AFRICAN AMERICANS, DEPEND ON (WHITES) FOR THEIR SURVIVABILITY, REGARDS TO SUSTAINABR LE EMPLOYMENT.

AND PRESIDENT BARACK OBAMA IS NO EXCEPTION, HOWEVER OUR NATION IS MARED IN A POLITICAL QUAGMIRE. V.I.A. THE DEMOCRATIC PARTY, IN MY WRITINGS, I HAVE INDICATED POLITICAL SELF DESTRUCTION OF MOST AFRICAN AMERICANS, ALSO THEIR HERDING PROCESS WOULD DEMINISH THE DEMOCRATIC PARTY.

IT IS POTHETICALLY ASTOUNDING

HOW GULLIBALE A LARGE SEGMENT OF (VOTERS) CAN BE IN AMERICA TODAY TO ELECT A CANADIATE OF THE

MOST POWERFUL NATION IN THE WORLD. BASED ON HIS CHARADE OF CHARACTERISTIC FRIVOLITY, RELATED TO HIS ETHNICS, AND SOCIALISTIC IDEOLOGY. PERTAINING TO THE UNITED STATES OF AMERICA.

IT IS CONCEIVABLE THAT WHEN HE AND HIS WIFE, IS IN PRIVACY THEY BUMP THEIR CLINCHED FIST TOGATHER, AND YELL THANK GOD FOR REV. WRIGHT. BECAUSE WE CONNED THESE SMALL DYSFUNCTIONAL BRAIN POLITICAL INEPT (WHITES) TO VOTE ME IN.

AND NOW THAT I AM PRESIDENT, MY INTENT IS TO BRING THE RICH ONES THAT CONTROL THIS COUNTRY, CHICKENS HOME TO ROOST.

THIS IS A POLITICAL PHENOMENON CAST ON OUR NATION, BASED ON POLITICAL IGNORANCE OF (WHITES) RELATED TO THEIR ILLITERACY OF BLACK CULTURE, MOST BLACKS ARE (NOT) OF THE SAME POLITICAL CONCEPT AS WHITES, THERE IS A INEVITABLE HOSTILITY PERTAINING TO PAST ISSURES, RELATED TO (ALL) WHITES.

AND IT IS PRIMARILY BASED ON GENETIC IGNORANCE, AFRICANS DERIVE FROM A CONTINENT OF TRIBAL (CHIEF) CONTROL. .

AND PRESIDENT BARACK OBAMA IS RESONATING TO THIS GENETIC DOCTRINE IN THE UNITED STATES OF AMERICA.

FOR INSTANCE JUST PAY ATTANTION TO HIS CONNED RHETORIC, SPEECHES HE DICTATE WITH SOCIALISTIC ARROGANCE.

MOST INTELLECT CITIZENS THAT RESIDE IN THE UNITED STATES OF AMERICA, ARE AWARE THAT THE VICE PRESIDENT SERVE AT THE REQUISITION OF DIPLOMACY TO THE PRESIDENT.

HOWEVER PRESIDENT BARACK OBAMA, (OWN) JOSEPH BIDEN, AS HE BLATANTLY REFER TO HIM AS (MY) VICE PRESIDENT.

DURING THE LATE FIFTIES, F.B.I. DIRECTOR J. EDGAR HOOVER, ACCESSED BLACKS AS HAVING BRAINS TWENTY PERCENT SMALLER THAN WHITES, UNFORTUNATELY HE NEGLECTED TO REALIZE THAT THIS IS A HORRIFIC CONTAGIOUS DISEASE.

BECAUSE A HERDING SEGEMENT OF (WHITES) IN THE UNITED STSTES OF AMERICA, IS TERRIBLY AFFECTED WITH THIS DYSFUNCTIONAL ABNORMALITY TO SUCH A DEGREE UNTIL THEY MAKE AFRICAN AMERICANS, LOOK LIKE POLITICAL (GENIUSES)

WITH BOUNCING CONGRESS REPRESENTATIVE NANCY POLOSI, LEADING THE CHARGE, WITH THIS POLITICAL INEPTNESS REGARDS TO PRESIDENT BARACK OBAMA.

APPLAUDING HIM AND GRINNING LIKE A JACKASS, EATING THORN BRIERS. THIS IS A PATHETIC BUFFOONISH, POLITICAL INEPT SYNDROME HAVING TO DO WITH (WHITE) PATRIOTISM, REGARDS TO (BLACK) DEMAGOGUERY ALSO THE NATION REBELLING AGAINST THE CLINTON PROPAGANDA. AND PRESIDENT GEORGE W, BUSH, ON A RAMPAGE GOVERNMENT SPENDING BINGE, AS IF HE HAD HIT THE SAUCE AGAIN.

ALSO A ROBOTIC OVER SEVENTY YEAR OLD, SENATOR JOHN MCCAIN, THAT WAS STUCK WITH THE HORSE AND BUGGY AGENDA, RELATING TO HIS MILITARY SERVICE, THAT HE HAD SERVED THIS COUNTRY SENSE SEVENTEEN YEAARS OLD, AND HAVE THE SCARS TO PROVE IT.

APPARENTLY SENATOR MCCAIN, IS DEVASTATED WITH SENILITY NOT TO REALIZE THAT MILLIONS OF RED BLOOD AMERICANS, HAVE SACRIFICED THEIR (LIVES)

TO DEFEND OUR DEMOCRACY, BASED ON PRESERVING CAPITALISM I WILL (FOREVER) SUSPECT THAT THERE WAS A COVERT POLITICAL CONSPIRACY INTERNALLY, REGARDS TO THE REPUBLICAN PRIMARY, TO OUSTS MITT ROMNEY, I WILL DEDICATE THIS LINE TO THE LATE PAUL HARVEY, MAY GOD BLESS HIS SOUL, YOU FIGURE THE REST OF THE STORY (GOOD DAY). HOWEVER THIS BOOK IS (NOT) WRITTEN TO COMPROMISE INTEGRITY. BUT TO EXPLOIT THE FUNDAMENTALS OF (REALITY); WE RESIDE IN THE GREATEST NATION ON GODS PLANET, OUR CONSTITUTION OFFER THE RIGHT TO MAINTAIN OR DESTROY THROUGH AN ELECTORIAL PROCESS, BASED ON A TWO PARTY SYSTEM, DEMOCRAT OR REPUBLICAN.

HOWEVER IF WE CHOOSE (NOT) TO ALLEVIATE, BASED ON THE FOUNDERING PRINCIPLES, IT IS A VERY DISTINCT

POSSIBILITY, THAT WE WILL SELF DESTRUCT AS A CIVIL NATION.

SIMPLY BECAUSE THE RADICAL SOCIALISTIC DEMOCRATS, ARE IN CONTROL OF ALL THREE FACTIONS OF OUR POLITICAL BRANCHES, LED BY A PRESIDENT, THAT HAS ILLUSTRATED BY AFFILIATIONS, OF HAVING RESERVATIONS REGARDS TO HIS PATRIOTISM FOR THE UNITED STATES OF AMERICA. THIS IS ONE OF THE MOST DEVASTATING TRAGEDIES, TO EVER OCCUR SENSE THE INCEPTION OF AMERICA.

SMALL DYSFUNCTIONAL BRAIN POLITICAL IDIOTS, HAVE ELECTED A PRESIDENT (WITHOUT) PRECISE CLARITY OF WHERE HIS PLACE OF BIRTH WAS. WHILE A SEGMENT OF POLITICAL INEPT MIS-FITS, ARE SLOBBERING OVER BARACK OBAMA, THERE ARE NATIONS PLANNING OUR DESTRUCTION. PARTICULARLY IRAN, AND RUSSIA, THE RUSSIANS ARE ALREADY PREDICTING OUR DEMISE INTERNALLY.

SIMPLY BECAUSE THEY UNDERSTAND AFRICAN CONGO IDEOLOGY, OF BEING CONTROLLED BY A TRIBAL CHIEF (NOT) A PRESIDENT.

THIS IS A COMPLEX GENETIC CONTROLLABILITY, THAT IS INEVITABLE. BASED ON AFRICAN (HERDING) FOR GENERATIONS, AND PRESIDENT BARACK OBAMA IS A RECENT POLITICAL AGRESSOR OF THIS PHILOSOPHY. MANY SMALL DYSFUNCTIONAL BRAIN (WHITES) ARE TORMENTED BECAUSE THEY SUDDENLY BEGINNING TO REALIZE THAT THEY VOTED FOR A (CHIEF) NOT A PRESIDENT THAT IS FOR AMERICA.

THE DEMOCRATIC TALKING HEADS, ARE TRYING TO SILENCE THIS ISSURE. BASED ON DEMAGOGUERY, AND IMPUGNING THE INTEGRITY OF REPUBLICANS IN AN EFFORT TO CAUSE CHAOS WITHIN THE REPUBLICAN PARTY, SO THEIR STUPID BLUNDER WILL GO UNNOTICED.

WHICH PRESIDENT FRANKLIN D. ROOSEVELT INITIATED OVER SEVENTY FIVE YEARS AGO. TO INDOCTRINATE (BLACKS) THAT HE WAS THEIR MESSIAH, AND OVER SEVENTEEN WERE LYNCHED ANUALLY. DURING HIS PERSIDENTAL REGIME.

HE ALSO (LOST) SOUTHERN DEMOCRATS TO THE REPUBLICAN PARTY. PRESIDENT BARACK OBAMA, IS USING THIS SAME TECHNIQUE ON SMALL DYSFUNCTIONAL BRAIN (WHITES) DIPLOMATICALLY, TO URINATE IN THEIR FACE, AND ATTEMPT TO CONVINCE THEM NOT TO WORRY, BECAUSE WE ARE HAVING A OVERCAST OF SHOWERS.

HOWEVER RUSH LIMBAUGH, SHAWN HANNITY, LAURA INGRUM, ANN COULTER, NEAL CAVUTO, CHARLES PAYNE, BEN FERGERSON, ANDREW CLARK SR. MIKE FLEMING, THESE ARE JUST A FEW, RADIO AND TELEVISION TALK SHOW HOST, (NOT) POLITICIANS, HOWEVER THEY LOVE THIS COUNTRY. THE GREATEST COUNTRY ON GODS EARTH, AND THESE TELEVISION AND RADIO, PERSONALITIES HAS TAKEN (FULL) RESPONSIBILITY UPON THEM SELVES, TO ALERT THE GENERAL PUBLIC, THAT THERE IS A CUNNING LYIING, DECEITFUL, IMPOSTURE, FUNGAS AMONG US.

THAT INTEND TO DESTROY CAPITALISM, REWRITE THE CONSTITUTION, AND RUIN OUR CREDIBILITY AS A SOLVENT NATION.

THAT INDIVIDUAL IS NONE OTHER THAN PRESIDENT BARACK OBAMA. AND THE SMALL DYSFUNCTIONAL BRAIN POLITICAL INEPT (WHITES) THAT IS SLOBBERING ALL OVER THEIR MESSIAH, IS TOTALLY IGNORENT TO HIS INTENT.

(ALL) AFRICAN AMERICANS, THAT RESIDE IN AMERICA IS OF (AFRICAN) HERITAGE AND BARACK OBAMA IS NO EXCEPTION, OUR GENETIC CONTROLLABILITY DICTATE THE SENTIMENT OF THE CONTINENT IN THE EASTERN HEMISPHERE. THAT IS CONTROLLED BY A CONGO TRIBAL CHIEF, OR A CRUEL DICTATOR, OVER NINETY PERCENT OF AFRICAN AMERICANS, THAT ARE CITIZENS IN AMERICA, HAVE CONTEMPT FOR THE CONSTITUTION.

BECAUSE MOST DEEM IT TO BE (WHITE MAN) WRITTEN LAWS, AND DOES NOT PERTAIN TO THEM. AND MOST ARE TO DAMN (STUPID) TO REALIZE THAT OUR ANCESTORS WERE BROUGHT INTO THIS CUSTOM FROM AFRICA. UNCIVILIZED, A HOSTILE ILLITERATE SAVAGE.

AND FOR OVER TWO HUNDRED YEARS ADHERED TO AFRICAN TRADITIONS, AND THAT CULPABLENESS STILL EXIST TODAY, AND MORE PREVALENT THAN EVER

HOWEVER JESSIE JACKSON, AL SHARPTON AND OTHERS, WOULD LIKE FOR OTHERS TO BELIEVE THAT OUR ANCESTORS, CAME FROM A COUNTRY OF EDUCATORS, AND THRUST INTO SLAVERY BECAUSE OF OUR COLOR. AND IF YOU BELIEVE THIS DEMAGOGUERY, YOU HAVE A SMALL BRAIN DISORDER, AS MANY (WHITES) HAVE CAUGHT THIS CONTAGION DISEASED DYSFUNCTION DILEMMA.

TIMES CHANGE BUT GENETIC HERITAGE WITHIN THE CHARACTERISTICS OF PEOPLE IS INEVITABLE.

FOR INSTANCE PRESIDENT ABRAHAM LINCOLN, FREED AFRICAN AMERICANS FROM BONDAGE, IN EIGHTEEN SIXTY FIVE, IN EIGHTEEN SIXTY SIX THE SOUTHERN DEMOCRATS FOUNDERED THE KU-KLUX-KLAN IN ORDER TO. CONTROL (BLACK) VIOLENCE, AND THE PUNISHMENT WAS QUITE SEVERE, WHEN THEY IMPOSED VIOLENCE ON OTHERS.

MANY TIMES THEY WERE LYNCHED, TO PROTECT INNOCENT CITIZENS. THIS ACT OF PERSECUTION WITH OUT PROOF OR TESTIMONY, WAS QUELLED BY REPUBLICAN PRESIDENT EISENHOWER DURING THE FIFTIES.

IN NINETEEN SIXTY FOUR AND FIVE, PRESIDENT LYNDON B. JOHNSON, SIGN THE CIVIL AND VOTING RIGHTS ACT FOR SOUTHERN AFRICAN AMERICANS FORTY FOUR YEARS LATER BLACKS ARE NOT (VARYING) FROM HORRIFIC VIOLENT DESTRUCTION IN AMERICA.

AND SATISTICS DONOT LIE, AS I HAVE REITERATED, THERE IS OVER THREE HUNDRED MILLION PEOPLE IN AMERICA, AFRICAN AMERICANS ARE ONLY APPROXIMATELT TWELVE PERCENT, WHICH CONSIST OF THIRTY SIX MILLION UNFORTUNATELY OPPOSE TO THE ENTIRE POPULATION IN THE UNITED STATES OF AMERICA, BLACKS ALONE HOLD INDIVIDUAL RECORDS OF SCORN, SUCH AS MOST PEOPLE INCARCERATED FOR CRIMINAL ACTIVITY, MOST BABIES BORN OUT OF WEDLOCK, MOST SCHOOL DROP OUT, MOST CONTRACTION OF THE AIDS VIRUS.

UNFORTUNATELY THERE HAS TO BE A MENTAL DEFICIENCY, BASED ON ECCENTRIC BEHAVIOR RELATED TO GENETICDYSFUNCTIONS,ACCORDINGTOCHRONOLOGICAL RECORDS OF SIGNIFICANT EVENTS, PERTAINING TO THE MAJORITY OF AFRICAN AMERICANS.

THIS IS A HERITAGE DYSFUNCTION, GENERATIONAL TAUGHT DILEMMA THAT IS INEVITABLE, RELATED TO MOST HERDING BLACKS.

UNFORTUNATELY SMALL DYSFUNCTIONAL BRAIN POLITICAL STUPID GUILT (WHITES) HAVE ELECTED A TYRANNICAL PRESIDENT FROM THIS HERD. AND WILL LIVE TO REGRET THE DAY THAT THEY BECAME ELIGIBLE TO VOTE BECAUSE OF AN INEPIITUDE REGARDS TO MOST BLACKS IDIOSYNCRASIES, PERTAINING TO THE FUNDAMENTAL CHEMISTRY OF OUR GREAT NATION PRINCIPLES, OF SUSTAINING LIBERTY, WHICH SHOULD BE EMBEDDED IN THE HUMAN MIND,.BASED ON CAPACITY, RELATED TO PRECEPTION. THAT IS WHY GOD GAVE EVERY LIVING HUMAN CREATURE A BRAIN, TO MANIFEST, BASED ON THEORY, RELATED TO CHOICE.

UNFORTUNATELY MOST BLACKS HAVE CHOSEN TO BE HOSTILE. THROUGHOUT THE SOUTH CASUAL, EVEN INTERRACIAL RELATIONSHIP WAS A CIVIL PRACTICE BETWEEN BLACK AND WHITE CHILDREN OF SLAVES, AND SLAVE OWNERS GREW UP AND PLAYED TOGATHER , BLACK WOMEN NURSED WHITE BABIES AND FORMED A AFFECTIONATE RELATIONSHIP.

UNFORTUNATELY MOST WERE ILLITERATE, AND THE ONLY THING THEY COULD DO WAS MAINTAIN AND CULTIVATE THE PLANTATION, THEIR POPULATION GREW BY EIGHTEEN THIRTY, THERE WERE APPROXIMATELY SIXTY SIX THOUSAND, WORKING IN HARMANY.

UNTIL A BLACK MAN NAME DAVID WALKER, DECLARED WAR ON THE SLAVE OWNERS, IN EIGHTEEN TWENTY NINE, AND INSINUATED LET SLAVE HOLDERS COME TO BEAT US FROM (OUR) COUNTRY AMERICA.

IT IS MORE OUR COUNTRY THAN THE WHITE MAN, LATER IN EIGHTEEN THIRTY ONE, NAT TURNER CLAIM HE SAW VISIONS OF BLOOD ON CORN, AND WHITE AND BLACK SPIRITS ENGAGED IN BATTLE, HE BELIEVED IT WAS A SIGN FROM GOD TO EXTERMINATE THE WHITE MAN.

AND STAGED ONE OF THE BLOODIEST VIOLENT MURDEROUS ACTS OF THAT ERA. THE CATASTROPHIC OF

THESE ATTACKS WERE FEARED NATION WIDE, NORTHERN STATES WERE ON THE ALERT.

SOUTHERN STATES PASSED LAWS TO PROHIBIT BLACKS FROM (ALL) GATHERINGS, ALSO WHITES REFUSE TEACHING BLACKS TO READ AND WRITE. BUT THE MOST HORRIFIC LAW PASSED IN THE SOUTH, TO SHOOT A BLACK DEAD WAS CONSIDERED TO BE A MISDEMEANOR.

ONE HUNDRED AND SEVENTY EIGHT YEARS LATER, MANY (WHITES) SUFFERING FROM POLITICAL IGNORANCE, AND BRAIN WASH BY SELF APPOINTED BLACK LEADERS, THEIR IMMUNE SYSTEM HAVE BEEN REDUCED TO THE EXTENT THAT THEY HAVE CAUGHT THIS CONTAGION SMALL BRAIN DYSFUNCTION DISEASE FROM BLACKS, AND ELECTED A CONSPIRATOR WITH A CONGO IDEOLOGY OF TYRANNICAL EXCURSIONS.

BUT TRUST ME IT DID (NOT) WORK FOR (NAT TURNER); AND IT IS NOT GOING TO WORK FOR PRESIDENT BARACK OBAMA, AND I WILL OFFER AN EXPLICIT ACCOUNT OF WHY NOT.

AND IT HAS (NOTHING) TO DO WITH RACISM, IT DEAL WITH THE SIMPLE PRINCIPLES OF (REALITY);

MOST BLACKS AND A LARGE SEGEMENT OF WHITES, IN RECENT YEARS ARE LIVING IN A POLITICAL DISTORTED PHANTASY WORLD, MOST BLACKS ARE NOT (INDEPTH) THINKERS, THEY RELY ON SELF APPOINTED BLACK LEADERS OR TELEPROMPTER TO ADVISE THEM.

AND MOST OF THESE ADVISERS ARE JUST AS STUPID AS THEY ARE, CONCERNING THE POLITICAL FUNDAMENTALS OF PRINCIPAL THAT THIS NATION WAS FOUNDERED ON.

SO THEY DISTORT (REALITY); BASED ON BEING TOTALLY IGNORANT TO FACTS, FOR INSTANCE MICHAEL BROWN, WAS ON NATIONAL TELEVISION CONTRADICTING THAT DR. MARTIN LUTHER KING, WAS WIRE TAPPED ON ORDERS FROM ATTORNEY GENERAL ROBERT KENNEDY, DURING THE SIXTIES, THERE IS AN OLD SAYING, IT IS UTTERLY IMPOSSIBLE TO TAKE A JACKASS, AND TRAIN TO BE A BREED RACE HORSE.

MOST AFRICAN AMERICANS ARE INEPT TO THE CONSTITUTION, ALTHOUGH THEY ARE SUBJECTS TO THE

VALIDITY, I WAS A KID IN ALABAMA, WHEN WHEN MY UNCLES WERE RANTING ABOUT PRESIDENT FRANKLIN D. ROOSEVELT NEW DEAL OF SOCIALISM.

THEY STATED OH MY GOD, HE IS LOOKING OUT FOR (US) WE LOVE THIS MAN, HE IS GIVING (US) OUR RIGHTS, BECAUSE HE IS (GIVING) US THE SAME AMOUNT IN (US) RELIEF CHECKS AS HE GIVE TO WHITE FOLKS. AND THEY WERE TO DAMN STUPID TO REALIZE, THAT IF IT WASNT FOR THE FOURTEENTH AMENDMENT OF THE CONSTITUTION, RATIFIED IN EIGHTEEN SIXTY EIGHT, THEY WOULD (NOT) HAVE GOTTEN A (TOKEN) PRESIDENT BARACK OBAMA, HAS TRULY STUDIED PRESIDENT LINCOLN, AND PRESIDENT ROOSEVELT BIOGRAPHY, AND COMBINED THEIR LITERATURES, BASED ON THEIR THEORIES.

HOWEVER HE IS UTALIZING LINCOLN AS A PROP, WHILE WHILE ATTEMPTING INITIATE A ROOSEVELT METHODOLOGY.

THIS IS A MIDDLE OF THE ROAD ATTEMPT TO DISTORT THE MIND OF THE GENERAL PUBLIC, AS TO WHOM HE REALLY IS, A RADICAL LIBERAL WITH THE INTENT TO IMPLEMENT TYRANNICAL SOCIALISM, WHILE IN ESSENCE DEMORALIZING THE WHITE HOUSE, AND OUR CREDIBILITY ABROAD,(NEVER) IN THE HISTORY OF OUR NATION HAS A SITTING PRESIDENT, FROLICED ON A COMEDIAN TALK SHOW.

SO YOU SMALL DYSFUNCTIONAL BRAIN (WHITES) THAT VOTED HIM IN, SUCK IT UP. BECAUSE THAT IS GENETIC CONGO IDEOLOGY OVERRULING, NEXT THER WILL BE GOATS, PIGS,AND CHICKENS ON THE WHITE HOUSE LAWN. AS I HAVE CONSTANTLY PREDICTED, THIS PRESIDENT DOES (NOT) HAVE LOYALTY FOR THE UNITED STATES OF AMERICA.

HOWEVER HE CONNED HIS WAY INTO THE WHITE HOUSE, PRIMALILY DUE TO HIS ABILITY TO READ EXPRESSIONS AND BODY LANGUAGE OF OTHERS. TO DETERMINE IF THEY ARE PRECEPTIVE TO HIS DEMAGOGIC RHETORIC. THE BRAIN IS THE MOST WONDERFUL ORGAN, THAT GOD CREATED FOR MAN KIND, IT CAN PERFORM MIRACLES, IF FUNCTIONING APPROPRIATELY, HOWEVER THERE ARE LIMITATIONS BASED

ON CHOICE OF BOUNDARIES. EVERY ONE PUZZLE OVER PRESIDENT OBAMA TELEPROMPTER MANNERISM, THIS IS A DESIGNED ARTICULATED AGENDA,

ONLY HE IS AWARE OF THE NECESSITY, HE TEST HIS AUDIANCE RESPONSE, NOTICE THE HEAD SWAGGER FROM SIDE TO SIDE, CONSTANTLY STARRING IN TO THE AUDIENCE, AND WILL KEEP TALKING UNTIL HE DEEM, HIS MESSAGE IS APPLAUDABLE TO HIS LIKING, THE BRAIN TEND TO OVERRIDE IN FAVOR OF INTELLECT PRIORITY, AND HIS NUMBER ONE PRIORITY IS TO READ THE AUDIANCE THAT HE IS ADDRESSING, AND STUDY THEIR DEMEANOR, IN AN EFFORT TO GRATIFY, AND IT DOSENT MATTER TO HIM IF HE IS LYING, AS LONG AS THEY RESPOND FAVORABLE.

HIS BRAIN IS (NOT) SYNCHRONIZED TO DRESS PEOPLE DOWN, AND MAINTAIN COMPOSED VERBIAGE, AND THAT IS THE IMPORTANCE OF THE TELEPROMPTER, BECAUSE BODY LANGUAGE AND EYE CONTACT IS HIS FORTE, TO COINCIDE WITH SPEECH DELIVERANCE.

THIS IS JUST A BRIEF REMINDER, TO YOU BRAIN DEAD POLITICAL INEPT BUFFOONS (WHITES) THE DEMOCRATS ARE IN UTTERLY SHAMBLES OF POLITICAL DISARRAY, AND THEIR LEADER PRESIDENT BARACK OBAMA, IS CHASING (JUBILANCE) FROM COMEDIC TALK SHOW HOAST.

AND GLOATING OVER HE BECOMING PRESIDENT, WHILE A FINANCIAL INFESTING CANCER IS EATING AWAY AT OUR NATION;

(STOP) REMEMBER REV. WRIGHT, PRESIDENT BARACK OBAMA PASTER FOR TWENTY YEARS, AND HIS INFERNOS STATEMENT ABOUT AMERICA, NOT GOD BLESS AMERICA, GOD DAMN AMERICA, AND RICH (WHITE) FOLKS CONTROL AMERICA, AND THEIR CHICKENS ARE COMING HOME TO ROOST. PRESIDENT BARACK OBAMA, IS HIS WISHFUL ELATED THINKING ANSWER, YOU WOULD HAVE TO BE SITTING ON YOUR BRAINS, (NOT) TO UNDERSTAND THAT IF YOU ARE A MEMBER OF (ANY) FORMAL ORGANIZATION FOR TWENTY YEARS, OF YOUR OWN CHOOSING, WITH OUT QUESTION YOU (ARE) THE EPITOME OF THEIR IDEOLOGY.

OUR NATION IS CONFRONTED WITH A DIRE CHRISIS, BECAUSE STUPID ASS (WHITES) HAVE VOTED A FOX, IN

CHARGE OF THE CHICKENS. I OFTEN THINK OF BILL AIRS, TERRORIZING AMERICA, AND STATED HE DIDNT DO ENOUGH AND NOW HE HAS HIS AFTER THE FACT ASSOCIATE AS PRESIDENT.

SO ALL OF YOU POLITICAL INEPT LEFT WING RADICALS, THAT ARE DEFENENDING PRESIDENT BARACK OBAMA AGENDA, JUST REMEMBER ONE THING.

YOU, YOUR FAMILIES, RELATIVES, FRIENDS AND LOVE ONES, RESIDE IN THE UNITED STATES OF AMERICA;

AND TERRORIST HAVE (NO) RACIAL BARRIERS, TO DISTORT REALITY IS A SELF MOTIVATION, THAT HAS A POLITICAL PREMEDITATED AGENDA. AND JUAN WILLIAMS IS THE EPITOME OF THIS IDOTIC SAGA, BECAUSE ON MARCH 07, 2009. HE WAS ON FOX NEWS, DEFENDING SMALL BRAIN IDEOLOGY, BY STIPULATING THAT RUSH LIMBAUGH, IS A (POLITICIAN) LEADING THE REPUBLICAN PARTY.

WHEN REALISTICALLY THE DEMOCRATIC PARTY IS IN DISARRAY, SEEKING ANY ONE TO PERSECUTE, IN ORDER TO DETER ATTENTION FROM THEM BEING MADE A DUNCE OF BY THEIR PRESIDENT ELECT.

WHICH IS A LOOSE CANNON IN THEIR PARTY, THAT EVENTUALLY WILL LEAD TO THEIR POLITICAL SELF DESTRUCTION, WHICH HAS BEGAN WITH SENATOR ROLAND BURRIS, AND PRESIDENT BARACK OBAMA IS (NOT) IMMUNE TO THIS FACTION.

HOWEVER MR. MICHAEL STEELE, I CONSIDER YOU TO BE A INDIVIDUAL OF INTELLECTUAL MORAL INTEGRITY, AND CAN BE A ASSET TO CONSERVATISM, IN ORDER TO ASSIST IN STABILIZING CAPITALISM IN AMERICA. YOU HAVE BEEN ELECTED TO CHANGE THE COURSE OF THE REPUBLICAN PARTY, WHICH IS QUITE A REMARKABLE HONORABLE OBLIGATION, THAT IS PROFOUNDLY DOABLE, WITH THE ASSISTANCE OF PRESIDENT BARACK OBAMA, AND THE DYSFUNCTIONS OF THE DEMOCRATIC CONGRESS.

HOWEVER YOU (MUST) UNDERSTAND THE VALIDITY OF YOUR RESPONSIBILITY A WORD OF ADVICE, PLEASE REFRAIN FROM (POLITICAL) DIALOGUES WITH SMALL DYSFUNCTIONAL BRAIN INEPT BUFFOONS, SUCH AS D.L. HAUGHLEY. THIS MAN IS SO POLITICALLY IGNORANT, AS THE

MAJORITY OF BLACKS ARE, PERTAINING TO DEMOCRATIC BRAIN WASH STRATEGY.

UNTIL IF YOU WERE TO ASK THIS IMITATION OF A PORCUPINE, WHICH PARTY FOUNDED THE KU-KLUX-KLAN, I SUSPECT HIS ANSWER WOULD BE DR. MARTIN LUTHER KING. MR. STEELE I BEG OF YOU PLEASE REFRAIN FROM DIALOGUES WITH BLACK T.V. AND RADIO, RADICAL LIBERAL BLACKS. BECAUSE THEY HAVE BEEN DEMONIZED BY DEMOCRAT CONSPIRATORS FOR OVER SEVENTY FIVE YEARS.

INDOCTRINATED BY NONE OTHER THAN THE SOCIALISTIC GENUS PERPETRATOR. PRESIDENT FRANKLIN D. ROOSEVELT.

AND DEMOCRAT IS EMBEDDED INSIDE OF THEIR (SMALL) DYSFUNCTIONAL BRAIN, AND THAT GENE IS PERMANENTLY AFFIXED.

ALL THEY ARE GOING TO DO IS RIDICULE YOU, AND ALWAYS REMIND YOUR SELF OF BLACK HERDING, WHICH HAS AND ALWAYS WILL BE A STIGMATIZATION RELATED TO MOST AFRICAN AMERICANS.

AND THAT IS INEVITABLE , BECAUSE OF AFRICAN GENETIC HERITAGE OF OF HERDING AROUND THEIR WITCH DOCTER OR TRIBAL CHIEF. YOU WERE CAUGHT OFF GUARD BY THESE TWO HERDING BLACK SMALL BRAIN POLITICAL IDIOTS, RELATED TO THE RUSH LIMBAUGH INCIDENT.

GUESS WHAT MR. LIMBAUGH, AUDIANCE OF RADIO LISTENERS DOUBLE, THIS IS TIPICAL DEMOCRATIC DCITFUL STRATEGY, THEY KNOW RUSH LIMBAUGH, IS (NOT) A POLITICIAN BUT YOU ARE.

INSTINCTIVELY LIBERAL BLACKS WILL POUNCE ON A CONSERVATIVE WHITE OR BLACK, IF YOU ARE WHITE YOU ARE A RACIST, IF BLACK YOU ARE A WHITE MAN BOOT LICK.

AND THEY ARE SO STUPID, THEY DO NOT REALIZE THAT THEIR TONGUES HAVE BEEN STUCK IN DEMOCRATS REAR END, JUST FOR THE SMELL FOR OVER SEVENTY YEARS.

HOWEVER THE REASON FOR RUSH LIMBAUGH, LISTENERS DOUBLING, THOSE WERE MOSTLY DEMOCRATS,

WAITING FOR RUSH TO DEMAGOGUE YOU. HE IS TO SMART FOR THAT TRAP, HE UNDERSTAND DEMOCRATIC DECITFUL BACK STABBING STRATEGY.

THE MAJORITY OF AFRICAN AMERICANS, EVENTUALLY WILL CAUSE THE DEMOCRATIC PARTY TO SELF DESTRUCT. IMPACTED BY THE SOCIALISTIC IDEOLOGY OF A CONGO DICTATOR, INSTEAD OF A PRESIDENT.

THE (WHITE) TRIBAL NATIVES THAT VOTED THIS IMPOSTER INTO OFFICE ARE BECOMING RESTLESS, BECAUSE THEY ARE (NOT) ACCUSTOM TO HIS GENETIC AFRICAN TRAITS.

AND THIS IS (NOT) A RACIST REMARK,IT IS THE ESSENCE OF CULTURAL (REALITY) THESE BEHAVIROL PATTERN ARE INEVITABLE, MOST BLACKS WILL NEVER ACKNOWLEDGE THIS DYSFUNCTION, BECAUSE THEY ARE A PART OF THE HERD, AND OTHERS ARE TO DAMN STUPID TO KNOW WHAT IT IS. THAT CAUSE HERDING, FOR INSTANCE MICHAEL STEELE ON A T.V. PROGRAM CONVERSING WITH ONE OR TWO BLACKS, ALL OF A SUDDEN HIS HERDING INSTINCTS KICKED IN AND HE STARTED BASHING RUSH LIMBAUGH, WHILE THEY WERE INSINUATING THAT THE REPUBLICAN PARTY WERE PARALLEL TO GERMANY NAZI PARTY.

MR STEELE THE REPUBLICAN PARTY NEED TO GROW UP AND GET BEYOND KISSING BLACK ASSESFOR VOTES. TRUST ME IT IS (NEVER) GOING TO HAPPEN SIMPLY BECAUSE OF A BRAIN DYSFUNCTION FOR THE DEMOCRATIC PATY. THEY HAVE (NOT) CHANGED THEIR THEORY IN SEVENTY FIVE YEARS. IF IT WAS ME I WOULD BE WORKING DILIGENTLY TO DISPEL THE NOTION OF BLACK RADICAL CYNICISM.

AND ALERT (WHITES) AND (HISPANICS) THAT VOTED FOR PRESIDENT BARACK OBAMA, THAT THEY WERE SUFFERING FROM A CONTAGIOUS BODY DISORDER THAT IS CALLED SMALL BRAIN DYSFUNCTION, HOWEVER NOT TO. WORRY, THE (CURE) IS IN THE WHITE HOUSE, ONCE THEY GET SICK TO THEIR STOMACH OF ARROGANT CONGO CHIEF SOCIALISM.

AND THROW UP, THEY WILL BE CURED OF THIS DREADED DISEASE, ALSO PAY VERY CLOSE ATTENTION

TO REV. WRIGHT REMARKS, ABOUT HOW RICH (WHITE) PEOPLE CONTROLL AMERICA.

HE IS TO STUPID TO REALIZE THAT HE WAS ON TO SOMETHING, BECAUSE THEY ARE GOING TO SIT ON THEIR FINANCIAL WEALTH, UNTIL THEY DISPOSE OF SOCIALISM, UNTIL THEN MILLIONS OF JOBS ARE GOING TO BE LOST, AND HOME FORECLOSURE, MANY ARE PITCHING TENTS (NOW) IN THE PARK, ALSO MANY (WHITES) THAT VOTED FOR PRESIDENT BARACK OBAMA WILL HAVE TIME TO CURE FROM THEIR SMALL BRAIN DYSFUNCTION AILMENT. WHILE INSECTS CHEW AWAY AT THEIR DERRIER, AND IF THIS BECOME UNPLEASANT, THEY CAN DIAL UP THE WHITE HOUSE,,TO SEE IF PRESIDENT OBAMA CAN GET A (HUT) IN AFRICA WHERE HIS BROTHER RESIDE. WE HAVE HAD OUR PROBLEMS IN AMERICA, PERTAINING TO RACISM, AND IT WAS THE (REPUBLICAN) PARTY THAT QUELLED (ALL) FOR THE BEST INTEREST OF OUR NATION.

PRESIDENT ABRAHAM LINCOLN FREED THE SLAVES, PRESIDENT DWIGHT EISENHOWER, WROTE THE FIRST CIVIL RIGHTS BILL IN EIGHTY FIVE YEARS FOR SOUTHERN BLACKS, DURING THE FIFTIES. HOWEVER IT WAS REJECTED BY THE DEMOCRATIC CONGRESS.

HOWEVER HE DID NOT GIVE UP, HE QUELLED THE VIOLENCE RELATED TO THE KU-KLUX-KLAN LYNCHING BLACKS.

AND MILITARY FORCED SCHOOLS TO INTEGRATE IN THE SOUTH., WHILE DEMOCRATS WERE BOMBING CHURCHES WITH LITTLE BLACK KIDS INSIDE. PRESIDENT RICHARD M. NIXON RATIFIED AFFIRMATIVE ACTION. I AM REQUESTING FOR SOME ONE TO CONTRADICT THESE (REALITES) AND PARAPHRASE IN DEMOCRATIC TERMINOLOGY, RELATED TO AFRICAN AMERICANS, OF ANY SORT OTHER THAN ESTABLISHING THE KU-KLUX-KLAN, THAT WAS LYNCHING BLACKS IN THE. SOUTH.

I HAVE OBSERVED MICHAEL STEELE ON MANY OCCASIONS, DURING TALK SHOWS, AND HE ALWAYS APPEARED TO BE A GENTLEMAN OF MORAL CHARACTER.

DIGNIFIED WITH PROUD TO BE AN AMERICAN, ALONG WITH A AGENDA OF CONSERVATIVE CAPITALISM.

UNFORTUNATELY HE CHOOSE TO HAVE A DIALOGUE WITH A CONGO REPLICA OF A PORCUPINE, THAT KNOWS (LESS) ABOUT THE POLITICAL FUNDAMENTALS OF OUR NATION, THAN THOSE TWENTY HOSTILE AFRICANS SAVAGES THAT WAS BROUGHT TO AMERICA IN SIXTEEN NINETEEN, REFERENCE RADICAL TALK SHOW HOST D.L. HAUGHLEY.

MILLIONS OF AFRICAN AMERICANS LIVE BY A CODE OF ETHICS, THAT IS CONSISTENT WITH CONSERVATIVE GUIDE-LINES, HOWEVER THEY VOTE DEMOCRATIC, BECAUSE THEY ARE TO DAMN POLITICAL STUPID TO COORDINATE PARTY PRINCPILES, BETWEEN DEMOCRAT AND REPUBLICAN, BASED ON THEIR GENETIC HERDING, THAT THE DEMOCRATS ARE AWARE OF.

SO AS A RESULT DEMOCRATS CONSTANTLY USE TACTICS OF SOCIALISTIC DISTORTION BEHAVIOR, SUCH AS REPUBLICANS ARE RESPONSIBLE FOR BLACKS BEING IN DESTITUTION, AND THAT ALL BLACKS WOULD BE EQUAL TO WHITES REGARDS TO FINANCIAL STATUS IF IT WASNT FOR RACIST NAZI REPUBLICANS.

THERE ARE MANY PRECEPTIONS IN LIFE, BASED ON A SENSE OF PROVERBIAL CONGLOMERATION.

HOWEVER THE VALIDITY IS IN CONJUNCTION WITH (REALITY); F.B.I. DIRECTOR J. EDGAR HOOVER, ASSESSED IN NINETEEN FIFTY SEVEN, THAT BLACKS BRAINS WAS TWENTY PERCENT SMALLER THAN WHITES, BASED ON HIS PRECEPTION THAT BLACKS WERE BEING LYNCHED IN THE SOUTH, BY THE SOUTHERN (DEMOCRATIC) FOUNDERS OF THE KU-KLUX-KLAN. AND THE NORTHERN CONSTITUENCE OF (BLACKS) THAT COULD VOTE, WERE VOTING FOR DEMOCRATS TO MAINTAIN POLITICAL POWER.

FIFTY TWO YEARS LATER, ATTORNEY GENERAL ERIC HOLDER, INSINUATE THAT AMERICANS ARE COWARDS.

AND I TOTALLY (AGREE) BASED ON MY ASSESSMENT, PERTAINING TO WHITES IN AMERICA, THEY HAVE ALLOWED SELF APPOINTED BLACK POLITICAL RADICAL INEPT DICTATORS, TO DEMORALIZE THEIR POLITICAL FORTITUDE. BASED ON INTIMIDATIONS OF UNREALISTIC INNUENDOS

TO GAIN SUPERIORITY, RELATED TO HISTORICAL RACIAL (DISTORTION)

AND TENTATIVELY AS A RESULT WITH TEARS IN MY EYES, I RELATE TO SWEET AMERICA PREDICAMENT AT THIS TIME.

AS A BIRD NEST ON THE GROUND, TO BE PICKED AWAY AT BY GLOBAL DICTATORS;

HOWEVER I AM OPTIMISTIC OF OUR ENDURANCE, MR. MICHAEL STEELE REMEMBER THE TITLE OF THIS BOOK, POLITICAL SELF DESTRUCTION OF MOST AFRICAN AMERICANS.

ALSO STORE THIS MESSAGE IN YOUR MEMORY BANK, OUR LORD JESUS CHRIST COULD DESCEND DOWN FROM THE HEAVENS, AND HE COULD (NOT) REMOVE THE MAJORITY OF POLITICAL IGNORANT BLACKS, NOSES AND HEAD FROM BEING STUCK INSIDE DEMOCRATS BUTTOCKS.

IT IS A GENETIC TRAIT THAT IS INEVITABLE, THE MAJORITY OF BLACKS DO NOT REPRESENT THE POLITICAL LANDSCAPE VERY WELL, SIMPLY BECAUSE OF A GENETIC BRAIN DISORDER THAT DICTATE ALOOFNESS, AND MISINTERPETING ALSO EVADING EXISTING POLITICAL MORALITY. WHITES ARE GUILTY OF THIS AGENDA ALSO, BUT SEEM TO MANAGE MORE PROFESSIONAL THAN BLACKS. BECAUSE OF THEIR FORTITUDE TO COMPREHEND AND ADJUST TO POLITICAL GUIDE-LINES, BASED ON DIVERSIFYING. BLACKS TEND TO BECOME ARROGANT WITH A DISPOSITION OF HEY MAMMA LOOK AT ME, (I) AM IN CHARGE.

MOST BLACKS ARE INEPT TO THE PRINCIPLES OF DIGNITY, RESPONSIBILILITY AND INDIVIDUAL CHOICE, MOST BLACKS PRECEIVE THAT AMERICA HAS BEEN UN_ JUST TO THEM, BECAUSE STANDARDS ARE NOT LOWERED TO THEIR EXPECTATIONS, OF AUTHORTATIVE, HERDING NEGLIGENCE.

PERTAINING TO THEIR INSIDIOUS AGENDA OF DEPRAVATIONS, AND THEY WILL REBEL BASED ON THEIR INCOMPTENCY.

OUR NATION IS SLOWLY DRIFTING INTO A PHANTASM OF BLIND BLACK HYSTERIA, OF NOT SEEKING INTELLECT

THROUGH EDUCATION, AND GAINFUL EMPLOYMENT IS FOR FOOLS, SO WHY NOT HERD TOGATHER ELECT BARACK OBAMA PRESIDENT, BECAUSE HE IS ONE OF US.

THAT IS GOING TO GET US REPARATION FOR SLAVERY, AND YOU IDIOTS THAT ARE GAINFULLY EMPLOYED, ESPECIALLY YOU SMALL DYFUNCTIONAL BRAIN (WHITES) FOLKS.THAT ASSISTED IN HIS WINNING THE ELECTION. GUESS WHAT YOUR EARNINGS ARE GOING TO HELP SUPPORT (US), THROUGH OUR BROTHER PRESIDENT BOO, INIATED SOCIAL PROGRAMS. BECAUSE YOU EVIL (WHITES) IS GOING TO PAY FOR BRINGING US HERE, FROM AFRICA US BEING SAVAGELY HOSTILE AND ILLITERATE, TEACHING US CIVILIZATION, AND TO READ AND WRITE..

NOT ONLY IT WAS TERRIBLY WRONG OF YOU RACIST WHITES, TO PREVENT US FROM EXTERMINATING YOU ALL, AND TAKING OVER AMERICA, AND SUBSTITUTING IT WITH CONGO IDEOLOGY, SO US COULD BE CONTROLLED BY A CHIEF, INSTEAD OF A PRESIDENT.

SO PRESIDENT BARACK OBAMA IS GOING TO SEE THAT WE ARE REWARDED FOR YOUR RACISM AGAINST US.

I AM IN THE PROCESS OF BRINGING THESE WRITINGS TO A CLOSE, BY PREDICTING THAT MOST BLACKS, WILL TAKE OFFENSE.

BASED ON THEIR HISTORICAL NATURE OF ENDEAVORS TO DISTORT (REALITY) IN ACCORDANCE WITH PHANTASIES.

THERE WAS A TRADITION IN WASHINGTON ON MARCH 21, 2009.THAT HAS BEEN CONGREGATED FOR ALMOST ONE HUNDRED AND FIFTY YEARS. (THE GRID IRON CLUB) THAT PRESIDENT BARACK OBAMA CHOSE TO SNUB WHICH (NO) SITTING PRESIDENT IN MODERN TIMES IF EVER. COULD IT BE BECAUSE THERE WERE AN ASSEMBLY OF REV. WRIGHT, RICH (WHITE) PEOPLE THERE, THAT CONTROL AMERICA. (HINT);

THERE IS AN ABUNDANCE OF POLITICAL SKILLED, INTELLECTUAL PEOPLE IN AMERICA, THAT NEED TO GET OFF THEIR KNEES, APPRAISING THIS ARROGANT MESSIAH PRESIDENT BECAUSE HE IS BLACK.

AND ADMIT THAT YOU HAVE BEEN HAD, THAT IT WAS A TERRIBLE MISTAKE TO ELECT BARACK OBAMA PRESIDENT.

AS THE SOUTHERN DEMOCRATS STATED IN EIGHTEEN SEVENTY ONE, AFTER REPUBLICAN PRESIDENT ULYSSES S. GRANT, SUSPENDED THE WRIT OF HABEAS CORPUSIN THE SOUTH, AND RELENTLESSLY PURSUED THE KU-KLUX-KLAN, IN ORDER TO QUELL THE VIOLENCE BEING PERPETRATED AGAINST AFRICAN AMERICANS.

DURING THIS TIME SIMULTANEOUS BLACKS BEGAN TO PERSUE POLITICS, WHEN THE SOUTHERN CLANNISH DEMOCRATS PREDICTED THAT BLACKS, WERE ARROGANT IGNORANT, AND INCOMPETENT PEOPLE.

HOWEVER I DISAGREE WITH THAT OMINOUS IRRESPONSIBLE ASSESSMENT, IT SHOULD HAVE BEEN ASSESED AS THE (MAJORITY) OF BLACKS. BECAUSE AT THAT SAME INTERVAL A (BLACK REPUBLICAN) HIRMAN RHODES REVELS BECAME THE FIRST AFRICAN AMERICAN U.S. SENATOR FROM MISSISSIPPI IN EIGHTEEN SEVENTY.

UNFORTUNATELY OUR NATION HAS ELECTED A PRESIDENT, THAT COINCIDE WITH THE MAJORITY OF BLACKS, ON DEIVATING FROM THE FOUNDING PRINCIPLES THAT OUR NATION WAS ESTABLISHED ON.

IN MY FINAL ANALYSIS, I AM GOING TO PAY TRIBUTE TO ONE OF THE MOST OUTSTANDING POLITICIAN OF MODERN TIMES, IN MY OPINION. THAT SERVED OUR COUNTRY WITH MORALISTIC DIGNITY, PERTAINING TO ETHNICS. IN TWO POLITICAL CAPACITIES AND (NEVER) FAULTED DURING HER REIGN. AND HAS POLITICAL ICE WATER IN HER VEINS, AND I SUSPPECT SENATOR BARBARA BOXER WOULD ACKNOWLEDGE THAT. SHE IS ONE OF

A KIND, AND THAT IS FORMER SECRETARY OF STATE DR CONDOLEEZZA RICE.

WITH A PRECISE CONTINUITY OF ESTEEM TO DOMINATE WITH OUT CONTROVERSY, AND IT IS QUITE OBIVOUS OF HER POLITICAL SKILLS, SHE IS NOT (ANY) PART OF A BLACK HERDING PROCESS.

THAT HAS ALIENATED THEM SELVES FROM THE CONSTITUTION OF THE UNITED STATES OF AMERICA.

HOPEFULLY ONE DAY AS WE SURVIVE THE ATTACK ON CAPITALISM, WITH HER ABILITY TO COMMUNICATE, SHE COULD BE AN ASSET TO REFORM POLITICAL INEPTNESS, REGARDS TO (ALL) PEOPLE THAT RESIDE IN OUR GREAT NATION.

BECAUSE SHE IS A LOYALIST TO HER NATION, WITH CONVICTIONS TO IMPROVE, RELATED TO COMPLEX ISSURES.

IN THE INTERIM IT WOULD SIMPLY BE UNPRECEDENTED NOT TO DIVULGE AN ANALYSIS OF PRESIDENT BARACK HUSSIAN OBAMA, SEEMINGLY HEALTH CARE REFORM DEBACLE.

I NOTICE ON SEPTEMBER 15, 2009. FORMER PRESIDENT JIMMIE CARTER DENOTED HIS IMPOSITION ON RACIST (WHITES) IN AMERICA, REGARDS TO AFRICAN AMERICANS AMBITIONS TO BECOME POLITICAL LEADERS. BY RELATING TO HIS (SOUTHREN) HERITAGE, WITH AN EXPLICIT EXPLANATION RELATIVE TO AFFIRMATION AS TO WHAT THE SOUTHERN KU-KLUX-KLAN ASSERTED IN EIGHTEEN SEVENTY.

WHEN HIRMAN RHODES REVELS, BECAME THE FIRST (REPUBLICAN) AFRICAN AMERICAN TO SERVE IN THE U.S. SENATE, FROM MISSISSIPPI FOR ONE YEAR, COMPLETING THE TERM OF JEFFERSON DAVIS, WHOM BECAME THE PRESIDENT OF THE CONFEDERACY IN EIGHTEEN SIXTY ONE. DURING THAT TIME MANY SOUTHERN (DEMOCRATIC) WHITES WAS ACTIVE IN THE KU-KLUX-KLAN BECAME BELLIGERENT DUE TO BLACKS INSPIRATION FOR POLITICS, AN ACCUSED BLACKS OF BEING IGNORANT.AND INCOMPETENT PEOPLE, ATTEMPTING TO RISE ABOVE THEIR NATURALLY SUBSERVIENT PLACE IN SOCIETY.

SO IT IS TRULY REMARKABLE AND ADMIRABLE. FOR THE FORMER PRESIDENT JIMMY CARTER TO ACKNOWLEDGE THE TRUE LEGACY AND REALITY OF (DEMOCRATIC); IDEOLOGY PERTAINING TO AFRICAN AMERICANS. BECAUSE AFTER ALL HE MR CARTER IS A (DEMOCRAT) FROM THE SOUTH, WHERE THE (DEMOCRATS) FOUNDERED THE (HOSTILE) KU-KLUX-KLAN, THAT LITERALLY LYNCHED, MAIMED AND INTIMIDATED, UNTIL (ALL) POLITICAL INSPITED

(REPUBLICANS) DEPARTED THE SOUTHERN STATES BLACK AND WHITE, SO THERE IS (NO) ONE BETTER TO ADVOCATE RADICAL DEMAGOGUERY THAN FORMER PRESIDENT JIMMY CARTER, BECAUSE IT IS A VERY DISTINCT POSSIBILITY THAT SOME OF HIS ANCESTORS WERE EMBEDDED WITH THE KU-KLUX-KLAN, THAT CAUSED THE DRAMATIC EXPULSION OF (REPUBLICANS) BLACK AND WHITE FROM THE SOUTHERN STATES. ONE HUNDRED AND THIRTY NINE YEARS AGO.

HOWEVER THE PREDICTIONS OF THE SOUTHERN (DEMOCRATS); DURING THE EIGHTEEN HUNDREDS, REGARDS TO POLITICAL INCOMPETENCY, PERTAINING TO MOST AFRICAN AMERICANS IS AUTHENTIC.

UNFORTUNATELY AND SADLY, WE AS A NATION IS BEING PLAGUED WITH A DIVISIVE CONSPIRACY INTENTIONALLY.

INSPIRED BY NONE OTHER THAN OUR NEWLY ELECTED (AFRICAN AMERICAN) PRESIDENT BARACK HUSSIAN OBAMA.

THE CHARACTERISTICS OF)MOST) BLACKS ARE RELEGATED TO (INEPT) DECEPTION AND DISTORTION, WITH A VINDICTIVE RADICAL HERDING CONSENSUS AND WHEN THEIR AGENDA IS EXPOSED, THEY SCREAM LIKE A PIG UNDER A FENCE WITH RACISM, IN AN EFFORT TO DISTORT THEIR INTENTIONS, OF BIAS DEMAGOGUERY, AS THE RADICAL (DEMOCRATS) ARE DOING UNDER THE ILLUSTRIOUS SUPERVISION OF PRESIDENT BARACK HUSSIAN OBAMA. FOR INSTANCE THE DEMOCRATS ARE AWARE THAT THEY ARE BEING LED TO POLITICAL CONDEMNATION OF SELF DESTRUCTION.

HOWEVER THEY ARE RELUCTANT TO VOICE THEIR OPINIONS BECAUSE HE IS (BLACK) AND FEAR OF BEING LABELED RACIST.

AND ALIENATE HERDING BLACK CONSTITUENCY, THAT HAS SUPPORTED THE DEMOCRATIC PARTY BY A MARGIN OF APPROXIMATELY NINETY FOUR OR SIX PERCENT IN A BLOC FOR OVER SEVENTY FIVE YEARS.

BUT TRUST ME THE DEMOCRATIC POLITICIANS ARE SOME OF THE MOST ASTUTE, CONTRIVING, DISTORTING AND RADICAL INDIVIDUALS IN AMERICA. THEY DID NOT

HOLD CONTROL OF CONGRESS FOR FORTY YEARS BEING POLITICALLY INEPT.

THEIR ELITE STRATEGY IS FOR OVER SEVENTY FIVE YEARS, ARE TO CONVINCE THE GENERAL PUBLIC, THAT REPUBLICANS ARE CONSPIRING AGAINST POOR PEOPLE, AND HAVE NO COMPASSION FOR DESTITUTION ESPECIALLY AFRICAN AMERICANS, AND THAT THEY ARE THE PARTY TO RESOLVE PROBLEMS FOR THE UNDER PRIVILEDGE.

THEY HAVE USED THIS COMBATIVE INDOCTRINATING AGENDA VERY AFFECTIVELY, THAT HAS ENABLED THEM TO CONTROL THE U.S. SENATE, THE HOUSE OF REPRESENTATIVES,AND THE ELECTION OF THE FIRST AFRICAN AMERICAN PRESIDENT.

THEIR ACCOMPLISHMENTS ARE TO BE COMMENDED. HOWEVER THERE IS A POLITICAL SOCIALISTIC BLACK VIRUS THAT IS CONTAMINATION THEIR PARTY WITH DECITFUL DISTORTED RHETORIC.

THAT IS CONTRIVED TO CHANGE THE CULTURE OF AMERICAFROM THE OBEDIENCE OF THE CONSTITUTION, TO A CONGO IDEOLOGY. WHERE HE CAN REMAIN (CHIEF) NOT PRESIDENT OVER (ALL) CITIZENS OF THE UNITED STATES OF AMERICA. HERDING BEHIND HIS POLITICAL INCOMPETENCE INDEFINITELY.

PUBLIC OPTION HEALTH CARE, IS HIS INITIAL CONTRIVED GOAL TO ACCOMPLISH HIS MISSION, HE DOSENT GIVE A DAMN ABOUT THE HEALTH OF CIRTZENS IN AMERICA.

(WAKE UP AMERICA); PUBLIC OPTION HEALTH CARE, IS NOTHING MORE THAN AN ENTRAPMENT TO SIPHON OFF WEALTH FROM THE ELDERY, TO SUPPORT (MIS-FITS)

PUBLIC OPTION HEALTH CARE. IS MANIPULATED BY A EGOTISTICAL POLITICIAN, PRESIDENT BARACK HUSSIAN OBAMA, FILLED WITH ZEAL, AND IS TOTALLY INEPT TO THE FUNDAMENTALS OF HUMAN PERCEPTION. HE IS ON THE VERGE OF POLITICALLY SELF DESTRUCTING, BECAUSE THE DIVERSITY INCORPORATED WITHIN THE AMERICAN PEOPLE, IS A CRITERIA OF INTELLECT, PATRIOTISM, COMPASSION, AND FORGIVING. HOWEVER AN ATTEMPT IS PERPETRATED TO INFRINGE ON THEIR CONSTITUTIONAL

RIGHTS, IT IS INEVITABLE THEY THEY ARE GOING TO RETALIATE. THIS HABITUAL LYING DECEITFUL PRESIDENT BARACK H. OBAMA, AND HIS BOOT LICKING SUPPORTING ORANGUTANS, HAVE INSULTED THE FABRIC OF OUR NATION (SENIOR CITIZENS)

THESE ARE THE PEOPLE THAT HAS PRODUCED MISCELLANEOUS BUISNESS PEOPLE, LAWYERS, DOCTORS, ENGINEERS, SCIENTIST, MINISTERS, ECT. FOR AMERICA AND ABROAD.

AND TO IMPUGN THEIR INTEGRITY, AND SUGGEST THAT THEY ARE RACIST AND DEMEANING OUR COUNTRY IS INEPTLY APPALLING SIMPLY BECAUSE MOST PEOPLE HAVE DISCOVERED THAT HE IS. A COVERT REPLICA OF THE EIGHTEEN THIRTY ONE (NAT TURNER) THAT IS HIGHLY SOPHISCATED WITH DISDAIN FOR THE CONSTITUTION OF AMERICA, RELATED TO THE TWENTY FIRST CENTURY.

THIS IS NOT ONLY POLITICAL SELF DESTRUCTION BUT SUCIDAL, IT ALSO SUBSTANTIATE THE PREDICTIONS OF THE SOUTHERN (DEMOCRAT) KU-KLUX-KLAN OF EIGHTEEN SEVENTY. ACCUSING BLACKS OF BEING POLITICAL IGNORANT, AND INCOMPETENT.

UNFORTUNATELY DURING THAT TIME THE MAJORITY OF SOUTHERN AFRICAN AMERICANS WERE ILLIERATE, APPROXIMATELY ONE HUNDRED AND THIRTY NINE YEARS LATER THE AMERICAN PEOPLE HAVE ELECTED A BLACK HARVARD

GRADUATE ATTORNEY FOR PRESIDENT OF THE UNITED STATES OF AMERICA. YET IT APPEAR THAT HE IS EMBEDDED WITH THAT SAME ACCESSED CATEGORY OF THE EIGHTEEN SEVENTIES, RELATED TO POLITICAL INCOMPETENCE MANY PEOPLE WOULD CONSIDER THIS TO BE A RACIST REMARK. FORTUNATELY SOUTHERN WHITES WORKED (VERY) CLOSELY WITH AFRICAN AMERICANS, TEACHING THEMTO READ AND WRITE.

IN DOING SO THE OPPORTUNITY WAS AVAILABLE TO EVALUATE THEIR MORAL EXCELLENCE, TRUST ME ALTHOUGH WHITE SOUTHERN (DEMOCRATS) WERE SLAVE OWNERS, PRESIDENT BARACK H. OBAMA, IS IN THE

PROCESS OF ELEVATING THEIR INTELLECTUAL STATUS TO EXCELLENT.

BECAUSE I SUSPECT THAT HE IS TOTALLY INEPT TO CHRONOLOGICAL RECORDS OF SIGNIFICANT EVENTS OF THE PAST,PERTAINING TO DEMOCRATS. DURING THE LATE FIFTIES (REPUBLICAN) PRESIDENT DWIGHT D. EISENHOWER, FORMULATED THE FIRST CIVIL RIGHTS BILL IN EIGHTY FIVE YEARS FOR SOUTHERN AFRICAN AMERICANS.

THE DEMOCRATS CONTROLLED THE SENATE LED BY NONE OTHER THAN SENATOR LYNDON B. JHONSON AND FORMER PRESIDENT.

THE (DEMOCRATS) DID NOT HAVE THE VOTES TO DEFEAT THIS BILL, HOWEVER TWELVE (REPUBLICANS) DEFECTED AND THE.BILL WAS DEFEATED. AT THIS JUNCTURE IN AMERICAN HISTORY, A SITTING REPUBLICAN PRESIDENT DWIGHT D. EISENHOWER, WERE TRYING TO RESTORE THE CONSTITUTIONAL FREEDOM FOR BLACKS, THAT WAS STOLEN BY THE SUPREME COURT IN EIGHTEEN NINETY FIVE, IN FAVOR OF THE SOUTHERN PLANTATION OWNERS. CALLED JIM CROW RULE, SEPARATE BUT EQUAL.

APPROXIMATELY ONE HUNDRED AND FOURTEEN YEARS LATER THERE IS ANOTHER SITTING (DEMOCRATIC) BLACK PRESIDENT BARACK H. OBAMA, THAT IS TRYING TO DECEIVE THE AMERICAN PEOPLE, IN THE NAME OF PUBLIC OPTION HEALTH CARE, IN AN EFFORT TO EVADE THE CONSTITUTION AND IJECT SOCIALISM.

THROUGH LYING ABOUT HIS CONCERNS FOR HEATH CARE, LETS JUST EVALUATE HIS INTENT, THERE ARE MILLIONS OF SENIORS OVER SIXTY FIVE, THAT IS ON MEDICARE, THE MAJORITY OF THESE PEOPLE RETIRED FROM SELF EMPLOYMENT, SMALL BUISNESSES, AND EVERY MAJOR CONGLOMERATE NATION WIDE.

AND MILLIONS HAVE SUBSTANTIAL BANK ACCOUNTS, LETS ASSUME OBAMA GET HIS PUBLIC OPTION HEALTH CARE PLAN, HIS INTENT IS TO SHIFT SENIORS SIXTY FIVE AND OVER TO THE PUBLIC OPTION PLAN. PRACTICALLY (EVERY) INDIVIDUAL THAT RESIDE IN AMERICA HAVE A FILE IN A DOCTOR OF MEDICINE OFFICE, AS OF TODATE

THOSE FILES ARE CONFIDENTIAL BETWEEN DOCTOR AND PATIENT.

IF THIS PUBLIC OPTION HEALTH CARE IS IMPLEMENTED, DOCTORS ARE GOING TO BE REQUIRED TO FORWARD YOUR FILE TO A GOVERNMENT CENTRAL DATA BASE. IN ORDER TO VIEW YOUR ILLNESS.

BUT MOSTLY TO ANALYZE RETIRED SENIOR CITIZENS BANK ACCOUNTS TO DETERMINE THEIR WEALTH, ONCE THIS OCCUR, SENIORS WILL BE SUBJECT TO A STANDARD SAME AS AID TO DEPENDENT CHILDREN. FOR INSTANCE IF TWO WOMEN HAVE FIVE CHILDREN EACH, AND ONE IS GAINFULLY EMPLOYED AND THE OTHER NOT, THE ONE NOT EMPLOYED WILL RECEIVE FULL GOVERNMENT ASSISTANCE, WHILE THE EMPLOYED ONE WILL BE SUBJECT TO ADJUSTMENTS BASED ON HER JOB INCOME. THIS SAME CRITERIA WILL BE APPLIED TO RETIRED SENIOR CITIZENS, UNFORTUNATELY THE ADJUSTMENT WILL BE IN ACCORDANCE WITH WHAT IS IN THEIR LIFE SAVINGS BANK ACCOUNT.

IN AN EFFORT TO DETERMINE IF THEY SHOULD BECOME ILL, HOW MUCH MEDICARE THEY ARE TO RECEIVE.(BASED ON THEIR BANK ACCOUNT)

SO WHEN THIS LYING SOCIALISTIC PRESIDENT BARACK H. OBAMA SPEAK OF MEDICARE WASTE HE IS REFERRING TO RETIRED SENIOR CITIZENS BANK ACCOUNTS, THE MAJORITY OF RETIRED SENIOR CITIZENS HAVE ALREADY PAID THEIR DUES.TO SOCIETY.

BY BEING GAINFULLY EMPLOYED FOR TWENTY, THIRTY, AND FORTY YEARS. AND FOR THIS VAMPIRE BLOOD SUCKING ARROGANT, DECITFUL, INCOMPETENT PRESIDENT BARACK HUSSAIN OBAMA, TO WAGE A COMPERSATION WAR ON THE ELDERLY, TO SPREAD THEIR ACCUMULATED WEALTH DUE TO HEALTH PROBLEMS.

IN CONSIDERATION FOR SOME MIS-FIT VIADUCT DWELLER, THAT HAS NEVER HELD A STEADY EMPLOYMENT, AND AWARD THEM ACCESS TO HEALTH INDEPENDENCE, UNDER THE PUBLIC OPTION PLAN, WHICH WILL OVER CROWD PHYSICIANS OFFICIES THROUGH THE NATION, WITH (ALL) KINDS OF PETTY AILMENTS.

AND THE PEOPLE THAT THIS IMPOSTER OF A PRESIDENT HAS CHOSEN TO SPONSER THIS APPALLING ACT ON, IS SENIOR CITIZENS, WHICH WILL PERISH DUE TO (NONE) ATTENTIVE CARE FOR THEIR HEALTH. THIS SOCIALISTIC PHILOSOPHY WILL BANK RUPT OUR NATION, ALONG WITH SENIOR CITIZENS.

HOWEVER ALWAYS REMEMBER, THE STATEMENT OF BARACK HUSSIAN OBAMA MINISTER FOR OVER TWENTY YEARS, RICH WHITE FOLKS CONTROL AMERICA. AND THEIR CHICKENS ARE COMING HOME TO ROOST, THIS IS THE AGENDA OF THE SITTING PRESIDENT BARACK HUSSIAN OBAMA. TO BANK RUPT AMERICA WHICH WILL DESTROY OUR IMAGE GLOBALLY.

SO YOU SMALL DYSFUNCTIONAL BRAIN SLOBBERING (WHITES) OVER SOPHISTICATED DIALECT, THAT VOTED THIS LYING DEMAGOGUE INTO OFFICE. YOU HAD BETTER GET OFF OF YOUR DEAD ASSES, AND HEAD TO THE POLLS IN TWO THOUSAND AND TEN, TO RECTIFY YOUR POLITICAL INEPT DISASTER I AM (NOT) INSINUATING ANY POLITICAL PARTY AFFILIATION, LEAVING IT TO YOUR DISCRETION. HOWEVER IF YOU WANT THE CONSTITUTION DESECRATED, CAPITALISM OMITTED, AND THE GOVERNMENT CONTROLLING YOUR LIFE, INCLUDING MONITORING YOUR CHOICE OF ATTENDING PHYSICIANS. IF YOU CAN NOT FIGURE OUT WHAT IS NECESSARY, THEN IT IS QUITE OBVIOUS YOU HAVE BEEN CONTAMINATED WITH THE SMALL BRAIN DISEASE THAT FORMER F.B.I. DIRECTOR J. EDGAR HOOVER MENTION IN NINETEEN FIFTY SEVEN. DESCRIBING AFRICAN AMERICANS.

HOWEVER THIS PRESIDENT HAS CREATED A DISCONNECT WITH THE AMERICAN PEOPLE, AND .MILLIONS ARE BEGINNING TO ALIENATE THEM SELVESFROM HIS DECITFUL CHICAGO BACK ALLEY DISTORTING SEDUCTION. UNFORTUNATELLY HIS SUPPORTERS ARE TRYING TO UTILIZE RACISM AS A TACTICAL DEPLOYMENT TO PERSUADE, BASED ON HE BEING BLACK. WHICH IS A BLATANT LIE, BECAUSE HE WAS ELECTED BY SMALL DYSFUNCTIONAL BRAIN (WHITES)

HE IS BEGINNING TO POLITICALLY SELF DESTRUCT, BECAUSE OF WHAT THE SOUTHERN DEMOCRATIC KU-KLUX-KLAN DISCOVERED AND PREDICTED ABOUT AFRICAN AMERICANS PERSUING A POLITICAL AGENDA IN EIGHTEEN SEVENTY THAT THEY WERE POLITICALLY IGNORANT, ALSO INCOMPETENT. PRESIDENT BARACK HUSSIAN OBAMA AFTER ONE HUNDRED AND THIRTY NINE YEARS, IS A FINE EXAMPLE THAT IS GIVING CREDENCE TO THEIR INTELLCT OF AFRICAN AMERICANS AND THE POLITICAL ARENA.

NOT TO MENTION REPRESENTATIVE MAXINE WATERS, GETTING INTO THE CARPET BAG ACT, AND SO DAMN STUPID NOT TO UNDERSTAND THAT THESE WERE THE NORTHERN REPUBLICANS, MANY WERE EDUCATORS THAT MIGRATED TO THE SOUTHERN STATES IN AN EFFORT TO TEACH FORMER SLAVES TO READ AND WRITE, IN ORDER TO BECOME INDEPENDENT, AFTER THEIR FREEDOM WAS RATIFIED BY (REPUBLICAN) PRESIDENT ABRAHAM LINCOLN, IN EIGHTEEN SIXTY FIVE.

IN EIGHTEEN SIXTY SIX THE SOUTHERN (DEMOCRAT) PLANTATION SLAVE OWENERS FOUNDERED THE KU-KLUX-KLAN, IN PULASKI, TENNESSEE, AND DROVE THE CARPET BAGGERS OUT OF THHE SOUTHERN STATES, AND SHOT AND KILLED, MAIMED, LYNCHED AND INTIMIDATED BLACKS, AND FORCED THEM FROM THE REPUBLICAN PARTY, INTO THE (DEMOCRAT) PARTY, SO MRS WATERS, YOU TWO CURRENT DAY BLACK POLITICIANS TO INCLUDE OBAMA, ARE SOLIDIFYING THE EVALUATION OF SOUTHERN (DEMOCRATS) DURING THE EIGHTEEN SEVENTYS, WHICH MEAN THAT THEY WERE ON TO SOMETHING, REGARDS TO BLACK POLITICAL INCOMPETENCY, NOT ONLY IS PRESIDENT BARACK HUSSIAN OBAMA INCOMPETENT,HE IS ASTONDINGLY ARRAGANT, ALSO VINDICTIVE.

HE.IS THE PRESIDENT OF (ALL) THE PEOPLE REGARDLESS OF THEIR IDEOLOGY, HE DEJECTED FOX NEWS ON SEPTEMBER 20, 2009. BECAUSE THE COMMENTATORS DO NOT SMELL THE SEAT OF HIS PANTS, UNLIKE THE MAJORITY OF OTHER NET WORK COMMENTATORS.

THIS IS CHILDISH, SELFISH AND EXTREMELY UNPROFESSIONAL, TO SHOW FAVOR OR DISFAVOR RELATED TO THE MEDIA.

UNFORTUNATELY PRESIDENT OBAMA, IS INEPT TO THE CHRONOLOGICAL RECORDS OF SIGNIFICANT EVENTS PERTAINING TO HIS PARTY, INDEED PRESIDENT BARACK H. OBAMA, HAS CONVINCED HIM SELF THAT HE IS INVINCIBLE, AND IT APPEAR THAT HE IS OF THE OPINION, THAT ALL HE HAVE TO DO IS APPEAR PUBLICLY, AND GIVE A SPEECH WITH GLOATING EVASIVE ERRONEOUS VERBIAGE.

AND THE AMERICAN PEOPLE WILL SWOON, WHICH IS AN INDICATION THAT HE HAS CHARACTERIZED U.S. CITIZENS AS BEING INEPT TO HIS FALLACIOUS FOLKLORE.

THIS PRESIDENT HAVE (NO) PERSPECTIVE OR RESPECT, FOR THE FUNDAMENTAL CHRONOLOGICAL EVENTS THAT IS THE STABILITY OF OUR NATION.

HE IS THE KIND OF INDIVIDUAL IF NOT APPEASED BY PEOPLE, IN ACCORDANCE WITH HIS OWN IDEOLOGICAL AGENDA. HE TEND TO REBEL, AND THIS TYPE OF ARROGANCE COULD VERY WELL DEMORALIZE AND JEOPARDIZE OUR NATION REGARDS TO CONSTITUTIONAL LIBERTIES, PRIME EXAMPLE. ON SEPTEMBER 20, 2009. HE STAGED A REBELLIOUS ACT OF DISCRIMINATION AGAINST ONE OF THE MOST FAIR AND BALANCE NEWS NET WORK. IN OUR NATION.

WITH A RATING THAT EXCEED (ALL) THE OTHER NEWS NET WORKS COMBINE, THIS WAS INTENDED TO BE A REPROOF, AND A WARNING TO FOX NEWS THAT HE (WILL) DO ANY THING TO DAMAGE THEIR CREDIBILITY, FOR EXPOSING HIS (NAT TURNER) RECKLESS IDEOLOGICAL AGENDA TO DRIVE AMERICA IN TO FINANCIAL DESTITUTION.

UNDER THE PRETENSES OF PUBLIC OPTION HEALTH CARE, THIS IS I HIDDEN COVERT AGENDA OF HIS (OWN) ACCORD, TO REDUCE AMERICA TO A THIRD WORLD STATUS. OMIT THE CONSTITUTION, EMPLEMENT LAWS TO FAVOR HIS SOCIALISTIC STANDARDS, IN ORDER THAT HE CAN REMAIN CONGO RULER ETERNALLY.

HOWEVER THE FORE FATHERS DESIGNED ONE OF THE MOST INCREDIBLE UNIQUE LEGISLATIVE DOCUMENTS ON

GODS EARTH, AND THAT IS THE CONSTITUTION AND THE DECLARATION OF INDEPENDANCE.

WHICH THE CONSTITUTION BEGIN WITH THESE WORDS. (WE THE PEOPLE) OF THE UNITED STATES, IN ORDER TO FORM A MORE PERFECT UNION, ESTABLISH JUSTICE, INSURE DOMESTIC TRANQUILITY, PROVIDE FOR THE COMMON DEFENCE, PROMOTE THE GENERAL WELFARE, AND SECURE THE BLESSSING OF (LIBERTY) TO OURSELVES AND POSTERITY, DO ORDAIN AND ESTABLISH THIS CONSTITUTION FOR THE UNITED STATES. OF AMERICA.

(ARTICLE ONE)

(ALL) LEGISLATIVE POWERS HEREIN GRANTED SHALL BE VESTED IN A (CONGRESS) OF THE UNITED STATES, WHICH SHALL CONSIST OF A (SENATE) AND HOUSE OF (REPRESENTATIVES);

THERE ARE FIVE HUNDRED AND THIRTY FIVE, CONGRESS PEOPLE, ONE HUNDRED SENATORS, FOUR HUNDRED AND THIRTY CONGRESS REPRESENTATIVES. EACH IS ELECTED TO SERVE BY THE FIRST WORDS OF THE CONSTITUTION.

(WE THE PEOPLE)

IF YOU NOTICE THERE IS (NO) MENTION OF A PRESIDENT IN THE FIRST ARTICLE OF THE CONSTITUTION.

HOWEVER THESE ARE THE PEOPLE THAT REPRESENT SETTING THE OBJECTIVES AND STANDARDS FOR THE UNITED STATES OF AMERICA, REGARDS TO THE CITIZENS.

THAT CONSIST OF TWO MAJOR PARTIES, DEMOCRAT AND REPUBLICAN, THAT BALANCE CONSTRUCTIVE OPINIONS, BASED ON AGENDAS.

WHICH RELATE TO LIBERAL AND CONSERVATIVE, MOST DEMOCRATS LIBERAL AND REPUBLICANS MOSTLY CONSERVATIVE.

HOWEVER THERE ARE ALTERNATIVES AS TO PARTY AFFILIATIONS, AND IT HAS TO DO WITH INDIVIDUAL DISCRETION, RELATED TO PERSONAL IDEOLOLOGY, PERTAINING TO CHOICE.

IN ORDER TO DETERMINE IN CHOOSING , SOLEY DEPEND ON FRAME OF MIND AND DEFINITELY ANALYZE THE DEFINITION OF EACH WORD CATEGORY.

(LIBERAL) IS DEFINED AS FAVORING POLITICAL REFORM, TENDING TOWARD DEMOCRACY AND PERSONAL FREEDOM FOR THE INDIVIDUAL PROGRESS.

AND CONFORMING TO ESTABLISHED DOCTRINES, WHICH MEAN TREATING (ALL) CLASSES OF PEOPLE THE SAME WAY ORTHODOXY.

WHICH IS A FORM OF (SOCIALISM);

(CONSERVATIVE) TENDING TO PRESERVE ESTABLISHED TRADITIONS, AND TO RESIST OR OPPOSE (ANY) CHANGES IN CONSERVATIVE POLICIES REGARDS TO THE STABILIZATION OF POLITICS.

WHICH MEAN PRESERVING THE INTEGRITY OF THE CONSTITUTION, AND MAINTAINING CAPITALISM.

UNFORTUNATELY A VAST MAJORITY OF AFRICAN AMERICANS, AND A LARGE SEGEMENT OF CAUCASIANS GENETICALLY ADHERE TO FAMILY TRADITIONS, PERTAINING TO POLITICAL!VOTE CASTING.

PARTICULARLY BLACKS, BECAUSE THEY ARE CONSTANTLY BEING SUBJECTED TO FENDISH, RACIST DEMAGOGUERY, FROM BLACK AND WHITE (DEMOCRATIC) POLITICIANS.

ALSO SELF APPOINTED BLACK LEADERS, WITH COMPELLING INNUENDO AND DISTORTED RADICAL RACISM. ALSO CONDEMMING (ALL) WHITES FOR THEIR INAPPROPRIATE FOOLISH INCOMPETENCE.

HOWEVER THE FUNDAMENTAL NATURE OF QUALITY. IS/ THERE ARE MILLIONS OF CITIZENS THAT RESIDE IN AMERICA, THAT ARE STAUNCH LIBERAL DEMOCRATS, BASED ON THEIR VOTING RECORD.

AND ARE TOTALLY (UNAWARE) THAT THEY ARE UTILIZING THE CONSERVATIVE (REPUBLICAN) PRINCIPLES OF STATUSQUO TO CAPITALIZE ON SUCCESS. VENTURING INTO THE BUISNESS WORLD, OWNING REALESTATE AND MISCELLANEOUS BUISNESSES. YET THEIR LOYALTY IS PREDICATED TO THE (LIBERAL) AGENDA.

GENERALLY (ALL) PEOPLE AND ANIMALS , ARE POSSESSED WITH GENETIC HERITAGE, THAT HAS DISTINCTIVE TRAITS

OF THEIR NATIVE CUSTOMS, REFERRING TO PEOPLE. I SUSPECT THAT IS WHY THE FORE FATHERS STIPULATED IN ARTICLE TWO, SECTION ONE OF THE CONSTITUTION, THAT (NO) PERSON EXCEPT A (NATURAL) BORN CITIZEN , OR A CITIZEN OF THE UNITED STATES, AT THE TIME OF THE ADOPTION, SHALL BE (ELIGIBLE) TO THE OFFICE OF PRESIDENT.

PRESIDENT BARACK HUSSIAN OBAMA, IS A MODERN DAY DIRECT GENETIC HERITAGE OF GFRICA, RELATED TO HIS FATHER.

AFRICA IS A CONTINENT OF MOSTLY UNCIVIL TRIBES, THAT IS GOVERN BY TRIBAL CHIEFS THIS IS THEIR NATIVE CUSTOMS.

UNFORTUNATELY OUR GREAT NATION HAVE ELECTED A PRESIDENT IN OBAMA, WITH THE INTENT OF BESTOWING, HIS AFRICAN HERITAGE ON OUR GREAT NATION THE UNITED STATES OF AMERICA.

CITIZENS OF AMERICA, DEMOCRATS, REPUBLICANS, INDEPENDANTS, AND GREENE PARTY ALIKE ECT.

PLEASE BE AWARE THAT WE ARE AT THE CROSS ROAD, OF OUR NATION AND FREEDOM;

THIS INFLAMATORY, EGOTISTICAL, NOISOME, AND NARCISSISM PRESIDENT, BARACK HUSSIAN OBAMA, THIS MAN HAS DISDAIN FOR AMERICA, WITH INTENTIONS OF POLITICAL CONDEMNATION, AND DESTRUCTION OF AMERICA. FOR INSTANCE THIS DELIRIOUS,INCOMPETENT PRESIDENT, ADDRESSED THE U.N. GENERAL ASSEMBLY ON SEPTEMBER 23, 2009.

AND BLATANTLY ACCUSED AMERICA OF BEING A NATION TORTURES AND IT WAS BROUGHT TO HALT BECOUSE OF HIS PRESIDENCY.

AFTER LISTENING TO THIS AMERICAN HATRED BASHING, MY HEAD BEGAN TO HURT, AND I HAD A SENSATION OF PUKING WHERE WAS THIS PSYCHOPATH OF A PRESIDENT, WHEN (TERRORIST) EXTERMINATED APPROXIMATELY THREE THOUSAND OF OUR INNOCENT AMERICAN CITIZENS.

THIS PRESIDENT IS CONSTANTLY BOASTING ABOUT (HIS) AMERICA AND HIS PEOPLE, BUT (NEVER) RAISE THE ISSURE OF (PRAISE);

REGARDS TO CHRONOLOGICAL GREATNESS,STABILITY AND FORTITUDE THAT IS EMBEDDED IN THIS WONDERFUL NATION CALLED THE UNITED STATES OF AMERICA.

PRESIDENT BARACK HUSSIAN OBAMA, IS THEORETICALLY ASSUMING THAT HE IS THE WISEST PERSON ON THE PLANET EARTH

WHILE OTHER NATIONS ARE UTILIZING HIS POLITICAL INEPTNESS, CHUCKLING WITH GLEE, AND IN THE INTERIM ADVANCING THEIR OWN CAUSES, TO SABOTAGE AMERICA.

HOWEVER CHRONOLOGICAL RECORDS OF SIGNIFICANT EVENTS DICTATE, THAT REGARDS TO DEROGATORY AND RADICAL ISSURES, THAT THREATENS OUR LIBERTIES, (WE THE PEOPLE) HAS ALWAYS RISEN TO THE OCCASION, IN AN EFFORT TO RECTIFY.

THE AMERICAN PEOPLE ARE EXTREMELY PATIENT, ALSO THEY ARE NOT POLITICALLY STUPID, BECAUSE THEY ARE SIGNALING VERY CLEAR, FROM EACH POLITICAL PARTY DEMOCRAT AND REPUBLICAN, FOR THEIR DESPERATION OF DISSATISFACTION TO BE ATTENTIVE. AND THESE ARE AMERICAN CITIZENS FROM EIGHTEEN TO NINETY YEARS OLD.

DEMONSTRATING AT TOWN HALL MEETINGS, ALSO TEA PARTYS ALL OVER THE NATION, AND YOU HAVE SMALL DYSFUNCTIONAL BRAIN PSYCHOPATHS. SUCH AS FORMER PRESIDENT JIMMY CARTER, BILL COSBY, FORMER PRESIDENT WILLIAM J. CLINTON AND WALTER MONDALE, THAT ARE ACCUSING BONA FIDE AMERICAN CITIZENS, THAT HAS CONCERNS ABOUT THE DEBT OF THE NATION, THEIR WELL FAIR RELATED TO SOCIALISM.

THEY ARE BEING IDENTIFIED AS RACIST BY THE ABOVE ARISTOCRATS. ALSO HARRY REID AND NANCY PELOSI, CLAIMING THAT THEY ARE TURF AND EXCITING VIOLENCE, SOLELY BECAUSE BARACK H. OBAMA IS A BLACK PRESIDENT, AS IF HE (WAS NOT) BLACK BEFORE (WHITE) PEOPLE ELECTED HIM TO THE PRESIDENCY.

I AM CERTAIN THAT I AM GOING TO BE CALLED A WHITE MAN NIGGER, BY LIBERAL BLACKS. JUST AS LIBERAL WHITES HAVE CALLED OTHER WHITES NIGGER HATERS COVERTLY.

HOWEVER I COULD CARE LESS, SIMPLY BECAUSE I LOVE MY COUNTRY AND WOULD DEDICATE MY LIFE TO SAVE MY COUNTRY FRON A CONGO IDEOLOGIST OF A SOCIALIST COVERT AGENDA TO FORFEIT OUR LIBERTIES. THROUGH DECEITFUL LYING AND DISTORTION, REGARDS TO PUBLIC OPTION HEALTH CARE.

SO I PLEADE AND BEG, OF YOU UNITED STATE CITIZENS, DEMOCRATS AND REPUBLICANS, IF YOU CARE ABOUT OUR CONSTITUTION, AND HOW IT REPRESENT THE MORAL FABRIC OF LIBERTIES, EMBEDDED IN OUR GREAT NATION PLEASE USE YOUR SELF INTELLECTUAL MORALITY, OF DISCRETION HEAD TO POLLS AND SAVE OUR NATION.

ON SEPTEMBER 24, 2009 WATCHED A SEGMENT OF FOX NEWS, THE OREILLY FACTOR, AND HE HAD A BLACK GUEST ON, WHICH WAS A CROSS BETWEEN A JACKASS AND BABOON, JEREMY LEVITT;

THAT ALL OF THE CONCERN CITIZENS PROTESTING, TO MAINTAIN THEIR LIBERTY, BY PROTECTING THE CONSTITUTION, FROM BEING RESCINDED BY PRESIDENT BARACK HUSSIEN OBAMA.

THIS JACKASS BABOON JERMEY LEVITT, INSISTED THAT (ALL) PROTESTERS CARRYING SIGNS WERE REPUBLICAN RACIST,AND AFFILIATED WITH THE KU-KLUX-KLAN.

IF I UNDERSTOOD IT CORRECTLY, HE IS A PROFESSOR AT A UNIVERSITY, AND HE IS SO DAMN POLITICALL INCOMPETENT, THAT IT WAS THE SOUTHERN DEMOCRATS THAT FOUNDERED THE KU-KLUX-KLAN, IN EIGHTEEN SIXTY SIX, AND SHOT, LYNCHED, AND MAIMED BLACKS, ALSO BLEW UP LITTLE BLACK GIRLS IN CHURCHES.

UNTIL (REPUBLICAN) PRESIDENT DWIGHT D. EISENHOWER, AUTHORIZED F.B.I. DIRECTOR J. EDGAR HOOVER, TO INFILTRATE THE KU-KLUX-KLAN. AND QUELL THE VIOLENCE AGAINST BLACKS.

ALSO PRESIDENT EISENHOWER, USED THE MILITARY TO INTEGRATE SCHOOLS IN THE SOUTH, FOR BLACKS. SO MR

HALF BREED JACKASS AND BABOON JEREMY LEVITT, ONE OF YOUR SITTING SENATORS A (DEMOCRAT) ROBERT BYRD IS A FORMER KU-KLUX-KLANSMAN.

IT IS PEOPLE LIKE YOU THAT PROMPTED F.B.I. DIRECTOR J. EDGAR HOOVER IN NINETEEN FIFTY SEVEN, TO IMPLY THAT BLACKS BRAINS WAS 20% SMALLER THAN WHITES. AND I MUST CONFESS WATCHING PEOPLE LIKE YOU MR. LEVITT, MAKE IT EXTREMELY DIFFICULT (NOT) TO AGREE WITH HIS IMPLICATIONS.

PRESIDENT BARACK HUSSIEN OBAMA, WERE ON SEVERAL NET WORKS TALK SHOWS, SEPTEMBER 20, 2009. WHEN ASKED BY ONE OF THE COMMENTATERS TO COMMENT ON (ACORN) HE BRISTLED WITH ARROGANCE, AND STATED THERE ARE MORE IMPORTANT THINGS TO DISCUSS, OTHER THAN ACORN. YET EARLIER THIS YEAR AT A PRESS CONFERENCE, WHEN ASKED BY A REPORTER HIS COMMENTS ON A (WHITE) POLICE ARRESTING A (BLACK) PROFESSOR.

HE ROARED AND CHIMED IN WITHOUT BEING AWARE OF AND BLURTED OUT THAT IT WAS STUPID, FOR A POLICE OFFICER TO ARREST THIS MAN IN HIS OWN HOME. DEMEANING THE BOSTON POLICE FORCE, WITH OUT KNOWLEDGE OF WHAT TRANSPIRED.

AMERICAN CITIZENS WAKE UP, YOU HAVE ELECTED A RACIST, RADICAL, COVERT, SOCIALIST, PEDESTAL, NARCISSISM PRESIDENT. THAT THINK HE IS INVINCIBLE, HOWEVER JUST AS JEREMY LEVITT, ON THE OREILLY FACTOR, WAS INEPT TO WHICH POLITICAL PARTY HAS STIMULATED RACISM.

PRESIDENT BARACK H. OBAMA , IS INEPT TO THE SAME PARTY, THAT IS CONTROLLING CONGRESS AND THE SENATE, HE HAS TRADITIONAL HERITAGE AFRICAN HIGH BUTTOCKS, BY THE TIME THE (DEMOCRATS) ARE FINISHED WITH HIM, HIS BUTTOCKS ARE GOING TO BE REDUCED TO (FLAT)

GEORGE WASHINGTON, WAS OUR FIRST PRESIDENT, I HAVE READ ABOUT HIM AND OTHERS AFTER HIM, I CALL PRESIDENT ROOSEVELT, AND THE OTHERS AFTER HIM,

AND AS OF TODATE THERE HAS (NEVER) BEEN A PRESIDENT ECCENTRIC AS BARACK HUSSEIN OBAMA.

HE IS (ASSUMING) THAT HE IS THE CONQUEROR OF ALL ILLS GLOBALLY, AND HAVENT THE SLIGHTEST IDEA WHAT IS COVERTLY TRANSPIRING IN HIS OWN CONGRESS.

THERE ARE REPETITIOUS STATEMENTS THROUGH OUT THIS BOOK, HOWEVER IT IS NECCESSARY TO OUTLINE DIFFERENT SCENARIOS, FOR INSTANT THERE ARE RACIST PERSONNEL IN EACH POLITICAL PARTIES, DEMOCRAT ALSO REPUBLICAN, AND THAT IS INEVITABLE.

AND THEY ARE (NOT) AILENATED FROM JOINING AT THE HIP TO CONQUER, AS I HAVE PREVIOUSLY STATED (REPUBLICAN) PRESIDENT EISENHOWER, DRAFTED THE FIRST CIVIL RIGHTS BILL FOR SOUTHERN BLACKS. IN EIGHTY FIVE YEARS, THE (DEMOCRATS) CONTROLLED CONGRESS AND DID NOT HAVE THE VOTES TO DEFEAT THE BILL.

IN RETROSPECT TWELVE (REPUBLICANS) RECONCILED ALONG WITH DEMOCRATS AND DEFEATED CIVIL RIGHTS FOR (ALL) SOUTHERN AFRICAN AMERICANS SO IN ESSENCE PRESIDENT BARACK HUSSIEN OBAMA, ARE ASSUMING THAT HE IS A POLITICAL GENIUS LORD OVER PEOPLE.

UNFORTUNATELY FOR HIM, HIS EGOTISTICAL ARROGANCE IS DISSIPATING. TO BORROW A PHRASE FROM THE LATE COUNTRY SINGER BUCK OWNES. HE HAS GOT A (TIGER) BY THE TAIL, AND HAVE NO IDEA AS TO WHAT IS GRADUALLY DEVELOPING WITHIN THE SENATE AND THE HOUSE OF REPRESENTATIVES, MEANING DEMOCRATS AND REPUBLICANS, HAVE COMBINE THEIR WITS COVERTLY. WHILE HE POLITICALLY DESTROY HIM SELF, WITH THE CITIZENS OF OUR NATION.

ALWAYS REMEMBER THE FIRST WORDS BEGINNING XN THE CONSTITUTION..THAT IS DETRIMENTAL TO MR OBAMA POLITICAL FUTURE.

(WE THE PEOPLE)

THERE IS A SEGMENT OF DEMOCRATS, ALSO REPUBLICANS, THAT HAS DETERMINED AND TEND TO REPUDIATE PRESIDENT BARACK HUSSIEN COVERT AGENDA, TO CAST AMERICA INTO HIS PERSONAL IDEOLOGY OF CONTROL.. NEITHER DEMOCRATS OR REPUBLICANS, ARE

GOING TO SIT SILENT AND HAVE OUR CONSTITUTIONAL LIBERTIES TERMINATED, AND BE SIPHONED INTO A MUSLIM FAITH, WHICH COVERTLY HE IS TRYING TO ACCOMPLISH. MOST CIVIL POLITICAL DEMOCRATS AND REPUBLICANS, HAS FIGURED THIS OUT LONG AGO.

HOWEVER NEITHER PARTY WOULD (NEVER) SPEAK OUT, FEAR OF BEING LABELED A RACIST, PARTICULARLY DEMOCRATS, THEY HAVE SEDUCE BLACKS TO VOTE FOR THEM FOR OVER SEVENTY FIVE YEARS, AT A RATE OF 90% AND. LYING ON REPUBLICANS, BY INSTIGATING THAT REPUBLICANS ARE RICH AND IS HOARDING FINANCES, AND ARE RACIST TOWARD BLACKS, AND THAT IS RESPONSIBLE FOR THE POVITY OF BLACKS.

HOWEVER THIS PRESIDENT THINK THAT (ALL) AMERICAN PEOPLE ARE STUPPID, AND ARE GLOATING OVER HIS CONTEXTUAL RADICAL SPEECHES. APPARENTLY HE MISS CHARACTERIZED THE INTELLECT OF WHITES, AND ASSUMED THAT THEIR THINKING WERE EQUIVALENT TO BLACK ANXIETIES, THE BODY OF BELIEFS FOR MOST AFRICAN AMERICANS ARE QUITE UNIQUE, MEANING THAT MOST HAVE CONTEMPT FOR THE CONSTITUTION, AND LAWS THAT GOVERN OUR NATION.AND APPROXIMATELY EIGHTY FIVE PERCENT HAVE SCORN FOR (WHITES) AND PRESIDENT BARACK HUSSIEN OBAMA, IS (NO) EXCEPTION. HE TEND TO CAPITALIZE ON HIS DOMINANCE BY TOUCHING AND STROKING DIGNITARIES. WHICH REPRESENT AUTHORITATIVE ECCENTRICITY.

AND THERE ARE POLITICAL (WHITE) MIS-FITS, THAT ARE INEPT TO THESE CULTURAL STANDARDS PREFERABLE USED BY BLACKS TO INDICATE HAUGHTINESS.

SUCH AS FORMER PRESIDENT WILLIAM JEFFERSON CLINTON, INSISTING THAT REPUBLICANS ARE TRYING TO DESTROY THE IMAGE OF BARACK OBAMA .

BY UTILIZING RACIST TACTICS, WOULD SOME ONE (PLEASE) INFORM THIS INFLAMMATORY PERVERT, THAT THE (DEMOCRATS) ARE IN CONTROL OF THE PRESIDENCY, THE SENATE ALSO THE CONGRESS, WITH MARGINS OF CONTROL TO DEFEAT OR PASS ANY THING THEY DEEM NECESSARY.

AS I HAVE REPEATEDLY INDICATED, THIS IS A STRATEGIC PLOT IMPLEMENTED BY ELEMENTS OF STOOGE (DEMOCRATS) LYING ON REPUBLICANS, IN AN EFFORT TO MAINTAIN THE STATUSQUO THAT EXIST, TO INDOCTRINATE SOCIETIES, PERTAINING TO A LIBERAL PHILOSOPHY.

HOWEVER WE AS A PEOPLE, LIVE IN A SOCIETY OF ADVANCE TECHNOLOGY, THAT SOME TIME CAUSE INFLAMITORY TENDENCIES, SIMPLY BECAUSE OF UNCERTANTY, BASED ON INEPTNESS REGARDS TO CHRONOLOGICAL RECORDS OF SIGNIFICANT EVENTS.

WHICH MEAN THE IDEOLOGY THAT OUR NATION WAS FOUNDED ON, UNLESS WE AS A CIVIL SOCIETY ADOPT THE SENTIMENTS OF MORALITY, AND REFRAIN FROM A SOCIALISTIC, LIBERAL,DOCTRINE, THAT IS INVADING OUR CIVIL COMMUNITY LIFE ON A DAILY BASIS.

FOR INSTANCE YOUNG SCHOOL PARTICIPANTS, MAULING EACH OTHER ON SCHOOL BUSES, AND FATALLY SLAUGHTERING INDIVIDUALS WITH WOODEN OBJECTS. THE SIGNIFICANCE OF THIS VIOLENCE IS BECOMING EXTREMELY PREVALENT, THROUGH OUT OUR NATION. ALSO SEVERAL ACTS OF TERRORISM WERE FOILED, DIRECTED AT MAJOR CITIES.

ALSO THERE ARE MASS GUN BATTLES IN URBAN CITIES, THAT EXTERMINATE PERSONS, NOT TO MENTION THE ENDURING CONFLICTS IN ASIA, IRAQ AND AFGHANISTAN, ALONG WITH THE IRANIANS NUCLEAR DEBACLE. AND WHERE IS OUR (DEMOCRATIC) CONTROLLING REGIME IN WASHINGTON. ESPECIALLY OUR PRESIDENT BARACK HUSSEIN OBAMA.

HE IS BUISY ADDRESSING THE BLACK CAUCUS, REGARDS TO BLACK URBAN POVITY, WHICH IS AND ALWAYS WILL BE INEVITABLE, BECAUSE OF EMBEDDED LIBERALIZE INDOCTRINATION, BASED ON DEMOCRATIC RACE BAITING. AND UNLESS WE ADOPT THE SENTIMENTS OF MORALITY, WE ARE GOING TO PERISH AS A VIABLE NATION OF HUMANE CIVILITY AND DIGNITY. AND BE FORCED TO ACCEPT A SOCIALISTIC CONGO IDEOLOGICAL WAY OF LIFE. HOWEVER I AM CERTAIN THAT MOST POLITICAL DEMOCRATS AND REPUBLICANS HAS EVALUATED THE INTENT OF PRESIDENT

OBAMA,LONG AGO.. UNFORTUNATELY NEITHER PARTY WILL ADMIT, NOR SPEAK OUT, FEAR OF BEING LABELED AS EXCITING.RACISM AGAINST BARACK OBAMA BECAUSE HE BLACK, THE BIBLE REVEAL THAT GOD CREATED MAN IN HIS OWN IMAGE, WHICH MEAN HE HAD A BRAIN, AND SO DOES HUMAN INDIVIDUALS, THAT IS IN CONTROL OF THEIR DESTINY, DURING THEIR STAY ON EARTH. WITHIN THE BRAIN CONSIST OF TWO CONTROLLING GENETIC FACTORS OF INHERITANCE, DISTINGUISHED FROM MALE AND FEMALE, WHICH IS MOST COMMONLY KNOWN AS MOTHER AND FATHER, AND THERE IS A DIVERSE GENETIC FACTOR WHICH INVOLVE EACH PARENT.

THAT IS UNIQUELY DISTRIBUTED THROUGH THE CHILD BODY, WHICH DICTATE THE IDENTY OF HUMANS, ALSO ANIMALS.

AS HUMANS BEGIN TO DEVELOP THEIR GENETIC SKILLS, PASSED ON FROM TRAITS OF EACH PARENT COMBINED, WHICH WILL DETERMINE THEIR DESTINY IN LIFE, THAT IS WHY THE RAISING OF CHILDREN, BY BOTH PARENT IS SO EVERLY IMPORTANT.

BECAUSE THE CHILD HAVE THE ADVANTAGE TO DETERMINE AND DISTINGUISH THE TRAITS OF EACH PARENT, IN ORDER TO FRAME THEIR FUTURE. AND THAT IS WHY (MOST) SINGLE PARENTS HAVE TREMENDOUS DIFFICULTY WITH RAISING CHILDREN, BECAUSE THE OTHER PARENT GENE IS EMBEDDED WITHIN THE CHILD, WHICH THE CHILD IS TOTALLY UNAWARE OF WHAT IS DICTATING AND DRIVING THEIR EMOTIONS FROM WITHIN. TRUST ME THIS IS THE CONTROLLING FACTOR IN THE LIFE OF PEOPLE IN VARIFYING THEIR IDENTY, BECAUSE OF A EMBEDDED GENE, THAT THEY ARE TOTALLY UNFAMILIAR WITH THE CHARACTERISTICS, WHICH COULD HAVE BEEN THE DOMINANT GENE THAT DICTATE IMPULSES.

AND WE AS A (GOD) CREATED PEOPLE GLOBALLY ARE IDENTIFIABLE IN ACCORDANCE WITH THE IDENTICAL CIRCUMSTANCES.OF REALITY WHICH IS INEVITABLE.

THAT IS ESSENTIAL TO NNP SURVIVAL AS A HUMAN RACE., GOD IS OUR CREATOR BUT DOES (NOT) ENDORSE IMPERFECTIONS PERTAINING TO PEOPLE HOWEVER MAN

HAS VIOLATED THE PRINCIPLES OF GOD, SENSE ADAM AND EVE. RECENTLY THE CRITERIA HAS BECAME MORE CYNICAL AND DRASTICALLY PREVALENTI.ENT. THROUGH OUT OUR NATION, AND ABROAD, SO IT IS ESSENTIAL THAT WE THECPEOPLEJ.BECOMEP.MOREEL NEOLMEPT FROM A INDIVIDUAL PRECEPTION, REGARDS TO THE PEOPLE THAT WE ELECT TO REPRESENT OUR HUMANITY AND FAITH IN THE CONSTITUTION, WHICH EIGHTY FIVE OR NINETY PERCENT OF AFRICAN AMERICANS, HAVE DISDAIN FOR.THE CONSTUTITION OF AMERICA.

WHICH INCLUDE SOME OF THE MOST HIGHLY EDUCATED AFRICAN AMERICANS IN CIVIL SOCIETY.

EVEN THOSE THAT GRAUTATED FORM PRESTIGIOUS INSTITUTIONS, IN AMERICA AND ABROAD.

UNFORTUNATELY THERE IS A INCONSISTENCY (UNREADABLE TEXT) AMERICA.

WHICH IS PRIMARILY DUE TO (DEMOCRATIC) UNRELENTING DECADES OF LYING AND DISTORTING REALITY, AND MOST AFRICAN AMERICANS INABILITY TO DECIPHER THEIR MOTIVES BASED ON POLITICAL INCOMPETENCE.

WHICH THE SOUTHERN DEMOCRATS DISCOVERED IN EIGHTEEN SIXTY EIGHT, SO IN ESSENCE MOST BLACKS HAVE A UNIQUE DISDAIN FOR THINGS THEY CAN NOT UNDERSTAND PERTAINING TO REALITY, AND WILL REBEL BASED ON THEIR OWN INEPTNESS, TO JUSTIFY THEIR INABILITY WITH DISTORTION. WHICH IS EMBEDDED FROM HERITAGE, AND A DEMOCRATIC LIBERAL PHILOSOPHY, OF MOTIVATED CYNICISM.

WHICH IS A CONDESCENDING REALITY OF (ALL) PEOPLE. HOWEVER BLACKS UTILIZE THIS EFFIGY TO STIGMATIZE THEM SELVES, MORE ABUNDING THAN OTHER NATIONALITY OF PEOPLE.

IN AN EFFORT TO DISGUISE FOR THEIR INAPPROPRIATE INTELLECT, BY CONSTANTLY APPEARING, IN ORDER TO CONVINCE WITH DECEITFUL DISTORTED NARCISSISM GLAMORIZATION.

PARTICULARLY IF THEY ARE INVOLVED IN POLITICS, MANAGING AFFAIRS OF GOVERNMENT.

WE AS A NATION UNDER THE GUIDANCE OF OUR CONSTITUTION HAVE ALLOWED A SLICK TALKING WEASEAL, TO CAST OUR NATION INTO DESPAIR. WHERE IN THE HELL HAVE YOUR SANITY DISSIPATED TO.

(REALITY) IS THE MOST ESTABLISHED WORD IN THE AMERICAN ENGLISH, ALSO GLOBALLY , IF ANY ONE DEFY REALITY THEY ARE A IMBECILE. THE STATE OF DEFYING IS A PARTICULAR FORM OF CIVILIZATION, HOWEVER IF USED INAPPROPRIATELY CAN BE DETRIMENTAL, EVEN THE SACRIFICE OF LIFE.

OUR GREAT NATION HAVE ELECTED A PRESIDENT BARACK HUSSIEN OBAMA. THAT IS INDICATIVE OF (ALL) THE ABOVE.

ALSO CONSTITUTE THE PREDICTIONS OF THE DEMOCRATIC KU-KLUX-KLAN OF EIGHTEEN SIXTY EIGHT, AND F.B.I. DIRECTOR J. EDGAR HOOVER OF NINETEEN FIFTY SEVEN, THE SOUTHERN KLAN, ACCESSED BLACKS IN EIGHTEEN SIXTY EIGHT OF BEING IGNORANT, AND POLITICALLY INCOMPETENT. DURING THE FIFTIES J. EDGAR HOOVER ASSERTED THAT BLACKS BRAINS AS BEING TWENTY PERCENT SMALLERTHAN WHITES.

APPROXIMATELY ONE HUNDRED AND FORTY ONE YEARS LATER, PRESIDENT BARACK HUSSIEN OBAMA, IS MAKING THE PSYCHOANALYSIS OF THESE PEOPLE. EQUIVALENT TO AN ANALYSIS OF ALBERT EINSTEIN.

IN ESSENCE I HAVE CAME TO THE CONCLUSION, THAT THESE REMARKS WERE (NOT) MEANT TO BE RACIST, UNFORTUNATELY OUT OF FRUSTRATION, SOME TIME PEOPLE WILL VENT WITH DEROGATORY REMARKS.

BASEDONTHEIRUNDERSTANDINGTHEFUNDAMENTALS OF REALITY, AND HAVING TO ENDURE THE LISTENING OF SOME ONE LYING AND DISTORTING THE ESSENCE OF TRUTH.

AND THIS HAS BEEN A REALISTIC FACTOR HISTORICALLY, HOWEVER THE PERSISTENCE OF DISTORTION HAVE BEEN UTILIZEDBYDEMOCRATICLIBERALS,ASAINDOCTRINATING POLITICAL PROCESS FOR HUNDREDS OF YEARS. THE INTEGRITY OF INTELLECT IS PROFOUND.

PERTAINING TO HUMANITY, UNFORTUNATELY MOST DEMOCRATS HAVE VIOLATED THE SANCTIMONY OF THESE PRINCIPLES, IN ORDER TO GAIN POLITICAL DOMINANCE.

AND THERE ARE MANY REPUBLICANS, THAT UTILIZE POLITICAL EXTREMITIES, TO DISTORT REALITY.

HOWEVER THE LIBERAL DEMOCRATS, HOLD THE CHRONOLOGICAL RECORDS OF SIGNIFICANT EVENTS, FOR THEIR RADICAL DECEITFUL AND INDOCTRINATING LIES.

SO IN ESSENCE TO EVALUATE THE VALIDITY OF THE EIGHTEEN SEVENTYS SOUTHERN DEMOCRATIC KU-KLUX-KLAN, PREDICTIONS REGARDS TO AFRICAN AMERICANS, BEING IGNORANT AND INCOMPETENT, RELATED TO POLITICS. THE OVERWHELMING DUPLICITY OF PRESIDENT BARACK HUSSEIN OBAMA. IS A CONFIRMING VALIDITY OF INCOMPETENCE.

REGARDS TO THE FUNDAMENTALS OF CHRONOLOGICAL EVENTS, AND THE ENDURANCE THAT AMERICA WAS ESTABLISHED ON.

PRESIDENT OBAMA, IS COCOON IN FICTITIOUS CONTEMPTIBLE NARCISSISM OF RADICAL LIES. HE HAS DISDAIN FOR (WHITES) ESPECIALLY THOSE THAT ARE WEALTHY, ALSO THE AMERICAN CONSTITUTION.

NOT ONLY THAT HE IS CONTRIVING TO DEMORALIZE OUR CREDIBILITY GLOBALLY. THE VALIDY OF MY FORECAST IS PROFOUND, BASED ON HIS OWN PRESUMPTIVE CONTAMINATED, RACIST LYING EFFIGY.

FOR INSTANCE HE LIED ABOUT HIS MINISTER, ATTENDING THE CONGREGATION FOR APPROXIMATELY TWENTY YEARS, AND (NOT) KNOWING THE MINISTER HAD RACIST DISDAIN FOR RICH WHITE PEOPLE, WHEN HE INDICATED THEIR CHICKENS ARE COMING HOME TO ROOST.

RECENTLY AT A NEWS CONFERENCE, HE SCOFFED WITH A DISDAINING DEROGATORY REMARK, REGARDS TO A (WHITE) POLICE OFFICER PERFORMING HIS DUTIES IN THE ARREST OF A (BLACK) MAN.

AND INADVERTENTLY REMARKED THAT THE OFFICERS WERE (STUPID) AND HAD (NO) IDEA WHAT THE ARREST WAS ABOUT.

HE CONNED THE AMERICAN CONSTITUENCY, WITH POLITICAL CONSTRUCTED BABBLE, MOST SUPPOSEDLY EDUCATEDBLACKS,USEAIMMORALUNIQUESOPHISTICATED BABBLE, IN AN EFFORT TO DISTRACT, REGARDS TO THEIR INCOMPETENCY.

MOST BLACKS ARE TREMENDOUS DECEIVERS AND EXPERT LIARS, THEY UTILIZE THESE SKILLS INSTEAD OF MORALITY, IN ORDER TO COMPENSATE FOR PARITY. ALSO MOST BLACKS ARE POTENTIALLY DEVIOUS, WHICH IS A GENETIC HERITAGE.WHICH THEY RELY ON AS A FORM OF DISTORTION. AMERICAN WHITES KNOW ABSOLUTELY NOTHING ABOUT THE GENETIC TRAITS OF MOST AFRICAN AMERICANS, AND MOST BLACKS COULD CARE LESS BECAUSE THEY ARE HERDING TOGETHER. WITH IDENTICAL CREDENTIALS. MOST BLACKS ARE LACKADAISICAL AND SHUN INDIVIDUAL RESPONSIBILITY, THEY WOULD RATHER PARASITE OFF OTHERS FOR PERSONAL GAIN, THEN BOAST ABOUT HOW SMART THEY ARE REGARDS TO THEIR ACCOMPLISHMENTS. AND THE MOST AFFECTIVE EXECUTIONER OF (ALL) TIMES PARALLEL TO THESE VINDICTIVE AND CYNICAL ACTS OF REPRISAL ON THE AMERICAN CHRONOLOGICAL RECORDS OF SIGNIFICANT EVENTS. IS PRESIDENT BARACK HUSSIEN OBAMA.

HIS INGENUITY OF DUPLICITY, HAS PERSUADED THE MAJORITY OF THE AMERICAN CONSTITUENCY INTO ELECTING HIM PRESIDENT.

AND THERE IS NO SUBSTANTIAL REGISTRY OF VALIDITY THAT HE WAS BORN IN AMERICA.

UNFORTUNATELY THE GULLIBILITY OF THE AMERICAN CONSTITUENCY IS PATHETICALLY ASTOUNDING. TO ELECT A BLACK MAN, BECAUSE HE CAN DELIVER CHARISMATIC SPEECHES FROM A TELEPROMTER.

THIS IS MIND BOGGLING, HOWEVER HE HAD MAJOR ASSISTANCE, FROM THE CLINTONS, THE COUNTRY WAS OBJECTING TO THEIR EIGHT YEAR BEHAVIOR ESCAPADES, FROM PRESIDENT CLINTON COMMITTING ADULTERY. IN THE WHITEHOUSE, AND SHE MRS CLINTON CONDONING IT, CLAIMING IT WAS A RIGHT WING CONSPIRACY.

AND OF COURSE JOHN MCCAIN, A CONVERT WITH TENDENCIES OF DYSFUNCTION RELATED TO THE AMERICAN PEOPLE.

AND FORMER PRESIDENT GEORGE H. BUSH, STAMMERING WITH DISSOLUTIONS REGARDS TO DEMOCRATS MOTIVATIONS OF DISTORTION, ALSO EXTENSIVE GOVERNMENT SPENDING.

WITH MILLIONS OF OLDER WHITES, THAT WOULD NEVER VOTE FOR A WOMAN, NOR A BLACK MAN, SO THEY LAID ON THEIR COUCHES, DID NOT VOTE, AND CAST OUR NATION INTO TURMOIL WITH THE ELECTION OF BARACK H. OBAMA AND NOW HE IS THE EPITOME, OF WHAT THE SOUTHERN DEMOCRATS PREDICTED IN EIGHTEEN SEVENTY, OF AFRICAN AMERICANS, REGARDS TO THE PURSUIT OF POLITICS. THAT THEIR EFFORTS WERE NONSENSICAL, BECAUSE OF IGNORANCE AND INCOMPETENCE.

MOST AFRICAN AMERICANS LIKE THE ABILITY TO RETAIN, OR THINK INDEPTH, SO IN ESSENCE IF THEY HAVE A COMPLEX PROBLEM, THEIR FIRST THOUGHT IS TO TEND TOWARD OPINIONS FROM OTHERS.

WHICH IS A GENETIC HERITAGE, PASSED ON FOR CENTURIES, IN ORDER TO BLAME SOME ONE ELSE FOR THEIR OWN INCOMPETENT IGNORANCE. IF I HAVE HEARD IT ONCE I HAVE HEARD IT A MILLION TIMES, HAVING TO DO WITH MANY MANY BLACKS.

MAN YOU KNOW I HAD THIS PROBLEM. I KNEW HOW TO SOLVE IT (BUT) I DISCUSSED IT WITH OTHER PEOPLE, OF COURSE I KNEW WHAT TO DO, HOWEVER I LISTEN TO THEM AND THEY REALLY MESSED ME UP. THIS IS A BONAFIDE ACT OF HYPOCRISY, TO DISTORT BASED ON INEPTNESS, THAT DOMINATE AFRICAN AMERICAN SOCIETY.

PRIME EXAMPLE AND LETS BEGIN AT THE TOP, WITH PRESIDENT BARACK H. OBAMA, HE IS INVOLVED WITH A DIPLOMATIC DECISION, WITH DECIDING TO ESCALATE TROOPS TO AFGHANISTAN. FOR THE SECURITY OF OUR NATION YET HE HAS CHOSEN TO IGNORE (HIS) APPOINTED GENERAL, AND BEGAN HAVING MEETINGS WITH STAFF.

PRIOR TO HIS DECISION, SO IF IT GOES WELL, HE WILL TAKE CREDIT, AND IF IT DOES (NOT) GO WELL, HE IS

GOING TO BLAME THE PEOPLE THAT HE WAS MEETING WITH, AND THIS IS TYPICAL FOR THE MAJORITY OF AFRICAN AMERICANS, PASSED ON THROUGH HERITAGE, AND EXEMPLIFIED BY COMPULSIVE LIBERAL DEMOCRATIC IDEOLOGY.

PRACTICALLY ON EVERY CONTINENT PEOPLE ARE COMMENTING ON WHY PRESIDENT BARACK HUSSEIN OBAMA WAS AWARDED THE NOBEL PEACE PRIZE. FROM OSLOW NORWAY, ALLOW ME TO OFFER AN EXPLICIT ANALYSIS OF THE MOTIVATIONS.

DIPLOMATS FROM EUROPEAN NATIONS, KNOW MORE ABOUT AFRICANSTHAN THEY KNOW ABOUT THEMSELVES, SLAVE TRADING FOR PROFIT BEGAN WITH THE EUROPEANS FROM GHANA AROUND THE FOURTH CENTURY, TO THE TWELFTH, AND IN MALI FROM THE THIRTEENTH, INTO THE LATE FIFTEENTH CENTURY, AT THAT TIME SLAVE TRADING INTENSIFIED BETWEEN EUROPE AND THE AFRICAN NATIONS, SONGHAY WAS ONE OF THE MAJOR TRADING EMPIRES IN WEST AFRICA,BECAUSE OF SUGAR CULTIVATION REQUEST FOR SLAVE LABOR INTENSIFIED.

SLAVE LABOR ACROSS THE ATLANTIC OCEAN TO BRAZIL AND THE WEST INDIES, MADE THE AFRICAN TRADING MORE LUCRATIVE FOR THE EUROPEAN NATIONS, UNTIL THEY ESTABLISHED A MULTITUDE OF SLAVE CASTLES ALONG THE AFRICAN COAST.

ONE OF THE FIRST SUCH FORTRESSES WAS ELMINA, ESTABLISHED BY THE PORTUGUESE IN FOURTEEN EIGHTY ONE, WHICH WAS TAKEN OVER BY THE DUTCH IN SIXTEEN THIRTY SEVEN.

AS THE SLAVE TRADE FLURISHED, THE EUROPEAN NATIONS CONSTRUCTED MORE THAN FIFTY FORTS ALONG THREE HUNDRED MILES OF COASTLINE, FROM THE SENEGAL RIVER TO ANGOLA.

WHILE THE AFRICAN NATIONS CONTROLED THE INTERIOR, AND SUPPLIED SLAVE LABOR, THESE PEOPLE WERE INVALUABLE TO COMMERICAL ENTERPRISES GLOBALLY.

SO IN ESSENCE THERE ARE (NO) PEOPLE ON GODS EARTH, THAT HAVE THE UNDERSTANDING OF AFRICAN CULTURE, REVELATIONS ACCREDITED TO THE EUROPEAN NATIONS.

THE CONTINENT OF EUROPE, WAS DEALING WITH AFRICA, REGARDS TO SLAVE SUPPLY THREE HUNDRED AND NINETY TWO YEARS BEFORE COLUMBUS DISCOVERED AMERICA. IN FOURTEEN NINETY TWO.

AFRICANS WERE BROUGHT TO AMERICA, ONE HUNDRED AND TWENTY SEVEN YEARS LATER, THE YEAR OF SIXTEEN NINETEEN.

ALSO EUROPE CONTROLLED AMERICA UNTIL THE WAR OF EIGHTEEN TWELVE, WHICH WE WON AND .OBTAINED OUR LIBERTIES. WHICH WE OWE A DEBT OF GRATITUDE TO OUR SEVENTH PRESIDENT ANDREW JACKSON, WHICH IS ON THE FACE OF THE TWENTY DOLLAR BILL.

HOWEVER I HAVE GIVEN A BRIEF SYNOPSIS OF PROPOUNDERS, RELATED TO EUROPEAN ETHNIC TRADITIONS, REGARDS TO AFRICAN SLAVE TRADING FOR PROFIT AS A LUCRATIVE COMMODITY.

UNFORTUNATELY AS OF TODATE, TWO THOUSAND AND NINE, OVER NINE HUNDRED YEARS AGO, AFRICA IS STILL A HOSTILE POVERTY STRICKEN NATION WITH THEIR LEADERS INDULGING IN GENOCIDE.

WHICH OFFER A DEFINITIVE INCLINATION PERTAINING TO CONGLOMERATION REGARDS TO THEIR THINKING CAPACITY, TO ENDURE MORALITY. A LARGE SEGEMENT OF AFRICAN AMERICANS, ARE STIGMATIZED WITH THE IDENTICAL MYSTIQUE.OF DESPAIR, RELATED TO INCOMPETENCY. A LARGE SEGEMENT OF SMALL BRAIN (WHITES) IN AMERICA, HAVE ASSUMED THAT THE THINKING CAPACITY OF BLACKS, IS EQUIVALENT TO THEIR PERSPECTIVE, PERTAINING TO THEI PHILOSOPHY OF (UNREADABLE TEXT), AND SELF ESTEEM.

UNFORTUNATELY THEY ARE LIVING IN A PHANTASY WORLD, OF AFRICAN AMERICAN DISTORTED HYPOCRISY, USING (RACISM) TO COMPENSATE FOR THEIR IGNORANT INCOMPETENCY.

THERE ARE GOING TO BE MANY, THAT WILL CONSIDER THESE STATEMENTS AS BEING (RACIST) HOWEVER THE

FACTS TO SUBSTANTIATE MY VALIDITY IS BASED ON RELAITY.

AS I HAVE WRITTEN THROUGH OUT THE BOOK, BLACKS AND SMALL DYSFUNCTIONAL BRAIN LIBERAL WHITES, ARE THOROUGHLY SKILLED AT LYING AND DISTORTING REALITY.

LETS CLARIFY MY ACCESSED ANALYSIS, OF AFRICANS AND AFRICAN AMERICANS, THE CONTINENT OF AFRICA IN SEGMENTS, ARE SOME OF THE MOST IMPOVERISHED LAND ON GODS EARTH.

THAT IS CONTROLLED BY SOME OF THE MOST EGOTISTICAL HOSTILE DICTATORS ON GODS EARTH.

THEY HAVE ABSOLUTELY NO COMPASSION FOR PEOPLE IN GENERAL, BECAUSE THEIR GENETIC HERITAGE IS SPONTANEOUS TO DOMINANCE OF A TRIBAL CHIEF, WHERE ONE MAN RULE INDEFINITELY.

LETS CHARACTERIZE IDIAMIN DADA, THAT CONTROLLED UGANDA FROM NINETEEN SEVENTY ONE TO NINETEEN SEVENTY NINE.

HE EMPHATICALLY STATED THAT HIS EXCELLENCY WAS PRESIDED FOR LIFE. THE ENTIRE WORLD IS AWARE THAT THIS IS A EMBEDDED AFRICAN HERITAAGE TRADITION. (ESPECIALLY EUROPE);

WITH AN ECEPTION OF AFRICA, (ALL) CONTINENTS IN THE HEMISPHERE, ARE AWARE OF THE GENETIC CHARACTERISTIC TRAITS OF AFRICANS ANDANS AFRICAN AMERICANS, BECAUSE THEY ARE INSTINCTIVELY DERIVATIVE. THIS IS A CRITERIA THAT APPLY TO (ALL) VARIOUS ETHNICS OF PEOPLE AND ANIMALS.

HOWEVER AFRICANS ARE UNIQUE, BECAUSE THEY CHOSE IFO SELL THEIR PEOPLE INTO SLAVERY FOR PROFIT. TO THE EUROPEAN NATIONS, THE DUTCH AND PORTUGUESE, FOR WOVEN MATS, BEDCOVERS, SPOONS, HORNS, AND SALTCELLARS INCIDENTALLY THE DUTCH BROUGHT THE FIRST CARGO OF AFRICANS TO VIRGINIA IN SIXTEEN NINETEEN.

SENSE THAT TIME THEY HAVE BLAMED (WHITES) AND RICH WHITE^PEOPLEHFOR THEIR INADEQUATE DEFICIENCY AND/INCOMPETENCE IN AMERICA. AFRICA IS THE SECOND

OLDEST CONTINENT IN THE EASTERN HEMISPHERE, WERE THERE BEFORE CHRIST, YET THEY ARE THE MOST POVERTY STRIKEN CONTINENT ON THE GLOBE.

AND THERE ARE (NO) RICH WHITE PEOPLE THERE PROHIBITING THEIR SUCCESSES. HOWEVER IT IS THE RICH WHITE PEOPLE FROM AMERICA,THAT IS ASSISTING WITH RELIEF IN ORDER TO PREVENT STARVATION AND GENOCIDE WHICH THEY HAVE EXECUTE WITH COMPASSION IN AMERICA, FOR HUNDREDS OF YEARS.FOR BLACK AND WHITE.

MOST BLACKS ARE A UNGRATEFUL SOCIETY OF PEOPLE, SIMPLY BECAUSE OF GLORIFIED INEPTITUDE IN THEMSELVES, BASED ON FICTION.

TO UNDERSTAND THE GRAPICS OF THE HUMAN BRAIN, AND HOW IT FUNCTION IS BASED ON LINE OF DESCENDENT, WHICH IS INEVITABLE, IT ALSO DICTATE THE ESSENCE OF ONES CHARACTER PERTAINING TO MORALITY OR IMMORALITY, ALL HUMAN BRAINS ARE FORMULATED ON THE SAME ORDER, THAT CONSIST OF CELLS WHICH CONTROL THE FUNCTIONS OF THE HUMAN BODY. HOWEVER THERE ARE DEIVATIONS REGARDS TO CELL CONTROL. THAT IS STIMULATED FROM PARENT HERITAGE, AND THAT IS THE REASON FOR SMART AND IGNORANCE, THAT IS PREVALENT IN (ALL) PEOPLE GLOBALLY. AMERICA IS ONE OF THE MOST COMPLEX ECONOMILAL SOCITIES ON THE GLOBE, BECAUSE OF HUMAN DIVERSITY.

HOWEVER EACH NATIONALLY IS EMBEDDED WITH THE TRAITS OF THEIR ORIGINAL CONTINENT OF HERITAGE, THAT GENERATE BACK TO THOUSAND OF YEARS.

IN ESSENCE THERE IS (NOT) ONE IMMIGRANT THAT MIGRATED TO AMERICA, CAME FROM A CONTINENT THAT (SOLD) THEIR PEOPLE INTO SLAVERY FOR TRINKETS AS THE CONTINENT OF (AFRICA) DID. AS A GLOBAL WHOLESALE COMMODITY.

PRESIDENT BARACK HUSSIEN OBAMA, IS A MODERN DAY DIRECT DESCENDENT FROM AFRICA I FIND IT TO BE AWFUL STRANGE, THAT THE MEDIA WOULD PRY INTO HIS WIFE AMERICAN CHRONOLOGICAL RECORDS, AND NOT ONE WORD ABOUT HIS AFRICAN GENETIC TRAITS. I

AM STUNNED AND PERPLEXED THAT POLITICAL (IDIOTS) WOULD ELECT A MAN FOR PRESIDENT OF UNE OF THE GREATEST COUNTRYS IN THE WORLD, AND (NOT) KNOW WHERE THE HELL HE IS FROM.

APPARENTY CRACK COCAIN, HAS TAKEN OVER OUR SOCIETY, REGARDS TO MORALITY. I AM GOING TO OFFER A BRIEF SYNOPSIS OF THE INTENT OF PRESIDENT BARACK HUSSIEN OBAMA AND TRUST ME WE ARE SITTING ON A POWDER KEG. AMERICA HAS (NEVER) BEEN SO VULNERABLE IN THE HISTTORY OF OUR NATION.

BECAUSE OF THE ELECTION OF THIS PRESIDENT, THAT HAVE DISDAIN FOR WHITES IN AMERICA, AND THE COUNTRY AS A WHOLE.

AS FAR AS WE KNOW HE COULD BE JOINED AT THE HIP WITH TERRORISM, TO CRITIQUE HIS STRATEGY, HE ALLOWED THE CONGRESS TO WRITE THE HEALTH CARE BILL. HE IS HAVING MEETING AFTER MEETING ON DECIDIDING TROOPS FOR AFGHANISTAN.

SO THAT HE IS (NOT) BLAMED FOR ANY DECISIONS, JUST HOW LONG ARE THESE SMALL DYSFUNCTIONAL BRAIN POLITICAL IDIOTS, ARE GOING TO ALLOW THIS DICTATOR TO MAKE A ASS OUT OF THEM.

THIS PRESIDENT OBAMA, IS A FACSIMILE OF NAT TURNER OF THE EIGHTEEEN THIRTIES, ALSO IDIAMIN DADA, THE UGANDA RULER OF THE SEVENTIES, IN AFRICA.

ALSO (NEVER) FORGET THE STATEMENT OF HIS MINISTER FOR AS REPORTED TWENTY YEARS, STATED RICH (WHITE) PEOPLE CHICKENS ARE COMING HOME TO ROOST, THIS PRESIDENT IS NOTHING MORE THAN A NARCISSISM BLACK ACTIVIST, WITH INTENTIONS OF SABOTAGING AMERICA TO A REPLICA OF AFRICA

AND THERE IS A FEW POLITICAL (WHITE) ALIMENTARY CANAL LICKS FOR (BLACKS) THAT IS INEPT TO HIS AGENDA, SUCH AS JOHN MCCAIN AND LINDSEY GRAHAM.

THEY ARE COMPROMISING WITH CONDONATION DISTORTED GIBBERISH, TO HIS DECITFUL ANARCHY, AND IS INEPT TO HIS INTENT TO SABOTAGE AMERICA, WHY DO YOU THINK OSLO NORWAY PRESENTED HIM WITH THE NOBEL PEACE PRIZE,BECAUSE EUROPE HAS DEALT WITH

AFRICANS FOR CENTURIES, THEY ARE AWARE OF THEIR PERSONA OF ILLITERATE HOSTILITY, FOR AMERICA, SO WHY NOT GIVE HIM A CONGRATULATED AWARD FOR SABOTAGING AMERICA TO A REPLICA OF AFRICA.

AMERICA HAS LOST DIGNITY AND CREDIABILITY GLOBALLY, BECAUSE OF THE ELECTION OF BARACK HUSSIEN OBAMA, NAME ME ONE NATION GLOBALLY OTHER THAN AFRICA, THAT HAS CHOSEN A AFRICAN TO HEAD THEIR POLITICAL AFFAIRS.

AMERICA HAS MADE A HORRIFIC MISTAKE, SIMPLY BECAUSE MOST BLACKS THINK IN A UNIQUE HERDING UNISON PHILOSOPHY, WHICH MOST ARE NOT AWARE OF, HOWEVER IT IS THE GENETIC HERITAGE FROM AFRICA, THAT DICTATE THEIR REACTIONS GENERATED FROM THE BRAIN.

AND IT IS MANIFESTED BASED ON COLOR, LETS JUST USE JUAN WILLIAMS TELEVISION AND RADIO PERSONALITY, HE HAS BEEN ON RADIO AND TELEVISION LIKE HORSE SHIT OVER A SMALL TOWN, IN ALABAMA DURING THE FORTIES, AND IF YOU NOTICE HE VERY SELDON CRITICIZE BLACKS, AND WHEN HE DOES THARE IS NO PRACTICAL EXCUSE TO DEFEND. THE ONLY TIME THAT HE WILL BE CRITICAL OF ANOTHER BLACK, IS WHEN WHAT EVER OCCURRED IT IS SO OBVIOUS UNTIL IT IS PATHETIC. HE WAS CRITICAL OF OBAMA, WITH THE POLICE OFFICER AND THE PROFESSSOR, AND HAD A SCOWL ON HIS FACE AS IF HE HAD JUST SWALLOWED A DOSE OF CASTOROIL.

THIS IS A GENETIC TRAIT PERTAINING TO THE MAJORITY OF AFRICAN AMERICANS, AND IT IS INEVITABLE, BASED ON TRIBAL AFFILIATIONS FROM AFRICA THOUSANDS OF YEARS AGO, AND THIS IS NOT RACIST INNUENDO IT IS REALITY, ONCE THERE WERE AFRICAN TRIBAL LIFE PORTRAYED ON HISTORY TELEVISION CHANNELS, THERE ARE NO MORE SENSE BARACK OBAMA BECAME PRESIDENT, HOWEVER THEY OFFERED A UNDERSTANDING OF AFRICAN CULTURE, THAT HAS BEEN PASSED ON TO AFRICAN AMERICANS. FOR INSTANCE EVERY TRIBE HAD A CHIEF, THAT THEY DEPENDED ON FOR GUIDANCE, NO ONE HAD A JOB, THEY SURVIVED OF THE LAND. AND THERE WERE CONSTANT

TRIBAL WARS.OF VIOLENCE, ALONG WITH TRADING HUMANS FOR ANIMALS.

AND MOST HAD SEVERAL WIVES, SECRETARY OF STATE HILLARY CLINTON, WAS ACCOSTED RECENTLY BY AN AFRICAN, REGARDS TO TRADING HUMANS FOR ANIMALS.

THIS IS A RENDITION OF AFRICAN TRADITIONS, THAT IS CUSTOMARY TO THEIR HERITAGE TRAITS, THEORETICALLY MY OPINIONS IS BASED ON HERITAGE, WHICH IS AS REAL AS THE SUN RISING IN THE EAST AND SETTING IN THE WEST.

THE TRANSITIONS OF HERITAGE IS INEVITABLE, ALSO ETERNAL. WHICH MEAN THE ELECTION OF BARACK HUSSIEN OBAMA AS PRESIDENT, IS DEVASTATING FOR OUR NATION, BECAUSE HE HAS DISDAIN FOR THE STRUCTURE OF THE CONSTITUTION. WHICH IS OUR GUIDANCE TO LIBERTY AND MORALITY, AND BASED ON HIS DIRECT AFRICAN HERITAGE, HIS IDEOLOGY IS TO ABOLISH THE CONSTITUTION, IN ORDER THAT HE CAN BECOME A INDEFINITE CONGO RULER OF AMERICA.

TODAY IS FRIDAY OCTOBER 15, 2009. AS I TURN ON MY TELEVISION PRESIDENT OBAMA IS ADDRESSING AN AUDIENCE IN LOUISIANA, I AM FULLY CONVINCED THAT THIS MAN IS A NARCISSISM PSYCHOPATH.

I WATCHED FOR A FIEW MOMENTS, AND HAD A SENSATION OF REGURGITATION, BECAUSE JUST TO OBSERVE AN ELECTED OFFICIAL SEDUCE AN AUDIANCE TO CHEER FOR HIM IS PERSISTENT APPEALING TO EMOTIONS. IN AN EFFORT TO COAX AN APPLAUSEIS A FORM OF INDOCTRINATING INSANITY, HE KEEP TALKING, MAKING JOKES UNTIL HE STROKE THE CROWD, WITH LYING TO THEM AS TO WHAT HE IS GOING TO DO FOR THEM. BECAUSE HE HAS COMPASSION FOR THEIR TOILS, THIS PRESIDENT IS ONE OF THE MOST LYING DECITFUL HOAXES OF MODERN TIMES, THE ONLY REASON THAT HE VISITED LOUISISNA, WAS TO PROMOTE PUBLIC OPTION HEALTH CARE, THIS IS THE (ONLY) MEANS OF HIS WELL CALCULATED AGENDA TO ACCOMPLISH HIS GOAL OF SOCIALISM, WHICH HE PLAN TO INDOCTRINATE YOUNG PEOPLE, AND GENOCIDE THE ELDERY.

BECAUSE THE ELDERY IS HIS LARGEST THREAT TO DESTROYOURLIBERTIESTHEMAJORITYOFSENIOR(WHITES) IN AMERICA IF NOT ALL, ARE BEGINNING TO REALIZE THAT THIS PRESIDENT OBAMA, IS A INCOMPETENT HOAX, THAT HAS THE INTIRE UNIVERSE LAUGHING, AND WONDERING ABOUT OUR SANITY, FOR ELECTING A DYSFUNCTIONAL BRAIN IDIOT, AS PRESIDENT. ON OCTOBER 15, 2009. HE WAS ASKED A SIMPLE QUESTION, PERTAINING GOVERNMENT ASSISTANCE, AND HE RESPONDED BY SAYING HE WOULD WRITE A CHECK, IF IT WASNT FOR THIS (THING) ABOUT THE CONSTITUTION AND CONGRESS. DENOTE THAT HE HAS (NO) RESPECT FOR THE CONSTITUTION BECAUSE IT IS A HINDRANCE, TO HIS DEPLOYING A CONGO IDEOLOGY OF SOCIALISTIC DOMINATING IDIAMIN DADA, RULE OF UGANDA AFRICA DURING THE SEVENTIES F ABOLISHING AMERICAN PRINCIPLES IN ORDER THAT HE CAN REMAIN AN INDEFINITE CONGO SOCIALISTIC PSYCHOTIC RULER OF AMERICA.

HOWEVER UNFORTUNATE FOR PRESIDENT BARACK HUSSIEN OBAMA, WHILE AT HARVARD AND BEING A COMMUNITY ORGANIZER, HE FIGURED OUT HOW TO MANIPULATE. PEOPLE F ALSO READ BODY LANGUAGE, AND GRAMMATICALLY ANALYZE WORDS TO APPEASE PEOPLE. BUT THERE ARE THREE STATEMENTS THAT WILL QUELL HIS INTENTIONS TO SABOTAGE AMERICA.

AND THAT IS DURING THE DEBATE IN EIGHTEEN FIFTY EIGHT, BETWEEN REPUBLICAN ABRAHAM LINCOLN AND DEMOCRAT STEPHEN A. DOUGLAS, WHICH DOUGLAS REPLIED AMERICA WAS FOUNDED BY WHITE MEN, FOR THE BENEFIT OF WHITE MEN AND THEIR POSTERITY FOREVER.

(SECOND) DURING EIGHTEEN SIXTY AND SEVENTY, SOUTHERN DEMOCRATIC (WHITE) KUKLUXKLUX, PREDICTED THAT AFRICAN AMERICANS WERE IGNORANT, INCOMPETENT AND TRYING TO RISE ABOVE THEIR NATURAL PLACE OF SERVITUDE IN POLITICS.

(THIRD) DURING NINETEEN FIFTY SEVEN THE LATE F.B.I. DIRECTOR J. EDGAR HOOVER, ON ORDERS FROM REPUBLICAN PRESIDENT DWIGHT DAVID EISENHOWER, TO

QUELL THE VIOLENCE MAIMING AND LYNCHING OF BLACKS IN THE SOUTHERN STATES, BY THE IMPLEMENTATION OF THE DEMOCRATIC FOUNDERED KU-KLUX-KLAN, WHICH HE DID AND FOR THE BETTERMENT OF BLACKS EDUCATION, PRESIDENT EISENHOWER DEMANDED THAT SCHOOLS BE INTEGRATED IN THE SOUTH, AT THE EXPENSE OF THE MILITARY NATIONAL GUARD.

UNFORTUNATELY BLACKS WITH A FREGEPTTJVE CONGO EMBEDDED IDEOLOGY OF HERDING BEHAVIOR, COMPARING WHITES WITH THE SAME ETHNOCENTRICITY, AND DEEM (ALL) WHITES TO BE AS SOLIDIFIED AS THEY ARE. AND IS TO DAMN STUPID TO REALIZE THAT AMERICA IS THE MOST DIVERSE NATION ON THE CONTINENT.

AND EACH ETHNIC OF WHITES IS ACCLIMATED TO THEIR NATION OF HERITAGE, AND THEIR DISPOSITION IS CONTRARY REGARDS TO MOTIVES. IN ESSENCE MOST AFRICAN AMERICANS ARE UNABLE TO DISTINGUISH THE DIFFERENCE BETWEEN LIBERAL AND CONSERVATIVE.

AND THIS IS WHY THE SOUTHERN DEMOCRATS DENIED THEM VOTING RIGHTS FOR DECADES, ALSO F.B.I. DIRECTOR J. EDGAR HOOVER, ACCUSED THEM OF HAVING BRAINS TWENTY PERCENT SMALLER THAN WHITES. THE MOTIVATED CRITERIA FOR WRITING THIS BOOK, IS TO CLARIFY A MISNOMER PERTAINING TO CHRONOLOGICAL EVENTS THAT OCCURRED HISTORICALLY IN AMERICA, REGARDS TO THE TRANSFORMATION OF AFRICANS. AT THE VERY BEGINNING AFRICANS REBELLED AGAINST CIVILIZATION, FOR TWO HUNDRED YEARS, THEIR INTENSIVE INITIATIVE WAS TO CHANGE AMERICA INTO A (UNREADABLE TEXT)

THE INTENSITY STILL EXIST TODAY, APPROXIMATELY THREE HUNDRED AND NINETY YEARS LATER, AND HAS BECAME MORE PREVALENT AMONG BLACKS, DUE TO THE ELECTION OF PRESIDENT BARACK HUSSIEN OBAMA. BECAUSE MOST ARE ELECTRIFIED WITH HIS ELECTION, AND ARE ASSUMING THAT HE WAS GOD SENT.TO RECTIFY WHAT THEY ARE TO DAMN STUPID TO COMPREHEND, AND THAT IS WHY F.B.I. DIRECTOR J. EDGAR HOOVER LABELED BLACKS AS HAVING BRAINS TWENTY PERCENT SMALLER

THAN WHITES. HOWEVER SYSTEMATICALLY MOST BLACKS ARE CHASING A MIRAGE OF INSIDIOUS ILLUSIONS OF HOPEFULNESS, BASED ON INCOMPETENCY. IT IS EXTREMELY UNFORTUNATE THAT MOST BLACKS HAVE DIFFICULTY CORRELATING AND DECIPHERING THE FUNDAMENTALS OF WHAT OUR NATION WAS ESTABLISHED ON REGARDS TO PRINCIPLES.

HOWEVER THEY ARE TUNED INTO SMALL DYSFUNCTIONAL BRAIN DEMOCRATIC LIBERAL (WHITES) THAT INTENTIONALLY OVERATE BLACKS TO MAINTAIN THEIR STATUS OF BLACK BLOCK VOTING FOR DEMOCRATS CONSTANTLY FOR OVER SEVENTY FIVE YEARS BY A MARGIN OF NINETY PERCENT. AND NOW THAT THE DECITFUL LYING, POLITICAL DEMOCRATIC INFRASTRUCTURE, HAS BEEN DUPED BY A POLITICAL IMPOSTER, BECAUSE HE SPEAKS APPROPRIATE ENGLISH, AND IS A PRODUCT OF AFRICAN CONGO IDEOLOGY. I AM ALMOST CERTAIN WE AS ANATION ARE BEING RIDICULED BEHIND CLOSED DOORS IMMENSELY GLOBALLY.

ALSO OUR STANDARDS OF MORAL INTEINTEGRITY HAS BEEN DIMINISHED GLOBALLY, SIMPLY BECAUSE THE ELECTION OF THIS ECCENTRIC POLITICAL INCOMPETENT PRESIDENT BARACK HUSSIEN OBAMA.

WHICH IS THE EPITOME OF AFRICAN HERITAGE, THAT HAS (NO) PRAGMATIC APPROACH TO RESOLVING THE CENTRAL ISSURES THAT COULD THREATEN THE STABILITY OF OUR AMERICAN NATION.

TRUST ME THIS IS NOT A COINCIDENT, IT IS A GENERATED DELIBERATE COVERT INCENDIARY ATTACK, TO DESTROY THE MORAL FABRIC OF AMERICA, ALL OF THE DIGNITARIES OF EUROPE, IS AWARE OF THE CONTEMPT THAT BARACK H. OBAMA HAVE FOR AMERICA.

HE DESPISE WEALTHY PEOPLE, ESPECIALLY (WHITES) ALSO ANY ONE THAT DISAGREE WITH HIS SOCIALISTIC AGENDA, IS VICIOUSLY VERBALLY ATTACKED. BY (HIS) WHITE AND BLACK ALIMENTARY CANAL LICKS AND SNORTS. WITH CHARGES OF RACISM, THIS PRESIDENT OBAMA IS A STAUNCH NARCISSISM INCOMPETENT RACIST.

FOR INSTANT HURRICANE KATRINA, WAS A DISASTER FOR MISSISSIPPI AND LOUISIANA, THE TWO STATES ARE ADJACENT TO EACH OTHER.

THE PRESIDENT DELIBERATELY CHOSE TO VISIT NEW ORLEANS, LOUISIANA AND GIVE ONE OF HIS SICK CHILDISH HYPERBOLIC SPEECHES. WHICH NEW ORELEANS HAVE A HEAVY POPULATION OF AFRICAN AMERICANS, WHICH THE CROWD WAS DOMINATED BY BLACKS.

AND LITERALLY SNUBBED MISSISSIPPI, SO IT IS QUITE OBVIOUS THAT (WHITES) HAVE ELECTED A PRESIDENT THAT DESCRIMINATE, BASED ON COLOR, WHICH INDICATE THAT HE IS (NOT) FOR ALL THE PEOPLE, JUST AREAS OF SEGMENTED BLACKS THAT WAS DECIMATED BY HURRICANE KATRINA AND IF ANY ONE DARE POINT OUT THIS OUTRAGEOUS RADICAL HYPOCRISY. THET ARE LABELED A RACIST AGAINST HIM.

FOR INSTANCE PRESIDENT OBAMA , HAS WAGED POLITICAL WAR ON ONE OF THE MOST FAIR AND ACCURATE NEWS OUT LETS IN AMERICA AND ABROAD. HE AND HIS RACIST SOCIALISTIC EXTREMIST, ARE ATTAMPTING TO SLANDER FOX NEWS WITH IDIOTIC MALICIOUS RACIST DEMAGOGUERY. SIMPLY BECAUSE HIS DECITFUL ADOLF HITLER LIKE SPEECHES DONT MAKE THEIR LEGS TINGLE.

AND THEY ARE ON TO HIS SOCIALISTIC AGENDA, THAT HE INTEND TO PROGRAM AMERICA INTO A REPLICA OF UGANDA OF THE SEVENTYS RULED BY A HOSTILE DICTATOR NAMED IDIAMIN DADA.

WITH BARACK H. OBAMA BEING THE FIRST BLACK ELECTED PRESIDENT OF THE UNITED STATES OF AMERICA, MANY AFRICAN AMERICANS ARE ASSUMING THAT THEY ARE GOING TO ACTIVATE A RADICAL MOVEMENT TO INTIMIDATE (WHITES) BY FALSELY ACCUSING THEM OF BEING RACIST.

IN AN EFFORT TO ALTER OPINIONS, FOR ENHANCEMENT TO ATTAIN FAVORABLENESS, TO DISCREDIT (WHITES) BASED ON RACISM.

AND MANY SPINELESS (WHITES) ARE COWARD TO THIS IDOTIC BUFFOONISH INCOMPETENT DEMAGOGUERY, FEAR OF BLACKS SCREAMING RACISM REPRISAL A PRIME EXAMPLE,

THERE IS NOT A FINER INTELLIGENT RESOURCEFUL, INTELLECTUAL PERSON IN OUR SOCIETY AND ABROAD, THAN MR. RUSH LIMBAUGH, WHICH HAVE THE UNIQUE ABILITY TO DECIPHER RADICAL DEMAGOGUERY, AND HE IS ON THE AIR WAYS ALERTING AND EXPOSING THEIR PROPAGANDA ON A DAILY BASIS. PERTAINING TO BLACK AND WHITE, WITH (NO) BIAS, AND FOR ANTIQUATED INCOMPETENT POLITICAL DEMOCRATIC LIBERAL CONGO DUNG LAPPING (BLACK) HYENAS. TO SCREAM ERRONEOUS DEROGATORY INSINUATIONS THAT THIS RADIO DISTINTIVE PERSON IS A RACIST, EVEN IF HE IS A RACIST, SENSE WHEN ARE RACIST IN AMERICA PROHIBIBITED FROM UTILIZING (THEIR) EARNINGS IN ACCORDANCE WITH THEIR DESIRES.

I WOULD BE WILLING TO BET THE RANCH IF THIS WAS DEMOCRATIC SENATOR ROBERT BYRD, WANTING TO INVEST IN (ANY) PROFESSIONAL SPORTS, YOU WOULD (NEVER) HEAR A WHISPER ABOUT HE BEING A FORMER KU-KLUX-KLAN, ALSO FILIBUSTERED FOR APPROXIMATELY SEVENTEEN HOURS AGAINST CIVIL RIGHTS FOR SOUTHERN BLACKS IN NINETEEN SIXTY FOUR, AND HE IS THE OLDEST SITTING SENATOR ON RECORD.

APPARENTLY THERE HAS BEEN (NO) BLACKS EVER VOTED FOR HIM TO MAINTAIN HIS SENATE SEAT. AND HE IS DAMN MORE IMPORTANT FROM WHERE HE SIT, THAN RUSH LIMBAUGH HAVING INTREST IN A PROFESSIONAL FOOT BALL TEAM. THIS LEGITIMACY IS WHY BLACKS ARE CALLED IGNORANT SMALL BRAINS I LIVED IN CHICAGO FOR APPROXIMATELY TWENTY FIVE YEARS, AND IS QUITE FAMILIAR WITH MAFIA TACTICS, WHICH IS EQUIVALENT TO MARXIST DOCTRINE, WHERE IF YOU SPEAK ILL AGAINST THE CONTROLLING GROUP, YOUR FATE COULD BE FROM SCOLDING, MAIMING, EVEN EXTERMINATION, FORTUNATELY WE SURVIVE IN A NATION THAT IS RATIFIED UNDER CONSTITUTIONAL RESTRAINT GUIDANCE, WHICH ELIMINATE SUCH PROVOCATION IF KNOWN, IN ORDER THAT WE SHALL REMAIN UNDER THE LEGITIMACY OF LIBERTIES AND FREE SPEECH.

I WAS TAUGHT OVER FIFTY YEARS AGO, THAT IF ONE PICK A FIGHT WITH LAW ENFORCEMENT, OR ESPICIALLY WITH THE NEWS MEDIA, THEY MIGHT AS WELL PUT THEIR HEAD BETWEEN THEIR LEGS AND KISS THEIR ASS GOODBY THERE IS A SEQUENCE OF DELIBERATE SHAMEFUL DISGUSTING POLITICAL ARROGANCE DEVELOPING IN OUR NATION, DUE TO SMALL BRAIN ABSURD DYSFUNCTIONS, AND IT IS DIRECTED AT THE AMERICAN PEOPLE. ASSUMING THAT AMERICANS ARE SO POLITICALLY IGNORANT, UNTIL THEY ARE UNABLE TO DETERMINE THE RADICAL STRATEGY OF PRESIDENT BARACK HUSSEIN OBAMA, TO RID THE NATION OF OUR CONSTITUTIONAL RIGHTS. IN AN EFFORT SO THAT HE CAN DEMINISH THE INTEGRITY OF AMERICANS TO A PROTEGE OF AFRICA.

IN ORDER TO REMAIN SOCIALISTIC DICTATOR OF AMERICA INDEFINITELY. I NOTICE THE MEDIA HAVE RESEARCHED HIS WIFE LINE OF DESCENT, BUT (NOT) HIS. HOWEVER I SUSPECT THAT HIS GENETICS IS RELATED TO THE WATUSI TRIBES OF BURUNDI OR RWANDA, A SO THE ZULU OF AFRICA. BECAUSE HE IS TALL, HIGH RUMP, BLACK MOUTH, AND LARGE EARS, WITH HAMMER SHAPED HEAD, ALL THAT IS MISSING IS THE DUNG MATTED BRAIDS MANY ARE GOING TO ATTEST THAT THIS IS RACIST.

BUT I SUGGEST CHECK YOUR HISTORY, AND IT WILL VERIFY THAT THIS IS (REALITY) PERTAINING TO SOME AFRICAN TRIBES.

HOWEVER THE PREDICTIONS OF THE SOUTHERN DEMOCRATS IN EIGHTEEN SEVENTY, THAT BLACKS WERE IGNORANT AND INCOMPETENT RELATED TO POLITICS, ALSO F.B.I. DIRECTOR J. EDGAR HOOVER, SUGGESTED THAT THEIR BRAINS WERE TWENTY PERCENT SMALLER THAN WHITES, DURING NINETEEN FIFTY SEVEN.

THIS IS TWO THOUSAND NINE, AND WE HAVE AN ELECTED BLACK OFFICIAL BARACK HUSSEIN OBAMA AS OUR PRESIDENT OF AMERICA.

THAT IS A GRADUATED ATTORNEY FROM HARVARD, ACCORDING TO THE NEWS MEDIA,WHICH IS THE STIGMATIC EPITOME OF TRANSPARENCY, THAT WAS PREDICTED ABOUT BLACKS AS BEING IGNORANT AND INCOMPETENTREGARDS

TO POLITICS, AND THAT WAS ONE HUNDRED AND THIRTY NINE YEARS AGO. APPARENTLY THEY HAD DISCOVERED THE (TRIBAL) INSTINCTS OF BLACKS, THAT STILL EXIST TODAY.

FOR INSTANCE THIS PRESIDENT IS A HABITUAL LIAR, AND IS CONSTANTLY LYING TO THE AMERICAN PEOPLE, WHICH IS A GENETIC TRAIT OF MOST BLACKS. FOR IMPRESSIVE FOLKLORE, TO PERSUADE THE SOME TIME NOTICEABLE DYSFUNCTION, IN AN EFFORT TO DISTORT AWAY FROM THEIR INCOMPETENCY. BY LYING TO GAIN THE CONFIDENCE OF OTHERS,THAT THEY ARE INTELLECTUALLY CLEVER, THIS IS A AUTHENTIC UNIQUE INEVITABILITY OF MOST AFRICAN AMERICANS, TO COMPENSATE FOR THEIR INABILITY TO ADEQUATELY RESOLVE OR DECIPHER ISSURES OF QUALITY, SO THEY LIE.

IN AN ATTEMPT TO CONVINCE PEOPLE THAT THEY HAVE A BETTER PLAN, AND IF THEY ARE .SUCCESSFUL, THE TALENTS OF. OTHER PEOPLE ARE UTILIZED | TO COMPENSATE FOR THEIR ECCENTRIC OF IGNORANCE AND INCOMPETENCY.

PRESIDENT BARACK HUSSEIN OBAMA, IS THE EPITOME OF THESE TRAITS. THAT IS A UNIQUE ORATION OF LIES.

FOR INSTANCE HE IS CONSTANTLY LYING TO THE AMERICAN PEOPLE ABOUT CERTAIN ISSURES, THE MOST OUTRAGEOUS LIE, WAS HE HAD NO IDEA THAT HIS PASTER WAS A RACIST BIGOT, WHEN HE IS AN ATTORNEY, AND A GRADUATE OF HARVARD, TWENTY YEARS UNDER THE GUIDANCE OF ANY ONE AND HAVE (NO) IDEA OF THEIR IDEOLOGY, IS TYPICAL LYING DEMAGOGUERY OF THIS PRESIDENT.

HE WAS GOING TO CLOSE GITMO IMMEDIATELY AFTER BEING ELECTED, THE LAST TIME I CHECKED, ALMOST A YEAR LATER GITMO IS STILL OPEN. THE STIMULUS PACKAGE WAS SUPPOSE TO CREATE JOBS, AND HOLD INFLATION TO APPROXIMATELY EIGHT PERCENT, AS OF TODATE OCTOBER 24, 2009 INFLATION HAS ESCALATED TO ALMOST DOUBLE DIGITS.

HE WAS (NOT) GOING TO HIRE LOBBYERS, AS OF TODATE THERE IS APPROXIMATELY THIRTY TWO ON BOARD, HE

WOULD NOT SIGN A BILL THAT HAD EARMARKS AND HE DID.

HE WAS GOING TO IMPLEMENT TRANSPARENCY, AND BIPARTISANSHIP, USE YOUR OWN JUDGEMENT IF HE LIED OR NOT.

HE WENT PUBLIC AND CLAIMED THE WAR IN AFGHANISTAN WAS A NECESSITY YET HE IS RELUCTANT TO SUPPORT HIS OWN APPOINTED GENERAL FOR MORE TROOP ASSISTANCE.

AT A PRESS CONFERENCE HE BECAME EMBROILED IN A (LOCAL) STATE INCIDENT, WHEN HE CONDEMNED (WHITES) AS BEING STUPID, BECAUSE THEY LAWFULLY ARRESTED A BLACK MAN, WHEN HE HAD (NO) IDEA WHAT CAUSED THE INCIDENT.

ALSO HE PRESIDENT H. OBAMA HAS WAGED ONE OF THE MOST CONTROVERSIAL BLATANT SABOTAGING ACTS, ON ONE OF THE MOST PRESTIGIOUS RENOWN NEWS MEDIA, NATIONALLY AND ABROAD, (FOX NEWS).

SIMPLY BECAUSE THEY ACCURATELY REPORT ON HIS IGNORANT INCOMPETENT DEFICIENCIES, OF CONSTANTLY LYING TO THE AMERICAN PEOPLE, TO CONCEAL HIS RADICAL DESTRUCTIVE MOTIVES TO SOCIALIZE AMERICA. WITH THE INTENT TO DESTROY THE MORAL FABRIC, BY REDUCING THE STANDARDS OF ITS CITIZEN.., TO A REPLICA OF AFRICAN CONGO IDEOLOGY. AND FOR THIS HE RECEIVED THE NOBAL PEACE AWARD FROM EUROPE. IF YOU NOTICE THE AWARDERS EMPHATICALLY STATED, THE AWARD WAS NOT FOR HIS CURRENT ACCOMPLISHMENTS, BUT FOR HIS PLANS FOR THE FUTURE AND I MUST ADMIT, THAT HE REALLY DESERVED IT.

BECAUSE HE REALLY DUPED AND MESMERIZED THE AMERICAN VOTING CONSTITUENCY, WITH CHARISMATIC LYING SPEECHES, WHICH THEY HAD (NEVER) HEARD COMING FROM A (BLACK) MAN WITH CALCULATED CHARISMA, AND HE WAS TOTALLY AWARE OF THAT, FRANKLY SPEAKING THIS WAS HIS METHOD FOR ACCOMPLISHING HIS AGENDA, OF MAKING A MESMERIZED (DUNCE) OUT OF THE (WHITE) VOTING CONSTITUENCY, BECAUSE HE KNEW BLACKS WERE GOING TO VOTE FOR HIM, EVEN IF HE HAD

BEEN JUST RECENTLY RELEASED FROM GITMO, SIMPLY BECAUSE HE IS BLACK.

APPARENTLY DURING HIS STAY AT HARVARD, HE UTILIZED MOST OF HIS NARCISSISM TIME, ON HOW TO MINIPILATE PEOPLE TO HIS ADVANTAGE. I TRULY COMPLIMENT HIM ON THAT.

HOWEVER THERE IS A DETRIMENTAL BACKLASH, WHEN PEOPLE SUDDENLY DISCOVER THAT THEY WERE DECEIVED BASED ON ISSURES OF RADICAL DISDAIN, PERTAINING TO THEIR COMPREHENSIBLE VALUES, THERE IS (NOTHING) CAN BEFORE (SEVERELY) DEVASTATING THAN LOOSING THE MERITS^OF THE AMERICAN PEOPLE.

BASED ON RADICAL TRICKERY, AND OMINOUS TACTICS TO DEPRIVE THEM OF THEIR CONSTITUTIONAL RIGHTS, CITIZENS OF AMERICA ARE THE GREATEST PEOPLE ON GODS EARTH, SIMPLY BECAUSE OF DIVERSE CHARACTERISTICS. THAT BLEND UNDER ONE MAJOR FACTOR, WE THE PEOPLE ADHERE TO THE CONSTITUTION AND THE DECLARATION OF INDEPENDENCE, BASED ON INTELLECTUAL MORAL VALUES.

AND THESE ARE THE SENTIMENTS, THAT HAS PROPELLED AMERICA TO BE THE GREATEST NATION ON GODS EARTH, AND IT IS QUITE OBVIOUS WE AS A NATION HAS ENDURED MANY CHALLENGES TO OBSOLETE OUR HUMANITY. AND THEY HAVE (NEVER) SUCCEDED.

AND FOR ANY ONE, EVEN A SITTING PRESIDENT, OR A SINGLE NATIONALOF PEOPLE, ALSO INDIVIDUAL PARTYS, EITHER DEMOCRATIC OR REPUBLICAN, THINK THEY ARE GOING TO ALTER THE FUNDAMENTAL TRAITS OF AMERICA, RELATED TO THE VALIDITY OF OUR LIBERTIES.

HAS TO BE UTTERLY CHAOTIC AND MENTALLY DERANGED, HOWEVER IT HAS BEEN TRIED, DURING THE FALL OF SEVENTEEN THIRTY NINE, A REBELLION WAS STAGED LED BY A AFRICAN NAMED JEMMY, FROM THE CONGO.

HIS RECRUITS MARCHED IN MILITARY RANKS, FLYING AFRICAN COLORS AND BEATING DRUMS IN SOUTH CAROLINA, ALONG THE STONO RIVER. THE COLONIAL

MILITIA,WAS SUMMONED, AND A VICIOUS BATTLE OCCURRED, FINALLY THE MILITIA WAS THE VICTORS.

DURING EIGHTEEN ELEVEN A AFRICAN NAMED CHARLES DESLONDES ORGANIZED A RADICAL MILITARY BRIGADE OF BLACK AFRICANS, AND MARCHED TO NEW ORLEANS, BEATING DRUMS, BURNING PLANTATIONS AND MURDERING WHS WHITES, UNTIL THE STATE AND LOCAL MILITIA QUELLED THE REBELLION, BY KILLING AND DISMEMBERING THEIR HEADS, AND PLACED THEM ON POLES ALONG THE MISSISSIPPI RIVER.

DURING EIGHTEEN TWENTY, A AFRICAN NAMED DENMARK VESEY, PLOTTED ONE OF THE MOST ELABORATE REVOLUTIONS IN AMERICA.

HOWEVER HIS PLOT WAS DISCOVERED BY AUTHORITIES, AND APPROXIMATELY THIRTY FIVE AFRICANS WERE HANGED, AND THEIR BODYS DISSECTED BY SURGEONS.

AND OF COURSE THE YEAR OF EIGHTEEN THIRTY ONE, THERE WAS THE REBELLION OF PSYCHOPATHIC BLACK AFRICAN,NAT TURNER FROM SOUTHHAMPTON COUNTY VIRGINIA, A DEEPLY RELIGIOUS MAN, THAT SAW VISIONS OF BLOOD ON CORN STALKS, ALSO WHITE AND BLACK SPIRITS, ENGAGED IN BATTLE, AND THE SKIES DARKENED, THE THUNDER ROLLED IN HEAVEN, AND THE STREAMS WERE FILLED WITH BLOOD.

HE ORGANIZED A BRIGADE OF REBELLIOUS BLACK REBELS, AND ROUTED THE WHITE MILITIA, SLAUGHTERING WHITES AT WILL, THIS WAS THE BLOODIEST REVOLT BY BLACKS IN U.S. HISTORY, IT CAUSED WHITES TO REINFORCE FROM TOWNS TO JOIN THE MILITIA FOR VICTORY.

AFTER THE QUELL NAT TURNER WAS TRIED AND LYNCHED SURGEONS REMOVED HIS SKIN, AND PURSES AND SHOES WERE MANUFACTURED FROM HIS SKIN, ALSO HIS BONES WERE UTILIZED FOR MANTEL TRINKETS.

THESE INCOMPETENT STAGED ACTS OF VIOLENT TERRORISM AGAINST WHITE CITIZENS BY BLACKS, WAS DEVASTATING FOR THE SURVIVAL OF MANY INNOCENT BLACKS IN THE SOUTH.

BECAUSE SOUTHERN STATES LEGISLATED LAWS TO PROHIBIT BLACKS FROM GATHERING AT CHURCH. ALSO IT

WAS A MISDEMEANOR FOR A WHITE TO MURDER A BLACK, THESE INITIAL OCCURRENCES OF VIOLENCE PERPETRATED (BY) BLACKS AGAINST WHITES CREATED A MULTITUDE OF VIOLENT ACTS AGAINST BLACKS.

SUCH AS MAIMING, SHOOTING, LYNCHING (UNREADABLE TEXT) HOWEVER MOST OF ALL WHITE WOMEN AND THEIR CHILDREN REFUSED TO TEACH BLACKS HOW TO READ AND WRITE.

HOWEVER AFTER THE NAT TURNER ATTACK, FEAR AND PANIC SPREAD THROUGH OUT THE ENTIRE REGION. THE GOVERNOR OF VIRGINIA CALLED OUT THE STATE INFANTRY, ALSO THE U.S. NAVY FOR ASSISTANCE, BECAUSE THERE WERE OTHER PLOTS DISCOVERED IN A NUMBER OF COUNTIES IN VIRGINIA. NORTH CAROLINA SUMMONED OUT THE STATE MILITIA, AND PLACED CITIES AND TOWNS UNDER HEAVY GUARD.

PRESIDENT ABRAHAM LINCOLN, SIGNED THE DECLARATION TO ABOLISH BONDAGE IN EIGHTEEN SIXTY FIVE.

THE SOUTHERN DEMOCRATS FOUNDERED THE KU-KLUX-KLAN, IN EIGHTEEN SIXTY SIX AS A DETERENT TO BLACK AGGRESSION AGAINST WHITES,FOR INSIDIOUS DOMINANCE,INSTITUTED FOR PERSONAL SATISFACTION AND GREED.

I GREW OP IN THE STATE OF ALABAMA, AND HAD THE OPPORTUNITY TO HAVE A PLAUSIBLE RELATIONSHIP WITH BLACK AND WHITE. I AM AN AMERICAN WITH AFRICAN HERITAGE, THAT IS EXTREMELY PROUD TO BE AN AMERICAN THAT LOVE MY COUNTRY.

AND TRULY UNDERSTAND AND ADORE THE MORAL FABRIC OF INTELLECT THAT AMERICA WAS FOUNDERED ON.

UNFORTUNATELY THERE WERE SOME OBJECTIONABLE OCCURRENCES IMPLEMENTED BY SOUTHERN DEMOCRATS, SUCH AS SEPARATE DRINKING FOUNTAINS, FOR BLACK AND WHITE, SITTING ON THE BACK OF THE BUS FOR BLACKS, AND SEGREGATED PUBLIC SEATING.

HOWEVER (NEVER) ONCE DID THIS DETER MY LOVE FOR AMERICA, BECAUSE I WAS SMART ENOUGH TO REALIZE

THAT THERE HAD TO BE A REASON FOR THIS KIND OF DILEMMA, OTHER THAN THE COLOR OF SKIN.

AS A KID GROWING UP IN ALABAMA, I PLOWED MULES, CHOP COTTON, PICKED COTTON, HARVESTED CORN, RAISED CATTLE AND PIGS, ALSO RODE HORSES AND MULES.

AND DRANK FROM SEPARATE PUBLIC WATER FOUNTIANS, WAITED IN SEPARARATE ROOMS FOR BUSSES, ALSO SAT ON THE BACK OF BUSSES. AND (NEVER) ONCE WAS ABUSED BY WHITES, IN DOING THIS I LEARNED THAT HISTORICALLY WHITES HAVE ALWAYS BEEN WILLING TO COMPROMISE WITH BLACKS REGARDS TO SUCCESS AND STABILITY.

PARTICULARY IF THEY PRESENTED A VIEW OF DISPLAYING SOME INTELLECT HOWEVER SOME BLACKS HAVE AN ODIOUS OPINION OF (ALL) WHITES. WHICH WILL (NEVER) BE ERADICATED, BECAUSE OF INSIDIOUS IGNORANT INCOMPETENCY, THAT EXTEND FROM HOME TAUGHT BIGOTRY FOR CENTURIES, AND INFLUENCED BY SELF APPOINTED BLACK LEADERS,FOR SELF CONVICTION BASED ON INEPTNESS RATIFIED WITH ERRONEOUS LIES.

MOST AFRICAN AMERICANS ARE SOME OF THE MOST UNGREATFUL, DISHONEST INTEGRITY IMPUGNING, NARCISSISM, HYPERCRITICAL, UNCHARITABLE, INTERRUPTIVE, UNDERMINING, FALSLEY ACCUSING, RADICAL EXTREMIST, VULGAR, ILLITERATE, IGNORANT, INCOMPETENT, (VIOLENT) LYING, AND HERDING PETTY THIEVERY, NATIONALITYRITHAT RESIDE IN THE UNITED STATES OF AMERICA.

ANDTHESEACCURACIESARESOMEOFTHEIMPEDIMENTS, THAT HAS CAUSED A VAST MAJORITY OF WHITES AND A SEGMENT OF BLACKS, TO AILENATE THEM SELVES FROM THESE EMBEDDED PHILOSOPHICAL ENDEAVORS,THAT HAS TRAITS OF THIEVERY AND EXTORTION .

THROUGHOUT MY WRITINGS I (NEVER) ACCUSE AND CLASSIFY (ALL) BLACKS AS HAVING THE IDENTICAL MENTAL CAPACITY, THE WORDING IS CHARACTERIZED AS EITHER MOST, SEGEMENT OR MAJORITY.

I AM ALSO OF THE OPINION THAT IF YOU MAKE A DEROGATORY ACCUSATION YOU MUST HAVE THE VALIDITY TO SUBSTANTIATE.

FOR INSTANCE ONE OF THE MOST AGONIZING BUFFOONISH, IGNORANT AND INCOMPETENT OCCURRENCES PERTAINING TO THE (MAJORITY) OF SOUTHERN BLACKS OCCURED IN EIGHTEEN NINETY FIVE, WHEN SOUTHERN DEMOCRAT, PLANTATION OWNERS, LITERALLY USED PRESTIGIOUS FOUNDER OF TUSKEEGEE INSTITUTE AND PRESIDENT, BOOKER T. WASHINGTON,TO TRAVEL THROUGH OUT POPULATED BLACK AREAS IN THE SOUTH, AND MANIPULATE THE MAJORITY OF INEPT BLACKS THAT THE JIM CROW RULE SEPARATE BUT EQUAL WAS INEVITABLE, AND WOULD BE AN ASSET TO BLACKS.

THE MAJORITY OF BLACKS APPLAUDED AND AGREED WITH HIS PROPAGANDA. BECAUSE HE WAS THE MOST INFLUNTIAL BLACK LEADER IN THE SOUTH, AND THE ALL WHITE SOUTHERN DEMOCRATS NEW THAT, ALSO THAT MOST BLACKS HERD BEHIND LEADERS ESPECIALLY IF THEY ARE BLACK.

SO IN ESSENCE THE CUNNING DEMOCRATS USED VERBIAGE TO INCITE BLACKS, (SEPARATE BUT EQUAL) KNOWING THAT THE MAJORITY OF BLACKS WERE SO IGNORANT AND INCOMPETENT, THEY WOULD (NEVER) DECIPHER THE TRUE FATE OF THE MESSAGE. AND ONLY GRASP THE WORD (EQUAL) AND ASSUME THAT WHITES HAD ACCEPTED THEM AS EQUALS, AND TOTALLY OMITTED THE WORD (SEPARATE) SO WITH A JUBLIANT ENDORSEMENT FOR THIS GUIDELINE SEPARATE BUT EQUAL, FROM THE MAJORITY OF SOUTHERN BLACKS.

THE SOUTHERN DEMOCRATS WENT TO THE SUPREME COURT,AND CONVINCED THE JUSTICES THAT IT SHOULD BECOME THE LAW OF THE SOUTH, AND IT WAS RATIFIED IN EIGHTEEN NINETY SIX, AS CONSTITUTIONAL LAW. THAT RACES OF PEOPLE COULD BE SEPARATED, BASED ON THEIR HAVING EQUAL FACILITIES PROVIDED.

WHITES KNEW THAT BLACKS DID (NOT) HAVE THE FINANCIAL RECOURSES IN THE SOUTH, AND WOULD HAVE TO USE THEIRS, SO THEY IMPLEMENTED RACIST

GUIDE-LINES OF DISCRIMINATION, IN PUBLIC PLACES AND BUISNESSES THAT THEY OWNED, SUCH AS BARRING BLACKS FROM EATING AT LUNCH COUNTERS, SEPARATE DRINKING FOUNTAINS, SITTING IN THE BALCONY AT THEATERS, AND RIDING IN THE BACK OF THE BUS.

THE RATIFIED FUNCTIONS OF THESE ACTIONS, WERE STIMULATED AND ENDORSED BY THE MAJORITY OF SOUTHERN IGNORANT AND INCOMPETENT BLACKS BY (NOT) BEING CAPABLE OF DECIPHERING AND GRAMMATICALLY ANALYZING THE MEANING OF SYLLABLELVERBIAGE (SEPARATE BUT EQUAL) SADLY THIS WAS THE STIGMATIZATION OF BLACKS THEN, ONE HUNDRED AND THIRTEEN YEARS LATER IT STILL EXIST, AND IS MORE PREVALENT TODAY. THERE WAS ANOTHER DISPARAGING NOTABLE INCIDENT THAT OCCURRED IN NINETEEN FIFTY SEVEN, REPUBLICAN PRESIDENT DWIGHT D. EISENHOWER, TRIED DESPERATELY TO REPEAL AND RESTORE CIVIL RIGHTS TO BLACKS IN THE SOUTHERN STATES, THAT BLACKS HAD SUPPORTED WITH CONVICTION, (SEPRATE BUT EQUAL) BEING TOTALLY UNAWARE OF THE CONSEQUENCES.HE DRAFTED A BILL TO ERADICATE.

HOWEVER THE DEMOCRATS CONTROLLED THE SENATE, AND REJECTED THE BILL. THIS DID NOT DETER HIS EFFORTS TO QUELL THE VIOLENCE AGAINST BLACKS BY THE SOUTHERN DEMOCRATIC FOUNDERED KU-KLUX-KLAN. THE PRESIDENT SUMMONED F.B.I. DIRECTOR J. EDGAR HOOVER, TO INFILTRATE THE KU-KLUX-KLAN, IN AN EFFORT TO ERADICATE THE VIOLENCE AGAINST BLACKS, ALSO INTEGRATE SCHOOLS, AFTER THIS WAS ACCOMPLISED, THE PRESIDENT LEARNED THAT NORTHERN BLACKS WHICH COULD VOTE, WERE AT THE DEMOCRATIC CONVENTION HELD IN PENNSYLVANIA, GIVING RECOGNITION AND VOTING FOR DEMOCRATS, IN ORDER THAT THEY COULD CONTINUE TO DENY THEIR RELATIVES IN THE SOUTH CIVIL RIGHTS AND INTIMIDATE WITH VIOLENCE, PRESIDENT EISENHOWER EMPHATICALLY STATED THAT ALL THE EFFORTS THAT WE AS REPUBLICANS, HAVE TRIED TO RESCUE BLACKS FROM THE GRASP OF THE VICTIMIZING VIOLENT SOUTHERN DEMOCRATS, THEY

STILL SUPPORT DEMOCRATS FOR CONGRESS AND THEF SENATE. AND THAT WAS OVER FIFTY YEARS AGO, AND THE MAJORITY OF BLACKS ARE STILL ASSOCIATING THEM SELVES WITH THE ALIMENTARY CANAL OF DEMOCRATS, AND IF YOU ASK WHY, THE ONLY ANSWER IS MY MOMMA AND DADDY WAS A DEMOCRAT, WHICH IS A IMPLICATION OF IGNORANCE AND INCOMPETENCE. BLACKS ARE THE (ONLY) NATIONALITY OF PEOPLE, THAT RESIDE IN AMERICA TO SUPPORT THE DEMOCRATIC PARTY BY A MARGIN OF NINETY FIVE PERCENT, FOR OVER SEVENTY FIVE YEARS.

EVEN THE IMMIGRANTS ARE (NOT) THAT SMALL DYSFUNCTIONAL BRAIN IGNORANT AND GULLIBLE.

AMERICA, WAS FOUNDERED ON ONE OF THE MOST DIPLOMATIC, COMPLEX, UNIQUE, SYSTEMATIC, ARRANGEMENTS OF PRINCIPLES ON GODS EARTH. AND IF ANY ONE RESIDE HERE AND IS A CITIZEN, BLACK OR WHITE, AND DO (NOT) ATTEMPT TO FOCUS ON THE LUCRATIVE OF WORTHINESS. IT QUIT AS A COMPREHENSIVE ADHERENCE.

THEN YOU ARE A IGNORANT,.WORTHLESS INCOMPETENT LYING IMBECILE THAT CONSTANTLY ACCUSE OTHERS FOR YOUR LIKE OF INTELLECT TO COMPREHEND THE FUNDAMENTAL GIST OF THE UNITED STATES OF AMERICA, AND THE COORDINATED STANDARDS THAT EXIST FOR (ALL) PEOPLE.

UNFORTUNATELY THE MAJORITY OF AFRICAN AMERICANS HAVE A GENETIC DISORDER EMBEDDED TRAIT OF DECEPTION,RELATED TO CONNING. BASED ON UTILIZING RACISM, AS A METHOD BY LYING TO DISTORT FOR EITHER EXTORTION, VENGEANCE, OR PERSONAL GAIN.

AND ANY THING THEY DO (NOT) UNDERSTAND, THEY WILL SEEK TO DESTROY PRIME EXAMPLE PRESIDENT BARACK HUSSEIN OBAMA, HAS DISDAIN FOR THE UNITED STATES OF AMERICA, AND THE GUIDE-LINES OF THE CONSTUTION. THAT IS PROFOUND REGARDS TO OUR LIBERTY, HE LIED DECEIVED AND DISTORTED HIS INTENTIONS TO THE AMERICAN PEOPLE.

THEY TRUSTED HIM, BASED ON HIS LYING HYPOCRISY, AND ONCE HE WAS ELECTED PRESIDENT, THE REAL OBAMA INITIATIVE IS APPEARING, RELATED THE TEACHING OF PASTER REV. WRIGHT.

THAT IS CONFIRMED BY THE PEOPLE THAT HE HAS (CHOSEN) TO SURROUND HIM SELF WITH.

HOWEVER THIS PRESIDENT BARACK HUSSEIN OBAMA, IS A NARCISSISTIC PSYCHOPATH, IRRESPONSIBLE, ARROGANT, INCOMPETENT IMBECILE. SIMPLY BECAUSE APPARENTLY HE HAS (FORGOTTEN) OR JUST PLAIN INEPT TO THE FACT THAT THE LEGITIMATE CONSTITUENT PRINCIPLE, WORDS OF THE CONSTITUTION IS (WE THE PEOPLE)

IN ESSENCE IT IS POLITICAL SUICIDE TO CONTINUE TRYING DECEPTIVE ACTS OF GIMMICKRY ON THE AMERICAN PEOPLE.

THE AUTHENTICITY OF OUR CONSTITUTION IS PROFOUND, THE FORE FATHERS KNEW THE COMPLEXITY.

THAT IS REASON THEY DEMANDED THAT TO BECOME PRESIDENT OF AMERICA YOU MUST BE BORN IN THE UNITED STATES.OE AMERICA WITHUCITIZENRY. SIMPLY BECAUSE YOUR LIFE WILL BE MOTIVATED OR DEMINISHED BY YOUR AFFILIATIONS, HOWEVER IT OFFER THE OPPORTUNITY TO ANALYZE THE PEOPLE THAT YOU CONGREGATE WITH ON A DAILY BASIS.

BECAUSE IF YOU SHOULD CHOOSE TO BECOME A POLITICIAN, AND GET ELECTED BY THE PEOPLE, BASED ON LIES AND DECEPTIVE PROMISES, ASSUMING YOU WILL BE GIVEN A PASS BECAUSE OF ETHNICS, AND WHEN QUESTION REGARDS TO DELIBERATELY LYING TO GET ELECTED.

WITH (NO) INTENTIONS OF DELIVERANCE ON YOUR PROMISES, AND WHEN QUESTIONED REGARDS TO YOUR MOTIVES,OR INTENTIONS.

YOU BECOME BELLIGERENT AND ATTEMPT TO INTIMIDATE THE NEWS MEDIA, ALSO DISTORT AND LIE ON THE PEOPLE THAT TRUSTED YOU BASED ON LIES AND ELECTED YOU.

TRUST ME THIS IS AMERICA, (NOT) AFRICA, YOU ARE PLAYING A CHILDISH GAME THAT IS EQUIALENT TO RUSSIAN ROULETTE.

THE UNITED STATES OF AMERICA, CONSIST OF A DIVERSE SOCIETY OF PEOPLE , WITH STRONG CONVICTIONS, THAT HAS ENDURED SOME BLEMISHES. HOWEVER MANY WERE FALSIFIED, BASED ON IGNORANCE AND INCOMPETENCE. WE (DO NOT) REPEAT (DO NOT) RESERVE THE RIGHT TO BE CASTIGATED BY YOUNG INSIDIOUS PATHETIC PUNKS.

THAT HAVE (NO) IDEA OF THE MORAL FORTITUDE THAT IS THE STABILITY OF OUR NATION, BASED ON INTELLECTUAL MORAL VALUES AND CAPITALISM. AS I HAVE RETIERATED I WAS BORN IN ALABAMA, PLOWED COTTON, PICKED COTTON, SLOPPED HOGS, RAISED CATTLE, ALSO CHICKENS.

SAT IN THE BALCONY OF THEATERS, DRANK FROM SEPARATED WATER FOUNTAINS, AND TRAVELED SITTING IN THE BACK OF PUBLIC BUSSING. HOWEVER I ROSE ABOVE THESE IDIOSYNCRASIES AND INVESTED MY TALENTS IN THE INTEGRITY OF WHAT THIS GREAT NATION WAS FOUNDERED ON. AND INTEGRATED INTO A DIVERSE SOCIETY OF INTELLECT, BASED ON MY INDIVIDUAL STANDARDS OF MORALITY.

(UNREADABLE TEXT) THESE ATTRIBUTES HAS BEEN AVAILABLE FOR HUNDREDS OF YEARS FOR (ALL) PEOPLE, BUT MOST BLACKS ARE TO INEPT AND INCOMPETENT TO GRASP. INSTANCE THROUGH OUT THE SOUTHERN STATES, WHITES GAVE THOUSANDS IF NOT MILLIONS ACRES OF LAND TO BLACKS, FOR THEIR LOYALTY, UNFORTUNATELY THEY SQUANDERED IT DUE TO IGNORANT INCOMPETENCY.

AND OVER THREE HUNDRED YEARS LATER BLACKS ARE STILL ACCUSING THE WHITE MAN FOR THEIR IMPOVERISHED SELF INFLICTED LUDICROUS, INORDINATE INEPT BEHAVIOR.

BLACKS ARE OF THE OPINION, THAT LAWS ARE TO BE BROKEN, BASED ON ON THEIR INTERPRETATION OF ASSUMPTIONS AS TO WHAT LAWS SHOULD BE. AND IF THEY ARE INVOLVED IN A CIRCUMSTANCE WHERE LAWS ARE BROKEN THEY SEEK A COMPROMISE, BASED ON THEIR BEING (BLACK) AND THIS IS A STIGMATIZATION OF MOST BLACKS IN THE UNITED STATES OF AMERICA.

IT IS AN ILLUMINATED OBSESSION WITH BLACKS TO DISTORT FOR ECCENTRIC AND VIOLENT INEPT BEHAVIOR.

FOR INSTANCE MOST ARE PROFESSIONAL MIMICS, THAT WILL LISTEN TO A DIALOGUE BETWEEN TWO PEOPLE, AND IF IT IS TO THEIR LIKING, THEY WILL UTILIZE AN ATTEMPT TO EXECUTE, AS IF THEY GENERATED THE IDEA AND WERE AND STILL IS TECHINICALLYIUNABLE TO DECIPHER THE MEANING OF VERBIAGE.

THESE GENETIC HERITAGE TRAITS WAS LARGELY RESPONSIBLE FOR MAIMING AND LYNCHINGS, FOR CENTURIES IN THE SOUTHERN STATES. WHITES INITIATED PETTY TRICKERY ON BLACKS, IN ORDER TO DETER THE4 IR VICIOUS INHUMAN VIOLENCE PERPETRATED BY BLACKS.

SOUTHERN WHITES BECAME ILLICIT EXTREMELY FEARFUL OF REBELLIOUS ATTTACKS FROM BLACKS, SO IN ESSENCE THEY IMPLEMENTED OUTRAGEOUS STRENUOUS GUIDE-LINES IN ORDER TO CONTROL THE HORRENDOUS REBELLIOUS VIOLENCE FROM BLACKS.

AND THIS HAD ABSOLUTELY (NOTHING) TO DO WITH RACISM OR BEING BLACK, IT WAS FOR THE SAFETY FOR THEM SELVES AND THEIR FAMILYS, THEY KNEW THAT BLACK MEN HAD AN OBSESSION FOR WHITE WOMEN. SO THEY IMPLEMENTED PETTY RULES TO QUELL BLACK VIOLENCE, SUCH AS IF A BLACK MAN WHISTLE OR INSULTED A WHITE WOMAN, ALSO SAID YES OR NO TO A WHITE MAN, THAT WAS A INDICATION OF ARROGANCE.

WHICH WAS REASON FOR WHITES TO SUSPECT THAT EITHER HE OR SHE WAS PART OF A REBELLIOUS GROUP OF BLACKS OR INITIATING ONE. HOWEVER (NO) BLACK WAS EVER LYNCHED BECAUSE HE WAS BLACK, IT HAD TO DO WITH FEAR AND PRECAUTIONAL MEASURES TO PREVENT REBELLIOUS VIOLENCE FROM BLACKS.

DURING THE YEAR OF SEVENTEEN SEVENTY FIVE, THERE WAS A AFRICAN NAMED COLONEL TITUS, THAT FORMED A BAND OF OVER EIGHT HUNDRED BLACK GUERILLAS, AND RAIDED PLANTATIONS VIOLENTLY FOR OVER FIFTY YEARS, CALLING THEM SELVES THE KING OF ENGLAND SOLDIERS. HOWEVER MODERN DAY SELF APPOINTED BLACK LEADERS,

BEING THE IDEOLOGICAL (INEPT) INCOMPETENT BUFFOONS THAT THEY ARE, MAINLEY SUCH AS JESSIE JACKSON AND AL SHARPTON, WOULD HAVE YOU BELIEVE THAT SOUTHERN BLACKS WAS A GROUP OF CHOIR BOYS, THAT WAS MAIMED AND LYNCHED BECAUSE THEY WERE (BLACK)

THE EGOTISTICAL LYING HYPOCRISY FORMULATED BY MOST BLACKS, IS ASTOUNDING , AND HAS STIGMATIZED THEIR PROGRESS FOR HUNDREDS OF YEARS, AND IS MORE PREVALENT TODAY THAN EVER.

SIMPLY BECAUSE, AFTER APPROXIMATELY TWO HUNDRED AND FORTY YEARS THE VIOLENCE AND LYING, HAVE BECAME PROGRESSIVELY WORSE, REGARDS TO BLACKS EXTERMINATING EACH OTHER ON A PREVALENTLY BASIS.

FOR INSTANCE THERE ARE APPROXIMATELY TWO AND A HALF MILLION PEOPLE INCARCERATED IN AMERICA, BLACKS (ALONE) ACCOUNT FOR APPROXIMATELY ONE AND A HALF MILLION.

AND NOTABLY IS ONLY THIRTEEN PERCENT OF THREE HUNDRED MILLION PEOPLE IN AMERICA.

THIS IS A PHENOMENON THAT BEARS SCRUTINY, HOWEVER IF ONE WOULD ASK SOME OF THE SMALL DYSFUNCTIONAL BRAIN, SELF APPOINTED (BLACK) OBJECTORS, THEY WOULD OFFER AN EXPLANATION THAT IT IS THE JUSTICE SYSTEM FALSE ACCURACIES,BECAUSE THEY ARE (BLACK) WE RESIDE IN A NATION OF IMPECCABLE STANDARDS, IF APPROPRIATELY APPLIED, HOWEVER THERE ARE MANY PEOPLE THAT IS IN DENIAL, AND ARE CONTENTIOUS OBJECTORS, REGARDS TO DISTORTING (REALITY) WITH LIES WHICH HAS BEEN THE ACHILLES HEEL, RELATED TO MOST BLACKS FOR HUNDREDS OF YEARS.

TECHNICALLY THEIR SADISTIC ALOOF PREMONITION IS ADVERSE TO CHANGE SIMPLY BECAUSE OF THEIR IDEOLOGY TO SET STANDARDS, PERTAINING TO THEIR SELF INDULGENCE RELATED TO THIEVERY, LYING, CONNING, AND VIOLENCE, ALSO NEGATING LAWS FOR JUSTICE.

BASED ON RELENTLESSLY CLAIMING THEY ARE BEING FALSELY PERSECUTED BECAUSE THEY ARE (BLACK);

AND THERE ARE SICK DYSFUNCTIONAL BRAIN HERDING PARASITIC SELF APPOINTED BLACK LEADERS, THAT ENDORSE THIS THEORY, AND WILL DEMONSTRATE ON THEIR LYING BEHALF, TO (NO) AVAIL , HOWEVER IT (NEVER) CEASE TO EXIST.

IN ESSENCE TO SUBSTANTIATE THE VALIDITY OF MY ACCUSATIONS, I WILL ELABORATE ON A FIEW MIND BOGGLING OCCURRENCES, OF OUTRAGIOUS LYING AND INORDINATE REPETITIOUS VIOLENT ACTS, PERPETRATED BY BLACKS, IN MODERN DAY SOCIETY.

THIS IS A BRIEF SYNOPSIS OF HIDEOUS IMPORTUNE CRIMES, RELATED TO BLACK AGGRESSION, THAT ALARMED THE NATION AND ABROAD. MOST BLACKS ARE TEMPERAMENTAL, AND LIKE THE ABILITY TO GRASP 0R DECIPHER AND EDIT CONSEQUENCES.

SO THEY COMMIT HIDEOUS (UNREADABLE TEXT) INNER , HATRED FOR LAW ENFORCEMENT, AND THE NATION IS BEWILDERED AS TO WHY.

UNFORTUNATELY IT HAS TO DO WITH GENETIC HERITAGE OF HERDING, AND NOTORIETY SUPERIORITY ATTENTIVENESS, WHICH IS A EMBEDDED TRAIT THAT IS INEVITABLE PERTAINING TO MOST BLACKS, EDUCATED OR (NOT) THEIR EMOTIONS ARE PARALLEL.

MOST BLACKS LIVE IN A PHANTASY WORLD OF DECEIT, IN AN EFFORT TO CAMOUFLAGE INCOMPETENCY, AND THERE IS (NONE) BETTER AT THIS FOLKLORE BECAUSE THE EVIDENCE IS IN THE WHITE HOUSE AS PRESIDENT OF THE UNITED STATES OF AMERICA.

THIS BOOK IS RITTEN TO OFFER A DEFINITIVELY CHRONOLOGICAL EXPLANATION TO BLACKS IN GENERAL.

THEY HAVE SUCCESSFULLY INDOCTRINATED (STUPID) ASS WHITES, BY CONSISTENTLY FOCUSING ON RACISM, THAT THEIR CREDIBILITY IS (BEYOND) REPROACH, WHILE THEY CONSTANTILY CONTINUE TO SLAUGHTER PEOPLE. AND DEMONIZE WHITES AS BEING RESPONSIBLE FOR THEIR ACTIONS. BECAUSE OF SLAVERY, THERE ARE THOUSANDS OF INNOCENT VICTIMS MURDERED BY BLACKS ANUALLY, IN

LOCAL TOWNS AND CITIES, THAT (NEVER) GET BROADCAST OVER THE NATIONAL NETWORK.

HOWEVER LETS ROLL BACK THE CLOCK ON SOME OF THESE VICIOUS CRIMES, THAT STUNNED THE NATION.

ALSO OUTRAGOUS LIES, BEGINNING WITH WAYNE BERTRAM WILLIAMS OF GEORGIA IN NINTEEN SEVENTY NINE, SLAUGHTERED TWENTY THREE INNOCENT CHILDREN AND TWO ADULTS, AS REPORTED.

JOHN MOHAMMAD AND LEE MALVO, IN TWO THOUSAND AND TWO, FROM WASHINGTON, STATE, DELIBERATELY PLANNED A UNIQUE WAY TO SLAUGHTER TEN INNOCENT PEOPLE, JUST BECAUSE THEY WERE THERE.

RECENTLY IN TWO THOUSAND AND EIGHT, CURTIS VANCE. IN THE STATE OF ARKANSAS, BROKE INTO A CAREER NEWS ANCOR WOMAN HOME, AND FATALLY BRUTALIZED HER, INCLUDING RAPE.

ACCORDING TO THE NEWS MEDIA REPORTING THAT THE PRESIDING JURORS OVER HIS TRIAL, WERE CONVINCED BY HIS DEFENCE AND HIS MOTHER THAT HE HAD A ROUGH CHILD HOOD, AND SHE WAS A DRUG ADDICT, ALSO HE IS SUSPECTED OF BEING PSYCHOTIC.

THAT IS ONE OF THE MOST DERANGED INEPT ASSUMPTIONS, FOR COMPASSION, UNTIL IT IS BEYOND INCOMPETENCE.

BECAUSE THERE ARE MILLIONS OF CHILDREN BORN, AND HAVE A HANDICAP. ROUGH CHILD HOOD, BLACK AND WHITE.

AND SOME ARE PSYCHOTIC, BUT THEY (NEVER) CHOOSE TO RAPE AND MURDER AND COMMIT HIDEOUS CRIMES AGAINST INNOCENT PEOPLE. THIS WAS TRULY A CRIME OF INCOMPETENT VILE IGNORANCE, THAT IS EMBEDDED IN THE GENETIC HERITAGE, THAT IS INEVITABLE WITH MOST AFRICAN AMERICANS.

AND CHRONOLOGICAL RECORDS OF SIGNIFICANT EVENTS, VALIDATE THE VALIDITY OF THESE UNWISE VICIOUS CRIMINAL ATTACKS, COMITTED BY BLACKS, THAT IS PREVALENT IN THE UNITED STATES OF AMERICA, FOR HUNDREDS OF YEARS.

FOR INSTANCE IT IS APPAULING AND INHUMAN, AS TO WHAT TRANSPIRED IN THE STATE OF OHIO, PERPETRATED BY ANTHONEY SOWELL, MURDERING APPROXIMATELY ELEVEN INNOCENT WOMEN, AND PLANTING THEIR BODIES OUTSIDE AND IN HIS HOME.

THERE IS (NO) EXPLANATION FOR THIS KIND OF GROSS BARBARIC ACT OF HUMAN SLAUGHTER, EXECUTED BY A BLACK MAN, OTHER THAN PERVERTED CYNICISM, ATTRIBUTED TO VULGAR MOTIVES, THAT IS WORSE THAN CARRION EATING HYENAS OF AFRICA, AT LEAST NOTHING IS LEFT TO CREATE A STENCH.

THE PSYCHOANALYSIS OF MOST AFRICAN AMERICANS ARE HOMOGENEOUS AND DISPARATE, BASED ON HERDING ASSUMPTIONS, TO FOLLOW SELF APPOINTED BLACK IDEOLOGUES.

HOWEVER IT IS CONSISTENT WITH AFRICAN TRADITIONS OF HERDING BEHIND A CONGO TRIBAL CHIEF.

THIS IS (NOT) A RACIST CONJECTURE BUT A FACT OF REALITY, PERTAINING TO AFRICAN HERITAGE.

THEIR PHILOSOPHY IS (ONE) INDIVIDUAL HAVE THE AUTHORITY TO SPEAK FOR AND CONTROL HIS TRIBE. AND STUPID ASS SMALL DYSFUNCTIONAL BRAIN DEMOCRATIC (WHITES) ARE ENDORSING THIS UNCIVILIZED THEORY, REGARDS TO PUBLIC OPTION HEALTH CARE.

HOWEVER IN ESSENCE LETS REVISIT SOME OF THE MOST OUTRAGEOUS RADICAL HOAXED LIES BY BLACK WOMEN.

NINETEEN EIGHTY SEVEN, NEWYORK, STATE. TWANA BRAWLEY, WENT MISSING, WHEN DISCOVERED SHE WAS COVERED WITH FECES, AND CLAIMED THAT FOUR WHITE MEN WERE RESPONSIBLE FOR THIS DEBACLE, INCLUDING RAPE. AL SHARPTON WENT PROJECTILE, AND DILIGENTLY SUPPORTED HER CLAIM, UNFORTUNATELY FOR HIM, A GRAND JURY RULED THAT IT WAS A HOAX.

(UNREADABLE TEXT)

THE STATE OF NORTH CAROLINA, TWO THOUSAND SIX. CRYSTAL GALE MANGUM, CAUSED A NATION WIDE RUCKUS, BY CLAIMING THREE DUKE LACROSS PLAYERS MOLESTED HER.

THOUSANDS OF BLACKS PREMATURLEY STORMED INTO NORTH CAROLINA, ACCUSING WHITES OF RACISM, AND THREATENING PEOPLE.

PRIOR TO A TRIAL TO LEARN THE FACTS, INSTEAD THEY CHOOSE TO INDITE/ AND TRY THESE YOUNG MEN, BASED ON ASSUMPTIONS.

WHICH IS TYPICAL TRAITS OF MOST BLACKS, WHEN THERE ARE FRICTIONS BETWEEN BLACK AND WHITE, MOST BLACKS ALWAYS ASSUME THAT IT IS THE FAULT OF THE WHITES.

IN ORDER TO VALIDATE THE VALIDITY OF MY ACCUSATION, I UTILIZE THE ACTION OF THE BLACK PRESIDENT OF THE UNITED STATES OF AMERICA. BARACK HUSSIEN OBAMA. WHEN IN A NEWS CONFERENCE, HE ASSUMED THAT WHEN (WHITE) POLICE OFFICERS OF MASSACHUSETTS ARRESTED A BLACK LAW PROFESSOR, THE PRESIDENT (INSISTED) THAT THE WHITE OFFICERS WERE (STUPID) ALTHOUGH HE KNEW (NOTHING) ABOUT THE CONSEQUENCES OF THE CHARGES RELATED TO THE PROFESSOR ARREST.

HOWEVER THE DUKE LACROSS YOUNG MEN WERE (ACQUITTED) BY A JURY BASED ON A LYING HOAX, AND DISTRICT ATTORNEY MIKE NIFONG, LOST HIS LICENSE TO PRACTICE LAW, FOR CONCEALING INFORMATION REGARDS TO A (HOAX);

ALSO I AM CERTAIN THAT THE ENTIRE NATION AND ABROAD, ARE AWARE OF THE LOUISIANA JENA SIX FIASCO, WHERE SIX BLACKS BASHED THE HEAD OF A YOUNG WHITE MALE INTO CONCUSSION.

BECAUSE OF A SYMBOLISTIC ROPE HANGING FROM A TREE, AND ALONG CAME HUNDREDS OF BLACK DEMONSTRATORS, IN AN EFFORT TO INTIMIDATE LAW ENFORCEMENT (AGAINST) LEGAL PUNISHMENT.FOR THIS VERY HIDEOUS ACT OF CRIMINAL ACTIVITY.

ALSO THE U.S. CONGRESSIONAL BLACK CAUCUS (DEMANDED) THAT LOUISIANA GOVERNOR KATHLEEN BLANCO, AT THAT TIME COMMUTE AND REPEAL ARREST AND TRIAL FOR THISI HELNQUS. CRIMINAL ACT.

LATELY IT WAS REPORTED ON NOVEMBER NINETEENTH, TWO THOUSAND NINE THAT JESSIE JACKSON CENSURED A BLACK CAUCUS CONGRESSIONAL MEMBER AURTHOR DAVIS OF ALABAMA, FOR USING HIS INDEPENDENT DISCRETION, AND WERE THE (ONLY) BLACK U.S.CONGRESSMAN TO (NOT) VOTE FOR PUBLLIC OPTION HEALTH CARE.

AND THE IMPLICATION FROM JESSIE JACKSON WAS OBJECTIONABLE, BECAUSE HIS PHILOSOPHY IS THAT (ALL) BLACKS SHOULD HERD TOGATHER AND NOT THINK INDEPENDENT FOR THEM SELVES.

MOST BLACKS HAVE AND ALWAYS WILL, LIVE IN COMPLACENCY, BIAS, NEGATIVE, PHANTASY WORLD, ADHERINGTOAIDEOLOGUEOFEMBEDDEDINCOMPETENCY, BEING OBSESSED WITH TRYING TO MONITOR WHITES ON RADIO AND TELEVISION , IN AN EFFORT TO DETERMINE IF A (WHITE) MAKE A DEROGATORY REMARK ABOUT A BLACK PERSON.

IN ESSENCE WHILE THEY ARE ENGAGED IN THIS PSYCHOPATIC INSANITY, BLACKS ARE SLAUGHTERING EACH OTHER, AROUND THE NATION, AS IF YOU WOULD FIRE A DOUBLE SHOT GUN INTO A FLOCK OF BLACK BIRDS. AND IT APPEAR THAT IT IS OF (NO) CONCERN FOR PRESIDENT BARACK H. OBAMA, OR THE U.S. CONGRESSIONAL BLACK CAUCUS, NEITHER JESSIE JACKSON OR AL SHARPTON.

FRANKLY SPEAKING THE BLACK CAUCUS, JESSIE JACKSON AND AL SHARPTON HAVE ENDORSED BLACK VIOLENCE,BY DEFENDING THE LOUISIANA (UNREADABLE TEXT) SIX BRUTALLY ATTACKING A WHITE YOUNGSTER.

ALLEN IVERSON IS A GENETIC REPLICA, OF HOW MOST AFRICAN AMERICANS ENVISION THEM SELVES, ALL NARCISSISTIC BRAUN, AND NO SENSE OF INDIVIDUAL MORALITY, AND SELF CONTROL OF INTELLECT, TO DETERMINE THEIR GUIDANCE IN LIFE.

AS REPORTED IVERSON IS GOING TO CONFER WITH HIS COLLEGE COACH, JOHN THOMPSON, IN ORDER TO DETERMINE HIS FUTURE, AS A BASKET BALL PLAYER.

IF THE BASKET BALL LEAGUE WASNT DOMINATED BY OUT STANDING (BLACK) PLAYERS, JESSIE JACKSON AND AL SHARPTON, WOULD BE MARCHING CLAIMING RACISM.

HOWEVER THIS IS A PRIME EXAMPLE THAT IS CONSISTENT WITH MOST BLACKS ,IN AMERICA.

TRYING TO DISTORT AND REFUSING TO ACCEPT (REALITY) BASKET BALL IS A GRUELING SPORT.ESPECIALLY FOR A GUARD, BECAUSE HE OR SHE IS CONSTANTANTLY MOVING MAKING PLAYS, AND WITH ANY BASKET BALL PLAYER THE LEGS IS THE FIRST TO GO, AND ONCE THAT HAPPEN, IT AFFECT YOUR ENTIRE COORDINATION IS AFFECTED, HOWEVER IVERSON IS STILL A CALIBER PLAYER, AND WOULD BE ASSET TO ANY TEAM, WITH LIMITED PLAYING TIME.

UNFORTUNATELY HE HAS ONLY THREE CHOICES, EXCEPT LIMITED PLAYING TIME, RETIREMENT, OR HAVE COACH JOHN THOMPSON, MANUFACTURE HIM A NEW SET OF (LEGS)

HOWEVER THIS IS TIPIGAL OF MOST BLACKS, BECAUSE THERE IS ONE IN OUR WHITE HOUSE, PRESIDENT BARACK HUSSIEN OBAMA, THAT IS OF THE IDENTICAL MENTALITY.

ALLEN IVERSON IS OF THE OPINION THAT A N.B.A. FRANCHISE SHOULD BE ORGANIZED AROUND HIM, WITH QUESTIONABLE LEGS.

PRESIDENT BARACK HUSSEIN OBAMA, IS ASSUMING THAT HE CAN BE THE LEADER OF THE GLOBE. WITH SMALL DYSFUNCTIONAL BRAINS

ALLEN IVERSON HAVE ONLY HIS PRIDE IN JEOPARDY. WE AS A NATION IS IN JEOPARDY, BECAUSE OUR NATION IS BEING SABOTAGED, WITH A COVERT EMBEDDED CALCULATED MOSLEM,OBAMA, PERPETRATED CONSPIRACY. HOWEVER THERE IS A SEGEMENT OF BLACKS,PARTICULARLY THOSE THAT HAVE A SUCCESSFUL ADAPTATION IN AMERICA. ARE BECOMING SKEPTICAL OF OBAMA MOTIVES, FOR INSTANCE ON NOVEMBER 29, 2009. TOM JOYNER STATED ON HIS RADIO SHOW, THAT THE PRESIDENT OF THE UNITED STATES OF AMERICA, WAS BENDING HIS BODY SO LOW TO THE EMPEROR OF CHINA, UNTIL HE WAS CONFUSED AS TO WHY THE PRESIDENT WOULD BE TYING THE EMPEROR SHOE LACES.

HOWEVER THE CONVENTIONAL WISDOM IS THAT THE PRESIDENT HAVE A VINDICTIVE REPLY FOR AMERICA HE THINK THE AMERICAN PEOPLE ARE STUPID. IN FACT APPROXIMATELY SIXTY FIVE MILLION OF THEM ARE, FOR VOTING HIM TO BECOME OUR PRESIDENT, HE HAS A VESTED PLAN TO CONTINUE INDOCTRINATING THE YOUNG VOTING IDIOTS OF AMERICA, THAT HAVE (NO) IDEA THAT THERE IS A CONSTITUTION, WHY DO YOU THINK THAT HE IS A PERMANENT FIXTURE ON RADIO TELEVISION,AND OTHER NEWS OUTLETS. ALSO TRAVELING ALL OVER THE GLOBE, HE THINK THAT HE IS BRAIN WASHING OTHER NATIONS, AS HE HAS THE BUFFOONS IN AMERICA. BUT OTHER NATIONS ARE GIGGLING A AMERICA FOR ELECTING A NARCISSISTIC INCOMPETENT PRESIDENT TO LEAD OUR NATION.

THIS BELLIGERENT PRESIDENT BARACK HUSSIEN OBAMA, IS A CONCEITED PHONY, THAT HAS INTENTIONS OF DESTROYING AMERICA, WHILE SOME STUPID ASS CONGRESSIONAL (WHITES) SIT BACK, AND ENDORSE HIS THEORY. FEAR OF BEING CALLED A RACIST, WHY DO YOU THINK HE IS TRYING THESE TERRORIST IN THE CITY OF NEW YORK.

ANY PUBLIC OFFICIAL DEMOCRAT OR REPUBLICAN, ENDORSE THIS CONTEMPTABLE ACT OF AGGRESSION, SHOULD BE VOTED OUT OF OFFICE. BASED ON CONSPIRING TO SABOTAGE AMERICA, BECAUSE THIS IS GOING TO BE A REVELATION GLOBALLY OF OUR TECHNIQUES, THAT KEEP OUR NATION SECURE FROM TERRORISM.

THEORETICALLY OBAMA IS AWARE OF THIS CONTEMPTUOUS ACT, WHICH WILL INCITE TERRORIST AROUND THE GLOBE AGAINST INNOCENT AMERICAN CITIZENS, PUBLIC HEALTH CARE AND COMPROMISING OUR SAFE GUARD TO THE ENEMY, IS HIS VINDICTIVE WAY OF PERSECUTING (WHITES) FOR WHICH HE ASSUME THEY DID TO BLACKS, AND ARE CURRENTLY PARTICIPATING IN, IN AN EFFORT TO PROHIBIT BLACK SUCCESS.

BLACKS HAVE CAPITALIZED ON RACISM IN AMERICA, AND CONVINCED WHITES, THAT THEY ARE SMART AS HELL, BUT HAVENT BEEN GIVEN A FAIR CHANCE, AND MILLIONS

OF WHITES HAVE FALLEN FOR THIS CONTEMPTIBLE NARCISSISTIC INCOMPETENCY,AND HAVE BECAME DOCILE.

PRESIDENT BARACK HUSSIEN OBAMA, IS PLAYING A MIND GAME WITH THE AMERICAN PEOPLE, JUST STOP AND THINK FOR A MOMENT, THERE HAS BEEN (NO) PRESIDENT IN AMERICAN HISTORY, PUBLICIZED TWENTY FOUR HOURS A DAY, HE IS TRAVLING GLOBALLY MEETING WITH FOREGIN DIGNITARIES, AND INVITING THEM TO THE WHITE HIUSE, AND HE HAVE THESE (WHITE) ALIMENTARY CANAL LICKS, SUPPORTING HIS CYNICAL TACTICS TO SABOTAGE AMERICA,AND HIS STAUNCH DEMOCRATIC SUPPORTERS, ARE GUILTY OF ACCESSORY TO CONSPIRE AGAINST THE AMERICAN PEOPLE.

AND HIS SUPPORTERS IS COMPLETELY INEPT TO HIS INTENTIONS, BECAUSE IF (ANYTHING) OCCUR OUT OF THE ORDINARY DURING THIS TRAIL OF THESE TERRORIST IN NEW YORK, HE HAS ALREADY PLANNED HIS EXCUSE, TO BLAME ATTORNEY GENERAL ERIC HOLDER, ANR THROW HIM UNDER THE BUS. THIS PRESIDENT IS COMPLETELY OUT OF TOUCH WITH THE AMERICAN PEOPLE EVEN HIS STAUNCH AFRICAN AMERICAN SUPPORTERS.

IT IS ALL ABOUT HIM, AND HIS ARROGANT RADICAL NARCISSISTIC CYNICIS DIRECTED AT THE AMERICAN PEOPLE, IN AN EFFORT TO DEMORALIZE THE UNITED STATES OF AMERICA. HOWEVER IF HE HAD STUDIED THE AFRICAN AMERICAN CULTURE IN AMERICA HE WOULD MOST CERTAINLY BE AWARE OF THEIR GENETIC CONTROLLABILITY WHICH DICTATE OF (NOT) BOWING TO (ANY) INDIVIDUAL.

THAT THEY DEEM TO BE SUPERIOR, SO IN ESSENCE MR BARACK HUSSIEN OBAMA HAS CROSSED THE LIME, WHICH IS CAUSING TRUE SPECULATIONS TO HIS TRUE IDENITY.

HOWEVER TRUST IN GOD , AND THE AMERICAN PEOPLE, BECAUSE THIS NATION COULD HAVE (NEVER) SUCCEEDED, FOR HUNDREDS OF YEARS WITHOUT THE PEOPLE AND THEIR BELIEF IN GOD.

ALTHOUGH, WE ARE A NATION OF COMPETITIVE INTUITIONS, WHICH IS ABSOUTELY NECESSARY TO PREVAIL WITH MORAL AND DIGNITY (UNREADABLE TEXT)

PERSONALLY I AM AN INDIVIDUAL, THAT HAVE VINDICTIVE REPRISAL AGAINST (UNREADABLE TEXT) TRULY BELIEVE (UNREADABLE TEXT) EXPERIENCED RADICAL RACISM PORTRAYED BY BLACKS, WHEN I WAS IN THE FIFTH GRADE, IN AN ALL BLACK SCHOOL IN ALABAMA.

MY FAMILY HAD CHICKENS GALORE, WHEN I STARTED SCHOOL AT SIX, I ASKED MY PARENTS IF I COULD TAKE SOME EGGS TO THE TEACHERS THEY SAID FINE, FOR AT LEAST THREE OR FOUR YEARS, I GAVE EGGS TO ALL OF THE TEACHERS, WHICH AT THAT TIME WAS ALL BLACK. LATER WE HAD A WHITE COME ABOARD NAMED MRS HOWARD, I WAS ONE OF HER STUDENTS, SO I BROUGHT HER TWO OR THREE DOZENS OF EGGS. THE VERY NEXT DAY, ONE OF THE BLACK TEACHERS MRS BLACKLEDGE, STOPPED BY MY PARENTS HOUSE, AND ACCOSTED MY MOTHER WITH INSINUATIONS OF RACISM, CLAIMING WHY WOULD YOU LET YOUR SON GIVE THAT OLD (WHITE WOMAN) EGGS BECAUSE SHE IS NOT ONE OF US, IS IT BECAUSE YOU ALL OWN LAND, AND TRYING TO BE WHITE.

MY MOTHER WAS A UNIQUE WOMAN WITH A TEMPER, THAT HAD A PERSONALITY TO RESOLVE MOST PROBLEMS PERTAINING TO MORALITY.

HOWEVER SHE WAS A EXPERT DEALING WITH IMMORALITY, SO SHE RESPONDED TO MRS BLACKLEDGE, YOUBEING A SCHOOL TEACHER, YOU OF ALL PEOPLE SHOULD KNOW THAT GOD CREATED ALL PEOPLE EQUAL. BUT THERE ARE SOME LIKE YOU THAT HAVE WEAK BRAINS, THAT TRY AND TELL OTHER FOLKS HOW TO LIVE THEIR LIVES, YOU ARE EDUCATED I AM (NOT) BUT I HAVE COMMON SENSE, AND MY TRUST IN GOD, THATS WHY I AM ABLE TO SUPPLY EGGS TO ALL OF THE TEACHERS AT THE SCHOOL. BECAUSE MY DEEDS IN LIFE IS TO TREAT ALL PEOPLE THE SAME. SO I WOULD LIKE VERY MUCH FOR YOU TO LEAVE (MY) PROPERTY, AND TELL YOUR FREINDS THAT MY HENS QUIT LAYING EGGS FOR DUMMIES.

MRS. HOWARD LIVED SEVERAL MILES AWAY IN THE CITY THE WHITE TEACHER, MY MOTHER WOULD GO TO THE CITY AT THAT TIME, MAYBE ONCE OR TWICE A MONTH, AND SHE WOULD ALWAYS LEAVE OR GIVE MRS. HOWARD DOZENS OF EGGS.

MY MOTHER EXPLAINED TO ME, THAT IF YOU TREAT PEOPLE KINDHEARTED, SKIN COLOR WILL NOT MAKE A DIFFERENCE, THEY WILL TREAT YOU EQUALLY, AND FOR GODS SAKES IF YOU CANT LEAD (NEVER) FOLLOW.

MANY MIGHT CONSIDER THIS AS BEING TRIVIA, BECAUSE AFTER ALL IT WAS OVER SIXTY YEARS AGO, HOWEVER I HAVE RAISED THE ISSURE PRIMARY BASED ON INTUITIONS OF THEOREMATIC REVELATIONS. BECAUSE THESE SAME EMBEDDED GENETIC TRAITS, ARE MORE PREVALENT IN MOST BLACK SOCIETY THAN EVER BEFORE.

MOST BLACKS HAVE A UNIQUE WAY OF DISGUISING THEIR VINDICTIVENESS FOR WHITES, BECAUSE THE MAJORITY OF TIMES WHITES HAVE THE ADVANTAGE, EITHER IN PRIVATE INDUSTRY EMPLOYMENT, THE POLITICAL ARENA ALSO SUPPLY AND DEMAND, THERE FORE BLACKS HAVE NO OTHER CHOICE THAN SUPRESS THEIR TRUE FEELINGS, AND THERE IS NONE BETTER. ALTHOUGH MY PARENTS MIGRATED TO THE STATE OF OHIO, MY MOTHER SAID TO GET ME AWAY FROM BLACK RACIST INSANITY.

HOWEVER MRS HOWARD RETIRED FROM TEACHING AND (NEVER) KNEW HOW HER BLACK COWORKERS FELT CONTEMPT FOR HER, BECAUSE THIS WAS DURING THE FORTIES, AND IF A BLACK REBELLED AGAINST A WHITE, WITH RACIST INNUENDO, THAT WOULD COST THEM THEIR JOBS, OR WERE PUNISHED MORE SERVILELY.

TODAY IS A DIFFERENT PEROID IN TIME, AND MOST BLACKS ARE TRUCULENT REGARDS TO WHITES, AND THAT IS ONE OF THE REASONS THEIR UNEMPLOYMENT RATE IS ABOVE FIFTEEN PERCENT.

BECAUSE FOR CERTAIN IT IS THE WHITES THAT SUPPLY MOST EMPLOYMENT.

AND TRUST ME NATIONALITY IS (NOT) A HINDERANCE, PROVIDING THAT YOU ADHERE TO INTELLECTUAL MORAL VALUES, AND THE ABILITY TO COMMUNICATE WITH

OTHERS PERTAINING TO DIGNITY, WHICH IS REQUIRED TO WASH DISHES.

HOWEVER IT IS SO OFTEN THAT DECEPTION CONTROL OUR LIVES, INTO BEING MANIPULATED BY SMALL DYSFUNCTIONAL BRAIN INCOMPETENT ARISTOGRATIC BUFFOONS, SUCH AS SENATOR HARRY REIDT A DEMOCRAT. EQUATING THE HEALTH CARE DEBATES TO SLAVERY, APPARENTLY HE IS SO INEPT TO REALITY, HE IS NOT AWARE THAT HIS PARTY THE DEMOCRATS ARE THE ORIGINATORS OF SLAVERY.

NOT ONLY THAT THE SOUTHERN (DEMOCRATS). FOUNDERED THE KU-KLUX-KLAN IN EIGHTEEN SIXTY SIX.

DURING THE YEAR OF NINETEEN THIRTY SEVEN , UNDER (DEMOCRATIC) PRESIDENT FRANKLIN DELANO ROOSEVELT REIGN, TWO BLACKS WERE BURNED TO DEATH WITH BLOW THORCHES, IN FRONT OF A CROWD OF APPLAUDING WHITED, IN DUCK HILL, MISSISSIPPI.

ALSO OVER A SEVEN YEAR PEROID, APPROXIMATELY EIGHTEEN BLACKS WERE LYNCHED ANUALLY.

WHILE (DEMOCRATIC) PRESIDENT ROOSEVELT, SAT SILENTLY WITH (NO) INTERVENTION TO QUELL.

DURING THE YEAR OF EIGHTEEN NINETY FIVE, THE SOUTHERN (DEMOCRATS) WERE SUCCESSFUL IN GETTING THE SUPREME COURT, TO RULE IN FAVOR OF THE JIM CROW RULE, SEPARATE BUT EQUAL, WHICH EXCLUDED BLACKS FROM ENTERING THE FRONT OF RESTAURANTS, THERE WERE SEPARATE QUARTERS IN PUBLIC PLACES, ALONG WITH SEPERATE WATER FOUNTAINSAND TRAVELING IN THE BACK OF PUBLIC TRANSPORTATION, SUCH AS BUSESSES. FOR APPROXIMATELY SEVENTY YEARS.

DURING THE YEAR OF NINETEEN FIFTY SEVEN, (REPUBLICAN) PRESIDENT DWIGHT D. EISENHOWER, GENERATED THE FIRST CIVIL RIGHTS IN EIGHTY FIVE YEARS, TO RELIEVE BLACKS OF THIS INSIDIOUS DELEMMA. HOWEVER THE (DEMOCRATS) CONTROLLED THE SENATE, GUIDED BY NONE OTHER THAN (DEMOCRATIC) SENATOR LYNDON BAINES JOHNSON, WHICH THEY REJECTED THE BILL.

AFTER THE ASSASSINATION OF PRESIDENT JOHN F. KENNEDY, LYNDON BAINES JOHNSON BECAME PRESIDENT, HOWEVER PRIOR TO HIS DEATH, PRESIDENT KENNEDY WAS INSTRUMENTAL IN RESTORING CIVIL AND VOTING RIGHTS FOR BLACKS IN THE SOUTHERN STATES.

SO THIS ORDEAL BECAME AN AGENDA FOR PRESIDENT LYNDON BAINES JOHNSON, SO HE RELUCTANTLY WENT TO THE (DEMOCRATIC CONTROLLED) SENATE AND SCOLDED THEM BY IMPLYING IF THEY REFUSED PASSAGE OF HIS BILL, THEY WOULD LOOSE THE NORTHERN BLACK VOTE.

SO THE CIVIL RIGHTS BILL WAS SUBMITTED, BUT (NOT) WITHOUT CONTROVERSY, MANY (DEMOCRATIC) SENATORS BALKED, ESPECIALLY FORMER KU-KLUX-KLAN SENATOR ROBERT BYRD, HE FILIBUSTERED FOR APPROXIMATELY SEVENTEEN HOURS, THE CIVIL RIGHTS BILL (NEVER) WOULD HAVE PASSED BUT THE(REPUBLICAN) SENATORS RALLIED AND HERDED TOGATHER, AND DEFEATED THE (DEMOCRATIC) FILIBUSTER.

IF NOT FOR THE (REPUBLICAN) SENATORS BLACKS WOULD HAVE SAT ON THE BACK OF THE BUS FOR MANY MORE YEARS.

AND FOR THIS OUT OF TUCH WITH REALITY AND THE AMERICANPEOPLE, IMBECILIC INCOMPETENT SENATOR HARRY REID.

IT IS A DISGRACEFUL DECITFUL DISTORTION FOR SENATOR HARRY REID TO STIPULATE THE EQUATING OF SLAVERY, AS IF IT WAS A REPUBLICAN AGENDA.

WHEN IT WAS (REPUBLICAN) PRESIDENT ABRAHAM LINCOLN, IN EIGHTEEN SIXTY FIVE WAS RESPONSIBLE FOR FREEING THE SLAVES FROM THE GRASP OF THE SOUTHERN (DEMOCRATIC) PLANTATION OWNERS.

ALSO PRIOR TO HE BEING ASSASSINATED, PRESIDENT LINCOLN HAD PLEDGED A PROCLAMATION, TO GIVE EVERY BLACK FAMILY IN THE SOUTH, FORTY ACRES OF DEMOCRATIC SOUTHERN PLANTATION SLAVE OWNERS LAND, AND A GOVERNMENT MULE.

PRESIDENT LINCOLN HAD CHOSEN A SOUTHERN (DEMOCRAT) FROM TENNESSEE TO BE HIS VICE PRESIDENT ANDREW JOHNSON, AFTER HE SUCCEEDED LINCOLN AS

PRESIDENT, HE RESCINDED THE PROCLAMATION, AND GAVE THE LAND BACK TO THE (DEMOCRATIC) SOUTHERN PLANTATION SLAVE OWNERS. ALSO DURING THE EIGHTEEN SEVENTIES, THERE WERE APPROXIMATELY THREE AFRICAN AMERICANS TO SERVE IN THE U.S. SENATE, AND AT LEAST TWENTY OR MORE U.S. HOUSE OF REPRESENTATIVES, TO SERVE FROM THE (REPUBLICAN) PARTY, REPRESENTING THE SOUTHERN STATES. HOWEVER THE SOUTHERN DEMOCRATIC KU-KLUX-KLAN, ACCUSED THEM OF BEING IGNORANT, INCOMPETENT AND TRYING TO RISE ABOVE THEIR NATURAL PLACE IN SOCIETY OF SERVITUDE.

AND SAVAGELY CHASED THE BLACK (REPUBLICANS) FROM THE SOUTH, SO FOR SENATOR HARRY REID TO EQUATE SLAVERY, TO ANY ONE OTHER THAN THE DEMOCRATIC PHILOSOPHY IS ASININE.

APPARENTLY HE IS EITHER A PSYCHOPATHIC DERANGED DYSFUNCTIONAL IDIOT, OR SUFFERING FROM PROGRESSIVE DEMENTIA.

HOWEVER THE HONORABLE CITIZENS OF THE STATE, THATRESIDEINNEVADA,DESERVEBETTERREPRESENTATION THAN THIS LYING DISTORTING INCOMPETENT WEASEL.

THEREARETHREEPOLITICALLEADERSINWASHINGTON. NAMELY PRESIDENT BARACK HUSSIEN OBAMA. SENATOR HARRY REID. AND CONGRESSIONAL WOMAN NANCY PELOSI, THAT ARE LIVING IN A VILE PHANTASY WORLD. ESPECIALLY PRESIDENT BARACK HUSSIEN. OBAMA. HE IS ACTING LIKE A AFRICAN (CONGO) TRIBAL CHIEF, SEEM TO THINK, ALL HE HAS TO DO IS GIVE INTERVIEWS ON TELEVISION AND GRIN, THROUGH THOSE (BLACK) LIPS. LIKE A JACKASS EATING THORNY BRIERS.

AND (ALL) AMERICANS SHOULD CURTSY TO HIS NARCISSISTIC INCOMPETENT LIES.

HE IS ON NATIONAL TELEVISION (RATING)5B PLUSV REGARDS TOHIS JOB PERFORMANCE. WHILE THE NATION IS EXPERIENCING DOUBLE DIGIT UNEMPLOYMENT, DEEPLY INDEBTED TO CHINA, TWO EXISTING TERRORIST CONFLICTS IN IRAQ AND AFGHANISTAN. THE IRANIANAS. AREDEVELSPINGNNHKES. OUR NATION IS IN SHAMBLES

REGARDS TO CRIMINAL ACTIVITY AND MURDER WHILE HE IS BRAGGING ABOUT HIS ACCOMPLISHMENTS.

OUR NATION IS AT THE CROSS ROAD, OF BEGINNING TO EXPERIENCE WHAT THE SOUTHERN (DEMOCRATS) PREDICTED IN EIGHTEEN SEVENTY, THAT BLACKS WERE IGNORANT AND INCOMPETENT. REGARDS TO POLITICS. ALSO THE LATE F.B.I. DIRECTOR J. EDGAR HOOVER, SUGGESTED THAT HE THOUGHT BLACKS BRAINS WAS TWENTY PERCENT SMALLER THAN WHITES. WHICH I TOTALLY DISAGREE WITH HIS APPRAISAL.

BECAUSE UNFORTUNATELY HE FAILED TO REALIZE THAT MILLIONS OF WHITES, HAVE SMALL DYSFUNCTIONAL BRAINS ALSO.

BECAUSE THEY VOTED THIS HYPOCRITICAL, DELIRIOUS, NARCISSISTIC INCOMPETENT PRESIDENT BARACK HUSSIEN OBAMA INTO OFFICE. FORMER PRESIDENT GEORGE W. BUSH, PREMATURELY STOOD ON THE DECK OF SHIP, WITH A BANNER STATING MISSION ACCOMPLISHED, REGARDS TO IRAQ AND HE WAS VICIOUSLY RIDICULED.

YET THIS MORON OF A PRESIDENT BARACK HUSSEIN OBAMA, IS PUBLICLY RATING HIM SELF. WITH A (B) PLUS AVERAGE REGARDS TO HIS PERFORMANCE, ARROGANTLY IGNORING THE THOUGHTS OF THE IDIOTS THAT VOTED FOR HIM TO BECOME PRESIDENT.

NOT ONLY THAT,HE HAS FORMALLY SENT A LETTER TO KIM JONG IL, OF NORTH KOREA. I DONT THINK THEY HAVE OUT HOUSES IN NORTH KOREA, SO MOST LIKELY THE LETTER WILL BE ATTACHED TO A ROLL OF TOILET PAPER AND USED FOR KIM JONG IL PERSONAL COMFORT.

THIS PRESIDENT OBAMA, IS TREATING THE AMERICAN VOTING CONSTITUENCY, LIKE KINDERGARDEN STUDENTS. CONTROLLING THEM WITH A MOB MENTALITY, WHILE HE IS DIAGRAMING METHODS TO SABOTAGE THE SCHOOL. HE IS ALL OVER THE PLACE, LIKE HORSE AND MULE SHIT, IN A SMALL COTTON GINNING TOWN IN THE SOUTH, DURING THE FORTIES.

THIS IS A STRATEGIC METHOD TO DISTRACT ATTENTION, WHIEE ADHERING TO HIS MINISTER IDEOLOGY FOR TWENTY YEARS, WITH STATEMENTS OF GOD DAM AMERICA,

AND THE RICH WHITE MAN THAT CONTROL IT. THEIR CHICKENS ARE COMING HOME TO ROOST, RELATING TO NINE ELEVEN AS A COMPATIBILITY.

DOOM IS SLOWLY BEING IMPLEMENTED FOR AMERICA, RIGHT UNDER YOUR NOSES, AND YOUR (DEMOCRATIC) CONGRESSIONAL LEADERS, ARE ACCESSORIES TO THIS DRASTIC AGENDA.

BEING PERPETRATED AGAINST OUR (UNREADABLE TEXT), WHILE THEY ARE GLOATING OVER ABLACK MAN BEING PRESIDENT, ANETKISSING HIS ALIMENTARY CANAL, IN ORDER TO MAINTAIN THE BLACK VOTING BASE

HOWEVER THIS IS A URGENT PLEAD, TO (ALL) CIVILIZE AMERICANS. OUR CONSTUTIONAL LIBERTIES ARE BEING THREATEN, AND ARE IN JEOPARDY. PERTAINING TO MARXIST SOCIALISM.

FOR INSTANCE THE FIRST EXECUTIVE LEGISLATION THAT PRESIDENT BARACK HUSSIEN OBAMA SIGNED INTO LAW WAS TO CLOSE GITMO. THIS IS CRUCIAL. REGARDS TO AMERICANS, BECAUSE OF HIS HIS CONGO IDEOLOGY,THAT AMERICA SHOULD HAVE A RULER, INSTEAD OF A PRESIDENT THIS IS DICTATED FROM HIS AFRICAN HERITAGE.

THIS IS GENETIC CONTROLLABILITY THAT IS EMBEDDED IN THE MAJORITY OF AFRICAN AMERICANS, RELATED TO HERDING INSTINCTS.

WATCH THE NEWS MEDIA PRACTICALITY EVERY AFRICAN AMERICAN IS IN T AGREEMENT WITH HIS PHILOSOPHY, ESPECIALLY MR HORSE SHIT JUAN WILLIAMS. WE AS A DIVERSE NATION, ARE ALLOWING MOST (DEMOCRATIC) OBSESSED AFRICAN AMERICANS STOOGES, ALONG WITH SMALL DYSFUNCTIONAL BRAIN JACKASS LIBERAL WHITES, ATTEMPTING TO ENGINEER DESTRUCTIVE FUNCTIONS, IN AN EFFORT TO VIOLATE OUR CONSTITUTIONAL LIBERTIES.

AS I HAVE INDICATED MANY MANY TIMES THROUGH OUT THIS BOOKVITHATE THIS ELECTED (DEMOCRATIC) OFFICIAL PRESIDENT BARACK HUSSIEN OBAMA IS ONE OF THE MOST CORRUPT IMPOSTERS IN THE HISTORY OF AMERICA. HE HAS A VINDICTIVE COVERT AGENDA AGAINST WHITES IN AMERICA, BASED ON ERRONEOUS BLACK GOSSIP

ASSUMPTIONS. AND AUTHORITATIVE GENETIC HERITAGE, TO DICTATE DISCIPLINE TO WHITES.

WHY DO YOU THINK HE CHOOSE HILARY CLINTON AS (HIS) SECRETARY OF STATE, SIMPLY BECAUSE SHE IS THE WIFE OS A FORMER PRESIDENT, THAT HAD SELECTIVE PRESIDENTIAL POLITICAL POWERS, THAT SERVED TWO TERMS, ALSO HIS DESPERATE ATTEMPT TO RATIFY HEALTH CARE, BECAUSE THERE HAS (NEVER) BEEN A WHITE PRESIDENT TO ACCOMPLISH THAT GOAL. HE IS ALSO TRAVELING ALL OVER THE GLOBE, TO BE (SEEN) AS A BLACK MAN DICTATING AND IN CHARGE OF WHITES IN AMERICA.

HE WANTS TO BE RECOGNIZED AS A LONE BLACK MAN, THAT DEGRADED RICH WHITES IN AMERICA, AND TUMBLED THEM INTO DISGRACE, AND HE WILL STOP AT (NOTHING)

AND WHILE YOU STUPID ASS WHITES, ARE GLOATING, WITH TINGLING LEGS AND SLOBBERING ALL OVER HIS ALIMENTARY CANAL, HE IS PLANNING OUR DESTRUCTION.

THE TRUE IDENTY OF ANY INDIVIDUAL IS THE SINGLE MOST IMPORTANT CRITERIA PERTAINING TO HUMAN LIFE, AND FOR ANYONE TO ENGAGE IN A ROLL OF BEING AN IMPOSTER, WILL EVENTUALLY SELF DESTRUCT. TO CAMOUFLAGE INTENTIONS IN POLITICS, IS A FORM OF INTENSE GRUELING DISAPPOINTMENT, NOT ONLY FOR THE PERPETRATOR, BUT ALSO FOR THOSE THAT ARE CONVINCED TO BE AN ACCESSORY TO COLLABORATION. FOR INSTANCE THERE IS A CONSPIRATORIAL POLITICAL DISASTER,DEVELOPING IN OUR NATION CAPITAL.

WITH TYRANT PRESIDENT BARACK HUSSEIN OBAMA LEADING THE CHARGE. WITH SENATOR HARRY REID AND CONGRESS WOMAN NANCY PELOST, AS HIS POLITICAL (WHITE) JUDAS GOAT SLAVE DRIVERS. WITH PERPETRATIONS OF CONGRESSIONAL ANARCHY BRIBES.

PRECEPTIONS IS PRIMARILY BASED ON THE ACTIONS OF OTHERS, PERTAINING TO THEIR INDIVIDUAL FUNCTIONS OR DYSFUNCTIONS, AND (EVERY) INDIVIDUAL BLACK OR WHITE. IS EVELUATED IN ACCORDANCE WITH THEIR

PERSONA. WE LIVE AND DIE, PRIMARILY BASED ON OUR OWN INDIVIDUAL CONVICTIONS.

IT IS A VERY DISTINCT POSSIBILITY, THAT MANY AMERICAN CITIZENS ARE (NOT) FAMILIAR WITH A JUDAS GOAT.

HE IS A TRAINED DECEIVER, THAT WAS INSTALLED IN MOST STOCK YARDS, TO DECEIVE CATTLE. LEADING THEM TO SLAUGHTER.

WITH A BELL ON, HIS PRIMARY FUNCTIONS IS TO GET THE CATTLE FORMULARY WITH THE BELL TO FOLLOW.

AND ONCE HE ACCOMPLISH HIS MISSION, THE CATTLE FOLLOW HIM INTO THE SLAUGHTER PIN, AND HE ESCAPE TO SAFETY THROUGH THEIR LEGS. AND THE CATTLE IS (NEVER) AWARE OF HIS TRAINED DECEIT.

HOWEVER GROWING UP ON MY FARM IN ALABAMA, THAT WAS INHERITED FORM MY GREAT, GREAT GRAND FATHER, IS WHAT INSPIRED ME TO WRITE THIS BOOK PERTAINING TO CAPITALISM AND INDIPENDANT THINKING. THAT IS CONTINGENCY OF WHAT OUR GREAT CONTURY THE UNITED STATES OF AMERICA CONSIST OF TODAY, AND WE (WILL) MAINTAIN THESE PRINCIPLES.

HOWEVER WE MUST CHARACTERIZE TRANSPIRING OCCURRENCES, THAT IS BEING FORMULATED BY OUR POLITICAL LEADERS IN WASHINGTON. I GREW UP ON OUR FARM IN ALABAMA, AND QUITE FAMILIAR WITH ANIMALS ESPECIALLY CATTLE AND GOATS, HOWEVER I FIND GOATS TO BE MOST INTRIGUING, BECAUSE OF THEIR SENSE OF CHARM.

MY UNCLES TAUGHT ONE TO DRINK BEER, WHICH WAS QUITE UNIQUE, YOU COULD SIT ON THE PORCH AND DRINK WATER ALL DAY, BUT ONCE YOU BROUGHT OUT A BOTTLE OR CAN OF BEER, HE WOULD COME AND STAND, OPEN HIS MOUTH WITH HEAD BACK, AND §WILL UNTIL DRUNK, AND STAGGER AWAY MANY TIMES I VISITED THE STOCK YARD CATTLE SLAUGHTER PIN, WHERE THE JUDAS GOAT WITH A BELL ON, WOULD MINIPULATE THEM TO SLAUGHTER FINALLY ONE DAY THE PIN KEEPER ASK ME TO WATCH THIS, AS THE JUDAS GOAT LED THE CATTLE TO SLAUGHTER, HE TURNER AND RAN TO THE GATE, AND THE

PIN KEEPER CLOSED THE GATE TO PREVENT HIS ESCAPE. NEVER IN MY LIFE HAD I EVER HERD A GOAT BELLOW SO LOUD. LADIES GENTLEMEN, AND (ALL) CITIZENS THAT RESIDE IN AMERICA, THERE IS A SIMILARITY OF THIS JUDAS GOAT METHOD BEING PRACTISED BY HUMANS IN WASHINGTON.

LED BY THREE JUDAS, BUT ONLY ONE HAS THE (BELL) ON. AND THAT IS PRESIDENT BARACK HUSSIEN OBAMA, WITH SENATOR HARRY REID AND REPRESENTATIVE NANCY PELOSI AS HIS ACCOMPLISHERS.

I BEG OF YOU LETS (CLOSE) THE GATE ON THE ONE WITH THE BELL, AND THE CATTLE WILL TRAMPLE ALL THE OTHERS.

TRUST ME IF WE DO NOT WORK DILIGENTLY, OUR NATION (WILL) BE LED TO SLAUGHTER.

CHRONOLOGICAL RECORDS OF SIGNIFICANT EVENTS, DICTATE THE FOUNDING FUNDAMENTALS OF OUR NATION. AND FOR HUNDREDS OF YEARS WHITES HAVE BEEN WILLING TO COMPROMISE WITH BLACKS. UNFORTUNATELY IT IS MOST BLACKS THAT DESTROY CONFIDENCE.

WITH LIES AND DISTORTION, AND WHEN THIS OCCUR WITH EITHER BLACK OR WHITE, YOUR CHANCES OF REGAINING THEIR TRUST IS NULLIFIED. PRESIDENT BARACK HUSSIEN OBAMA, HAS (LOST) THE TRUST OF MOST AMERICANS. BASED ON THINKING THAT HE IS INVINCIBLE, WITH A RADICAL ARROGANT VINDICTIVE COVERT AGENDA FOR (WHITE) AMERICANS. ADHERING TO AUTHORTATIVE GENETIC HERITAGE MOTIVES, TO DICTATE DISCIPLINE TO WHITES.

WHY DO UOU THINK THAT HE CHOOSE HILLARY CLINTON FOR HIS SECRETARY OF STATE, SIMPLY BECAUSE IT IS A FIRST, FOR A FORMER PRESIDENT WIFE TO SERVE AS SECRETARY OF STATE, NOT ONLY THAT HER HUSBAND HAD PRESTIGIOUS SELECTIVE POLITICAL POWER.

HE DOSENT GIVE A DAMN ABOUT HEALTH CARE, IT IS THAT (NO) WHITES HAVE (EVER) ACCOMPLISHED THAT MISSION.

HE IS TRAVELING ALL OVER THE GLOBE, TO BE SEEN AS A BLACK MAN IN C5AR?E^7?F, WHITES IN AMERICA, HE WANTS TO BE RECOGNIZED AS THE (UNREADABLE TEXT)

THAT DEGRADED RICH WHITES IN AMERICA, AND TUMBLED THEM INTO DISGRACE, WHILE SOME OF YOU STUPID ASS WHITES ARE GLOATING WITH TINGLING UP THE LEGS, AND SLOBBERING OVER HIS ALIMENTARY CANAL, AS HE BEING THE FIRST BLACK PRESIDENT.

WHILE HE IS PLANNING MARXIST DESTRUCTION FOR OUR NATION. FOR INSTANCE HE HAS CHOSEN TO BRING FOREGIN TERRORIST TO AMERICAN SOIL. FOR TRIAL IN NEW YORK AND INCARCERATED HOUSING NEAR CHICAGO. WHICH IS THE TWO LARGEST POPULATED CITIES IN AMERICA. HOWEVER THERE IS STILL TIME TO CLOSE THE GATE ON THIS IMPOSTER JUDAS GOAT. AND IT HAS TO DO WITH OUR CONSTITUTION. ARTICLE TWO, SECTION FOUR WHICH STATE.

THE PRESIDENT, VICE PRESIDENT AND ALL CIVIL OFFICERS OF THE UNITED STATES, SHALL BE REMOVED FROM OFFICE ON IMPEACHMENT FOR, AND CONVICTION OF, (TREASON) BRIBERY, OR OTHER HIGH CRIMES AND MISDEMEANORS.

THERE SHOULD BE AN AMENDMENT ADDED BY CONGRESS, TO STATE IF ANY SITTING PRESIDENT AUTHORIZE FOREGIN TERRORIST TO BE TRIBUNAL OR HOUSED ON AMERICAN SOIL, AND IF A TERRORIST ATTACK OCCUR, IN THE DESIGNATED AREA, OR THE IMMEDIATE DISTANCE OF HIS CHOOSING. AND THOUSANDS OF INNOCENT AMERICAN CITIZENS LOOSE THEIR LIVES. THE PRESIDENT AND HIS ACCOMPLICES (WILL) BE CHARGED IN ACCORDANCE WITH SECTION FOUR OF THE CONSTITUTION. EVEN (AFTER) THEY LEAVE OFFICE.

AMERICA PLEASE WAKE UP, BECAUSE WE ARE SITTING ON A POWDER KEG. IN CLOSING I WOULD LIKE TO PAY TRIBUTE TO THREE OF THE MOST HUUMBLE, POLITICAL INTELLECTUAL AND PATRIOTIC AFRICAN AMERICANS, IN MY OPENION THAT RESIDE IN AMERICA TODAY.

AND THAT IS FORMER SECRETARY OF STATE, MISS CONDOLEEZZA RICE, RADIO PERSONALITY MR ANDREW

CLARK SENIOR AND TELEVISION COMMENTATOR MR CHARLES PAYNE.

AND OF COURSE I DEDICATED THIS BOOK TO MY GREAT, GREAT GRAND FATHER, WHICH WAS AN AMERICAN PATRIOT. THAT WAS BORN PRIOR TO PRESIDENT ABARAHAM LINCOLN. ABOLISHED SOUTHERN (DEMOCRATIC) SERVITUDE. TRAINED HIM SELF TO BE A PROFESSIONAL CARPENTER, AND MOST LIKELY BUILT THE FIRST COTTON GIN HOUSE IN MARENGO COUNTY ALABAMA. PURCHASED HIS OWN LAND IN EIGHTEEN EIGHTY THREE, HE ALSO WAS A STORE OWNER WHICH HE BUILT..

DOWEN JONES WAS MARRIED TO AMANDA, WHICH HE FATHERED ONE SON, BEN JONES, BEN FATHERED SIX CHILDREN, BEN JR, SYLAS, HORACE, PERCY, DOWEN AND MARY, WHICH WAS MY MOTHER. ALSO A NAME SAKE FORM GRANNY THEY ALL WERE FARMERS, BUT HAD SPECIAL TALENTS TO COMPENSATE, FOR INSTANCE BEN JR. WAS A PROFESSIONAL BASKET MAKER, THAT WAS ON THE COVER OF LIFE MAGAZINE DURING THE EARLY EIGHTIES. SYLAS INVESTED HIS TALENTS IN GROWING COTTON, RASING CATTLE AND HOGS FOR SALE. HORACE WAS A CARPENTER AND OWNED HIS GUN REPAIR SHOP, ALSO A BARBER. PERCY WAS A EXTRAODINARY WATCH REPAIRMAN, I WAS HIS HELPER I REMEMBER VERY VIVIDLY OF HIM DISASSEMBLING WATCHES AND CLOCKS, FLUSH THE PARTS TOGATHER, SORT OUT THE DEFECTIVE PART, EVEN HAIR SPRINGS, AND ASSEMBLE WITH ACCURACY.FOR PERFECT PERFORMANCE. I RECALL A VERY UNIQUE CIRCUMSTANCE, A JEWISH GENTLEMAN HAD A CLCK, THAT WAS A FAMILY INHERITANCE FROM HIS COUNTRY. AND HE HAD GONE TO WATCH AND CLOCK REPAIR SHOPS ALL OVER, AND NONE COULD REPAIR. HE STATED THAT SOME ONE HAD GIVEN HIM MY UNCLE PERCY ADDRESS. AND ASKED IF HE COULD REPAIR HIS CLOCK, MY UNCLE STATED THAT YOU CAN PICK IT UP WEDNESDAY, THE GENTLEMAN STARED AT HIM AS IF HE WAS JOCKING.

HOWEVER HE LEFT THE CLOCK, MY UNCLE TORE THE CLOCK APART, PLACED ALL PARTS IN A LARGE BOWL, HE WOULD CALL ME MAN, HE SAID MAN WE HAVE OUR WORK

CUT OUT FOR US HERE, BECAUSE WHOM EVER TRIED TO REPAIR THIS CLOCK LOST A PART THAT IS MISSING.

SO LETS GO LOOK THROUGH ALL THOSE OLD CLOCKS, AND FIND A PIECE OF METAL THAT MATCH HIS CLOCK METAL, AND I AM GOING TO MAKE THE MISSING PART, HE WAS A PERSON THAT WOULD TALK TO HIM SELF, BUT WOULD (NEVER) TELL WHAT HE WAS SAYING, WE LOCATED THE PIECE OF METAL. HE SPENT HOURS MANUFACTURING A REPLACEMENT PART, THAT HE HAD NEVER SEEN, THE GENTLEMAN RETURNED WEDNESDAY. MY UNCLE HAD THE CLOCK ON THE PORCH RUNNING.

WITH TEARS WELLED IN HIS EYES,HE ASKED MY UNCLE PERCY WHAT WAS THE CHARGE, HE SAID THREE DOLLARS. HE PULLED THIRTY DOLLARS FROM HIS WALLET, GAVE IT TO MY UNCLE. AND STATED YOU ARE THE (UNREADABLE TEXT) PROFESSIONAL CLOCK REPAIRMAN EVER AND GAVE MY UNCLE HIS ADDRESS, AND.SAID IF YOU NEED ANYTHING EVER YOU KNOW WHERE I LIVE.

MY UNCLE DOWEN WAS A CONSTRUCTION SUPERVISOR, ALSO A CARPENTER FOR A CAUCASIAN COMPANY.

THE TRUE IDENTY OF (ANY) INDIVIDUAL IS THE SINGLE MOST IMPORTANT CRITERIA PERTAINING TO HUMAN LIFE.

AND FOR ANYONE TO ENGAGE IN A ROLL OF BEING AN IMPOSTER (WILL) EVENTUALLY SELF DESTRUCT.

PRECEPTIONS IS PRIMARILY BASED ON THE ACTION OF OTHERS, PERTAINING TO THEIR FUNCTIONS OR DYSFUNCTIONS, AND EVERY INDIVIDUAL BLACK OR WHITE, IS EVALUATED IN PARITY WITH THEIR PERSONA. WE LIVE AND DIE IN ACCORDANCE TO OUR CONVICTIONS, WHICH IN ESSENCE DETERMINE WHO WE ARE OR WERE.

IT ,IS PARAMOUNT THAT WE AS A SOCIETY OF PEOPLE, BLACK AND WHITE, DELVE INTO GENETIC ANCESTRY, IT (WILL) DICTATE YOUR PROSPERITY OR DEFICIENCY, AND THERE IS NO DOUBT.

BECAUSE IT IS INEVITABLE, PERTAINING TO ALL MAN KIND ALSO ANIMALS I PARTICULARLY DELVE INTO THE CHRONOLOGICAL TRAITS OF MY LATE ANCESTORS, IN

AN EFFORT QUELL AND DISPEL. THE OUTRAGEOUS (LIES) PERPETRATED BY MOST AFRICAN AMERICANS.

THAT IT IS ALWAYS SOME ONE ELSE THAT PROHIBIT THEIR SUCCESSFUL FUNCTIONS IN AMERICA. BECAUSE THEY ARE BLACK, PARTICULARY WHITES, MOST BLACKS HAVE CONSISTENTLY USED THIS DECEITFUL DYSFUNCTIONAL TACTIC. FOR HUNDREDS OF YEARS (UNREADABLE TEXT) FOR THEIR ILLITERATE, INNEPT INCOMPETENT IGNORANCE.

MOST BLACKS HAVE APPALLING DISDAIN, FOR ANYONE THAT HAS USED THEIR GOD GIVEN TALENTS TO ATTAIN A DESIRED OBJECTIVE IN LIFE, BASED ON THEIR INITATIVE TO RESOLVE PSYCHOLOGICAL PROBLEMS. PERTAINING TO THE FUNDAMENTALS OF WHAT OUR FORE FATHERS RESTABLISED, REGARDS TO INTELLECTUAL (MORAL) VALUES, WHICH IS THE DOMINATING FACTOR IN ALL HUMAN LIVES, LIKE IT OR NOT. BECAUSE IT IS INEITABLE PERTAINING TO THE FUNDAMENTALS OF AMERICA, IN ACCORDANCE WITH REALITY.

HOWEVER THERE ARE SUFFERING CONSEQUENCES AHEAD LIKE (NEVER) BEFORE, BUT AS A CIVILIZE NATION, WE MUST UNDERSTAND THE CONFRONTING PROBLEMS, THAT IS BEING CREATED BY EMBLEMATIC JUDAS GOATS IN WASHINGTON.

IS TO DEPRIVE AMERICA OF OUR CONSTITUTIONAL LIBERTIES, LED BY A BIG EARED JUDAS, WITH A BELL ON. HOWEVER THROUGH OUR VOTING PROCESS, WE MUST, REPEAT WE MUST SILENCE THIS BELL.

RECENTLY THERE HAS BEEN A SEEMINGLY RACIST CONTROVERSY, REGARDS TO STATEMENTS FROM (DEMOCRATIC) SENATE LEADER , HARRY REID, PERTAINING TO NOW PRESIDENT BARACK HUSSIEN OBAMA, DURING HIS CAMPAGIN WHICH SENATOR REID SUGGESTED THAT BECAUSE OF HIS LIGHT SKIN COLOR AND THE (ABSENT) OF NEGRO DIALECT HE COULD BECOME PRESIDENT. ACCORDING TO THE MEDIA FORMER PRESIDENT WILLIAM JEFFERSON CLINTON IMPLICATIONS WERE, A FIEW YEARS BACK, BARACK H. OBAMA WOULD BE SERVING THEM COFFEE. EVEN VICE PRESIDENT JOSEPH BIEDEN LABELED HIM AS BEING A CLEAN AFRICAN AMERICAN.

I DONT KNOW WHAT ALL THE FUSS ABOUT, BECAUSE THIS IS TIPICAL (DEMOCRATIS) TRADITIONS, THAT CARRY BACK ONE HUNDRED AND FIFTY TWO YEARS AGO, WHEN IN EIGHTEEN FIFTY EIGHT, DURING THE SENETORIAL ELECTION BETWEEN (REPUBLICAN) ABRAHAM LINCOLN AND STEPHEN A. DOUGLAS. SLAVERY WAS ONE OF THE GENERAL TOPICS. (REPUBLICAN) ABRAHAM LINCOLN DENOUNCED SLAVERY, AS UN-JUST. HE QUOTED THE DECLARATION OF INDEPENDANCE, AND DECLARED THAT SLAVERY WAS A TOTAL. VIOLATION OF PRINCIPLE, BECAUSE THE SLAVE OWENRS CONTROL SLAVES WITHC OUT CU CONSENT, THAT CASTIGATE. WITH A SET OF- GUIDE-LINES TOTALLY DIFFERENT FROM WHAT HE DICTATE FOR HIM SELF.

STEPHEN A. DOUGLAS A STAUNCH (DEMOCRAT) ARGUED THAT SIGNERS OF THE DECLARATION OF INDEPENDANCE HAD (NO) REFERENCE TO (NEGROES) WHAT SO EVER. AND AMERICA WAS (UNREADABLE TEXT) BY WHITE MEN AND (UNREADABLE TEXT)POSTERITY FOREVER.

I WAS INTERRUPTED BY A SEGEMENT ON FOX NEWS, JANUARY 11, 2010. 9 00 AM. WITH MR HORSE SHIT ALL OVER TOWN, DURING THE FORTIES, AT A COTTEN GIN MR JUAN WILLIAMS TRYING TO CHASACTERIZE SENATOR HARRY REID STATEMENT OF LIGHT NEGRO.

AND ACCUSING (REPUBLICANS) OF NOT REACHING OUT TO BLACKS AND HISPANICS, I WOULD LIKE TO REMIND THIS POLITICAL SMALL BRAIN DYSFUNCTIONAL IDIOT. JUAN WILLIAMS, THAT IT WAS THE (REPUBLICANS) CONGRESS THAT PASSED THE CIVIL RIGHTS ACT OF EIGHTEEN SIXTY SIX, AND AND THE FOURTEENTH AMENDMENT GUARATEEING BLACKS CITIZEN SHIP TO TO THE CONSTITUTION, AND THE SOUTHERN (DEMOCRATS) NULLIFIED IT THROUGH THE SUPREME COURT.

UNTIL NINETEEN SIXTY FOUR, HIRMAN RHODES REVELS WAS THE FIRST BLACK (REPUBLICAN) U,S. SENATOR TO REPRESENT MISSISSIPPI IN EIGHTEEN SEVENTY. BLANCH K. BRUCE WAS THE FIRST AFRICAN AMERICAN (REPUBLICAN) TO SERVE A FULL TERM AS A U.S. SENATOR ELECTED FROM LOUISIANA IN EIGHTEEN SEVENTY FOUR.

ALSO THERE WERE TWENTY BLACK REPUBLICANS ELECTED TO THE U.S. HOUSE OF REPRESENTATIVES. AND THE (DEMOCRAT) FOUNDERED KUKLUX KLAN ERADICATED THEIR POLITICAL POTENTIAL, BY ACCUSING THEM OF BEING IGNORANT INCOMPETENT AND TRYING TO RISE ABOVE THEIR NORMAL PLACE OF SERVITUDE. AND VIOLENTLY DROVE THEM FROM THE SOUTHERN STATES. SO MR HISTORIAN (DEMOCRATIC) ALMENTARY CANAL LICK. JUAN WILLIAMS, NAME ME ONE DEMOCRAT AFRICAN AMERICAN THAT ,WAS ELECTED (UNREADABLE TEXT) EIGHTEEN SEVENTIES FOR ANY THING OTHER THAN AT DEMOCRAT KU-KLUX-KLAN LYNCHING.

DEMOCRAT SENATOR ROBERT BYRD FORMER KU-KLUX-KLANSMAN, HOLD THE LONGEST FILIBUSTER IN WHITE HOUSE HISTORY, AGAINST AFRICAN AMERICANS CIVIL RIGHTS BEING RESTORED IN NINETEEN SIXTY FOUR. AND IT WAS THE (REPUBLICANS) RESPONSIBLE FOR HIS DEFEAT. HOWEVER THE MOST DEVASTATING BLOW TO AFRICAN AMERICANS BY A (DEMOCRAT) WAS AT THE END OF THE WAR IN EIGHTEEN SIXTY FIVE, WHEN ANDRED JOHNSON BECAME PRESIDENT. AFTER THE ASSASSINATION OF PRESIDENT LINCOLN. THE (DEMOCRATIC) PRESIDENT JOHNSON RESCINDED THE PROCLAMATION THAT PRESIDENT LINCOLN HAD SET FORTH TO GIVE EVERY AFRICAN AMERICAN FAMILY, FORTY ACRES OF SOUTHERN CONFEDERATE LAND, AND A GOVERNMENT MULE, (REPUBLICAN) PRESIDENT DWIGHT DAVID EISENHOWER DESEGREGATED SCHOOLS IN THE SOUTH FOR BLACKS, WHILE DEMOCRTS WERE BLOWING UP CHURCHES WITH LITTLE BLACK GIRLS INSIDE. THE LATE F.B.I. DIRECTOR J. EDGAR HOOVER, IMPLIED THAT HE THOUGHT BLACKS BRAINS WERE TWENTY PERCENT SMALLER THAN WHITES, THIS WAS NOT A RACIST REMARK, BUT OUT OF PURE FRUSTRATION, HE PRECEIVED THAT (ALL) THE COMPASSION THAT (REPUBLICANS) HAD ENDORSED FOR BLACKS, OVER NINETY TWO YEARS, AND THAT WAS IN NINETEEN FIFTY SEVEN TODAY IT IS ONE HUNDRED AND FORTY FIVE YEARS LATER.

AND MOST AFRICAN AMERICANS ARE STILL MESMERIZED WITH (DEMOCRATIC) SICK SOCIALISTIC WELFARE PROPAGANDA.

HOWEVER ITS A VERY POOR WIND THAT NEVER CHANGE, PRESIDENT BARACK HUSSEIN OBAMA IS IN THE PROCESS OF CHANGING THE WIND FOR THE DEMCRATS, THEY WENT OUT ON A LIMB, AND ELECTED HIM PRESIDENT, NOT REALIZING THAT HE IS A NARCISSISTIC BLACK JUDAS IMPOSTER. AND THEY ARE JUST BEGINNING TO PERCEIVE THAT, SO NOW THEY ARE JUMPING LIKE RATS FROM A SINKING SHIP.

THEY WERE UNDER THE IMPRESSION THAT BARACK HUSSEIN OBAMA, WAS JUST ANOTHER LITTLE INNOCENT BLACK, THAT WAS LIGHT SKIN, WENT TO HARVARD, AND HAVE A DIALECT DIFFERENT FROM OTHER (NEGROES) WHEN WANTED, AND THEY COULD PUPAL HIM TO THEIR AGENDA OF INDOCTRINATING BLACK SOCITEY.

THE DEMOCRATS (ASSUME) THAT HE WOULD BE THEIR POLITICAL PUPPET TO SOLICIT BLACK AND HISPANIC VOTERS, AND THEY WOULD LIVE HAPPY EVER AFTER ACCUSING REPUBLICANS OF BEING RACIST.

(STOP) IT HAS TAKEN ONE YEAR FOR THESE DEMOCRATIC (WHITE) POLITICAL BLACK SLAVE DRIVERS TO DETERMINE, THAT THEY ARE BEING LED TO POLITICAL SLAUGHTER BY A REPLICA OF A JUDAS GOAT WITH A BELL ON. WHILE THEY ARE GLOATING OVER HIS NOT SPEAKING (NEGRO) AND TINGLING UP THEIR LEGS WITH HIM BEING LIGHT SKIN.

(NO) ONE WILL ATTEND AND SIT IN ANY CONGREGATION, ESPECIALLY CHURCH, FOR TWENTY YEARS AND (NOT) ADHERE TO THE IDEOLOGY OF THE LEADER.

REMEMBER GOD DAMN AMERICA, AND THE RICH WHITE MAN, AND THEIR CHICKENS ARE COMING HOME TO ROOST, AND THE COMMENTS ABOUT NINE ELEVEN, LADIES AND GENTLEMEN CITIZENS OF AMERICA. BARACK HUSSEIN OBAMA HAS MADE A (ASS) OUT OF (DEMOCRATS)

AND THEY ARE SO STUNNED UNTIL THEY ARE ACTING LIKE ZOMBIES, THEY (NEVER) EXPECTED HIM TO BE THIS CONTRADICTORY WITHOUT THEIR CONSENT, WERE THEY EVER SURPRISED.

BARACK HUSSEIN OBAMA FORMULATED HIS (OWN) AGENDA THROUGH HERITAGE YEARS AGO. IF HIS FATHER WAS A MUSLIM, HE IS EMBEDDED WITH THOSE GENETIC TRAITS, THAT DICTATE HIS PHILOSOPHY PERTAINING TO AMERICA YOU WOULD HAVE TO BE A COMPLETE IDIOT NOT TO NOTICE HIS SLY COMPASSION TO PEOPLE THAT WANT TO DESTROY AMERICA.

MILLIONS OF STAUNCH (WHITE) DEMOCRATS AROUND THE NATION ARE BEGINNING TO REALIZE THAT THEY HAVE CREATED A NARCISSISTIC MONSTER. THAT IS A DERIVATIVE OF AFRICA, THAT DATE BACK THOUSAND OF YEARS AGO.

WHEN TRIBES BECAME VILOENT, THE CONGO TRIBAL CHIEF OR DICTATOR WOULD SETTLE THE DISPUTE. DURING BONDAGE IN AMERICA, THE APPOINTED (BLACK) SLAVE DRIVER WOULD QUELL THE PLANTATION TURMOIL. SENATOR HARRY REID, AFTER HIS REMARK ABOUT LIGHT NEGRO DIALECT. HE UTILIZED THE IDENTICAL PREHISTORIC AFRICAN RENDITION TO HERD AMERICAN, AFRICAN AMERICAN TRIBES TO HIS AIDE, FOR THIS DEMOCRATIC EMBEDDED RIDICULOUS BLUNDER.

HE HARRY REID SUMMONED THE AMERICAN TRIBAL CHIEFS TOGATHER, IN AN EFFORT TO JUSTIFY HIS RADICAL REMARK.

BARACK HUSSEIN OBAMA, AL SHARPTON, THE CONGRESSIONAL BLACK CAUCUS AND THE NAACP.

AND OF COURSE THE MAJORITY OF HERDING BLACKS, THROUGH OUT AMERICA RALLIED AROUND HARRY REID WITH GLEE.

THIS IS AN OLD PLANTATION GIMMICK UTILIZED VERY EFFECTIVELY, BY SOUTHERN (DEMOCRATS) IN EIGHTEEN NINETY FIVE, WHEN THEY SUMMONED BOOKER T. WASHINGTON, THE FOUNDER OF TUSKEEGEE INSTITUTE IN ALABAMA, TO SUGGEST TO HERDING BLACKS OVER THE SOUTHERN STATES, THAT THE JIM CROW RULE SEPARATE BUT EQUAL, WAS INEVITIBLE, BLACKS THROUGH OUT THE SOUTHERN STATES APPLAUDED HIM.

THE U.S. SUPREME COURT RATIFIED IT LAW, WHICH ELIMINATED THE STATUS OF EQUAL RIGHTS FOR BLACKS, UNDER THE THIRTEENTH AMENDMENT OF THE

CONSTITUTION, WHICH THE (REPUBLICAN) CONGRESS HAD RATIFIED IN EIGHTEEN SIXTY SIX, ABOLISHING SERVITUDE DESCRIMINATION FOR (ALL) PEOPLE IN AMERICA.

PRESIDENT FRANKLIN DELANO ROOSEVELT DELT THE MAJORITY OF AFRICAN AMERICANS NATION WIDE A SERIOUS POLITICAL BLOW. DURING THE THIRTIES, WHEN HE UTILIZE THE GENETIC TRAITS OF BLACK HERDING BEHIND OTHER AFFLUENT BLACKS, WHICH HE EXALTED AND PROMOTED TWO BLACKS IN THE MILITARY, AND GAVE SOUTHERN BLACKS THE (SAME) AMOUNT IN SOCIALISTIC RELIEF CHECKS AS HE DID WHITES.

AND THE MAJORITY OF AFRICAN AMERICANS NATION WIDE ABANDONED THEIR CONSERVATIVE PRINCIPLES, THAT IS EMBEDDED WITHIN THE REPUBLICAN PARTY THAT PRESIDENT ABARAHAM LINCOLN WAS SO PROUD OF. AND CHOOSE TO HERD BEHIND (DEMOCRATIC) LIBERAL PRESIDENT FRANKLIN DELANO ROOSEVELT, FOR THE PROMOTION OF TWO (BLACK) MILITARY PERSONNEL AND A WELFARE CHECK.

AND SEVENTY SIX YEARS LATER, THE MAJORITY OF BLACKS ARE STILL HERDING BEHIND ELECTED AND SELF APPOINTED BLACK LEADERS, INTO THEHIGH RISE GHETTO SLUM DWELLING UNIVERSAL FOR A SEGMENT OF BLACKS IN THE UNITED STATES OF AMERICA. AND DECEIVING THEIR GOVERNMENT SUPPLIED WELFARE CHECKS, AND SERVILETY IS PRONOUNCED WITH (NO) HOPE.

THE ALIENATION OF THE HUMAN MIND IS DETRIMENTAL, BECAUSE GOD CREATED MAN KIN IN HIS OWN IMAGE, WHICH HE CHOOSE THE BRAIN TO CONTROL THE BODY OF MAN KIND IN EVERY ASPECT RELATED TO HERITAGE, PERTAINING TO MALE AND FEMALE.

PRESIDENT BARACK HUSSIEN OBAMA IS A UNIQUE BLACK MAN, THAT HAVE TRANSPARENT AFRICAN GENETIC HERITAGE, THAT DICTATE HIS MOTIVATIONS, WHICH DOES (NOT) FORMULATE WITH THE TRADITIONS OF THE AMERICAN PEOPLE. WHICH CONSIST OF INTELLECTUAL MORAL VALUES AND LIBERTY THAT IS DRIVEN BY A CAPITALISTIC AGENDA.

WHITES IN AMERICA FOR HUNDREDS OF YEARS, HAVE BEEN WILLING TO COMPROMISE WITH BLACKS, PERTAINING TO MORAL ISSURES, UNFORTUNATELY IT IS THE MAJORITY OF BLACKS THAT VIOLATE PRINCIPLES, WITH ACCUSATIONS OF DECITFUL RADICAL ISSURES TO COMPENSATE FOR INCOMPETENCE FOR INSTANCE WHITES GAVE A BLACK MAN THE OPPORTUNITY TO BECOME PRESIDENT. ONCE ELECTED HE ASSUMED THAT (WHITES) WOULD CONTINUE CATERING TO HIS RADICAL DECITFUL LIES.

MOST BLACKS ARE EMBEDDED WITH ASSUMING DISTORTIONS. AND ONCE WHITES BECOME AWARE OF THEIR CUNNING INCOMPETENCY THEY (WILL) RETALIATE BASED ON SCENARIO.

OUR FORE FATHERS FORMULATED THE CONSTITUTION IN ORDER THAT THE PEOPLE COULD CONTROL THEIR OWN POLITICAL DESTINY, THROUGH A VOTING PROCESS.

PERTAINING TO TO A TWO PARTY SYSTEM, WHICH IS THE DETERMINING FACTOR, LEFT ENTIRLEY TO THE AMERICAN PEOPLE.

APPARENTLY PRESIDENT BARACK HUSSIEN OBAMA IS (UNFAMILIAR) WITH THIS PROCESS, BECAUSE HE IS TRYING TO MODERNIZE THE AMERICAN PEOPLE TO ADJUST TO HIS CONGO PHILOSOPHY OF ONE SIZE FIT ALL. BECAUSE AMERICANS ARE SO POLITICALLY STUPID, UNTIL THEY CANT DECIPHER HIS NARCISSISTIC DECITFUL LYING RADICAL DISDAINING TACTICS TO SABOTAGE LIBERTIES IN AMERICA.

I HAVE EXPERIENCED MANY POLITICAL EVENTS DURING MY LIFE, EVEN THE CIVIL RIGHTS MARCHES OF DR MARTIN LUTHER KING, DURING THE SIXTIES WHEN HE WAS TRYING TO GET SOUTHERN BLACKS LIBERTIES RESTORED, THAT THE (REPUBLICAN) CONGRESS RATIFIED IN EIGHTEEN SIXTY SIX. WHICH THE SOUTHERN (DEMOCRATS) NULLIFIED, DURING EIGHTEEN NINETY FIVE.

BUT (NOTHING) LIKE THE INTENSITY OF WHITE AMERICA INGAGED IN TODAY, IN ORDER TO SAVE OUR RIGHTS UNDER THE CONSTITUTION. CHRONOLOGICAL RECORDS OF SIGNIFICANT EVENTS DICTATE, THAT BLACKS HAVE ALWAYS STARTED NEGATIVE ENCROACHMENTS

AGAINST WHITES, BUT TRUST ME PRESIDENT BARACK HUSSEIN OBAMA, THEY WILL RISE TO THE OCCASION AND RETALIATE.

JUST IN CASE YOU ARE NOT AWARE MR PRESIDENT, MOST WHITES ARE TOTALLY CONTRARY TO THE CHARACTERIZATION AND DEMEANOR OF MOST BLACKS AND YOU ARE OUT OF TUCH WITH THIS REALITY.

ONCE WHITES SUPPORT YOU, AND YOU DECEIVE THEM BEING A BLACK MAN. THEY WILL (NEVER) RECONCILE WITH YOU.

NOT ONLY THAT YOU HAVE SET OTHER BLACKS BACK FIFTY YEARS, BECAUSE OF YOU WHITES ARE GOING TO TAKE THEIR FRUSTRATION OUT ON OTHER INNOCENT BLACKS.

JUST AS THE SOUTHERN DEMOCRATS, RETALIATED AGAINST NAT TURNER FOR HIS AGGRESSION IN EIGHTEEN THIRTY ONE. THEY DEPOSED OF HIS FOLLOERS, REMOVED HIS SKIN AND MADE SHOES. PURSES FROM IT AND TRINKETS FROM HIS BONES.

AND SLAUGHTERED OVER ONE HUNDRED AND THIRTY INNOCENT BLACKS IN ONE DAY. I AM (NOT) ADVOCATING VIOLENCE, JUST WRITING ABOUT REALITY. BECAUSE VIOLENCE OF THIS MAGNITUDE, COULD (NEVER) OCCUR TODAY, BECAUSE OF OUR CONSTITUTION.

HOWEVER DO NOT KID YOUR SELF, HIDES ARE STILL BEING STRIPPED OF TODAY IN EFFIGY, BUTR MT THEF BALLOT. BOX.

THERE WAS A LAND MINE THAT EXPLODED IN THE FACE OF THE (DEMOCRATIC) OBAMA ADMINISTRATION ON JANUARY 19, 2010. WITH NOW (REPUBLICIAN SENATOR SCOTT BROWN WINNING THE ELECTION IN MASSACHUSETTS. WHICH IS JUST THE BEGINNING, BECAUSE THERE IS A SCENARIO DEVELOPING NATION WIDE WITH (WHITES)

THEY TRUSTED THIS BLACK MAN THAT IS LIGHT SKIN AND DO (NOT) SPEAK (NEGRO) VOTED HIM INTO THE OFFICE OF PRESIDENT. AND HE HAS DECEIVED OUR NATION. WITH MARXIST PROPAGANDA,AND CATERING TO THE WELFARE OF TERRORIST THAT INTEND TO EXTERMINATE (ALL) AMERICANS. BUT TRUST ME MR PRESIDENT OBAMA, I CANT

REPAIR WATCHES AND CLOCKS MAKE BASKETS, REPAIR GUNS, OR RAISE PIGS AND CATTLE FOR SALE. BUT THERE IS ONE DAMN THING FOR CERTAIN THAT I AM GOOD AT, AND THAT IS COOKING FOOD, ALSO IDENTIFYING WHITE AND BLACK JUDAS GOATS. WITH BELLS ON.

I GREW UP IN THE SOUTH, ALSO THE NORTH. AND PRACTICALLY ALL OF MY LIFE, I HAVE CONCENTRATED ON BLACK AND WHITE DISPOSITIONS RELATED TO GENETIC HERITAGE, AND THERE IS (NO) COMPARISON.

(UNREADABLE TEXT) HERD BEHIND LEADERS, PREDOMINATELY EMBEDDED WITH IN THEIR GENETIC HERITAGE AND ADHERE TO THEIR GUIDANCE. AND WHITE SOUTHERN DEMOCRATS HAS UTILIZED THIS IGNORANCE TO THEIR ADVANTAGE FOR OVER SEVENTY YEARS V.I.A. SENATOR HARRY REID.

MOST WHITES ARE INVOLVED IN RESOLUTIONS, PERTAINING TO INDIVIDUAL BEST INTEREST, REGARDS TO PRECEPTIONS AND COLLABORATE WITH OTHERS TO DETERMINE RELEVENT ISSURES, AND ACT ACCORDANTLY.

AND IF IT HAS BEEN DETERMINED THAT THEY HAVE BEEN DECEIVED OR AUTHORITATIVELY ABUSED THEY WILL (NEVER) TRUST YOUR AMBITIONS AGAAIN.

NOT ONLY THAT THEY WILL RETALIATE BASED ON THE CIRCUMATANCES OF HUMILIATIONS.

I REALIZE THE REDUNDANCY IS NECESSARY BASED ON DIFFERENT SCENARIOS, IF THERE IS ANYTHING BLACK AND WHITES DETEST IS LYING DECEITFUL THIEVERY, RELATED TO ARROGANCE AND VIOLENCE.

WHICH IS A EMBEDDED TRAIT OF MOST AFRICAN AMERICANS GENETIC HERITAGE, COMBINE WITH IGNORANT INCOMPETENCY. WHICH HAS PROVEN TO BE DETRIMENTAL TO BLACKS FOR CENTURIES.

JUST IN CASE YOU ARE NOT AWARE MR PRESIDENT, THE DEMEANOR OF MOST WHITES ARE TOTALLY DIFFERENT FROM MOST BLACKS, AND YOU ARE OUT OF TUCH WITH THIS REALITY, ONCE WHITES ARE SUPPORTIVE, AND YOU DECEIVE THEM, BEING A BLACK MAN, SIR THEY WILL (NEVER) RECONCILE WITH OR FOR YOU.

NOT ONLY THAT YOU HAVE SET A LARGE SEGMENT OF BLACKS BACK FIFTY YEARS, BECAUSE OF YOUR RADICAL DISPOSITION, WHITES ARE GOING TO TAKE THEIR FRUSTRATION OUT ON OTHER OTHER INNOCENT BLACKS, JUST REMEMBER IT IS THE WHITES THAT SUPPLY THE MAJORITY OF EMPLOYMENT IN AMERICA FOR BLACKS WHITES AND HISPANICS.

AND THEY DONT HAVE TO HIRE BLACKS, BECAUSE THE HISPANIC POPULATION HAS EXCEEDED BLACKS, AND THEY ARE KNOCKING THE DOOR DOWN TO BE EMPLOYED. WHILE BLACKS ARE DEPENDING ON (YOU) TO TAKE OVER AMERICA AND PRODUCE REPARATION FOR SERVITUDE, WHILE THEY LAY BACK AND BRAG ABOUT NOW IT IS WHITEY TURN ON THE BACK OF THE BUS. ACCORDING TO SENATOR HARRY REID, THE NATION ELECTED ITS FIRST BLACK PRESIDENT, BECAUSE HE WAS LIGHT SKIN, AND DID NOT SPEAK (NEGRO) UNLESS HE WANTED TO.

HOWEVER COUPLED WITH LIES, NARCISSISTIC ARROGANCE AND TREATIJSFCTHE AMERICAN PEOPLE AS IF THEY ARE HIS CONGO TRIBE, SIMPLY BECAUSE HE IS INEPT TO THE FUNDAMENTALS STANDARDS THAT AMERICA WAS FOUNDERED ON OR HE COULD CARE LESS.

TRUST ME ONCE YOU POLITICALLY DECEIVE THE AMERICAN PEOPLE, ESPECIALLY WHITES, IT IS YOUR TURN IN THE BARREL, AND THEY WILL NEVER LET YOU OUT, EVEN IF YOU DO NOT SPEAK (NEGRO);

THIS PRESIDENT IS OUT ON A LIMB, AND THE AMERICAN PEOPLE ARE SAWING IT OFF, BECAUSE HE HAS INSULTED THEIR INTEGRITY BY IGNORING THEIR STANDARDS WITH ARROGANCE.

AS IF HE IS A CONGO CHIEF OF AMERICA NOT A PRESIDENT. I WATCHED SOME SEGEMENTS OF HIS STATE OF THE UNION DEBACLE, AND NEVER ONCE DID HE COMMENT ON WHY HE CHOOSE TO TRY AND HOUSE FOREGIN TERRORION AMERICAN SOIL, IN AND NEAR TWO OF THE LARGEST POPULATED CITIES IN OUR NATION, NEITHER THE GITMO FLOP.

ALSO PUBICALLY REPROOF OUR U.S. SUPREME COURT TO THEIR FACE, THIS PRESIDENT BARACK HUSSIEN OBAMA,

IS ACTING LIKE A BACK ALLEY CRACK HEAD FROM THE GHETTO ON THE STREETS OF CHICAGO.

HE IS THE FIRST PRESIDENT IN THE HISTORY OF OUR NATION, TO BECOME A LAME DUCK, ALSO A COOKED GOOSE IN ONE YEAR. APPARENTLY HE IS SO NARCISSISTIC, AND INEPT TO THE TRADITIONALPRINCIPLES OF THE AMERICAN PEOPLE, THIS MAN HAVE SERIOUS DYSFUNCTIONAL PROBLEMS, IN ESSENCE HIS GENETIC AFRICAN HERITAGE IS DICTATING HIS PHILOSOPHY, AND THAT IS INEVITABLE.

WHICH I DOUBT VERY SERIOUSLY THAT HE IS AWARE OF, BECAUSE GENETIC CONTROLLABILITY CAUSES ONE TO REACT SUBCONSCIOUSLY.

THE PERSONA OF PRESIDENT BARACK HUSSEIN OBAMA, IS DOMINATED WITH HIS FATHER GENETIC TRAITS, I HAVE (NOT) READ OR HEARD ANY THING ABOUT HIS FATHER, BUT YOU CAN BET THE RANCH THAT HE WAS CHARISMATIC, EGOTISTICAL, WITH AN APPEALING AFRICAN TRAIT.

RELATED TO PRESUPPOSITIONS OF INCOMPETENT ARROGANCE, WITH A DESIRE FOR THE LADIES.

BECAUSE DURING THE SIXTIES FOR A BLACK MAN, TO CONVINCE A WHITE WOMAN TO SLEEP WITH HIM, HE HAD TO BE QUITE A CONNING ORIENT. PRESIDENT BARACK HUSSIEN OBAMA, UTILIZED THIS IDENTICAL GENETIC HERITAGE TRAIT, TO CHARM THE MAJORITY OF THE AMERICAN CONSTITUENCY TO ELECT HIM PRESIDENT.

HOWEVER THERE ARE DIRE CONSEQUENCES FOR THIS KIND OF FOOLERY, DECEPTION AND IT IS A VERY DISTINCT POSSIBILITY WHY OBAMA GREW UP WITHOUT A FATHER IMIAGE, BECAUSE HIS MOTHER DISCOVERED DECEPTION IN HIS FATHER IDEOLOGUE, AND DUMPED HIM.

BASICALLY THE SAME SCENARIO THAT THE AMERICAN PEOPLE IS IN THE PROCESS OF DOING TO HIS HIS SON. BARACK HUSSIEN OBAMA, POLITICALY DUMPING HIM.

BECAUSE OF HIS RADICAL LYING (UNREADABLE TEXT) ON THE AMERICAN PEOPLE AT HIS DISCRETION. IF PRESIDENT OBAMA WAS A (CONSERVATIVE) THE LIBERAL NEWS MEDIA WOULD HAVE EXHUMED HIS FATHER TO DETERMINE WHAT KIND OF NOSE BONE OR LIP DISK HIS ANCESTORS INSERTED.

LEFT WING DEMOCRATS HAVE A UNIQUE WAY OF DISTORTING ISSURES, THEY WILL ONLY TELL PART OF A STORY, TO JUSTIFY THEIR CONCERNS.

SUCH AS THIS BOTTOM CARRION FEEDING YELLOW BELLY CAT FISH, ALL MOUTH AND NO BRAINS. KEITH OLBERMANN, WENT BERSERK ON JANUARY 21, 2010. COMPARING U.S. SUPREME COURT JUSTICE JOHN ROBERTS, TO U.S. CHIEF SUPREME COURT JUSTICE ROGER B. TANEY OF EIGHTEEN FIFTY SEVEN, WHEN THE SUPREME COURT SEVEN TO TWO RELAY AGAINST DRED SCOTT, A BLACK MAN TRYING TO OBTAIN HIS LIBERTIES.

BUT WHAT THIS DYSFUNCTIONAL BRAIN KEITH OLBERMANN, (NEGLECTED) TO EXPLAIN WAS THAT U.S. CHIEF JUSTICE ROGER B. TANEY, WAS A (DEMOCRAT) HE AND HIS FAMILY WAS SLAVE OWNERS, HE ALSO DECLARED THAT CONGRESS HAD NO AUTHORITY TO EXCLUDE SLAVERY FROM THE TERRITORIES AND ATTACKED (ALL) AFRICAN AMERICANS, CLAIMING THEY WERE (NOT) NEVER BEEN AND COULD NEVER BE AMERICAN CITIZENS, BECAUSE THEY HAD NO RIGHTS UNDER THE CONSTITUTION.

DURING THIS SAME TIME PEROID THE NEWLY FORMED (REPUBLICAN) PARTY WAS FIGHTING DILIGENTLY TO QUELL SLAVERY, WHICH THE (REPUBLICAN) CONGRESS ANSWERED BACK ON JULY 9, EIGHTEEN SIXTY EIGHT, WHEN THEY RATIFIED THE FOURTEENTH AMENDMENT TO THE CONSTITUTION. I AM CONSTANTLY REMINDED OF THE PREDICTIONS OF SOUTHERN DEMOCRATS OF EIGHTEEN SEVENTY, WHEN THEY STATED BLACKS ARE IGNORANT, POLITICALLY INCOMPETENT, AND (NOT) APPROPRIATE FOR INVOLMENT IN THE POLITICAL ARENA.

I AM CERTAIN THEY BASED THEIR OPINION ON BLACKS SUCH AS PRESIDENT BARACK HUSSEIN OBAMA. THE FOUNDING FATHERS OF THE CONSTITUTION FOR AMERICA, WERE SOME OF THE MOST SHREWDEST PEOPLE ON GODS EARTH IN ESSENCE THEY DEALT WITH THE HUMAN MIND, AND CHARACTERIZED PHILOSOPHICAL MOTIVES. AND THAT IS WHY THE FIRST PHRASE OF THE CONSTITUTION IS WE THE PEOPLE.

THEY INTENDED FOR THE UNITED STATES OF AMERICA TO BE THE BED ROCK OF MORALITY, AND THE PEOPLE IN CONTROL OF THEIR OWN DESTINY.

NOT SOME SLEAZY GROUP OF RADICAL POLITICIANS.

MANY PRESIDENTS HAVE CHALLENGED THE WISDOM OF OUR FOUNDING FATHERS, AND CAME UP BUFFOONISH (LOOSERS).

BUT NONE MORE AGGRESSIVE THAN PRESIDENT BARACK HUSSIEN OBAMA, IT IS TRULY REMARKABLE HOW FORTY ONE MEN, TWO HUNDRED AND TWENTY THREE YEARS AGO, CAN CAUSE JUDAS GOATS TO SELF DESTRUCT POLITICALLY

TODA I.

WITH THE RATIFICATIONS OF THE CONVENTIONS OF NINE STATES SHALL BE SUFFICIENT FOR ESTABLISHMENT OF THIS (CONSTITUTION) BETWEEN THE STATES, SO RATIFIED THE SAME DONE IN CONVENTION BY THE UNANIMOUS CONSENT OF THE STATES PRESENT THE SEVENTEENTH DAY OF SEPTEMBER IN THE YEAR OF OUR (LORD) ONE THOUSAND AND EIGHTY SEVEN, AND OF THE (INDEPENDANCE) OF THE UNITED STATES OF AMERICA. THE TWELFTH IN WITNESS WHERE OF WE HAVE HEREUNTO SUBSCRIBED OUR NAMES. GEORGE WASHINGTON PRESIDENT AND DEPUTY FROM VIRGINIA. LADIES AND GENTLEMEN OF AMERICA UNDER THIS FORMAT CAME MANY AMENDMENTS, WHICH REPRESENT THE GREATEST (NATION) ON GODS EARTH, WHICH WE THE PEOPLE (WILL) SUSTAIN.

TO GROW UP IN A FREE SOCIETY WITH THE OPTION TO THINK, BASED ON YOUR (OWN) PHILOSOPHY AND RELATE TO REALITY, IS A FORM OF ATTENTIVE GRATITUDE, BUT TO ALLOW SOME ONE OR OTHERS TO CAPTIVATE YOUR PRINCIPLES WITH ERRONEOUS LIES, IS A HINDERANCE TO YOUR PROSPERITY, WHICH IN ESSENCE ILLUMINATE YOU AS A DYSFUNCTIONAL IMMORAL INCOMPETENT IDIOT.

SUCH AS RADIO AND TELEVISION PERSONALITY JUAN WILLIAMS, ON FOX NEWS JANUARY 11, 2010. 9 00 AM. HE WAS TRYING TO CHARACTERIZE SENATOR HARRY REID STATEMENT OF LIGHT SKIN BLACK NOT SPEAKING NEGRO UNLESS HE WANTED TO.

IN AN ATTEMPT TO PACIFY, HE ACCUSED REPUBLICANS OF (NOT) REACHING OUT TO BLACKS AND HISPANICS, WILL SOMEONEPLEASEADVISETHISBUFFOONTHATREPUBLICANS HAVE BEEN RECHING OUT TO BLACKS FOR ONE HUNDRED AND FORTY FIVE YEARS, PRESIDENT ABRAHAM LINCOLN A REPUBLCAN ABOLISHED SERVITUDE IN EIGHTEEN SIXTY FIVE, ALSO AWARE OF BLCKS AT THAT TIME WERE MOLSTY IGNORANT. SO HE CHOOSE TO OFFER STABILITY BY GIVING THEM FORTY ACRES OF SOUTHERN CONFEDRATE LAND AND GOVERNMENT MULE, UNFORTUNATELY HE WAS ASSASSINATED, HIS VICE PRESIDENT WAS A DEMOCRAT FROM TENNESSEE ANDRED JOHNSON,RESCINDED THE PROCLAMATION AND GAVE THE LAND BACK TO THE SLAVE OWNERS OF THE PLANTATIONS.

DURING THE DRED SCOTT DEBACLE CHIEF JUSTICE ROGER B. TANEY SCOFFED AT BLACKS AND PREDICTED THEY (NEVER) BE U.S. CITIZENS BECAUSE THEY WERE NOT IN THE CONSTITUTION.

THE REPUBLICAN CONGRESS RALLIED TO ADD THE FOURTEENTH AMENDMENT TO THE CONSTITUTION, WHICH WAS RATIFIED IN EIGHTEEN SIXTY EIGHT, WHICH GAVE BLACKS EQUAL RIGHTS.

THE HERITAGE OF IGNORANCE IS BLAME, PRIMARILY BASED ON INTEGRITY REGARDS TO THE HUMAN MIND TO DETRMINE FATE.

PRESIDENT DWIGHT DAVID EISENHOWER A REPUBLICAN, REACHED OUT TO BLACKS IN NINETEEN FIFTY SEVEN, TO RESTORE THEIR CIVIL RIGHTS IN THE SOUTH, UNFORTUNATELY THE DEMOCRATIC CONTROLLED CONGRESS BLOCKED IT.

HOWEVER HE NEVER STOP REACHING OUT FOR BLACKS, HE WEAKEN THE KU-KLUX-KLAN, AND INTEGRATED SOUTHERN SCHOOLS FOR BLACKS.

THE DEMOCRATS CONTROLLED THE CONGRESS IN NINETEEN SIXTY FOUR, WHEN DEMOCRAT SENATOR ROBERT BYIRD FORMER KU-KLUX-KLAN.

FILIBUSTERED THAT STILL HOLD THE LONGEST IN WASHINGTON TODATE, AGAINST CIVIL RIGHTS FOR SOUTHERN BLACKS.

THE REPUBLICAN CONGRESS REACHED OUT FOR BLACKS AND OVERTURNED THE DEMOCRATIC FILIBUSTER. IN ORDER FOR BLACKS TO HAVE EQUALITY. REPUBLICAN PRESIDENT GEORGE W. BUSH, REACHED OUT AND APPOINTED THE SECOND AFRICAN AMERICAN TO THE U.S. SUPREME COURT, WHILE THE DEMOCRATS WAS TRYING TO PEEL THE HIDE OF JUSTICE CLARENCE THOMAS, ESPECIALLY DEMOCRATIC SENATOR JOSEPH BIEDEN.

U.S. SUPREME COURT JUSTICE THOURGOOD MARSHALL WAS A (DEMOCRAT) ALSO A STAUNCH ADVOCATE FOR AFRICAN AMERICAN PARITY, HE FORMED AN AGENDA SUCH AS FAIR HOUSING, TRANSPORTATION, VOTING, TO END SEGREGATION, BROWN VS BOARD OF EDUCATION, AND AFFIRMATIVE ACTION. (REPUBLICAN) PRESIDENT RICHARD MILLHOUSE NIXION, REACHED OUT AND MOST OF JUSTICE MARSHALL CONCERNS WERE RATIFIED INTO LAW. (REPUBLICAN) PRESIDENT GEORGE W. BUSH, REACHED OUT AND SELECTED THE FIRST TWO AFRICAN AMERICANS (EVER) TO SERVE IN HIS CABINET, DURING HIS ENTIRE TERM IN OFFICE. WHICH WAS SECRETARY OF STATE COLEN POWELL, AND LATER SECRETARY OF STATE CONDOLEEZZA RICE.

IN CLOSING. IT IS TERRIBLY ASTOUNDING WITH POLITICAL INEPTNESS, THAT APPROXIMATELY NINETY TWO PERCENT OF AFRICAN AMERICANS ARE DESPERATELY LOYAL TO THE DEMOCRATIC PARTY.

WHEN THE DEMOCRATS FOUNDED THE KU-KLUX-KLAN, DURING EIGHTEEN SIXTY SIX. IN PULASKI, TENNESSEE. AND EXPLOITED THEIR BRUTALITY FAR NORTH AS THE STATE OF INDIANA, ON A TEMPORARY BASIS, AND RETURNED TO THE SOUTHERN STATES, (ONLY) REACHING OUT TO SOUTHERN BLACKS WITH BLOW TORCHES AND ROPES WITH NOOSES AT THE END.

ALSO DOCTRINE BLACKS INTO THINKING, IT IS THOSE RICH RACIST REPUBLICANS THAT DESPISE YOU BECAUSE YOU ARE BLACK.

WHEN THEY THE DEMOCRATS HAVE BEEN THE CULPRITS, FOR OVER ONE HUNDRED AND FORTY YEARS.

BEGINNING DURING THE EIGHTEEN SEVENTIES, WHEN THE SOUTHERN DEMOCRATS VIOLENTLY EXPELLED WHITE AND BLACK REPUBLICANS FROM THE SOUTHERN STATES, AND LITERALLY FORCED THE REMAINING BLACKS TO JOIN THE DEMOCRATIC PARTY.

WHICH IS THE SAME UPTATED ANALYSIS MINAS THE VIOLENCE, THAT PRESIDENT BARACK HUSSEIN OBAMA, IS TRYING TO DUPE AND ACCOMPLISH ON THE AMERICAN PEOPLE TODAY.

WITH PUBLIC OPTION HEALTH CARE. AND AS THE LATE PAUL HARVEY WOULD SAY AND NOW YOU KNOW THE REST OF THE STORY.